[redacted]

F

PSYCHOLOGY
in
TEACHING READING

PSYCHOLOGY
in
TEACHING READING

HENRY P. SMITH

School of Education
The University of Kansas

EMERALD V. DECHANT

Division of Education and Psychology
Fort Hays Kansas State College

1961
Englewood Cliffs, N. J.
PRENTICE-HALL, INC.

PRENTICE-HALL PSYCHOLOGY SERIES

LIBRARY OF CONGRESS
CATALOG CARD NO.: 61–8230

PRINTED IN THE UNITED STATES OF AMERICA
73666—C

PREFACE

The purpose of this book is to provide teachers with an understanding of the psychological bases of the reading process. As teachers, we need to know the facts and principles behind our classroom methods. But facts and principles presented in isolation are difficult to understand and unlikely to be used; we must see how they apply to the teaching of boys and girls.

Psychologists have made numerous attempts to systematize what is known about behavior. In this work, we seek to identify and organize the facts concerning reading behavior. In order effectively to guide the child who is learning to read, the teacher should understand both those general principles that govern all learning and those special principles that govern learning to read.

Just what is a psychology of reading? There is a vast amount of data and carefully considered theory to be found in psychology and related fields. But frequently it is expressed in technical language and those portions of it that have educational implications are interwoven with much that has little or no direct application to education. Out of this wealth of information, a psychology of reading selects what is relevant to the teaching of reading and attempts to organize it in logical form. But it must do more than this. It must suggest applications of the findings and theories of the psychologist to classroom situations.

In a very real sense this book is an introduction to educational methods and materials as well as a basic course in the psychology of the reading-learning process. However, the methods and materials discussed are used primarily to illustrate the application of psychological principles. We cannot hope to include in one book both a psychology of reading and an account of all the numerous and complex methods and materials of teaching reading. We have therefore emphasized the essential psychological data and introduced only those applications that are needed for an understanding of the place of psychology in the reading process.

This book was not written for the *reading* teacher alone. It is rather for all teachers, because *all* share the responsibility for improving reading. It is for the prospective teacher, the active teacher, and, indeed, for the administrator who wishes to gain a better understanding of the psychology of reading. In a broad sense, it is a psychology of teaching directed specifically toward reading. At all levels of development, reading is perhaps our best example of the effective teaching-learning process and, at the same time, one of its most important products.

In our society, helping every person attain proficiency in reading skill is an important educational goal. Even adult reading programs are becoming so numerous that the National Society for the Study of Education found it worthwhile to devote a recent yearbook entirely to adult reading. Unfortunately, teachers too often have insufficient knowledge of the reading process. Too few teacher-training schools offer courses in the psychology of reading. And many teacher-certifying agencies require no formal training in the teaching of reading.

In attempting to analyze and synthesize the available psychological and educational data and theory, some 2,500 studies have been examined. From this vast literature, we have tried both to organize what is known of the psychology of reading and to identify at least a portion of those problems that require further investigation.

This book has three major goals:

1. To *select* those data that are most relevant to the teacher's understanding of the reading process.

2. To *interpret* these data in terms of the problems that the teacher will encounter.

3. To *apply* the interpretations to the specific classroom problems that teachers meet.

HENRY P. SMITH
EMERALD V. DECHANT

TABLE OF CONTENTS

1

THE TEACHER'S INTEREST IN THE READING PROCESS

Everyone in the civilized areas of the world —child, adolescent, and adult—has a personal need for being an effective reader. Reading is a primary avenue to all knowledge. It offers access to the information, ideas, ideals, aspirations, and happenings of both the past and the present. Through reading one extends his environment from home and community to the world as a whole.

For the child, reading is a key to success in school, to the development of out-of-school interests, to the enjoyment of leisure time, and to personal and social adjustment. It helps him to adjust to his age mates, to become independent of parents and teachers, to select and prepare for an occupation, and to achieve social responsibilities. As our culture becomes more complex, reading plays an increasingly greater role in satisfying personal needs and in promoting social awareness and growth. Through reading we acquire many of our standards of behavior and morality; we may broaden our interests, our tastes, and our understanding of others. In the modern school, effective reading is the most important avenue to effective learning.

Reading is one of the few academic areas in which we demand success from all children. Unfortunately, we know that success is not always possible. Reading retardation probably will vex educators always. There are far too many poor readers or even non-readers in both the elementary and the secondary schools. And too many of our children leave school with insufficient competence in this most important means for learning.

The evidence is clear. We know that we are not producing as many effective readers as we should like. Too frequently even the so-called good readers have not developed their reading skill to the extent of their capabilities. And, whereas slow learners will commonly evidence reading difficulties, there are far too many instances of general reading retardation and, particularly, of deficiencies in comprehension and rate skills among our most intelligent students.

The reasons for failure in reading are many. Some children have inferior learning capacity, poor memory and attention spans, defective vision or hearing, weak language and experiential backgrounds, neurological or physiological handicaps, and emotional or social immaturities. Some have narrow recognition spans, inadequate recognition skills, and insufficient knowledge of phonics. Some show directional confusion. Some lack interest in reading. And, some have received inadequate instruction in important phases of effective reading.

Unfortunately, the criticisms leveled at the inadequate reading of children frequently imply that inadequate instruction alone is responsible. And, even in those many cases where inadequate instruction is responsible, the critics generally fail to recognize that there are forces beyond the control of the teacher that must share the burden. Some students fail to receive adequate instruction because they have not attended school regularly, have changed schools frequently, or have been placed in classes that are too large.

Nevertheless, certain failures are directly attributable to unskillful teaching. Sometimes, for example, too much emphasis is placed on rôte drill, word analysis, oral reading, or reading rate. Or there may be too little emphasis on readiness or insufficient adjustments for individual differences in ability. Teachers need to know why certain children learn to read and why others do not. We must know how to develop and promote reading interests. We must know how to make reading a goal for which each child clamors. To identify inadequacies and the forces responsible for them is only a beginning step. We must know how to help each child, whatever his present level of reading skill, achieve his maximum growth in reading.

THE TEACHER'S SPECIAL INTEREST IN READING

The professional teacher recognizes that effective teaching must mean effective learning by each child. Whenever the students' reading abilities lag behind their learning abilities, we must reappraise the quality of our teaching.

Let us stop here to examine the general significance of reading in the teaching-learning process. At one time we were inclined to believe that the ability to read was acquired, if at all, in the elementary grades. Formal instruction in reading was limited to the first six grades or at best continued only to the end of the eighth grade. We recognized, of course, that remedial reading must be offered to those who failed to learn to read, but the high school and the college teacher felt no major responsibility for teaching reading skills.

Today we remain greatly concerned with the quality of reading instruction in the primary and elementary school grades. At those levels we strive constantly to improve reading instruction. But our interest in reading has been extended and broadened. Now developmental programs begin in the nursery schools and kindergartens, and we emphasize that reading development should continue into adult life. During the early school years the focus is upon the *basic skills,* but throughout the school years we seek to develop those *special skills* required for effective reading at the higher levels.

We no longer aim to develop merely a general reading ability. We have become concerned with those special skills that are demanded by each subject in the curriculum. We recognize that there are specific reading skills for specific reading tasks. For example, a child develops gradually his ability to skim and scan, to read critically, to interpret graphs, maps, and tables, and to understand the special vocabulary of each subject that he studies. A child must acquire specific reading skills for each of the content areas.

In recent years the unique reading demands of each subject matter area have increased. For example, the atomic and space age has introduced numerous concepts and vocabulary terms that were unheard of just a few years ago. Wittich [24] points out that as early as 1954 the *Biennial Survey of Education in the United States* reported that more than 800 different courses were being offered by some 24,000 American high schools.

The child's need for effective reading increases as he advances through school. In fact, a student's over-all scholastic progress can almost be gauged by his reading competence. This is to be expected. Reading offers opportunities to deliberate over facts and principles; it permits one to learn independently and to acquire new areas of interest. No other avenue of learning offers as much in these directions as does reading.

The pupil's development in reading, then, must not become static with the ending of the elementary grades. With each year he must become increasingly able to read for the purpose of learning. Reading is his principal tool for mastering the varied curriculum of the modern school.[19]

Since reading is so important, we cannot be concerned merely with those factors that contribute to deficiencies and difficulties in reading. To do so would focus our attention on the below-average reader. We must give equal attention to the factors that are basic to high excellence in reading.

Perhaps, in our attempt to offer education to all youth regardless of their abilities and interests, we have introduced barriers to the optimum education of our more gifted children. In too many cases our desire for equality of educational opportunity has led us to offer no more than a middle standard of education.[8] This is unfortunate. A middle standard is fair only to middle-ability children. Individuals are different and should achieve differently. To be different is normal, not abnormal.

As we strive for the optimum development of every child, we must be concerned with his total physical, emotional, social, and intellectual development. We must locate his specific strengths and weaknesses. We must provide for his advancing at his own rate and as far as his ability permits. We must recognize that different children become ready to learn certain skills, including reading skills, at different ages. Our practical decisions on the teaching of reading must be based on sound psychological and physiological principles.

We must know when to introduce reading and when to direct the child toward other forms of learning. All children do not learn equally well through all media. The language arts are not separate disciplines. Speaking, listening, and writing often are important aids to reading development. Observational abilities, too, play a part in reading readiness and reading achievement. Frequently we must decide whether to concentrate upon the repair of a pupil's limitations in reading or to emphasize his potentialities in the areas of listening or observing.

There was a time when the term, "reading readiness," was used only to refer to the pre-primer child. Today we see that readiness applies to every child. Even the college teacher must be concerned with the student's readiness to interpret and discriminate as he reads.

Our deep concern with readiness at all levels does not imply that reading is being taught poorly in the elementary school. On the contrary, it reflects the broadening of our knowledge of both the nature of the reading process and the nature of the reader. We now recognize what formerly we ignored: every student at every level in his development encounters new reading problems and his development of reading skills is a continuing process.

This newer interpretation of reading presents each teacher with an additional professional responsibility. Teachers at all levels and in all subjects share responsibility for teaching reading. Each must accept his portion of the task of continually improving each child's ability to read.

This means, of course, that whatever subject and at whatever level we teach, we will need to acquaint ourselves with all that is known about both the nature of the reading process and the nature of the reader. We must understand the psychological data and theory as well as the methodology and materials that have grown from the applications of psychology to the teaching of reading. We must understand reading as a learning process, indeed, as basically a psychological process. And it is not enough merely to know the psychology and methodology of the age and grade levels at which we teach. We must understand the goals and methods of reading instruction from the preliminary readiness acquired in the home and kindergarten to the finely developed reading skills that should be taught and applied at the high school and college level. Each teacher must see his part in the cooperative project of developmental reading throughout the educational life-span of the pupil.

For a thorough understanding of the teaching-learning process, the elementary school teacher must foresee clearly the goals and problems of the child as he advances through the school years and into adult life. And high school and college teachers need to have some acquaintance with the methods, materials, and problems of teaching at the elementary level. Only with such knowledge can the "upper-school" teachers see fully the needs and opportunities for individualized adjustments and utilize fully the methods and materials of diagnosis and remediation that are necessary for competent instruction.

In 1880 only about three per cent of American youth between the ages of fourteen and seventeen attended secondary school. Until well after the beginning of the twentieth century our teachers taught a rather homogeneous group, especially at the secondary level. They worked with children who were well above average intellectually. Generally speaking, they taught those who wished to be taught. Their students were preparing for professions and for leadership.

Today a variety of strong pressures virtually compel children of all levels of ability to attend not only elementary but secondary school as well. And because of this tremendous increase in school attendance, many compromises both in methods and materials are made at all educational levels. The teacher cannot always teach what he wants to teach nor as well as he would like to teach. In an ideal educational environment our poorer students, and our better students as well, almost certainly could learn more and apply their learnings to a much better advantage than they now can. Neither the student, the teacher, nor society in general can be completely happy with the compromises that have been made to meet the problems of universal education.

Although the school is a product of society, it is also an instrument of society and as such it shares a major part of the responsibility for transmitting its society's culture to the new generation. It must educate as well as possible each pupil entrusted to its jurisdiction.

In past ages man communicated through gestures and simple sounds and signals. Primitive man was not "educated" unless he understood and was able to assign meaning to signals. Today's youth is not educated until he becomes an effective reader.

Reading is so interrelated with the total educational process that educational success requires successful reading. Experience has taught us that those who fail in school usually have failed first in reading. Giordano Bruno pointed out that if the first button of a man's coat is wrongly buttoned, all the rest are certain to be crooked. Reading is that first button in the garment of education.

To assure the greatest possible number of successful readers, the teacher must know how to proceed toward his goal. He must become a student of methodology. No one method succeeds with all children. And no one teacher can employ all methods equally well. Thus, a psychology of reading must include an examination of the psychological principles underlying the various methods of teaching reading and offer some suggestions as to their strengths and weaknesses. The choice of methods must be made on the bases of the needs of the individual child. And the identification of these needs is a basic element in the psychology of reading.

RESEARCH IN READING

Reading's importance in our modern schools is indicated by the amount of research that has been devoted to it. Over the past fifty years no single problem has received more attention from the educational and psychological laboratories than the problem of understanding the reading process. Both teachers and research specialists have sought to understand what reading is; how reading facility may be developed; and what adjustments in method and material must be made in order that all pupils may profit optimally from reading instruction.

AMOUNT OF RESEARCH

Actually, the first quantitative investigation in reading did not appear in print until 1884 [2] and by 1912 the total number of studies printed was but sixty-five. By 1945, however, 2,600 studies on reading had been published[20] and in recent years such studies have become progressively numerous.

Three Educational Records Bulletins, *Ten Years of Research in Reading* (1930–1940),[21] *Another Five Years of Research in Reading* (1940–

1945),[22] and *Eight More Years of Research in Reading* (1945–1953),[23] cite and annotate 1,905 studies that appeared during a twenty-three year period.

Between 1950 and 1954 almost 1,500 studies in reading were mentioned in *Psychological Abstracts, Education Digest,* and in the yearly summaries by William S. Gray in the *Journal of Educational Research.* Even though there is considerable duplication among the studies cited, this is an amazing amount of attention to one area of inquiry. However, the tremendous body of research has in some ways added to the teacher's problem. It is almost impossible for him to read all the material, weigh the evidence, and thereby form opinions that will serve as his basis for effective teaching procedures.

Scott,[17] for example, observes that the research has been voluminous, but that often it is quite unrelated. It appears to leave many important areas untouched and fails to provide a system or theory that integrates the data. He calls for a greater coordination of effort by clinical psychologists, child-development workers, physicians, and psychiatrists. He suggests that research has been so concerned with practical aspects that numerous theoretical questions have been left unanswered. Gray (pp. 1087–1088) [7] notes that the research on reading often has been fragmentary and incomplete. He suggests that research workers have failed to co-ordinate their efforts. Betts [1] states that there is a "need for carefully considered *critiques,* rather than a mere summarizing of research in order to identify valid conclusions and implications." These authors are calling for an organization of what is known. The research in reading has become so voluminous that perhaps some digestion is required before further ingestion may be worthwhile.

Indeed some attempts have been made to integrate the vast research in reading. Since the time of his 1925 monograph [6] collating the results of 435 studies done prior to July, 1924, William S. Gray has been well known for his reviews of the research in reading. Beginning in 1924 and continuing until 1932, the *Elementary School Journal* carried his annual annotated references to reading research. Since 1932 his annual summaries * have appeared in the *Journal of Educational Research.*

Beginning in October, 1931, *The Review of Educational Research* published summaries on reading every third year. The tenth of these appeared in 1958. In this summary, McCullough reported on 77 studies made in the years 1955 through 1957. The 1955 summary contained articles by several different authors. For example, the research on the psychological aspects of reading was summarized by Gilbert and Holmes.[5] They reported on 129

---

* Dr. Gray died during the summer of 1960. His February, 1960 summary, reviewing 120 studies, covers the period July 1, 1958 to June 30, 1959.

studies that appeared between 1952 and 1955. Sheldon [18] reported on studies concerning the instructional aspects of reading that appeared during the same years. In the 1952 summary Keyser [9] dealt with the research on the elementary school level and Davis [3] did the same thing for reading research on the high school and college level.

Traxler and his co-workers prepared the three monographs mentioned previously which trace twenty-three years of research that is of interest to the reading teacher. Essentially these three monographs are a collection of annotated references classified under various topics. The 1955 publication contains 760 references grouped under twenty-three headings.

ORGANIZATION OF RESEARCH

In addition to the reviews mentioned above, several attempts have been made to organize the data and theory concerning some specific phase of the general reading area. Most notable of these are those yearbooks of the National Society for the Study of Education that have been devoted to the field of reading.

The first of these, the *Report of the National Committee on Reading,*[12] appeared in 1924. In 1937, the society published *The Teaching of Reading: A Second Report* [13]; in 1948, it sponsored *Reading in the High School and College* [14]; in 1949, *Reading in the Elementary School* [15]; in 1956, *Adult Reading* [16]; and in 1961, *Development in and through Reading.*

Each of these compilations brings together the knowledge and thinking of the period in which it was written. In general, each summarizes the research as it was being applied or should have been applied to the teaching of reading. The volume, *The Teaching of Reading: A Second Report,* gives the following three reasons for its preparation (p. 1–2) [13]:

> . . . (a) to trace briefly the developments in the field of reading during the last decade and to identify the major problems that schools face today; (b) to provide in specific and nontechnical terms the information needed by teachers and school officers in reorganizing and improving instruction, especially by making specific constructive recommendations that are supported both by experience and by the results of experiments reported during the last decade; and (c) to provide, as a guide in the case of debatable issues, tentative suggestions to be formulated after careful and deliberate study by a group of qualified experts.

Gates stated that the purpose of the N.S.S.E., 48th yearbook on *Reading in the Elementary School* was (p. 1–2) [4]:

> . . . to present practical principles and procedures for the classroom teacher and supervisor and to illustrate them sufficiently to make them clear. In par-

ticular the yearbook undertakes to express the consensus of the national committee's views on all significant controversial issues.

Thus the purposes of these yearbooks were to report the findings and opinions of the experts, to evaluate the research, and to provide answers to controversial issues.

The *Reading Teacher,* a publication of the International Reading Association, also provides recent summaries of research in selected areas of reading plus extensive bibliographies. The December, 1958 issue of this journal was entitled "New Frontiers in Reading," and the December, 1959 issue was called "Research in Reading."

Another important attempt to synthesize the research is William S. Gray's article on reading in the *Encyclopedia of Educational Research.*[7] He summarizes the research relevant to the sociology of reading, the physiology and psychology of reading, and the teaching of reading. The historical contributions to our knowledge of reading are more clearly portrayed in this article than in any of those previously mentioned in this chapter.

RESEARCH'S CONTRIBUTION TO PROFESSIONALISM

Unfortunately, most of the comprehensive reviews of research mentioned above were written for the benefit of research workers. They are not in a form particularly usable by the teacher. A purpose of this book is to identify and organize the findings of the researchers is such a way that the teacher can become acquainted with the most useful facts and principles.

Although most of us, reading specialists as well as classroom teachers, are much more interested in the practical problems of developmental and remedial reading than in the philosophical and psychological bases for these applications, it is worthwhile for us to consider those data upon which we must depend for sound applications.

Professionalism is based on sound theory and experimental research. The physician anchors his art in biology, anatomy, and chemistry. The engineer anchors his art in mathematical and physical theory and research. The teacher cannot be merely a practitioner; he must anchor his teaching art in psychological, physiological, and educational research.

New concepts and theories give meaning and direction to our professional activities. They help us to see the reasons for our methodology and to predict its success (pp. 33–37).[11] For example, theories form the basis for hypotheses about the child's deficiencies; they help us to identify causes, choose remediation, and make prognoses.

Much of this book is devoted to an understanding of the psychological bases of the reading process. When the light rays reflected from the printed page hit the retinal cells of the eyes, signals are sent along the optic nerve to the visual centers of the brain. But this physical process does not constitute reading. The mind must function in the reading process. The signals must be interpreted. In a psychology of reading we are concerned with the nature of the reading process and the nature of the reader. We are interested in the difficulties encountered in learning to read and in the differences in individual performance.

In the psychology of reading we also are interested in physiological factors. Factors such as visual and hearing defects, malnutrition, speech impairment, and handedness are intimately related to the psychology of reading. A child's psychology is not insulated from his physiology.

Evidently we cannot restrict our analysis to the findings of psychology. We are concerned with findings in the fields of biology, physiology, and neurology. We are also interested in the writings of professional educators who many times have clearer insight into the problems facing the teacher in the classroom than has the researcher.

THE FACETS OF READING

The psychology of reading is a complex and vast field primarily because reading can be viewed from so many different vantage points. Each view and its array of problems has appealed to the curiosity of research workers. For example, we can focus upon the sensory bases of reading. Research on visual difficulties and on eye movements alone has been voluminous. Or we can focus our attention upon reading as a perceptual process. Here the psychological research and theory concerning all types of perception have a bearing on our understanding of reading. As a third facet of reading we see that it is a response and, as such, is influenced by motivation, physical well-being, fatigue, and habit.

From a fourth viewpoint, we see that reading is a learned process and is subject to the same rules as other learned processes. The laws of learning and the causes of forgetting apply to learning to read. Or we can look upon reading as a developmental task. We find that if the child does not learn to read at the appropriate time, other aspects of normal development are blocked and future success in reading becomes more difficult. Also we can view reading as a portion of the total growth process. Data concerning all phases of the child's growth have implications for our understanding of reading as a growth process. The child's intellectual, emotional, physical, and social development, and his attitudes and ideals have a bearing on reading.

From still another viewpoint, reading may be regarded as an interest in its own right and it may provide clues to the other interests of the individual. Much study has been devoted to the development of reading interests and to other interests that are related to reading. And, reading is a means for learning. It is a learning process. Although originally the child learns to read, soon he reads to learn. Many data are available concerning basic study skills and the particular reading skills demanded for specific learning tasks.

These eight viewpoints of reading may be likened to the facets of the cut gem. The brilliance of the total is dependent on the perfection of each facet. Figure One illustrates this.

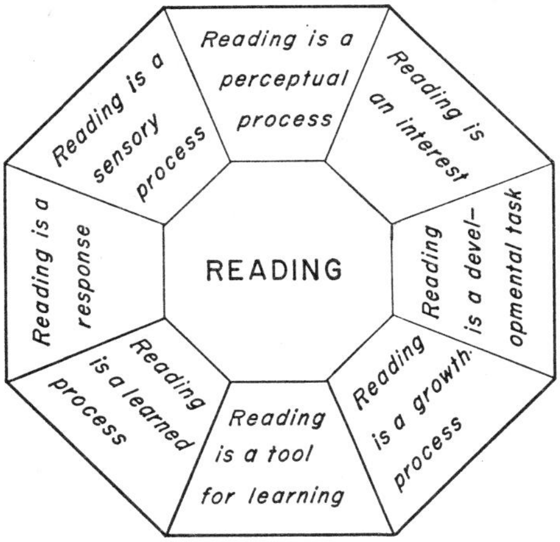

Adding to the complexity of our task of understanding the psychology of reading is the fact that these eight facets of reading are not independent. Each depends upon and each contributes to the others. Each represents a point of view rather than the total process of reading. To understand reading, we must see it from each point of view and further we must see the interrelationships.

THE INFORMATIONAL NEEDS OF THE TEACHER

Because this book is intended for both the active and the prospective teacher, it is only reasonable that the informational needs of the teacher should guide the selection of the topics that are discussed. A book designed to help teachers become acquainted with the facts and principles concerning the psychology of reading must be built around the specific interests of teachers.

There are numerous questions that a psychology of reading should help teachers to answer. The following seem especially important:

1. What is the nature of the reading process?
2. What performance and learning variables are involved in reading?
3. What are the psychological bases of reading readiness?
4. What are the sensory bases of reading?
5. What other physiological variables, besides hearing and vision, are basic to reading?
6. What word recognition skills are important and how may they be developed?
7. What comprehension and rate skills are important and how may they be developed?
8. How do readability and legibility factors influence reading achievement?
9. What are the effects of motivation and interest on reading readiness and achievement?
10. How does personal adjustment affect reading and how does reading affect personal development?
11. How does reading become a means for learning and how may the child best learn to use reading for learning?
12. What are the special demands of reading in the content areas?
13. What developmental processes and sequences characterize a good reading program?
14. How do diagnosis and remediation function in the reading program?
15. What interrelationships can be found among the vast body of knowledge concerning reading?

The questions above identify fifteen informational needs of the teacher. In this book a separate chapter has been given to finding answers to each of them. Brief paragraphs about each question provide a preview of the successive chapters of the book. They are numbered here to correspond to the chapters that they introduce.

Second: The teacher must understand the basic nature of reading. Reading is a perceptual rather than merely a sensory process and, as such, it includes more than mere recognition of words. Neither printed pages nor orally spoken words transmit meaning. The essence of meaning comes from the reader's fund of experience. Reading includes thinking as well as understanding. We are concerned with what the psychologist has discovered about the general nature of perception and how perceptual abilities are developed.

Third: Reading is a process that must be learned. The laws of learning and the facts concerning such topics as motivation, reinforcement, practice, interference, transfer, and conditioning apply to learning to read. The tremendous body of knowledge on the learning process must not be reserved for specialized books on learning, but must become a part of the reading teacher's professional equipment.

Fourth: As teachers, we are intimately concerned with the readiness of individuals for learning. As teachers of reading, we wish to know the most favorable moment for beginning to teach a child to read and for the teaching of each specific reading skill. The readiness concept is not reserved for the period of beginning reading; it applies to all levels of reading development.

Fifth: The reading teacher needs to understand the sensory processes of reading. Efficiency in reading frequently depends on the oculo-motor habits of the reader. Reading begins with visual stimuli; the eyes bring the stimuli to the reader. Auditory factors, though perhaps not as significant as visual factors, under certain conditions also are determinants of reading success.

Sixth: There are numerous physiological factors in addition to vision and hearing that play significant roles in the reading process. Thus general physical health, speech development, glandular and neurological functioning, and cerebral dominance become of professional interest to the reading teacher.

Seventh: To a large extent at least, the development of reading ability is the acquisition of a series of skills. The reading teacher is interested in how these skills meet the specific demands of both oral and silent reading and how they may best be fostered. The first of these are the word-recognition skills.

Eighth: Word recognition is but one of the basic reading skills. Comprehension and rate are at least as important. Meaning is the *sine qua non* of reading but effective reading emphasizes economy which includes comprehension and rate. These two skills are so interrelated that we speak of them as rate of comprehension.

Ninth: We wish to put the right book in the right hands at the right time. To accomplish this we need to know how to recognize the materials that best fit the needs of each child. A knowledge of readability formulas, which gauge the difficulty level of reading materials, will be useful to us. We also need to know the legibility factors which either promote or hinder reading. Readability and legibility have been studied extensively and the data that have accrued should be useful in detecting and eliminating some of the barriers to effective reading.

Tenth: We know that performance is closely dependent upon motivation. Without motivation learning seldom, if ever, occurs. The reading teacher employs his knowledge of motivated learning to direct children first toward learning to read and later toward reading to learn. Interests are closely related to motivation: they develop from attempts to satisfy basic motives. The teacher wants to know the factors that direct interest toward reading and that attract the child to specific reading content. Effective reading not only creates interests, it can be a product of interests as well.

Eleventh: The children in our classroom differ greatly in personality. To plan appropriate educational experiences, we must understand the nature of personality development and become able to recognize the common emotional and maturational deviations. We are especially concerned with the personality patterns that are related to success or failure in reading. We must know what adjustments can be made for personality differences and, further, how reading may be used to influence personality development.

Twelfth: Learning to read is not an end in itself. Reading must become a tool for learning. Much is known about reading for effective learning which includes a composite of special skills beyond those commonly labeled basic reading skills. Among these are locating and organizing information and planning for its retention.

Thirteenth: In reading for learning each content area requires its own specific skills. The teacher must know the unique reading needs of social studies, science, mathematics, and the language arts. Special problems are posed by the vocabulary, symbolism, and concepts of each area.

Fourteenth: Reading and the entire process of growth and development are interdependent. Data concerning the typical patterns of development of boys and girls, as well as individual differences among members of the same sex, are of particular interest to teachers. Differences among children of the same age in physical, social, emotional, and attitudinal development guarantee that we cannot successfully use a patent-medicine approach to teaching children to read. When we add to the problems generated by these divergencies the tremendous problems stemming from differences in intellectual development, we see why the teaching of reading at all grade levels is so extremely complex and why we must make individual diagnoses and prescriptions for each child.

Fifteenth: We know that, in learning to read, all children do not progress at the same rate. Even among those of adequate ability some meet problems that delay or block their learning. We must strive constantly to discover these deterrents to learning and plan individualized work to further each child's development. An effective developmental reading program is built on a foundation of early diagnosis of inadequacies, careful evaluation of needs and abilities, and the utilization of professionally designed materials and methods.

Sixteenth: After examining these many areas of knowledge concerning reading and the reader, we must find the interrelationships that are involved. We wish to apply our knowledge to our professional tasks. To make wise application of our knowledge, its discrete parts must be integrated.

SUMMARY

The major purpose of this chapter has been to outline the scope and goals of this book. We cannot be content to find out merely what is known about the psychological bases of the reading process. We must go further and learn how such knowledge may be applied to the teaching that we do in our classrooms. Although we must become acquainted with facts, opinions, and principles, we will be equally concerned with applications.

The challenge to improve the reading skills of our children is an important one. Reading proficiency is important to all ages. Both the teacher who has reading as a specific responsibility and the teacher of the content areas must be capable of helping children to progress in reading. It is hoped that this book will help you in the successful performance of your professional task.

SUGGESTED READING

There will be wide variations in purpose among the users of this book. Yet, unfortunately, it cannot be all things to all people. Many of its readers will be teachers, but some teachers are most concerned with the elementary level whereas others are most concerned with the secondary level. And even among its teacher-readers, some will come to it for a first view of the psychological bases of the reading process and others will have a background of numerous courses in psychology, educational psychology, and teaching methods. Thus, some will find it desirable to review principles and theory commonly found in early courses in a teacher-preparation program; others will wish to pursue certain topics in a depth or detail greater than can be provided by a single book.

With these widely divergent needs in mind, each chapter includes a list of suggested readings that vary from those designed to offer background understandings to those planned for the special interests of advanced students.

Since, to a major extent, this book is an *educational psychology* of reading, the chapter list of suggested reading frequently includes, as background reading, a selection from a general textbook in educational psychology. The specific book mentioned was written by the senior author of this book, but nearly any such introductory book in general educational psychology gives an adequate and worthwhile discussion. At least thirty fairly recent such textbooks are available.

Actually most of the readings are drawn from a relatively small group of sources. Generally, the suggested readings have been chosen from sources likely to be available in the libraries of teacher-training colleges.

For the college class or individual undergraduate student wishing to review or to acquire a background on topics in educational psychology, specific readings are suggested for most chapters from a single elementary textbook (Smith, *Psychology in Teaching*). For the graduate student or the undergraduate who wishes to go beyond the elementary text, several chapters have suggested reading from a commonly used advanced book in educational psychology (Stroud, *Psychology in Education*). For the class or the individual student, either at undergraduate or graduate level, wishing to develop a broader view of the fields of reading and psychology, selections from professional journals and yearbooks are provided for nearly all chapters. Most of these selections, however, may be found reprinted in a single readily available book (Causey's, *The Reading Teacher's Reader*).

For still greater depth or breadth of study additional readings have been selected from the *Encyclopedia of Educational Research,* a few specialized text or reference books, and certain professional monographs and yearbooks. In addition, the extensive chapter bibliographies offer wide possibilities for the satisfaction of special interests.

***

For a discussion of the specific understandings of the reading process and competencies needed by teachers at the high school and college level:

Anderson, Harold A., Chapter 13, "Teacher-Education in the Field of Reading," pp. 276–293, in *Reading in the High School and College,* 47th Yearbook of the National Society for the Study of Education, Part II, 1948.

***

For a general discussion of the teacher's professional knowledge, skills, and problems and the place of psychology and, particularly, educational psychology in meeting teacher needs:

Smith, Henry P., Chapter 1, "The Professional Needs of the Teacher," pp. 1–19, in *Psychology in Teaching.* Englewood Cliffs, N. J.: Prentice-Hall, Inc., 1954.

***

For reviews of recent trends and research in improving college and adult level reading (with extensive bibliographies) see articles by Emery P. Bliesmer in the yearbooks of the National Reading Conference for College and Adults (prior to 1958 this was the Southwest Reading Conference for Colleges and Universities). For example:

Bliesmer, Emery P., "Review of Research on College and Non-College Adult Reading," pp. 49–62 in *Research and Evaluation in College Reading,* Ninth Yearbook, The National Reading Conference for College and Adults. Fort Worth: Texas Christian University Press, 1960.

***

For a discussion of the history of research in reading, the influence and extent of reading, adult reading and the materials read, and the psychological aspects of reading (with extensive bibliographies):

Gray, William S., "Reading," "Sociology of Reading," and "Physiology and Psychology of Reading," pp. 1086–1114 in *Encyclopedia of Educational Re-*

search, Chester W. Harris (Ed.), 3rd Edition. New York: The Macmillan Company, 1960.

***

For current discussions of research in reading with implications for teaching, generally with articles by various authorities (with bibliographies) see recent issues of *The Reading Teacher.* For example:

"New Frontiers in Reading Research," Vol. 12, Number 2, December, 1958, and "Research in Reading," Vol. 13, Number 2, December, 1959, *The Reading Teacher,* International Reading Association.

QUESTIONS FOR DISCUSSION

1. How would you define reading?
2. What are the elements of professionalism? What makes one a professional teacher?
3. What portion of a teacher's knowledge may be classed as *professional*? How would you classify his general cultural background and his knowledge of subject matter?
4. A knowledge of what psychological, sociological, and physiological topics would be basic to an understanding of the reading process?
5. What uses do we have for reading? Are different kinds of reading required for different purposes? Explain.
6. How does our American goal of a single track educational system and higher education for nearly all complicate our problem of teaching reading?
7. What are some of the possible reasons for failing to learn to read?
8. Why is a high school teacher concerned with reading?
9. Where may you look for review and integrations of research in reading? What sources?
10. Is it possible that reading instruction in the elementary grades is far better than it was thirty years ago even though we may have far more poor readers in our high schools? Explain.
11. What are some of the special reading skills that should be emphasized during the junior and senior high school levels? When and where should they be taught?
12. Is excellent instruction in reading during the elementary school years likely to result in an increase or a decrease in the range of differences in reading ability among high school students? Explain.
13. List as many as you can of the questions that a study of the psychology of reading should help you to answer.

BIBLIOGRAPHY

[1] Betts, Emmett A. "Unsolved Problems in Reading: A Symposium I." *Elementary English,* 31 (October, 1954) 325–338.

[2] Brownell, William A. "The Growth and Nature of Research Interest in Arithmetic and Reading." *Journal of Educational Research,* 26 (February, 1933) 429–441.

[3] Davis, Frederick B. "Research in Reading in High School and College." *Review of Educational Research,* 22 (April, 1952) 75–88.

[4] Gates, Arthur I. "A New Yearbook on Reading in the Elementary School." *Teachers Service Bulletin in Reading.* The Macmillan Company, New York, No. 4, 10 (March, 1949).

[5] Gilbert, Luther C., and Holmes, Jack A. "Reading: Psychology." Language Arts and Fine Arts, *Review of Educational Research,* 25 (April, 1955) 77–91.

[6] Gray, William S. *Summary of Investigations Relating to Reading.* Supplementary Educational Monographs, No. 28, University of Chicago Press, Chicago, 1925.

[7] Gray, William S. "Reading." *Encyclopedia of Educational Research,* Chester W. Harris (Ed.). The Macmillan Company, New York, 1960, 1086–1135.

[8] Kandel, I. L. "Some Unsolved Issues in American Education." *Educational Forum,* 20 (March, 1956) 269–278.

[9] Keyser, Margaret L. "Research in Reading in the Elementary School." Language Arts and Fine Arts, *Review of Educational Research,* 22 (April, 1952) 65–75.

[10] McCullough, Constance M. "Reading." Language Arts and the Fine Arts, *Review of Educational Research,* 28 (April, 1958) 96–106.

[11] McDonald, Frederick J. *Educational Psychology.* Wadsworth Publishing Company, Inc., San Francisco, 1959.

[12] National Society for the Study of Education. *Report of the National Committee on Reading,* Twenty-fourth Yearbook, Part I. Public School Publishing Company, Bloomington, 1925.

[13] National Society for the Study of Education. *The Teaching of Reading: A Second Report,* Thirty-sixth Yearbook, Part I. Public School Publishing Company, Bloomington, 1937.

[14] National Society for the Study of Education. *Reading in the High School and College,* Forty-seventh Yearbook, Part II. University of Chicago Press, Chicago, 1948.

[15] National Society for the Study of Education. *Reading in the Elementary School,* Forty-eighth Yearbook, Part II. University of Chicago Press, Chicago, 1949.

[16] National Society for the Study of Education. *Adult Reading,* Fifty-fifth Yearbook, Part II. University of Chicago Press, Chicago, 1956.

[17] Scott, C. Winfield. "A 'Forest' View of Present Research in Reading." *Educational and Psychological Measurement,* Supplement on Reading Research, 14 (Spring, 1954) 208–214.

[18] Sheldon, William D. "Reading: Instruction." Language Arts and Fine Arts, *Review of Educational Research,* 25 (April, 1955) 92–106.

[19] Sheldon, William D. "Curriculum Problems Presented by Poor Readers." *The Reading Teacher.* 11 (February, 1958) 175–178.

[20] Smith, Lawrence J. "Research Workers in Selected School Subjects." *Journal of Educational Research,* 45 (December, 1951) 255–273.

[21] Traxler, Arthur E., and Seder, Margaret. *Ten Years of Research in Reading.* Educational Records Bulletin, No. 32, Educational Records Bureau, New York, 1941.

[22] Traxler, Arthur E., and Townsend, Agatha. *Another Five Years of Research in Reading.* Educational Records Bulletin, No. 46, Educational Records Bureau, New York, 1946.

[23] Traxler, Arthur E., and Townsend, Agatha. *Eight More Years of Research in Reading: Summary and Bibliography.* Educational Records Bulletin, No. 64, Educational Records Bureau, New York, 1955.

[24] Wittich, Walter A. "Reading and Audio-Visual Materials." *The Reading Teacher,* 11 (February, 1958) 151–157.

2

THE PERCEPTUAL NATURE OF READING

The teacher must understand the basic nature of reading. Reading is a perceptual rather than merely a sensory process and, as such, it includes more than mere recognition of words. Neither printed pages nor orally spoken words transmit meaning. The essence of meaning comes from the reader's fund of experience. Reading includes thinking as well as understanding. We are concerned with what the psychologist has discovered about the general nature of perception and how perceptual abilities are developed.

Chapter 1 furnished evidence of the vast amount of research that has been done in reading. However, too frequently educational research has been concerned with *"what works"* rather than with *"why it works."* Probably this is as it should be. As teachers we are interested in creating effective learning situations. We wish to help children learn. The fact that they do learn better under one approach than under another seems much more important than why they learn better. But professional teaching is a science as well as an art. We may be content to give first place to the art of effective teaching; but, for highest excellence in our art, we must know also its scientific basis. We must know the *why* in order best to perform the *how.*

In examining the *why,* let us begin with the basic nature of the reading process.

THE NATURE OF READING

It would seem that before we spend the greater part of a textbook discussing reading, we should attempt to agree on just what is meant by reading. Everyone has had numerous experiences with reading: he has read, he has seen or heard others read, perhaps he has taught reading. Therefore one might conclude that forming a definition of reading would be relatively easy. But we know that reading has so many facets that a simple definition cannot adequately encompass all of them.

Reading means many things to many people.The psychologist is interested in reading as a thought process. The semanticist is concerned with meaning and considers the printed page to be the graphic representation of speech. The linguist concerns himself with the relationships between the sounds of a language and its written form. The sociologist studies the interaction of reading and culture, and the litterateur reacts to the artistic nature of the production before him.[49]

THE ROLES OF LANGUAGE AND THOUGHT

Perhaps our first concern should be with the communicative aspects of reading. The term "communication" indicates that reading involves much more than the mere ability to pronounce or recognize the words printed on the page. The purpose of all communication is the sharing of meanings. And it is the symbol that must carry the burden of meaning between the communicators. The symbol is the writer's or speaker's tool for awakening meaning in the reader or listener.

According to Dewey,[10] anything deliberately employed as a symbol or sign is language—gestures, monuments, pictures, totems, smoke signals, music, or finger movements.

James (p. 356) [28] defined language as ". . . a system of signs, different from the things signified, but able to suggest them." The phrase "able to suggest them," emphasizes the relationship of language and thought. If the communicators deliberately use symbols for "things signified," thought must be involved. This is true whether the things signified are suggested by gestures, pictures, or by written or spoken words.

Many years ago Abelard wrote that language is generated by the intellect and generates intellect. Later, Muller (p. 56) [36] remarked: "It has always seemed incredible that language should ever have been conceived as something that could exist by itself, apart from our whole intellectual nature, or that thought, on the other hand, should have been considered as possible without language." And Sapir (p. 235) [43] has said that language is the most massive and inclusive art we know, an anonymous work of countless unconscious generations.

Long ago Kant suggested that "To think is to speak with oneself." And, though we may not wish to go so far as to refer to thought as "subvocal behavior," or the "subvocal use of language," or just simply subvocal speech,[57] the inseparability of language and thought seems to be well established.

Although, as we have seen, the term "language" has extensive meanings, here we will consider it within the framework of two communication skills: "(1) the *expressional skills,* involved in writing and speaking, and (2) the *receptive skills,* involved in reading and listening. Each presents somewhat different problems in the analysis and appraisal of meanings" (p. 175).[22]

Although this book is devoted to the receptive aspects of communication, reception always is dependent on expression. Thus we are concerned with accuracy and clarity of expression as we choose materials that are readable for each child.

THE DIMENSIONS OF READING

The receptive skill of reading certainly involves much more than recognition of the graphic symbol; it includes even more than the arousal of meaning or the gaining of meaning from printed symbols. Effective reading includes experiencing, learning, and thinking. It frequently requires reflection, judgment, analysis, synthesis, selection, and the critical evaluation of what is being read. The reader is stimulated by the author's printed words, but in turn he vests the author's words with his own meaning. And frequently the reader must select one specific meaning from the numerous meanings that he has acquired.[5]

Reading typically is the bringing of meaning *to* rather than the gaining of meaning *from* the printed page. Horn points out that the author ". . . does not really convey ideas to the reader; he merely stimulates him to construct them out of his own experience" (p. 154).[26] Numerous studies have demonstrated that our past experiences form a basis for our new experiences. Thus the one who takes the most to the printed page gains the most. Chall,[6] for example, gave an information test about tuberculosis to about one hundred sixth and eighth graders. She then had them read a selection on tuberculosis and gave them a test on the selection. Those children who already knew the most about tuberculosis also made the best comprehension scores on the reading selection. As Chall (p. 230) says, "We read in order to gain experience, and yet we get more out of reading if we have more experience."

Certainly the printed symbols and the sense of sight are necessary elements in reading. But they are by no means the only elements, nor even the first elements requisite to reading. Experience is the basic prerequisite. For the printed symbols to arouse meaning, recognition and perception must occur. Gray,[21] discussing the reading act, suggests that its dimensions include perception, understanding, reaction, and integration. So delineated, reading is a responsive and an interpretative process. It is indeed a complex process. The entire child, not his eyes or his voice, reads. He reads with his muscles, his senses, his experiences, and his cultural heritage. Thus our study of the psychology of reading must emphasize the *nature* of the reader.

Recognizing the fact that there can be no simple but adequate definition of reading, as teachers we may choose to use a broad, comprehensive definition of the term. We may define reading as *interpretation of the printed page.* In the process of interpretation the reader relates graphic symbols to his own fund of experience. Interpretation requires both *recognition and perception.*

THE PERCEPTUAL PROCESS

Previously we indicated that the critical element in the reading act is the organism's *meaningful response* to the stimulus (the written symbol). Such a response requires *perception.* Hebb (p. 182) [23] has defined perception as a setting up or modification of "mediating processes" in preparation for an adequate response. From first to last, perception includes initiation by a stimulus, preparation for a response (perception itself), and culmination in a response. Reading, in its simplest form, conforms to this same pattern. It includes the stimulus (graphic symbol), the meanings and interpretations drawn from the reader's past experiences, and the response of relating meaning to the symbol.

In reading as in all perception, the arousal of meaning is an integral portion of the process, and the selection of an appropriate meaning forms the basis for an adequate response.

In reading, an *adequate response* demands much more than the mere recognition of the meaning of the configuration of the written word. It requires interpretation through some mediating process that can utilize whatever we see, taste, hear, smell, touch—everything to which we react through our senses. And this interpretation requires information not presently available to the senses: those meanings which, in the past, we have given to various stimuli to which we have reacted. Perception is a cumulative process. In reading, the critical element is not what is seen on the page but, rather, what is *signified* by the written symbol.

Because perception plays such a major rôle in reading, it is important that we have some acquaintance with the theories of the perceptual process.

The ancient Greeks interpreted the perceptual process as one in which "copies" of objects passed down sensory tubes. In the early 1700's Berkeley interpreted perception as *habit* involving both the sensory experience and memories. In later years the phenomenon of apparent movement, generally called the phi-phenomenon, gave impetus to other interpretations of the nature of perception. Motion pictures are an excellent example of apparent movement. The projected images from the individual frames of the film have no movement; the movement is only apparent. Certainly what is apprehended by the viewer involves sensory data not *presently* available to the senses. There is an implication here that, in some way, the incoming sensory data are retained, processed, and reorganized by the viewer. Some intermediary step takes place between the sensory input and the response. This process could be termed a readying or a preparation for a response and as such it conforms to Hebb's (p. 182) [23] definition of *perception.* However, Hebb (p. 187) is not satisfied with an introspective approach to explaining the phi-phenomenon. His explanation takes into consideration the motor effects of perception. He indicates that the conditions of stimulation (the successive projection of the individual film-frames of the movementless images) which cause apparent movement must produce, at some level in the brain, the same process that would be produced if the images actually were in motion. Basing his theory on data from anatomy and physiology and on the subject's responses, he attributes the "apparent" movement to the arousal of the same neural cell-assembly activities whether the retina is stimulated by actual movement of the images or by proper timing in the projection of succeeding still images.

Although the phi-phenomenon emphasizes perception in its relation to visual stimulation only, perception may be generated through other sensory avenues such as hearing, taste, and touch as well. And our percepts (the end-products of perceiving) may vary in their complexity as well as in their origins. An elementary percept such as from a black dot on white paper is dependent almost entirely on the physical characteristics of that stimulus plus the perceiver's physiological functioning which includes brain function and the properties of the receptors. This simple process goes little beyond *sensation.* The more complex processes in which percepts involve values, word connotations, estimation of character and definition of complex ambiguous stimulations, frequently are called *apperception, cognition,* or *imagination.*

The Gestalt psychologists (field theorists) have used the phi-phenomenon to demonstrate that the individual's response is not determined directly by the stimulus. They emphasize that a central process is a co-determiner of behavior.[45] This central cerebral process is a representational process. As Leeper (p. 36) [33] points out these cerebral processes ". . . represent or reflect or 'stand for' properties which may not be present in the immediate stimulus-situation at all, and which are now represented merely because of past learning experiences." Scheerer [46] defines the central processes as the perceptual representation of distal objects.*

In Gestalt psychology two points are emphasized: (1) a central process intervenes between the stimulus and the response; (2) this process modifies the incoming sensory data. The important point is that the organization given to the sensation comes from within the organism.

One group of psychologists sometimes called stimulus-response theorists tend to emphasize habit formation as a basis of perception. Leeper, citing articles by various stimulus-response theorists, interprets their position as follows (p. 35) [33]:

> When the afferent neural materials come into the brain, each discriminable aspect of this afferent material tends to keep its independent and separate existence. All of the discriminable stimulus aspects which act on the organism, shortly before a response is made and a reinforcement is secured, get habit-linkages with the response.

Hebb,[23] though admitting to speculation, bases his discussion of mediating processes on physiological hypotheses. He theorizes (p. 103) that the mediating process consists of activity in neuron groups or in a series of such groups. He refers to the neuron groups, arranged as a set of closed pathways, as *cell-assemblies* and to a series of such groups as *phase sequence* and he uses these terms in discussing the physiological aspects of the mediating process. He suggests that each time an impulse crosses a synapse it becomes increasingly easy for later impulses to accomplish that crossing. He indicates that the increasing ease may be due to enlargement of synaptic knobs or to some chemical change. Although in proposing this theory he states (p. 108) that it is "suggested by present anatomical, physiological and psychological evidence," he recognizes the presently incomplete fund of physiological knowledge.

Cole (pp. 503–504) [7] † has commented on the various views of perception thus:

> Nearly all views of learning, perceiving, and thinking advance the notion of some type of 'trace' in the nervous system. . . . Commonly these traces are

---

* Scheerer distinguishes between the distal stimulus which is the object and the proximal stimuli which are the light rays.

† Cole, Lawrence E., *General Psychology,* (New York: McGraw-Hill Book Co., Inc., 1939).

thought of as some type of change in neural tissue and are usually referred to the synaptic junctions of the central nervous system.

Then he proceeded to disagree somewhat with such views:

It is impossible, in the present state of our knowledge, to secure any support for this simple mechanical view of things from neurological studies. . . .

Outer events do not make their impression on any waxlike substance. On the contrary, they evoke active responses. The perceiving and attending individual is busy selecting, evaluating, remolding his environment. . . .

He adds that, "The evidence which we have examined suggests that there is a great deal of resemblance in all the 'higher' mental processes. All show a determination by the past, and all show constructions, inventions, transpositions" (p. 517). [7] *

Although, as we have seen, there is diversity in the theories of perception and even some disagreement among their adherents, the theories are not necessarily competitive. The divergences in theories lie mainly in the specific interpretation and orientation of each. Actually, this discussion of the general nature of the perceptual process and some of the theories of perception cannot pretend to be either comprehensive or conclusive. It is presented only for the purpose of giving an overview of the subject to serve as a background for discussing perception in reading. The various viewpoints of perception emphasizing, as they do, the roles of representation, intervention of a central cerebral process, organization and modification of sensory data, and individualization of understandings and meanings do seem to be in agreement with what we know of the nature of the reading process. The perception of a graphic symbol must, of necessity, involve a simple perception of certain forms (the printed word) as a means of learning to read. But the more complex perception of the word must come to include the organization and modification of various sensory data in order that a particular series of printed letters (the word) may evoke meaning. And the meanings the word will evoke depend greatly on acquiring "differentiated perceptions of stimuli" (p. 942).[15]

Although the earlier psychologists used somewhat different terminology than those writing in recent years, they noted similar characteristics of perception. Lange (p. 8) [31] wrote: "The mind apprehends outer impressions in accordance with its wealth of knowledge gained through former activity." William James (p. 103) [28] noted that *"whilst part of what we perceive*

---

* Cole, Lawrence E., *General Psychology,* (New York: McGraw-Hill Book Co., Inc., 1939).

comes through our senses from the object before us, another part (and it may be the greater part) *always comes . . . out of our head.*" Lange (p. 21) [31] added that "we see and hear not only with the eye and ear, but quite as much with the help of our present knowledge, with the apperceiving content of the mind."

Many contemporary psychologists continue to emphasize that interpretation is a critical element in perception. For example, Stroud (p. 114) [51] writes:

> The brave who reads the moss on the trees, hoofprints of horses, bent twigs, twisted grass, smoke signals, pictographs inscribed on the face of a rock, is in each case making a similar psychological reaction. He is going beyond the sense data actually given. He is reacting upon the basis of the signal properties of the stimuli. His reactions are dependent upon his optical mechanism, but not determined by it, as are brightness and color; he is 'seeing' with his existing store of knowledge.

Perception is a very personal thing. If a group of persons were to look at the same object, there would be as many different interpretations (perceptions) of that object as there were viewers. Lange (p. 3)[31] said:

> It is a well-known experience that one and the same object seldom occasions precisely similar perceptions in the minds of different people. Of the same landscape the poet's image would differ greatly from that of the botanist, the painter's from that of the geologist or the farmer, the stranger's from that of him who calls it home. . . . And the artist, does he not perceive in a work of art a thousand things that escape the closest attention of the ordinary observer? Has not each of us the sharpest kind of an eye for the objects with which our calling makes us best acquainted?

Munn (pp. 320–321) [37] discusses perceiving in terms of the three interrelated processes involved: receptor, symbolic, and affective. In most perception more than one of the receptor processes (visual, olfactory, auditory, kinesthetic, etc.) are simultaneously activated. However, he points out that (p. 320):

> When perceiving is narrowed to a particular receptor process, such as vision, there is still much more to it than reception. The reception which is involved sets off in turn a complicated pattern of events which represents former stimulation. For example, the picture of a skunk (visual stimulation) may remind us (symbolic process) of how skunks smell, or give us an image (symbolic process) of the odor . . . neural activities aroused by stimulation leave their 'trace' or 'record' in the nervous system. This trace may represent, or act as a substitute for, the original situation, activity, and experience.

But, in addition to the receptor and symbolic processes involved, each perceptual experience may have, also, its affective aspects. Munn continues with, "We not only see an object and perhaps have images of former sensory stimulation, but the object impresses us as pleasant, unpleasant, or perhaps neither." The nature of the impression made upon us depends upon the *tenor* of our past experiences.

It is easy to understand that, due to the personal nature of perception, there are many possibilities for faulty communication between writer and reader, and there is little likelihood that any two readers ever will give *exactly* the same interpretation to any given paragraph.

The simple fact is that our perceptions are determined almost exclusively by our experiences. And everything that has contributed to making the organism what it is influences its response to the printed page.

THE MAJOR DETERMINANTS OF MEANING

To this point we have concluded that reading is a perceptual process and that without perception there is no true reading. *It is through perception that the graphic symbol achieves meaning.* We have discussed the personalized pattern of perception and have considered some of the theories of the perceptual process. The evidence suggests that perception is a form of behavior that results in an organization of incoming sensory data. Perception has biological pre-determinants but its personalized characteristics are due in great part to the individual's past experiences.

It seems appropriate, then, that we discuss further some of the factors which influence perception. What are some determinants of the meanings which the individual will bring to the graphic symbol? Are there ways in which we can help a group of persons to have similar understandings of the materials they read? And how can we reduce "discommunication" between reader and writer? It may be worth noting at this point that much of the discussion of the determinants of meaning pertains almost equally well to the formation of concepts which will be discussed later in the chapter.

BIOLOGICAL-NEUROLOGICAL FACTORS

The biological-neurological factors which were mentioned in a preceding section certainly are among the determinants of meaning. Although meaning must develop from experience, the process is "rooted in biology" (p. 3).[1] And, if the organism lacks the ability to organize the stimuli (Gestaltists), or to develop habit linkages (S-R Theorists), or if there is a breakdown in the "phase cycle" (Hebb), or if no "trace" or "record" is left by the neural activities (Munn), there is little hope that perception will reach a level adequate for thinking, reasoning, reading, or even for simple recall or rote memorization.

CULTURE

The culture in which one has lived surely is a major determinant of what a word will mean to him. Smith states that ". . . our interpretation of what we read, in fact our very readiness to *learn* to read, is largely a function of those human groups and institutions with which we have been associated" (p. 23).[47] Stroud (p. 189) [51] points out that both our thoughts and our everyday perceptions have a social origin. And the stereotype—that socially molded, and often imperfectly cast form of perception—also demonstrates the influence of culture on the meanings which an individual will take to his reading and listening.

Language and culture are closely related. Sapir (p. 69),[44] for example, says that:

> The understanding of a simple poem, for instance, involves not merely an understanding of the single words in their average significance, but a full comprehension of the whole life of the community as it is mirrored in the words, or as it is suggested by their overtones. Even comparatively simple acts of perception are very much more at the mercy of the social patterns called words than we might suppose.

It is obvious that the culture delimits the character of individual behavior.[35] It does this in part by determining the individual's self-concept. A primitive culture passes on a primitive self-concept. And unquestionably the self-concept tends to produce behavior that corroborates the self-concept with which the behavior originated.[9] Behavior may be less directly determined by the actual organic or cultural factors in a situation than by the individual's interpretation of these factors.[41] Thus culture governs the acquisition of perceptions. As Russell (p. 323) [42] has pointed out: "The adult's concepts determine what he knows and believes and therefore, to a great extent, what he is."

PAST EXPERIENCES

The individual's specific life experiences are another important determinant of the nature of the interpretation that he will give to a stimulus. This has been referred to in Munn's (p. 320) [37] discussion of the symbolic process of perception. He wrote, as have many other authors, of the "trace" or "record" which is left in the nervous system. When neural activities are aroused by stimulation of a particular receptor process, a pattern of neural events representing former stimulation of various receptor processes may be set off. These stimuli could, in a broad sense, be termed basic experiences because it is through stimuli that one acquires experiences. Thus the individual becomes a storehouse for his past experiences. Each new experience relates to and becomes a part of previous experiences which, in turn, are the bases for interpretation of the new experiences or stimuli.

The backwoods boy who has known a "road" to be the painfully rocky mule-path along a gullied hillside might give an unusual interpretation of the sentence, "All roads lead to Rome." And, the child who has lived all his life in the city or near a superhighway is likely to take to the lines of the poem, "Let me live in my house by the side of the road and be a friend to man" numerous memories of the roar of speeding vehicles and the odors of gas fumes and speed-heated tires, hardly the peaceful atmosphere the poet intended to project.

Although each child's interpretation of the two quotations will become more accurate as his experiences, real or vicarious, become more extensive, there will always remain some elements of his original perceptions. This topic will be discussed further in the section on veridicality.

PHYSICAL AND EMOTIONAL FACTORS

The physical state of the individual also influences his perceptions. The child who is ill and the healthy, normally hungry youngster will have quite different reactions to such phrases as "hot dogs and mustard" or "turkey stuffed with dressing."

Earlier we referred to the affective aspects of perception. Perception also may be dependent on the *emotive* quality of our past experiences. The word "cave," for example, will be interpreted differently by the boy who has enjoyed security while digging or exploring caves and by the boy whose experience with a cave was one of terror and panic. During World War II it would have been exceedingly difficult for a youngster to obtain an undistorted meaning from a story about a Japanese family if his brother or father had been killed by the Japanese. Leeper (p. 37) [33] points out that "Our representational mechanisms create a psychological environment or apparent reality which seems so real—so inexorably given by our objective environment—that we do not dream that *we* are producing such effects." In fact, the emotional state of the reader may distort, color, or completely change meaning to such an extent that communication becomes impossible.

There is no suggestion here that the factors which influence perception

—and thereby the meanings which will be taken to the printed page—are to be considered in isolation. Their influence is the greater because of their interrelation. Lange (p. 4) [31] said, "Were we in perception chiefly passive, could the things of the outer world impress themselves immediately upon our minds and thus stamp their nature upon it, they would necessarily always leave behind the same ideas, so that a variety of apprehension would be impossible and inexplicable." However, because the individual's interpretations of stimuli (his perceptions) are inexorably influenced by some or most of the factors discussed above, it is obvious that his perceptions can attain only relative accuracy.

PERCEPTUAL VERIDICALITY

The discussion of factors which influence perception indicates that no two persons will have exactly the same perceptions of the same object, or, as applied to reading, of the same word. However, the individual does seem to strive to achieve the closest possible agreement between the realities of his environment and his own perceptions of them. In other words, the individual is striving for perceptual veridicality. Perception, unfortunately, rarely is totally veridical. Due to the various and varying factors which influence it, perception is, at best, an inadequate and approximate representation of concrete reality.

Herrick (p. 340) [25] suggests that the validity of a perception is its predictive value as a guide for action. The perceiver calls upon his previous experience and generally assumes that the perception that was most successful in the past is most likely to be correct now. He interprets the sensory data on the basis of his past experience. When he finds his perception to be in error, he must change his interpretation even though his retinal image has not changed. Weiner,[58] for example, demonstrated that through experience individuals *learn* how to perceive. A cigarette box was moved away from the subject along a distorted wall and was perceived as shrinking in size instead of as receding into distance. As the subject became familiar with the room he gradually began to see the cigarette box in proper perspective and, when he was tested in another experimental room, he did not make his former error. Ittelson and Kilpatrick (p. 55) [27] stated the following relationship between experience and perceptual veridicality:

> When we have a great deal of relevant and consistent experience to relate to stimulus patterns, the probability of success of our prediction (perception) as a guide to action is extremely high, and we tend to have a feeling of surety. When our experience is limited or inconsistent, the reverse holds true.

In reading, veridicality generally is difficult to attain. Words are abstractions that have acquired their meaning from specific experiences. And if the symbolic or affective processes of perceiving have caused inaccuracies or have left deeply entrenched inaccurate interpretation, a high degree of veridicality will be even more difficult to attain.

Pupils commonly make substitutions when they read. Studies have shown that when the good reader errs he tends to substitute words that harmonize with the context. The poor reader, on the other hand, substitutes words that do not fit contextually. Perhaps this is because of the greater variety of experience underlying the good reader's perception. As Norberg has said (p. 24) [38]: *"Given objective conditions and associated retinal stimulation, the observer perceives whatever represents, for him, the most likely prognosis for action based upon his experience."* Thus the good reader's prognosis is superior to that of the poor reader primarily because his experience is superior.

Words permit the writer to share experiences with the reader. The reader does not see nor experience directly the object, person, place, sensation, or event of which the author writes. He sees or experiences them through the symbols that stand for them and evoke his perception of them. There is no direct or invariable connection between the symbol and the datum or sensation. In fact, language does not represent objects but, rather, concepts that the mind has formed of them. Communication through reading is most difficult when the reader's experience is inadequate. And the degree of accuracy of perceptions depends greatly upon the number and variety of experiences that the reader has had.

CONCEPT FORMATION

We have discussed the development of the individual's experience-based understanding as a growth from sensation (the basic experiences) to perception. Perception can range from the concrete and specific to the abstract and generic. At the latter extreme it is properly called conceptualization and may involve categorization, generalization, analysis and synthesis, and insight—all of which are dependent upon experience. Russell (p. 329) [42] says that "percepts, memories, and images are combined into concepts."

Concepts permit a massive economy in communicating and in thinking. Lawther (pp. 365–366) [32] states:

> Successful advancement in the fields of human learning would be impossible without concepts as tools of thought. Only by their means can experience be

labeled, identified, classified, and organized. . . . Unorganized masses of factual material can neither be comprehended nor retained. They must be classified under their appropriate concepts, and mentally filed for use.

Freeman and Conklin (pp. 267–268) [13] extend this idea:

. . . for without the use of symbols and conceptualization, a person's behavior would not be able to transcend the immediate situation. He would be limited to reasoning with the concrete and specific materials before him.

And they later add:

Attitudes can, of course, be formed with respect to a series of rather discrete situations; but if behavior and attitudes are to exhibit the characteristics of reflection and integration, the individual must have reached the level of generalization and conceptual thinking, principally in terms of language and number.

What, then, are we to understand by this important term "concept"? Munn (p. 297) [37] says "A concept is a process which represents the similarities in otherwise diverse objects, situations, or events." Vinacke (p. 527) [55] refers to concepts as ". . . cognitive organizing systems which serve to bring pertinent features of past experience to bear upon a present stimulus-object." In short, the development of a concept requires a distillation of the essential and unvarying similarities from a series of related objects or events.

To form an adequate concept of "dog" there would have to have taken place the activation of some (and probably several) of the receptor processes in response not only to one dog but to several kinds of dogs. Indeed, communication would be seriously jeopardized if John's concept of dog was based on his responses to St. Bernard dogs alone and Fred had had experience with Chihuahuas only. It is necessary, also, that there be a recognition that numerous creatures which bear fur, walk on four feet, and have pads on their feet are *not* dogs.

Smoke (p. 8) [48] suggests that "the *sine qua non* of concept formation is a response to relationships common to two or more stimulus patterns." He adds: "By 'concept formations' . . . we refer to the process whereby an organism develops a symbolic response (usually, but not necessarily, linguistic) which is made to the members of a class of stimulus patterns but not to other stimuli."

Scheerer (p. 126),[46] * discussing the symbolic nature of words, writes:

---

* Gardner Lindzey (Ed.), *Handbook of Social Psychology,* Addison-Wesley Publishing Company, Reading, Mass., 1954, reprinted by permission.

First, the sound patterns come to represent something different from what they are as mere sounds. Second, the word is an expression of generalizing thought which culminates in genuine concept formation. Concepts are psychologically operative when the invariant relationship between the properties of an object, an action, or an idea is grasped, and when the communality of characteristics that is invariant can be abstracted from a variety of changing aspects. This process in turn makes the word a conceptual symbol. The name for an individual object in daily life does not refer to the specific uniqueness of the object; the name signifies the object as a representative of a category—an exemplification of all the possible variations allowed for by its invariant characteristics.

For example, in the development of a concept of the word "house," the child's first understanding of the term (or experience with it) may have been through a picture of a house in an alphabet book. From this, of course, he cannot have developed an adequate concept of the term "house." Ideally his experience should include first-hand as well as vicarious encounters with various types of houses. His understanding of the written or spoken symbol "house" must be broadened through experience so that it includes cottages, mansions, native huts, houses made of various materials and of different colors, and a knowledge that the term implies a structure for people to live in. It also includes the realization that there are somewhat similar structures (hospitals, office buildings) which are not termed houses. His concept of "house" develops from his various experiences with the object and the term. And the impact of his culture will, of course, have an influence on his concept.

Many years ago, Dewey (p. 125) [10] defined a concept as "any meaning sufficiently individualized to be directly grasped and readily used, and thus fixed by a word. . . ." Conversely, one may say that the word evokes a concept. Also, words may be used to express the concepts of one person and stir up those of another.

Lawther (p. 365) [32] has said that concepts organize experience. He traces the evolution of a concept thus:

The earlier perceptions are of gross similarities, which seem to transfer response patterns. Like responses to similar situations do not fit exactly. Readjustments are necessary. Responses that fit are kept; others are discarded. The next similar experience is acted on by the revised responses. With successive experiencing, responses suitable for the common elements gain in development. Responses suitable only for individual examples are discarded. Attaching word symbols to the successively appearing aspects epitomizes the experiences and organizes them into meaning units. There is some evidence that the normal process of forgetting tends to eliminate specific details, but to retain the ideas of the general traits. Rechecking the similar experiences tends to bring out the common aspects in the differing total patterns.

We see, then, that the development of a concept involves two major steps: *abstracting* or seeing the similarities within a framework which involves dissimilarities and *generalizing* or evolving a general principle from the many experiences of the individual. And it seems logical to conclude that the larger and more abstract the concept, the greater is the requirement for wide experience and ability to utilize insight.

PROGRESS IN CONCEPT DEVELOPMENT

Piaget has suggested that the child advances through various stages of concept formation. In the beginning his thinking is characterized by realism. There is ". . . a spontaneous and immediate tendency to confuse the sign and the thing signified, internal and external, and the psychical and physical" (p. 124).[39] The child confuses his own thought with the object itself. At another stage the child has ". . . the tendency to regard objects as living and endowed with will" (p. 170).[39] This Piaget calls animism. A third stage, artificialism, is marked by the tendency to regard ". . . things as the product of human creation . . ." (p. 253).[39] Children commonly conclude that the sun was put in the sky by man.

Although Piaget suggests that specific stages of thought coincide with specific ages in a child's life, this is difficult to establish. However, it does seem certain that there is a definite progression in the development of concepts (pp. 454 ff.).[40]

Children generally advance in their ability to conceptualize in proportion to their experiences, and thus their ability to conceptualize generally improves as they grow older. Vinacke [56] points out that the child becomes less unique and more conventional in the meaning that he ascribes to words. As he grows older, his concepts usually become more similar to those of the people with whom he associates. Here again we see the influence of culture on the development of concepts.

Vinacke (pp. 532–533) [55] summarizes the important factors related to progress in concept development:

1. Increasing age (signifying accumulation of experience) is the single most important variable in concept formation.
2. Progress in learning concepts is a continuous and cumulative affair, rather than occurring in distinct phases. . . .*

---

* Vinacke (p. 532) [55] points out, however, that the research of Werner and Kaplan [64] indicates that: "Many of the immature uses of words show a sudden disappearance or reduction at about age ten to eleven."

3. Earlier concept learning provides a preparation for later development. . . .
4. Among the most important specific changes which take place with increasing age . . . are the following:
   a. Progression from simple to complex concepts. . . .
   b. Progression from diffuse to differentiated concepts. . . .
   c. Progression from egocentric to more objective concepts. . . .
   d. Progression from concrete to abstract concepts. . . .
   e. Progression from variable to more stable concepts. . . .
   f. Progression from inconsistent to more consistent and accurate concepts. . . .
5. Concept formation involves processes which cannot be inferred from either mental age or vocabulary.

Just as perceptions to a great extent are determined by experience, so also are concepts. These three: experience, perceptions, and concepts might be called the triumvirate of understanding. Indeed, within this triumvirate will be found the elements of reasoning, insight, meaning, comprehension, generalization, abstraction, logic—in fact, all the terms that are associated with thinking.

ABSTRACT THINKING IN CONCEPT FORMATION

Conceptualization involves the ability to think on an abstract level. Individuals differ in ability to handle the events they encounter. Some typically seek to form conceptual groupings whereas others deal with events in simple categories.[3] Those taking the first approach tend to think on an abstract level and the latter on a concrete level.

The difference in approach is not dependent entirely upon the maturity and experiences of the individuals. There is evidence that not all individuals, though mentally capable, achieve concept development commensurate to their maturity and experiences. Then, too, there are those who are victims of either structural or functional disturbances such as brain lesions and emotional blockings. For example, studies with aphasics * indicate that frequently they are able to use symbols in a concrete sense but are unable to categorize and thus, to abstract. An aphasic may call a knife a knife only when it is presented with a fork. If the knife is presented with an apple he may call it an apple peeler; with a pencil he may call it a pencil sharpener. When given the Holmgren color-sorting test, the aphasic can choose a red yarn that matches another red yarn but he is unable to select other reds

---

* Aphasia is the loss or impairment of the ability to use or to understand language symbols. It more commonly refers to the loss or impairment of the power to speak or to understand speech.

of varying tints and brightness. When asked to give the names of the animals he saw at the zoo, he may reply, "a polar bear, a brown bear, a black bear, a lion, and a monkey." Each name represents a specific animal and he is unable to generalize "bears." [19]

In their monograph, *Abstract and Concrete Behavior,*[20] Goldstein and Scheerer suggest that the aphasic is incapable of abstracting, of planning ahead, and of symbolizing. He cannot use a word in its generic sense. Young children tend to be like aphasics in the level of their interpretations. A child learning the word "flower" associates the word with a specific flower. Lukina [34] reports that a child, aged 12 to 14 months, associated the word 'ribbon' with the ribbons of her bonnet but not with a ribbon from which dangled a celluloid parrot. The same child referred to a small, pink cup with white spots as a cup, but not to a larger white cup. Liublinskaya (p. 201) [34] comments thus:

> Only as his experience becomes richer does the child relate one and the same word to many different objects of the same kind. . . . Initially, every cup is perceived by the child as a new and special object, whereas later he perceives any cup as a representative of a whole known group of objects; in the particular he sees the general. Later, he will be able, on this basis, to isolate the particular.

The research also indicates (1) that the lower the mental age of the child, the more specific his reaction to a word tends to be; and (2) that the development of facility in conceptualization is a function of previous experience in concept formation. Younger children tend to perceive words as concrete and older children turn more to the abstract features of word meaning. Feifel and Lorge,[12] for example, studied the responses of children between the ages of six and fourteen and found that younger children interpret words on a concrete level and emphasize particular aspects, whereas older children stress "class" features.

Research in the area of reading, too, suggests that there are two general levels of interpretation of stimuli, and that the good reader characteristically interprets on an abstract level. Burks and Bruce [4] studied 31 poor readers and 11 good readers as determined by their being one or more years either below or above the average for their grade on the reading section of the *Wide-Range Achievement Test.* Each of the subjects had an I.Q. of above 90. The average I.Q. for the good readers was 117; that for the poor readers was 101. It was found that the scores for the poor readers on the *Wechsler Intelligence Scale for Children* tended to be high on the Comprehension, Block Design, and Picture Arrangement scales. They suggest that the common elements in these three subtests include: (a) "relative lack of need for long or short term, symbolic memories," and (b) "the immediate availability of a structured stimulus" (p. 491). On the Picture Arrangement scale the poor readers showed their greatest superiority of performance.

Less abstract thinking was required to answer the specific questions in the above three scales than was required for answering questions on some of the other subtests of the *Wechsler Intelligence Scale for Children.* The poor readers performed significantly lower on the Information scale (.01 level), on Arithmetic (.05 level), and on Coding (.01 level). It appears that the poor readers as a group did not handle abstractions as well as did the good readers.

Kress,[29] studying 25 poor readers and 25 good readers, found that poor readers lacked adequate labels for common concepts; they lacked adequate concepts for dealing with reading; and they tended to be more concrete and less abstract in their responses.

Thorndike (p. 331) [52] concluded that reading a textbook paragraph and, to a lesser extent, reading a narrative involve the same sort of organization and analytic action as that which occurs in thinking of "supposedly higher sorts." We may assume, then, that the effective reader will employ most or all of the elements of perception, conceptualization, abstract and concrete thinking, selection, integration, generalization, analysis—in fact, all of the elements which are included in "thinking of supposedly higher sorts." It seems logical to assume, also, that the readers who employ these elements to the greatest extent will be the most effective readers.

The evidence concerning concept formation suggests certain general conclusions:

1. The greater the number of concepts that the reader has fixed through words, the better tends to be his understanding of what he reads.
2. The more specific the reader's reaction to printed words, the less effective tends to be the communication between writer and reader; and the more generic the reaction, the more effective tends to be the communication.
3. Differences in abstracting ability or in the ability to think in categories generally differentiate the superior reader from the poor reader.

As we examined the topic of concept formation considerable point was made of the differences between concrete and abstract levels of interpretation. The ability to form categories and thus to conceptualize seems essential for effective reading. The written word cannot awaken a generic meaning within the reader who is unable to conceptualize. Although such a reader takes a meaning to the printed symbol, too frequently it is an incorrect or inadequate meaning. Let us examine some of the teacher's responsibilities in the development of effective readers.

THE TEACHER'S RESPONSIBILITIES

The important role of perception and conceptualization in reading delineates the teacher's responsibilities for their development and utilization in the classroom.

The teacher must be aware first of the perceptual readiness of each individual child. Only thus can he estimate the child's total readiness for reading—an important factor in all grades, in all subjects, and at all ages. The teacher should know what level of conceptual development he can expect of his pupils. He should be able to determine whether a child lags excessively behind expected development. And when he finds that a child is hampered, he should know how to proceed. He must be able to assist *all* of his pupils toward maximum reading development.

PERCEPTUAL READINESS

Data concerning the perceptual development of poor readers indicate that often they have not learned to notice the details of objects. They tend to have difficulty selecting the common elements from among a group of different objects or finding the essential differences among similar objects.[18] Coleman [8] used the non-verbal portion of the Alpha Form of the Otis Quick-Scoring Tests to obtain a measure of the perceptual age of 33 retarded readers. He compared this measure with the mental age score obtained on individual intelligence tests (Stanford–Binet and W.I.S.C.). He found that 27 of the 33 retarded readers were retarded an average of two years in perceptual age.

Thurstone (pp. 127–129) [53] used factorial analysis to search for perceptual differences between fast and slow readers chosen from a group of university freshmen. He found some evidence that the fast readers excel in word fluency, in verbal associations, and in reasoning. Interestingly enough, he found the slow readers generally superior in sensory judgments and in performance on a "hidden digit" test. This provides evidence that the difference between fast and slow readers goes far beyond differences in the quality of the sense organs.

If we may conclude that perceptual development is a major determinant of reading achievement, what are the implications for the teacher? Of course, he must recognize that certain children will be perceptually retarded because of physical, mental, or emotional inabilities. But he must also accept a responsibility for fostering perceptual development whenever it is possible to do so. What are some of the ways in which he will be able to assist the child toward perceptual readiness? Bruner (p. 148) [2] points out that perception depends on ". . . the construction of a set of organized categories in terms of which stimulus inputs may be sorted, given identity, and given more elaborated, connotative meaning." And he adds: "Perceptual readiness refers to the relative accessibility of categories to afferent stimulus inputs. The more accessible a category, the less the stimulus input required for it to be sorted in terms of the category. . . ."

Although general level of maturation is one determinant of reading readiness, appropriate experiences are essential if the child is to gain a perceptual readiness commensurate to his over-all capabilities. Stephens (p. 366) [50] emphasizes this in the following statement. "Meanings can never far outrun direct concrete experience. At least they can never do so safely. A meaning that is not closely anchored to some clear experience is likely to be wide of the mark."

At best, reading is a second-hand experience. The writer can communicate with the reader only to the extent that the reader has had experiences (real or vicarious) similar to those of which the author writes. Meaning requires at least some awareness of the idea or experience a word connotes (p. 38).[54] Author-reader communication can be greatly improved through rich experiences, real and vicarious (discussion, pictures, background reading, movies and field trips). Only thus can the pupils attain a high degree of perceptual veridicality.

Certainly teaching method can influence the child's perceptual development. To a degree at least, the child will come to see relationships and gain understandings if the teacher emphasizes these aspects in learning situations. In short, we can teach children what to look for.

CONCEPTUAL READINESS

There is, of course, a close relationship, even an overlapping one, between perception and conceptualization. Bruner [2] suggests that categorization is a basic part of perception. Certainly, it is a basis also for concept formation. He (p. 124) [2] notes that "All perception is generic in the sense that whatever is perceived is placed in and achieves its 'meaning' from a class of percepts with which it is grouped." And it has been said (p. 349) [24] that "some conception enters into every perception."

Let us examine some of the general levels of conceptual development that teachers can expect—and equally important, those which, due to children's immaturity or lack of experience, they can not expect. For example, it would be as unreasonable to expect a normal second-grade child to have formed a concept of a term such as "liberty" as it would be to expect the "toddler" to execute the Swan Lake Ballet. Obviously, that is an exaggerated illustration. But the basing of classroom instruction on conceptual developments that pupils have not attained is almost as unreasonable.

Welch and Long, [60, 61, 62] have shown that children normally learn to conceptualize by proceeding from simple to complex levels. In the early years there is concretistic behavior. This is gradually followed by the development of hierarchical concepts such as that all men and women are people. This phase is likely to occur around the twenty-sixth month. By the middle of the fourth year the child should be able to produce concepts of slightly higher order. Potatoes are seen to be vegetables; apples are recognized as fruits, and both vegetables and fruits are food.

Simple size relationships are acquired by the fifteenth month.[59] Gellerman [17] reports that two-year-old children generally have a concept of "triangularity." Wenzel and Flurry [63] indicate that concepts tend to be acquired in stages. Words referring to the present are more easily understood than those denoting the future or the past. Thus "today" may be understood by age two but "tomorrow" waits until about age two and one-half and an understanding of "yesterday" comes at about three years of age. By the age of four most children can distinguish between "morning" and "afternoon." At age five children may know what day it is, and at seven what time it is, but an understanding of the general system of chronology probably comes much later, sometime around the sixth grade.[14]

Wesley (pp. 301–302) [65] points out that we must make a clear distinction between *time* and *chronology*. Children early become familiar with moment, hour, day, week, month, season, year, century, past, present, future, night, summer, late, now, after, again, tomorrow, and yesterday; but until about grade six they show little understanding of events in sequence (chronology). The average child will need to be at least eleven or twelve years of age before he has a fair degree of understanding of time in the historical sense. And it has been suggested that: "Knowledge of the sequence and duration of historical periods is likely to be quite spotty and limited, well into the high school grades" (p. 187).[16]

Wesley (p. 307) [65] suggests that attempts to introduce concepts of latitude, sphericity, date line, zone, altitude, and longitude before grades six or seven probably are futile. Dixon [11] found that as early as age three or four children generally understood the principle of contradiction—for example, the idea that a color cannot be both black and white. Cause and effect relationships, however,[30] are rarely well understood before the age of eight or nine and complex social concepts generally must wait until the sixth or seventh grade. Russell (p. 327) [42] has pointed out that social concepts develop first from family experiences, later from play with peer groups, and that by the fifth or sixth grade adult prejudices and labels are learned.

This resumé of conceptual readiness, although brief, indicates that there are maturational levels of conceptual development that may be expected from children and that a teacher should not expect effective learning if concepts are required that are beyond the child's maturational level. For example, it may be quite unreasonable to teach systematic history before the child has acquired conceptions of chronology or to teach mathematics before adequate number concepts are developed. Certainly, it is quite unrealistic to present symbols in abstract categories before the child's experiences are mature enough to enable him to deal with them.

Knowledge of conceptual readiness must be applied in classroom procedures. A teacher should expect from his pupils the maximum but never the impossible. It's been said (p. 183) [16] that

> . . . a child is likely to be naive and inconsistent, to be sure, but when adults are confronted with unfamiliar problems they make much the same kind of mistakes as does a child. Give him a problem that ties in with his own information and experience, and the child will use good logic within the limits of his understanding and patience.

There are some general procedures which the teacher will follow if he is to assist his pupils to remove those limitations of understanding. Lawther (p. 366) [32] states that "The organization of experience into meaningful material depends upon concept formation; completeness of understanding depends on adequate experience to permit precision and exactness." The word "experience" as used here, certainly includes the structured experience that may be given within the classroom.

For concepts to be taught effectively they must be presented in such a manner that the common aspects or basic relationships will appear in numerous situations and in a fairly prominent manner. To form a concept of "soft" it is necessary that the child discern its properties as they pertain to a variety of objects or terms: soft fur, soft music, soft materials, soft colors, soft fruit. If the term soft were consistently presented in one context, the concept of soft would never emerge. Also it is necessary that he see the term in relation to its antithetic meanings: wiry, loud, stiff, harsh, firm, and with its similar, but not precisely the same, meanings such as gentle, mellow and ripe.

Verbalization of an idea such as the use of the word "soft" (a form of the linguistic response which Smoke [48] referred to as a symbolic response made to members of a class of stimulus patterns but not to other stimuli) is of value because ". . . the use of these word symbols enables him to *think about* things which are not present to the senses, and to communicate these meanings to other persons" (p. 416).[16] Such verbalization also gives the teacher an opportunity to check the validity of the child's concept—a very important step. The same general plan holds true for concept formation whether the concept be of "softness" or such terms as justice, art, charity, holiness, liberty, plus, death, prejudice, four, rhythm, gravity, square, religion, or etiquette.*

In connection with the link between concept formation and experience, Stevens (p. 368) [50] says that ". . . our grasp of those concepts which go beyond our experience is very uncertain and vague. Typically we cannot go many steps beyond concrete experience if we are to understand an idea in a defendable manner."

Lawther (p. 366) [32] suggests that "The teacher should keep in mind that concepts (1) develop through numerous specific experiences from everyday life; (2) grow slowly from the concrete, perceptual level to the abstract, relationship-of-common-elements level; (3) must await educational readiness for learning on a higher, abstract level."

Almost certainly we would all accept a statement that a word not in an individual's vocabulary cannot call forth appropriate meanings. Until the word is known one cannot associate experiences with it. Spoken words acquire their meaning in the same manner that other sounds in our environment become meaningful—a footstep, a scream, or the song of a bird. And written words acquire meaning in the way that other visual stimuli acquire meaning—a table, a bed, or the face of one's mother.

A written word's meaning generally is acquired through association with a spoken word which previously has acquired meaning through the individual's experiences. By such a process the child becomes ready to read. And when the child discovers that printed words talk, his readiness for reading has taken a giant stride.

Although the emphasis here has been that reading development must await conceptual development, the relationship is one of interdependence rather than a one-sided dependence. As reading development progresses, conceptual development will be fostered through the experiences gained from the reading. Actually, the child's reaction to or use of the ideas he gains through reading differs little, if any, from his reactions to what he sees or hears.

SUMMARY

This chapter has sought to define reading by discussing the nature of the reading process. The stress has been on perception rather than sensation and on meaning rather than on the symbol.

---

* There is an excellent discussion of this general topic in Gates, *et al.*,[16] Chapter XIII, "The Development of Meanings," pp. 412–441.

Our recognition of the perceptual nature of the reading process has a number of applications to our understanding of reading. We know that the printed word itself possesses no meaning. And we know that the perceiver's reaction to the word depends on the quality and number of his prior experiences, his ability to reconstruct and combine these experiences, and the general nature of the culture in which he has lived.

We know that perception always involves an interpretation. This is so because words can only "stand for" experiences; they are substitutes that must be interpreted in terms of the perceiver's experiences. Rarely do words communicate perfectly.

We have seen that reading involves meaningful interpretation of sensory data; that this interpretation is greatly influenced by one's culture and one's experiences; and that the interpretation has degrees of accuracy. Interpretation that is consistently on a concrete level and interpretation that is restricted by lack of experience are not adequate for meaningful reading.

The teacher needs to become especially familiar with the levels of interpretation made by any given child. To a great extent, a child's understanding of what he reads depends on his level of concept development. Conceptualization must occur in thinking of higher sorts.

Reading is the perception of graphic symbols. It is the process of relating graphic symbols to the reader's fund of experience.

The symbol without the perceiving individual is meaningless. It is his biological inheritance and his present physical status, his learnings and his immediate environment, his culture and his needs that make a word meaningful. In this sense every reaction to a word is specific to the reactor. Yet, it is these same forces that permit the individual to acquire generic meanings.

The individual's experiences cumulated through the interaction of his physiology with his environment results in his conceptual development. An abstract level of perception requires the summing up of a vast number of sensory impingements. Yet only at this level of perceptual development does one take sufficient meaning to the printed page to allow for true communication via reading.

SUGGESTED READINGS

For a general background discussion of the psychology of reading:

Smith, Henry P., Chapter 11, "Reading, Thinking, and Communicating," pp. 297–327 in *Psychology in Teaching*. Englewood Cliffs, N. J.: Prentice-Hall, Inc., 1954.

***

For a discussion of reading as a perceptual act and an overview of the history of reading and writing, see:

Stroud, James B., pp. 113–122 in Chapter 5, "Psychology of Reading," *Psychology in Education.* New York: Longmans, Green and Co., 1956. (Pages 123–163 of this chapter are devoted to such topics as reading readiness, eye-movement data, reversals and laterality, basic skills, and typography. Since each of these topics is given considerable space either in separate chapters or as major subtopics in your book, Stroud's entire chapter can profitably be read as an introduction to the psychology of reading.)

***

For a brief discussion of theories of perception and a detailed discussion of concepts and their development (with extensive bibliographies):

Gage, N. L. "Perception," pp. 941–945, and Russell, David H., "Concepts," pp. 323–333, in *Encyclopedia of Educational Research,* Chester W. Harris, (Ed.), 3rd Edition, New York: The Macmillan Company, 1960.

***

For an extremely interesting discussion of the nervous system and its mode of operation and a detailed review of the nature of perception, see:

Hebb, Donald Olding, Chapter 4, "The Nervous System," pp. 66–87, Chapter 5, "Neural Transmission," pp. 88–108, and Chapter 9, "Perception, Knowledge and Response," pp. 178–199 in *A Textbook of Psychology,* Philadelphia: W. B. Saunders and Company, 1958.

***

For short journal or yearbook articles on specific topics discussed in this chapter see the following as reprinted in Oscar J. Causey, (Ed.) *The Reading Teacher's Reader,* New York: The Ronald Press, 1958.

Article 1, Staiger, Ralph C. "What Is Reading?" pp. 5–13. Fifth Yearbook of the Southwest Reading Conference for Colleges and Universities, Texas Christian University Press, Fort Worth, 1956.

Article 3, Smith, Henry P. "The Sociology of Reading," pp. 23–28. Fifth Yearbook of the Southwest Reading Conference for Colleges and Universities, Texas Christian University Press, Fort Worth, 1956.

Article 6, Carner, Richard L. and William D. Sheldon, "Problems in the Development of Concepts Through Reading," pp. 226–229, *Elementary School Journal,* 55 (December, 1954).

QUESTIONS FOR DISCUSSION

1. What is meant by culture? How does culture influence perception? Illustrate.
2. What are the implications of the statement "Reading is the bringing of meaning *to* the printed page?" (In regard to the beginning reader, the slow reader, reading rate increase, and the reading of technical material.)
3. How should the socio-economic level and structure of your school influence your plan for a reading program?
4. Discuss the statement: "The whole child reads."

5. What is difference between sensation, recognition, and perception?
6. Illustrate from your own experience the *personal* nature of perception.
7. What are some of the problems involved in determining the *size* of one's vocabulary?
8. Who gets most from a single reading about a topic? One who already knows much or one who knows little?
9. What is meant by "apparent movement"?
10. What is a Gestalt?
11. What do we mean by veridicality?
12. What are some of the concepts we use that come from recent additions to our culture? Show how culture refines concepts (as of time, distance, etc.).
13. What factors within the perceiver determine how an object or a word is perceived?
14. What is the difference between an intensional and an extensional meaning?
15. What are some of the most commonly observed differences between good and poor readers?
16. What materials do we use for thinking?
17. Show how the *concept loading* of reading materials is of concern to the teacher.

BIBLIOGRAPHY

[1] Anderson, Irving H., and Dearborn, Walter F. *The Psychology of Teaching Reading.* The Ronald Press Company, New York, 1952.

[2] Bruner, Jerome S. "On Perceptual Readiness." *Psychological Review,* 64 (March, 1957) 123–152.

[3] Bruner, Jerome S., Goodnow, Jacqueline J., and Austin, George A. *A Study of Thinking.* John Wiley and Sons, Inc., New York, 1956.

[4] Burks, Harold F., and Bruce, Paul. "The Characteristics of Poor and Good Readers as Disclosed by the Wechsler Intelligence Scale for Children." *Journal of Educational Psychology,* 46 (December, 1955) 488–493.

[5] Burton, W. H. "The Characteristics of a Good Reading Program." *Developing Personal and Group Relationships Through Reading.* Fifteenth Yearbook of the Claremont College Reading Conference, Claremont, Calif., 1950, 3–15.

[6] Chall, Jeanne S. "The Influence of Previous Knowledge on Reading Ability." *Educational Research Bulletin,* Ohio State University, 26 (December 10, 1947) 225–230.

[7] Cole, Lawrence Edwin. *General Psychology.* McGraw-Hill Book Co., Inc., New York, 1939.

[8] Coleman, James C. "Perceptual Retardation in Reading Disability Cases." *Journal of Educational Psychology,* 44 (December, 1953) 497–503.

[9] Combs, Arthur W. "Intelligence from a Perceptual Point of View." *Journal of Abnormal and Social Psychology,* 47 (July, 1952) 662–673.

[10] Dewey, John. *How We Think.* D. C. Heath and Company, Boston, 1910 (New York, 1933.)

[11] Dixon, James Cannon. "Concept Formation and Emergence of Contradictory Relations." *Journal of Experimental Psychology,* 39 (April, 1949) 144–149.

[12] Feifel, Herman, and Lorge, Irving. "Qualitative Differences in the Vocabulary Responses of Children." *Journal of Educational Psychology,* 41 (January, 1950) 1–18.

[13] Freeman, Frank S., and Conklin, Edmund S. "From Childhood to Adolescence." Charles E. Skinner (Editor) *Educational Psychology,* 3rd Edition. Prentice-Hall, Englewood Cliffs, N. J., 1951, 255–277.

[14] Friedman, Kopple C. "Time Concepts of Elementary School Children." *Elementary School Journal,* 44 (February, 1944) 337–342.

[15] Gage, N. L. "Perception," Chester W. Harris (Editor) *Encyclopedia of Educational Research,* 3rd Edition, The Macmillan Company, New York, 1960, 941–945.

[16] Gates, Arthur I., Jersild, Arthur T., McConnell, T. R., and Challman, Robert C. *Educational Psychology,* 3rd Edition, The Macmillan Company, New York, 1950.

[17] Gellermann, Louis W. "Form Discrimination in Chimpanzees and Two-Year-Old Children, I. Form (Triangularity) Per Se." *Journal of Genetic Psychology,* 42 (March, 1933) 3–27.

[18] Goins, Jean Turner. "Visual and Auditory Perception in Reading," *The Reading Teacher,* 13 (October, 1959) 9–13.

[19] Goldstein, Kurt. "The Problem of the Meaning of Words Based Upon Observation of Aphasic Patients." *Journal of Psychology,* 2 (July, 1936) 301–316.

[20] Goldstein, Kurt, and Scheerer, Martin. "Abstract and Concrete Behavior: An Experiment With Special Tests." *Psychological Monographs,* Vol. 53, No. 2, Whole No. 239, 1941.

[21] Gray, William S. "Growth in Understanding of Reading and Its Development Among Youth." *Keeping Reading Programs Abreast of the Times.* Supplementary Educational Monographs, No. 72, University of Chicago Press, Chicago, 1950, 8–13.

[22] Greene, Harry A., and Gray, William S. "The Measurement of Understanding in the Language Arts." *The Measurement of Understanding,* Forty-fifth Yearbook of the National Society for the Study of Education, Part I, University of Chicago Press, Chicago, 1946, 175–200.

[23] Hebb, Donald Olding. *A Textbook of Psychology.* W. B. Saunders Company, Philadelphia, 1958.

[24] Helson, Harry. "Perception." *Theoretical Foundations of Psychology.* D. Van Nostrand Company, Inc., New York, 1951, 348–389.

[25] Herrick, Judson. *The Evolution of Human Nature.* University of Texas Press, Austin, 1956.

[26] Horn, Ernest. *Methods of Instruction in the Social Studies.* Charles Scribner's and Sons, New York, 1937.

[27] Ittelson, W. H., and Kilpatrick, F. P. "Experiments in Perception." *Scientific American* (August, 1951), 50–55.

[28] James, William. *Principles of Psychology.* Holt, Rinehart and Winston, Inc., New York, 1890.

[29] Kress, Roy A., Jr. "An Investigation of the Relationship Between Concept Formation and Achievement in Reading." Temple University, 1955, *Dissertation Abstracts,* 16 (March, 1956) 573–574.

[30] Lacey, John Irving, and Dallenbach, Karl M. "Acquisition by Children of the Cause-Effect Relationship." *American Journal of Psychology,* 52 (January, 1939) 103–110.

[31] Lange, Karl. *Apperception: A Monograph on Psychology and Pedagogy,* Charles De Garmo (Ed.), D. C. Heath and Company, Boston, 1902.

[32] Lawther, John D. "Development of Motor Skills and Knowledge." Charles E. Skinner (Editor) *Educational Psychology* (3rd Edition) Prentice-Hall, Inc., Englewood Cliffs, N. J., 1951, 335–373.

[33] Leeper, Robert W. "What Contributions Might Cognitive Learning Theory Make to Our Understanding of Personality." *Journal of Personality,* 22 (September, 1953) 32–40.

[34] Liublinskaya, A. A. "The Development of Children's Speech and Thought." *Psychology in the Soviet Union.* Brian Simon (Ed.), Routledge & Kegan Paul, London, 1957, 197–204.

[35] Métraux, Rhoda. "Anthropology and Learning." Alexander Frazier (Editor) *Learning More About Learning,* Association for Supervision and Curriculum Development, National Educational Association, Washington, D. C., 1959, 21–37.

[36] Müeller, F. Max. *The Science of Thought: Three Introductory Lectures.* The Open Court Publishing Company, Chicago, 1877.

[37] Munn, Norman L. *Psychology: The Fundamentals of Human Adjustment.* Houghton Mifflin Co., Boston, 1956.

[38] Norberg, Kenneth. "Perception Research and Audio-Visual Education." *Audio-Visual Communication Review,* Vol. 1 (Winter, 1953), 18–29.

[39] Piaget, Jean. *The Child's Conception of the World.* (Translated by Joan and Andrew Tomlinson) Harcourt, Brace, and Company, 1929.

[40] Piaget, Jean and Bärbel Inhelder. *The Child's Conception of Space* (Translated by F. J. Langdon and J. L. Lunzer). Routledge and Kegan Paul, London, 1956.

[41] Rogers, Carl R. "Some Observations on the Organization of Personality." *The American Psychologist,* 2 (September, 1947) 358–368.

[42] Russell, David H. "Concepts," Chester W. Harris (Editor) *Encyclopedia of Educational Research,* 3rd Edition. The Macmillan Company, New York, 1960, 323–333.

[43] Sapir, Edward. *Language.* Harcourt, Brace, and Company, New York, 1921.

[44] Sapir, Edward. "The Status of Linguistics as a Science." *Culture, Language, and Personality: Selected Essays.* University of California Press, Berkeley, Calif., 1957, 65–77.

[45] Scheerer, Martin. "Personality Functioning and Cognitive Psychology." *Journal of Personality,* 22 (September, 1953) 1–16.

[46] Scheerer, Martin. "Cognitive Theory." *Handbook of Social Psychology,* Vol. I. Gardner Lindzey (Ed.), Addison-Wesley Publishing Company, Reading, Mass., 1954, 91–142.

[47] Smith, Henry P. "The Sociology of Reading." *Exploring the Goals of College Reading Programs.* Fifth Yearbook of the Southwest Reading Conference for Colleges and Universities, Texas Christian University Press, Fort Worth, 1956, 23–28.

[48] Smoke, Kenneth L. "An Objective Study of Concept Formation." *Psychological Monographs,* Whole No. 191, Number 4, 42 (1932) 1–46.

[49] Staiger, Ralph C. "What is Reading?" *Exploring the Goals of College*

Reading Programs. Fifth Yearbook of the Southwest Reading Conference for Colleges and Universities, Texas Christian University Press, Fort Worth, 1955, 5–13.

[50] Stephens, J. M. *Educational Psychology,* Revised Edition, Holt, Rinehart and Winston, Inc., New York, 1956.

[51] Stroud, James B. *Psychology in Education.* Longmans, Green and Company, New York, 1956.

[52] Thorndike, Edward L. "Reading as Reasoning: A Study of Mistakes in Paragraph Reading." *Journal of Educational Psychology,* 8 (June, 1917) 323–332.

[53] Thurstone, L. L. *A Factorial Study of Perception.* University of Chicago Press, Chicago, 1944.

[54] Vernon, M. D. *A Further Study of Visual Perception.* The University Press, Cambridge, England, 1952.

[55] Vinacke, W. Edgar. "Concept Formation in Children of School Ages." *Education,* 74 (May, 1954) 527–534.

[56] Vinacke, W. Edgar. "Concepts and Attitudes in the Perception of Words." *Education,* 75 (May, 1955) 571–576.

[57] Watson, John B. "Is Thinking Merely the Action of Language Mechanisms?" *British Journal of Psychology,* 11 (October, 1920) 87–104.

[58] Weiner, Melvin. "Perceptual Development in a Distorted Room: A Phenomenological Study." *Psychological Monographs,* 70 (No. 423, 1956) 1–38.

[59] Welch, Livingston. "The Development of Size Discrimination Between the Ages of 12 and 40 Months." *Journal of Genetic Psychology,* 55 (December, 1939) 243–268.

[60] Welch, Livingston. "A Preliminary Investigation of Some Aspects of the Hierarchical Development of Concepts." *Journal of General Psychology,* 22 (April, 1940) 359–378.

[61] Welch, Livingston, and Long, Louis. "The Higher Structural Phases of Concept Formation of Children." *Journal of Psychology,* 9 (January, 1940) 59–95.

[62] Welch, Livingston, and Long, Louis. "A Further Investigation of the Higher Structural Phases of Concept Formation." *Journal of Psychology,* 10 (October, 1940) 211–220.

[63] Wenzel, Bernice M., and Flurry, Christine. "Sequential Order of Concept Attainment." *Journal of Experimental Psychology,* 38 (October, 1948) 547–557.

[64] Werner, Heinz, and Kaplan, Edith. "Development of Word Meaning Through Verbal Context." *Journal of Psychology,* 29 (April, 1950) 251–257.

[65] Wesley, Edgar Bruce. *Teaching Social Studies in Elementary Schools.* D. C. Heath and Company, Boston, 1957.

3

LEARNING PRINCIPLES AND THE READING PROCESS

Reading is a process that must be learned. The laws of learning and the facts concerning such topics as motivation, reinforcement, practice, interference, transfer, and conditioning apply to learning to read. The tremendous body of knowledge on the learning process must not be reserved for specialized books on learning, but must become a part of the reading teacher's professional equipment.

In Chapter 2 we examined the perceptual nature of reading. Since reading, and in fact all types of perception, is learned, we shall be concerned here with the principles that guide learning. Every teacher needs to know and understand how the child learns to read. Effective learning is the only criterion of effective teaching. We must know the principles of effective learning so that we can apply them in effective teaching.

As we study what is known about learning we find a maze both of theory and of suggested practice. Sometimes it seems that the theories conflict with one another. And too frequently educational practice is based on the momentary intuition of the teacher rather than on sound research or carefully considered theory. In many instances the gap between theory and practice is unbridged. Perhaps this is because much of the experimental data is rat-oriented. However, we have little interest in teaching rats; we wish to build effective learning situations for human children.

Actually the psychologist finds it difficult to extend and to apply learning theory to school situations. The basic reason for this is that learning theory must be founded on carefully controlled experimentation, but, unfortunately, experimentation with children is often a complex and forbidding task. Rigidity and control, which are the major strengths of laboratory research, are the very factors that often make accurate research in the classroom forbidding if not impossible. Certain applications, however, can and should be made. Much that we would like to know about human learning is unknown, but surely we must understand what is known.

DEFINING LEARNING

Before examining the factors that are involved in learning to read we must define the term "learning." What do we mean when we say that an individual is learning? What are those elements that are common to *all* learning?

All definitions of learning embody the idea that it requires some interaction of the organism and its environment. In short, experience is a necessary condition for learning. Actually we are unable to observe learning itself; we must be content to infer from changes in performance that learning has taken place. Yet to define learning merely as change in performance would be inaccurate for not all changes in performance are learned changes; performance changes also as an organism matures, becomes fatigued, is injured, or is drugged. For example, an injured baseball player may not swing his bat effectively, but we would not attribute this change in performance to learning. And the log rotting in a stream certainly is changing, but we would not say that it is learning. Furthermore, learning goes beyond current changes in performance. It is a determinant of both present and future performance. What we learn today provides a basis for future learning.

What kinds of changes in performance signify that learning has taken place? Theorists have tended to reserve the term "learning" for changes in performance that are occasioned by experience.

Let us examine definitions of learning that have been proposed. Smith (p. 210) [29] suggests that learning is "the acquisition of new behavior patterns, or the strengthening or weakening of old behavior patterns as the result of practice." Kingsley and Garry (p. 12) [13] state that "Learning is the process by which behavior . . . is originated or changed through practice or training . . ." These definitions tend to focus our attention on the observable behavior that indicates that learning has taken place.

Frequently psychologists identify learning with the formation, strengthening, or weakening of associative connections between stimuli and responses. This focus upon associative connections tends to emphasize the mental process that is involved. Some psychologists say, however, that the development of insights is the critical element in learning. This interpretation will be discussed in more detail later in the chapter.

DETERMINANTS OF LEARNING

There is little doubt that teachers need to be concerned with effective learning. Our classrooms contain evidence of inadequate instructional methods and materials. Too many boys and girls are not reading and many more are not reading as well as they should. We can be certain that at least some of these reading disabilities can be traced to the teacher's lack of understanding of the principles of learning or his failure to apply these principles.

The teacher needs to understand the factors that aid or hinder successful achievement in reading. In this chapter, therefore, we will identify and discuss elements of general learning theory that apply to the specific problem of learning to read.

Laboratory experiments have suggested a number of determinants of learning in general. Do these same determinants influence the child's attempts to learn to read or to progress successfully in reading? For example, what does the research in reading suggest concerning the importance of practice? And are motivation and reinforcement necessary or are they merely beneficial conditions for learning to read?

Hull,[10] in a highly scientific analysis of the learning process, suggests that performance is determined by previous habit strength, motivation and drive, and the amount and nearness of reinforcement. Reading is a performance; it is a performance that occurs in response to a printed page. Furthermore, it is a learned performance. What, then, are the implications of Hull's statements as they are transposed to the problem of learning to read?

Certainly the research in the area of reading indicates that the more reading a child has done in the past, the greater is his tendency to do still more reading in the future. It suggests that when reading satisfies the child's personal needs, in short, when reading is a rewarding experience, he will read. As he does more reading, the act itself becomes more rewarding and thus the goal becomes more immediate. Children, even more than adults, are most highly motivated by goals that are close at hand.

Hull points out that an organism's tendency to respond or act is reduced by certain forces that he calls *inhibitory factors*. Poor health, low physical energy, the amount of energy required by the reading act, and the number of times one reads without reward are general examples of inhibitory factors. A number of specific inhibitory factors have been investigated. We know, for example, that handicaps such as glandular dysfunction, vitamin deficiencies, and nutritional and digestive problems may reduce a child's tendency to read. Studies also have shown that difficult or uninteresting materials may reduce the child's devotion to reading.

Hull has suggested another principle of significance to reading. He states that there is variability in performance. A child does not and, in fact, cannot respond in the same way or with equal efficiency every day. He may bring the appropriate meaning to a word 99 out of 100 times, but once in a while he cannot do so. And, on certain days, a child may not care to read even though the class schedule calls for reading.

As one of the determinants of performance, we must be concerned with motivation. Smith's (p. 211) [29] comments concerning the importance of blocks between motives and goals are pertinent. He writes:

> Motives or drives . . . are fundamental to the learning process. If we are to learn, we must first have some goal and then encounter some block that prevents us from attaining that goal. If we encounter no block—no difficulty of any kind—the chances are that we have already learned the behavior necessary to reach the goal or that we will not learn it until our goal becomes more attractive and more demanding. The block or problem then, rather than the number of repetitions of the experience, is the essential element in the learning situation.

To learn, then, one must recognize that the attainment of a certain goal will prove satisfying. And, equally important, one must identify and try to surmount those problems that bar his way to the goal. The reason that we learn little from certain of our often repeated experiences is that they have included no block to the reaching of our goals.

Materials are learned most easily when they belong in a situation. Relational elements are likely to be perceived as needed and thus as meaningful. Research tends to show that a child learns a word more readily when he needs to know the word in order to understand a passage that he is reading than when it is given as an isolated word to be learned by rote.

Thorndike's Law of Belonging relates in part to motivation. Stroud (pp. 340–341) [30] points out that belonging may be thought of as the seeing of relationships; the noting that one event is caused by or belongs with another. Although belonging is not essential to all learning, it is extremely important for most of the learning that is done in school situations.

There are numerous examples of the importance of both motivation and belongingness not only in the teaching of reading but in the teaching of all school subjects. For example, the learning of the meaning or the spelling of words such as harbor, island, strait, peninsula, and canal is little more than mental exercise when approached out of context. However, when such learnings stem from a need to know, they become both meaningful and rewarding. Even the rôte memorization of multiplication facts is seen as needed when the usefulness of multiplication as a short-cut to addition is fully understood.

We have surveyed briefly some of the determinants of performance—the variables which determine how the child will perform. They influence the child in making the responses needed for learning to read and in performing the reading act itself. If the child is to learn to read, he must make certain responses. If he cannot make the appropriate responses, we can hardly expect him to learn.

The determinants of performance mentioned above—motivation, problems, meaningful goals, and reinforcement—form the theoretical bases of effective learning and teaching. Those and other factors related to learning will be discussed in detail later in this chapter. However, first we should consider a topic which is fundamental to the subject of learning: How does learning take place?

HOW LEARNING TAKES PLACE

In Chapter 2 we saw that true reading is a perceptual process. In this chapter we shall see that it is also an associative process. These concepts of reading are not contradictory. Although the crucial element in reading is what we take to the printed page, learning to read requires the occurrence of a stimulus and a response which results in new associative connections. Let us see how these two views of the reading process fit into the various learning theories.

Explanations of how learning takes place (sometimes called learning theories) generally focus on specific aspects of the problem. Some emphasize the observable actions, some focus on the perceptual process, and others are most concerned with the neural bases. For example, Hull [10] suggests that learning is the acquisition of habits, Tolman [35] says that the learner acquires expectancies, and Hebb [8] proposes that the learner forms cell assemblies and phase sequences. Each viewpoint may contribute to our understanding of the general principles of learning. Let's examine some of these explanations.

Many American psychologists focus their attention on the observable stimulus and response aspects of learning and consequently are called S-R theorists. They suggest that what the organism learns is a response. Generally they consider association to be the basis for learning and in so doing they are concerned with the individual's present needs and past experiences.

Hull, explaining learning as the formation of habits, has developed an elaborate system of postulates to account for differences among individuals as well as for moment-to-moment variations in the behavior of each learner. Since Hull has attempted to account for what happens within the organism (the stimulus trace and neural interaction are important parts of his theory), his theory might better be described as an S-O-R theory. The inclusion of O, standing for organism, emphasizes its motives, goals, previous experiences, and abilities.

Another group, the field theorists (sometimes called Gestalt psychologists), emphasize the learner's cognitive structures and the meaning given by the learner to certain signs. Thus in field theory the response is an indication that "insight" has taken place and that learning has occurred. The field theorists maintain that the nature of the response is determined by the individual's perceptual organization and that cognition is an indispensable ingredient of this organization. According to them the organized structure of a person's past and present experience is a crucial determinant in learning.

Attempting to explain the process of association in physiological terms, Hebb [8] proposes that a system of cell assemblies and phase sequences is developed during learning. His explanation of a cell assembly is most easily shown by a diagram. In Figure 1, cells or cell systems A, B, and C are functionally related. When a stimulus activates A and B,* C is fired. As a result connections are formed between both A and C and B and C. Subsequent firing of A alone may lead to the firing of a new cell X, because X is functionally related either to B or to C.

Hebb suggests that the repeated excitation of cell assembly sequences makes each cell assembly easier to arouse whenever any one of the assemblies is triggered by a stimulus. In short, he suggests that a neural circuit starts operating as soon as any portion of it is excited. Thus, an individual eventually may come to perceive a word or group of words by attending only to certain parts of the word or to only certain words in the group of words. Hebb suggests that initially the growth of cell assemblies and phase sequences is slow, and thinking and learning are tedious. With the organization of elaborate phase sequences, conceptual and insightful learning becomes easier, often being triggered by only one stimulation.

Hebb deals with the development of a structural relationship among neural connections by suggesting that frequent stimulation leads to the

---

* Hebb assumes that initially two cells must fire simultaneously in order to activate a third cell.

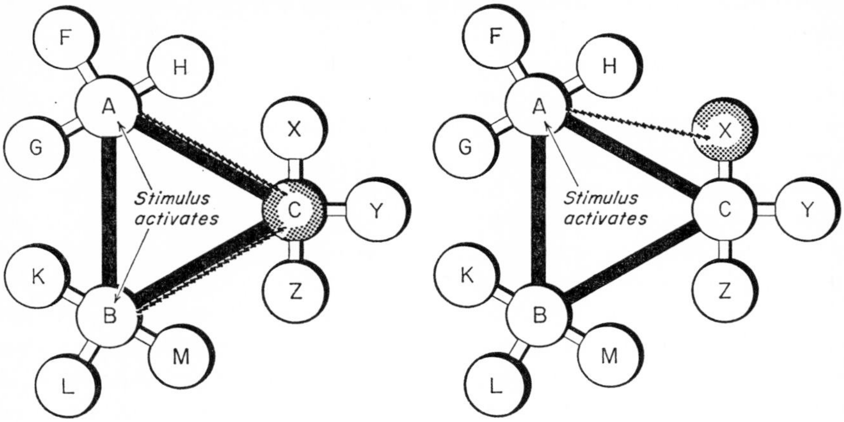

growth of synaptic knobs and that these knobs result in a larger area of contact between the axon and the neural tissue into which it fires. Knobs thus lower the resistance between two neurons and result in an easier transmission of nerve impulses.

Closely related to Hebb's suggestions are those of Donald E. P. Smith [27, 28] who suggests that poor reading may result from faulty function at the synapse. The chemicals, acetylcholine (Ach) and cholinesterase (Che), seem to control the transmission of nerve impulses from one neuron to another.* Ach crosses from the first to the second neuron causing it to fire. The firing continues until Che breaks the circuit by reducing Ach to its component parts.

It has been observed that many readers cannot blend phonemes and have a very slow reading rate even when they know the words. Smith suggests that an overproduction of Ach leads to continuous firing of the nerve cells and to an inability to change rapidly one's locus of attention. To blend phonemes the simultaneous activity of two networks is necessary. Unfortunately, by the time a second circuit has been aroused, the activity in the first has ceased. An overproduction of Che leads to rapid breaking of circuits and to inaccurate perception.

This brief resumé of learning theories shows that there is some disagreement among psychologists as to just what happens within the organism when learning takes place. Fortunately such disagreement as exists does

---

* The endocrine system seems to control the supply of Ach and Che. The concentration of cholinesterase is especially heavy in the axon, the nerve endings, and in the thin hull of the core surrounding the nerve ending.

not preclude general agreement as to the educational procedures that best promote effective learning.

LEARNING TO READ AS ASSOCIATIVE LEARNING

Psychologists frequently have maintained that learning grows from the repeated occurrence of a stimulus and response and that consequently it is a gradual process. The *initial response* to a stimulus might be likened to the birth of a new association; *practice* or *repetition,** to its maturation. Learning thus involves both a stimulus and a response. However, Guthrie, as well as the Gestalt theorists, feels that learning is a sudden process. Their view is that practice merely prepares for learning. Gestalt psychologists suggest that once insight is attained, it is not improved by frequency of stimulation.

Certain concepts are basic to an understanding of what is meant by association. Conditioning is one of these. Pavlov (1849–1936) [19] called attention to what is now referred to as classical conditioning. He found that a dog salivated immediately when food was placed in its mouth. This he referred to as an unconditioned reflex. In a simple experiment, a tone was sounded (conditioned stimulus), and this was followed by presenting a plate of powdered food (unconditioned stimulus). Originally the tone did not bring a salivary response, but after frequent associations between the tone and food the sound alone resulted in salivation.

Shaffer and Shoben [24] show how conditioning may be used in a simple learning problem. If we wish a dog to learn to rise on his haunches, we offer him something that normally causes him to sit up (perhaps a piece of meat held over his head) while giving the command, "Sit up!" In time, the words alone will make the dog sit up.

In both examples learning through conditioning takes place. In the first a dog learns to salivate at the sound of a tone. In the second he learns to "sit-up" at the sound of a spoken command. In each instance a dog responds to a stimulus that previously did not produce that response.

This is what is meant by conditioning. Historically it is a term used ". . . to denote the behavioral fact that a stimulus inadequate for some response could become adequate by virtue of being combined one or more times with a stimulus adequate for the response . . ." (p. 173).[21] This definition presupposes that all conditioning requires some association.

As we examine how a child learns to read, we can see a striking sim-

---

* Based on Kingsley and Garry's (p. 12) [13] and Smith's (p. 210) [29] definitions of learning stated earlier in this chapter.

ilarity between learning to read and learning by conditioning. Generally, for a six-year-old child the spoken word is a familiar stimulus; the written word is the new stimulus. Gradually, with repeated associations between the written and the spoken word, the child brings to the written word those meanings that he attached to the spoken word. Stimulus substitution has taken place. Through association, meaning has become attached to the written word.

Figure 2 outlines the parallels between the learning process in reading and in classical conditioning.

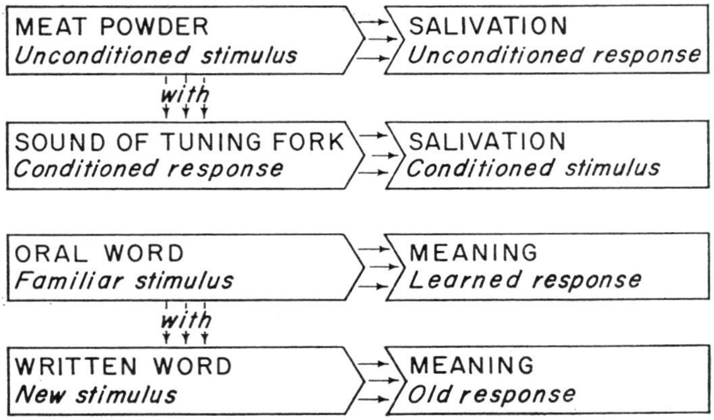

In both learning experiences one stimulus is substituted for another. The dog has become "conditioned" when he makes a salivary response to the tuning fork. A child has learned to read when he makes the physical, emotional, and mental responses to the written word that he previously made to the spoken word.

In 1928 Hollingworth used the term, *redintegration,* to refer to a situation in which a portion of a complex stimulus gave rise to the total response which originally was made only to the stimulus as a whole. In the beginning the dog responded to the meat, later he responded also to the more complex stimulus of the meat and the words, "Sit-up!" Finally his response was evoked by only a part of the complex stimulus, the words. In similar manner the principle of redintegration applies to reading. A child learns to bring to the printed word the same response pattern that was previously evoked by the spoken and the written word together. And even more significant, the written word comes to evoke all the affective and emotional concomitants of the experience suggested by the spoken word.

Association of the spoken * and the written word seems essential in learning to read. Whether learning to read always or ever involves only the classical conditioning described in Pavlov's experiments is not certain. The latter is a special and rather simple type of association. Certainly much of the learning done in the school has properties that are much more complex. This more complex type of learning frequently is described as *insightful.*

The development of an association between the spoken and the written word requires some care on the part of the teacher. For the easy formation of associations, it seems necessary that the child's eyes be on the written word at the same time that he says the spoken word. Guthrie (p. 25) [5] notes that "Many nonreaders among children foil our efforts because they have established habits of looking away from the printed word to which we point." For this reason Anderson and Dearborn (p. 141) [1] suggest that the "look-and-say" method might better be called the "look-while-you-say" method. The Fernald kinesthetic method which includes tracing the word may be useful precisely because it forces the child to look at the word.

Pestalozzi suggested that the written word be accompanied by a picture; others present it with an object. The object or picture is then the familiar stimulus and the written word is the new stimulus to a concept that the child already possesses.

The association of printed words with their auditory equivalents sometimes presents special difficulties. The child may not hear the word correctly or he may not have learned to pronounce it accurately. In such cases a child may not readily associate the word with his background experiences. Also he may not know the precise meaning of the word as it is used in the materials that he is expected to read. Thus the formation of correct associations between the spoken word and the written word depends on the child's ability to hear and to speak as well as upon the general richness of his experiences with the word in its various meanings.

As we have examined the problem here, it appears that the act of learning to read is very much an associative process. Learning to read requires an association of a stimulus and a response.

PRACTICE AND LEARNING

We have seen that, if a child is to learn, he must make at least one response to a stimulus. To this extent practice is necessary for all learning.

---

* The association also may be between the written word and a firsthand experience, a picture, or any activity or object that arouses the appropriate meaning.

However, rarely is learning completed with but one experience. Children generally require numerous experiences with a word in order to learn it. Thorndike recognized the need for practice when he first proposed the Law of Exercise some half century ago. Later in his 1930 edition of *Educational Psychology,* he discussed the place of exercise:

> When a modifiable connection is made between a situation and a response, that connection's strength is, other things being equal, increased. . . . When a modifiable connection is not made between a situation and response during a length of time, that connection's strength is decreased (pp. 2–4).[32]

This law asserts that practice is necessary for learning and that when practice is discontinued, performance deteriorates. Thorndike's law of exercise sometimes is called the law of "use and disuse."

Thorndike recognized, however, that practice is not the sole determinant of learning. Practice does not itself *cause* learning. It is important only because of the conditions that operate during practice. He recognized that improvement in performance requires certain motivations. He listed these as interest in one's work; interest in improving oneself; the significance of the material for the learner; the learner's attentiveness to the situation; and, finally, a problem-solving attitude.

THE EFFECTS OF PRACTICE

Certainly not all stimuli result in learning, but all learning seems to require both a stimulus and a response. For learning to occur, the stimulus must somehow pose a problem that requires us to respond. A response is a practice. This much seems clear. The specific effects of practice are perhaps not so clear. As teachers we ask a number of questions concerning the effects of practice. We wish to know whether equal amounts of practice tend to increase or decrease individual differences in achievement between bright and dull children and whether massed or spaced practice is preferable.

Numerous investigations have been made of these problems and a variety of somewhat contradictory data has been obtained. Whenever improvement is shown as a percentage of the original performance, the answer has always been that differences between bright and dull children decrease as a result of practice. Unfortunately, when the amount of initial difference between A (good performer) and B (poor performer) is compared with the gross amount of difference after practice, A ordinarily will have put a greater distance between himself and B. Stroud (p. 383) [30] has pointed out that, in general, equalizing practice has been found to increase individual differences in performance except in experiments in which the results are expressed *erroneously* as when percentage of gain is used as the criterion.

The complexity of the response to be learned also must be considered. When the behavior that is to be acquired is so simple that both the good and the poor performers can achieve mastery, the differences decrease with practice and the variability within a group of learners becomes less. If the task is complex the slow tend to stand still while the gifted advance and the variability in the group increases.

EDUCATIONAL SIGNIFICANCE OF PRACTICE

As teachers our major question concerning practice is how the child's time can best be used. The evidence seems to indicate that distributed practice is generally superior to massed practice. This is especially true for the learning of motor skills such as typewriting, skating, and dancing. And learning that is gradual and spaced seems to be retained for a longer period of time. True, cramming right before an examination is effective if one wishes to acquire a lot of information in a short time and for an immediate purpose only, but retention is poor and transfer to later tasks seems to be minimized.

In planning the effective learning situation, the teacher must make numerous decisions concerning the most valuable use of classroom time. Sometimes, as in the case of practice on a school play or in the learning of a poem, interest would be lost if the learning were spread over too long a time. But for most classroom learning, distributed practice offers more advantages. By using frequent short examinations rather than infrequent longer ones, we can guarantee that practice will be spread over a longer period of time. And we distribute practice as well as encourage recall when we see that the child uses previous learning to attack new problems. For example, in the primary grades we teach the child to use initial sounds and endings of words as a cue to pronouncing new words. Rather than spending one long period of time in learning all these sounds, the effective teacher distributes their learning over many weeks, introducing one initial sound every day or two and seeing that the child develops his understanding of them by letting him give the initial sound and the ending of various words. Similarly, teachers find that distributed practice is most effective in teaching large units such as the names and properties of the various elements studied in a chemistry class or in teaching foreign language vocabulary.

There have been many suggested explanations of why distributed practice is and should be better than massed practice. Certain of these explanations appear to have educational significance. Massed practice, especially if kept up for any amount of time, tends to become fatiguing and boring. Both fatigue and decrease in motivation result in lowered performance.

Finally, the teacher should be aware that not all children need the same amount nor even the same kind of practice. Underwood's [37] study indicates that there are genuine differences between fast and slow learners in the effectiveness of distributed practice. With slow learners distributed practice frequently is less effective than massed practice.

This point needs clarification. It is quite conceivable that the slow learner may need more time to gain a framework of understanding. His memory span generally is not good; and, when he is interrupted, he has difficulty in recovering the mental set and the motivation that are necessary for effective learning. Studies suggest that he is not as easily bored by repetition and drill. For him each repetition is a new experience because on the first exposure he became aware of but few of the available relationships and ideas. He may find it necessary to read a paragraph several times whereas the fast learner generally profits little from a second reading.

Actually, the slow learner needs a longer period of time to become aware of relationships or belongingness. If his learning is interrupted before he has had the time to profit from the experience, it is hardly possible for him to attain insight.

One of the causes of poor reading is that the pupil frequently is given too much to learn. We advance his learning tasks faster than his capabilities will allow. Inadequate learnings are confusing. By tailoring the slow-learner's task to his ability, more is accomplished in the long run. The learner needs to complete a task. To gain a feeling of success he needs to find solutions to the problems he encounters.

GENERALIZATIONS REGARDING PRACTICE

The teacher of reading must learn to use practice to promote learning. The learning situation must be structured so that practice is suited to the needs and the abilities of the individual child. Practice is necessary for learning, but it must be motivated practice. The following characteristics of practice are worth considering:

1. Practice does not itself cause learning, it merely provides time for whatever does cause learning.
2. In general, distributed practice is more efficient than massed practice.
3. Members of a group tend to keep the same relative position during practice.
4. Members of a group tend to become more different rather than more alike as a result of practice.

5. Generally, the greater a child's rate of learning, the less practice is necessary for learning to read.

REINFORCEMENT

For the S-R theories of learning, the Law of Exercise (Practice) is a significant learning principle. However, Thorndike recognized that still other factors must be considered.* His Law of Belonging has already been mentioned, but perhaps most important for current psychological theory is his Law of Effect. It reads:

> When a modifiable connection between a situation and a response is made and is accompanied or followed by a satisfying state of affairs, that connection's strength is increased; when made and accompanied or followed by an annoying state of affairs, its strength is decreased (p. 4).[32]

At the time of the formulation of this law in 1913 Thorndike conceived of pleasure and pain as opposites in their influence on learning. His interpretation of the Law of Effect seems to have implied a large element of "affect." In later years he became convinced that either reward or punishment may reinforce behavior.

The Law of Effect has gradually evolved toward an emphasis on reinforcement. Hull has maintained that without reinforcement learning does not take place. Thorndike introduced the principle of "multiple response" to account for the initial occurrence of the correct act. He suggested that the organism uses a trial and error approach until it hits upon the correct response. This correct response tends to be repeated because of the operation of the Law of Effect (Reinforcement).

Stimulus-Response theorists are not in complete agreement among themselves as to whether or not reinforcement is always required for learning. Guthrie implies that contiguity of association is sufficient. Mowrer (p. 416 ff.) [16] and Skinner,[26] although emphasizing the importance of reinforcement for most forms of learning, deny that it is necessary for all learning.

Lewin, the field theorist, suggests that if the teacher wishes to get a pupil to learn, he must place learning between the pupil and his goal.

We have already seen that through association the printed word becomes a substitute for the spoken word. This is the initial step in learning to read. Reinforcement theorists maintain that before the printed word

* Because motivation is the central theme of a separate chapter, we introduce it in this chapter only when it is essential to the present discussion.

can become an adequate substitute for the oral word, reinforcement must occur.

THE NATURE OF REINFORCEMENT

The various learning theorists differ somewhat in their explanations of the exact nature of reinforcement. Hull identified reinforcement with physiological drive reduction; Guthrie, with the termination of stimulation; Tolman, with the confirmation of expectancies; and Sheffield, with consummatory responses. Stroud (p. 346) [30] writes:

> A drive is a condition of want, need, anxiety, and so on that arouses activity and demands satisfaction or reduction depending upon its strength. Thus the satisfaction of a motivating condition is, of necessity, rewarding. Furthermore, the only mechanism of rewarding an act is by the satisfaction of a motivating condition.

Hebb and Bugelski base their explanation on the findings of neurology and physiology. In fact, Bugelski defines motivation as a disturbance of the normal rhythms of the brain (p. 260).[3] When this neural disturbance is terminated, the drive or motivation dissipates and reinforcement occurs.

TOLMAN'S THEORY

There are a number of suggested explanations or theories as to why reinforcement operates as it does. Tolman's is one of the best known.[35] He suggests that the learner *expects* the meaning to "appear" when the printed word is presented on subsequent trials. If it does appear, the learner's expectancy is "confirmed."

Expectancy is represented by $S_1R_1S_2$ much as an association is represented by S-R. The following example illustrates how an expectance is formed. "When this *button* (S_1) is pressed (R_1), I *expect* to hear the ringing *doorbell* (S_2)" (p. 446).[9] When the bell rings, my expectancy is confirmed and the attractiveness (cathexis) of the button is increased. The next time one wishes to ring the doorbell, he pushes the button. Thus the incentive power of the doorbell (its valence) will depend on one's need to ring the doorbell as well as on the cathexis of the button.

Tolman's theory is supported by certain experimental evidence. Tinklepaugh,[34] for example, found that a monkey, when "expecting" a banana, rejected a lettuce leaf although usually he was well satisfied with it. Woodworth cites the seeking behavior of a dog (p. 41).[41]

That there is a persistent inner tendency towards the consummatory reaction is seen when, for instance, a hunting dog loses the trail; if he were simply carried along from one detail of the hunting process to another by a succession of stimuli calling out simple reflexes, he would cease hunting as soon as the trail ceased, or follow it back again; whereas what he does is to explore about, seeking the trail, as we say. This seeking, not being evoked by any external stimulus (but rather by the absence of external stimulus), must be driven by some internal force; and the circumstances make it clear that the inner drive is directed toward the capture of the prey.

Tolman's expectancy theory posits that in the presence of certain signs we expect to find a certain goal if we follow our customary behavior route. We learn what leads to what. If we do this, we may expect this to happen. If, as expected, we reach our goal, our behavior is confirmed. If we do not, we must vary our behavior. According to this point of view, immediate knowledge of results becomes important to learning. Confirmation of correct responses tends to perpetuate them and knowledge of incorrect responses should lead the pupil to vary his behavior until correct responses are obtained.

SECONDARY REINFORCEMENT

Psychologists have tried repeatedly to explain how drives can become attached to objects. Wolfe [39] trained chimpanzees to obtain grapes by inserting a poker chip in a vending machine. The chimps learned to value the chips and, in a later experiment, Cowles [4] found that the chips alone could be used to motivate learning. The poker chips had indeed taken on some of the qualities of primary motivation and reinforcement. A chimp, for example, would learn "position habits" * for tokens.

These and other experiments have demonstrated that when a stimulus has been associated with a primary reinforcer, the stimulus may itself become a reinforcer. Whenever this occurs, it is customary to speak of secondary reinforcement.

Reinforcement certainly offers some explanation of the child's learning to read. In the beginning he wishes to read because he wants to know how, because his brothers and sisters read, because his parents want him to learn to read, or because learning to read is the acceptable group activity of his

* In two-position learning the chimp must locate a token in one of two cups. The cups themselves are in separate wooden boxes closed by a horizontal lid. In five-position learning there are five wooden boxes. The tokens apparently are adequate incentives. The chimps learn not only the rather simple right and left position of the box containing the token, but also the much more complicated problem required in the five-box arrangement.

class. For the motivating condition to be satisfied, he reads. Gradually, reading may become a secondary reinforcer. When it does so, reading becomes an interest in itself. Although a later chapter discusses reading as an interest, we can see here that a part of the process by which it becomes an interest is secondary reinforcement.

INCENTIVES

Through the teacher's knowledge of the theoretical bases for effectual teaching and learning (the *Why*) comes his understanding of the value of certain procedures in the classroom. For example, he comes to realize how the principles of reward and incentives may become operative for effective learning (the *How*).

We know that motivation plays an important role in learning. A child's early speech responses, for example, are rewarded in many ways. At first, he speaks to get the esteem and recognition that satisfy his own special needs. He gains social approval or his physical demands are satisfied. Gradually, other less direct incentives become sufficient, and indeed the drive to speak eventually becomes self-sustaining. Stroud writes (p. 173) [30]:

> . . . inward drives that have little to do directly with social approval or the satisfaction of bodily needs seem to come into the picture. Such a child may talk when alone or when no one is listening, or about things that seem to have nothing to do with the satisfaction of his primary needs.

Ryans [22] suggests that rewards and punishments, praise and blame, group recognition, and knowledge of progress may be used as incentives for learning. In general, studies [11, 31, 40] have shown that praise is a somewhat more powerful incentive than blame, but that blame seems to reinforce more strongly than no recognition at all. Actually, both praise and blame if overdone tend to lose their power. Smith points out that "Both praise and blame, like certain drugs, lose their effectiveness as we become tolerant of them, but our tolerance varies in relation to the individual from whom we receive them" (pp. 200–201).[29]

Menchinskaya (pp. 190–191) [15] after stating that censure and approval, in themselves, have no real significance, adds:

> . . . these become important only when the pupil understands *why* his reply received a particular evaluation.
>
> In contemporary psychological literature, a great deal of attention is paid to the so-called 'law of effect,' which is regarded as the basis of learning. It is taken to imply the necessity of reinforcing the pupil's correct or incorrect actions by means of approval or censure. But, in the treatment of this law, an

extremely important point is ignored, namely that the real power of 'reinforcement' is only brought to bear when knowledge of a result is accompanied by understanding of the reason for the evaluation.

Thompson and Hunnicutt [31] report that praise resulted in greater improvement with introverted children, but that blame was more powerful with extroverted children. Sims [25] found that individual motivation was a stronger incentive than group motivation but that group rivalry was better than none.

Ryans [22] has observed that *knowledge* of one's success or progress facilitates learning. Success generally leads to a desire for more success; failure leads to a fear of further failure. However, the extent to which knowledge of success improves learning depends largely upon the needs of the child to find success in the specific task in which he is engaged. And, the feeling of success that accompanies any given performance depends greatly upon the level at which the child is expected to perform.

Numerous other incentives may play a role in the learning situation. Briggs,[2] for example, found that students were most influenced by friendly conferences, public commendation, praise, encouragement, and by being excused from work. It seems also that helping students to identify definite goals, helping them to develop appropriate attitudes, encouraging a set for learning and frequent evaluation of progress are all helpful motivating devices.

Some general conclusions can be drawn from what is known of the effect of incentives. The child strives for goals that appear likely to satisfy one or more of his needs. He will learn when he must do so to reduce his physical drives, when it will satisfy his need for security, self-esteem or the esteem of others, when his curiosity is aroused, or when his habit motives demand satisfaction.

GOALS AS INCENTIVES

Goals and incentives are much the same thing so long as the goals are set by the child himself. The teacher can help each child identify personal reading goals, but he cannot give ready-made goals to the child and expect them to be attractive merely because society generally thinks them to be worthwhile. "Goals are *defined objectives* which the individual seeks to attain" (pp. 295–296).[22] Goals, to be effective, must seem achievable to the child. They must be within his ability. A goal, no matter how attractive, can operate as an incentive only when the child sees it as attainable.

Obviously children differ greatly from one another. This in itself is sufficient reason to dissuade the teacher from setting up the same goal or incentive for all children. Some children strive for praise, the esteem of others, or high test marks; other children are most stirred by blame, by low test marks, or even by the disapproval of others. What is rewarding to one child may not be rewarding to another child, or at least not to the same extent. Many social and emotional phenomena are explained on this basis. For example, you chose the teaching profession because you have certain incentives and goals. These might not appeal at all to the industrialist, the military man, the truck driver, or the comedian.

IMMEDIACY OF REWARD

The immediacy of reward, sometimes referred to by psychologists as the gradient of reinforcement, is another concept of interest to teachers. Reinforcement is effective in direct proportion to its nearness to the response. "Closeness to the goal is an important factor in learning, and learning behavior is facilitated as the goal is more closely approached" (p. 325).[22] Children, especially, strive hardest for goals that are close at hand. The chances are that the further the child is removed from the attainment of his goal, the less will be his interest in reaching it. This, of course, has many implications for teaching. The child works far harder for a word of praise attainable *now* than he works toward a college degree which is many years in the future.

TRANSFER OF LEARNING

No educator questions the importance of transfer of learning. If transfer were not possible, the learner would have to acquire new behavior for each new situation. The important questions are how, when, where, and why transfer occurs. Unfortunately too often the learnings of the classroom seem designed only for use within the classroom. They do not appear to fit directly into life situations. In short, they lack belongingness and have little influence on the out-of-school behavior of the learner.

Transfer may be defined as the effect of previous learnings upon our later proficiency under different conditions or upon the ease with which we later acquire some other performance. In short, it is the application of our previous learnings to our current problems.

As we study transfer we wish to know what effect the learning done in one circumstance will have on performance in other circumstances. Transfer is said to have occurred when something that is learned affects later relearning of the same thing or the acquisition of new responses. When one utilizes his past experience in reacting to a situation that has in it some element of newness, we conclude that there has been transfer of learning.

The learner originally makes specific responses to specific stimuli. When he learns to apply these responses in other situations, he has generalized his behavior. This generalization of behavior is a most important kind of transfer. Frequently generalization and transfer are used synonymously. Judd (p. 441) [12] pointed out that

> . . . mental development consists . . . in equipping the individual with the power to think abstractly and to form general ideas.
>
> When the ends thus described are attained, transfer . . . has taken place because it is the very nature of generalization and abstraction that they extend beyond the particular experiences in which they originate.

The experimental evidence offers no support for a belief once commonly held that the mind is strengthened or the memory is improved merely by *exercise* such as memorizing poetry or factual material. The muscles of the body may thus be strengthened but not the organs of the mind. Learning experiences are rather specific in their educational values. Learning to reason in mathematics is somewhat different from learning to reason in social sciences. This holds also for the development of reading ability. In the past, reading programs tended to be based on an assumption that the child develops a general reading ability. Unfortunately, it has been found that a child may be a far better reader in one area than in another.

However, even though educational experiences do not result in a general strengthening of the mind or even in the general development of specific faculties such as memory and ability to reason, transfer of learning has tremendous educational significance. Somehow the learnings acquired in our classrooms must be made to transfer to later and often quite different problems. And we know that such transfer is possible. As teachers we wish to know how to guarantee that a maximum amount will occur.

GENERAL NATURE OF TRANSFER

In seeking to understand transfer, psychologists have recognized that there are numerous levels at which transfer may or may not operate. Generally it has been accepted that specific skills and knowledge transfer readily from one situation into another of the same type. For example, knowledge of how to subtract and how to spell specific words should transfer directly from the school to life. However, the transfer of broad understandings, methods of attacking problems, general scholarly habits, and scientific attitudes from one school subject to another and from school to life situations is much more difficult to guarantee.

Thorndike once suggested that all learning is specific and that such generalization as occurs is merely a by-product of new learning that is similar in some way to old or previous learning. On the other hand Harlow [7] speaks of learning how to learn. Under certain circumstances it appears that a general learning skill may transfer.

There is also a vast middle ground between the direct transfer of specific knowledge or skills and the transfer of complex understandings and scholarly habits or attitudes to quite different situations. For example, it seems well established that a child's facility in attacking new words improves as he amasses experience in word attack. And an ability to develop new concepts is positively related to the number and complexity of concepts one already has acquired. Also we know that a child reads most effectively in the area in which he has had the most experience. Let us examine some of the more specific rules governing transfer and then seek to define the relationships between transfer and such topics as insight, generalization, and meaning.

EFFECTS OF TRANSFER

Unfortunately transfer does not always operate to favor learning. Poffenberger [20] has suggested that where no identical bonds existed between two processes no transfer would take place; where there were identical processes, transfer would be positive; and when the learning of the new process necessitated the breaking of a previous bond, the transfer would be negative and interference would occur. Positive transfer has been interpreted as a phase of stimulus generalization. If stimulus A leads to response B, then other stimuli A_1, A_2, similar to A will also tend to lead to B. On the other hand, if we have learned that stimulus A should lead to response B and are forced to learn that A no longer leads to B but now requires a new response C, we find negative transfer. In positive transfer the stimulus is changed, but the response called for is within the repertory of the organism's behavior; in negative transfer the organism must learn a new response to an old stimulus. Naturally, the closer the new situation is to the original training situation, the greater are the chances that the training will be applied. It is also true that the more dissimilar the new stimuli A_1 and A_2 are from the original stimulus A, the less are the chances of transfer.

INSIGHT AND TRANSFER

As we have seen previously, Gestalt psychology emphasizes the place of insight in learning. Insight involves the seeing of relationships. It is a reorganization of mental process (p. 41).[8] It is a recombination of pre-existent perceptions. The Gestaltists do not use the term "insight" as an explanation of what takes place in learning. Koehler says that the concept of insight is used in a "strictly descriptive fashion" (p. 342).[14] Yerkes[42] in 1927 listed the evidences for insight and from these Hilgard (p. 238)[9] selected the following items as most indicative of insightful behavior:

> *First,* the interruption of movement for a period, referred to by Yerkes as one of survey, inspection, attention, followed by a critical solution. . . . *Second,* the ready repetition of the solution after a single critical solution. . . . *Third,* solution with insight should be generalized to new situations that require mediation by common principles, or awareness of common relationships.

That insightful behavior does occur is generally accepted. There is considerable lack of agreement, however, as to whether or not all human learning is insightful.

Hilgard (pp. 234–237)[9] makes the following observations:

1. A more intelligent organism is more likely to achieve insight. . . . Thus older children are more successful at insight problems than younger ones . . . and apes more successful than guinea pigs.
2. An experienced organism is more likely to achieve insightful solutions than a less experienced one. . . . Thus, a child cannot get insight into a mathematics problem stated symbolically unless he understands the conventional signs, even if the problem is otherwise suited to his capacity.
3. Some experimental arrangements are more favorable than others for the elicitation of insightful solution. . . . [The nature of the *environment* as well as the nature of the learner is a factor in the occurrence of insight. For example if the various parts needed for the solution are arranged so that they can be seen at the same time, insight is most likely to occur.]
4. Trial-and-error behavior is present in the course of achieving insightful solution. . . . [Before achieving insight, the learner may do considerable searching for a solution. This may appear to be relatively blind trial and error but for the more intelligent learner it is likely to be the trying out of various hypotheses.]

For insightful solutions to occur past experiences must be utilized. Somehow a transfer of past learnings must be made to a present problem. Relationships must be seen among past and present events so that generalizations may result. Meaningfulness always depends both on prior learning and on the perceiving that the prior learnings *belong* in the present situation.

GENERALIZATION

Studies on transfer have stressed the value of generalization. Generalization provides for applications to new learning situations. The child who has learned the principles of word attack and can generalize can apply those principles in learning to identify new words. Unfortunately, not all learning is transferred even when identical elements are present. For transfer to occur the learner must perceive the identities. He must *recognize* that the new situation is similar to the situations for which he learned the behavior. The more intelligent the child, the more likely he is to perceive relationships between new and old situations. This broadens our conception of transfer.

It seems probable that much of the apparent generalization by young children is not true generalization. It may be generalization by default. Children often appear to be generalizing when in reality they are unable to perceive the differences. Scheerer [23] suggests that

> It is conceivable that 'transfer' occurred not because the initial reaction (to A) became generalized, but because the differences between A and A_1 are not yet discriminated. The early phases of child language abound in instances of such undiscriminating transfer responses to 'equivalent stimuli,' a process better described as undifferentiated cognition of phenomenal or perceptual sameness.

For example, the young child may use the word cat to refer to a domestic cat and also to a baby leopard. This pseudo-generalization may be due to his inability to note differences between the two.

Frequently, generalization is confused with transposition. Experiments by Koehler and by Yerkes showed that animals can transpose and that they can apply previous learnings to the solution of a new problem. Scheerer suggests that transposition is a special type of generalization that occurs without the accompanying discrimination found in human learning. True generalizations require that differences as well as likenesses be discriminated. In short, abstraction of relationship is involved. This latter process has been observed only in human learning. Actually, as Menshinskaya [15] has suggested, abstraction requires that the essential features of the members of a category not only be separated from inessential ones, but they must actually be *set over against them.*

MEANING AND TRANSFER

Meaning is closely related to transfer. Meanings are *perceived* relationships. Meaningful materials are transferable to a maximum number of situations. We already have suggested that the field theorist believes that cognition or perceptual organization is the indispensable ingredient of meaning. Meaning for the field theorist is essentially a central mental process. In the associationistic or S-R point of view, meaning is identified with the responses that can be made about something. The responses denote the meaning.

In his study with 119 USAF recruits Noble concluded that meaning increases as the connections between the stimulus and response increase in number. He states (p. 429) [17]:

> A neutral S, by the present definitions, is meaningless; an S conditioned to twenty R's is more meaning*ful* (*i.e.*, has more meanings) than is one conditioned to ten, and so on. Speaking quite non-technically, meanings are habits. And as more habits accrue to a particular stimulus situation, so does its meaningfulness increase.

Noble [17] points out that a single word such as *home* can be a stimulus for a wide variety of meanings: family, spouse, children, friends, love, and many others. Thus the meaningfulness of a word depends upon the number of appropriate responses that have become associated with it.

EDUCATIONAL SIGNIFICANCE OF TRANSFER

The educational implications of the findings concerning transfer are certainly important. For one, the teacher knows that the greater the child's experience, the more meaningful his responses are likely to be. Meaning is a perception of the relationship between two situations. Experience tends to increase meaning because it increases the possibilities for transfer.

Transfer has still further values in education. Stroud (p. 527) [30] has summarized these. He says:

1. We can predict the level at which it is profitable to undertake to learn, and explain why it is that the student must start at a given level and work upward in steps.
2. We can explain how meaningful material becomes meaningful.
3. We can explain how meaningful material is more readily learned and will have greater usefulness when learned.
4. We can explain how mental development takes place under the molding

processes of education and predict that a given type of education will produce given results.

5. We can explain why an educated person's behavior differs from that of an undisciplined person.
6. Knowledge of how education produces its effect tells us a great deal about the kinds of educational experiences that should be sought after and the kinds of educational procedures we should strive to put into practice.

Trow (pp. 1–2) [36] has summarized those educational procedures which the teacher should strive to put into practice. The teacher should:

1. Determine the skills, abilities, and attitudes to be taught by means of school subjects or other school experiences. In other words, clarify the objectives of instruction.
2. Provide numerous 'similar' situations which call for the response taught. . . .
3. Teach the students to perceive the significant (similar) stimuli to which response is to be made.
4. Provide experience in learning the response, involving motivation, repetition (in various situations), and reward (satisfying).
5. And lastly, emphasize and provide practice in considering the consequences of making the response R to S's as against making some other response learned in some other situation—in other words, provide practice in problem solving.

Educationally we are equally concerned with the attitudes, the scholarly habits, and the interests and values that may be developed through school experiences and be transferred to new situations. A child's feeling of success in reading may well generalize to personal confidence in approaching his problems later in life. Watson and Rayner [38] found that Albert's fear, originally conditioned to a furry animal, generalized to other furry animals, to wool, to a fur coat, and Santa Claus's whiskers. The attitudes, interests, concepts, habits, and values of childhood certainly do transfer to adult situations.

LEARNING THEORY AND TEACHING

Each of the topics discussed in this chapter has certain direct educational applications. Still other applications seem to depend upon the interaction of all or part of the topics discussed in this and the preceding chapter. Let's consider some of these.

Educators have long been interested in the formal steps of teaching developed by Herbart. Although other terms frequently have been substituted for those used by Herbart, his steps of preparation, presentation, association, systematization, and application remain a basic part of current educational methods. Today no one applies them in the formal manner suggested by Herbart, but they do illustrate the essential elements of an effective learning situation.

PREPARATION

In his first step Herbart states that the child must be prepared for learning. In reading this requires that his interest be aroused, that he have a mental set or readiness to learn, and that an adequate experiential background be provided before the materials are presented.

Thorndike identified this process with the Law of Readiness. Hilgard (p. 18) [9] paraphrases a portion of Thorndike's law thus:

> When an action tendency is aroused through preparatory adjustments, sets, attitudes, and the like, fulfillment of the tendency in action is satisfying, non-fulfillment is annoying. Readiness thus means a preparation for action.

There are many children who come to school with a "set" to read. They are psychologically ready. Certainly, it would be poor procedure to ignore this feeling of readiness. An extended program of readiness training, rather than actually beginning reading, may thwart the action tendency which these children brought to school.

On the other hand (p. 233) [29]

> If he does not have a felt need to learn—in short, if he is not ready—it is unlikely that he will learn very much. Preparing the pupil for learning is the first step in good teaching procedure. It is for this reason that many skilled teachers spend so much classroom time in presenting assignments. They set the stage, arouse curiosity, and in other ways appeal to the needs of the child. Once the child feels a readiness to learn, the teacher may need to do little more than offer occasional guidance and encouragement.

An effective learning situation is one in which the child strongly desires to find the solution of a problem. If learning satisfies his personal needs, the child will learn, provided he has the capacity to do so. A child will learn to read if by doing so he can get the esteem of his parents, his teacher, his peers, or if he can increase his own self esteem. The teacher must create a *need* and a *desire* to learn to read.

Bugelski (pp. 460–461) [3] points out that the teacher functions in the classroom as a motivator of learning. Motivation does not necessarily mean that the student *consciously desires to learn.* Rather it implies that he is "set" to react to stimuli. The first obligation of the teacher is to create "an appropriate level of anxiety" or curiosity within the student. The learner must come to feel uneasy or distressed in situations where his knowledge is inadequate. Bugelski suggests that the teacher must develop "controlled degrees of anxiety or curiosity" even by artificial means, if necessary. In this way he employs the learner's attention and interest as positive forces to foster learning.

Educators have found that positive identification with the teacher is a powerful motivator toward learning. When the child feels the need to learn what is taught because of the "worth" of the teacher and the "esteem" that the child has for him, he is ready to have the teacher lead him beyond his immediate interest. The child usually must work for goals that are near at hand. However, since children readily identify themselves with their teacher, he can use this identification to direct the child toward long range goals. He can see to it ". . . that the child's activity takes him in a desirable direction and at the same time fulfills needs that he feels at the moment . . . goals with high social utility can be made as rewarding to the needs of the child as goals with little or no utility" (p. 196).[29]

PRESENTATION

Herbart's second step is presentation. The teacher provides learning opportunities as well as motivation. He provides the stimuli to which the pupil reacts. Teachers have always wished to know the most effective methods of presenting classroom material. Stroud (pp. 407–408) [30] says:

> While we can say that pupils in general can learn through one sense avenue about as well as through another, it does not necessarily follow that any given pupil can do so . . . one would be inclined to suspect, however, that individual differences in the sensory mode of presentation are not great. . . .

Stroud points out that since the mental reactions rather than the sensory stimulations are the basis for learning, the only differences that we should expect to find between various sensory methods of presentation would be due to the work habits of the learner or to the fact that one type of presentation (a motion picture film, for example) might be more interesting or more available than another.

There is a variety of experimental evidence relating to presentation. In a study of college students Hall and Cushing [6] found that there were no significant differences in achievement whether students used a reading approach, a lecture approach, or a film approach in learning materials. The personality of the learner had as much influence on achievement as had the method itself. Odom and Miles,[18] studying 200 sophomore psychology students, likewise found that superior college students seem to do about equally well on true-false examination questions when they listened to the questions as when they read the questions themselves, but there was some tendency to score slightly higher when they read the questions themselves. Inferior students, however, did considerably better when the questions were read to them by the instructor. It may well be that the superior students were better able to use the opportunity to reconsider their answers when the questions were presented in printed form. Inferior students, on the other hand, may rely more on classroom discussion and develop an "ear-mindedness" for learning. Auditory presentation also seems to be somewhat superior at the primary and intermediate levels.

ASSOCIATION

Herbart proposed that the third step in teaching is association. The mastery of the new materials grows from a previous mastery of similar materials. As we have seen earlier in the chapter materials are meaningful to the extent that they have been learned or partially learned previously. However, this is not enough. The learner must be able to recognize that the materials are familiar or have familiar elements. There must be a transfer of the previous learnings to the present problem. Somehow the new must be integrated with the old. New learnings must be presented where possible in terms of the old learnings. This is a necessary preliminary to abstraction.

SYSTEMATIZATION

Herbart's fourth step has been called *organization* by some educators, *generalization* by others. It is through a process of abstraction that generalization occurs. To learn, the child must react. As he reacts he draws on his fund of meanings, but, through relating ideas, he integrates new meanings with the old with a resultant new systematization of his knowledge. It is this phase in learning that encourages insight.

APPLICATION

For learnings to become the full property of the learner, he must *use* them. So long as his knowledge is a passive thing, it is immature and impermanent. Its maturation depends on its active use in new situations. Application promotes generalization and thus encourages transfer. Our modern educational emphasis on science laboratories, current problems in the social sciences, and the speaking rather than the reading of foreign languages are but a few examples of our concern for application.

SUMMARY

We conclude this chapter with a summary of the applications of learning research to teaching in the classroom. Hilgard (pp. 486–487),[9] author of two books specifically devoted to the theories of learning and other books and many articles related to learning theory, seems to be eminently qualified to propose such a set of application techniques. To Hilgard's fourteen principles, we have added certain statements from Thorpe and Schmuller (pp. 449–464).[33] The following principles, with which many theorists agree, are proposed:

1. In deciding who should learn what, the capacities of the learner are very important. Brighter people can learn things less bright ones cannot learn; in general, older children can learn more readily than younger ones; the decline of ability with age, in the adult years, depends upon what it is that is being learned. [Thorpe and Schmuller state the principle thus: "Learning proceeds most rapidly and tends to be most permanent when the activity involved is geared to the learner's physical and intellectual ability to perform that activity." *]

2. A motivated learner acquires what he learns more readily than one who is not motivated. The relevant motives include both general and specific ones, for example, desire to learn, need for achievement (general), desire for a certain reward or to avoid a threatened punishment (specific). [Thorpe and Schmuller write: "Learning proceeds most effectively and tends to be most permanent when the learner is motivated, that is, when he has a stake, as it were, in the activity being undertaken." *]

3. Motivation that is too intense (especially pain, fear, anxiety) may be accompanied by distracting emotional states, so that excessive motivation may be less effective than moderate motivation for learning some kinds of tasks, especially those involving difficult discriminations.

4. Learning under the control of reward is usually preferable to learning under the control of punishment. Correspondingly, learning motivated by success is preferable to learning motivated by failure. Even though the theoretical issue is still unresolved, the practical outcome must take into account the social by-products, which tend to be more favorable under reward than under punishment.

5. Learning under intrinsic motivation is preferable to learning under extrinsic motivation.

---

* Louis P. Thorpe and Allen M. Schmuller, *Contemporary Theories of Learning* (New York: The Ronald Press Co., 1954).

6. Tolerance for failure is best taught through providing a backlog of success that compensates for experienced failure.

7. Individuals need practice in setting realistic goals for themselves, goals neither so low as to elicit little effort nor so high as to foreordain to failure. Realistic goal-setting leads to more satisfactory improvement than unrealistic goal-setting.

8. The personal history of the individual, for example, his reaction to authority, may hamper or enhance his ability to learn from a given teacher.

9. Active participation by a learner is preferable to passive reception when learning, for example, from a lecture or a motion picture.

10. Meaningful materials and meaningful tasks are learned more readily than nonsense materials and more readily than tasks not understood by the learner. [Thorpe and Schmuller state: "Learning proceeds most effectively and tends to be most permanent when the learner is provided with the opportunity of perceiving meaningful relationships among the elements of the goal toward which he is working." *]

11. There is no substitute for repetitive practice in the overlearning of skills (for instance, the performance of a concert pianist), or in the memorization of unrelated facts that have to be automatized.

12. Information about the nature of a good performance, knowledge of his own mistakes, and knowledge of successful results, aid learning. [Thorpe and Schmuller write: "Learning goes forward with relatively greater effectiveness when the learner is provided with some criterion for indicating specifically what progress he is making." *]

13. Transfer to new tasks will be better if, in learning, the learner can discover relationships for himself, and if he has experience during learning of applying the principles within a variety of tasks.

14. Spaced or distributed recalls are advantageous in fixing material that is to be long retained.

15. [As an additional point, Thorpe and Schmuller suggested that learning is encouraged when it takes place under conditions that enhance the personality adjustment and social growth of the learner.*]

SUGGESTED READINGS

For a general background discussion of learning principles and applications to teaching:

Smith, Henry P., Chapter 8, "How We Learn," pp. 208–239 and Chapter 9, "Learning in the Classroom," pp. 240–269 in *Psychology in Teaching.* Englewood Cliffs, N. J.: Prentice-Hall, Inc., 1954.

***

---

* Louis P. Thorpe and Allen M. Schmuller, *Contemporary Theories of Learning* (New York: The Ronald Press Co., 1954).

For a discussion of associationistic psychology, laws of learning, practice and learning, reinforcement psychology and field psychology:

Stroud, James B. Chapter 10, "Approaches to the Psychology of Learning," pp. 330–369 in *Psychology in Education.* New York: Longmans, Green and Co., 1956.

***

For detailed discussions of transfer of learning and the literature on the general topic of learning (with extensive bibliographies):

Stephens, J. M. "Transfer of Learning," pp. 1535–1542 and Estes, William K. "Learning," pp. 752–770 in *Encyclopedia of Educational Research,* Chester W. Harris (Ed.), 3rd Edition, New York: The Macmillan Company, 1960.

QUESTIONS FOR DISCUSSION

1. Define learning, forgetting, meaning, perception, and transfer.
2. What are the major factors determining the effectiveness of a learning situation?
3. Why might S-R theory better be called S-O-R theory?
4. What does Hebb mean by a cell assembly? How is it related to learning?
5. Show how reading is both a perceptual and an associative process.
6. What is meant by conditioning? How is conditioning related to learning to read?
7. Why is look-while-you-say better than look-and-say?
8. Discuss the idea that practice makes perfect. Does practice *cause* learning?
9. What is the effect of practice on the range of individual differences in a group?
10. What seem to be the relative effects of massed and distributed practice for fast and slow learners?
11. What does Hull mean by previous habit strength and amount and nearness of reinforcement? What is the nature of reinforcement as seen by various learning theorists?
12. What does Tolman's expectancy theory have to do with learning?
13. What is meant by secondary reinforcement? What is meant by the *gradient* of reinforcement?
14. Discuss the relative strength of various incentives.
15. What is meant by transfer of training? What are the interests of the teacher in transfer?
16. What is meant by insight? How is it related to transfer?
17. Discuss generalization among children. What is meant by generalization by default?
18. What is the current status of Herbart's steps as related to effective teaching procedure?

19. What is the basic criterion of effective teaching?
20. Define reading in terms of various definitions of learning.
21. How may a teacher best use incentives to teach reading?

BIBLIOGRAPHY

[1] Anderson, Irving H., and Dearborn, Walter F. *The Psychology of Teaching Reading.* Ronald Press Co., New York, 1952.

[2] Briggs, Thomas H. "Praise and Censure as Incentives." *School and Society,* 26 (November, 1927) 596–598.

[3] Bugelski, B. R. *The Psychology of Learning.* Holt, Rinehart and Winston, Inc., New York, 1956.

[4] Cowles, John T. "Food Tokens as Incentives for Learning by Chimpanzees." *Comparative Psychology Monographs,* 14 (September, 1937) 1–96.

[5] Guthrie, E. R. "Conditioning: A Theory of Learning in Terms of Stimulus, Response, and Association." *The Psychology of Learning,* Forty-first Yearbook of the National Society for the Study of Education, Part II, Public School Publishing Company, Bloomington, 1942, 17–60.

[6] Hall, William E., and Cushing, James R. "The Relative Value of Three Methods of Presenting Learning Material." *Journal of Psychology,* 24 (July, 1947) 57–62.

[7] Harlow, Harry F. "The Formation of Learning Sets." *Psychological Review,* 56 (January, 1949) 51–65.

[8] Hebb, Donald Olding. *A Textbook of Psychology.* W. B. Saunders Company, Philadelphia, 1958.

[9] Hilgard, Ernest R. *Theories of Learning.* 2nd Edition, Appleton-Century-Crofts, Inc., New York, 1956.

[10] Hull, Clark L. *A Behavior System.* Yale University Press, New Haven, 1952.

[11] Hurlock, Elizabeth B. "An Evaluation of Certain Incentives Used in School Work." *Journal of Educational Psychology,* 16 (March, 1925) 145–159.

[12] Judd, Charles Hubbard. *Psychology of Secondary Education.* Ginn and Company, Boston, 1927.

[13] Kingsley, Howard L., and Garry, Ralph. *The Nature and Conditions of Learning,* 2nd Edition, Prentice-Hall, Inc., Englewood Cliffs, New Jersey, 1957.

[14] Koehler, Wolfgang. *Gestalt Psychology.* Liveright Publishing Company, New York, 1947.

[15] Menchinskaya, N. A. "Some Aspects of the Psychology of Teaching." *Psychology in the Soviet Union,* Brian Simon, (Ed.) Routledge & Kegan Paul, London, 1957, 190–196.

[16] Mowrer, O. Herbert. *Learning Theory and Behavior,* John Wiley & Sons, New York, 1960.

[17] Noble, Clyde E. "An Analysis of Meaning." *Psychological Review,* 59 (November, 1952) 421–430.

[18] Odom, Charles L., and Miles, R. W. "Oral versus Visual Presentation of True-False Achievement Tests in the First Course in Psychology." *Educational and Psychological Measurement,* 11 (Autumn, 1951) 470–477.

[19] Pavlov, Ivan P. *Conditioned Reflexes.* G. V. Anrep (Transl.), Oxford University Press, London, 1927.

[20] Poffenberger, A. T., Jr. "The Influence of Improvement in One Simple Mental Process Upon Other Related Processes." *Journal of Educational Psychology,* 6 (October, 1915) 459–474.

[21] Razran, Gregory. "A Note on the Use of the Terms *Conditioning* and *Reinforcement.*" *American Psychologist,* 10 (April, 1955) 173–174.

[22] Ryans, David G. "Motivation in Learning." *The Psychology of Learning,* Forty-first Yearbook of the National Society for the Study of Education, Part II, Public School Publishing Co., Bloomington, Ill., 1942, 289–331.

[23] Scheerer, Martin. "Personality Functioning and Cognitive Psychology." *Journal of Personality,* 22 (September, 1953) 1–16.

[24] Shaffer, Laurance Frederic and Shoben, Edward Joseph, Jr. *The Psychology of Adjustment.* 2nd Edition, Houghton Mifflin Company, Boston, 1956.

[25] Sims, Verner Martin "The Relative Influence of Two Types of Motivation on Improvement." *Journal of Educational Psychology,* 19 (October, 1928) 480–484.

[26] Skinner, B. F. "Reinforcement Today." *American Psychologist,* 13 (March, 1958) 94–99.

[27] Smith, Donald E. P. "The Neurophysiology of Reading Disability." *Significant Elements in College and Adult Reading Improvement,* Seventh Yearbook of the National Reading Conference for Colleges and Adults, Texas Christian University Press, Fort Worth, 1958, 54–59.

[28] Smith, Donald E. P., and Carrigan, Patricia M. *The Nature of Reading Disability.* Harcourt, Brace and Company, New York, 1959.

[29] Smith, Henry P. *Psychology in Teaching.* Prentice-Hall, Inc., Englewood Cliffs, 1954.

[30] Stroud, James B. *Psychology in Education.* Longmans, Green & Co., New York, 1956.

[31] Thompson, George G., and Hunnicutt, Clarence W. "The Effect of Repeated Praise or Blame on the Work Achievement of 'Introverts and Extroverts'." *Journal of Educational Psychology,* 35 (May, 1944) 257–266.

[32] Thorndike, Edward L. *Educational Psychology II, The Psychology of Learning.* Teachers College, Columbia University, New York, 1930.

[33] Thorpe, Louis P., and Schmuller, Allen M. *Contemporary Theories of Learning.* Ronald Press Co., New York, 1954.

[34] Tinklepaugh, Otto Leif. "An Experimental Study of Representative Factors in Monkeys." *Journal of Comparative Psychology,* 8 (June, 1928) 197–236.

[35] Tolman, Edward C. *Collected Papers in Psychology.* University of California Press, Berkeley, 1951.

[36] Trow, William Clark. "What Is the Transfer Value of Certain School Experiences?" *Letters to Schools,* University of Michigan, 4 (May, 1952) 1–2.

[37] Underwood, Benton J. "Studies of Distributed Practice: XII. Retention Following Varying Degrees of Original Learning." *Journal of Experimental Psychology,* 47 (May, 1954) 294–300.

[38] Watson, John B., and Rayner, Rosalie. "Conditioned Emotional Reactions." *Journal of Experimental Psychology,* 3 (February, 1920) 1–14.

[39] Wolfe, John B. "Effectiveness of Token Rewards for Chimpanzees." *Comparative Psychology Monographs,* 12 (May, 1936) 1–72.

[40] Wood, Theodore W. "The Effect of Approbation and Reproof on the Mastery of Nonsense Syllables." *Journal of Applied Psychology,* 18 (October, 1934) 657–664.

[41] Woodworth, Robert S. *Dynamic Psychology.* Columbia University Press, New York, 1918.

[42] Yerkes, Robert M. "The Mind of a Gorilla." *Genetic Psychology Monographs,* Vol. 2, No. 142 (1927) 1–156.

4

THE PSYCHOLOGICAL BASES OF READINESS

As teachers, we are intimately concerned with the readiness of individuals for learning. As teachers of reading, we wish to know the most favorable moment for beginning to teach a child to read and for the teaching of each specific reading skill. The readiness concept is not reserved for the period of beginning reading; it applies to all levels of reading development.

In the three previous chapters we have been concerned with the significance and importance of reading, the basic nature of the reading process, and the learning principles that should guide us in the teaching of reading. Here we wish to identify the determinants of reading readiness at all levels. Our basic question is: When is the child ready to learn to read?

We know that in our culture all children must attempt to learn to read. Society demands that the child be a reader. A child who cannot read risks insecurity, loss of self-esteem, and an inability to pursue his future interests to fullest satisfaction.

THE NATURE OF READING READINESS

Havighurst has proposed that there are certain tasks that every child needs to accomplish. These he calls developmental tasks. He writes (p. 2) [44]:

A developmental task is a task which arises at or about a certain period in the life of the individual, successful achievement of which leads to his happiness and to success with later tasks, while failure leads to unhappiness in the individual, disapproval by the society, and difficulty with later tasks.

Certainly reading qualifies as a developmental task. It is a task that the child must perform to satisfy his own needs and the demands of society. And reading readiness commonly is understood to be a developmental stage at which constitutional and environmental factors have prepared the child for reading.

Originally, the concept of readiness was reserved for readiness for initial reading. Lamoreaux and Lee, however, have emphasized that each stage of reading is a step toward readiness for further reading (p. 1).[56] And Betts (p. 104) [11] points out that "A mental, emotional, and physical readiness for sustained reading activities possesses as much significance in a modern secondary school as it does in a modern primary school." Thus the reading readiness concept applies not only to initial reading instruction but to the teaching of every specific reading skill. And our interest in readiness continues throughout the developmental reading program. A child may become ready for learning to read by age six; he will not become ready to read to learn until much later.

What are the factors that determine or characterize the teachable moment of reading? And which of these factors are most significant?

In attempting to answer the first question, authorities generally have suggested that a child's readiness for reading is dependent upon the following eleven factors:

1. Perceptual development
2. Intellectual development
3. Maturational adequacy, including the reader's sex
4. Background of personal experience
5. Auditory and visual discrimination
6. Language development
7. Sensory development
8. Health and freedom from neurological disturbances
9. Attitudes and motivation: interest in and desire for reading
10. Social and emotional development
11. Instructional methods and procedures

In this chapter our emphasis will be on factors two through six, namely the child's intellectual, maturational, and experiential readiness and his growth in sensory discrimination and language facility. Factors seven through eleven are discussed in later chapters. Chapter 2 emphasized the importance of perceptual readiness and at this time you may wish to review

"The Perceptual Process," "The Major Determinants of Meaning," and "Concept Formation," in that section.

THE CORRELATES OF READING READINESS

Reading readiness is a complex of many abilities, skills, understandings, and interests, each of which contributes in some measure to the process of learning to read. A knowledge of the child's developmental level from each of these points of view can help us to predict his readiness for reading.

Research workers have searched for the multiple and often somewhat unexpected factors that may be related to reading readiness. For example, Sutton [89] studied 150 children and compared reading readiness test scores with numerous other measures. In all, he computed 246 correlation coefficients. The measures that showed the highest degree of relationship with readiness scores were: mental maturity ($r = .51$); language factors ($r = .51$); enjoyment of listening ($r = .44$); taking trips ($r = .42$); marital status of parents ($r = .36$); social adjustment ($r = .36$); reading stories at home ($r = .34$); private instruction ($r = .33$); age in months ($r = .30$); parents' education ($r = .29$); Sunday school attendance ($r = .27$); independent play ($r = .27$); record player in home ($r = .26$); interest in magazines ($r = .26$); occupation of father ($r = .25$); number of books ($r = .21$); and nursery school attendance ($r = .21$). Each of the above intercorrelations was significant at the .01 level of confidence.

The determinants of reading readiness are inextricably interrelated. Obviously, many factors will be found to correlate with readiness not because they are causes but, perhaps, because they are symptoms of a causal factor. For example, father's occupation, possession of a record player, and even interest in books and magazines may or may not directly affect readiness. They may serve merely as clues to the cultural level of the child's home. And studies have indicated that the presence or absence of specific factors may not be as important as the general pattern of the factors—the complex of correlates—in affecting the development of readiness.

INTELLECTUAL READINESS

Numerous writers have emphasized that intelligence is an extremely important determinant of reading readiness and general reading achievement.[91, 84] We should expect this to be true. Reading is a thinking process. Essentially intelligence implies the ability to learn and to apply what is learned. Both the reading skill itself and the background necessary for the reading-thinking process must be learned.

Harrison (pp. 8–9) [43] has suggested that certain specific mental abilities are necessary for success in reading.

> . . . (1) the ability to see likenesses and differences, (2) the ability to remember word forms with freedom from aphasia and word-blindness, (3) memory span of ideas, (4) ability to do abstract thinking, and (5) the ability to correlate abstractions with definite modes of response as this ability is related to the reading process.

To understand a discussion of intellectual readiness two important concepts, mental age and intelligence quotient, must be understood.

Mental age (M.A.) refers to the *level of mental growth* that has been achieved. An average six-year-old child will have a mental age of six; an average child of 10, a mental age of 10; an average youth of 15, a mental age of 15. And any child making the same score on the test that was made by the average child of any given age is assumed to have that *mental age*. Mental growth has been assumed to continue at a fairly constant pace until about age 15 or 16 after which time scores on intelligence tests no longer increase significantly. Thus an average youth of 20 will still have a mental age of but 15 or 16.*

The intelligence quotient (I.Q.) is a statement of the *rate of mental growth*. We all remember the simple rate, time, and distance formulas: distance equals rate multipled by time ($D = R \times T$) and rate equals distance divided by time ($R = D \div T$). Just as the mental age of a child is the distance or level to which he has traveled mentally, so the intelligence quotient is the rate at which he must have grown mentally to have reached that level. Thus, the I.Q. is derived by dividing the child's mental age by his life age in years and months. For example, if a six-year-old child obtains a score on a test that is equal to the average score obtained by eight-year-olds, he is said to have a mental age of eight. Since his level of mental growth is two years higher than that of the average six-year-old, it is evident that his rate of intellectual development was faster than that of the average six-year-old. By dividing his mental age (8) by his chronological age (6), we obtain his rate of growth (I.Q.). We see that for every year that he has lived he has advanced 1.33 mental age years. For convenience we remove the decimal point by multiplying his rate of growth by 100 and arrive, in this case, at an I.Q. of 133. The formula for computing the I.Q. is usually given as $\text{I.Q.} = \frac{MA}{CA} \times 100$.

Wechsler (p. 24) [99] defines the intelligence quotient as

---

* Some studies indicate that mental age scores may continue to increase beyond the chronological ages of 15 or 16.

. . . the ratio between a particular score which an individual gets (on a given intelligence test) and the score which an average individual of his life age may be assumed to attain on the same test, when both scores are expressed in the same notation (*e.g.*, in terms of months and years).

The definition of intelligence quotient necessarily indicates the relative nature of the concept. In the example above, the I.Q. of 133 is relative to the I.Q. of the average six-year-old which, of course, is 100. A child's mental age (M.A.) increases as he grows older but the I.Q., representing as it does his past rate of growth, is assumed to be our best prediction of the rate at which he will continue to grow until mental maturity is reached somewhere around the age of fifteen or sixteen.

It is readily seen that *rate* of mental growth (the I.Q.) is not a sufficient criterion for reading readiness. Reading readiness is related to level of mental development rather than to rate. Thus a one-year-old child may have an exceptionally high I.Q. but certainly he will not have attained the necessary mental level to learn to read.

Harris (p. 32) [42] has prepared a table showing the relationship between mental age, I.Q., and chronological age. This table is useful for finding the correct combinations of I.Q. and chronological age that result in a mental age "adequate" for beginning to read.

TABLE 1

READING READINESS: RELATION OF MENTAL AGE TO CHRONOLOGICAL AGE AND INTELLIGENCE QUOTIENT

	Intelligence Quotient						
	70	80	90	100	110	120	130
Chronological Age	Corresponding Mental Age						
5 yrs. 3 mos.	3–8	4–2	4–9	5–3	5–9	6–4	6–10
5 yrs. 9 mos.	4–0	4–7	5–3	5–9	6–4	6–11	7–6
6 yrs. 3 mos.	4–5	5–0	5–8	6–3	6–9	7–6	8–2
6 yrs. 9 mos.	4–9	5–5	6–1	6–9	7–5	8–1	8–9
7 yrs. 3 mos.	5–1	5–10	6–6	7–3	8–0	8–8	9–5
7 yrs. 9 mos.	5–5	6–2	7–0	7–9	8–6	9–4	10–1

Since all individuals—bright, average, and dull—cease improving in mental age score at about the same time, the I.Q. does indicate the ultimate level of a child's mental development and thus allows us to predict his maximum reading development. Witty and Koppel (p. 227) [103] suggest that individuals with a Binet I.Q. below 25 ordinarily will never reach a level of mental development sufficient to learn to read; those with an I.Q. below 50 will experience difficulty in reading abstract material as well as other types of difficult material; and those with an I.Q. between

50 and 70 ultimately could become able to learn to read, but rarely above a fourth-grade level.

Mental age scores have been found to be closely related both to reading readiness and to reading achievement. Generally, mental age scores correlate highly with reading-readiness test scores. In numerous studies and summaries of research the correlation between these two sets of scores has been found to range from about .35 to .80. We know that reading-achievement test scores also correlate highly with intelligence-test scores. This leads us to conclude that to a large extent reading-achievement and reading-readiness tests measure the same factors that are measured by intelligence tests.

Bond and Tinker, however (p. 42),[14] report that by the end of the first grade the correlation between intelligence and reading ability (achievement) is generally around .35, but by the sixth grade it increases to .65. Manolakes and Sheldon,[61] studying children in grades one to twelve, found support for this conclusion. They found that the correlation between reading achievement and intelligence was greater after the fourth grade. These findings suggest that mental age actually is a more basic determinant of reading success when children have reached the stage at which they *read to learn* than it is when they are *learning to read.*

Although there is a high relationship between mental age scores and readiness test scores, it also is true that a high correlation is quite different from a perfect correlation. So long as the interrelation between two factors is imperfect, we expect to find that other factors are operating. Clearly, we cannot expect to predict reading readiness on the basis of intellectual development alone.

A mental age of about 6½ has been suggested by some authorities as optimal for reading readiness. For example, Dean,[19] studying 116 first-grade entrants, concluded that a mental age of 6½ is needed for average success in the first grade. Only when the mental ages at the beginning of the first grade were 6½ or above did the greater percentage of children make "average progress" in reading. Of those children with mental ages between 6 and 6½ only 29 per cent made average progress. Furthermore, Dean obtained a correlation of .62 between Stanford–Binet mental age at the beginning of the first grade and reading achievement on the Metropolitan Achievement Test as measured after six months of instruction.

There is some evidence also that such reading skills as may be acquired by children with mental ages well below 6½ are relatively impermanent. Keister [53] found that five-year-old children of average ability generally could attain the first-grade norm in reading by the end of the one year, but, unfortunately, they forgot considerably more than did older children by the following September, and by the end of the second year of school they were below the norms for the second grade.

Finally, although a mental age of 6½ may be our best choice as a point for beginning reading instruction, that mental age does not guarantee success in reading. Many bright children find learning to read difficult and as they grow older many read at a level far below that which their level of mental development appears to promise. Witty and Kopel (p. 228) [103] report that 90 per cent of the poor readers have an I.Q. between 80 and 110. And in a study of 155 children with reading defects Monroe (p. 5) [64] found an I.Q. range from 60 to 150.* There are many possible reasons for poor reading. Binet [12] emphasized that a child's desire and will to learn, his attentiveness, his habits of work, and his persistence are important traits. Various problems of emotional and physiological development also may contribute to reading failure.

Although he recognizes that there is a positive correlation between reading achievement and mental age and that this correlation is highest when instruction is at its best, Gates (p. 506) [31] points out that

> . . . statements concerning the necessary mental age at which a pupil can be entrusted to learn to read are essentially meaningless. The age for learning to read under one program or with the method employed by one teacher may be entirely different from that required under other circumstances.**

He examined the results of four studies and concluded that the mental age required for learning to read is directly related to the provisions for individual differences that are made within the classroom. It seems likely that in those instances in which very young children are taught to read there is a combination of favorable circumstances and that both high intelligence and extreme individualization of instruction are most important factors.***

However, Harris (pp. 32–33) [42] draws the following conclusions concerning the relationship of mental ability to reading:

> (1) There is a substantial relationship between mental age and ease of learning to read; most children who fail in reading in the first grade have mental ages below six years. . . .
> (2) Most children who have normal I.Q.'s, have M.A.'s above six years, and are free from special handicaps, can be successfully taught to read in the first grade. However, a delayed start does these children no harm.
> (3) It is not possible to set a definite minimum mental age for learning to read because too many other factors are involved. . . .
> (4) Schools which provide a first-grade program which is rich in experi-

---

* These children were referred to a clinic primarily because of their reading difficulties.

** Copyright 1937 by the University of Chicago, reprinted by permission.

*** *Time,* "Education," November 7, 1960, p. 103 reports reading by three-year-old children.

ences and social activities, with no formal reading instruction, avoid many problems of reading failure and achieve as good or better reading in the higher grades as the schools which teach reading from the beginning of the first grade.

Gray (p. 124) [39] points out that

. . . (a) a mental age of 6½ years is usually accompanied by rapid progress in learning to read, if pupils are well prepared for reading in other respects; (b) a mental age of 6 is usually accompanied by satisfactory progress if pupils have developed normally in other readiness factors; (c) many pupils who have not acquired a mental age of 6 can learn to read provided the reading materials are very simple and based on interesting, familiar experiences and the methods used are adapted to the specific needs of the learners. Indeed, studies made in Scotland and the experience of several other countries show that children who have developed normally can learn to read at the age of 5 if instruction is adapted to their level of maturity.

In general, the evidence concerning intellectual development and readiness to read cautions us that no single index can guarantee success in reading. The child's wants, interests, and attitudes, and his levels of physiological maturation may be at least as important as his level of mental development in determining whether or not he will learn to read.

SEX DIFFERENCES AND MATURATIONAL FACTORS

It is commonly observed that girls do better than boys in reading achievement. As a group, they learn to read earlier and fewer of them become reading disability cases.

Numerous studies support the observation that boys have more difficulty with reading than do girls. Alden, Sullivan, and Durrell,[1] studying 6,364 children in grades two to six inclusive, found that 18.6 per cent of the boys and 9.8 per cent of the girls were retarded in reading. Schonell [78] reports that of 15,000 school children in the city of London, five per cent of the boys and two and one-half per cent of the girls were retarded more than one and a half years. Macmeeken,[60] studying 383 Scottish children between the ages of 7½ and 10½, found that 12.2 per cent of the boys but only 6.2 per cent of the girls were retarded in reading. In this study a child was considered to be retarded * in reading if his reading age was no more than 85 per cent of his mental age.

* The term "retarded" is used by some writers to mean that a child is performing below the average of his chronological-age group whereas other writers use it to indicate that he is performing below what his mental age appears to promise. Other writers reserve the terms "disability" or "special disability" for cases in which reading age is well below mental age.

Monroe (p. 98) [64] notes that of her 155 disability cases, 86 per cent were boys. Fernald (p. 149) [27] in a study of 69 reading disability cases reported that 67 were boys, and Durrell states that the ratio of boys to girls at the Boston University Educational Clinic has been ten to one. He writes (p. 281) [22]:

> Boys have much more difficulty in reading than do girls. In the study of 1130 children using Stanford–Binet as the criterion, 20 per cent of the boys were retarded in reading, while only 10 per cent of the girls were similarly retarded. Among the six thousand children given the Durrell-Sullivan Reading Capacity and Achievement Tests, 18 per cent of the boys were retarded as compared to 9 per cent of the girls. . . . Among children brought to the Boston University Educational Clinic for study, the ratio of the boys to girls is ten to one.

The evidence also seems to indicate that there are sex differences in general educational achievement. Stroud and Linquist [88] found differences favoring the girls on the *Iowa Every-Pupil Tests of Basic Skills* for grades three to eight. Except in arithmetic the girls maintained a consistent and fairly significant superiority over the boys in all subjects tested. However, on the high-school level the differences as shown by the *Iowa Every-Pupil Tests of High School Achievement* favored the boys except in algebra and reading comprehension.

In general, the girls establish a definite superiority in educational achievement during the elementary grades, but much if not all of their advantage disappears by the time high school is reached. Perhaps this is because different elements are emphasized in high school. History and science tend to replace some subjects such as spelling and handwriting in which girls generally excel. However, girls do maintain their superiority in English usage throughout the high-school years.

Certainly the facts are impressive. The differences between girls and boys in reading readiness and achievement seem genuine and we must look for reasons. An examination of certain related data may help us to come to a better understanding of the problem as well as to arrive at useful conclusions.

Generally, by the twentieth month of life, girls show some superiority in the production of speech sounds. McCarthy [62] states that in the pre-linguistic or babbling stage no appreciable differences are noticeable, but she cites evidence that differences appear in the second year of life. Louttit (p. 409),[59] pointing out that the estimates of the ratio of boy to girl stutterers vary all the way from 2 to 1 to 10 to 1, says that, wherever the true ratio may be, the incidence of stuttering certainly is much greater among boys than girls. Burt (pp. 364–365) [17] reports that there also is a greater incidence of lisping and lalling * among boys. Durrell (p. 281) [22] found that even when children are equated on oral language achievement there are still twice as many reading disability cases among boys as among girls.

Monroe (p. 99),[64] trying to account for the differences between boys and girls, suggests that the incidence of those constitutional factors that hinder progress in reading may be greater among boys. Gallagher [29] indicates that the difference might be explained on the basis of heredity and suggests that a substantial deviation in the language mechanism may be a primary cause of reading disability. Sheridan (p. 8) [83] also suggests that girls, even those of lesser intelligence, have a superior language sense. Some writers stress maturational differences, particularly in emotional and intellectual development. Others intimate that girls possess a natural advantage of interest in verbal rather than mechanical or athletic activities.

It has been suggested that the prevalence of women teachers may be a determining factor. Back in 1909 Ayres (p. 158) [8] concluded that schools were better fitted to the needs and natures of girls than of boys. He felt that the poorer showing of the boys was the result of over-feminization. St. John (p. 668) [85] studying some 500 boys and 450 girls in Grade One to Six, agreed with this, and pointed out that

> . . . the consistent inferiority of the boys in school progress and achievement is due chiefly to a maladjustment between the boys and their teachers which is the result of interest, attitudes, habits, and general behavior tendencies of the boys to which the teachers *(all women)* fail to adjust themselves and their school procedures as well as they do to the personality traits of girls.

Betts (p. 137) [11] observes:

> First, there is some evidence to the effect that girls are promoted on lower standards of achievement than boys are. Second, girls use reading activities for recreation more often than boys do. Third, there is a need for more reading materials to challenge the interests of boys.

Harris (p. 27) [42] suggests that the girl's weaving, sewing, and doll-play activities may help to develop fine manual skills and improve near-point vision. A related factor is the different rôles society expects of boys and of girls. Boys are supposed to be athletic and aggressive; girls are expected to be physically inactive and docile. And the non-reading boy's aggressiveness

---

* The laller substitutes easier sounds for more difficult ones made with the tongue. For example, he may pronounce "rice" as "lice."

leads him to create trouble in school whereas the non-reading girl's tractability causes her to suffer in silence! Thus it may be that boys tend to be referred to clinics in greater numbers because their aggressive symptoms bring them so sharply to parent and teacher notice.

Of course, it is entirely possible that differences in maturational rate at least partially explain the greater number of reading problems found among boys. Girls generally reach maturity about a year and a half earlier than boys. However, Anderson, Hughes, and Dixon [6] report that there are few if any differences in achievement when boys and girls of high I.Q. (130 or more) are compared. On the other hand, when comparisons are made among children of 100 I.Q. or less, the girls tend to show superior achievement.

Some studies have indicated that intelligence is more variable among boys than among girls—more boys than girls have extremely low as well as extremely high intelligence quotients. This would lead us to expect that the reading ability of boys might also be more variable and that a larger number of boys would be poor readers (p. 112).[96]

Unfortunately, the mere knowledge that there are sex differences in readiness and reading achievement does not tell us what action to take in adjusting the educational program to these differences.

It has been suggested that boys should enter school later than girls. Anderson and Dearborn (p. 42) [3] point out, however, that this approach is not a feasible adjustment to the problem of individual differences. They reported the results of standardized reading tests given in the University of Michigan Elementary School. Their findings are given in Figure 1 and allow us to compare the average reading ages of boys and girls at various chronological ages and at the same time see the wide range in achievement among children at each chronological age. For example, at 132 months (11 years) there is a ten-year range in reading achievement among the boys. In all instances the average performance of the girls was superior to that of the boys, but the boys showed greater variation among themselves. Certainly the differences in achievement among boys are greater than the differences between girls and boys.

Obviously, starting all girls in school earlier than all boys would not solve the problem of individual differences. Many six-year-old boys are more mature than the average six-year-old girl. And although girls may tend to excel in some academic areas, boys, at least by the high school years, do so in others. Thus, recommendations that might appear logical when we consider group averages may be most illogical when we consider the individual boys and girls within the group.

However, the variations among children in readiness for reading demand that educational adjustments be made. Delayed entrance to school would

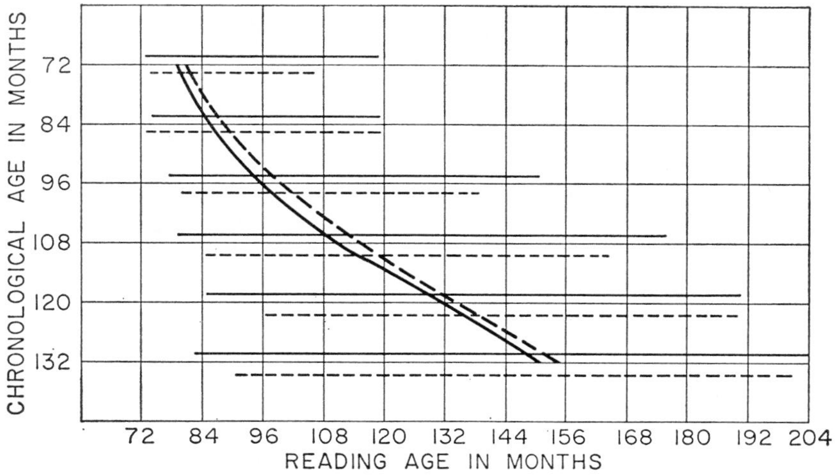

Irving H. Anderson and Walter F. Dearborn, *The Psychology of Teaching Reading*. Copyright 1952, The Ronald Press Company.

be a negative approach whether the variations are due primarily to differences in rate of maturation or to differences in the cultural stimulation of the home. The school must somehow offer a planned program of experiences that will build a framework of readiness as rapidly as possible on whatever abilities the child possesses. The solution probably lies in a delay of formal reading instruction until the child is ready for it and in an early provision of experiences that will prepare him for reading.

EXPERIENTIAL READINESS

In Chapter 2 we discussed the importance of experience as a determinant of perceptual readiness. An early step toward readiness for reading is an awareness of the representative function of symbols. An incident in the life of Helen Keller shows how a child becomes aware that printed words talk (pp. 23–24).[54]

We walked down the path to the well-house, attracted by the fragrance of the honeysuckle with which it was covered. Someone was drawing water and my teacher placed my hand under the spout. As the cool stream gushed over one hand she spelled into the other the word *water*, first slowly, then rapidly. I stood still, my whole attention fixed upon the motions of her fingers. Suddenly I felt a misty consciousness as of something forgotten—a thrill of returning thought; and somehow the mystery of language was revealed to me. I knew then that 'w-a-t-e-r' meant the wonderful cool something that was flowing over my hand. That living word awakened my soul, gave it light, hope, joy, set it free! . . . I left the well-house eager to learn. Everything had a name, and each name gave birth to a new thought.

Experience provides the basis for all educational development. We know that the function of symbols is to call forth or evoke meaning. The meanings themselves spring from the mind of the reader as he brings "meaningful concepts to the symbols in terms of his own experience. Symbols are but empty shells. It takes experience to fill them with the meat of meaning." [84] The most important reason for the difference between children's concepts and those of adults is the differential in experience.

Studies have shown that the greater the child's experience, the greater are his possibilities for success in reading. Hilliard and Troxell (p. 263) [47] in a study of kindergarten children concluded that:

. . . children with rich backgrounds are more strongly equipped to attack the printed page than are pupils of meager backgrounds because of enriched meanings and thought which the former bring to the task.*

Hildreth,[46] using her own information tests with 47 first-grade pupils, observed that children made the best scores on topics with which they were most familiar. She points out that this demonstrates the impact of experience. Children can learn only what their environment provides and what is most often seen or heard is most likely to be learned thoroughly.

Almy studied the school records of 106 first-grade pupils and compared school success with various facts revealed during interviews with the parents of each child. She found a significant positive relationship between success in reading and such experiences as looking at books and magazines, having someone to read to them, and interest in words, letters, and numbers. She writes (p. 111) [2]:

While experiences which are usually thought of as 'reading,' such as looking at books and magazines, or being read to, contribute to the positive relationship between reading success and responses to opportunities for reading, interests in words, letters, numbers, wherever they may be found, as on signs, cans, packages, and table games, are also important factors in the relationship.

It has been observed that children from lower-class homes generally do not achieve as well in school as do children of the middle and upper classes. Granzow [36] selected three groups of sixth- and seventh-grade children equated on the basis of I.Q. He had forty each of underachievers, overachievers, and normal achievers in reading. An investigation of the home backgrounds of the individuals composing the groups showed that the underachievers in reading tended to come from homes of lower socio-economic background. And Engle [25] found that "privileged" high school youths received higher grades than "underprivileged" youths. Milner (p. 110) [63] reports that performance in reading also is positively related to family social status. Comparing children of middle-class homes with those from lower-class homes, she concluded that children entering school:

> . . . had already had specific, 'patterned,' family-based experiences which had influenced their degree of readiness to read. . . . This study . . . shows again that the middle-class child has a superior verbal advantage even before he enters school—an advantage which the school apparently enhances and reinforces.

Loevinger,[58] in reviewing numerous studies, actually found an average correlation of .40 between test intelligence of children and the occupational level of their fathers. She also found that children from professional and executive families had an average I.Q. of 116, whereas those of day-laborers had an average I.Q. of 92. Since social status correlates significantly with intelligence, one would expect to find a high correlation between reading achievement and social class status.

The differences in test intelligence are not surprising when one considers the intellectual stimulation possible in the upper-class home as compared with the dearth of stimulation in the lower-class home. The upper-class child has opportunities to make trips, go to summer camp, and has the encouragement, facilities, and time to read books and magazines. The language used and the topics discussed in the upper-class home are likely to be on a more advanced level.

Sheldon and Carrillo [82] report that as the number of books in the home increases, the percentage of good readers increases. Their study of advanced (one year), average, and retarded readers (one year) indicates that the retarded readers generally (1) come from families of lower socio-economic status; (2) come from large families; (3) tend to be among the later children rather than among the first children; (4) have fewer books available; (5) have parents who left school sooner than the parents of advanced readers; and (6) tend to dislike school.

The evidence is clear that intelligence is closely related to cultural background of the home. And in addition there is some evidence that even when children of the same intelligence but from different levels of cultural background are compared, the child with the more stimulating home background has an advantage both in readiness for reading and for later achievement in reading.

However, the correlation between reading achievement and cultural background is far from perfect. Cases of severe reading disability occur among children from all socio-economic levels. This cautions us against an extreme emphasis on the influence of cultural factors but leaves us with a responsibility to do everything possible to enrich the experiences of the less fortunate children.

If the child's environment fails to stimulate perceptual growth, the school must attempt to provide the necessary experiences. This implies that we should be particularly eager to supply stimulating nursery school and kindergarten experiences as well as such physical facilities as neighborhood reading centers, bookmobiles, group trips, and day-camp organizations to children from the lower socio-economic groups. The provision of these opportunities for cultural experiences has long been recognized as a social responsibility of the community. It may be that it is even more precisely an educational responsibility.

Studies generally have shown that readiness programs have value. There is some doubt, however, that reading-readiness training is equally effective with all children. Anderson and Dearborn (p. 93) [3] write *: "Surprisingly or not, the literature does not show that kindergarten experience has any great effect in facilitating the process of learning to read, possibly because the right children have not been involved." Basing their conclusion on studies by Fuller [28] and Herr,[45] they point out that reading-readiness training seems to be particularly successful in the case of children handicapped by a foreign language background or coming from the poorer socio-economic classes.

Gates and Russell [34] found that dull-normal underprivileged children (I.Q. 75–95) profit especially from pre-reading activities and they recommended that such children be given at least two semesters of such training. Studies generally suggest that the lower the intelligence, the longer must be the period of readiness training before beginning reading.

Pratt,[73] studying 226 children, found that there was a significant superiority of kindergarten pupils over non-kindergarten pupils when both were tested on reading readiness and on achievement tests at the end of the first grade. Herr [45] selected two groups of five-year-old Spanish-speaking children from nine New Mexico towns. One group received readiness training and the other did not. Results showed that pre-first-grade training promoted success in learning to read. Scott [80] studied two groups of thirty-four pupils each and found that readiness classes are a better preparation for the first grade than are either no preparatory work or attend-

* Irving H. Anderson and Walter F. Dearborn, *The Psychology of Teaching Reading*. Copyright 1952, The Ronald Press Company.

ance at kindergarten alone. And Fast [26] reports that first-grade children who had attended kindergarten obtained significantly higher scores on reading tests than did children who had not.

These studies indicate that if there is no kindergarten program the first-grade teacher should be especially careful not to hurry children into a formal reading program. Children must have an opportunity to prepare for reading. Children of families in the lower socio-economic levels, those with foreign language backgrounds, and slow learners generally find pre-reading experiences especially beneficial.

Although experiences such as radio and television may actually lessen the amount of reading, we are not certain that they hinder reading readiness. It is difficult to know what is implied by Sutton's [89] finding that possession of a television set is negatively correlated with reading readiness. Several attempts have been made to assess the effects of television on reading achievement. Witty,[102] in summarizing the data, suggests that excessive viewing generally is associated with lower achievement. However, he points out that whereas earlier studies showed that children generally read less when TV became available, more recently the amount of reading being done by children is increasing. Scott [81] found that sixth- and seventh-grade pupils who watched television from 22¾ to 69½ hours per week achieved significantly less in arithmetic, reading, and total achievement than a matched group of those who watched TV from 0 to 9¾ hours per week.

The educational effect of television is difficult to gauge. It is of course possible that television viewing helps a child to acquire better readiness for reading; but, after the child has learned to read, it may rob him of his interest in reading. It may even rob him of his desire to learn to read. Excessive watching is rather certain to take some of his time away from reading and there are strong possibilities that it may deprive him of first-hand experiences and even influence his social and emotional adjustment.

AUDITORY AND VISUAL DISCRIMINATION

Skills in auditory and visual discriminations certainly are major factors in perceptual development. Recent studies have indicated that these skills also are closely related to readiness for reading.

Harrington and Durrell [41] have concluded that auditory and visual discrimination of word elements appears to be more closely related to the acquisition of the primary-grade reading vocabulary than is mental age which frequently has been used as almost the sole criterion of reading readiness. Tests were administered to 500 primary children. The children were matched as to visual discrimination, phonic ability, and mental age, but one child in each pair was superior in auditory discrimination. It was found that, by the end of the second grade, superiority in auditory discrimination resulted in a mean difference of 18 words on the reading vocabulary test used. In another portion of the experiment one child in each pair was superior in visual discrimination. This resulted in a mean difference of 32 words. Superiority in phonics resulted in a mean difference of 33 words. Surprisingly, however, a mental age difference * of a year and a half was accompanied by a mean difference of only three words in reading vocabulary.

The study cautions one against placing too great a stress on intelligence as the major factor in reading readiness. Its authors suggest that most children entering the first grade have sufficient speaking and listening vocabulary for success in first-grade reading and that additional excellence in vocabulary has little influence on success in the beginning stages of reading. However, their conclusions that skill in visual and auditory discrimination and in phonics is highly related to the development of a sight vocabulary is of major interest in our search for the determinants of reading readiness.

Sister Nila [68] concluded that the four chief factors related to reading readiness were auditory discrimination, visual discrimination, range of information, and mental age, in that order.

Recent studies suggest that we must give increasing consideration to auditory and visual factors in reading. Nicholson [67] for example, concluded that a knowledge of the names of letters is the best guarantee that a child will learn to read. Tests measuring ability to associate the name of a letter with its form showed the highest correlations with learning rate ** for words.

In a summary of four studies involving more than 2,000 first-grade children Durrell (p. 5) [24] points out that certain forms of visual-discrimination training are not useful.

> All children were able to match capital letters as well as lower-case letters. Exercises in this ability should be omitted from reading readiness materials.

---

* The mental age used in this study was obtained from the *Otis Quick Scoring Mental Abilities Test, Alpha,* Form A, which is largely a test of ability to understand oral language and orally-given directions.

** As a part of the *Murphy-Durrell Diagnostic Reading Readiness Test,* ten words are taught by means of flash cards. Each word is discussed and practiced for one minute. This is followed by ten minutes of practice on the ten words as a group. The child's retention is then tested three times during the day and his percentage score on the third test is considered to be his *learning rate.*

It appears to follow that matching of non-word forms and pictures as preliminary instruction for letter and word perception is relatively useless.

Durrell adds:

The average child in this population of first-grade children could, in September: give the names of 12 capital letters and 9 lower-case letters; identify 17 capitals named and 12 lower-case letters named; write 10 letters from dictation. . . .

In discussing one of the studies summarized by Durrell, Nicholson (p. 24) [67] writes:

High mental age does not assure a high learning rate in beginning reading. Although children with very high mental ages have better letter knowledge, it is apparently the letter knowledge rather than the mental age which produces the high learning rate.

Olson (p. 36),[69] studying 1,172 first-grade children, drew a number of similar conclusions. He states:

September tests which measure knowledge of letter names provide the best predictions of February success in reading. All such tests show higher correlations with reading achievement than does mental age.

He found that February tests of various phonic abilities yielded the highest correlations with reading achievement.

He adds:

All findings are consistent with the conclusion that early teaching of letter names and of various aspects of phonics is essential to rapid progress in reading. There is no support for the assumptions that a sight vocabulary of 75 words should be established before word analysis instruction is given or that a mental age of seven is necessary for the use of phonics.

Gavel,[35] studying 1,506 first-grade children, found those September tests that best predicted June achievement to be: writing letters dictated, naming letters, identifying letters named, and learning rate for words. September tests that showed less than a .50 correlation with June achievement were: I.Q., mental age, ability to give the sound of letters, identification of words shown, identification of sounds in words, and matching of letters. She found that chronological age showed a slight negative correlation (— .06) with achievement. February tests that predicted June reading achievement with correlations higher than .60 included hearing of sounds in words, applied phonics, and ability to give the sound of lower-case letters.

Linehan [57] compared an experimental group of 314 pupils with a control group of 300. Each group was chosen on a random basis but the pre-tests showed the control group to be somewhat superior in mental age, learning rate, and letter knowledge. The experimental group began with training in letter knowledge and ear training and later used the sight method for learning words; the sequence of training in the control group was just the reverse. In the experimental group phonics training was started as soon as children had a mastery of letter names and could identify sounds in spoken words (p. 45).

The phonics program emphasized sounds accompanying printed words, but practice was given on sounding letters separately. In addition, there was much practice in applied phonics which emphasized word meaning. For example, the words *call, fall,* and *tall* were presented; children were told that every word said *all* at the end, then were asked, "Which word describes a big man?" "Which does your mother do when she wants you to come?"

As measured by tests given at mid-year and again at the end of the year, the experimental group excelled in oral reading, in silent reading, in applied phonics, in hearing sounds in words, and in tests of letter knowledge.

The evidence is clear that auditory and visual discrimination are closely related to initial success in learning to read. The reasons for this relationship are not so easy to identify. However, general level of perceptual development appears to be a determinant of both skill in sensory discrimination and success in learning to read. And perceptual development, although certainly dependent in part on the accuracy of the sensory mechanism, is dependent also on the child's ability to profit from what he hears and sees and upon the richness and variety of experiences to which he is exposed.

However, to an extent at least, skill in auditory and visual discrimination can be improved by direct training. One of our major responsibilities will be to see that such training is given early in the child's reading program.

LANGUAGE DEVELOPMENT

The acquisition and use of language is closely related to auditory and visual discrimination. But language is more than a basis for hearing, seeing, and taking meaning to words. It is the very basis of the thinking process, and though related to auditory and visual discrimination, language development plays a significant and unique rôle in reading readiness.

Buckingham [16] asserts that many pupils who seem deficient in reading actually are deficient in general language ability. And Harris (p. 38) [42] believes that the major aspects of language that are significant for reading readiness are: the child's vocabulary, the child's mastery of sentence structure, and his clarity of pronunciation.

Artley (pp. 325–326) [7] has outlined the language areas in which the child should have special preparation before beginning to read. He asserts that readiness teaching involves the following:

1. *"Developing awareness of oral words as language units."* [For example, "gimmethe" is three separate words.]
2. *"Enriching oral vocabulary."*
3. *"Strengthening meaning associations."*
4. *"Formulating sentences."*
5. *"Organizing ideas into language units."*
6. *"Using narrative expression."*
7. *"Improving articulation."*
8. *"Developing sensitivity to inflectional variants."*
9. *"Developing awareness of sentence structure."* *

Not all children have equal proficiency in these areas. The slow learner has had a difficult time in learning to interpret speech, and he frequently finds it extremely hard to express himself. Children from the lower socio-economic levels and from homes in which English is spoken only part time may lack opportunity to develop a good vocabulary and to acquire skill in sentence construction. Inaccuracies of pronunciation learned in their homes also may bar them from effective communication and thus reduce still further the stock of meanings that they can take to the task of learning to read.

WHEN IS THE CHILD READY?

To this point we have examined six of the factors that help to determine reading readiness. Although other factors considered in later chapters must contribute to our final decisions, let us, on the basis of our examination of six of the correlates of reading readiness, ask ourselves at this point: when is a child ready to read?

EVIDENCE FOR DELAYING INSTRUCTION

Numerous authorities caution us against hurrying the child too much. Real harm may come from pushing the child beyond his stage of readiness. Is it not better to delay reading instruction for a time and concentrate on other aspects of the child's development?

This is essentially what Schonell was requesting in 1945 (p. 6).[79]

---

* Copyright 1953 by the University of Chicago, reprinted by permission.

My strongest plea in the teaching of reading is, don't hurry the children, don't expect too much in the early stages—do all you can to provide a language background. This slower, wider approach will repay doubly later on. The teaching of both reading and number would greatly benefit if we allowed children time to really understand and assimilate, indirectly and informally, at their own pace and through carefully planned experiences, the fundamental concepts in these two subjects, namely, the meaning of language and the meaning of numbers.

Rousseau (p. 83) [76] found occasion to write:

I would much rather he (Émile) would never know how to read than to buy this knowledge at the price of all that can make it useful. Of what use would reading be to him after he had been disgusted with it forever?

And much more recently Stroud (p. 127) [87] has cautioned teachers not to rush the child into reading. He has pointed out that it is difficult to find any benefit from spending a year making little progress and it is easy to see that much harm may result.

The too early introduction to reading may create a situation in which the child actually learns *not* to read. This is quite different and far more serious than not learning to read.

The experimental evidence indicates that we should be deeply concerned with this problem. Whipple,[100] studying 83 disabled readers from Detroit schools, concluded that in 59 cases the early introduction to reading led to reading difficulties later on. Jensen,[50] studying 22 cases of reading disability, concluded that nine were driven to neuroses because of the unrelenting pressure to force the child to read when he was not capable of reading. Numerous other writers and reading specialists list the early introduction to reading as one of the prime causes for reading disability.

Bond and Tinker (p. 115) [14] suggest that

Reading disability is frequently caused by starting a child in a standard reading program before he has acquired the readiness which will assure success in classroom reading activities. Due to his lack of experience, verbal facility, intellectual or emotional maturity, or a combination of these, he is unable to achieve enough of the learnings day by day to handle satisfactorily what is coming next. He gets farther and farther behind as time goes on. Inability to cope with the assignments produces frustration which leads to feelings of inadequacy, inferiority, insecurity, and perhaps even rebellion. Such a child is likely to develop an attitude of indifference to reading. He may even come to hate reading and all persons and activities connected with reading activities.

Witty (p. 55) [101] points out that the child's life-long attitudes toward reading may be colored by his first experiences with it. Strang and

Bracken (p. 7) [86] suggest that it is extremely difficult to teach reading to a child who has failed in reading. And Doll [21] goes so far as to say that the *principal* cause of poor reading is premature instruction. He recommends that formal pressure to learn the three R's should be postponed until the third grade.

Morphett and Washburne [65] reported that success in reading among first grade pupils in Winnetka, Illinois, increased sharply up to mental age 6½ and that among children who were past that level of mental development at the beginning of school there were relatively few failures. Their findings led many teachers to conclude that reading should be postponed until the child's mental age is six or even six and a half. However, Harris (pp. 28–29)[42] has cautioned against a too literal interpretation of these data. The first-grade reading materials available in 1930 were more difficult and generally less interesting than today's materials. In addition "satisfactory progress" tended to be evaluated on an absolute scale rather than in relation to the child's abilities.

King,[55] studying the relationship between age at entering school and subsequent achievement, used two groups of children entering the first grade. The first group consisted of 54 children whose ages were between five years, eight months and five years, eleven months. In the second group were 50 children between six years, five months and six years, eight months. She found that the majority of children who entered grade 1 before the age of six years did not realize their optimum academic achievement at the end of six years of school. Only one child who entered the first grade after age six was retained in a grade, but ten of the younger children were held back. The study indicated also that members of the younger group had more adjustment problems.

Baer [9] compared two groups of 73 intellectually superior children (average I.Q. 111) matched on intelligence quotient and sex. One group had entered first grade at an average age ten months older than that of the other group. After eleven years in school the older group was found to have received significantly higher grades and achievement-test scores over the entire period. The children in the older group also received significantly higher ratings from teachers on such traits as dependability, emotional stability, initiative, and participation in group activity.

EVIDENCE AGAINST DELAYING INSTRUCTION

Although the evidence suggests that it is unwise to push a child into reading and that a mental age of 6½ may be optimum for beginning reading, there is little basis for choosing a specific chronological age as a criterion. However, as we shall discover in a later chapter, there is some evidence that the eyes may be harmed by an emphasis on close work before the age of eight.

That children, particularly those of higher than average ability, can learn to read at an early age is well established. And, since generally children come to school to learn to read, psychologically it makes little sense to delay those who are ready.

Hollingworth (pp. 69–192) [48] describes a group of children who learned to read at the age of three. Terman and Oden (p. 25) [90] found that nearly 50 per cent of the children with an I.Q. above 140 learned to read before they began school; twenty per cent read before the age of five; six per cent before the age of four; and approximately two per cent before the age of three.

Barbe,[10] studying a group of 103 high-school freshman and sophomores with a mean I.Q. of about 135, reports that forty-seven per cent of the girls and thirty-three per cent of the boys had learned to read before they entered school. And Roslow [75] provides evidence that children below a mental age of six can perform successfully if the instruction is designed to cope with their specific needs.

Thus it seems obvious that numerous factors must be considered before we decide that a general delay in starting reading instruction is the best solution to our problem. Authorities generally suggest that a decision as to when reading instruction begins requires a complex appraisal of the child's developmental level and his psychological needs.

THE ORGANISMIC AGE CONCEPT

We are interested in identifying all of the factors that may be useful predictors of reading readiness. Are there factors such as height, weight, dental age, and various body measurements which in addition to knowledge of the child's mental and chronological age and visual and perceptual discriminatory skills will indicate the child's readiness to read?

Among the numerous proposals for determining when reading instruction should begin is the organismic age hypothesis generally associated with the names of Olson and Hughes.[70] Their premise is that reading is a function of the child's total development. And Olson [71] has suggested that we should delay formal reading instruction until the child's organismic age has reached an appropriate level. Organismic age is defined as an average of mental, physiological, and anatomical age scores and it provides an index of the child's present developmental level.

The theory assumes that there is a systematic relatedness between the structure and the functions of the human organism.[93] Studies indicate that a slight relationship does in fact exist between structures (height, weight, etc.) and functions (reading achievement), but rarely do the correlation coefficients exceed .20.

Tyler [92] raises some serious doubts as to the validity of the organismic age concept, and Stroud [87] suggests that it is based on a spurious relationship. He points out that all aspects of growth require time. For example, one could find a relationship between size of shoe and mental age and in turn with reading ability. He feels that little is gained by adding physical growth measurements to mental age.

Studies by Dearborn and Rothney, Gates, and Blommers, Knief and Stroud support this evaluation. Dearborn and Rothney (p. 270) [20] found that intelligence has some relationship to various physical factors. They obtained correlations with standing height of approximately .22; weight, .14; chest width, .14; iliac, .08; and chest depth, .06. However, the correlation between intelligence and a combination of these five measures still was only about .25.

In 1924 Gates [30] found that the addition of data concerning bone ossification, height, weight, grip, lung capacity, chest girth, and nutritional status to the mental age score, raised the correlation between mental age and certain scholastic achievement measures only from .60 to .63. A more recent investigation [13] of the relationship between mental age and reading and mental age and arithmetic achievement indicates that the addition of three physical measures to the mental age score increased the coefficient by only about .01. The physical measures used were weight, height, and dental age.

THE PRINCIPLE OF SELF-SELECTION

Olson [71] proposes that seeking and self-selection are basic to effective learning. He points out that each child constantly seeks experiences that fit his needs. We have already noted that it is unsound to hurry the child into reading. Self-selection is proposed for preventing undue haste. It is suggested that the child will show his readiness for reading through spontaneous manifestations of readiness activities. Proponents of self-selection suggest that the teacher should look for "seeking behavior." We know that the child generally does not have to be encouraged to speak. If the environment provides proper stimulation for speech, the child, without excessive exhortation or push, learns to speak. The inference is: he need not be exhorted or pushed into reading.

Attempts have been made to plan reading instruction around the principles of seeking and self-selection.[95] Such procedures require considerable individualization of instruction. Children are encouraged to explore materials and make their own selections. They read independently and proceed to new or more difficult materials at their own pace. Brief and frequent teacher-pupil conferences are used to discuss needs and difficulties and to interpret progress. Group activities may be planned to meet needs identified during the individual conferences.

Numerous studies of the effectiveness of individualized reading programs have been reported during the past few years. Some have had positive findings; in others the findings were inconclusive or negative. Let us examine two of them.

Jenkins [49] concluded that second grade children following an individualized approach made significantly greater gains in reading vocabulary and in comprehension than did a comparable group following a more traditional type program. Another study [5] reports that 66.8 per cent of the 223 boys and 86.3 per cent of the 211 girls who received group instruction attained a reading age of 84 months at or before the time they were 84 months of age. Only 44.9 per cent of the 109 boys and 60.8 per cent of the 102 girls who participated in an individualized program achieved a reading age of 84 months at or before the time they reached a chronological age of 84 months. This finding is especially significant because the mean I.Q. of the children in the individualized program was ten I.Q. points above the mean I.Q. of the control group. In the individualized program the children were permitted a choice of basal readers and frequently switched from one set to another. The control group followed a systematic approach to reading. The gains for the systematic approach, however, were not maintained. The children in the individualized program, once they had learned to read, advanced more rapidly and by the age of 132 months the reading achievement of both groups was similar.

As long as we do everything possible to provide experiences that will advance the child's readiness for learning, an individualized approach seems to have certain advantages. It is in harmony with what we know about individual differences in readiness. It seems possible also that individualization can result in more interest in reading. There are important questions, however, that must be answered before one could choose to base reading instruction almost *solely* on the child's *existing* interests. Surely a major responsibility of the teacher is to help the child *extend* his present interests and develop *new* ones.

Stroud (p. 8) [87] has pointed out that:

> It is by teaching children things that they do not, or did not, spontaneously wish to know as a natural consequence of their social life, that we have raised the whole cultural and intellectual level of mankind.

Finally, in any individualized reading program the teacher is faced with almost impossible tasks. He must be familiar with the content and the reading difficulties presented in *numerous* books. Only in this way can he guide children to books written for their level and provide the necessary readiness training.

Actually, the best reading programs encompass both basic skill development and self-selection. Fortunately, as Gates [33] has noted, we are not forced to choose between two antagonistic systems. We are allowed a third and probably a much better option. We can encourage individualized choice of reading matter. In short we can utilize self-selection, but we need not wait passively for it.

INDIVIDUAL DIFFERENCES IN READINESS

The question, "When are children ready to read?" has no decisive answer. There is no single criterion that applies to all children. The teacher must determine *for each child* what program would result in hurrying too much and what would result in too much delay; he must decide when the child is ready to be self-selective and when it is appropriate for the teacher to assume most of the initiative.

We know that children grow toward readiness for reading at different rates. And numerous studies have shown that children who are unready for reading make little or no progress. However, as we have seen, the prediction of readiness is an extremely complex problem. The facts concerning individual differences require that the teacher consider at least three different factors before he can decide on the readiness of a child for beginning reading.

First: The range of differences in level of mental development among first grade children may be as much as four or even six years. Some who enter the first grade may need as much as three years before they are ready to learn to read, but others already may be reading second or third grade material. Differences in achievement within the same age group increase rather than decrease as children advance through school. Harris (p. 16) [42] has suggested that the typical fifth grade exhibits a range of reading proficiency from second or third grade norm to secondary level. Gray [38] reports that a study made in a Chicago suburban area disclosed that 22 per cent of almost 6,000 ninth graders fell below the seventh grade norm in reading achievement. About four per cent attained scores approximating those of the average second or third grader. Waite [98] in 1948 reported a range of over six years among third-grade pupils in the Omaha schools.

Of the 2,212 pupils tested, 33.6 per cent had a reading level appropriate to their grade, 36.2 per cent were better, and 30.2 per cent were below.

Second: The same child may show variations in the development of his various abilities that are as great as are the differences between two children in the same grade. These vast growth differences within the child pose special problems. Readiness for reading requires that a child has achieved at least a minimum level of growth in all essential characteristics. A child may be intellectually ready for reading and have a sufficient background of experiences and yet not be emotionally or, perhaps, physiologically ready.

Third: Individual growth patterns frequently are marked by spurts and plateaus. Even children who appear to be at the same stage of development advance in reading achievement at different rates. A child may lag behind his classmates in the early stages of reading development and catch up with them later on or he may precede them and later fall behind. And variations in rate of growth and variations between boys and girls at different periods of life may be of considerable importance in determining the effectiveness of reading instruction.

In summary, the data concerning individual differences suggest that children develop at different rates; that it is natural to expect a wide range in achievement and that this range widens with age and education; that there are intra-individual differences in growth; and that individual growth frequently is marked by spurts and plateaus.

IDENTIFYING READINESS TO READ

Certainly some aspects of readiness can be measured, but at present no single measure or known combination of measures is fully adequate. Unfortunately, as yet we have no adequate criterion for readiness and no measuring device gives us a complete answer. Betts avers (p. 107) [11] that as yet,

> No scientist has been able to devise any one single basis for a *yes* or *no* answer to the question of when is a child ready for reading instruction.

Thus authorities differ somewhat in their recommendations for determining reading readiness. The clinician tends to place his confidence in a case study approach; the psychometrist generally restricts his study to specific pencil and paper tests; and the teacher is preoccupied with such data as he can gather from group tests and careful observation of each child in the classroom. Lack of time for gathering data and lack of certain specialized clinical skills will bar many teachers from information they might wish to attain. With this in mind, let us examine some specific recommendations concerning how teachers may estimate readiness for reading.

Petty [72] reports that mental age, eidetic ability, the ability to draw, and the ability to distinguish between visual symbols are all positive indications of reading readiness.

Durrell (pp. 49–51),[23] although admitting that reading readiness tests predict readiness fairly well, suggests a very simple method. He recommends teaching the child some words and then seeing if he can remember them. He suggests that children be taught three to ten words printed on individual cards which bear no identifying marks that may be associated with individual words. After an hour each child is tested individually to see how many words he remembers. Durrell says that the child who can remember the words is ready for reading.

Strang and Bracken [86] feel that reading readiness scores when combined with the teacher's day-by-day observation predict the child's success in reading quite reliably. Generally, experienced teachers gauge a pupil's readiness by informal observational techniques, available records, and by scores on readiness and intelligence tests.

Betts (pp. 229–233) [11] and Lamoreaux and Lee (pp. 89–93) [56] provide check lists on which the teacher can record and classify his observations.

Gray (p. 126) [39] presents a *Reading Readiness Chart* based on Schonell [79] that helps the teacher to gauge a child's readiness. This chart is reproduced below.

FIGURE 2

READING READINESS CHART

Name of child ....
Date of Birth .... Age in years .... and months ....
Results of tests, if any are given:
  Mental age .... Intelligence Quotient ....
  Reading Readiness score ....

Estimates of child's development:	1	2	3	4	5
General mental ability					
Background of previous experience					
Range of speaking vocabulary					
Accuracy of pronunciation and related speech habits					
Ability to express oneself clearly to others					
Habit of observing details and forming associations with things seen or heard					
Ability to perceive likenesses and differences					
Ability to recognize relationships					
Ability to keep in mind a series of events or other items					

FIGURE 2 (*Continued*)

Ability to think clearly and in sequence ....
Ability to make good choices and decisions ....
Good health ....
A well nourished body ....
Freedom from undue fatigue ....
Visual efficiency and discrimination ....
Auditory efficiency and discrimination ....
Emotional balance ....
Social adjustment and feeling of security ....
Ability to focus on specific learning activities ....
Ability to follow directions ....
Ability to work effectively in a group ....
Interest in pictures and the meaning of written printed symbols ....
A desire to learn to read ....

1 = *well below average;* 2 = *below average;* 3 = *average;* 4 = *above average;* 5 = *well above average.*

Gray (p. 126) [39] suggests that the teacher use this chart to record the characteristics and behavior of children in their play activities; his observations of the pupil's responses in various learning activities; and the reports of parents and previous teachers concerning the child's interests, language ability, and his mental, physical, social, and emotional development.

A somewhat simpler appraisal chart is given by Gray and Reese (p. 113).[37] Their chart, however, does not provide for gradations in the estimates of the child's development. Instead of giving a rating of 1, 2, 3, 4, or 5, one makes either a "yes" or "no" judgment.

The teacher's ability to co-ordinate various appraisal techniques will be an important determinant of his success in providing for individual differences. At present no single index is sufficient and we must base our judgments on an understanding of numerous factors. Determining reading readiness requires a continuous diagnosis of progress.

SUMMARY

This chapter has been concerned with the broad scope of reading readiness. We have found that readiness is not a unitary trait, but rather that it results from the interaction of many factors. Readiness for beginning reading is an important type of readiness, but the concept of readiness applies to reading on any level. Reading readiness has been identified with a *"teachable moment"* for all phases of learning to read.

We recognize that many factors determine or characterize the teachable moment for reading. At least eleven factors were proposed.

Among these were mental age, the child's sex and general maturity, his background of experience, his language and perceptual development, and his skill in auditory and visual discrimination. It has been our experience that the complex of correlates was more important than any single correlate.

The most teachable moment is different from child to child. In searching for a specific determinant of when a child is ready to read, we found that our decision on when to introduce reading must be based on our knowledge of the individual.

SUGGESTED READINGS

For a general background discussion of the nature of intelligence:

Smith, Henry P., Chapter 6, "The Nature and Development of Intelligence," pp. 151–182 in *Psychology in Teaching*. Englewood Cliffs, N. J.: Prentice-Hall, Inc., 1954.

***

For a detailed discussion of the correlates of intelligence, effect of practice on individual differences, promotion policies, sex differences in achievement and the relationships of chronological age and achievement:

Stroud, James B. Chapter 11, "Individual Differences," pp. 370–405 in *Psychology in Education*. New York: Longmans, Green and Co., 1956.

***

For a discussion of the history of educational interest in readiness, factors related to readiness, readiness tests, and building readiness (with bibliography):

Blair, Glenn M., and R. Stewart Jones, "Readiness," pp. 1081–1086 in *Encyclopedia of Educational Research*, Chester W. Harris (Ed.), 3rd Edition, New York: The Macmillan Company, 1960.

***

(Causey, *The Reading Teacher's Reader*)

Article 8, Duggins, Lydia A. "Theory and Techniques of Auditory Perception as an Approach to Reading" (from an unpublished paper)

Article 16, Sochor, Elona. "Readiness and the Development of Reading Ability at All School Levels," from *Education*, 54 (May, 1954), pp. 550–560.

Article 19, Parkin, Phyllis. "An Individual Program of Reading," from *Educational Leadership* (October, 1956), pp. 34–38.

Article 31, Harrington, Sister Mary James and Donald D. Durrell, "Mental Maturity Versus Perception Abilities in Primary Reading," from *Journal of Educational Psychology*, 46 (October, 1955), pp. 375–380.

QUESTIONS FOR DISCUSSION

1. What is meant by *readiness*? Is it a concept that is of interest to the high-school teacher?

2. What general types of problems can arise from failure to learn to read?
3. What is a developmental task? Discuss.
4. What factors are found to be related to reading readiness?
5. What is meant by mental age? Intelligence quotient? How are they different? Which is more closely related to reading readiness?
6. Discuss the range of mental ages that you would find among a large group of unselected children of age 6. Of ages 8, 10, 12, 14. Give specific data as to the percentages of various mental age levels in each of the above groups.
7. What are the advantages and disadvantages of group tests of intelligence? Individual tests?
8. Suggest as many reasons as you can why girls as a group are better readers than are boys.
9. Why should reading readiness be related to socio-economic status?
10. What are some of the reasons for and against delaying reading instruction? What are the reasons for and against self-selection as a guide for reading instruction?
11. Why might intelligence be more closely related to reading ability at the high-school than at the elementary-school level?
12. What factors in reading readiness should be most amenable to training?
13. How are mental ages and intelligence quotients obtained? How valid and how reliable are they? What is the general shape of the curve of mental growth?
14. Define, discuss, or otherwise show understanding of the following measurements concepts: standard deviation, average deviation, percentile level of confidence, longitudinal and cross-sectional studies, control group, probable error, mean, median, and mode.
15. Discuss the idea that boys may show greater ranges in both I.Q. and scholastic achievement than girls.
16. Should good teaching tend to increase or decrease the range in educational achievement in a class? Should good teaching increase or decrease the size of the correlation between mental age and educational achievement?
17. Suggest solutions to the problem presented by sex difference in readiness to read.
18. What are the implications of the relationship between home background and intelligence for nursery school and kindergarten training? (What children most need such training?)
19. How is home background measured? What are some of its correlates?

BIBLIOGRAPHY

[1] Alden, Clara L., Sullivan, Helen B., and Durrell, Donald D. "The Frequency of Special Reading Disabilities." *Education,* 62 (September, 1941) 32–36.

[2] Almy, Millie Corinne. *Children's Experiences Prior to First Grade and Success in Beginning Reading.* Contributions to Education, No. 954, Bureau of Publications, Teachers College, Columbia University, New York, 1949.

[3] Anderson, Irving H., and Dearborn, Walter F. *The Psychology of Teaching Reading.* Ronald Press Co., New York, 1952.

[4] Anderson, Irving H., Hughes, Byron O., and Dixon, W. Robert. "Age of Learning to Read and Its Relation to Sex, Intelligence, and Reading Achievement in the Sixth Grade." *Journal of Educational Research,* 49 (February, 1956) 447–453.

[5] Anderson, Irving H., Hughes, Byron O., and Dixon, W. Robert. "The Relationship Between Reading Achievement and the Method of Teaching Reading." *University of Michigan School of Education Bulletin,* 27 (April, 1956) 104–108.

[6] Anderson, Irving H., Hughes, Byron O., and Dixon, W. Robert. "The Rate of Reading Development and Its Relation to Age of Learning to Read, Sex, and Intelligence." *Journal of Educational Research,* 50 (March, 1957) 481–494.

[7] Artley, A. Sterl "Oral-Language Growth and Reading Ability." *Elementary School Journal,* 53 (February, 1953) 321–328.

[8] Ayres, Leonard P. *Laggards in Our Schools.* Russell Sage Foundation, New York, 1909.

[9] Baer, Clyde J. "The School Progress and Adjustment of Underage and Overage Students," *Journal of Educational Psychology,* 49 (February, 1958) 17–19.

[10] Barbe, Walter B. "A Study of the Reading of Gifted High-School Students." *Educational Administration and Supervision,* 38 (March, 1952) 148–154.

[11] Betts, Emmett Albert. *Foundations of Reading Instruction.* American Book Co., New York, 1957.

[12] Binet, A., and Simon T. "Le développement de l'intelligence chez les enfants." *L'année psychologique,* 14 (1908) 1–94.

[13] Blommers, Paul, Knief, Lotus M., and Stroud, J. B. "The Organismic Age Concept." *Journal of Educational Psychology,* 46 (March, 1955) 142–150.

[14] Bond, Guy L., and Tinker, Miles A. *Reading Difficulties: Their Diagnosis and Correction.* Appleton-Century-Crofts, Inc., New York, 1957.

[15] Boney, C. Dewitt, and Lynch, Julia E. "A Study of Reading Growths in the Primary Grades." *Elementary English Review,* 19 (April, 1942) 115–121, 133.

[16] Buckingham, B. R. "Language and Reading—A Unified Program." *Elementary English Review,* 17 (March, 1940) 111–116.

[17] Burt, Cyril. *The Backward Child.* Appleton-Century-Crofts, Inc., New York, 1937.

[18] Burton, William H. "Basic Principles in a Good Teaching–Learning Situation." *Phi Delta Kappan,* 39 (March, 1958) 242–248.

[19] Dean, C. D. "Predicting First-Grade Reading Achievement." *Elementary School Journal,* 39 (April, 1939) 609–616.

[20] Dearborn, W. F., and Rothney, J. W. M. *Predicting the Child's Development.* Sci-Art Publishers, Cambridge, Mass., 1941.

[21] Doll, Edgar A. "Varieties of Slow Learners." *Exceptional Children,* 20 (November, 1953) 61–64, 86.

[22] Durrell, Donald D. *The Improvement of Basic Reading Abilities.* World Book Company, Yonkers, N. Y., 1940.

[23] Durrell, Donald D. *Improving Reading Instruction.* World Book Company, Yonkers, N. Y., 1956.

[24] Durrell, Donald D. "First-Grade Reading Success Study: A Summary." *Journal of Education,* Boston University, 140 (February, 1958) 2–6.

[25] Engle, T. L. "Home Environments and School Records." *The School Review,* 42 (October, 1934) 590–598.

[26] Fast, Irene. "Kindergarten Training and Grade I Reading." *Journal of Educational Psychology,* 48 (January, 1957) 52–57.

[27] Fernald, G. M. *Remedial Techniques in Basic School Subjects.* McGraw-Hill Book Company, Inc., New York, 1943.

[28] Fuller, Lorraine. "The Effect of Kindergarten Speech Training on Primary Grade Progress and Achievement of Children with Foreign Language Handicaps." *California Journal of Elementary Education,* 4 (February, 1936) 165–173.

[29] Gallagher, J. Roswell. "Can't Spell, Can't Read." *Atlantic,* 181 (June, 1948) 35–39.

[30] Gates, Arthur I. "The Nature and Educational Significance of Physical Status and of Mental, Physiological, Social and Emotional Maturity." *Journal of Educational Psychology,* 15 (September, 1924) 329–358.

[31] Gates, Arthur I. "The Necessary Mental Age for Beginning Reading." *Elementary School Journal,* 37 (March, 1937) 497–508.

[32] Gates, Arthur I. "Some Characteristics of Research in the Teaching of Reading." *Classroom Techniques in Improving Reading,* Supplementary Educational Monographs, No. 69, University of Chicago Press, Chicago, 1949, 17–22.

[33] Gates, Arthur I. "Improvement in Reading Possible in the Near Future." *The Reading Teacher,* 12 (December, 1958) 83–88.

[34] Gates, Arthur I. and Russell, David H. "The Effects of Delaying Beginning Reading a Half Year in the Case of Underprivileged Pupils with I.Q.'s 75–95." *Journal of Educational Research,* 32 (January, 1939) 321–328.

[35] Gavel, Sylvia R. "June Reading Achievements of First-Grade Children." *Journal of Education,* Boston University, 140 (February, 1958) 37–43.

[36] Granzow, Kent Rayburn. "A Comparative Study of Underachievers, Normal Achievers, and Overachievers in Reading." Unpublished doctoral dissertation, State University of Iowa, 1954; *Dissertation Abstracts,* 14 (No. 4, 1954) 631–632.

[37] Gray, Lillian, and Reese, Dora. *Teaching Children to Read.* Ronald Press Co., New York, 1957.

[38] Gray, William S. "The Nature and Extent of the Reading Problem in American Education." *Educational Record,* 19, Supplement No. 2 (January, 1938) 87–104.

[39] Gray, William S. *The Teaching of Reading and Writing.* UNESCO, Scott, Foresman and Company, Chicago, 1956.

[40] Gray, William S. "Role of Group and Individualized Teaching in a Sound Reading Program." *The Reading Teacher,* 11 (December, 1957) 99–104.

[41] Harrington, Sister Mary James, and Durrell, Donald D. "Mental Maturity versus Perception Abilities in Primary Reading." *Journal of Educational Psychology,* 46 (October, 1955) 375–380.

[42] Harris, Albert J. *How to Increase Reading Ability,* 3rd Edition. Longmans, Green and Company, New York, 1956.

[43] Harrison, M. Lucille. *Reading Readiness,* Revised Edition. Houghton Mifflin Company, Boston, 1939.

[44] Havighurst, Robert J. *Human Development and Education.* Longmans, Green and Company, New York, 1953.

[45] Herr, Selma E. "The Effect of Pre-first-grade Training upon Reading Readiness and Reading Achievement among Spanish-American Children." *Journal of Educational Psychology,* 37 (February, 1946) 87–102.

[46] Hildreth, Gertrude. "Information Tests of First Grade Children." *Childhood Education,* 9 (May, 1933) 416–420.

[47] Hilliard, George H., and Troxell, Eleanor. "Informational Background as a Factor in Reading Readiness and Reading Progress." *Elementary School Journal,* 38 (December, 1937) 255–263.

[48] Hollingworth, Leta S. *Children Above 180 I.Q.* World Book Company, Yonkers, N. Y., 1942.

[49] Jenkins, Marian. "Self-Selection Reading." *The Reading Teacher,* 11 (December, 1957) 84–90.

[50] Jensen, Milton B. "Reading Deficiency as Related to Cerebral Injury and to Neurotic Behavior." *Journal of Applied Psychology,* 27 (December, 1943) 535–545.

[51] Karlin, Robert. "The Prediction of Reading Success and Reading-Readiness Tests." *Elementary English,* 34 (May, 1957) 320–322.

[52] Karlin, Robert. "Some Reactions to Individualized Reading." *The Reading Teacher,* 11 (December, 1957) 95–98.

[53] Keister, B. V. "Reading Skills Acquired by Five-Year-Old Children." *Elementary School Journal,* 41 (April, 1941) 587–596.

[54] Keller, Helen. *The Story of My Life.* Doubleday & Company, New York, 1920.

[55] King, Inez B. "Effect of Age of Entrance into Grade I Upon Achievement in Elementary School." *Elementary School Journal,* 55 (February, 1955) 331–336.

[56] Lamoreaux, Lillian A., and Lee, Dorris May. *Learning to Read Through Experience.* Appleton-Century-Crofts, Inc., New York, 1943.

[57] Linehan, Eleanor B. "Early Instruction in Letter Names and Sounds as Related to Success in Beginning Reading." *Journal of Education,* Boston University, 140 (February, 1958) 44–48.

[58] Loevinger, Jane. "Intelligence as Related to Socio-Economic Factors." *Intelligence: Its Nature and Nurture,* Thirty-ninth Yearbook of the National Society for the Study of Education, Part I, University of Chicago Press, Chicago, 1940, 159–210.

[59] Louttit, C. M. *Clinical Psychology of Exceptional Children,* 3rd edition. Harper & Brothers, New York, 1957.

[60] Macmeeken, A. M. *Ocular Dominance in Relation to Developmental Aphasia.* University of London Press, London, 1939.

[61] Manolakes, George, and Sheldon, William D. "The Relation Between Reading-Test Scores and Language-Factors Intelligence Quotients." *Elementary School Journal,* 55 (February, 1955) 346–350.

[62] McCarthy, Dorothea A. "Some Possible Explanations of Sex Differences in Language Development and Disorders." *Journal of Psychology,* 35 (January, 1935) 155–160.

[63] Milner, Esther. "A Study of the Relationship Between Reading Readiness in Grade One School Children and Patterns of Parent-Child Interaction." *Child Development,* 22 (June, 1951) 95–112.

[64] Monroe, Marion. *Children Who Cannot Read.* University of Chicago Press, Chicago, 1932.

[65] Morphett, Mabel Vogel, and Washburne, Carleton. "When Should Children Begin to Read?" *Elementary School Journal,* 31 (March, 1931) 496–503.

[66] Nally, Thomas P. F. "The Relationship Between Achieved Growth in Height and the Beginning of Growth in Reading." *Journal of Educational Research,* 49 (October, 1955) 153–154.

[67] Nicholson, Alice. "Background Abilities Related to Reading Success in First Grade." *Journal of Education,* Boston University, 140 (February, 1958) 7–24.

[68] Nila, Sister Mary, O.S.F. "Foundations of a Successful Reading Program." *Education,* 73 (May, 1953) 543–555.

[69] Olson, Arthur V. "Growth in Word Perception Abilities as it Relates to Success in Beginning Reading." *Journal of Education,* Boston University, 140 (February, 1958) 25–36.

[70] Olson, Willard C., and Hughes, Byron O. "The Concept of Organismic Age." *Journal of Educational Research,* 35 (March, 1942) 525–527.

[71] Olson, Willard C. *Child Development* (2nd edition). D. C. Heath & Co., Boston, 1959.

[72] Petty, Mary Clare. "An Experimental Study of Certain Factors Influencing Reading Readiness." *Journal of Educational Psychology,* 30 (March, 1939) 215–230.

[73] Pratt, Willis E. "A Study of the Differences in the Prediction of Reading Success of Kindergarten and Non-Kindergarten Children." *Journal of Educational Research,* 42 (March, 1949) 525–533.

[74] Rose, Florence C. "The Occurrence of Short Auditory Memory Span Among School Children Referred for Diagnosis of Reading Difficulties." *Journal of Educational Research,* 51 (February, 1958) 459–464.

[75] Roslow, Sydney. "Reading Readiness and Reading Achievement in the First Grade." *Journal of Experimental Education,* 9 (December, 1940) 154–159.

[76] Rousseau, Jacques. *Émile,* W. H. Payne (trans.). Appleton-Century-Crofts, Inc., New York, 1899.

[77] Samuels, Fra. "Sex Differences in Reading Achievement." *Journal of Educational Research,* 36 (April, 1943) 594–603.

[78] Schonell, Fred J. *Backwardness in the Basic Subjects.* Oliver and Boyd, Ltd., Edinburgh, 1942.

[79] Schonell, Fred J. *The Psychology and Teaching of Reading.* Oliver and Boyd, Ltd., London, 1945.

[80] Scott, Carrie M. "An Evaluation of Training in Readiness Classes." *Elementary School Journal,* 48 (September, 1947) 26–32.

[81] Scott, Lloyd F. "Television and School Achievement." *Phi Delta Kappan,* 38 (October, 1956) 25–28.

[82] Sheldon, William D., and Carrillo, Lawrence. "Relation of Parents, Home, and Certain Developmental Characteristics to Children's Reading Ability." *Elementary School Journal,* 52 (January, 1952) 262–270.

[83] Sheridan, Mary D. *The Child's Hearing for Speech.* Methuen & Co., Ltd., London, 1948.

[84] Smith, Nila Banton. "Readiness for Reading, II." *Elementary English,* 27 (February, 1950) 91–106.

[85] St. John, Charles W. "The Maladjustment of Boys in Certain Elementary

Grades." *Educational Administration and Supervision,* 18 (December, 1932) 659–672.

[86] Strang, Ruth, and Bracken, Dorothy Kendall. *Making Better Readers.* D. C. Heath & Company, Boston, 1957.

[87] Stroud, James B. *Psychology in Education.* Longmans, Green and Company, New York, 1956.

[88] Stroud, James B., and Lindquist, E. F. "Sex Differences in Achievement in the Elementary and Secondary Schools." *Journal of Educational Psychology,* 33 (December, 1942) 657–667.

[89] Sutton, Rachel S. "A Study of Certain Factors Associated with Reading Readiness in the Kindergarten." *Journal of Educational Research,* 48 (March, 1955) 531–538.

[90] Terman, Lewis M., and Oden, Melita H. *The Gifted Child Grows Up.* Stanford University Press, Stanford, Calif., 1947.

[91] Tinker Miles A. "Diagnostic and Remedial Reading, I." *Elementary School Journal,* 33 (December, 1932) 293–306.

[92] Tyler, Fred T. "Concepts of Organismic Growth: A Critique." *Journal of Educational Psychology,* 44 (October, 1953) 321–342.

[93] Tyler, Fred T. "Organismic Growth: Sexual Maturity and Progress in Reading." *Journal of Educational Psychology,* 46 (February, 1955) 85–93.

[94] Tyler, Ralph W. "The Curriculum—Then and Now." *Elementary School Journal,* 57 (April, 1957) 364–374.

[95] Veatch, Jeannette (Ed.). *Individualizing Your Reading Program: Self-Selection in Action.* G. P. Putnam's Sons, New York, 1959.

[96] Vernon, M. D. *Backwardness in Reading.* The University Press, Cambridge, 1957.

[97] Vernon, P. E., O'Gorman, M. B., and McLellan, A. "A Comparative Study of Educational Attainments in England and Scotland." *British Journal of Educational Psychology,* 25 (November, 1955) 195–203.

[98] Waite, William. "The Improvement of Reading in the Omaha Public Schools." *Elementary School Journal,* 48 (February, 1948) 305–311.

[99] Wechsler, David. *Measurement of Adult Intelligence.* The Williams and Wilkins Company, Baltimore, 1944.

[100] Whipple, Gertrude. "Remedial Programs in Relation to Basic Programs in Teaching." *Elementary School Journal,* 44 (May, 1944) 525–535.

[101] Witty, Paul A. *Reading in Modern Education.* D. C. Heath & Company, Boston, 1949.

[102] Witty, Paul A. "Children, TV and Reading." *The Reading Teacher,* 11 (October, 1957) 11–16.

[103] Witty, Paul A. and Kopel, David. *Reading and the Educative Process.* Ginn and Company, Boston, 1939.

5

THE SENSORY BASES OF READING

The reading teacher needs to understand the sensory processes of reading. Efficiency in reading frequently depends on the oculo-motor habits of the reader. Reading begins with visual stimuli; the eyes bring the stimuli to the reader. Auditory factors, though perhaps not as significant as visual factors, under certain conditions also are determinants of reading success.

In Chapter 4 we were concerned with six determinants of readiness for reading. Here we will continue our interest in readiness by examining the sensory bases of reading. As in Chapter 4, our concern goes far beyond readiness for beginning reading. At all levels of development reading achievement is related to sense-organ efficiency.

VISION AND READING

Obviously, reading must begin as a sensory process. The reader must react visually (in the case of Braille, kinesthetically) to the graphic symbols.

The teacher of reading is concerned with the significant facts of seeing and vision. Frequently, writers make some distinction between these two terms. Generally the term seeing is used to include phases of perception as well as sensation whereas vision refers more directly to the efficiency of the eyes.[27] Writers, however, are not always consistent in their use of these words.

Gesell and his collaborators take the position that vision involves the body as a whole. They stress the organismic nature of vision and insist that we not restrict our attention too sharply to the eyes (p. 14).[36] And a publication of the American Optometric Association states (p. 3) [1]:

> Participating in the visual act is the visceral component regulating the focusing of the eye which allows clear vision at the various distances; the skeletal component, regulating the change in position of the eye, which allows single vision at the various distances; and with all of this there must be cortical participation for unification of the resulting visual impressions and for interpretation of the objects perceived.

The act of seeing includes all of what is meant by vision but it goes much further. Ewing (p. 87) [29] writes: "Seeing is mind seeking knowledge. Seeing is mental interpretation. Seeing is the learned skill of interpreting the environment of the organism."

In this chapter, however, our first concern is with the physiological aspects of vision. We shall begin with a focus upon the sensory rather than the perceptual nature of the seeing process. We wish to know: When is a child physiologically ready to read? When are his eyes mature enough for reading?

VISUAL READINESS

We know that a child must have attained certain levels of visual maturation before he is ready to begin reading. He should have become able to focus his eyes at distances of 20 inches or less as well as be able to focus at 20 feet or more. He should have acquired some skill in depth perception, binocular co-ordination, ability to center, and ability to change fixation at will.

Harris (pp. 231–232) [42] points out that for clear vision the eyes must be able to adjust to the amount of illumination and to the distance of the object and be able to focus so that the object is in the most sensitive portion of the visual field. Betts (pp. 131–132) [9] says that visual efficiency means three things in the school:

> First, the child must be able to see clearly at all working distances. . . . Second, the child must be able to see singly at all working distances. . . . Third, the child must be able to see singly and clearly for periods of sustained attention.

Our concern, then, is with the age at which a child achieves sufficient proficiency in these visual skills to begin reading. Our cumulative question now may be phrased: When are the child's seeing processes sufficiently mature for learning to read?

There is some indication that we should question our current educational procedures concerning the age for beginning formal instruction in reading. For example, Jacques,[80] addressing the 1956 Oklahoma Optometric Associtation Convention, stated that the eyes of children are generally not mature enough to cope with the printed page before the age of eight.

There are some data supporting his position and certain others take a similar stand. Cole (p. 282) [19] has said that if the eyes develop normally, the six-year-old is still too farsighted to see clearly such small objects as the printed word. She indicated that a child must be eight years old before we can be reasonably certain that his eyes are ready for reading.

Children are born farsighted. As the eyeball lengthens farsightedness gradually decreases and the child becomes capable of adapting to the demands of near vision. Gray and Reese (p. 99) [40] indicate that some children are unable to focus their eyes on objects at close range until they are seven or eight years old.

It is possible that too early attempts to use the eyes in reading tends to produce myopia (nearsightedness). Leverett,[59] using the Massachusetts Vision Test with some 6,000 elementary and secondary school pupils, found that vision tends to deteriorate markedly from kindergarten through grade twelve. Typically the 20/30 level of visual acuity * is achieved at about age three and the 20/20 level at age five or six. At the kindergarten level 90 per cent of the children passed 20/20 monocular acuity tests. Unfortunately, about the time that children attain 20/20 acuity, deterioration seems to begin. By age 17 about 39 per cent are unable to demonstrate 20/20 acuity in both right and left eyes. This progressive deterioration in vision occurs among children who had achieved only the 20/30 and 20/40 levels of acuity as well as among those achieving the 20/20 level. Figure 1, taken from Leverett (p. 514), plots this process.

Leverett suggests the following explanation for this decrease in acuity (p. 514).

> At school ages, the most obvious potential source of losses in acuity would appear to involve changes in refraction. A trend toward an increase in refraction, less hyperopia and more myopia, during the school years has been reported by many authors. . . . there is evidence that refraction may shift in the hyperopic direction in the early school years. It seems to be agreed, however, that the average refraction moves in the myopic direction after ages seven or eight.

---

* Visual acuity is sharpness of vision. A person is said to have 20/20 acuity if he can read at 20 feet a symbol that the average person can read at 20 feet; he has 20/30 acuity if he needs to read at 20 feet a symbol designed to be read at 30 feet.

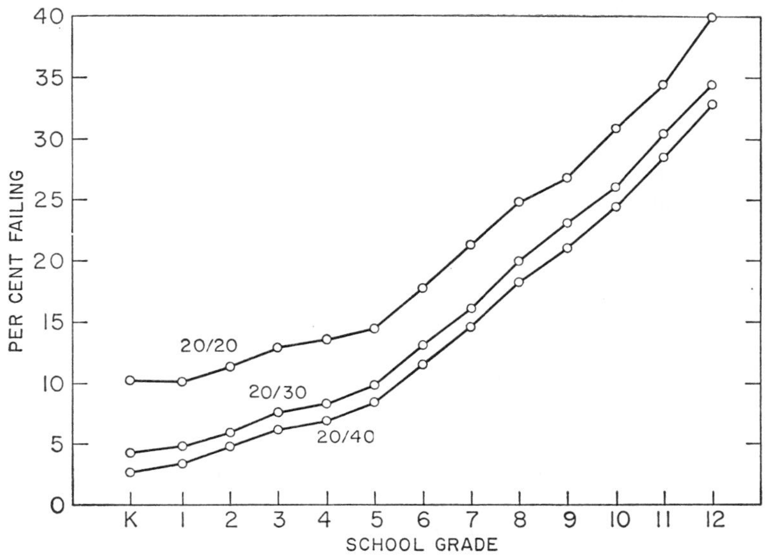

Whether the early introduction to reading actually is a major causal factor in the continuous loss of far-point acuity is not yet certain. Kosinski [52] believes that myopia is a symptom of a general weakness of connective tissue, which manifests itself also in hernias and varicose veins. He suggests that in reading the sweep of the eye from the end of one line to the beginning of the next causes waves of congestion and pressure which may affect the eye's posterior pole.

VISION AND ACHIEVEMENT

Much evidence has accrued that visual skills are related to school achievement.[38, 98] Kephart, for example, tested 2,200 children in grades three through twelve and concluded that four of ten had visual skills below those required for good school work. He also found a positive relationship between visual skill and school achievement.

In a follow-up study, Lowder gave a test of ability to copy seven simple geometric forms (circle, square, horizontal and vertical diamond, cross, divided rectangle, and triangle) to 1,510 first, second, and third graders in Winter Haven, Florida. Lowder concluded that performance on this test was more closely related to school achievement than were scores on an intelligence test.[72] Kephart and Lowder have concluded that visual skills can be improved and that such improvement should lead to better school achievement.

McQuarrie and McQuarrie,[60] analyzing the work of Lowder, adduce evidence that skill in form perception is necessary for successful achievement in reading. They also cite the findings of Ammons, Siegel, and Hebb as illustrations of how perceptual skills are acquired. It seems that a child can be taught to perceive form. The question consequently is: Would children, during the first year in school, find training designed to improve their basic perceptual skills more profitable than conventional reading instruction? Certainly, such data as are available emphasize that these skills are important.

EYE-MOVEMENT RESEARCH

Much of our knowledge of how the eyes react during reading has come from the early work of Javal who was the first to report on the nature of eye movement during reading. He described the eyes as moving "par saccades"—by jumps or jerks.

In reading there is no continuous sweep of the eyes across the page. The eyes proceed in quick, short, movements with pauses interspersed. Eye movements are characterized by fixations, interfixation movements, regressions, and return sweeps. The time required for reading has two elements: fixation time and movement time.

A fixation is the stop the eye makes so that it can react to the stimuli.* It is the pause for seeing. Tinker suggests that the fixation varies from about 220 milliseconds (.22 seconds) for easy reading material, 236 milliseconds for scientific prose, and from 270 to 324 milliseconds for reading objective test items. Fixations account for approximately 92 to 94 per cent of the reading time, whereas eye-movement time accounts for about six to eight per cent of the reading time. The eyes tend to converge during the return sweeps and the interfixation movements and to diverge during the fixation that follows.[18] The interfixation eye movements require from 10 to 23 milliseconds.

During the fixation pause the reader recognizes letters, words, or possibly phrases. The size of the unit recognized during a single fixation depends upon the reader's facility in word recognition, his familiarity with the material being read, the physical characteristics of the material, and his ability to assimilate ideas. Perry and Whitlock [69] have emphasized vocabulary level and the familiarity with the content as determinants of the duration of the fixation pause. Each reader develops his own individual oculomotor habits and is differentiated by them from other readers.

* Tinker [94] found that photographs of eye movements record the approximate center of the field of vision. This "fixation field" is called the point of fixation. However, when "fixating" on this point, one also sees and recognizes a part of the peripheral visual field.

After examining the research data Spache (p. 123) [85] concludes that:

> . . . fixation frequency is not highly related to reading speed. Differences between good and poor readers are not consistently large or significant. While some individuals, particularly good readers, tend to be consistent or tend to show an habitual fixation pattern, fixation frequency is markedly influenced by the purposes of the reader and a number of his individual characteristics. Difficulty of the material, familiarity of the content, as well as format also influence the pattern of fixations. If these elements of the reading situation and the reader modify fixation frequency to a significant degree, training intended to produce a fixed pattern seems unrealistic.

A regression is a return to a previously fixated syllable, word, or phrase for a repeat fixation or a return to material that was missed because the eye movement over-reached the perceptual span. Eye deficiencies that prevent accurate sensation often cause regressions (p. 17).[27] Sometimes, however, the reader regresses out of habit or because he lacks confidence. He feels the need for constant re-reading. Bayle [5] reports that regressions are likely to occur when the flow of thought is interrupted or when perceptions are recognized as inaccurate. The flow of thought may be broken in a number of ways; failure to recognize the basic meaning of a word; failure to recognize the meaning suggested by the context; failure to relate the meaning of one word to that of other words; or failure to relate the meaning of a word to the conditions under which it is used.

Buswell (pp. 33–36) [14] reported that regressions result in immature reading but Bayle [5] has suggested that a certain amount of regression is desirable. Regressions for verification, for phrase analysis, and for re-examination of a previous sentence seem especially useful. However, Hildreth (p. 70) [46] reports the findings of Gilbert [37] and Taylor.[92] Taylor found that senior high school students made on the average 15 regressions per 100 words and college students made 11. Gilbert found that ninth-graders averaged 18.5 regressions per 100 words and college students made 13.6.

After a line is read the eyes make a return sweep to the beginning of the next line. Tinker [97] says that the return sweep takes from 40 to 54 milliseconds. Inaccuracies here may require refixation. For example, the proper line may be missed entirely or the eyes may fix on a point before or after the first word of the new line.

Buswell (p. 26) [14] reported that the average child in grades IB and IA made 18.6 and 15.5 fixations respectively per 3½ inch (21-pica) line. The average college student made 5.9 fixations on a line of the same length. Walker,[103] studying the eye movements of 50 superior readers among freshmen at the University of Iowa, obtained an average of slightly more than eight fixations per four-inch line on material of moderate difficulty.

Buswell photographed the eye movements of 186 subjects ranging from the first grade to the college level. His data suggests that eye-movement skills develop rapidly during the first four grades and that after this little improvement occurs. A slight rise occurs in the sophomore and junior years of high school (p. 27).[14] However, Ballantine (pp. 105–106) [3] discussing his own and Buswell's data writes:

> Both Buswell's and the present study have shown growth beyond the fourth grade. There are differences revealed in the pattern of growth between the two studies, but, if wide enough intervals are used on Buswell's data, then both studies indicate that growth may continue as far as the tenth grade. It is extremely doubtful that, in the case of average groups, any change in growth would prove significant after Grade X.

Various suggestions have been made concerning the relationships between eye-movement characteristics and reading achievement. Some have suggested that eye movements are the major determinants of reading facility; some hold that they are only symptoms of good or poor reading; and still others, indicate that they may be either causes or symptoms or both.

When researchers in reading first succeeded in recording eye movements, many concluded that to improve reading it was necessary merely to improve eye movements. The reasoning was that, generally, poor readers had many more regressions and required more fixations per line than did good readers. It seemed logical that if the number of regressions and fixations could be reduced, reading would be improved. Tinker [95] early questioned the desirability of attempting to improve reading through exercises designed to correct faulty eye movements. He believed that eye movements do not cause, but merely reflect efficient or poor reading performance. Spache [85] takes the position that if attempts are made to reduce undesirable types of regressions some of the desirable ones also are likely to be removed.

In a study of 54 fifth-graders and 54 seventh-graders Morse [64] found that eye movements varied little in proportion to the difficulty of the passage. The eye movements of children at these grade levels seem to be more dependent on individual characteristics than on the difficulty of the reading material. Previously Morgan [63] had proposed that eye movements were hereditary. He obtained photographic records of the eye movements of 33 pairs of fraternal twins, 35 pairs of identical twins, and 40 pairs of unrelated children who were matched on the basis of C.A., I.Q., reading age, grade position, and socio-economic factors. Correlations between the eye-movement scores (regressions, fixations, and average pause duration) for the pairs within each group ranged from .04 to .24 for the pairs of unrelated children, from .24 to .53 for the fraternal twins, and from .66 to .72 for the identical twins.

Other studies, however, seem to indicate that the eye-movement patterns are more directly determined by the difficulty of the reading material. Ledbetter,[57] studying the eye-movement records of 60 eleventh graders tested with five 300-word selections from various fields, found that eye movements varied with the nature of the material. He found that comprehension also varied and concluded that for the average student meanings are more crucial than are vocabulary, sentence length, or sentence structure.

Tinker [96] summarizes past research on this point and concludes that as the difficulty of the material increases and as the individual takes greater pains to read well, the fixation pauses become more frequent and grow longer. Thus the proportion of time required for eye movement becomes relatively smaller. In a later analysis [97] he points out that eye-movement patterns reflect the efficiency of the central processes of comprehension. He suggests that when eye movements do not vary with the difficulty of the reading matter, the readers are immature. Oculo-motor behavior is a symptom of the underlying perceptual and assimilative processes. Efficient reading results in efficient eye movements rather than vice-versa.

Laycock [55] reports that the more flexible reader is distinguished from the less flexible reader both by his rate of eye movement and by the width of his fixation span. He used an experimental group of 37 college students who could shift their rate easily and a control group of 35 who had more difficulty in doing so. He felt that his evidence suggested that rate of progression and width of the fixation span are the eye-movement characteristics that training programs might best emphasize.

Spache (p. 119) [85] suggests that

> . . . eye movements reflect the difficulties of the reader in sight word recognition, word analysis, and comprehension. There is little reason to believe that irregular eye movements cause poor reading. Secondly, irregularities are present in the eye-movement patterns of both good and poor readers, particularly when they are attempting to read difficult or unfamiliar material. Gilbert again stresses the fact that eye-movement records do not accurately predict reading-test performances. They do not discriminate adequately between good and poor readers. Perfect rhythmical eye-movement patterns exist only theoretically, or possibly when one is reading fluently in extremely simple material. Therefore, the concept that eye movements should be subjected to training in the hope of improving reading is extremely tenuous.

MEASURING EYE MOVEMENT

Among the most commonly used means for recording eye movements are the various types of ophthalmographs and special movie cameras, the first of which was invented by Dodge in 1901. In this process, as the individual reads a selection, small beams of light are reflected from his eyes to a photographic film. However, electrical recordings of eye-movement pattern are becoming a common technique. Bond and Tinker (p. 253) [11] suggest that a small mirror can satisfy most needs for observing eye movements. By placing a mirror on a table between the child and the examiner, the number of fixations per line can be counted.

Witty, while at the University of Kansas, checked students' eye movements by placing a mirror on the left side of a mimeographed page. While one student read the page another counted the number of fixations and regressions. Miles [62] suggested a similar method. A hole was punched in the center of a page of reading material. As one person read, another looked through the hole and observed the eye movement. This method was called the "peephole method."

TYPES OF DEFECTIVE VISION

General visual acuity seems to have less significance for reading than do numerous other visual factors. First: reading is a near-point task and near-point acuity becomes far more important than general acuity. Second: reading the average book requires far less visual acuity than the average child possesses.

There are, however, two major types of visual deviation with which we will be concerned. In one, refractive dysfunction, there are defects in the conformation of some portion of one or both eyes. In the other, binocular failure, there is an inability of the two eyes to co-operate successfully.

It is difficult to evaluate the specific effect of these visual difficulties. Children are able to make numerous adjustments to overcome problems. A child can learn to ignore a distortion from one eye if he sees clearly with the other or he may be able to compensate by adjusting his reading position. In some cases he may be able to suppress or suspend the vision in one eye or alternate from one eye to another. However, most such adjustments result in monocular vision, whereas generally for most efficient vision the child should be able to use his eyes in unison. As we shall see, some visual abnormalities create little difficulty if present in minor amounts and still others seem to be associated with reading excellence rather than with reading disability.

REFRACTIVE DIFFICULTIES

Refractive difficulties may be due to injuries, disease, or to hereditary deviations in the lens or other portion of one or both eyes. Generally, refractive errors, if not too severe, can be corrected by glasses. Myopia or nearsightedness is one of the most common refractive errors. The myopic eyeball is too long from front to back. The result of this condition is that at normal reading distance the light rays come into focus in front of the retina. This compels the child to hold his book closer than the normal fourteen to sixteen inches.

Eberl [25] has suggested that a child may become myopic through attempts to adapt his eyes to the demands of close vision before they are ready for it. And, perhaps as important, she concludes that children who do not become myopic may tend to avoid reading (and other tasks demanding near vision) and turn to activities that are more pleasant for them.

Hyperopia is the term used to designate farsightedness. Where the myopic eye was too long, the hyperopic eye is too short. In this condition, at reading distance the image tends to focus at a point behind the retina.

Another type of refractive difficulty, astigmatism, is caused by an uneven curvature of the front or cornea of the eye. The light rays cannot be brought to a single focal point. Vision is blurred. Unless the distorted image is corrected with glasses, reading fatigues the child.

BINOCULAR DIFFICULTIES

The double image is a phenomenon common to all binocular difficulties. In certain cases the two eyes do not aim correctly, in others they give conflicting reports. When the differences are minor, the individual may make adjustments for them. If the differences are major the child sees either two clear images or one blurred image. Somehow he must suppress the image from one eye. When he can suppress it only partially or only temporarily, he is likely to lose his place, omit words, regress, or become confused.

Strabismus (from a Greek word meaning to squint) or muscular imbalance results from an inco-ordination of the muscles that move the eyeball. This defect sometimes is corrected by surgery. In strabismus the eyes actually aim in different directions. One eye aims too far outward, inward, or upward to co-ordinate properly with the other eye. A mild case of strabismus may result in a blurring of the image; a more severe case results in two images.

Special names are given to each of the three types of strabismus. The general tendency of the eyes to deviate is called *heterophoria.* When the deviation is outward, it is called *exophoria;* when inward, *esophoria;* and when one eye focuses higher than the other, it is called *hyperphoria.* Even a moderate amount of heterophoria is likely to result in fatigue. And as the child tires, the deviations tend to increase. As they increase, his attempts to compensate for them heighten his fatigue. He may suppress one image temporarily, but frequently he will lose his place, omit, and regress. His fatigue is likely to be accompanied by inattention and irritability.

A special type of fusion problem, aniseikonia, occurs when there is a difference in the size or shape of the two ocular images. Figure 2 illustrates the different types of aniseikonia.

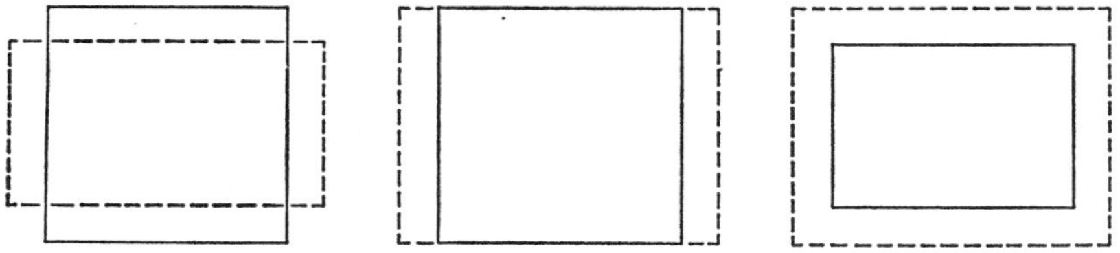

For clear vision, the two eyes must so focus that the images fuse. Inability to fuse correctly is likely to result in the mixing of letters and words, inability to follow the line across the page and frequent loss of place. Fusion problems also may create tension and result in fatigue and headaches.

EYE DEFECTS AND READING PROFICIENCY

Eye defects of one kind or another are rather common. Farris,[30] for example, reports that 44 per cent of the 1685 seventh graders studied had eye defects of varying degree. He also cites two other studies which reported that 42 per cent and 63 per cent of the children studied had some eye defects. A teacher's logical question would be, are there significant differences in visual skills between good and poor readers?

Studies of a general nature do not offer conclusive evidence. Fendrick,[31] for example, comparing 64 poor readers with 64 good readers in grades two and three, reports that the optometrist's examination revealed that 44 per cent of the poor readers and 30 per cent of the good readers had visual deficiencies. This does not appear to be a highly significant difference.

Edson, Bond, and Cook, studying 188 fourth-grade pupils,[26] found no significant relationship between reading proficiency and visual acuity, fusion difficulty, and defective stereoscopic vision. Jackson and Schye [48] studied 640 ninth graders and found that the mean of the mental ability scores on the *Kuhlmann-Anderson Intelligence Test* and the mean reading scores on the *New Stanford Reading Test* actually were slightly higher in the cases of pupils with defective vision than for those with normal vision. Robinson (pp. 217–218, 220–221),[75] studying 22 reading disability cases between the ages of six and fifteen, found visual anomalies present in 73 per cent of these cases but concluded that these contributed to the reading difficulties in only eleven of the cases.

Evaluating the various studies of the relationship between reading deficiency and eye defects, Austin [2] points out that at the high school and college level there are few indications of visual differences between good and poor readers, but on the elementary level more poor readers seem to have visual defects than do good readers. It is possible that by the high school years many of those with poor vision have left school, and that those who remain have been able to adapt their reading habits to compensate for their visual inadequacies.

Certain investigators have focused their attention on the possible relationships between reading proficiency and specific visual factors. First let us examine some of the studies that deal primarily with the refractive errors (myopia, hyperopia, and astigmatism).

Eames,[24] Taylor (pp. 167, 183),[91] Farris,[30] and Witty and Kopel [107] were unable to differentiate the good reader from the poor reader on the basis of incidence of myopia, and in general the research indicates that myopia is not closely related to reading difficulties. In fact, Farris suggests that myopia tends to be associated with better than normal reading progress.

The evidence on hyperopia (farsightedness) seems somewhat more positive. Farris,[30] Taylor (pp. 167, 183) [91] and Eames [24] report that farsightedness is more common among poor readers than among good readers. However, Stromberg,[88] in a study on the college level, suggests that there is little if any relationship between farsightedness and reading proficiency.* And Swanson and Tiffin [90] in another study on the college level, and Witty and Kopel [107] in a study of 100 pupils in grades three to six, reached a similar conclusion.

There also is lack of agreement concerning the effect of astigmatism on reading. Robinson (p. 19),[75] after a summary of the research, concluded that astigmatism may even be associated with superior reading performance. She notes, however, that Betts and Eames have suggested that higher degrees of astigmatism might be a serious handicap to a reader.

There has been considerable research on the effect of muscular imbalance and lack of fusion. The evidence indicates that some pupils are handicapped in reading by muscular imbalance. Harris (p. 235) [42] suggests that lack of binocular coordination is a definite handicap. He points out that of the visual defects poor near-point acuity and poor eye-muscle balance are most significantly related to reading problems. When the devia-

---

* Reading proficiency in Stromberg's study refers to proficiency as measured by the Chapman-Cook Speed of Reading Test.

tions are vertical (in hyperphoria one eye focuses higher than the other), the reader frequently loses his place. This condition appears to occur with equal frequency among both good and poor readers. When the deviations are lateral in nature, the convergence may be insufficient (exophoria) or excessive (esophoria) as in cross-eyes. The former condition seems to occur more frequently in poor readers than does the latter.

Comparing 143 unselected school children with 114 reading disability cases, Eames [23, 24] found fusion difficulty in 44 per cent of the disability cases but in only 18 per cent of the unselected group. Exophoria, and far-sightedness as well, were far more frequent among the disability cases. Dearborn and Anderson,[21] comparing 100 severely retarded and 100 unselected readers, found that 51 per cent of the poor readers and 23 per cent of the controls showed significant amounts of aniseikonia.

Bond and Tinker, summarizing the research on the relation of vision to reading, suggest that even though eye defects do not clearly differentiate good and poor readers this does not indicate that good vision is unimportant to reading. Perhaps, the good reader who has poor vision would have been a far better reader if he had had good vision. There seems to be considerable evidence that at least in certain cases farsightedness, binocular inco-ordination, difficulty of fusion, and aniseikonia contribute to reading difficulty (pp. 89–90).[11]

In searching for possible relationships between visual defects and reading achievement, we must consider the likelihood of multiple causation. In many cases an eye defect alone might not reduce reading efficiency, yet the same defect combined with other factors might do so. And it is quite possible that certain eye defects affect reading performance only when their severity is beyond certain critical points.

SYMPTOMS OF VISUAL DEFICIENCY

A teacher will not be satisfied with mere general information on the incidence of eye defects and their relationship to reading ability. He must have sufficient knowledge of the specific nature of defective vision and of the symptoms of defective vision that he can identify those children whose reading difficulties may be due to visual deficiencies. Particularly, he must become able to detect those defects that should be referred to a specialist.

Prompt referral may result in retarding the progress of some types of defects, and early corrective measures (*e.g.* glasses) may prevent the development of reading problems. Also, if the teacher detects a visual defect, he may be able to adjust his teaching for that individual and thereby avoid a possible reading problem.

The symptoms of visual difficulty are many. Numerous writers have tried to categorize them. Knox (p. 98) [51] counted 94 and from these selected 30 that optometrists and ophthalmologists approved. These are: *

1. Inflammation, reddening, or thickening of the lids and watering of the eyes
2. Assumes poor sitting position
3. Attempts to brush away blur
4. Blinks eyes often
5. Changes distance at which book is held
6. Deviation in one eye
7. Drooping of upper lid
8. Excessive head movement while reading
9. Facial contortions: scowls, puckers forehead, squints, etc.
10. Forward thrusting of head
11. Rubs eyes often
12. Shuts or covers one eye while reading
13. Tilts head
14. Very restless or nervous
15. Alignment in penmanship unsatisfactory
16. Apparently guesses words from quick recognition of parts of words
17. Avoids as much close work as possible
18. Confuses letters such as *o* and *a*, *e* and *c*, *n* and *m*, etc.
19. Holds book far from face while reading
20. Holds book close to face while reading
21. Holds body tense while looking at distant objects
22. Is inattentive in reading lesson
23. Is inattentive during a group lesson on a chart, map, or blackboard
24. Makes errors when copying from board or works slowly while copying from the board
25. Reads smoothly and accurately at first, then jerkily and with errors
26. Skips words or lines while reading orally
27. Has tendency to reverse in reading, spelling, or arithmetic
28. Has tendency to lose place in reading
29. Is tense during close work
30. Tires quickly upon beginning to read or to do other close work

Certainly, early detection of a child's visual difficulty may depend upon our alertness to these danger signs. The child's comfort and the ease and interest with which he approaches reading may be affected. And, in particular cases where a child's reading progress has been delayed by a now-corrected visual handicap, we may need to give him temporary remedial help to restore him to his proper level of reading performance. Although poor vision does not always result in poor reading, good vision certainly will mean more comfortable reading and it will increase the likelihood that the child will find reading rewarding.

SCREENING TESTS

Screening tests are used by the eye specialist as well as by the classroom teacher or school nurse to detect visual problems. The teacher or school nurse uses these tests to locate visual difficulties that require referral to a specialist. Robinson [76] says that one of the first needs of any reading clinic is to provide for a visual screening test.

The *Snellen Chart Test* was one of the first to be used for this purpose. It was designed by Snellen in Utrecht in 1862. The Snellen test identifies nearsightedness and measures visual acuity at a distance of twenty feet, but it fails to detect astigmatism and farsightedness. Since nearsightedness frequently is associated with good reading rather than with poor reading, the test is not too helpful and, generally, it has been replaced by more recent and better tests. The *American Medical Association* (A.M.A.) *Rating Reading Card* can be used with the Snellen test. It is similar to the Snellen but is read at a distance of fourteen inches. One who fails on this test and succeeds on the Snellen Chart probably is farsighted; when the results are reversed the person probably is nearsighted.

The *Keystone Visual Survey Test* requires a telebinocular and a number of special slides. It may detect nearsightedness, astigmatism, muscular imbalance, lack of near- and far-point fusion, and farsightedness. It also tests for stereopsis or depth perception. It is particularly useful as a screening test and does not require highly specialized training.

The *Eames Eye Test* identifies most of the same deficiencies as the *Keystone Visual Test.* It tests for farsightedness, nearsightedness, dimness of vision, eye coordination and fusion. It provides tests also for eye-dominance and astigmatism. It is easy to give and inexpensive. The *Massachusetts Vision Test* and the *Ortho-Rater Visual Efficiency Test* also are coming into greater use. The *Massachusetts Vision Test* requires permanent installation and trained personnel. The *Ortho-Rater* test is difficult to interpret and it is intended for use only by an eye specialist.

We must be cautious in interpreting all visual screening tests. As Rosenbloom puts it (p. 30) [77]: *

> Visual screening tests do not identify every child who has a visual problem, for they are inadequate in identifying certain less common visual difficulties, such as aniseikonia, incipient myopia where acuity is normal, intermittent strabismus, and peripheral and central defects of the visual field.

As has been mentioned, when screening tests are used by the school nurse or the teacher with specialized training, the purpose is to identify those children who should be referred to an eye-specialist.

Since the tests are for screening purposes and frequently lack somewhat in reliability, in doubtful cases the child's welfare is better served if we err in referring him to the specialist than if we err in not referring him.

Not only must the teacher know when to seek the help of the eye specialist, he must know how to co-operate with the specialist for the greatest good of the child.

As Strang and Bracken (p. 163) [87] have pointed out, after children have been referred to an eye specialist, the teacher will wish to know the answers to such questions as the following:

> Should the student return to the eye specialist for further examination?
> Should his reading activity be restricted?
> Have glasses been prescribed? Should they be worn for near work, for distance, or all the time?
> Does the student require any special lighting? If so, what kind and how much?
> Can he do a normal amount of reading and study?
> Should he have a special seat where he can see more easily?
> Does he require a special desk, books, large sheets of paper, large black pencils?

HEARING AND READING

We have already discussed the significance of auditory discrimination in reading. The child must be able to distinguish sounds so that he can learn to speak correctly and to associate the appropriate sound with the printed symbol (p. 276).[17] The ability to discriminate between the various phonetic elements of a word is a skill essential in reading. Auditory factors are particularly important because imperfect hearing causes the child to confuse words and this confusion results in a progressive inability to discriminate among words and their meanings.

The evidence generally indicates that (p. 302) [17]

> Any substantial loss of hearing which exists at birth or occurs soon thereafter will hinder both language development and the establishment of adequate speech habits. Two factors are responsible. First, the hearing loss reduces sharply the number of listening experiences that the child has and thus slows up the process of learning to talk. Second, losses of certain types make it impossible for the child to distinguish some of the elements in speech. No child will learn to pronounce distinctions he does not hear, unless, of course, he has special guidance.

The child who has not made the distinctions in his speech will find it difficult to make the appropriate associations between the spoken word and the written word. Hearing may bear as close a relationship to reading proficiency as does vision.

AUDITORY FACTORS AND READING ACHIEVEMENT

Dahl's (p. 49–51) [20] summary of studies of the relationship between hearing and intelligence indicates that the I.Q. of hard of hearing children when measured by verbal intelligence tests is about seven points below that of the normal child. Wade, for example, found a mean I.Q. of 99.6 for 466 children with good hearing and a mean I.Q. of 92.1 for 86 children with poor hearing (p. 116).[102] However, when the hard of hearing and the normal person are measured on a non-verbal test, the I.Q. differences tend to disappear.

The differences between the normal and the hard of hearing child in educational achievement are much more impressive. Dahl (pp. 51–53) [20] reports on the following studies: Newhart found that retardation occurs three times more frequently among children with defective hearing than among children with normal hearing. Warwick, studying 18,864 school children, found that repeaters were three times as frequent among the hard of hearing as among normal children. Dahl (p. 52)[20] on the basis of data gathered by Wade and Aretz [102] drew the following conclusions:

1. The deafened child in regular school classes is retarded seven-tenths of a school year, in comparison with the normal hearing child.
2. In terms of the Stanford test, these defective hearers are slightly over a whole year below the good hearers in educational achievement.
3. Those pupils who have unilateral defects are one half-year below the average in educational achievement, while those with bilateral defects are slightly more than a whole year below the average.
4. Defective hearing interferes with achievement in all subjects and in all grades. . . .
5. There is a difference of nearly one year's retardation between a group of poor hearers and a group of very good hearers.
6. For every five repetitions among good hearers, there are nine among poor hearers.

Deaf children are handicapped educationally much more than are the hard of hearing. Even minimal perception of sounds appears to allow for most of those experiences that are essential to normal speech and language development. La Grone [53] found that deaf children were far below normal in reading age. For example, the reading scores of her fifth-grade deaf children were at the 2.9 to 3.0 grade level and those of the tenth-grade children were at the 4.7 to 6.6 grade level. Sheridan (pp. 47–48) [82] reports that as hearing loss increases reading achievement becomes poorer. Ewing and Ewing (pp. 245–248),[28] however, report on twelve deaf children who with special training made substantial progress in reading.

Durrell and Murphy [22] in analyzing previous research found that auditory discrimination is closely related to reading achievement.* Gates [35] studying 173 pupils reports a correlation of .28 between the ability to rhyme words and reading achievement, but he believes that the true correlation is even higher since the test he used was a short and consequently fairly unreliable form. The ability to name letters and numbers showed a correlation of .46 with reading achievement.**

Robinson (p. 229) [75] concluded that inadequate auditory acuity is one of the less frequent causes of reading disability.*** She found it to be a contributing factor in but nine per cent of her disability cases. Auditory discrimination and auditory memory span were more significant. However, she does mention that losses in high-frequency acuity are prominent among reading disability cases and Kennedy [50] has offered some support for this. Reynolds,[74] studying 188 fourth grade pupils, reported that the addition of measures of auditory acuity to the mental age scores provided no significant increase in the accuracy of predicting general reading achievement. However, he found indications that auditory-acuity measures may be highly predictive of ability to learn the sounds of common word elements and to acquire certain word-recognition skills.

Henry [44, 45] studied children in the first six grades and found a significant difference in reading scores between those pupils with poor acuity for high-frequency tones and those with normal acuity. She implies that this loss may affect both vocabulary development and reading progress. Actually the 62 sub-normal readers (46 boys and 16 girls) in this group had a greater average hearing loss at all frequencies, but their loss was greatest at high frequencies. Dahl (p. 14) [20] cites six studies which indicate that the boys show a greater incidence of high-frequency loss than do girls. Sheridan (p. 14) [82] notes that

---

* Auditory discrimination refers to the ability to distinguish differences between sounds (as *m* and *n*, *d* and *t*). Auditory acuity refers to the ability to hear sounds. Acuity is likely to vary with the frequency of the sound. Thus a high-frequency hearing loss means that an individual has lowered acuity for sounds of high pitch (frequency).

** This is in agreement with the more recent studies at Boston University reported in the previous chapter.

*** Kennedy found that the auditory acuity of six-year-old children generally is lower than that of eight-year-old children. This point may be quite significant when we remember that the *eyes* may be physiologically unready for reading until about age eight.

If the 'high frequencies' (4,096 and 8,192 cycles) are lost . . . many of the finer sounds, for example '*s*,' '*f*,' and '*θ*' * are so distorted as to become unrecognizable, and the vowel sounds, deprived of their distinctive upper harmonics, acquire a flattened unmusical quality, so that eventually they tend to become indistinguishable from one another.

Hearing losses may be due to inadequate development or deterioration of specific portions of the ear. End-organs for sound are located in the cochlea. Speech sounds of higher frequency such as *f, v, s, z, sh, zh, th, t, d, p, b, k,* and *g,* have been referred to by Berry and Eisenson (p. 448) [8] as the critical determiners of intelligibility. Cole (p. 282) [19] notes that the average six-year-old does not distinguish consistently between *g* and *k, m* and *n,* and *p* and *b.* Metraux's [61] report that the auditory memory span for vowels increases to age ten whereas memory span for consonants increases to age twelve may indicate also that consonants are more difficult to distinguish than are vowels.

However, as Pugh [71] has cautioned, acoustical handicaps do not automatically lead to reading difficulties. Thus immaturities or general weaknesses in auditory discrimination may or may not block progress in reading.

Witty and Kopel (p. 214) [108] suggest that auditory factors are related to reading disability when the method of instruction puts a premium on auditory perception or when the auditory defect is of a gross nature. Bond (pp. 26 and 43) [10] states that auditory acuity is particularly important when the "oral phonetic" method is used. Since auditory acuity seems to be less important when the look-and-say method is stressed, we may have here another important reason for adjusting instruction to the pupil's strengths and limitations.

DEFINITION OF HEARING LOSS

Normal hearing is variously defined. Some authorities suggest that a hearing loss of six decibels ** makes one hard of hearing; others believe the loss must equal fifteen or more decibels. Because of this variation in definition writers have reported proportions of hearing deficiencies varying from three to twenty per cent. Bond and Tinker (p. 92),[11] Silverman (p. 355),[83] and O'Connor and Streng (p. 156) [67] estimate that five per cent of school children suffer from auditory deficiencies that interfere with their school

* "th" as in thin.

** The decibel is a unit in the measure of sound intensity variation. Normal conversation has an intensity of about 60 decibels above a sound that is barely audible. Thus if an individual has a sixty decibel hearing loss in the speech range of sound, he would be aware of conversation only as a barely audible sound.

progress. Other estimates are considerably higher, ranging upward to ten per cent. Dahl (p. 14) [20] identifies several factors that may lead to variations in the estimates of the number of hard-of-hearing children. Among these are the following:

1. The incidence of impaired hearing is higher in the elementary school than in the high school.
2. Hearing impairments occur more frequently among children from homes of low socio-economic groups than among children of high socio-economic levels.
3. Hearing acuity is better among Negro than among white children.
4. Children of superior intelligence make better scores on the audiometer than do children of low intelligence even when their hearing loss actually is the same.

SYMPTOMS OF HEARING DEFICIENCIES

There are certain symptoms of hearing difficulty with which we should be familiar. Hard of hearing children are likely to be inattentive and to ask that questions be restated. They tend to tilt the head so the best ear is toward the speaker. They also tend to look closely at the speaker to get additional clues or they may cup a hand behind the ear. At times their facial expressions may indicate an inability to perceive sounds. Parents may suspect hearing difficulty if the child needs to have the radio, record player, or TV exceptionally loud or if he complains of ringing or buzzing in the ears.

The hearing of every child showing such symptoms (indeed that of any reading disability case) should be tested. Bond and Tinker (p. 94) [11] suggest a number of methods for doing this. A loud-ticking watch may be used as a simple test. Normally a child can hear the ticking up to a distance of about 48 inches. Anything below 20 inches probably indicates hearing deficiency. For a more accurate test an audiometer may be used. Newby (p. 39) [66] suggests that the audiometer used in testing should provide for both air-conduction and bone-conduction testing and for introducing masking tones. There are two general types of audiometers: *discrete* frequency, providing tones in half- or full-octave steps, and *sweep* frequency, providing a continuous variation of frequencies. Hearing loss usually is measured in five-decibel steps. Some audiometers are similar to a portable phonograph with several connected telephone receivers that permit individual testing or the simultaneous testing of as many as 40 children. For group testing with such a machine children must be able to write numbers, although in individual testing a teacher could record a child's answers.

EDUCATIONAL SIGNIFICANCE OF THE RESEARCH ON AUDITORY FACTORS

O'Connor and Streng [67] divide the hard of hearing into four groups. Those with an average loss of 20 decibels or less in the better ear require no special treatment although it would be wise to seat them advantageously in the classroom. Children in the 25 to 55 decibel loss group may need speech training and those with a loss of 35 decibels may need a hearing aid. A third group with losses ranging from 55 to 75 decibels usually cannot learn to speak without aid. The individuals in this group are considered educationally deaf. A fourth group consists of those who are suffering more than a 75 decibel loss. Members of this group cannot learn speech through sound, and ordinarily the public school is unable to meet their needs. They require special treatment. Frisina (p. 3 ff.) [34] notes that children with a 40 decibel loss across the speech range will have particular difficulty with *ch, f, k, s, sh, t, th,* and *z.*

Certainly loss of hearing, if severe enough, can aggravate a reading difficulty, but we must remember that causes often are complex rather than simple, multiple rather than single. It may be that auditory deficiencies and reading disability are closely related only under certain circumstances: if the hearing loss is severe, if the specific hearing loss involves high-tone deafness, and if instruction puts a premium on auditory factors.

We cannot be satisfied, however, with the mere detection of auditory deficiencies. Although there may be little we can do to improve auditory acuity, auditory discrimination at least in part may be learned. We can train the child to become more aware of sound, to make gross discriminations such as between the sound of a bell and a horn, to discriminate among simple speech patterns such as differences between the vowels, and we can help him to recognize the phonetic elements of words (p. 284).[17]

LISTENING AND READING

In the preceding portions of this chapter we have focused our attention on the sensory processes of vision and hearing. We have discussed them at length because sensation is a first step toward perception. However, we cannot divorce the sensory phases from the perceptual phases. We must seek to integrate our knowledge of sensation with our understanding of the total process of perception.

We have already examined the perceptual aspects of vision. Let us now examine the perceptual aspects of hearing. These generally are referred to as listening.

Listening, although dependent on the ability to hear, involves more than the physical process of hearing. Listening is learned early in life, and listening habits are acquired and perfected through experiences. Carhart (p. 279)[17] points out that

> . . . *the capacity for mastering new sound discriminations diminishes with age.* It is common knowledge that a child will learn to speak fluently the language he hears, regardless of his race or nationality. By contrast, when an adult learns a new language, he finds that he has what native speakers call a 'foreign accent.' The fault is partly that he has fixed his habits of speech and partly that he has fixed his habits of listening. The latter interests us here. What happens is that he does not notice subtle differences in the phonetic elements and cadences of the two languages. He 'hears' the elements in the new language as though they were identical with those of his native tongue. When he talks, he puts the old patterns in the new language. Unless he is taught to notice the subtle differences, he may go through life without even realizing that they exist.

The implications for reading are obvious. The child cannot say what he hasn't heard. He cannot learn to associate the visual stimulus with the proper oral-aural equivalent if he has neither heard nor spoken accurately.

THE NEED FOR LISTENING ABILITY

Caffrey[16] uses the term "auding" to encompass the process of hearing plus the interpretation or comprehension of spoken language. Fessenden[32] theorizes that there are seven levels of listening. From simplest to most complex they are: isolation of sounds, ideas, arguments or facts; attribution of meanings to the factors we have isolated; integration of them with our past experience; inspection of them for relationships; interpretation of them for implications; interpolation of the statements that we have heard; and introspection for an understanding of what effect they have on us.

In the past, listening was a most important communicative skill. For ages communication of ideas was by word of mouth. Indeed, as Overstreet suggests, in the long preliterate stages of history, the person who was not a good listener must have been a prisoner within his own small cell of experience.[68] We realize that today many children fail to develop proficient listening skills. Some of this inefficiency results from inattention or an unwillingness to listen to what is contrary to certain preconceived notions.

Only recently has it been recognized that the development of the listening skill of pupils is an important concern to the modern classroom teacher. We know that some children benefit more, at least during certain portions of their educational program, from an emphasis on listening rather than on reading. With the advent of radio, movies, and television listening has become increasingly important.

Teachers, unfortunately, frequently fail to see the importance of skillful listening. Wilt [106] questioned teachers from 42 states in an effort to determine the amount of time that they believed pupils devoted to listening activities and, in addition, personally visited 19 classrooms and recorded pupil listening time. Teachers estimated that listening occupied only 74 minutes per day, but actually, on the elementary level, 158 minutes per day were so occupied. She concluded that most elementary teachers are not fully aware of listening as a basic communication skill.

THE LISTENING PROCESS

Listening and reading involve the same mental process. Both call for the reception of ideas from others; both are basic means of communication. Reading demands sight and comprehension; listening calls for hearing and comprehension. Essentially the spoken and the written word should result in the same meaning. The listener or reader first receives the stimulus. He then identifies it and gives it meaning through integration with his past experiences. Berg (p. 55) [7] adds:

> Reading, verbal expression, and listening are a part of the central thought processes of language symbolization. Thus, comprehension, being largely a centrally-determined function, operates independently of the mode of presentation of the material.

Studies show a high correlation between ability to listen and ability to read. This should be expected. The correlations range from approximately .30 to .80. Generally, they lie between .60 and .80. Brown,[13] for example, reports a study at the University of Minnesota in which those who graduated "with high distinction" had an average percentile rank of 78 in reading and of 92 in listening. Those who graduated "with distinction" also had an average percentile rank of 78 in reading, but only 81 in listening. The extreme importance of listening ability is further emphasized by the finding that only two students in these two groups came to the university with listening ability below the 50th percentile.

However, there are certain important differences between reading and listening. In reading, the child can proceed at his own rate. He may pause for reflection. In listening the personality and "delivery" of the speaker become important. He contributes to the child's "set" to listen much as the writer contributes to the reader's "set," but he goes beyond this, for face-to-face contact offers the listener a clearer picture of the emotions, the emphasis and shadings of meaning, and the attitudes that the speaker strives to impart.

Listening has a dimension that reading does not possess. This dimension is the speaker's control of emphasis and timing which offers potentialities for increased perceptual veridicality. And the skilled speaker can perceive audience reaction and adjust to it with added explanation when necessary. Whereas the writer's action must precede the reader's reaction; the speaking-listening situation can be a directly interactive process.

Harris (pp. 396–397) [42] mentions some of the special demands made on the reader:

> Reading, however, imposes additional tasks which are absent when one listens. For one thing, the words must be recognized if their meaning is to be appreciated. A second difference is that, in reading, one must organize the material into meaningful phrase and thought units, while in listening this is to a large extent done for the listener by the phrasing and expression of the speaker. A third point of difference is that in listening, the rate of comprehension is set by the rate of speech of the speaker while in reading one has to learn to govern one's rate of reading so as to go fast enough to catch the flow of ideas, but not so fast as to miss too many of the details.

As we discuss the importance of listening we have certain questions. How efficient is listening as a means for learning and what are its limitations? Can listening actually be taught? Does teaching the child how to listen help him in his reading? Does the concept of readiness apply to listening as well as to reading? If so, when is a child ready to listen?

THE RELATIVE EFFECTIVENESS OF LISTENING

Teachers have long been concerned with the comparative effectiveness of listening and reading. Early studies suggested that listening might be the better means for learning. Young,[110] studying some 2,000 students in grades four, five, and six, found that a child's reading comprehension skills tend to catch up with his listening skills during the fifth or sixth grade. He also reports that children learn only a very small proportion of orally presented materials. In Grade Four, for example, the comprehension scores ranged from 21 to 33 per cent depending on the selection used. In the later elementary years the child may profit more by reading than by listening. However, Berry [6] suggests that learning acquired through listening may be remembered for a longer period of time.

The slow learner, especially, finds listening beneficial, and the retarded reader frequently expresses a preference for listening as a mode of learning. Larsen and Feder [54] found that the lower the reading ability and the lower the scholastic aptitude, the greater is the advantage of listening over reading. And the higher the scholastic aptitude the more definitely superior is reading over listening. Lazarsfeld (p. 138 ff.) [56] states that the lower the cultural level of the home, the more emphasis is put on listening. He points out, however, that the greater one's interest is in certain information, the greater is the tendency to use the means of communication that can provide the most data.

Larsen and Feder,[54] in a study already referred to, report that as the difficulty of material increases the scores in reading comprehension are increasingly higher than the scores in listening comprehension. They recommend that orally presented material should be less difficult than material to be read if it is to be comprehended with equal effectiveness.

Russell's [79] study of the relative effectiveness of reading and listening of 690 fifth, sixth, and seventh graders permits the following conclusions:

1. In grade five, students learn more from having material read to them than by reading it themselves.
2. In grade seven, the relative effectiveness of the two methods is practically equal.
3. In grade nine, learning by reading has a slight advantage.

Bond and Tinker (p. 233) [11] summarize the findings relative to listening thus:

1. In the lower grades, listening comprehension is equal to or better than reading comprehension. This holds true also for pupils of low ability.
2. However, when pupils have become more skilled in reading, reading comprehension is equal or superior to listening comprehension. The same trend is evident for pupils of relatively high academic ability.

Caffrey's [15] study is particularly interesting in that he has proposed specific rules governing the relationship between listening and reading. He states (p. 310):

1. When auding ability is low, reading ability tends more often to be low.
2. When auding ability is high, reading ability is not predictable.
3. When reading ability is low, auding ability is not predictable.
4. When reading ability is high, auding ability is to a very small extent predictable, likely to be high.

THE TEACHER'S INTEREST IN THE LISTENING PROCESS

Listening certainly is a method for learning and as such should be developed and used to advantage in the classroom. Its role in promoting reading readiness may not be fully understood. If a child is immature in near-point vision, it seems that we might find it advantageous to focus more attention on his listening ability. Thus we may help him gain a background of experiences for his later development in reading. And we need to become better acquainted with the uses that can be made of listening as a diagnostic tool. We have come to recognize that a child may be expected to read at a level comparable to his listening level. Thus, if a child is known to be able to learn effectively through listening but not through reading, we may conclude that he should benefit greatly from special help in reading. The slow learner especially may have needs for learning that should be nurtured through listening before he can be ready to read effectively. Also films, slides, and film strips seem to offer unique opportunities for broadening the child's experiences and increasing his stock of usable concepts.

Film-readers [58] appear to have special values. Not only can the child see and hear while using the film, but he can then read the same words and content in a correlated reader. The opportunity to hear speech and to see it in print at the same time may greatly encourage learning. At present at least three sets of film-readers are available. D. C. Heath & Company, under the series title, "It's Fun to Find Out," provides one set for the second grade and one for the third grade. Row, Peterson & Company provides a series of readers that correlates with the Britannica film series entitled "Children of Many Lands."

Just as perception is much more complex than sensation, so listening is more complex than hearing. Listening goes beyond the mere recognition of sound. Berg (p. 59) [7] stresses that training in listening

> . . . must consider the thought processes which are necessary for comprehension and attempt to instruct in ways of improving these, rather than dealing exclusively with the peripheral and mechanistic aspects of the media. Such attention to thought processes should certainly include work in the pragmatic use of language and thinking in general.

From Barbe and Myers' [4] discussion of the data on listening it may be concluded (1) that listening is an effective means for learning; (2) that listening ability is governed by the physical, emotional, and mental status of the individual; (3) that listening is an acquired skill and its growth advances in an orderly fashion through developmental levels; (4) that listening is of three kinds: appreciative, critical, and discriminative; and (5) that how one listens is determined by his purpose for listening.

Hackett [41] suggests that our present knowledge of how to teach listening is extremely inadequate. Sister Mary Kevin Hollow,[47] however, in a study involving 302 fifth graders reports that listening skills can be appreciably improved through a planned program of instruction. Needham [65] recommends that as a first step youngsters must learn that communication involves the *reception* as well as the transmission of ideas. Among the procedures he suggests for accomplishing this is the provision for pupil practice in carrying out oral instructions. Hatfield (p. 555) [43] says that listening should be taught and he lists seven approaches:

1. Listening for the answer to a definite question
2. Listening to a question, with the intention to answer
3. Listening to form an opinion on a controversial question
4. Listening for news . . .
5. Listening to an argument in order to answer it
6. Listening to directions which one expects to follow
7. Listening for unspecified information on a topic one is interested in.

SUMMARY

Reading is a visual skill, but success in reading depends more on the underlying perceptual and assimilative processes than on visual efficiency and the peculiar oculo-motor habits of the individual reader. Faulty eye movements are not so much a cause of poor reading as a symptom of poor reading. Eye defects, even though they are of a fairly gross nature seldom are an absolute bar to a child's becoming a good reader. However, they may result in uncomfortable and inefficient reading.

Auditory defects are most likely to hinder reading success when there is a severe hearing loss, when hearing loss involves deafness for high tones, and when instruction puts a premium on auditory factors.

Closely related to auditory factors is listening. Listening requires a cultivation of auditory abilities. It involves the same basic perceptual and mental processes as reading and, indeed, in certain cases may be a more suitable method of learning than is reading. The child of low intelligence as well as the average child in the lower grades may find it more profitable to listen than to read.

The teacher needs to be aware of the possible deficiencies of vision and hearing and be able to recognize their symptoms. Aware of pupils' problems, he may more efficiently arrange his classroom for the benefit of any who may be handicapped. If the symptoms and the school's physical testing service so indicate, the child's parents should be consulted and they should be advised to seek medical aid.

SUGGESTED READINGS

(Causey, *The Reading Teacher's Reader*)

Article 5, Berg, Paul C. "Reading in Relation to Listening," from Fourth Yearbook Southwest Reading Conference (1955) pp. 52–59.

Article 17, Pratt, Edward. "Auditory Disabilities Related to Reading."
Article 30, Brown, James I. "The Measurement of Listening Ability," from *School and Society*. (February, 1950) pp. 102–104.

***

For short adapted articles, see the following as reprinted in C. W. Hunnicutt and William J. Iverson, *Research in the Three R's,* New York: Harper and Brothers, 1958.

Chapter 3, "How We Read," contains three articles on the general nature of eye movements.

QUESTIONS FOR DISCUSSION

1. What distinctions may be made between the terms *seeing* and *vision*?
2. Discuss the question of when the child's eyes are ready for reading.
3. What are the data concerning deterioration in vision as children grow older?
4. What relationships are observed between form perception and reading?
5. What is known about the nature of eye movements during reading? What are some of the factors that result in variations in eye movements? Should training designed to improve eye movements result in reading improvement?
6. What are the general types and symptoms of defective vision?
7. What relationships have been observed between eye defects and reading proficiency?
8. What tests are used for detecting visual defects?
9. What are the relationships between hearing and reading?
10. How is hearing loss measured?
11. What relationships have been observed between reading and listening?
12. What may be done to improve listening skill?
13. In what ways are reading and listening the same process? How do they differ?
14. What are the common refractive errors and binocular difficulties?
15. What auditory and visual screening tests would you choose? Why?
16. Discuss visual readiness for reading.

BIBLIOGRAPHY

[1] American Optometric Association. *Manual on the Visual Care of the Non-Achieving Child.* Committee on Visual Problems in Schools, St. Louis, 1956.

[2] Austin, Mary C. "Personal Characteristics that Retard Progress in Reading." *Keeping Reading Programs Abreast of the Times,* Supplementary Edutional Monographs, No. 72, University of Chicago Press, Chicago, 1950, 112–117.

[3] Ballantine, Francis A. "Age Changes in Measures of Eye-Movements in Silent Reading." *Studies in the Psychology of Reading,* Monographs in Education, No. 4, University of Michigan Press, Ann Arbor, 1951, 67–111.

[4] Barbe, Walter B., and Myers, Robert M. "Developing Listening Ability in Children." *Elementary English,* 31 (February, 1954) 82–84.

[5] Bayle, Evalyn. "The Nature and Causes of Regressive Movements in Reading." *Journal of Experimental Education,* 11 (September, 1942) 16–36.

[6] Beery, Aletha. "Interrelationships between Listening and Other Language Arts Areas." *Elementary English,* 31 (March, 1954) 164–172.

[7] Berg, Paul. "Reading in Relation to Listening." *Evaluating College Reading Programs,* Fourth Yearbook of the Southwest Reading Conference for Colleges and Universities, Texas Christian University Press, Fort Worth, 1955, 52–60.

[8] Berry, Mildred F., and Eisenson, Jon. *Speech Disorders: Principles and Practices of Therapy.* Appleton-Century-Crofts, Inc., New York, 1956.

[9] Betts, Emmett Albert. *Foundations of Reading Instruction.* American Book Company, New York, 1957.

[10] Bond, Guy L. *The Auditory and Speech Characteristics of Poor Readers.* Contributions to Education, No. 657, Bureau of Publications, Teachers College, Columbia University, 1935.

[11] Bond, Guy L., and Tinker, Miles A. *Reading Difficulties: Their Diagnosis and Correction.* Appleton-Century-Crofts, Inc., New York, 1957.

[12] Boykin, Leander L. "Who is the Exceptional Child?" *Elementary School Journal,* 58 (October, 1957) 42–47.

[13] Brown, James I. "Evaluating Student Performance in Listening." *Education,* 75 (January, 1955) 316–321.

[14] Buswell, Guy Thomas. *Fundamental Reading Habits: A Study of Their Development.* Supplementary Educational Monographs, No. 21, University of Chicago Press, Chicago, 1922.

[15] Caffrey, John. "The Establishment of Auding-Age Norms." *School and Society,* 70 (November 12, 1949) 310–312.

[16] Caffrey, John. "Auding." *Review of Educational Research,* 25 (April, 1955) 121–138.

[17] Carhart, Raymond. "Auditory Training," and "Conservation of Speech," pp. 276–317 in Davis, Hallowell. editor. *Hearing and Deafness: A Guide for Laymen.* Murray Hill Books, Inc., New York, 1947.

[18] Carmichael, Leonard, and Dearborn, Walter F. *Reading and Visual Fatigue.* Houghton-Mifflin Company, Boston, 1947.

[19] Cole, Luella. *The Improvement of Reading with Special Reference to Remedial Instruction.* Farrar & Rinehart, Inc., New York, 1938.

[20] Dahl, L. A. *Public School Audiometry: Principles and Methods.* The Interstate Printers and Publishers, Danville, 1949.

[21] Dearborn, Walter F., and Anderson, Irving H. "Aniseikonia as Related to Disability in Reading." *Journal of Experimental Psychology,* 23 (December, 1938) 559–577.

[22] Durrell, Donald D., and Murphy, Helen A. "The Auditory Discrimination Factor in Reading Readiness and Reading Disability." *Education,* 73 (May, 1953) 556–560.

[23] Eames, Thomas H. "A Comparison of the Ocular Characteristics of Unselected and Reading Disability Groups." *Journal of Educational Research,* 25 (March, 1932) 211–215.

[24] Eames, Thomas H. "A Frequency Study of Physical Handicaps in Reading Disability and Unselected Groups." *Journal of Educational Research,* 29 (September, 1935) 1–5.

[25] Eberl, Marguerite. "Visual Training and Reading." *Clinical Studies in Reading, II,* Supplementary Educational Monographs, No. 77, University of Chicago Press, Chicago, 1953, 141–148.

[26] Edson, William H., Bond, Guy L., and Cook, Walter W. "Relationships between Visual Characteristics and Specific Silent Reading Abilities." *Journal of Educational Research,* 46 (February, 1953) 451–457.

[27] Educational Developmental Laboratories, Inc. *The Evolution and Growth of Controlled Reading Techniques.* Huntington, New York, 1958.

[28] Ewing, Irene R. and Ewing, A. W. G. *Speech and the Deaf Child.* The Volta Bureau, Washington, 1954.

[29] Ewing, J. Ralph. "Visual Disabilities in Regard to Reading Problems." *Exploring the Goals of College Reading Programs,* Fifth Yearbook of the Southwest Reading Conference for Colleges and Universities, Texas Christian University Press, Fort Worth, 1956, pp. 87–92.

[30] Farris, L. P. "Visual Defects as Factors Influencing Achievement in Reading." *Journal of Experimental Education,* 5 (September, 1936) 58–60.

[31] Fendrick, Paul. *Visual Characteristics of Poor Readers.* Contributions to Education, No. 656, Bureau of Publications, Teachers College, Columbia University, 1935.

[32] Fessenden, Seth A. "Levels of Listening—A Theory." *Education,* 75 (January, 1955) 288–291.

[33] Frank, Helene. "A Comparative Study of Children Who Are Backward in Reading and Beginners in the Infant School." *British Journal of Educational Psychology,* 5 (February, 1935) 41–58.

[34] Frisina, D. Robert. *Hearing: Its Interrelation With Speech.* Bulletin No. 1, Gaullaudet College, Kendall Green, Washington 2, D. C., 1957.

[35] Gates, Arthur I. "A Further Evaluation of Reading-Readiness Tests." *Elementary School Journal,* 40 (April, 1940) 577–591.

[36] Gesell, Arnold, Ilg, Francis L., and Bullis, Glenna E. *Vision: Its Development in Infant and Child.* Paul B. Hoeber, Inc., New York, 1949.

[37] Gilbert, Luther C. *Functional Motor Efficiency of the Eyes and Its Relation to Reading.* Publications in Education, No. 3, University of California Press, 1953, 159–232.

[38] Goins, Jean Turner. *Visual Perceptual Abilities and Early Reading Progress.* Supplementary Educational Monographs, No. 87, University of Chicago Press, Chicago, 1958.

[39] Goldstein, Kurt. *The Organism.* American Book Company, New York, 1939.

[40] Gray, Lillian, and Reese, Dora. *Teaching Children to Read.* The Ronald Press Company, New York, 1957.

[41] Hackett, H. "A Null Hypothesis: There is Not Enough Evidence." *Education,* 75 (January, 1955) 349–351.

[42] Harris, Albert J. *How to Increase Reading Ability,* 3rd Edition. Longmans, Green and Company, New York, 1956.

[43] Hatfield, W. Wilbur. "Parallels in Teaching Students to Listen and to Read." *English Journal,* 35 (December, 1946) 553–558.

[44] Henry, Sibyl. "Children's Audiograms in Relation to Reading Attainment: I. Introduction to and Investigation of the Problem." *Journal of Genetic Psychology,* 70 (June, 1947) 211–231.

[45] Henry, Sibyl. "Children's Audiograms in Relation to Reading Attainment: II. Analysis and Interpretation." *Journal of Genetic Psychology,* 71 (September, 1947) 3–63.

[46] Hildreth, Gertrude. *Teaching Reading.* Holt, Rinehart and Winston, Inc., New York, 1958.

[47] Hollow, Sister Mary Kevin. "Listening Comprehension at the Intermediate Grade Level." *Elementary School Journal,* 56 (Dec., 1955) 158–161.

[48] Jackson, Thomas, and Schye, Virginia. "A Comparison of Vision with Reading Scores of Ninth Grade Pupils." *Elementary School Journal,* 46 (September, 1945) 33–35.

[49] Kasdon, L. M. "Some Characteristics of Highly Competent Readers Among College Freshmen." *Dissertation Abstracts,* 15 (October, 1955) 1785–1786.

[50] Kennedy, Helen. "A Study of Children's Hearing as It Relates to Reading." *Journal of Experimental Education,* 10 (June, 1942) 238–251.

[51] Knox, Gertrude E. "Classroom Symptoms of Visual Difficulty." *Clinical Studies in Reading, II,* Supplementary Educational Monographs, No. 77, University of Chicago Press, Chicago, 1953, 97–101.

[52] Kosinski, W. "Die Myopie als variköses Syndron Der Augen." Klinische Monatsblätter für Augenheilkunde, 130 (1957) 266–270. Cited by Linksz, Arthur. "Optics and Visual Physiology." *A. M. A. Archives of Ophthalmology,* 59 (June, 1958) 901–969.

[53] La Grone, Truda Gough. "An Analytical Study of the Reading Habits of Deaf Children." *Journal of Experimental Education,* 5 (September, 1936) 40–57.

[57] Larsen, Robert P., and Feder, D. D. "Common and Differential Factors in Reading and Hearing Comprehension." *Journal of Educational Psychology,* 31 (April, 1940) 241–252.

[55] Laycock, Frank. "Significant Characteristics of College Students with Varying Flexibility in Reading Rate: I. Eye-movements in Reading Prose." *Journal of Experimental Education,* 23 (June, 1955) 311–319.

[56] Lazarsfeld, Paul F. *Radio and the Printed Page.* Duell, Sloan, and Pearce, New York, 1940.

[57] Ledbetter, Frances Gresham. "Reading Reactions for Varied Types of Subject Matter: An Analytical Study of the Eye Movements of Eleventh Grade Pupils." *Journal of Educational Research,* 41 (October, 1947) 102–115.

[58] Leestma, Robert. "The Film-Reader Program." *Elementary English,* 33 (February, 1956) 97–101.

[59] Leverett, Hollis M. "Vision Test Performance of School Children." *American Journal of Ophthalmology,* 44 (October, 1957) 508–519.

[60] McQuarrie, Charles W., and McQuarrie, Esther Ingram. "Perceptual Ability and School Achievement." *Journal of the American Optometric Association,* 28 (January, 1957) 335–338.

[61] Metraux, Ruth Watt. "Auditory Memory Span for Speech Sounds: Norms for Children." *Journal of Speech Disorders,* 9 (March, 1944) 31–38.

[62] Miles, W. R., and Segel, David. "Clinical Observation of Eye-Movements in the Rating of Reading Ability." *Journal of Educational Psychology,* 20 (October, 1929) 520–529.

[63] Morgan, David H. "Twin Similarities in Photographic Measures of Eye-Movements While Reading Prose." *Journal of Educational Psychology,* 30 (November, 1939) 572–586.

[64] Morse, William C. "A Comparison of the Eye-Movements of Average Fifth- and Seventh-Grade Pupils Reading Materials of Corresponding Difficulty." *Studies in the Psychology of Reading.* Monographs in Education, No. 4, University of Michigan Press, Ann Arbor, 1951.

[65] Needham, Arnold. "Listening Exercises with a Purpose." *Education,* 75 (January, 1955) 311–315.

[66] Newby, Hayes A. *Audiology: Principles and Practice.* Appleton-Century-Crofts, Inc., New York, 1958.

[67] O'Connor, Clarence D., and Streng, Alice. "Teaching the Acoustically Handicapped." *The Education of Exceptional Children,* Forty-ninth Yearbook of the National Society for the Study of Education, Part II, University of Chicago Press, Chicago, 1950, 152–176.

[68] Overstreet, Bonaro W. "After This Manner, Therefore Listen . . ." *Wilson Library Bulletin,* 20 (April, 1946) 597–598.

[69] Perry, William G., Jr., and Whitlock, Charles P. "A Clinical Rationale for a Reading Film." *Harvard Educational Review,* 24 (January–December, 1954) 6–27.

[70] Petty, Mary Clare. "An Experimental Study of Certain Factors Influencing Reading Readiness." *Journal of Educational Psychology,* 30 (March, 1939) 215–230.

[71] Pugh, Gladys S. "Appraisal of the Silent Reading Abilities of Acoustically Handicapped Children." *Volta Review,* 43 (April, 1946) 197–198.

[72] Radler, D. H. "Visual Training Hopeful—Now Johnny Can Read." *Horizon,* Purdue Research Foundation, 3 (September, 1956) 1–4.

[73] Rankin, P. T. "Listening Ability: Its Importance, Measurement, and Development." *Chicago Schools Journal,* 12 (January, 1930) 178.

[74] Reynolds, Maynard C. "A Study of the Relationships Between Auditory Characteristics and Specific Silent Reading Abilities." *Journal of Educational Research,* 46 (February, 1953) 439–449.

[75] Robinson, Helen M. *Why Pupils Fail in Reading.* University of Chicago Press, Chicago, 1946.

[76] Robinson, Helen M. "Diagnosis and Treatment of Poor Readers with Vision Problems," *Clinical Studies in Reading, II.* Supplementary Educational Monographs, No. 77, University of Chicago Press, Chicago, 1953.

[77] Rosenbloom, A. A., Jr. "A Critical Evaluation of Visual Diagnostic Materials." *Elementary School Journal,* 56 (September, 1955) 27–31.

[78] Rossignol, Lois J. *The Relationships Among Hearing Acuity, Speech Pro-*

duction, and Reading Performance in Grades 1A, 1B, and 2A. Contributions to Education, No. 936, Bureau of Publications, Teachers College, Columbia University, 1948.

[79] Russell, R. D. "A Comparison of Two Methods of Learning." *Journal of Educational Research,* 18 (October, 1928) 235–238.

[80] Schubert, Delwyn G. "Visual Immaturity and Reading Difficulty." *Elementary English,* 34 (May, 1957) 323–325. (Schubert quotes Dr. Louis Jacques, Sr.)

[81] Seibert, Earl W. "Reading Reactions for Varied Types of Subject Matter." *Journal of Experimental Education,* 12 (September, 1943) 37–44.

[82] Sheridan, Mary D. *The Child's Hearing For Speech.* Methuen & Co., Ltd., London, 1948.

[83] Silverman, S. R. "Hard-of-Hearing Children," pp. 352–356 in Davis, Hallowell (Ed.). *Hearing and Deafness: A Guide for Laymen.* Murray Hill Books, Inc., New York, 1947.

[84] Spache, George D. "The Role of Visual Defects in Spelling and Reading Disabilities." *American Journal of Orthopsychiatry,* 10 (April, 1940) 229.

[85] Spache, George D. "A Rationale for Mechanical Methods for Improving Reading." *Significant Elements in College and Adult Reading Improvement,* Seventh Yearbook of the National Reading Conference for Colleges and Adults, Texas Christian University Press, Fort Worth, 1958, pp. 115–132.

[86] Still, D. S. "The Relationship between Listening Ability and High School Grades." *Dissertation Abstracts,* 15 (October, 1955) 1761–1762.

[87] Strang, Ruth, and Bracken, Dorothy Kendall. *Making Better Readers.* D. C. Heath and Company, Boston, 1957.

[88] Stromberg, E. L. "The Relationship of Measures of Visual Acuity and Ametropia to Reading Speed." *Journal of Applied Psychology,* 22 (February, 1938) 70–78.

[89] Stroud, James B. *Psychology in Education.* Longmans, Green and Company, New York, 1956.

[90] Swanson, Donald E., and Tiffin, Joseph. "Betts' Physiological Approach to the Analysis of Reading Disabilities as Applied to the College Level." *Journal of Educational Research,* 29 (February, 1936) 433–448.

[91] Taylor, Earl A. *Controlled Reading: A Correlation of Diagnostic Teaching and Corrective Techniques.* University of Chicago Press, Chicago, 1937.

[92] Taylor, Earl A. *Bulletin of the Washington Square Reading Center,* New York, 1954.

[93] Teegarden, Lorene. "Tests for the Tendency to Reversal in Reading." *Journal of Educational Research,* 27 (October, 1933) 81–97.

[94] Tinker, Miles A. "The Use and Limitations of Eye-Movement Measures in Reading." *Psychological Review,* 40 (July, 1933) 381–87.

[95] Tinker, Miles A. "The Role of Eye Movements in Diagnostic and Remedial Reading." *School and Society,* 39 (February, 1934) 147–148.

[96] Tinker, Miles A. "Time Relations for Eye-Movement Measures in Reading." *Journal of Educational Psychology,* 38 (January, 1947) 1–10.

[97] Tinker, Miles A. "Recent Studies of Eye Movements in Reading." *Psychological Bulletin,* 55 (July, 1958) 215–231.

[98] Triggs, Frances Oralind. "A Study of Visual Discrimination and Its Relationship to Success in Reading." *Reading in a Changing Society*. International Reading Association Conference Proceedings, 4 (1959) 82–84.

[99] Vernon, M. D. *The Experimental Study of Reading*. The University Press, Cambridge, England, 1931.

[100] Vernon, M. D. *Backwardness in Reading*. The University Press, Cambridge, England, 1957.

[101] Vernon, M. D. "The Development of Visual Perception in Children." *Education,* 78 (May, 1958) 547–549.

[102] Waldman, John L., Wade, Francis A., and Aretz, Carl W. *Hearing and the School Child*. Volta Bureau, Washington, 1931.

[103] Walker, Robert Y. "The Eye-Movements of Good Readers." *Studies in Experimental and Theoretical Psychology; Psychological Monographs,* No. 3, 44 (1933) 95–117.

[104] Wheeler, Lester R., and Wheeler, Viola D. "A Study of the Relationship of Auditory Discrimination to Silent Reading Abilities." *Journal of Educational Research,* 48 (October, 1954) 103–113.

[105] Wiksell, Wesley. "The Problem of Listening." *Quarterly Journal of Speech,* 32 (December, 1946) 505–508.

[106] Wilt, Miriam E. "A Study of Teacher Awareness of Listening as a Factor in Elementary Education." *Journal of Educational Research,* 43 (April, 1950) 626–636.

[107] Witty, Paul and Kopel, David. "Factors Associated with the Etiology of Reading Disability." *Journal of Educational Research,* 29 (February, 1936) 449–459.

[108] Witty, Paul A., and Kopel, David. *Reading and the Educative Process*. Ginn and Company, Boston, 1939.

[109] Wood, Louise and Shulman, Edythe. "The Ellis Visual Designs Test." *Journal of Educational Psychology,* 31 (November, 1940) 591–602.

[110] Young, William E. "The Relation of Reading Comprehension and Retention to Hearing Comprehension and Retention." *Journal of Experimental Education,* 5 (September, 1936) 30–39.

~ 6

THE PHYSIOLOGICAL CORRELATES OF READING

There are numerous physiological factors in addition to vision and hearing that play significant roles in the reading process. Thus general physical health, speech development, glandular and neurological functioning, and cerebral dominance become of professional interest to the reading teacher.

Whereas, in the previous chapter, we were most concerned with the sensory bases of the reading process, here we will examine a variety of general physical conditions—speech defects, brain injuries, and those facts concerning cerebral dominance that may have a bearing on reading readiness and achievement.

Learning requires experience. Yet defects of any kind, whether in hearing, vision, speech, or general physical health, tend to restrict experiences and hinder learning.

GENERAL PHYSICAL CONDITIONS

Numerous studies have dealt with the relationships of reading disability and glandular dysfunction, hemoglobin variations, vitamin deficiencies, nerve disorders, nutritional and circulatory problems, and heart conditions. Other studies have stressed conditions such as adenoids, infected tonsils, poor teeth, rickets, asthma, allergies, tuberculosis, rheumatic fever, and prolonged illnesses. For example, Johnson noted in one report [41] that 65 per cent of her clinical reading cases had had serious or recurrent illnesses.

Physical problems may result in mental or at least cultural retardation, lowered vitality, and slower physical development. Naturally, any condition that hinders vigorous performance can affect reading development. We should expect a lowering of the child's vitality to affect his reading success. Fatigue alone can make it difficult to enjoy and become interested in a reading task; attention suffers and comprehension is certain to be lowered. As nervous tension due to failure experiences builds up, disinterest, disgust, and possibly even reading disability may result. Illness also may cause the child to miss school and thus miss important phases of instruction.

Now let's consider some specific types of physical deviations. Mateer [52] points out that vitamin deficiencies may be associated with reading difficulties. Experimenting with orphanage children, Harrell [30] found that adding two milligrams of thiamine to the daily diet of one group of children for a year resulted in improvement in 15 different areas as compared with a matched control group of orphaned children who received a placebo. The most noticeable improvements were in vision, recall, code substitution, memorization, intelligence, reaction time, reading, vocabulary, arithmetic, weight, and height.

Harris (p. 244) [31] suggests that more poor readers than good readers have endocrine disturbances. Witty and Kopel (p. 216) [82] also believe that the apparent association of reading deficiencies and motor inco-ordination may have as an underlying cause the dysfunction of the endocrine glands. Mateer [51] indicates that the underfunctioning of the pituitary gland is a common cause of reading difficulty. She suggests that pituitary dysfunction may cause intellectual retardation, speech defects, eye disturbances, motor inco-ordination, and reversal tendencies.

Cavanaugh [12] reports that of 660 children in the Santa Barbara County schools 18 per cent had thyroid deficiency sufficiently severe to result in two or more years of retardation in physical maturity. He concluded that thyroid deficiency accounted for 75 per cent of all behavior, performance, and social-adjustment problems in children.

Eames [19] examining the blood specimens of thirty reading failures, found one-fifth of the group presenting abnormal cell forms and one-third low in hemoglobin. The significance of the abnormal cell forms is not clear. However, the low hemoglobin may indicate that anemia is a factor in some cases of reading disability. Hemoglobin is a determinant of the brain's oxygen supply and hemoglobin deficiency has been found to be associated with diminution of visual and auditory acuity and even with personality variations and impaired writing performance.

Watts,[75] studying twenty students with reading difficulties at Fresno State College, found that six had nutritional and digestive problems, five had respiratory and heart disorders, two suffered from glandular imbalance, and two showed nervous disorders.

These findings must be interpreted with caution. Even though a relationship may be found between certain physical conditions and reading, we can not conclude that a causal relationship has been established. Many variables are involved. The data merely tell us to pay special attention to the physical health of our students and to recognize that certain physical deviations may be accompanied by educational problems. Thus Burt (p. 170) [10] indicates that bodily weaknesses and bodily ill health generally are contributory factors rather than basic causes of reading disability.

SPEECH DISORDERS AND READING

Speech disorders * frequently are accompanied by reading disabilities. Possible reasons for this will be discussed after a brief review of the types of speech disorders.

TYPES OF SPEECH DISORDERS

Some authorities place the speech disorders into four general classifications: articulation, rhythm, phonation (voice conditions), and symbolization.

Studies indicate that approximately 75 per cent of all speech problems are *articulatory* in nature. Such speech disorders are characterized by the imperfect production of phonetic elements (p. 304 ff.) [11] and are accompanied by distortions, substitutions, or omissions of certain speech sounds. These disorders include baby talk, lisping, lalling (may be due to inactivity of the tongue tip), delayed speech (unintelligible or narrow repertoire of consonants), and weakly stressed consonants (in some circumstances these seem to be omitted consonants). Some of the above may be due to structural or organic impairment and some may be due to careless speech habits. Still others may be remnants of attention-getting mechanisms.

The speech disorders which are related to *rhythm* are stuttering (stam-

---

* Speech is considered to be defective when it is not easily audible, not easily intelligible, is vocally unpleasant, deviates in respect to specific sound reproduction, is labored in production, lacks conventional rhythm, stress, tonal quality or pitch, or is inappropriate in terms of the age, sex, or physical development of the speaker. Berry and Eisenson (p. 1) [4] say that speech is defective if more attention is paid to *how* one speaks than to *what one says.*

mering), cluttering, and spastic speech. Stuttering may be present only to the extent of causing vaguely hesitant or unrhythmic speech. Or it may be so severe that the stutterer has spasms of the throat muscles or the diaphragm and is unable to produce voiced sounds.[37] Its causes may be emotional and/or organic. Cluttering is rapid, jerky, stumbling speech accompanied by slurring and distortion of words. In spastic speech the voice quality and articulation may be normal, but the speaker, unable to control air flow, lacks fluency.

In speech defects related to *phonation* there are problems of pitch, intensity, timbre, and possible combinations of these. The first of these includes monotony, extremes of pitch, and stereotyped inflection (probably most often appearing in the bilingual individual). Problems of intensity include the too loud- or too weak-voiced individual and the aphonic who is voiceless or speaks in a strained whisper. There are at least seven problems of timbre (quality). These include hypernasality (cleft-palate speech is an extreme form), hyponasality (adenoidal speech), throaty or pectoral, guttural, harsh, hoarse, and husky. Some voice problems include more than one phonation disorder. Falsetto voice, for example, involves both pitch and timbre.

Symbolization, the fourth classification of speech disorders, involves fewer classroom cases than the others, but its relationship to reading disabilities may be closer than the other three. Dysphasia is the general term for the disorders of symbolic formulation and expression. In its mild form it may evidence itself as a pronounced reading, writing, and speaking disability. The aphasic has difficulty in using and understanding both written and spoken language symbols.

An individual's speech difficulty may involve more than one classification of speech disorders, and speech disorders may be either organic (structural) or emotional (functional), or both. While imperfectly developed vocal cords and cleft or malformed palate, brain abnormalities or damage, and inadequate hearing can all physically block language or speech development, many speech disorders are symptomatic of personal and emotional problems. Overstreet and Overstreet (p. 34) [59] suggest that all emotional problems have some effect on the speech of the person who suffers them. In some cases it is impossible to make a clear-cut separation between the organic and emotional determiners of speech disabilities.

SPEECH DISABILITIES AND READING ACHIEVEMENT

Speech disabilities may affect the child's reading in a number of ways. Their effect on oral reading is obvious. Moreover, they may have a decidedly deleterious effect on reading in general, and further important indirect effects of speech disorders are likely to be underestimated. The child who is forced to concentrate on his speech cannot contribute his full attention to the social-learning situation. And he is handicapped in a "look and say" approach to learning words. He may even try to avoid being heard by others while he tries to appear to be saying the words.

The average child of eight years of age is able to articulate 90 to 95 per cent of the sounds needed in speech. However, numerous children have articulatory disabilities in which they may substitute or omit sounds (say "mudder" for "mother," "pay" for "play") or may distort sounds (perhaps emit laterally or whistle the S sounds). Monroe (p. 93) [55] says that faulty articulation may confuse the child because words sound one way when he says them and another way when he hears them spoken by someone else. This leads him to faulty word recognition and comprehension.

Harris (p. 244) [31] suggests that the two speech defects most frequently associated with reading are *indistinctness,* characterized by blurred consonant sounds and 'thick' quality, and *cluttering*. However, Monroe (p. 92) [55] indicates that stuttering, too, is related to reading disabilities. She reported that stuttering was exhibited in nine per cent of her 415 reading disability cases but in only one per cent of a 101 case control group.

Travis (pp. 42–43) [72] concluded that many speech defects are caused by lack of cerebral dominance. He notes that 61 per cent of 200 cases of stuttering studied by Bryngelson tended to be ambidextrous. Hildreth (p. 44) [37] says:

> . . . stuttering and left-handedness are correlated. Stuttering is more noticeable in young children who lack consistent handedness, those who are delayed in establishing dominance or children at beginning school age who are abruptly 'shifted over' for writing. . . . Persons with high dextral dominance are relatively free of stuttering. Sinistrals and ambilaterals are more subject to it.

Burt (p. 288) [10] found that only 1.7 per cent of the right-handed children but 6.5 per cent of the left-handed children tended to stammer. He adds that stammering is nearly twice as frequent among left-handed children who are right-eyed as among left-handed children who are left-eyed.

Other psychologists have stressed the emotional causes of stuttering: vocabulary taboos, feelings of inferiority, fear of speaking, shock, and various symbolic factors.

Wendell Johnson [42] suggests that stuttering may develop because of parental disapproval of "normal non-fluency." Vernon (p. 99) [74] states that speech defects may be more common among completely left-handed individuals because such children have been under pressure to change from the left to the right hand. Rotter,[63] studying eight stutterers, suggests that pampering predisposes the would-be stutterer to use stuttering as a rationalization for failure. He suggests (p. 165) that stuttering is *"a rhythmic disorder in speech in a person who is aware of his speech as being different from that of other people and who reacts to it as if it were a handicap."*

The origin, organic or emotional, of a stuttering difficulty is important in that knowledge of the origin may suggest the proper approach to remediation of the disorder. The remediation may in turn affect, positively, a stuttering-caused reading difficulty. Perhaps one of the greatest problems of the stutterer is that his disability causes a lack of proper communication vocally and socially. His inability to communicate may erect emotional barriers to his normal social progress as well as to his progress in reading.

Neurologically, speech and reading are closely related. Both the speech center and the center for other motor processes involved in reading are usually located in the language area on the left side of the brain. In right-handed individuals this is certainly so. Vernon (p. 107) [74] cites evidence that the speech center for left-handed persons usually will be in the right hemisphere. When handedness is changed this does not alter the location of the language center.

Eames,[18] reviewing 24 studies, concludes that neurological lesions in the language centers may impair both speech and reading. And he adds that inadequacy of auditory association and discrimination (the sounds of words are not associated with the muscular movements required to produce them) may predispose an individual to both speech and reading difficulties. In oral reading, particularly, the association pathways between the various areas of the brain assume importance.

Studies of reading disabilities tend to show a relationship between speech and reading. Monroe (p. 92) [55] found that 27 per cent of 415 reading disability cases but only eight per cent of her 101 controls had speech defects. Sister Nila (p. 549) [56] reports that of 38 children with speech defects 40 per cent of the boys and 23 per cent of the girls failed to learn to read during the first grade. However, of the 72 reading failures studied, 50 were bilinguals.

Noall [57] states that students who have both speech and reading defects need special training in auditory discrimination. She refers to the findings of a recent study at the University of Utah that 70 per cent of the freshmen falling below the 15th percentile on the Cooperative General Achievement Test were deficient in phonics.

Eames (p. 53),[18] after reviewing the research, draws the following conclusions:

1. Neurological lesions in the language centers or their inter-connections [in the brain] may impair both speech and reading.
2. Failure or inadequacy of auditory association and discrimination may predispose to either speech or reading trouble.

3. Speech defects occur in a certain proportion of reading failures and *vice versa*.
4. Emotional reactions to speech difficulties may impair reading.
5. Oral reading is more difficult for a person with a speech defect.

Hildreth,[35] summarizing a number of studies, concludes that reading success may be hindered by immature and inadequate articulatory coordination, by indistinct and inaccurate articulation, by emotional conflicts resulting from speech defects, by poor auditory discrimination, by sensory and motor aphasia, by spasms and stuttering, and by bilingual background. She takes the position that a speech defect alone generally does not cause reading difficulties, but that it presents enough of an obstacle that when it accompanies some other blockage, reading difficulties are likely to result. She suggests that mentally slow children tend to be retarded in speech development and that the speech defects, along with reading failure, may be only added symptoms of mental retardation.

The evidence of a relationship between speech defects and reading deficiencies is certainly sufficient to warrant our early attention to any speech difficulties. Like errors in reading, they may be symptoms of underlying problems that need the teacher's, and frequently the specialist's, immediate attention.

THE BRAIN AND READING

Research by Gall, Dax, Broca, Jackson, Head, Wernicke, Goldstein, Halstead, Sherrington, and Penfield have given us detailed information concerning the projection areas of the brain. Figure 1 shows the auditory, visual, motor, and olfactory areas.

The sense organs connect with their special projection areas of the brain's cortex, and the essential sensory processes occur there. Injury to the visual area in the occipital lobe, for example, may cause blindness.

The functions of the brain, however, are not restricted to localized areas. More than three-fourths of the brain is occupied by association areas. The actual associations that are formed between the various sensory and motor areas are learned. As George W. Gray (p. 34) [28] points out, the reason that a child avoids fire is not because of the sharp signal of pain received in the sensory area, but because he *associates* the pain with the sight of fire.

The brain must have memory in order to relate the information of the moment with that of the past and to recognize its significance. This means millions

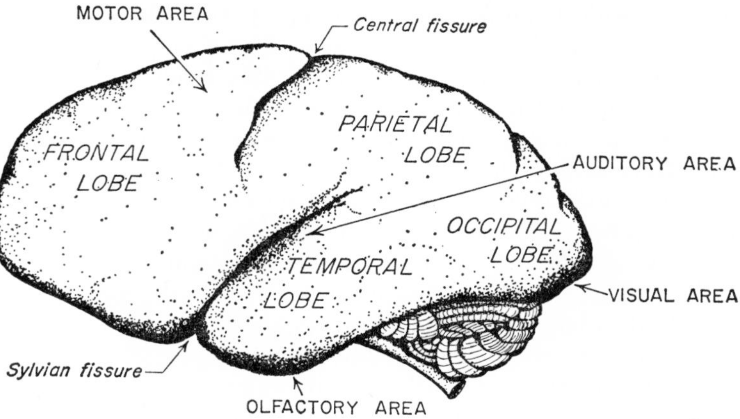

of functional correlations, countless hookups of sensory centers with one another and with motor centers, repeated exchanges of data for analysis, comparison, and synthesis. These elaborative functions of the cortex are performed by the association areas.

The visual projection area in the occipital lobe, for example, is surrounded by an association area known as the parastriate cortex. A second association area, known as the peristriate cortex, surrounds the latter. Gray [28] says that if the parastriate cortex is injured, the person is unable to recognize or identify what he sees. Gray adds that

> If it is the peristriate (second association) area that suffers the injury, the mind may have no difficulty recognizing objects but cannot recall their appearance when they are not in view. This kind of disability was early recognized in disturbances of the use of language, when the patient was unable to associate the printed or written word with any meaning. So the loss of function of the second visual association area is commonly called word blindness. . . .*

There have been attempts to make pinpoint localizations of the brain functions. This is rarely possible. It has been suggested (p. 472) [78] that injuries to the same areas in two different brains would not necessarily produce similar symptoms. This is true because life experience so conditions and changes each person's brain that it is unique. Some authorities believe that intellectual activities are a function of the brain as a whole. Nevertheless, some generalizations regarding local brain damage can be made.

The brain is subject to many injuries and to certain internal deviations

---

* This condition occurring either as alexia (structural) or dyslexia (functional) is discussed at length later in the chapter.

that interfere with its proper functioning (p. 453).[78] One deviation is the inadequate development of the brain tissue. This is termed aplasia. Microcephaly and mongoloidism are examples of this condition. In less severe cases we may find epilepsy or mental retardation.

Sometimes physical injuries—a severe blow on the head, cerebral tumors, infections, and changes accompanying old age—occur to the nervous system. Tumors may crowd brain tissue and restrict the metabolism of the nerve cells. Infections such as encephalitis and paresis may damage neural tissue or interfere with its normal development. Pick's disease, Alzheimer's disease, and arteriosclerosis and other degenerative diseases also may lead to impaired functioning.

Finally, the brain may be damaged by vitamin deficiences, endocrine disorders, and toxins. Vitamin deficiencies, for example, may lead to pellagra and an endocrine disturbance may lead to cretinism. Toxic conditions resulting from excessive intake of lead, alcohol, carbon monoxide, or opium may damage brain tissue. Extremely high fever or lack of oxygen may lead to irreparable damage of brain cells.

Brain injuries that result in aphasia are especially significant for reading. There is some disturbance of the thought processes and there may be a loss of speech. In Chapter 2 it was noted that the thought of the aphasic tended to be restricted to a concrete level. Hebb (pp. 85–86) [33] points out that the lesions (damage to brain tissue) producing aphasia are

> . . . usually in the middle regions of the left cerebral cortex, close to the Sylvian fissure: more often somewhat posterior, but sometimes slightly anterior. A few left-handed persons may get aphasia with lesions of the right hemisphere, but these are rare, except in cases in which there was damage to the left hemisphere before the age of two years; then, at maturity, damage to the right hemisphere may produce aphasia. There appears also to be a group of persons, mostly left-handed, for whom damage to both sides is necessary to cause aphasia. In these persons, that is, 'speech localization' is bilateral.

Hebb continues:

> The relation of speech area and handedness bears on the topic of *cerebral dominance*: the conception that one hemisphere controls the other, or is more important in behavior. Thus a large majority of the human race are right-handed, with a higher level of skill for most tasks in the hand which is controlled by the left hemisphere: the same hemisphere which, as we have just seen, is usually involved in speech. For most persons, therefore, the left hemisphere is dominant. However, older ideas of dominance implied that hand-control and speech-control would necessarily be localized together, and this appears not to be true (since left hemisphere lesions can produce aphasis in left-handed persons). . . .

The facts of cerebral dominance then are: in most persons the left hemisphere is dominant in handedness and speech control, but some persons (the ambidextrous ones) do not show handedness (or show it to a less than usual degree), and speech sometimes has a bilateral localization.

Now let us consider certain hypotheses concerning reading deficiencies and brain damage.

Hinshelwood (pp. 40–63)[39] used the term "congenital word-blindness" to indicate a reading disability due to localized brain defect though not necessarily associated with lack of intelligence. He suggested that abnormality in specific portions of the cortex of the left parietal lobe (in right-handed persons) might cause severe problems in learning to read. He proposed that such conditions required that a new center for visual memory be established in the opposite hemisphere.

Word-blindness refers to the inability to remember word forms. The condition may be either structural or functional in nature.* Structural defects may be either hereditary or the result of brain damage.

Schilder[65] concluded that severe reading disability frequently is characterized by an inability to analyze the spoken word into its sounds and to synthesize sounds into words. He studied intensively seven cases of retarded reading, ranging from eight to 14 years of age. All exhibited some confusion between *b* and *d*, *B* and *D*, *g* and *p*, *Y* and *G*, *p* and *d*, *M* and *N*, *m* and *n*, *b* and *g*, *A* and *S*, *d* and *t*, *C* and *S*, *A* and *M*, *I* and *L*, *T* and *L*, and *H* and *D*. In nearly all cases letters and words were confused, but not numbers. Two cases had a tendency toward mirror writing and reading. In evaluating his data Schilder says (p. 86):

> We do not doubt that the congenital reading disability can and must be interpreted from a neurological point of view. We, therefore, consider the opinion of Gates that reading disability is due to faulty habits in learning as contradictory to the facts.

Hallgren[29] compared 122 children with reading difficulties with 212 children without such difficulties. He discovered that, with the exception of thirteen cases, the reading disabilities showed a familial history of reading disability. He concluded that a primary disability in reading is inherited as a dominant characteristic. He believed that secondary disabilities could be explained on the basis of poor intelligence, environmental conditions, or emotional disorders. Burt (p. 381),[10] too, reports that speech defects also frequently run in families.

Vernon (p. 81)[74] states that there is inadequate evidence for Hallgren's

* The general symptoms of the two forms of word-blindness are the same.

conclusion that reading disability is linked to a single congenital disability. She suggests that reading disability may be a sign of deficient cortical maturation and that there may be a congenital disposition toward the occurrence of certain related defects such as reading disability, speech defects, motor inco-ordination, and ambidextrality.

It has already been suggested that speech defects may be caused by brain injuries. Severe brain injury may result in paralysis or mental retardation. Lesser injuries, especially birth injuries, may lead to motor inco-ordination, to speech defects, or to reading disabilities.

Gesell (pp. 238–239) [26] says:

> In many instances the symptoms of minimal injury are so benign that they escape attention. . . .
>
> The type which expresses itself in speech difficulties, poorly defined unilateral dominance, and in delayed integration may later result in serious difficulty in the acquisition of reading. . . . The surprising prevalence of reading disabilities, so-called, and their frequent association with minimal birth injuries tends to support our thesis that these injuries are more common than is ordinarily supposed.

Jensen [40] has suggested that the term "reading disability" be restricted to reading cases resulting from organic injury. He uses the term "reading inability" for those cases whose reading difficulties are functional in nature. His 22 cases of reading disability showed a high frequency of difficult birth, awkward gait, speech defects, faulty eye co-ordination, lack of auditory discrimination, and neurotic symptoms. Of course, many of these conditions as well as the reading difficulty could be hereditary rather than the result of brain injury.

Johnson [41] reports that 21 per cent of 34 clinical reading disability cases had had accidents resulting in brain injury. Preston and Schneyer [60] report on nine severely retarded readers. Five of these were non-readers, ranging in age from eight to fifteen. Seven showed evidence of significant reversal tendencies. Neurological examination indicated that three had damage to the nervous system, four had difficult births, three had head injuries in childhood, and two had suffered high fever in childhood. Neurologists suggested that it was possible that in all cases brain injury might have induced the reading retardation.

Although, as can be seen here, there has been considerable interest in the possibility that hereditary brain defects and brain damage are basic causes of reading disability, not all psychologists agree that these are the most general causes. Blau (pp. 149–166),[5] for example, argues against hereditary and neurological explanations. He emphasizes personality and emotional disturbances and considers reading disability as a symptom of a basic personality maladjustment. He believes that a child may unconsciously discharge hostile and rebellious feelings against reading content.

CEREBRAL DOMINANCE AND READING

The research in this area has been more concerned with cross laterality and lack of dominance than with lateral dominance. Lateral dominance refers to the consistent use of and preference for the muscles of one side of the body. Cross laterality (mixed laterality) refers to the condition in which the dominant hand and the dominant eye are on opposite sides. A third possibility is lack of dominance resulting in ambidexterity.

Orton [58] has suggested that in learning to read the child develops memory traces of "engrams" for words both in the dominant and the non-dominant sides of the brain, but that those in the non-dominant hemisphere normally are mirror images of the former and are suppressed. He points out that injury to the non-dominant hemisphere usually does not lead to reading disability. Furness (p. 39) [23] summarizes Orton's [58] position:

> It is assumed then that the inactive (or non-dominant) hemisphere is stimulated as freely as the active (or dominant) side and that such stimulation leaves memory traces, or engrams, behind it in the nerve-cells of both hemispheres. . . . When the right-sided person reads, only the memory traces on the dominant or active side are stimulated. When the left-sided person reads, the right hemisphere is dominant. . . . According to Dr. Orton, the failure to establish the normal physiological habit of using exclusively the memory traces of one hemisphere may easily result in a confusion in orientation, reversal errors, and hence difficulty in learning to read and spell.

Orton hypothesized that if cerebral dominance were well-developed by the time reading began, reading difficulty would not occur. If, however, no special dominance had been developed, reading difficulties would occur. In this latter case the child sometimes would read a word with a left orientation and at another time with a right orientation depending on whether the right or left hemisphere predominated at the moment. The result would be numerous incidences of reversals.

Orton proposed his theory in 1925. Unfortunately the evidence for it is inconclusive. In the first place dominance itself is not an either-or proposition; rather it is a matter of degree. To some extent every one is two-handed. Burt (pp. 280–281),[10] Hildreth [36, 37] and Burge [9] show that the development of a dominant hand is a gradual process and that the dominance of one hand over the other increases with age.

At one time it was thought that the preferred use of one eye over the other was an indication of the dominance of one cerebral hemisphere. More recent knowledge of eyedness has furnished little evidence for this belief. The nerves from each eye are connected to both hemispheres of the brain. In each eye the right half of the visual field in the retina is related to the right cerebral hemisphere, and the left half is related to the left hemisphere. The theory that eye dominance is related to hand dominance resulted in part from a misunderstanding of the data. For example, studies indicate that not more than five to ten per cent of the population is left-handed, whereas about 30 per cent is left-eyed. These data make Orton's theory suspect.

Since left-handedness, a symptom of right-cerebral dominance, frequently is associated with poorer reading, the data concerning the incidence of left-handedness also have been taken as evidence for Orton's position. Milne [53] reports that about four per cent of the general population is left-handed. Burt (p. 281),[10] studying some 600 children, found that 5.2 per cent were left-handed. Of these children only four out of five of the boys and three out of five of the girls wrote with the left hand. Brain,[8] after examining numerous studies, states that between 5 and 10 per cent of the population in Britain and America is left-handed. He adds, however, that right- or left-handedness does not necessarily prove there is a natural predisposition to be so. Innate tendencies frequently are obscured by training.

Studies generally have indicated that handedness may be a familial trait. Burt (p. 296) [10] reports that 14 per cent of his left-handed cases had a left-handed parent and 31 per cent had left-handed relatives. Certainly there is some evidence that handedness generally is a hereditary trait with right-handedness behaving as does a Mendelian dominant trait and left-handedness as a recessive trait.[8] However, not all children are left-handed even when both parents are left-handed. And, if handedness were determined strictly by a simple dominant and recessive rule, we might expect to find right-handedness equally frequent among girls and boys. Burt (p. 282) [10] and Brain [8] report that left-handedness is more common among males than among females. In fact, Brain suggests that the ratio is about two-to-one although Burt reports that about six per cent of the boys and almost four per cent of the girls are left-handed.

The main point in investigating cerebral dominance is that handedness may be found to show some demonstrable relationship with intelligence and/or motivation favoring or hindering the learning situation. And in fact, in examination of both children and adults, Burt,[10] Fitt and O'Halloran,[22] Karlin and Strazzula,[45] Blau,[5] Milne and Milne,[53] and Gordon [27] have all found strong correlations between left-handedness and various undesirable traits such as low I.Q. or unqualified mental deficiency and, frequently, even psychopathy, as well as explicit speech and reading disabilities.

Speaking to this point, Blau (pp. 182–183) [5] believes that there are personal, dynamic explanations for left-handedness other than that it is related to brain dominance or to heredity. He (p. 86) points out that left-dominance is more prevalent among males than females. He suggests that it is acquired through imitation of left-handed parents and/or older children; through a temporary physical injury to the right hand that compels the child to use his left hand; and through emotional negativism. In this last case left-handedness may be an expression of hostility, resentment, or aggression. He takes the position that sinistrality is an expression of infantile negativism due to maternal rejection in early infancy. In fact, it is suggested that maternal rejection or similar unfortunate experiences may be the antecedent of numerous conditions, including the personal and language disorders just discussed.

Harris (pp. 255–256) [31] has concluded that for the teacher the significant question is not the child's specific pattern of lateral dominance but whether or not he shows directional confusion. He says that if the transition is completed before reading instruction is begun, a left-handed child ordinarily may be converted to right-handedness with no serious effect upon his ability to learn to read. However, if the change-over is attempted just before or during the early stages of reading instruction, the child is likely to experience directional confusion and, consequently, to exhibit reversal symptions in reading and in writing, spelling, and numbers, as well. Smith,[68] studying 100 children within an age range of 9 to 11, reports that 12 per cent of the retarded readers had been forced to change handedness whereas only four per cent of the good readers had been forced to do so. Hildreth [37] reports a study by Scheidemann in which 184 left-handed children between the ages of four and five were trained to use the right hand. No speech defects developed among those that were taught to write with the right rather than with the left hand.

However, Lauterbach,[49] studying 37 left-handed adults with speech defects, found that fifty per cent had been forced to write with the right hand. He says that it is not the transfer itself that causes the speech defect. It is, instead, the method used coupled with a particular type of child personality. In instances of paralysis or amputation, transfer from one hand to another occurs without the development of speech disorders. Mintz,[54] after citing studies that suggest correlations between unstable cerebral dominance and stuttering, psychosis, psychopathy, drug addiction, and feeble-mindedness, suggests that the basic cause of the relationship may be the harsh measures taken by certain parents or teachers to make children right-handed.

Although the evidence suggests that change of handedness and left-handedness may bear some relationship to the development of speech problems, its relationship to cerebral dominance is not clear. Brain (p. 841) [8] points out that cerebral dominance is not in itself a function.

. . . it is simply a name for the fact that speech and allied functions are located in the left hemisphere. The abnormal handedness which so often goes with congenital speech disorders means in my view that incomplete development of speech pathways has left the child without normal hemisphere dominance on either side—a condition incidentally quite different from 'natural' left-handedness.

Dearborn [14] suggests that the left-handed person has difficulty proceeding from left to right in his eye movement because it is more natural for him to move his dominant left hand from right to left and consequently his eyes also tend to move in that direction. This natural tendency of the left-handed person must be reversed when he is called upon to write or read and it precipitates reversals and orientational confusion.

Studies of reading disability cases have provided some evidence for a relationship between poor reading and cross laterality and lack of dominance. Eames,[17] studying 100 disability and 100 unselected cases, found that poor readers showed a greater frequency of crossed dominance than did the unselected cases, although the difference was not great. Monroe (p. 85) [55] reported that the incidence of crossed dominance among 101 normal children was 27 per cent; among 155 reading disability cases, 38 per cent; and among 44 intellectually defective cases, 50 per cent.

In a study using the Harris Tests of Lateral Dominance, Harris (p. 254) [31] concluded that:

The present data show quite dramatically that a very high proportion of young reading disability cases show mixed dominance on these tests, and that the development of a fairly consistent preference for one hand takes place later than the age of nine in a far higher proportion of reading disability cases.

Schonell,[66] studying 104 readers who were retarded more than one and a half years and 75 normal readers, found a greater incidence of reversals among the retarded readers. In another phase of his study [67] he compared the handedness of 73 backward readers with 75 normal readers. He found that more backward readers than normal readers are either right-handed and left-eyed or left-handed and right-eyed. He concludes that the disability of some backward readers is due in part to their mixed eyedness and handedness. This occurs especially with those who are left-handed but who are right-eyed.

Not all studies show a positive relationship between mixed laterality or lack of dominance and poor reading. Woody and Phillips [85] found that among 136 pairs of right- and left-handed children handedness had little or no relation to reading success. Wittenborn,[79] studying college freshmen, found that ambidexterity and confused or undetermined handedness had very little or no significance for language ability. He suggests, however, that consistent use of the left hand may result in mechanical inconvenience and have some emotional consequences. Wolfe,[84] studying two matched groups of eighteen pupils each, one group of which was average in reading achievement and the other retarded, reports the same proportion of right, left, and mixed laterality among the retarded as among the normal readers.

Stevenson and Robinson [70] studied 60 kindergarten children of generally superior intelligence and from homes of high socio-economic level for more than two years at the Laboratory School of the University of Chicago. Of the group about 50 per cent preferred the right hand and eye, about 30 per cent the right hand and the left eye, and about 20 per cent exhibited other combinations of eye-hand preference. They stated that children who prefer the right hand and the left eye tend to move from right to left when performing physical activities and thus that it is extremely important for first-grade teachers to emphasize left to right progression in readiness activities and in reading. However, when this was done they found that for bright children there seemed to be no relationship between right-hand preference and either reversal errors or reading achievement. Mintz [54] made an intensive study of 95 intellectually subnormal seven to seventeen year old boys (I.Q. 47 to 87) and concluded that a lack of unilateral cerebral dominance seemed unrelated to reading deficiencies.

Hildreth,[36, 37] summarizing the research, found no evidence for a causal relationship between handedness and either speech difficulties or success in reading. She notes (p. 50) [37]:

> Whether the relationship between speech and handedness is causal or only associative has not been fully established. . . . Those who have reported on the incidence of stuttering and left-handedness, lack of dominance or enforced changes in dominance in early childhood are impressed with the relationship; those who report on older subjects, 10 to 12 and older, particularly adults, find little relationship. . . . There are certainly many causal factors in the stuttering complex of which manual inconsistency may be only one.

Nevertheless, Harris (p. 251) [31] states that he has become convinced that there is a significant relationship between lateral dominance and reading disability.

In a later study Harris [32] suggests that, if tests are sufficiently discriminative, genuine relationships between reading disability and laterality are found. Testing 316 children with severe disability and 245 unselected children, he found that among seven- to eight-year-old children there were twice as many cases of lack of hand dominance among the disability cases as among the unselected cases. Among the nine to ten year old children the proportion was three to one.

Harris also reports that at age seven 38 per cent of the disability cases, as opposed to five per cent of the controls, had difficulty distinguishing right from left. At age nine the groups no longer were differentiated on this point. Crossed-dominance was not significantly more frequent among reading disability cases, but such cases showed a greater tendency to "strong-left" dominance.

Thus the evidence concerning the relationship between dominance and reading disability seems to present some lack of agreement. When relationships are found, they are ordinarily based on cases of severe reading disability. Little evidence of relationship has been found when large groups are studied.

However, there has been enough interest in the problem that certain tests have been devised. One complete set of tests of lateral dominance is the Harris *Tests of Lateral Dominance*. Van Riper's *Critical-Angle Board Test* [73] identifies tendencies toward directional confusion. The Simultaneous Writing Test of the Harris set performs the same function.

Eyedness can be tested through the use of the Miles *A-B-C Vision Test of Ocular Dominance*. In addition, many simple tests have evolved. For example, the tester holds an object (perhaps a pencil) about 15 feet from the subject and tells him to look at it. The subject is told to keep his eyes focused on the object and not to turn his head. Then he is asked to point to the object. Almost invariably the subject will bring the finger directly in front of one eye, thus indicating that eye is the dominant one and showing that he is neglecting the image from the other eye.

REVERSALS AND READING

The topic of reversals is closely related to the topic of dominance. Reversals (or strephosymbolia, a term originated by Orton) may be defined (p. 38) [23] as:

> . . . the tendency certain individuals have to reverse letters, parts of words, or even whole words. This inversion tendency is not limited to seeing words in reversed order, or writing letters backward or upside down. "It may be observed occasionally in the very young child who has difficulty in putting on his garments the right way; who fails to remember right and left distinctions; and who loses his bearings within his own home when looking for something he knows is in a certain place."

THE CAUSES OF REVERSALS

Orton inferred that in the case of crossed dominance the child on one occasion would attack the written word with a left and, at another time, with a right orientation. The implication was that reversals result from crossed dominance.[58]

Spache takes a quite different position on the meaning of reversals. He wrote (pp. 50–51) [69]:

> They are a universal phenonenon present among learners of all ages who are attacking a new and strange group of symbols. Reversals are not related to handedness or eyedness or cerebral dominance, nor are they indicative of laterality or visual handicaps. In my opinion, their only meaning is as an indication of the unfamiliarity of the individual with the particular symbols he is trying to learn.*

Although Dearborn [14] believed that reversals tend to result from the difficulty a left-eyed child has in looking from left to right, Gates (p. 107) [24] minimizes the effects of eyedness and handedness on reading. In his book, *The Improvement of Reading,* he writes (p. 308) [24]:

> . . . left-handed children in general do not show markedly greater difficulty in reading in general and no markedly greater tendency in particular to make reversal errors than right-handed; that of those who make reversal errors the percentage of left-handed is not much greater than in the population at large; and that among those subject to serious difficulties in reading the percentage is similar to that found among representative readers.

After an intensive study Krise [47] decided that reversals result from a lack of familiarity with the relationship that exists between symbols and their background. He implies that some persons find it more difficult than others to differentiate between certain similar symbols. In a later study of 20 adult subjects Krise [48] concluded that everyone exhibits some reversal tendencies. He found a correlation of .62 between reversal tendencies and inability to perceive space relations. This seems to support the thesis that reversals may be due to difficulties in perceiving space relations or, more specifically, figure-ground relations.

Actually, Fildes [21] made this suggestion as long ago as 1923. She concluded that the tendency of younger children toward mirror-writing was only part of their general tendency to reproduce forms of any kind without apparent heed to the position that they occupy in space.** Anderson and Anderson [1] report that a rotation of the entire figure in the *Thematic Apperception Test* indicates disturbance in spatial orientation and add that this is not uncommon in young children, in some left-handed subjects, and in children with reading disabilities.

Bond and Tinker (p. 308),[6] in summarizing the research, point out that

---

** Additional evidence for this was given in Chapter 5.

studies of groups of children reveal little relation between dominance and reversals, but in individual clinical cases left-handedness, left-eyedness, mixed dominance, lack of dominance, or behavioral habits developing from one of these factors may be involved in reversals. Other causes of reversals advanced by various writers are: lack of maturation, visual defects, a habit of perceiving objects from right to left, and improper teaching methods which involve the exclusive use of the whole-word method and over-emphasizing the final sounds of words by concentrating on word families. In interpreting the data it may be necessary to take the position that both good and poor readers encounter problems but the good readers somehow have overcome their difficulties better than the poor readers.

THE RELATION OF REVERSALS TO READING ABILITY

There have been numerous studies of the possible relationship of reversals to poor reading achievement. Even though the causes of reversals are not firmly identified, we recognize that reversals do occur. We are concerned as to how, if at all, they influence reading.

During the early school years reversals are normal. They become a serious problem in reading only when they continue beyond the second or third grade. The research tends to show that children with continuing reversal tendencies do not make normal progress in reading. For example, Monroe (p. 86) [55] found reversal tendencies more frequently among reading disability cases than among normal readers. Tinker [71] notes that severely retarded readers or non-readers have difficulty in progressing perceptually from left to right in their reading, and Harris (p. 188) [31] maintains that 10 per cent of reading disability cases show reversal tendencies.

Wolfe,[83] studying 18 boys averaging nine years of age and with two years retardation in reading and a matched group of 18 normal readers, found more reversals of letters, words, and letters within words among the retarded readers. They could read mirrored words better than could the normal readers.

Spache (p. 50),[69] however, in a 1953 article took this stand regarding reversals:

> As pointed out in the earlier summary in 1941, reversals are not causal in poor reading or even related to it.*

THE TYPES OF REVERSALS

Let us examine some of the different types of reversals. The term static reversal refers to the reversal of letters showing right-left symmetry (*p* and *q, b* and *d*).[23] Children tend to have more difficulty with the lower-case letters than with capitals. Gates (pp. 318–319) [24] questions whether letter confusions such as these are really cases of reversal error. He found that confusion of these letters did not necessarily imply confusion in left to right orientation.

In another type of reversal, the "kinetic reversal," the sequence of letters is reversed and a new word is formed, as for example, *was* for *saw*. Other types of reversals involve various transpositions of letters. There are numerous kinds of transposition (initial letter to an internal position, terminal letter to an initial position, internal letter to a different internal position, etc.) that have been observed (p. 161).[46]

Also the parts of phrases and compound words may be reversed as when "in the house" becomes "house in the," or "barnyard" becomes "yardbarn."

The following tests may be used to identify reversals:

1. *Durrell Analysis of Reading Difficulty:* detects reversals of *b* and *d, p* and *q*.
2. *Monroe Diagnostic Reading Test:* detects reversals of *b* and *d, p* and *q, w* and *m,* reversals of the sequences of letters within words, and reversals of the order of words.
3. *Gates Reading Diagnostic Tests:* detects reversals of the sequences of letters in words.

REVERSALS AND THE TEACHING OF READING

The child must learn to proceed from left to right not only in reading a line, but also in reading a word. Yet a child's early experiences in perception required no such directional sequences. The teacher must emphasize the order and direction of letters in words. Writing the word serves to call the pupil's attention to this order.

A child should early learn to identify his right and left hand, to experience objects on the right and objects on the left so that gradually the concepts of "leftness" and "rightness" will acquire meaning. Hester (pp. 123–128),[34] as well as Russell and Karp,[64] gives examples of training the child in this skill. Although Hildreth (p. 287) [38] is not at all certain that this training is beneficial on a pre-reading level, Gates (p. 304) [24] suggests that the concepts of left and right should be established before the child begins actual reading. It seems possible that equipment such as a controlled reader, or a reading film which presents a few words at a time with a beam of light moving from left to right, could be helpful in training the eyes to move from left to right.

In addition to the general causes of reversals discussed above, certain writers emphasize specific causes. For example, Bond and Tinker (p.

309) [6] say that reversals may arise from an undue emphasis on sounding in the development of word-analysis techniques. Dolch (pp. 350–352) [15] notes that the most important part of sounding is the use of initial sounds, especially consonants. The good reader attacks any word that is not in his sight vocabulary by beginning with the first sound in left to right progression. Perhaps a too early emphasis on the endings of words may result in confusion of movement direction.

OVERCOMING REVERSAL TENDENCIES

Writing practice may be used to develop left to right progression and discourage mirror writing (p. 317).[6] The recommended approach is to have the child start at the extreme left edge of the paper. If he has a strong tendency toward mirror writing, he may be asked to write one word under another with only one word to a line. Apparently some success is also obtained by teaching the child what a reversal is, how it is made, and what the results look like.

Fernald [20] recommends a *tracing-sounding-writing* method. The teacher writes or prints a meaningful word on a piece of paper and the child then traces the word while saying it aloud. This is repeated until the child can reproduce the word without looking at it. The child should pronounce the word aloud, and should never be allowed to erase or rewrite the word. This procedure trains not only in left to right movement but in word perception as well.

Monroe (p. 128) [55] says that the child may be taught how to move from left to right by using his finger to help him direct his eyes. She suggests that for best results the finger should slide from left to right rather than merely point.

Barger,[2] basing his recommendations on the theory that "mixed laterality" results in "biaxial confusion" and eventually in reversals, advocates a method of training these cases. His procedure requires that a mirror be so placed that the word is reversed both vertically and horizontally. He feels that children with reversal symptoms have a functional disturbance that makes them see print in the way that the average person sees it in a mirror. The mirror may help to correct this functional difficulty and may be discarded after a few weeks. Leavell,[50] advocating another method, suggests that in the "unadjusted" crossed-dominance cases the non-dominant eye should be trained to co-ordinate with the dominant hand. For this purpose he uses a small stereoscope with a design so placed that but one eye can see it. However, it appears to the child that he sees the design with both eyes and for the purpose of visual training he "traces" the design in the position of the "projected" image.

Harris (pp. 371–372) [31] suggests the following methods for overcoming reversal tendencies:

1. Tracing, writing, and sounding words which are frequently confused. These procedures automatically enforce using the correct sequence of letters.
2. Covering a word with a card and removing the card slowly to the right so that the letters are exposed in proper sequence.
3. Underlining the first letter in the word. . . .
4. Encouraging the child to use finger or pencil as a guide in reading along a line. While this practice is to be discouraged in good readers, it is very helpful as a means of teaching the proper direction for eye movements.
5. Exposing a line of print a little at a time by means of a card, or by means of an opening cut in a card, or by opening a zipper.
6. Drawing an arrow pointing to the right under words which are frequently reversed.
7. Allowing the child to use a typewriter. . . .

Other writers have listed additional techniques. Some of these are:

1. Stress the beginnings of words while at the same time seeing to it that the child pronounces the whole word.
2. Practice choral reading—this develops reading from left to right in a line of material.
3. Use mechanical devices that permit thought units to appear in a left to right progression.
4. Demonstrate reversal errors to the child to show him how reversal falsifies the context.
5. Provide alphabetizing and dictionary exercises.

SUMMARY

In this chapter we have examined those reading problems that accompany certain physical deviations, speech defects, brain defects and injuries, and incomplete dominance.

Physical conditions that lower vitality, such as glandular dysfunction, vitamin deficiencies, and nutritional and digestive problems generally are associated with a reduction in efficiency.

Speech defects also tend to be related to reading deficiencies and poorer achievement, especially in oral reading. Such defects make word recognition and word comprehension more difficult. Speech defects rarely seem to cause reading failure but more often are symptoms of underlying disturbances; reading failure seems to be an additional symptom.

Neurological lesions or cerebral imbalance may impair both reading and speech and may influence handedness. There is a high incidence of brain injury among clinical reading disability cases. And left, lack of, or mixed cerebral dominance seems to have some relation to reading disability. Mixed laterality frequently seems to be related to retarded speech and retarded linguistic development. The left-handed child and the ambidextrous child find it less natural to proceed from left to right and consequently may find it harder to understand the orientation of words.

Reversals that continue beyond the second grade are associated with poor reading achievement. Regardless of their interpretation—as symptoms of incomplete, left, or crossed dominance, or as spatial disorganizations and figure-ground disturbances—they are nevertheless symptoms of underlying difficulties.

There is also much evidence that certain children seem to be congenitally predisposed to a group of correlated defects. Reading disability is usually found in combination with one or more additional problems such as speech defects, motor inco-ordination, left-handedness, crossed-dominance, or ambidexterity.

The teacher will need to be familiar with the physiological correlates of reading so that he can recognize those factors which may contribute to the child's reading disabilities. He will then know if it is necessary for the child's family to ask for the help of a specialist. His knowledge will be of value to him in his general classroom approach to teaching reading and also aid him in his individualized work with the child.

SUGGESTED READINGS

For a review of the literature on incidence, theories, and educational implications of handedness (with bibliography):

Wills, Betty J. "Handedness," pp. 613–616 in *Encyclopedia of Educational Research,* Chester W. Harris (Ed.), 3rd Ed., New York: The Macmillan Company, 1960.

***

For a unique point of view emphasizing relationships between mixed laterality and reading disability with suggestion that prevention and treatment of reading disability require management, from birth, of behaviors such as sleep patterns, handedness, tonality:

Delacato, Carl H. *The Treatment and Prevention of Reading Problems: The Neuro-Psychological Approach,* Springfield, Illinois: Charles C. Thomas, 1959, 122 pp. (See also review of Delacato: Henry P. Smith, "Laterality before Literacy," *Contemporary Psychology: A Journal of Reviews,* 5 (March, 1960) 91.)

***

For an emphasis on chemical factors in reading disability and suggestions for combined medical treatment and teaching as a remedial approach:

Smith, Donald E. P., and Patricia M. Carrigan. *The Nature of Reading Disability,* New York: Harcourt, Brace, and Co., 1959, 149 pp. (See also review of Smith: Thomas W. Richards, "Chimerical Chemistry," *Contemporary Psychology: A Journal of Reviews,* 5 (July, 1960) 235.

***

(Causey, *The Reading Teacher's Reader*)

Article 32, Furness, Edna Lue. "Perspective on Reversal Tendencies," from *Elementary English,* 33 (January, 1956) 38–41.

Article 33, Shea, Dorothea P. "The Case for the Kinesthetic Method," from *The Grade Teacher,* 74 (October, 1956) 60, 108, 110.

QUESTIONS FOR DISCUSSION

1. How may physiological defects reduce the meaningfulness of printed materials? How are defects and perception related?
2. List and discuss types of physiological defects commonly found related to reading failure.
3. What are the general types of speech disorders? How (causes or symptoms) are these related to reading?
4. What is meant by functional disorder? Structural? Which type should be most closely related to reading problems?
5. What if any relationships exist between speech disorders and brain localization? Reading and brain localization? Handedness and reading problems?
6. What are some of the more common causes of brain damage?
7. What is meant by word-blindness?
8. What relationships appear to exist between brain damage and reading retardation?
9. What relationships appear to exist between dominance and reading?
10. What educational methods are used to prevent reversals?
11. What is cerebral dominance and what is its importance?
12. Of what concern is left-handedness to the reading teacher?
13. Discuss the origin of reversals.
14. Why should there be some overlap among speech and reading disorders?
15. What physical conditions may be expected in relation to reading difficulties? Why?

BIBLIOGRAPHY

[1] Anderson, Harold H., and Anderson, Gladys L. *An Introduction to Projective Techniques.* Prentice-Hall, Inc., Englewood Cliffs, N. J., 1951.

[2] Barger, William C. "An Experimental Approach to Aphasic and to Nonreading Children." *American Journal of Orthopsychiatry,* 23 (January, 1953) 158–170.

[3] Bender, Lauretta. *A Visual Motor Gestalt Test and Its Clinical Use.* Research Monographs, No. 3, The American Orthopsychiatric Association, New York, 1938.

[4] Berry, Mildred Freburg, and Eisenson, Jon. *Speech Disorders: Principles and Practices of Therapy.* Appleton-Century-Crofts, Inc., New York, 1956.

[5] Blau, Abram. *The Master Hand.* American Orthopsychiatric Association, New York, 1946.

[6] Bond, Guy L., and Tinker, Miles A. *Reading Difficulties: Their Diagnosis and Correction.* Appleton-Century-Crofts, Inc., New York, 1957.

[7] Boykin, Leander L. "Who Is the Exceptional Child?" *Elementary School Journal,* 58 (October, 1957) 42–47.

[8] Brain, W. Russell. "Speech and Handedness." *The Lancet,* 249 (December 29, 1945) 837–842.

[9] Burge, Ivor C. "Some Aspects of Handedness in Primary School Children." *British Journal of Educational Psychology,* 22 (February, 1952) 45–51.

[10] Burt, Cyril. *The Backward Child.* University of London Press, London, 1937.

[11] Carhart, Raymond. "Conservation of Speech," pp. 300–317 in *Hearing and Deafness: A Guide for Laymen.* Murray Hill Books, Inc., New York, 1947.

[12] Cavanaugh, Lyman A. "Reading Behavior With Regard for Endocrine Imbalances." *Implementing the Process of Reading,* Thirteenth Yearbook of the Claremont College Reading Conference, Claremont, 1948, 95–102.

[13] Crosland, H. R. "Superior Elementary-School Readers Contrasted With Inferior Readers in Letter-Position, 'Range of Attention,' Scores." *Journal of Educational Research,* 32 (February, 1939) 410–427.

[14] Dearborn, Walter F. "The Nature of Special Abilities and Disabilities." *School and Society,* 31 (May, 1930) 632–636.

[15] Dolch, Edward W. *Teaching Primary Reading,* 2nd Edition. The Garrard Press, Champaign, 1950.

[16] Douglass, Leigh C. "A Study of Bilaterally Recorded Electro-Encephalograms of Adult Stutterers." *Journal of Experimental Psychology,* 32 (March, 1943) 247–265.

[17] Eames, Thomas H. "The Anatomical Basis of Lateral Dominance Anomalies." *American Journal of Orthopsychiatry,* 4 (October, 1934) 524–528.

[18] Eames, Thomas H. "The Relationship of Reading and Speech Difficulties." *Journal of Educational Psychology,* 41 (January, 1950) 51–55.

[19] Eames, Thomas H. "The Blood Picture in Reading Failures." *Journal of Educational Psychology,* 44 (October, 1953) 372–375.

[20] Fernald, Grace M. *Remedial Techniques in Basic School Subjects.* McGraw-Hill Book Company, Inc., New York, 1943.

[21] Fildes, Lucy G. "Experiments on the Problem of Mirror-Writing." *British Journal of Psychology,* 14 (July, 1923) 57–67.

[22] Fitt, Arthur B., and O'Halloran, K. H. "The Relation Between Handedness and Some Physical and Mental Factors." *Journal of Educational Psychology,* 25 (April, 1934) 286–296.

[23] Furness, Edna Lue. "Perspective on Reversal Tendencies." *Elementary English,* 33 (January, 1956) 38–41.

[24] Gates, Arthur I. *The Improvement of Reading,* 3rd Edition. The Macmillan Company, New York, 1950.

[25] Gates, Arthur I., and Bennett, C. C. *Reversal Tendencies in Reading: Causes, Diagnosis, Prevention, and Correction.* Bureau of Publications, Teachers College, Columbia University, 1933.

[26] Gesell, Arnold, and Amatruda, C. S. *Developmental Diagnosis: Normal and Abnormal Child Development.* Paul B. Hoeber, Inc., New York, 1941.

[27] Gordon, Hugh. "Left-Handedness and Mirror Writing, Especially Among Defective Children." *Brain,* 43 (January, 1921) 313–368.

[28] Gray, George W. "The Great Ravelled Knot." *Scientific American,* 179 (October, 1948) 26–39.

[29] Hallgren, Bertil. "Specific Dyslexia (Congenital Word Blindness)." *Acta Psychiatrica Et Neurologica,* Supplement No. 65, Copenhagen, 1950.

[30] Harrell, Ruth F. *Further Effects of Added Thiamin on Learning and Other Processes.* Contributions to Education, No. 928, Bureau of Publications, Teachers College, Columbia University, 1947.

[31] Harris, Albert J. *How to Increase Reading Ability,* 3rd Edition. Longmans, Green and Company, New York, 1956.

[32] Harris, Albert J. "Lateral Dominance, Directional Confusion, and Reading Disability." *Journal of Psychology,* 44 (October, 1957) 283–294.

[33] Hebb, Donald O. *A Textbook of Psychology.* W. B. Saunders Company, Philadelphia, 1958.

[34] Hester, Kathleen B. *Teaching Every Child to Read.* Harper & Brothers, New York, 1955.

[35] Hildreth, Gertrude. "Speech Defects and Reading Disability." *Elementary School Journal,* 46 (February, 1946) 326–332.

[36] Hildreth, Gertrude. "The Development and Training of Hand Dominance: I. Characteristics of Handedness; II. Developmental Tendencies in Handedness; III. Origins of Handedness and Lateral Dominance." *Journal of Genetic Psychology,* 75 (December, 1949) 197–220, 221–254, 255–275.

[37] Hildreth, Gertrude. "The Development and Training of Hand Dominance: IV. Developmental Problems Associated with Handedness; V. Training of Handedness." *Journal of Genetic Psychology,* 76 (March, 1950) 39–100, 101–144.

[38] Hildreth, Gertrude. *Readiness for School Beginners.* World Book Company, Yonkers, N. Y., 1950.

[39] Hinshelwood, James. *Congenital Word-Blindness.* H. K. Lewis and Company, Ltd., London, 1917.

[40] Jensen, Milton B. "Reading Deficiency as Related to Cerebral Injury and to Neurotic Behavior." *Journal of Applied Psychology,* 27 (December, 1943) 535–545.

[41] Johnson, Marjorie S. "A Study of Diagnostic and Remedial Procedures in a Reading Clinic Laboratory School." *Journal of Educational Research,* 48 (April, 1955) 565–578.

[42] Johnson, Wendell. *Children With Speech and Hearing Impairment.* U. S. Department of Health, Education, and Welfare, Bulletin No. 5, Washington, 1959.

[43] Johnson, Wendell, and King, Arthur. "An Angle Board and Hand Usage Study of Stutterers and Non-Stutterers." *Journal of Experimental Psychology,* 31 (October, 1942) 293–311.

[44] Karlin, Isaac W. "Speech- and Language-Handicapped Children." *Diseases of Children,* 95 (April, 1958) 370–376.

[45] Karlin, Isaac W., and Strazzula, Millicent. "Speech and Language Problems of Mentally Deficient Children." *Journal of Speech Disorders,* 17 (September, 1952) 286–294.

[46] Kennedy, Helen. "Reversals, Reversals, Reversals!" *Journal of Experimental Education,* 23 (December, 1954) 161–170.

[47] Krise, Morley. "Reversals in Reading: A Problem in Space Perception?" *Elementary School Journal,* 49 (January, 1949) 278–284.

[48] Krise, Morley. "An Experimental Investigation of Theories of Reversals in Reading." *Journal of Educational Psychology,* 43 (November, 1952) 408–422.

[49] Lauterbach, C. E. "Shall the Left-Handed Child Be Transferred?" *Journal of Genetic Psychology,* 43 (December, 1933) 454–462.

[50] Leavell, Ullin W. *Manual of Instructions for Users of the Leavell Language-Development Service.* Keystone View Company, Meadville, Pennsylvania, 1960.

[51] Mateer, Florence. "A First Study of Pituitary Dysfunction in Cases of Reading Difficulty." *Psychological Bulletin,* 32 (November, 1935) 736.

[52] Mateer, Florence. "The Constitutional Basis of Alexia." *Physiological Factors Affecting the Reading Process,* Eleventh Yearbook of the Claremont College Reading Conference, Claremont, 1946, 143.

[53] Milne, Lorus J., and Milne, Margery J. "Right Hand, Left Hand." *Scientific American,* 179 (October, 1948) 46–49.

[54] Mintz, Alexander. "Reading Reversals and Lateral Preferences in a Group of Intellectually Subnormal Boys." *Journal of Educational Psychology,* 37 (November, 1946) 487–501.

[55] Monroe, Marion. *Children Who Cannot Read.* University of Chicago Press, Chicago, 1932.

[56] Nila, Sister Mary, O.S.F. "Foundations of a Successful Reading Program." *Education,* 73 (May, 1953) 543–555.

[57] Noall, Mabel S. "Reading in Relation to Speaking." *Evaluating College Reading Programs,* Fourth Yearbook of the Southwest Reading Conference for Colleges and Universities, Texas Christian University Press, Fort Worth, 1955, 61–68.

[58] Orton, Samuel T. "An Impediment to Learning to Read—A Neurological Explanation of the Reading Disability." *School and Society,* 28 (September, 1928) 286–290.

[59] Overstreet, Harry, and Overstreet, Bonaro. *The Mind Alive.* W. W. Norton and Company, Inc., New York, 1954.

[60] Preston, Ralph C., and Schneyer, J. Wesley. "The Neurological Back-

ground of Nine Severely Retarded Readers." *Journal of Educational Research,* 49 (February, 1956) 455–459.

[61] Rheinberger, Margaret B., Karlin, Isaac W., and Berman, Abraham B. "Electro-encephalograpic and Laterality Studies of Stuttering and Nonstuttering Children." *Nervous Child,* 2 (January, 1943) 117–133.

[62] Robinson, Helen M. *Why Pupils Fail in Reading.* University of Chicago Press, Chicago, 1946.

[63] Rotter, Julian B. "The Nature and Treatment of Stuttering: A Clinical Approach." *Journal of Abnormal and Social Psychology,* 39 (April, 1944) 150–173.

[64] Russell, David H., and Karp, Etta E. *Reading Aids Through the Grades: Three Hundred Developmental Reading Activities,* Revised Edition. Bureau of Publications, Teachers College, Columbia University, 1952.

[65] Schilder, Paul. "Congenital Alexia and Its Relation to Optic Perception." *Journal of Genetic Psychology,* 65 (September, 1944) 67–88.

[66] Schonell, Fred J. "The Relation of Reading Disability to Handedness and Certain Ocular Factors." *British Journal of Educational Psychology,* 10 (November, 1940) 227–237.

[67] Schonell, Fred J. "The Relation of Reading Disability to Handedness and Certain Ocular Factors." *British Journal of Educational Psychology,* 11 (February, 1941) 20–27.

[68] Smith, Linda C. "A Study of Laterality Characteristics of Retarded Readers and Reading Achievers." *Journal of Experimental Education,* 18 (June, 1950) 321–329.

[69] Spache, George D. "Factors Which Produce Defective Reading." *Corrective Reading in Classroom and Clinic,* Supplementary Educational Monographs, No. 79, University of Chicago Press, Chicago, 1953, 49–57.

[70] Stevenson, Lillian P., and Robinson, Helen M. "Eye-Hand Preference, Reversals, and Reading Progress." *Clinical Studies in Reading, II,* Supplementary Educational Monographs, No. 77, University of Chicago Press, Chicago, 1953, 83–88.

[71] Tinker, Miles A. "Remedial Methods for Non-Readers." *School and Society,* 40 (October, 1934) 524–526.

[72] Travis, Lee Edward. *Speech Pathology.* Appleton-Century-Crofts, Inc., New York, 1931.

[73] Van Riper, C. "The Quantitative Measurement of Laterality." *Journal of Experimental Psychology,* 18 (June, 1935) 372–382.

[74] Vernon, M. D. *Backwardness in Reading.* The University Press, Cambridge, England, 1957.

[75] Watts, Phyllis W. "An Application of Clinical Diagnostic Techniques in the Classroom Situation for the Improvement of Reading at the College Level." *Journal of Educational Research,* 42 (March, 1949) 513–524.

[76] Weber, C. O. "Strephosymbolia and Reading Disability." *Journal of Abnormal and Social Psychology,* 39 (July, 1944) 356–361.

[77] Wheeler, Lester R., and Wheeler, Viola D. "Dyslexaphoria: Symptoms and Remedial Suggestions." *Elementary English,* 32 (May, 1955) 305–311.

[78] White, Robert W. *The Abnormal Personality.* Ronald Press Company, New York, 1956.

[79] Wittenborn, J. R. "Correlates of Handedness Among College Freshmen." *Journal of Educational Psychology,* 37 (March, 1946) 161–170.

[80] Witty, Paul, and Kopel, David. "Factors Associated with the Etiology of Reading Disability." *Journal of Educational Research,* 29 (February, 1936) 449–459.

[81] Witty, Paul, and Kopel, David. "Sinistral and Mixed Manual-Ocular Behavior in Reading Disability." *Journal of Educational Psychology,* 27 (February, 1936) 119–134.

[82] Witty, Paul, and Kopel, David. *Reading and the Educative Process.* Ginn and Company, Boston, 1939.

[83] Wolfe, Lillian S. "An Experimental Study of Reversals in Reading." *American Journal of Psychology,* 52 (October, 1939) 533–561.

[84] Wolfe, Lillian S. "Differential Factors in Specific Reading Disability: I. Laterality of Functions." *Journal of Genetic Psychology,* 58 (March, 1941) 45–56.

[85] Woody, Clifford, and Phillips, Albert J. "The Effects of Handedness on Reversals in Reading." *Journal of Educational Research,* 27 (May, 1934) 651–662.

7

BASIC READING SKILLS: WORD RECOGNITION

To a large extent at least, the development of reading ability is the acquisition of a series of skills. The reading teacher is interested in how these skills meet the specific demands of both oral and silent reading and how they may best be fostered. The first of these are the word-recognition skills.

In this and in the succeeding chapter, we detour somewhat from the pattern set in the previous chapters. In Chapters 2 through 6, as we examined the perceptual nature of the reading process, the nature of learning, and the determinants of readiness and achievement—we focused on the nature of the *reader*. In Chapters 7 and 8 our focus will be upon the nature of the *skills* that are required for effective reading.

For even a low level of reading development numerous basic skills must be acquired. And the development of the more advanced reading skills depends upon the successful acquisition of these basic skills. Thus skill development proceeds both vertically and horizontally. New and more complex skills are built upon the foundation of earlier and simpler skills while at the same time the basic foundation skills are perfected and enlarged. Growth in skills is gradual but it must be continuous. As new learnings are added, old learnings are practiced and strengthened.

How the basic reading skills are developed is a tremendously large topic. Our long-range goal is to develop those basic skills that make reading a means for learning and for enjoyment. And this is our criterion for deciding whether or not a reading skill is basic: does it function primarily in "learning to read" rather than in "reading to learn?" It is not until about the fourth-grade level that "reading to learn" begins to replace "learning to read." Concerning this topic Lee [34] concluded that a level of reading ability equal to that achieved by the *average* child in the fourth grade is prerequisite to success during the fifth or sixth grade. Studying 204 fourth, fifth, and sixth graders, she found that those pupils who had one or more reading scores below the average for the fourth grade were more likely to be non-achievers than achievers (p. 58).[34] In short, we see here that the acquisition of the basic skills tends to be a developmental task in that if it is not accomplished, later development is impeded or blocked.

READING SKILLS—A GENERAL VIEW

Although this chapter is concerned mainly with the basic reading skills, we may best see the scope of the problem by examining a list of general reading skills. Numerous lists of general reading skills have been made. The one given here is a compilation and selection from numerous previously published lists.

1. Independence in word recognition
2. Accuracy of comprehension
3. Speed in silent reading
4. Development of vocabulary; recognition of words and their meanings
5. Ability to read critically and to evaluate what is read
6. Flexibility in reading including skills in skimming and scanning
7. Ability to locate, select, and record material
8. Recognizing and understanding the organization of what is read
9. Ability to draw inferences, to relate ideas to one another, and to read between lines
10. Ability to recognize literary devices
11. Ability to determine the writer's purpose and the general feeling and tone of the article
12. Ability to interpret the printed page to another
13. Ability to follow directions
14. Ability to survey materials, to get at the main idea, and to determine the purpose of the reading
15. Ability to choose an appropriate reading technique
16. Ability to handle graphs, charts, maps, and other diagrammatic materials
17. Ability to use library and reference materials
18. Ability to retain and apply what has been read

19. Fluency in oral reading
20. Ability to read a textbook
21. Knowledge and use of study skills
22. Ability to read in specific content areas
23. Growth in reading interests, tastes, and appreciations

Perhaps not all of these skills can be considered specific to reading. Items 17 and 18, for example, may be general learning or study skills, and yet study skills are so integrated with higher-level reading that they should be included in any discussion of reading skills. However, the "basic reading skills" considered in this and the following chapter have been limited to (1) word-recognition skills, (2) comprehension skills, and (3) rate skills. The reading skills that do not fit into these three classifications are discussed later with the topics to which they are most closely related.

ORAL READING

Before we examine specifically the basic reading skills, let's consider some of the general relationships between silent and oral reading.

Recently there has been renewed emphasis on oral reading as an essential portion of a reading program. There are definite reasons for this. Studies have indicated that the young people of today are not as proficient in oral reading as those of thirty years ago. Just as complaints that pupils today generally are less proficient than those of former years in attacking new words led to an added emphasis on phonics, so the recognition of deficiencies in oral-reading skills has led to renewed efforts in that area. A second reason for the added emphasis on oral reading is our awareness of its importance as an avenue to learning.

Oral reading has social, cultural, and educational values. Among the major uses for oral reading are: providing enjoyment in a social group; substantiating answers challenged by others in a group; sharing content to which all do not have access; making reports, announcements or presenting other information to a group; reading radio and television program schedules and commercials; and reading prepared speeches at meetings. W. S. Gray [25] refers to oral reading as a fine art which conforms to certain aesthetic standards. Veatch [55] suggests that, in an individualized reading program, oral reading is a *culmination* of the child's study.

As suggested in earlier chapters, oral reading may be useful also as a diagnostic tool. It provides clues to the fluency and accuracy of the child's silent reading. Bond and Tinker (p. 347) [7] point out some other educational values of oral reading:

When the teaching of oral reading is done properly, not only is interpretive reading enhanced, but also oral language patterns are improved and better silent reading results. . . . His [the child's] silent reading will be improved because, in his preparation for oral reading, he will be concerned with the meaning, the characterizations, and the action which he is to interpret to others. His concern with thought units in oral reading will teach him to cluster words together properly in his silent reading.

GENERAL RELATIONSHIPS TO SILENT READING

McKee (p. 598) [37] believes that oral reading is merely a vocal expression of silent reading; that if the pupil can read silently with sufficient skill, reading orally to others is a problem in speech rather than a problem in reading.

However, most writers suggest that there are basic differences between oral and silent reading. And the non-oral method of teaching reading, as advocated by McDade, assumes that oral and silent reading are distinct processes. McDade [36] recommends that the child refrain entirely from saying the word to himself and suggests that the oral and the printed symbol should never be presented at the same time. In the non-oral method vocalization is avoided. Silent reading is considered to be a "see and comprehend process" rather than a "see, say, and comprehend" process. Buswell,[8] too, sees value in the non-oral method of teaching reading. He says that silent reading should be a process of association between perceptual stimulation and meaning *"without a mediating subvocalization."*

The research on eye-movement has identified certain differences between silent and oral reading. In oral reading there are more fixations, more regressions, and longer pauses. And we become concerned with another factor—eye-voice span.* This is the space (measured in words) between the word being vocalized and the word being fixed by the eye (the eye fixation). Good readers tend to have a much wider span and more moment-to-moment variations in span than do poor readers. Thus the good reader's voice can proceed smoothly even though his eyes may stop for a time on difficult words with his eye-voice span dropping to near zero. But the poor reader's voice flow will show hesitation as he meets difficult words because he has little or no eye-voice span.

It is, of course, possible to consider oral and silent reading to be overt

* Quantz (pp. 46–47) [41] was the first to measure eye-voice span and found that, on the average, this was 5.4 words. His method was to have the subject read aloud and as he was reading, a card was slipped over the page. The number of words the subject could then add was his eye-voice span. C. T. Gray (p. 106) [23] developed a technique that permitted the simultaneous photography of eye-movements as the voice was recorded on a dictaphone. Tiffin and Fairbanks [52] installed a sound-wave recorder in the ophthalmograph.

and implicit expressions of the same basic mental processes. It seems likely that speech traces are a part of all, or nearly all, silent reading. Gray and Reese (p. 240) [24] point out that tiny throat vibrations are present in even the best silent reading.

Actually implicit speech seems to accompany thinking as well as reading. When one thinks, the muscles of the tongue or upper-lip vibrate as if he were saying the words. Jacobson [32] found evidence that the muscles controlling the eyes, for example, contract during imagination as though the subject were looking at the object. And when the subject imagines that he is performing a muscular act, contractions occur in the muscle fibers which would be used in the actual performance of the act. It seems also that deaf mutes accompany their reading with finger and hand movements. Although persons who are unable to speak frequently do learn to read, it is much more difficult for them to do so.

These data suggest that although vocalization may not be essential to reading, it may well aid beginning reading. However, after silent reading attains the maximum speed of oral reading, vocalization tends to block further increases in rate.*

McKee (p. 606) [37] sees some disadvantages in the non-oral methods. He suggests that a non-oral approach would lead the pupil to disregard voice intonations and would deprive him of the use of much of the achievement in language that he has acquired as a listener. This would tend to divorce printed from spoken language.

However, four distinct objections [19] have been raised to a classroom emphasis on oral reading. It is contended that oral reading encourages the child to develop faulty silent-reading habits. His inadequate sight vocabulary forces him to hesitate and interrupt his thinking. Second, the child's inadequate eye-voice span leads to choppy, halting, and non-rhythmic reading. Third, even the mature reader may be forced to pay too much attention to word pronunciation and not enough to meaning. And, fourth, the emphasis on vocalization, lip movement, laryngeal movement, and the need for auditory imagery leads to slow reading.

It seems possible that each of these objections can be met by one or more constructive approaches. Generally the problem centers on the student's lack of ability with words. This can be remedied through the acquisition of a sufficient sight vocabulary and well-developed recognition skills

---

* Gray and Reese (24, p. 247) present data from the Boston University Education Clinic for the number of words read per minute by children in grades one through six on materials of average difficulty.

Grade	1	2	3	4	5	6
Oral reading	45	80	110	135	150	170
Silent reading	45	78	125	156	180	210

before oral reading is emphasized and by the proper choice of oral-reading materials.

It is, of course, true that oral reading generally is slower than silent reading. In oral reading the rate is limited by pronunciation; in silent reading the only limitation is the reader's ability to grasp the meaning. That oral reading is slower is hardly a valid reason for its exclusion from the program. Generally the purposes of oral and silent reading are quite different. However, the over-lapping purpose to develop skills and appreciations in reading would seem to justify the use of both approaches.

A study by Edwards [18] suggests that an oral-reading approach can further the acquisition of word recognition skills. Studying 126 college freshmen and sophomores who learned pronounceable nonsense dissyllables, he found that words were learned more readily if they were seen, heard, and spoken. If the words were only seen, many more contacts with the word were required.[19]

It has already been suggested that oral reading could be used as a diagnostic device in giving clues to a child's eye movements and speech defects. The teacher can observe the student's mispronunciations, repetitions, omissions, additions, and reversals. These reflect many of the mistakes he makes in his silent reading. Oral reading also provides practice in pronouncing words and in grammatical usage. Through it the child's speaking vocabulary may be developed, and poise and voice control may be fostered. The teacher, of course, wishes to discover deficiencies and improve the oral reading itself as well as to find clues to silent-reading errors.

Deficiencies in oral-reading skills are shown (p. 343) [7] by an inappropriate eye-voice span, improper phrasing, improper rate and timing, and emotional tenseness. Actually an eye-voice span may be too wide as well as too narrow. Improper phrasing results in word-by-word reading or in a clustering of words that do not fit into thought units. An improper rate may be either too slow or too fast. Emotional tenseness shows in inappropriate pitch, mounting increase in speed, an increase in number and types of errors, or possibly a tendency for a non-stutterer to show signs of stuttering.

SKILLS OF ORAL READING

Gray and Reese (p. 222–223) [24] point out that at the time of the War of Independence, teachers demanded dramatic expression in oral reading. "Expression" was the goal:

> . . . replacing the functional motive of reading to perceive and then project meaning. The elocutionary aim set a pattern, and during the decades that fol-

lowed, teachers continued to admonish their pupils to read in a flamboyant and oratorical style.

But expression cannot be considered apart from thought. It cannot be gained from superficial drill. If a child comprehends what he is reading, if he recognizes the meaning or emotion of a passage, good expression follows naturally.

The latter paragraph indicates our present emphasis in teaching oral reading. The oral reader must have a purpose for reading aloud; he must want the listener to hear and understand clearly; and he must convey to his audience those meanings that he previously obtained through careful silent reading. He reads in thought units, he avoids mumbling and slurring; and he progresses at a rate appropriate both to the materials and to the abilities of his audience. He uses his voice to transmit the emotions and feelings that he gains from the printed words.

Worthington (p. 5) [61] has provided a checklist giving the following characteristics of the good oral reader:

1. Comprehension
   - a) Transmits meaning successfully
   - b) Interprets feeling effectively (humor, surprise, suspense, etc.)
   - c) Knows many sight words
   - d) Uses word-recognition techniques easily

2. Fluency
   - a) Reads in thought units
   - b) Phrases correctly
   - c) Observes punctuation
   - d) Reads smoothly, without jerkiness or hesitation

3. Voice and speech characteristics
   - a) Can be heard easily
   - b) Enunciates clearly and distinctly
   - c) Uses suitable pitch
   - d) Has pleasing voice quality
   - e) Is free from strain or tension
   - f) Reads at appropriate rate

4. Avoids most common errors
   - a) Does not omit words
   - b) Does not substitute words
   - c) Does not transpose words
   - d) Does not repeat
   - e) Does not have a pronounced accent
   - f) Does not lisp
   - g) Does not stutter
   - h) Holds book properly
   - i) Keeps the place without difficulty
   - j) Has good posture

W. S. Gray (p. 10) [25] summarizes the elements most to be desired in the oral reader's attitude toward his listeners and toward the author's words: For transmitting meaning to others, the oral reader must be (1) "motivated by a keen desire . . . to share with others something to which he attaches real significance"; (2) he must understand "the purposes to be achieved and the interests, needs, and probable attitudes of the listeners"; (3) he must have "both a penetrating grasp of the meaning and a vivid sensing of the mood and feeling intended by the author"; and (4) he must use "varied techniques in conveying both meaning and feeling to his audience." * It might be said that the oral reader bears the same relationship to his listener as the author bears to his reader.

CONCLUSIONS

The following list of specific skills needed for proficiency in oral reading emphasizes the difference between oral and silent reading.

1. Oral reading calls for interpreting to others; silent reading only to oneself.
2. Oral reading demands special skill in projecting the mood and feeling intended by the author.
3. Oral reading demands skills in delivery, voice, tempo, and gesture.
4. Oral reading requires special eye-movement skills—there are more fixations, more regressions, and longer pauses than in silent reading.
5. In oral reading, speed is limited by pronunciation; in silent reading, by one's ability to grasp the meaning.
6. Eye-voice span is important in oral reading. Good readers have a wider eye-voice span than do poor readers.

Oral reading certainly is not a basic reading skill in the same way that word recognition, comprehension, and rate are. Instead, oral and silent reading are two approaches to reading, and children must become proficient in both. Both require skill in word recognition, comprehension, and rate. Thus oral reading requires all the skills of silent reading and some special ones of its own. Seen in this light, oral reading may itself be termed a special reading skill.

PRINCIPLES OF WORD RECOGNITION

The terms "word recognition" and "word attack" are used somewhat interchangeably as applied to reading skills. Although, as a first step in learn-

---

ing to read, children are commonly taught a basic sight vocabulary, we cannot leave to sight vocabulary the burden of learning and remembering the thousands of words needed for higher-level reading. Thus we early begin to develop special skills that permit the child to advance rapidly in vocabulary development and to proceed far beyond what could be achieved if he were forced to learn by sight each new word form. Word-recognition skills, then, act both as memory clues to familiar words and as a means for attacking completely new or at least unknown words. Thus the word-recognition skills also are commonly referred to as word-attack skills.

Unquestionably the word-recognition skills are important basic reading skills. It is in word-recognition skill that retarded readers most commonly are deficient. Although comprehension is the primary goal of reading instruction, word recognition is prerequisite.

It is a common observation that the major emphasis in Grades One and Two is on recognizing and identifying words. Generally, the pupil already knows the meaning of most words that he learns to read in these grades. This point deserves some elaboration. If children already know the meaning of most words they meet in the first and second grades—in short, if reading readiness depends primarily on being ready to recognize words—do not abilities in auditory and visual discrimination possibly become more significant than mental ages for predicting reading readiness? Are we not primarily concerned, then, with finding the method of teaching that best advances the pupil in auditory and visual discrimination?

Bond and Tinker (p. 265) [7] identify word recognition with the following basic skills:

1. Associating the appropriate meanings with the printed symbols.
2. Using context clues and other meaning aids to anticipate the words to be recognized and then checking the accuracy of the recognitions.
3. Becoming flexible and efficient in visually analyzing the words into usable recognition elements.
4. Developing knowledges of visual, structural, and phonetic elements (knowledge such as what the visual element, *ight* says in *fright, right, night,* etc.), knowledge of consonant and vowel sounds, blends and digraphs, prefixes, and suffixes, etc.
5. Learning skill in auditory blending and visually synthesizing word parts to rapidly pronounce or recognize the word as a whole.
6. Forming the habit of using the more analytical and the pronunciation techniques when and only when needed.

In Chapter 3 reading was identified as a process of association. The printed word is associated with the oral word (or some picture, object, or event) until the child can make the same physical, emotional, and mental responses to the written word that he previously made to the spoken word. Thus it appears that *the basic word recognition skill is the ability to associate the sound* (spoken word) *with the visual stimulus* (the written word). When the child becomes able to do this, the meaning that the spoken word elicits may then be elicited by the written word.

Above all, in learning to read, the child must become aware of the relationships between the spoken and the written language. He must learn that what can be said can also be written.[45] Soffiètti [49] points out that reading is a vocal or subvocal response to visual symbols. At least in the early stages of learning to read, the meaningful reactions that accompany this process are responses to the vocalization.

In initial reading instruction (at least in word recognition) we are not teaching the child meaning so much as we are teaching how to look. We are more interested in visual and auditory discrimination than in the perceptual aspects of the seeing and hearing processes. We find that some children confuse words because they are focusing on the similarities rather than upon the differences. This may be an important reason that reversals are made and why we find that words similar in form are reversed most frequently.

Actually, recognition of differences is an essential phase of learning at all levels.* For example, to many of us rocks are rocks, weeds are weeds, and bugs are bugs. The geologist, botanist, and entomologist expend a great deal of their educational effort in recognizing how each rock, weed, or bug is *different.* They learn what to look for. In other words, they learn *how to look.*

In Chapter 5 we saw that children generally can see likenesses when they come to school. Thus there seems to be little value in teaching children to match geometric forms, pictures, and objects. The majority are already able to do this, and any difficulty in transferring this ability to the process of word recognition is minimal. Apparently we must, in our teaching, emphasize how words differ. When, then, should the training in "what-to-look-for" begin?

It seems reasonable that such instruction should be made a part of readiness training. The child must be taught to differentiate word sounds. This requires careful planning on the part of the teacher. The child cannot readily learn sound differentiation if he is forced to deal with the phonetic inconsistencies with which our language abounds. Soffiètti [49] suggests that we present materials made up of monosyllabic words in which each letter has *only one phonetic value* (get). The materials should have no words containing silent letters (knit), double letters (add), or peculiar letter

---

* As was indicated in an earlier chapter, young children frequently give the impression of thinking on an *abstract* level when actually they are reacting to similarities as identities and failing to perceive the differences.

combinations (tea). He recommends that initial instruction be based on words composed of combinations of seventeen consonants, *b, c, d, f, g, h, j, l, m, n, p, r, s, t, v, w, y,* and the vowels. Sight words such *I, is, the,* and *has* are introduced only as needed in sentence formation.

The goal of this approach to reading instruction is to familiarize children with the phonetically consistent letter combinations (presented in words) as a basis for generalizations to new words. The success of Soffiètti's method depends on the lawfulness with which the phonetic elements are introduced. The child acquires a set of whole words from which he learns to associate the form of a letter or letter combination with a particular sound. He learns to make visual discriminations and matches these with certain auditory discriminations. The economy of the method depends on the child's ability to make the necessary transfer to similar visual stimuli. In efficient word attack he is able to associate a specific sound with a visual symbol that he recognizes as similar to one with which he previously associated the sound.

Learning is most efficient and permanent "*. . . when the learner is provided with the opportunity of perceiving meaningful relationship among the elements of the goal toward which he is working*" (p. 455).[50] * All our emphasis upon "learning through insight" is useless unless we make it possible for a child to develop insights.

Not only is learning inferred from present performance; it forms the basis of future performance. Learning how to recognize words according to this method certainly has transfer value. It would seem that when word recognition is divorced from association with the spoken word transfer is minimized. Transfer is fostered when the child recognizes that what he is learning fits into the framework of what he already knows.

METHODS OF TEACHING WORD RECOGNITION AND WORD ATTACK

As indicated earlier, word attack is a special application of the techniques of word recognition. It may be defined as the utilization of all those skills that enable one to recognize and master the meaning of new words.

When should instruction in word attack begin? If "word attack" is limited to the acquisition of "sight words," most authorities are willing to begin word attack in kindergarten. If word attack is understood to include the study of "phonics," authorities are more cautious. Generally it is suggested that phonics should be introduced only after the child has learned a certain number of sight words. The teacher is told by some to wait until

---

* Louis P. Thorpe and Allen M. Schmuller. *Contemporary Theories of Learning,* Copyright 1954, The Ronald Press Company.

the child has learned three or four words by sight whereas others recommend as many as a hundred words or more.

Phonics, however, has come to mean different things to different people. Harris, using the term to mean the study of the speech equivalents of printed symbols, suggests that the essential element in learning phonics is the association of the appearance of a letter or letter combination with a particular sound (p. 330).[28] In this sense the teaching of sight words certainly includes sounding. We look upon it as a *see, say,* and *comprehend* process, and we stress the importance of *saying* the word.

Children progress at different rates through the stages of word-attack development and vary widely in the levels they ultimately attain.

We have identified certain guiding principles in both the development of word-recognition skills and in the teaching of reading; now let us examine the various word-attack methods. Methods that begin with the elements of words (letters, phonetic sounds or syllables) generally are called synthetic methods. They are so called because the letters, syllables, and sounds are sooner or later combined to form words. The analytic methods, discussed later in the chapter, begin with large units (words, phrases, or sentences) and later break these down into their basic elements.

THE ALPHABETIC METHOD

Probably the earliest formal attempt to teach the reading of our language was a synthetic method—the alphabetic approach. Each new word was spelled out. Even the Greeks and the Romans appear to have used this method. The *New England Primer* in 1690 was based on the ABC method. The child first learned to recognize the letters and gradually proceeded toward the word.

Although the letter may be the crucial unit in writing and spelling, its validity as a unit for reading is not easily established. Certainly the chief weakness in the alphabetic method is that the sounds of the names of the letters do not always indicate the sounds to be used in pronouncing the words.

An extension of the alphabetic method, the syllabic method, has been used. However it has achieved little acceptance although it may be especially adaptable to the teaching of certain languages.

THE PHONIC METHOD

The second synthetic method to be advocated was the phonic method, originated by Ickelsamer in 1534. Whereas the alphabetic method starts with the name of the letter, the phonic method starts with the phonetic sound of the letter. Unfortunately, sounds as well as letters lack meaning and most of the various letters in the English language may be used to suggest many different sounds. We see a portion of the problem involved when we consider the "ou" sound in the following words: sour, pour, would, tour, sought, couple (p. 209).[1]

However, a modern version of the phonic method has become the most acceptable of the synthetic methods. That phonics have a place in the reading program is now generally accepted. The question is not whether to teach or not to teach phonics, but rather when and how to introduce and use phonetic principles most effectively.[46]

In Chapter 4 we saw the role of visual and auditory discrimination in reading readiness. We also observed the general superiority of girls in readiness. Cordts [11] states that unless children learn to discriminate between the sounds in words, they will have an inadequate groundwork in phonics. Durrell and Murphy [17] found that training in auditory discrimination not only increased the rate of learning words, it increased general reading achievement as well. When combined with training in visual perception the gains were even greater. When both boys and girls received training in auditory discrimination, girls no longer had a faster rate of learning words than had the boys. They point out that children who notice the separate sounds in spoken words generally find it easy to learn to read.

In his list of criteria for phonic readiness Harris (pp. 330–331) [28] emphasizes the auditory factors. He states:

(1) The child should be able to hear that there is a difference between words that sound somewhat alike, such as *man* and *men,* or *had* and *hat.*

(2) He should be able to detect whether two words begin with the same sound or not. . . . He should also be able to listen to a word and supply two or three other words that begin with the same sound.

(3) He should be sensitive to rhymes, should be able to pick out words that rhyme, and should be able to supply words to rhyme with a given word. This ability is fundamental to the construction of "word families."

(4) He should be able to hear similarities and differences in word endings.

(5) He should be able to hear similarities and differences in middle vowels; *e.g.,* he should be able to tell whether *rub* and *rob,* or *hill* and *pit,* have the same middle sound.

(6) He should be able to listen to the pronunciation of a word sound by sound and fuse or blend the sounds mentally so as to be able to recognize the word intended.

Tinker (p. 141) [53] says that phonic readiness has been reached when

. . . the child has acquired the visual and auditory discrimination adequate for differentiating between letter forms and between letter sounds, when the child has acquired a considerable stock of sight words, when he has attained a mental age of approximately seven years, and when he is making some progress in formal reading situations.

Let us examine the recommendations of some writers concerning the most desirable age or grade level for beginning instruction in phonics.

Dolch and Bloomster [15] found that among first and second grade pupils there was a close relationship between mental age and ability to use phonics. They concluded that a mental age of seven seemed to be required for effective use of even relatively simple phonics. In short, a higher level of mental development is required for applying phonics than for learning sight words. They (pp. 204–5) point out that their results

> . . . do not tell, however, exactly when the teaching of phonics should be started. Ear training, which is the basis of phonics, may begin early. Children may be taught to notice the similarities between sounds some time before they are expected actually to use sounding generalizations.*

Watts (p. 96) [59] says that with from 100 to 200 words learned by sight, a normal child of six and a half generally is ready for phonic instruction. And Betts [6] cautions that if children are required to memorize a "large" sight vocabulary before phonics are introduced, they are likely to begin confusing one word with another.

Beltramo [4] suggests that first grade children can learn not only the phonic readiness skills but, with systematic instruction, they can gain proficiency in the basic phonic skills as well. Harris (p. 329) [28] remarks that the Dolch and Bloomster study mentioned above underestimates the phonic readiness of first graders. He seems to agree with McKee (p. 200) [37] that, once two or three sight words have been learned in which a phonic element occurs, the phonic element can be learned.

The value of phonics is indicated in many studies. Already in 1913 Valentine [54] had concluded that, except with very dull children,** the phonic method gave "far better results" than the "look and say" method. He suggested that interest was not lost by the necessary plodding, letter-by-letter, through certain words; but, if there was too great a focus on the content of the reading material before the child's word-recognition skills were adequate, interest in the act of reading was more likely to be lost. Focus on content (p. 112)

> . . . may tend to divert attention from the words themselves and cause not only wild guessing and misreading of words but also such a very fleeting atten-

---

** He pointed out that no doubt the "look and say" method also is the better method for the dull teacher.

tion even to words properly read, that they are not remembered on future occasions.

In short, he was pointing out that interest in learning to read may be hindered by a too early emphasis on reading to learn or on reading for entertainment purposes.

The above recommendations suggest that word-attack training should begin early. Certainly we should help the child to develop fundamental auditory and visual discrimination skills (basic phonic skills) in the kindergarten. One way for doing this is by familiarizing him with phonetically consistent words. At first the emphasis should be on the discrimination and association of auditory and visual cues. More advanced phonic skills may need to be reserved for a later time. Because ability in auditory and visual discrimination frequently shows a higher correlation with reading achievement in the first grade than does mental age, training in these skills is not only beneficial but may compensate somewhat for otherwise inadequate mental development.

Garrison and Heard [22] studied the reading progress of an experimental group (given training in phonics) and a control group of children for three consecutive years. They began their study when the children were first grade entrants who could neither read nor spell. These were the reported conclusions (pp. 13–14):

1. Training in phonetics makes children more independent in the pronunciation of words.
2. Children with no phonetic training make smoother and better oral readers in the lower grades.
3. In teaching children to read in the early part of the primary grades, first and perhaps second, bright children seem to be helped more by training in phonetics than are dull.* For all children, phonetic training seems to be more effective in the latter part of the primary grades.
4. In the teaching of reading it seems probable that much of the phonetic training now given should be deferred till the second and third grades. It appears that work in meaningful exercises which are planned to increase comprehension and to teach discrimination of words is more important than phonetics.
5. Children who have had training in phonetics have some advantage in learning to spell over children who have had no such training. . . .
6. First grade children with no phonetic training seem to lose less during vacation than do children with such training. Apparently, phonetic training makes a young child, particularly a young dull child, dependent upon

* Students of superior intelligence frequently are found to profit less from word-recognition training than do children of average or low intelligence. Bedell and Nelson [3] have concluded that this is also true of training in phonics. Superior pupils learn to attack words as a result of their usual reading experiences, many of which begin before they enter school.

a device of word analysis which is more difficult to retain than is his own peculiar method. With the older children, children at the end of the second grade, phonetic training seems to be an aid in retention during vacation.

Currier and Duguid (p. 452) [13] reported on a five-year study of primary children. They concluded: *

1. Phonetic drills have very real value but are not essential to every child as a part of the daily program in primary grades.
2. Phonetic drills should at all times be employed with discretion and adapted to the needs of the individual child or special groups.
3. Do not use one system for every case. What is food for one may be poison for another. . . .

Sexton and Herron,[44] working with nearly 1,000 children in Grades 1A and 1B, found that phonic training was a definite help, but that the differences between the phonic and non-phonic group were less than the differences between groups having different teachers. A good teacher produced good results, phonics or no phonics.

In summarizing the data concerning the phonic method it may be said that many of the criticisms of phonics have stemmed from a misconception of its basic contribution to word recognition. When elaborate phonetic systems are used in experimental studies, it is only reasonable to expect that there is little emphasis upon understanding of what is read. The children tend to recognize words piecemeal and interest in reading may be lost.

Phonics need not necessarily imply that we start with the parts of the word. As a matter of fact, we have seen that the initial association of a sound with visual symbols should be an association between a sound and a monosyllabic word. Certainly phonic elements need not be learned in isolation, and meaning need not be ignored.

Numerous studies have demonstrated that phonic instruction has value. Some indeed have indicated that the phonic method is the only legitimate way to teach word recognition. Generally, however, it has been shown that an extreme emphasis on phonics has definite limitations. It seems clear that the phonic method is highly desirable but it is far from sufficient as the sole method for a reading program.

THE ANALYTIC METHOD

The method of using the words, phrases, or sentences as the unit of teaching is called the analytic method. The "word" method was introduced

---

* Copyright 1916 by the University of Chicago, reprinted by permission.

in Europe in 1658 by Comenius through his book *The Orbis Pictus.* Samuel Worcester advocated the use of the method in America in 1828 (p. 86).[47, 48] According to Smith (p. 87),[48] Josiah Bumstead, an early author of school readers, after describing the alphabet method, wrote:

> This method, so irksome and vexatious to both teacher and scholar, is now giving place to another, which experience has proved to be more philosophical, intelligent, pleasant, and rapid. It is that of beginning with familiar and easy *words* instead of *letters.*

In 1885 Cattell and in 1898 Erdmann and Dodge demonstrated that in a given unit of time only a few unrelated letters could be recognized; but in the same unit of time it was possible to recognize familiar words containing two to four times as many letters (pp. 212–213).[1] In 1885, Cattell,[9] using a tachistoscopic technique, found that in 10 ms. of exposure time (.01 seconds) a child could comprehend equally well three or four unrelated letters, two unrelated words (up to 12 letters) or a short sentence of four words. Obviously, in recognizing entire words the reader was not reacting to the individual letter in the word.

Others have suggested that if we desire to proceed from simple to complex in learning a language we must go from the meaningful wholes to the component parts, and that the words and phrases rather than their letters or syllables are the simplest meaningful elements in reading. Claparède (p. 177) [10] pointed out that

> . . . the mind proceeds from the simple to the complex; the fact that the child sees the whole before perceiving its parts does not contradict this statement. For the child, the whole not being a collection of parts, but, on the contrary, a block, a unity, to go from the simple to the complex is to proceed from the whole to its part.

Consequently, educators have suggested that the best way to teach a word is to present it as a whole. They have generally maintained that the perception of shape or form tends to be syncretistic. In short, they suggest that the child sees the word as a unit, not as a bundle of parts. Certain studies (p. 127) [51] indicate that rapid readers especially are form dominant: they tend to see words as wholes.

Discussing visual perception on an adult level, Vernon (pp. 118–119) [56] wrote:

> The conclusion seems to be that some general form or contour is perceived, with certain dominating letters or parts arising out of it, as the 'figure' rises out of the "ground." The ascending letters seem to play an important part, and an alternation of vertical and curved letters may also help in structuralizing the form. It is improbable that any individual letters or parts of words are rec-

ognized as such. But they are the details, standing out from the rest of the field, which differentiate its flat clearness, and finally produce perception of the "specific object." The words are not necessarily recognized and named individually, but the structuralized visual percept of the whole phrase or sentences arouses the more or less subliminal auditory or kinesthetic imagery of the sounds appropriate to that percept, or in some cases an incipient vocalization of these sounds. This total percept is then interpreted directly in accordance with the general meaning of the reading content.

However, some research indicates that although the child generally approaches the word as a unit, if the whole is complex or relatively meaningless to the perceiver, the details then tend to dominate.

When the global approach is unsuccessful the child resorts to other techniques. Petty,[40] for example, found that some first-graders focus on the general shape when they draw whereas others tend to emphasize and select details. Young children (four- and five-years old) and poor readers commonly identify words by certain key letters, letter arrangements, or other outstanding characteristics, and for this reason confuse them with other words having the same letters or characteristics. The poor reader can perceive shapes, but perhaps he has a greater tendency to be attracted by specific details than has the normal reader.

Young children and poor readers frequently do not perceive clearly either the total configuration of the word or the details of the letters. The word tends to be a jumble of lines, and unless it contains some striking characteristic the child has difficulty in perceiving it.[58] Vernon (p. 29) [57] suggests that children and also retarded readers have not acquired an understanding of the importance of particular details in letter shapes and of their relationship to one another within the total word. And even if they can perceive these details, they fail to remember their significance.

Hildreth,[29] writing in 1957, says that the word method is the most accepted approach today. Letters or combinations of letters are taught as sounds *within words*. She adds that the introduction of word cards by Nila B. Smith and S. A. Courtis helped to promote the analytic method.

The phrase, the sentence, and the story methods are extensions of the word method. The phrase method has not been widely used. Perhaps this is because even mature readers seldom read by phrases. However, this would seem to be even more true for sentences, but for some reason the sentence method has received more attention than the phrase method.

A special weakness of analytic methods is that children tend to confuse similar words. Gray [26] mentions that with the word method, pupils frequently become ineffective in attacking new words. When basic word-attack skills are ignored, the pupil frequently becomes a retarded reader. A word method, stressing drill on isolated words apart from context, may result in no more meaning than comes with an alphabetical approach. Somehow the child must be led to look for the meaning that is expressed in thought units. Finally, a strict adherence to the word method frequently is uneconomical. Teaching children to learn *all* words by sight is neither possible nor does it lead to independence in word recognition (pp. 35–36).[24]

As yet no one method can claim to have solved all problems. Effective reading requires a flexibility of behavior. One needs a basic sight vocabulary, but he also needs skill in analyzing those words that are in his sight vocabulary, so that they may serve as examples in attacking unfamiliar words.

THE ANALYTIC-SYNTHETIC METHOD

There are certain objections to the exclusive use of either the synthetic or the analytic method. We have just summarized the limitations of the analytic method. The synthetic methods also seem to have certain weaknesses. They are said to (1) disregard the child's natural mode of learning; (2) ignore the fact that not all children learn the same way; (3) result in slow development of recognition span; and (4) fail to develop fluent readers (p. 77).[27] It is frequently charged that synthetic methods lead to "word-calling" without comprehension of meaning.

However, as we study the synthetic and the analytic methods for teaching word recognition, we can see the contributions of both. And recent trends in teaching reading appear to be in the direction of combining them.

The combined analytic-synthetic approach uses sentences and short selections based on a carefully selected group of words. Almost from the beginning the child learns both to analyze and to synthesize the words and simple sentences.

Daniels and Diack [14, 42] compared for one year two methods of teaching reading to nearly 100 totally illiterate seven and eight year olds. The first method, referred to as a modified phonic method, was developed for their own reading series known as the *Royal Road Readers*. It starts with words that are phonetically regular and at all times emphasizes the phonetic sounds of the letters. Under this method, the phonetic sounds are stressed in meaningful words rather than as isolated letters. The second method, called a mixed method, begins with a look-and-say approach and is supplemented with phonics. They concluded that those children who had been taught by "Method One," the modified phonic method, displayed the following characteristics: (1) they excelled significantly in ability to pronounce both isolated words and words in sentences; (2) they excelled significantly in the ability to recognize new words; and (3) when unfamiliar words were presented to them they failed to make responses less often than did the group taught by "Method Two," the mixed method. The children in "Method One" failed to respond to 16.3% of the total words whereas the children in "Method Two" failed to respond to 46% of the words. This latter finding suggests that the children taught by "Method One" showed more confidence in attacking words.

Naeslund,[39] in a controlled experiment with eight pairs of fraternal and ten pairs of identical twins, compared a phonic method (in which the pupil begins "by mastering the smallest components" and proceeds towards greater units) with a sentence method (in which the pupil begins with whole sentences, first analyzing the words and then the sounds). One member of each pair of twins was taught by the phonic method and the other by the sentence method. He concluded that with pupils of average or above intelligence there was no significant difference. However, with twins of below average intelligence, the phonic method seemed superior in promoting both reading and spelling achievement. The sentence method promoted more interest in reading with children of all levels of ability.

Certainly, the evidence presented in these two studies indicates that it is unwise to rely totally on an analytic method. The word and the phonic methods supplement each other. Word recognition is superior when the pupil can use both techniques. Even these two methods, however, are not always sufficient. Russell and Karp [43] point out that word recognition utilizes the shape and configuration of the word; the idiosyncrasy of a word, as, for example, the double "o" in moon; picture clues; context clues; recognition of a basic sight word in a compound or affixed word; phonetic analysis or sound clues; and structural analysis into prefix, root, and suffix. One of these alone or a combination of them can help the child to recognize the word.

WORD CONFIGURATION AND WORD ELEMENTS

Although we have examined the relative merits of the whole-word and the phonic methods, perhaps it should be worthwhile to see how each contributes to word recognition.

When the reader uses the form of the entire word to recognize it, he is using configurational clues. For example, even if the word "dad" were written like this: dad, and the word "butterfly" like this: butterfly, a reader would be likely to recognize these words.

Unfortunately, the shape and configuration of a word frequently depends on certain key letters. The ascenders and descenders have special configural significance to the learner. Thus, a word such as "trunk" has its configuration mostly determined by the *t* and *k* and has an over-all appearance of 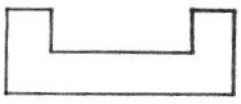 whereas in a word such as monkey the descending *y* gives it a unique form 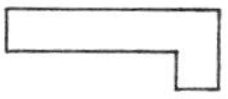 Wiley [60] indicates that in recognizing words children tend to depend more on certain letters, especially initial and final letters and ascenders and descenders, than on the general form. For this reason similarities in these significant elements most frequently lead to word confusion.

This dependency on configuration should have important implications for choosing the words that are to form a child's basic sight vocabulary. Generally the words will be easier to learn and will be less likely to be confused with one another if they differ in configuration. Variations in length are an additional configurational clue to be considered in making the choice of sight vocabulary words. Crosland [12] studied 31 superior and 34 retarded readers with matched mental ages and of average chronological age of 11.5 years who had learned to read under similar methods. He found that the superior readers were attracted to the beginning of the word but the retarded readers were better in their recall of the last letter of a word. He noted that in this tendency defective readers are similar to left-eyed college students, and in fact the majority of the retarded readers were found to be left-eyed.

Confusion of word elements is probably the most frequent cause of word-recognition errors. Bennett,[5] analyzing 34,274 errors by retarded readers, found that most errors resulted from a confusion of final letters, initial letters, median vowels, reversals of initial consonants, reading of a whole word or part in right-to-left sequence, final–S errors, and substitutions. Confusion of letter or syllable sounds as "ketch" for catch; and the omission of letters, syllables, and words have also been mentioned by writers as examples of word-recognition errors.

A child also can be helped in word recognition if he is taught how to use structural analysis in conjunction with other word-recogntion skills.[20] When the child recognizes the endings of words such as *ing, er, or, ed, s, ate,* when he is dividing a compound word into simpler words, when he looks for prefixes, roots, and suffixes, or when he divides the word into syllables, he is doing structural analysis.

Thus a knowledge of the most commonly used prefixes, roots, and suffixes can be a basic tool for word recognition. However, it is an even more powerful aid in understanding the meaning of new words. For this reason a list of important affixes and roots is included in Chapter 8, in the section on "Teaching Word Meaning," rather than in the present section.

Usually a child can be introduced to simple syllabication as early as the third grade. However, the average student should not be taught more advanced syllabication before the sixth grade (pp. 340–341).[28]

KINESTHETIC AND COMBINATION METHODS

Methods of teaching word recognition frequently have taken their name from the sensory modalities most stressed in their use. Thus we find mention of an auditory method, a visual method, a kinesthetic method, and various combination approaches.

The kinesthetic method is described by Fernald.[21] Here the learner traces the word on a model that the clinician or teacher has written for him on a large piece of paper. He pronounces it by syllables as he traces and he continues until he can reproduce the word without copying. One advantage of this method is that the direction of movement from left to right is automatically controlled. The kinesthetic method seems especially effective with severe reading disability cases.

Harris (pp. 320, 321) [28] describes a combination approach that he calls the *Visual-Motor Word Study* method. It is designed for retarded readers and combines seeing the word, saying the word, and writing it from memory. First the teacher presents the word visually in context (possibly in a sentence on the chalkboard). He then shows the single word on a card and pronounces it. The pupils look at it and pronounce it softly. They repeat this a few times. Then with eyes closed each child tries to form a visual image and checks this image with the card. Next the card is removed and each child tries to write or print the word from memory. He then checks his written word against the card. The process is repeated as needed.

Mills [38] experimented with groups of children, 39 boys and 19 girls, in grades two to four. Four methods, visual, phonic, kinesthetic, and a combination approach, were compared. His findings were that children learn to recognize words by different methods, and that no one method is superior for all children. For children of low intelligence (65–80 I.Q.) the phonic method proved least effective; the kinesthetic and the visual, most effective. For children of I.Q. 85–100 the kinesthetic method proved least effective, whereas the phonic method showed no statistically significant advantages or disadvantages. For these children the visual method or a combination of the three proved best. Superior learners (105–120 I.Q.) learned words regardless of the method used. The study suggests that a variety of approaches is needed—structural analysis, phonics, word-form analysis, and kinesthetic techniques.

Gray (p. 17) [26] summarizes the conclusions that can be drawn from the research on the methods of teaching word recognition skills. He writes: *

---

1. The same method does not secure equally satisfactory results in all schools and classrooms. This indicates that other factors, such as the teacher, the pupils, and the materials used, exert a vital influence on progress in learning to read.
2. Contrasting methods emphasize different aspects of reading. A phonic method gives most emphasis initially to word recognition. A word method gives most emphasis from the beginning to the meaning of what is read.
3. Contrasting methods start pupils toward maturity in reading over different routes. Sooner or later any specialized method must be supplemented to insure growth in all essential aspects of reading.
4. Best results are secured when both meaning and word-recognition skills are emphasized from the beginning. This finding lends definite support to the eclectic trends described earlier.

Gray (p. 16),[26] discussing a world-wide survey of reading by UNESCO, points out that most reading programs use a variety of approaches. He says: *

> This not only makes possible the use in a given reading program of all the techniques of established worth, but it insures balanced emphasis from the beginning on all the essential aspects of reading: a thoughtful reading attitude, a clear grasp of meaning, accuracy and independence in word recognition, thoughtful reaction to the ideas read, and interest in personal reading.

SUMMARY

As a summary of this chapter, let us identify the principles of word recognition that have been established or at least strongly indicated by the research in the area:

1. The *basic* word-recognition skill is the ability to associate the sound (spoken word) with the visual stimulus (written word).
2. Skill development in reading proceeds both vertically and horizontally.
3. An optimum reaction in reading is global in nature. Reaction is to the bigger meaningful unit, the word. The letter, syllable, or phonetic sound does not suggest meaning.
4. When the global reaction to the meaningful unit fails, the reader turns to synthetic methods. Some readers show a marked tendency to react to details rather than to the larger unit.
5. More poor readers than good readers react to the letter or a specific pecularity of the word rather than to the whole word.
6. The younger the child, the more he tends to react to peculiar characteristics of words rather than to the general form or shape of the word.

---

7. The rate of recognition in reading begins to surpass the rate of articulation in about the third or fourth grade. The student becomes able to read faster silently than orally.
8. The perception of a word is dependent both upon the meaning of the word and upon the relationship between the elements that make up the word.
9. The context of words functions positively in word recognition. Recognition is easier when the word is presented with other words that give a clue to its meaning.
10. Poor readers make more recognition errors than do good readers.
11. Word recognition is best taught in context, but practice is necessary for thorough learning and this frequently is reduced if context situations alone are used.
12. Word-attack training results in relatively greater improvement for the average pupil than for the bright pupil. The bright pupil generally acquires word-attack skills through his everyday reading experiences.
13. The analytic-synthetic method better provides for growth in reading than do either the analytic or synthetic methods alone because
    a. it can be adjusted to the individual needs of the pupil;
    b. it permits emphasis on meaning;
    c. it stresses accuracy and independence in word recognition; and
    d. it encourages an interest in reading.

    Best results are secured when both meaning and word recognition are emphasized from the beginning.
14. Synthetic methods alone do not provide adequately for the reader's needs because
    a. they disregard the child's natural way of perceiving: wholes to parts;
    b. they ignore the fact that not all children learn the same way;
    c. they result in slow development of word-recognition span;
    d. they fail to develop fluency in reading; and
    e. they lead to "word-calling" without comprehension of meaning.
15. The word or analytic method, if used alone,
    a. tends to result in confusion of similar words;
    b. may result in inaccurate perception of the word; and
    c. fails to develop independence in word recognition.
16. Phonic training is most effective when it grows out of a functional need.
17. Auditory discrimination is the chief determinant of phonic readiness. Becoming able to recognize differences is an important facet

of learning at all levels. The child who notices the separate sounds in spoken words is likely to learn to read easily.

18. The phonic method is essential for reading achievement because
    a. it increases independence in word attack;
    b. it makes it easier for a child to learn new words;
    c. it leads to better oral reading;
    d. it promotes correct pronunciation; and
    e. it promotes spelling and alphabetizing.
19. Pupils taught by a phonic method achieve significantly higher on a word-recognition test than those taught by a look-and-say method.
20. Pupils differ in the benefits they derive from phonic training. When intelligence is held constant, phonic training is more effective with poor readers than with good readers.
21. A higher level of mental development is required for applying phonics than for learning sight words.
22. Poor readers make less application of their phonic skills to new words than do good readers.
23. The more intelligent pupils tend to use their word-analysis skills more than do the less intelligent pupils.
24. Extreme emphasis on phonics frequently is associated with lower scores on tests of comprehension.
25. The lower the intelligence and the more severe the reading disability, the more effective is the kinesthetic method.
26. The same method will not secure equally satisfactory results with all children. Thus an eclectic approach appears to provide more flexibility in method and promises better results.

SUGGESTED READINGS

For a detailed discussion of oral reading (language readiness, pertinent motives, oral expression, classroom procedures, choral reading, appreciation of orally-presented materials—from kindergarten through college level):

Robinson, Helen M. (Ed.) *Oral Aspects of Reading, Supplementary Educational Monographs,* No. 82, Chicago: University of Chicago Press, 1955.

***

(Causey, *The Reading Teacher's Reader*)

Article 10, Dolch, E. W., "Four 'Methods' of Teaching Reading," from *Elementary English,* 31 (February, 1954), pp. 72–76.
Article 45, Morris, William and Emmett A. Betts, "Teaching Johnny To Read," from *Saturday Review,* July 30, 1955.
Article 48, Tronsberg, Josephine "The Place of Phonics in Basal Reading Instruction," from *The Reading Teacher,* 8 (October, 1954), pp. 18–20, 38.

QUESTIONS FOR DISCUSSION

1. What specific reading skills must be learned early in the child's development? How do you define *basic* skill?
2. What are the values of oral reading? What place does oral reading have in basic instruction in reading?
3. What is the non-oral method? What values might it have?
4. What are the advantages and disadvantages of vocalizing during reading?
5. What are word-recognition skills? How are they developed?
6. How should phonic instruction be started and developed?
7. Discuss the alphabetic and phonic approaches to reading. What is an analytic method?
8. What advantages may be found in an analytic-synthetic approach?
9. What is structural analysis? How do configurational clues operate? What is meant by a kinesthetic approach?
10. What basic skills should a mature reader possess?
11. What seem to be the most significant factors in phonic readiness?
12. What is word attack? When and how should it be taught?
13. In beginning reading what emphasis should be placed on meaning?
14. Why should skill in auditory discrimination be related to reading readiness?

BIBLIOGRAPHY

[1] Anderson, Irving H., and Dearborn, Walter F. *The Psychology of Teaching Reading.* Ronald Press Company, New York, 1952.

[2] Artley, A. S. "Oral-Language Growth and Reading Ability." *Elementary School Journal,* 53 (February, 1953) 321–328.

[3] Bedell, Ralph, and Nelson, Eloise Schott. "Word Attack as a Factor in Reading Achievement in the Elementary School." *Educational and Psychological Measurement,* Supplement on Reading Research, 14 (Spring, 1954) 168–175.

[4] Beltramo, Louise. "An Alphabetical Approach to the Teaching of Reading in Grade One." Unpublished doctoral dissertation, University of Iowa, 1954; *Dissertation Abstracts,* 14 (Fall, 1954) 2290.

[5] Bennett, Annette. "An Analysis of Errors in Word Recognition Made by Retarded Readers." *Journal of Educational Psychology,* 33 (January, 1942) 25–38.

[6] Betts, Emmett Albert. "Phonics: Syllables," *Education,* 79 (May, 1959) 557–564.

[7] Bond, Guy L., and Tinker, Miles A. *Reading Difficulties: Their Diagnosis and Correction.* Appleton-Century-Crofts, Inc., New York, 1957.

[8] Buswell, G. T. "Perceptual Research and Methods of Learning." *The Scientific Monthly,* 64 (June, 1947) 521–526.

[9] Cattell, James McKeen. "Ueber die Zeit der Erkennung und Benennung von Schriftzeichen, Bildern und Farben." *Philosophische Studien,* 2 (1885) 635–650. Cited in Anderson,[1] p. 212.

[10] Claparède, Edouard. *Psychologie de l'Enfant et Pédagogie Expérimentale.* 4th Ed., Champel, Geneva, 1910. *Experimental Pedagogy and the Psychology of the Child,* Mary Louch and Henry Holman (trans.). Longmans, Green and Company, New York, 1911.

[11] Cordts, Anna D. "And It's All Known as Phonics." *Elementary English,* 32 (October, 1955) 376–378, 412.

[12] Crosland, H. R. "Superior Elementary-School Readers Contrasted With Inferior Readers in Letter-Position, 'Range of Attention,' Scores." *Journal of Educational Research,* 32 (February, 1939) 410–427.

[13] Currier, Lillian Beatrice and Duguid, Olive C. "Phonics or No Phonics." *Elementary School Journal,* 23 (February, 1923) 448–452.

[14] Daniels, J. C. and Diack, H. *Progress in Reading.* University of Nottingham, Institute of Education, 1956.

[15] Dolch, E. W., and Bloomster, Maurine. "Phonic Readiness." *Elementary School Journal,* 38 (November, 1937) 201–205.

[16] Donnelly, Helen E. "The Growth of Word Recognition Skills in Grade One." *Education,* 56 (September, 1935) 40–43.

[17] Durrell, Donald D., and Murphy, Helen A. "The Auditory Discrimination Factor in Reading Readiness and Reading Disability." *Education,* 73 (May, 1953) 556–560.

[18] Edwards, Thomas J. "The Role of Meaning, Frequency of Contact and Auditory-vocomotor Stimulation in the Visual Perception of Verbal Stimuli." Unpublished doctoral dissertation, Temple University, 1955; *Dissertation Abstracts,* 16 (1956) 382–383.

[19] Edwards, Thomas J. "Oral Reading in the Total Reading Process." *The Elementary School Journal,* 58 (October, 1957) 36–41.

[20] Feldmann, Shirley C., and Merrill, Kathleen K. *Ways to Read Words* and *More Ways to Read Words.* Bureau of Publications, Teachers College, Columbia University, New York, 1959.

[21] Fernald, Grace Maxwell. *Remedial Techniques in Basic School Subjects.* McGraw-Hill Book Company, Inc., New York, 1943.

[22] Garrison, S. C., and Heard, Minnie Taylor. "An Experimental Study of the Value of Phonetics." *Peabody Journal of Education,* 9 (July, 1931) 9–14.

[23] Gray, Clarence T. *Types of Reading Ability as Exhibited Through Tests and Laboratory Experiments.* Supplementary Educational Monographs, No. 5, University of Chicago Press, Chicago, 1917.

[24] Gray, Lillian, and Reese, Dora. *Teaching Children to Read.* Ronald Press Company, New York, 1957.

[25] Gray, William S. "Characteristics of Effective Oral Reading." *Oral Aspects of Reading,* Supplementary Educational Monographs, No. 82, University of Chicago Press, Chicago, 1955, 5–10.

[26] Gray, William S. "Current Reading Problems: A World View." *Elementary School Journal,* 56 (September, 1955) 11–17.

[27] Gray, William S. *The Teaching of Reading and Writing.* UNESCO, Scott, Foresman and Company, Chicago, 1956.

[28] Harris, Albert J. *How to Increase Reading Ability,* 3rd Edition. Longmans, Green and Company, New York, 1956.

[29] Hildreth, Gertrude. "New Methods for Old in Teaching Phonics." *Elementary School Journal,* 57 (May, 1957) 436–441.

[30] Horn, Ernest. *Methods of Instruction in the Social Studies.* Charles Scribner's Sons, New York, 1937.

[31] Huey, Edmund B. *The Psychology and Pedagogy of Reading.* The Macmillan Company, New York, 1912.

[32] Jacobson, Edmund. "Electrophysiology of Mental Activities." *American Journal of Psychology,* 44 (October, 1932) 677–694.

[33] Johnson, Eleanor M. "The Nature and Scope of Reading Programs Adapted to Today's Needs: Discussion." *Better Readers For Our Times,* Conference Proceedings, International Reading Association, Scholastic Magazines, New York, 1956, 29–30.

[34] Lee, Dorris M. *The Importance of Reading for Achieving in Grades Four, Five and Six.* Contributions to Education, No. 556, Bureau of Publications, Teachers College, Columbia University, 1933.

[35] Loevinger, Jane. "Intelligence as Related to Socio-Economic Factors." *Intelligence: Its Nature and Nurture,* Thirty-ninth Yearbook of the National Society for the Study of Education, Part I, University of Chicago Press, Chicago, 1940, 159–210.

[36] McDade, James E. "A Hypothesis for Non-Oral Reading: Argument, Experiment, and Results." *Journal of Educational Research,* 30 (March, 1937) 489–503.

[37] McKee, Paul. *The Teaching of Reading in the Elementary School.* Houghton Mifflin Company, Boston, 1948.

[38] Mills, Robert E. "An Evaluation of Techniques for Teaching Word Recognition." *Elementary School Journal,* 56 (January, 1956) 221–225.

[39] Naeslund, Jon. *Methods of Teaching Primary Reading: A Co-Twin Control Experiment.* Research Bulletins from the Institute of Education, No. 4, University of Stockholm, 1955.

[40] Petty, Mary C. "An Experimental Study of Certain Factors Influencing Reading Readiness." *Journal of Educational Psychology,* 30 (March, 1939) 215–230.

[41] Quantz, J. O. "Problems in the Psychology of Reading." *Psychological Review Monograph Supplements,* 2 (December, 1897) 1–51.

[42] Russell, David H. "Progress in Reading: A Special Review." *Elementary English,* 34 (April, 1957) 242–244.

[43] Russell, David H., and Karp, Etta E. *Reading Aids Through the Grades: Three Hundred Developmental Reading Activities,* Revised Edition. Bureau of Publications, Teachers College, Columbia University, 1959.

[44] Sexton, Elmer K., and Herron, John S. "The Newark Phonics Experiment." *Elementary School Journal,* 28 (May, 1928) 690–701.

[45] Simon, J. "Contribution à la Psychologie de la Lecture." *Enfance,* No. 5 (November–December, 1954) 431–447.

[46] Simpson, Elizabeth A. "Classroom Procedures in Correcting Reading Deficiencies in High School and College." *Better Readers For Our Times,* Conference Proceedings, International Reading Association, Scholastic Magazines, New York, 1956, 140–146.

[47] Slover, Vera. "Reading—Then and Now." *The Education Forum,* 21 (May, 1957) 413–420.

[48] Smith, Nila B. *American Reading Instruction.* Silver Burdett and Company, New York, 1934.

[49] Soffiètti, James P. "Why Children Fail to Read: A Linguistic Analysis." *The Harvard Educational Review,* 25 (Spring, 1955) 63–84.

[50] Thorpe, Louis P., and Schmuller, Allen M. *Contemporary Theories of Learning.* Ronald Press Company, New York, 1954.

[51] Thurstone, L. L. *A Factorial Study of Perception.* University of Chicago Press, Chicago, 1944.

[52] Tiffin, Joseph, and Fairbanks, Grant. "An Eye-Voice Camera for Clinical and Research Studies." *Psychological Monographs,* 48 (No. 3, 1937) 70–77.

[53] Tinker, Miles A. *Teaching Elementary Reading.* Appleton-Century-Crofts, Inc., New York, 1952.

[54] Valentine, Charles W. "Experiments on the Methods of Teaching Reading." *Journal of Experimental Pedagogy,* 2 (June, 1913) 99–112.

[55] Veatch, Jeannette (Ed.). *Individualizing Your Reading Program: Self-Selection in Action.* G. P. Putnam's Sons, New York, 1959.

[56] Vernon, M. D. *The Experimental Study of Reading.* The University Press, Cambridge, England, 1931.

[57] Vernon, M. D. *Backwardness in Reading.* The University Press, Cambridge, England, 1957.

[58] Vernon, M. D. "The Development of Visual Perception in Children." *Education,* 78 (May, 1958) 547–549.

[59] Watts, A. F. *The Language and Mental Development of Children.* George G. Harrap and Company, Ltd., London, 1946.

[60] Wiley, Will E. "Difficult Words and the Beginner." *Journal of Educational Research,* 17 (April, 1928) 278–289.

[61] Worthington, Louise Willson. *Oral Reading? Certainly!* Ginn and Company Contributions in Reading, No. 16, Ginn and Company, Boston, 1954.

8

BASIC READING SKILLS: COMPREHENSION AND RATE SKILLS

Word recognition is but one of the basic reading skills. Comprehension and rate are at least as important. Meaning is the sine qua non *of reading but effective reading emphasizes economy which includes comprehension and rate. These two skills are so interrelated that we speak of them as rate of comprehension.*

In the preceding chapter we examined various phases of the problem of teaching word recognition. But recognition of the word is not the ultimate goal in reading. Without comprehension reading is mere verbalism. We know that in beginning reading the printed word is associated with the spoken word until the child can make the same physical, emotional, and mental responses to the written word that he previously made to the spoken word. *A basic word-recognition skill is the ability to associate the sound* (spoken word) *with the visual stimulus* (the written word). This recognition process is, of course, fundamental to reading comprehension, but it is only a first step.

COMPREHENSION

Strangely enough, comprehension is difficult to define. In fact, Traxler (p. 92) [77] suggests that no adequate definition of reading comprehension has been offered. He writes:

Specialists in the reading field think of 'reading' as anything from a set of more or less mechanical habits to something akin to the 'thinking' process itself. No one has yet been able to identify the components of reading comprehension. . . .

Yoakam (p. 32) [86] describes comprehension as follows:

Comprehending reading matter involves the correct association of meanings with word symbols, the evaluation of meanings which are suggested in context, the selection of the correct meaning, the organization of ideas as they are read, the retention of these ideas, and their use in some present or future activity.

Edwards (p. 38) [20] points out that *

. . . continuous development toward greater reading proficiency is a process with many phases, the goal of which is the comprehension of ideas. Success in the process depends on adequate motivation, a substantial background of concepts, word-perception skills, and the ability to reason one's way through smaller idea elements and to grasp, as a whole, the meaning of a larger unitary idea.

In the reading process comprehension may be likened to the cake which must include a proper combination of ingredients *plus* the kitchen chemistry of their reaction upon exposure to heat (or exposure, in the case of reading, to the mind's active and thoughtful reaction to its stimulation by the ingredients, the printed words).

COMPREHENSION SKILLS

Writers have suggested that the following abilities are basic to understanding and may be called comprehension skills.

1. Ability to associate meaning with the graphic symbol
2. Ability to understand words in context and to select the meaning that fits the context
3. Ability to read in thought units
4. Ability to understand units of increasing size: the phrase, clause, sentence, paragraph, and whole selection
5. Ability to acquire word meanings
6. Ability to select and understand the main ideas
7. Ability to follow directions
8. Ability to draw inferences

---

9. Ability to understand the writer's organization
10. Ability to evaluate what is read: to recognize literary devices and to identify the tone, mood, and intent of the writer
11. Ability to retain ideas
12. Ability to apply ideas and to integrate them with one's past experience.

Actually the identification of these various abilities or comprehension skills is only a preliminary step. We wish to know whether they can be taught and, if so, how we can best teach them. Davis (p. 542),[16] discussing five comprehension skills, makes the following comment:

> Underlying all five skills are two general mental abilities: ability to remember word meanings and ability to reason with verbal concepts. Basically, neither of these general abilities lends itself to specific teaching; they are probably part of the pupil's native endowment. However, the gradual building up of experiential background and of associations with words tends to augment an individual's store of usable word meanings; and conscious attention to methods of attack on problems and to logical steps in reasoning tends to improve an individual's ability to think.

This statement implies that certain limitations are imposed on training in comprehension. Skills can be developed only within the potentials that already exist. Sommerfeld[66] suggests that the basic problem of reading is not that of getting the material to the brain, but of assimilating it after it gets there.

THE SIGNIFICANCE OF COMPREHENSION

There are a number of reasons for our concern with reading comprehension. For one thing, we know that it is highly related to academic grades. We should expect this to be true because intelligence and vocabulary skills are basic determinants of school achievement. They also correlate highly with comprehension.

However, comprehension and reading performance are related in still other ways. Fairbanks[21] found that poor readers made an average of 5.8 oral errors per 100 words, but that good readers made only 2.1 errors per 100. More relevant is the fact that in 51 per cent of the cases the errors of the poor readers tended to change the meaning, but the errors of the good readers never did. The good readers also corrected their own errors more often than did the poor readers. This indicates that the basic problem of the poor reader is lack of comprehension.

DEVELOPING COMPREHENSION SKILLS

In Chapter 2 we say that words are symbols. They can do no more than suggest meaning. In this chapter we are concerned with how a child *learns* to bring the proper meaning to the word.

Although the word symbol itself has no meaning it provides a focal point for concept formation, and comprehension certainly depends on the adequacy and accuracy of one's concepts. The reader builds his store of meanings both from his direct experience and from the new meanings he is able to form by combinations of his previously acquired meanings. Meaning then is acquired from experience, and comprehension cannot be more adequate than experience.[71] Yoakam pointed out that the comprehending of reading matter "involves the correct association of meanings with word symbols. . ." (p. 32).[86] Bond and Tinker (7, p. 231) add that for a word to be serviceable in reading, meaning must be attached to it. And it is only by the use of word meanings that comprehension may be attained.

VOCABULARY AND COMPREHENSION

Studies generally indicate that vocabulary is highly related to comprehension. Without an understanding of words comprehension is impossible. In a factorial study of comprehension, Davis [15] found that a knowledge of word meanings and the ability to select the correct meaning from the context were essential factors.

Fortunately, it appears that children have a far greater knowledge of the meaning of words than we usually credit to them. Hughes and Cox [32, 33] studied the speaking vocabulary of 45 first graders and compared this with the language used in a number of primers and preprimers. They concluded that the speaking vocabulary included many additional words, was more descriptive, contained more verbs and verb forms, and utilized more words denoting a relationship. Madorah Smith,[63] studying 273 children, found that the one-year-old child speaks about three words; the two-year-old, 272 words; the four-year-old, 1,540 words; and the six-year-old, 2,562 words. Rinsland,[53] studied more than 200,000 individual writings of first to eighth graders (the writings included a total of 6,012,395 words) and found a total of 25,632 different words. The writings of the first graders contained 5,099 different words. Seashore and Eckerson [59] report that the average college student knows about 155,736 words, including derivatives.

Hartmann [30] estimates that the average undergraduate student at the University of Alabama can recognize the meanings of 215,040 words.

Figures on vocabulary growth obtained by Mary K. Smith [64] suggest that when derived words are included the average first grader has a total vocabulary of about 24,000 words; the average sixth grader, about 50,000 words; and the average twelfth grader, about 80,000 words.* However, Dolch [18] says that these figures appear to be too high in that children demonstrate no such facility with words.

Whether these studies are providing accurate data concerning the size of children's vocabularies is relatively unimportant. The important point is that even entering first-grade children have large vocabularies. Certainly children acquire a major portion of their vocabularies without formal instruction. And such facts as we have regarding vocabulary size cause us to question the necessity for the extremely restricted vocabularies used in many basal readers. Perhaps we have set our goals in vocabulary development too low. Certainly, vocabulary studies indicate as much. Smith [64] suggests that we have underestimated the vocabulary ability of our better students and have overestimated that of our poorer students. She also notes that generally the best first and second graders know more words than do the poorest student in every other grade except Grade Twelve.

GROWTH TOWARD COMPREHENSION

There are certain basic skills that assist the reader's comprehension. Although no single basic procedure or method has been identified for developing comprehension skills, writers recommend the following procedure: survey the main headings, check the key words and ideas, and try to relate what is being read to what is already known. Some speak of thought-unit reading; some stress that reading should be done to answer specific questions that the student formulates for himself or that the teacher has formulated for him; and others emphasize outlining.

Spache,[67] however, suggests that children benefit little from being told to read for the main ideas and prepare to answer general questions. Instead of general drill in comprehension, the student should be taught how to read for differing degrees of comprehension. Spache feels that training for intelligent reading requires five steps (p. 23):

1. Planning each reading and its purpose in relation to the whole area of study, the demands and general purposes of the instructor, and the specific purposes of the reader.

---

* Smith used the Seashore-Eckerson English Recognition Vocabulary Test. It requires only auditory recognition knowledge of words. A word is assumed to be known if the pupil can give some correct meaning for it.

2. Teaching the student different ways or rates of reading and their effect upon comprehension.
3. Instructing him in a systematic approach to difficult materials, such as Robinson's SQRRR (Survey, Question, Read, Recite, Review) [56] or some similar study procedure which will promote thorough retention.
4. Training in critical reading, as in social science and propaganda materials. This involves practice in identifying the facts given, evaluating the ideas offered, and detecting bias, omission, distortion, and the like.
5. Giving the student practice in applying his reading skills in the various content fields.*

The good reader is not limited to word-by-word reading. He has become proficient in seeing meaningful relationships among the words that he reads. Such reading may be called thought-unit reading. The good reader reacts to a word and its modifiers or to the phrase or clause as a unit rather than to the individual words. Thus, "the small white house" and "during the spring semester" are individual thought units. Bond and Tinker suggest that some beginning in learning to read in thought units generally has taken place by the end of Grade One and that the average reader is fairly proficient in this skill by the time he reaches the sixth grade.

Comprehension certainly depends somewhat on understanding the structure of the sentence. In addition it demands an understanding of the vocabulary, an awareness of the organization of the reading material, and above all an ability to attend to what is read.[19] For full comprehension the reader must get both the main and the minor ideas and be able to relate them to one another.

Harris [29] carries this proposal a step further. He says (pp. 422–423):

> Even at the preprimer level, however, the sentence is not a complete, self-sufficient unit; from the beginning, each sentence is a part of a sequence that tells a little story. The word has meaning as part of a phrase; the phrase, as part of a sentence; the sentence, as part of a paragraph; the paragraph as part of a story. Gradually the children learn to grasp the meanings of larger and larger units.

We may trace the development of comprehension as follows:

1. As the child grows in general experience his ability to take meanings to words will increase and his potential for comprehension increases.
2. As his proficiency in recognizing words (and their meanings) grows, his ability to comprehend develops.
3. As his comprehension develops, his skill in reading larger and larger thought units develops.
4. As his skill in reading larger thought units develops, his skills of

comprehension and his ability to understand more involved (complex) thoughts will increase.

5. And as his ability to read larger and more complex thought units increases, his comprehension and potential for comprehension develop.

At this point, let us summarize the methods that have been suggested for developing reading comprehension. As a basis for good comprehension the child must learn to associate with the written word symbol the meanings that he has acquired through experience. He may improve his comprehension by such techniques as surveying the main headings, reading for the main ideas, reading in thought units, and forming the habit of grouping supporting details about main ideas in a thought-outline form. He should have a purpose for his reading and he should read critically, identifying the facts and evaluating them in the light of his own experience. He should organize what he learns and attempt to retain it. In Chapters 12 and 13 we will consider in detail the topics of intensive reading and critical reading. These topics also are related to the problem of developing good comprehension.

TEACHING WORD MEANINGS

Since the meaning of words comes from experience, meaning is fostered by enlarging the child's experience. We must make the child word-conscious; we must help him see the importance of words; we must make him *curious* about words. We can provide both direct and vicarious experiences. We may provide trips to a farm, a museum, a factory, and a baseball game, but we can also broaden his experience through films, pictures, maps, charts, radio, TV, and newspapers.

Bond and Tinker (p. 246) [7] point out that word study should deal with new words as they are met in context. Then learning a word's meaning fulfills the child's desire to understand some passage. This is true in the upper elementary grades as well as in the lower grades. Leary [41] points out the value in teaching a word in context (p. 25):

> Train a child to anticipate probable meaning, to infer an unknown word from its total context, to skip a word and read on to derive its probable meaning, to check the context clue with the form of the word, to search the context for a description or explanation that will identify the word, and he will have acquired the most important single aid to word recognition. For, regardless of what word he perceives, if it doesn't 'make sense' in its setting, his perception has been in error.

Fay (p. 18) [22] suggests that:

> . . . the most effective clue to recognition is meaning or context. As more detailed analysis of a word is required, over-all efficiency of reading decreases. Therefore, making readers *meaning conscious* is as much a part of word recognition as it is of comprehension.

Context offers the reader many types of clues to word meaning. It may help to define the word, relate it to previous experiences, associate it with a word whose meaning is known, provide a synonym; and context usually indicates, furthermore, the mood and the tone the writer attaches to the word.

However, the child will not always gain the correct meaning of a word from the context. Sometimes errors or vagueness results. The intended meaning may be contaminated by personal experience. Witty (p. 148)[84] makes the following suggestions:

> *First,* whenever possible, new words should be associated with firsthand experience; *second,* the meanings of new words obtained by examination of context should be systematically checked to insure that they are reasonably clear and correct; and *third,* new words should be introduced gradually in contexts containing familiar words.

The norms of the Durost-Center Word Mastery Test indicate that the average high school graduate uses the context to derive meanings in only about 50 to 60 per cent of the words that are unknown to him (p. 109).[69] For one to profit most from context clues, the reading material must not be too difficult, nor contain too many new words. Thus the vividness of contextual clues is proportionate to the ease of the material and the reader's familiarity with the subject.

There are numerous ways other than first-hand experience and context for developing meaning for words. One may explain the word to a child by giving a synonym, by classifying the word, by pointing out differences, and by indicating similarities. Also, the meaning of the word may be obtained from picture clues, language rhythm clues, and the dictionary. Wide reading experience is valuable, of course. Vocabulary notebooks and exercises, index cards, contests, games, pupil-dictated experience charts, and creative writing are all legitimate motivational aids.

In Chapter 7 we examined the basic skills of *word recognition* and we saw that there are practical limitations on the number of words that can be learned and retained as sight vocabulary. For independence in word recognition, the child must acquire phonic skills. These skills lead him to understand the lawfulness of word pronunciation. Similarly, as we examine the development of *word understanding,* we can see that there are limitations on the number of word meanings that can be learned and remembered if each word's meaning must be acquired through specific experiences and retained within an unorganized mass of discrete elements. For independence in word understanding, the child must become aware of the lawfulness of word meaning. He must learn to gain meaning from word components. For example, an analysis of words into roots, prefixes, and suffixes helps the child to understand their origins, substance, and usage. Roots give the basic meaning of the word; the prefix frequently serves as a modifier altering the meaning of a root much as the adjective modifies the noun. The suffix often identifies the word as a part of speech.

Stauffer [70] reports that 24 per cent of the words in the Thorndike Teacher's Word Book have prefixes and that fifteen prefixes account for 82 per cent of all the prefixes in the 20,000 words. A list of those fifteen prefixes appears below (p. 455):

ab (from)	dis (apart)	pre (before)
ad (to)	en (in)	pro (in front of)
be (by)	ex (out)	re (back)
com (with)	in (into)	sub (under)
de (from)	in (not)	un (not)

Brown and Wright [8] found that 14,000 words in the desk dictionary and some 100,000 words from the unabridged dictionary contain one or more of the elements found in fourteen master words. The master words contain two Greek roots, twelve Latin roots, and 20 prefixes. The list of 14 words appears below:

Master-words	*Prefix*	*Common meaning*	*Root*	*Common meaning*
Precept	pre-	(before)	capere	(take, seize)
Detain	de-	(away, from)	tenere	(hold, have)
Intermittent	inter-	(between)	mittere	(send)
Offer	ob-	(against)	ferre	(bear, carry)
Insist	in-	(into)	stare	(stand)
Monograph	mono-	(alone, one)	graphein	(write)
Epilogue	epi-	(upon)	legein	(say, study of)
Aspect	ad-	(to, towards)	specere	(see)
Uncomplicated	un-	(not)	plicare	(fold)
	com-	(together with)		
Nonextended	non-	(not)	tendere	(stretch)
	ex-	(out of)		
Reproduction	re-	(back, again)	ducere	(lead)
	pro-	(forward)		
Indisposed	in-	(not)	ponere	(put, place)
	dis-	(apart from)		
Oversufficient	over-	(above)	facere	(make, do)
	sub-	(under)		
Mistranscribe	mis-	(wrong)	scribere	(write)
	trans-	(across, beyond)		

Training in the elements of word analysis may begin as early as the first grade. McKee (p. 200) [45] suggests that

> . . . any one of certain structural elements which need to be taught—a suffix such as *ed, es, ing* added to a base word to make a variant—will be taught as soon as the list of words already learned by sight includes two or three words which contain that element and which, therefore, can be used for introducing the element.

The evidence clearly indicates that vocabulary skills can be taught and Addy,[1] in a questionnaire study directed to 250 teachers, principals, and supervisors, obtained the following recommendations for learning vocabulary: examine the context; note the way the word is used in the sentence; associate the word with one's past experiences; have the meaning of the word demonstrated through activities, concrete objects, and visual aids. Other suggestions were: use a dictionary, study the origin of words, study synonyms and antonyms, study prefixes and suffixes, and study word combinations and word compounds. Although procedures for learning new words are important, provision for retaining them is equally so. It was recommended that practice and conversation using the correct word to describe a given meaning would result in fixing the word into one's vocabulary.

Jenkins [35] experimented with five seventh-grade English classes, each of which was equated with the others in factors of age, intelligence test scores, and scores on a silent reading test. In one class no special emphasis was given to vocabulary. A second group used a reading workbook with vocabulary exercises; a third stressed individual word study using a dictionary and index cards. A fourth group stressed synonyms, antonyms, and word lists. And a fifth group studied prefixes, roots, and suffixes. The third and fourth groups showed the most improvement in vocabulary. Miles [46] conducted an experiment with 50 tenth-grade pupils. After teaching the meanings and uses of words on the Alpha form of the Inglis Vocabulary test during one semester, she found a median gain on the Beta form of about one year. Thirty of these pupils were retested at the end of Grade Twelve and the median score still was higher than that of a control group.

In summary, the teacher has many opportunities to help the child comprehend words as well as to expand his vocabulary. Both first-hand and vicarious experience may be utilized. Context clues, picture clues, structural analysis, dictionary practice, and synonyms and antonyms are helpful. Formal drill in vocabulary may be valuable. Certainly concepts must be fixed by words, and the ability to handle concepts is basic to comprehension.

RATE AND COMPREHENSION

To discuss rate of reading adequately, we must emphasize that it means rate of *comprehending* printed or written material. Although comprehension thus remains of primary importance, and rate has no meaning apart from comprehension, rate of reading is worth considering. No one actually reads faster than he comprehends, but many read much more slowly than their comprehension would permit. Generally the limiting factor to rate improvement is the mind rather than the vision.

The good reader is not only a comprehending reader; he comprehends at a satisfactory rate. The good reader, however, does not read all materials at a certain fixed rate. He is a *flexible* reader. His rate is governed by the difficulty and organization of the material, his purposes, his intelligence, his background for understanding the materials, and his proficiency in basic reading skills.

It is important that we examine the relationship between rate and comprehension if for no other reason than to destroy two common misconceptions. As Harris has pointed out (p. 504),[29] many believe that fast readers have a tendency to be inaccurate and that slow readers make up for their plodding by getting more out of their reading. However, there is also a common belief that fast reading is good reading, and slow reading is poor reading. Thus the first of these viewpoints would indicate a high negative correlation between rate and comprehension and the second viewpoint is that there is a high positive correlation. Actually both of these viewpoints are wrong or at best they are inaccurate and need qualification.

Let's examine some data concerning the relationship between comprehension and reading rate. Studies generally indicate that the degree of relationship varies with the nature of the reading task, the techniques of measurement that are used, the difficulty of the material, and the purposes of the reader. We shall see that intelligence also influences the relationship between rate and comprehension.

Shores and Husbands [61] used biological science reading materials to test 90 children in grades four through six. The correlations between rate and comprehension scores were either low or negative. The writers note that the relationship between speed and comprehension depends to a large extent upon the purpose set for the reading and upon the nature of the material read. Studying twenty-three rapid and twenty-three slow readers, Thurston (p. 126) [75] found that reading rate correlated positively with comprehension scores on social science materials (.44), on literary materials (.42), and on physical science materials (.11). Lanigan [40] reports that reading rate is more closely associated with success in the areas of English, language, and science than it is in the areas of social studies, mathematics, and fine arts. Bond (p. 35)[6] reports that among ninth-graders slower reading tends to be associated with high achievement in general science, Latin, and algebra. And others have reported an inverse relationship between rate and comprehension in mathematics and science. This means that with at least certain types of reading materials the students with the highest reading comprehension scores and achievement scores in the area tend to be the slowest readers.

Correlations between the rate score and the comprehension score generally range from slight negative to high positive. We have already suggested that the procedures used in testing and the general mental set of the reader are factors in determining the correlation that is obtained. Whenever the comprehension score is obtained from questions over the entire test (even though the reader may not have completed the test selection), the relationship is necessarily high. Obviously, the reader cannot be expected to answer correctly questions that refer to material that he has not read. Thus, Preston and Botel[50] found that the correlation between rate and *timed* comprehension was a statistically significant coefficient of .48. However the correlation between rate and *untimed* comprehension was but .20 and was not statistically significant.

Studies (p. 376)[7] likewise suggest that:

> With elementary school children, the correlations between speed and comprehension tend to be negligible. However . . . rapid readers are more efficient in comprehension at the upper levels of intelligence, and slow readers more efficient at the lower levels of intelligence.

Carlson[11] found that individuals with high intelligence tend to comprehend better when reading rapidly than when reading slowly; those with average or low intelligence comprehend better when reading slowly than when reading rapidly. This tendency was even more clear when the purposes for reading were made more exacting and the difficulty of the material was increased. Carlson's conclusions that the teacher should try to determine at what speed the individual's comprehension begins to deteriorate caution us not to press all students to increase their reading rate.

Blommers and Lindquist point out that good comprehenders tend to reduce their reading rate as the material increases in difficulty. Poor comprehenders apparently read easy and difficult materials at much the same rate.[5] And McKee (pp. 109–110)[45] points out that *every pupil should adjust his reading rate to the purpose for which he is reading and to the difficulty of the reading matter.* A reader should have several speeds, each to be used as needed. And the mature reader has a variety of approaches at his command. He may read an article once slowly, then rapidly or vice versa. Or he may choose to skim or to scan.

Flexibility appears to point to a critical difference between good and poor readers. The good reader sets comprehension as his goal and adjusts his rate rather automatically. The poor reader mechanically plods from word to word and such comprehension as he obtains seems to be a by-product of the process rather than the central goal of his reading. Since children in the upper grades and those with higher intelligence generally are more mature in their reading, one expects to find them better able to vary their rate with the demands of the material.

These relationships between rate and comprehension are important to the teacher for he must decide when to stress rate improvements and when to emphasize comprehension skills. A reader who is low in both comprehension and rate generally will not benefit from an emphasis on speed. He needs training in basic comprehension skills. One who reads rapidly but with low comprehension likewise needs comprehension training. However, one who reads all materials slowly but with good comprehension may well profit from training in speed. The intelligence of the reader also is a significant factor. The intelligent reader tends to perform better when reading rapidly. Perhaps this is because rapid reading requires his full attention whereas, when he plods along, his attention wanders. On the other hand, the slow learner's rate is limited by his comprehending or thinking rate.

IMPROVEMENT OF RATE

Rate improvement programs have become commonplace in recent years. We should know what, if any, values they offer. Obviously there is economy in being able to read at a rapid rate. Our concern here is with the benefits derivable from intensive training in rapid reading. Most writers agree that rate of reading can be improved with training. Harris (p. 537) [29] suggests that rate training should be included in developmental reading programs and should begin at or above the sixth grade. Betts has indicated that most readers cease improving in rate, if no attempts are made to increase it, by about the sixth grade. Ordinarily they read from 200 to 300 words per minute at that time.

Numerous studies have indicated that not only can rate be improved, but that the comprehending reader can learn to read effectively at many times the rate he will use if he does not receive such training. Some investigators report additional values from training in rapid reading: increased accuracy of perception, more accurate and more rapid visual discrimination, better visual memory, orderly left to right progression, wider span of apprehension, better attention organization and concentration, better work habits, better visual focus, shorter reaction time, greater self-confidence, fewer regressions, a decrease in number and duration of fixations, reduction of vocalization, more rhythmical reading, and better comprehension.

At present various methods are used to increase rate. Harris mentions tachistoscopic training, paced reading, timed reading, and extensive reading without specific emphasis on speed (p. 525 ff).[29] There is considerable disagreement as to whether a machine-centered or a book-centered approach results in most improvement. Some apparently have greatest confidence in tachistoscopes and pacers of various types.* Others recommend book-centered programs.

EXPERIMENTAL EVIDENCE ON RATE IMPROVEMENT

There are certain somewhat technical terms that are used in the experimental research on reading rate. Let's define some of these before proceeding to the research itself. Among these are visual field, visual span, and recognition span.

Taylor [73] says that, unless there are impairments, the visual field generally consists of a lateral arc of approximately 180 degrees. The visual field includes both peripheral and foveal (spot of clearest) vision and depth of vision.

The visual span ** is the amount (usually in terms of the number of digits or letters) that can be *seen* by the eye in a single fixation. It might well be called the seeing span. This is measured by a tachistoscopic exposure and usually is more than what would be seen during a single fixation in normal reading. Taylor points out that poor readers frequently have a wider visual span than good readers because they do not organize what they see.

The recognition span is the amount that a reader *sees and organizes* during a single fixation pause. It is the number of words that are *recognized or understood* at a single fixation and it is computed by dividing the number of words in a selection by the number of fixation pauses made by the reader.

A wide span of recognition contributes to a wide eye-voice span in oral reading and to a wide eye-memory (organization) span in silent reading.

---

* Reading pacers are also called rate controllers or accelerators. Guy T. Buswell originated the device. It consists of a shutter that slides down a page at a regulated speed.

** Taylor refers to this as "span of apprehension." Other writers sometimes refer to it as "perceptual span."

Taylor (p. 505) [73] points out that a narrow span of recognition contributes to narrow eye-voice span and forces the child

> . . . to pronounce each word as it is recognized in order to obtain meaning from the text. He has little ability to keep his eyes several words ahead of his voice, to carry the context in his mind, and to make the suitable pause and voice inflections that accompany colorful reading.

Thought-unit reading sometimes is wrongly identified with the number of words read per fixation. Even though a child may be engaging in thought-unit reading, he rarely recognizes more than one word per fixation. Indeed, very few adult readers have an average recognition span of as much as two words. Table 1 illustrates this. The data were obtained by Taylor (p. 503) [73] in a study of the eye-movements of over 5,000 children.

TABLE 1

MEASURABLE COMPONENTS OF THE FUNDAMENTAL READING SKILL

Grade Level	1st	2nd	3rd	4th	5th	6th	JHS	HS	College
Fixations per 100 words	240	200	170	136	118	105	95	83	75
Regressions per 100 words	55	45	37	30	26	23	18	15	11
Average span of recognition (in words)	.42	.50	.59	.73	.85	.95	1.05	1.21	1.33
Average duration of fixation (in seconds)	.33	.30	.26	.24	.24	.24	.24	.24	.23
Average rate of comprehension (in words per minute)	75	100	138	180	216	235	255	296	340

Because there is lack of agreement as to the best methods for improving reading rate, let us examine some of the experimental evidence.

Numerous studies indicate that tachistoscopic training broadens the visual span. Weber [80] reports that the visual span can be increased both horizontally and vertically.* Fink,[23] using sixteen subjects, concluded that tachistoscopic training in digit perception does not change significantly the duration of reading fixations nor the number of fixations required per page. He suggested that such rate gains as do occur are due to the elimination of regressive eye movements. Luckiesh and Moss (pp. 480–481),[43] however, suggest that attempting to enlarge the area of acute vision may result in visual damage. Mills [47] suggests that memory itself is related to foveal

---

* Although the recognition span can be increased through tachistoscopic training, this does not guarantee that such training improves reading.

vision and material learned through peripheral vision is not easily retained. He also takes the position

> . . . that the production of myopia, with its characteristic exophoria, which usually becomes evident at about that period of life when school affairs begin to press, is bound up with the hurried and abnormal use of peripheral vision. . . .

Paterson and Tinker,[49] on the other hand, suggest that peripheral vision has an important role in reading and determines the width of the recognition span. They point out that the proficient reader tends to make maximum use of cues in peripheral vision at least in reading easy material.

Other studies suggest that training on mechanical devices frequently is accompanied by improvement in reading rate. Sutherland,[72] for example, besides finding a relationship between visual span and rate of visual perception as well as visual span and reading rate, indicates that both rate of perception and reading rate can be increased through improvement of the perceptual span.

Robinson,[55] working with college freshmen for ten weeks, found that by gradually increasing the length of the training phrases he obtained a 58 per cent gain in reading rate and a five per cent increase in comprehension. Renshaw [52] reports that tachistoscopic training with digit patterns results in an increased rate of reading.

Cosper and Kephart [14] report that 38 college students were given a reading program consisting of about 28 to 30 hours of training of which about half was on an accelerator. The group tachistoscope was used from ten to fifteen minutes per session. In addition a film was shown once a week, and every two weeks a difficult essay was read. The reading rate of this group increased significantly more than that of a comparable control group of 28 students. Comprehension did not change significantly. Retesting after 14 months showed that approximately 60 per cent of the gains in speed were retained.

Weeden,[81] working with Brooklyn College freshmen, used two experimental groups and one control group. One experimental group trained with a rate controller, the other used a book-centered approach. Both experimental groups improved significantly in reading rate with the controller-trained group gaining more than the book-centered group. Unfortunately, the rate gains were apparent only on a test using the machine, and not on ordinary reading tests. Spache [68] comments that Wedeen's results may well indicate that practice on a rate controller results in ability to read faster *when using the controller*. However this does not guarantee that mechanical training transfers all of its effects to ordinary reading.

Jones [37] reports significant gains from a Reading and Study Skills Program combining machine and book-centered techniques. Before training, the 98 students had an average comprehension percentile on the *Iowa Silent Reading Test* of 45. By the end of the program the average percentile rank had increased to 96. The number of words read per minute increased from 212 to 570. Eye-movement photographs showed that the fixation pause had decreased and the span of recognition had increased from 1.16 words to 2.38 words.

Smith and Tate [62] report substantial rate gains for a small group of students at the University of Kansas. All subjects participated in at least 25 fifty-minute sessions using both rate controllers and tachistoscopes. A part of the findings showed that gains as measured by tests were less than gains as measured by controller settings. Allen,[2] in a study involving army personnel, found that the subjects preferred a rate controller to the tachistoscope. However, the overwhelming majority of participants did not believe that the exercises on the mechanical devices were as beneficial as the practical work exercises for developing ability to handle specific reading problems. Wilson,[83] using six high school groups, failed to find a perceptible increase in rate resulting from tachistoscopic training. However, the group using the controller did make significant gains in rate.

The above are only a few of the many reports of gains in reading rate with machine-centered programs. The basic question then is: are mechanical devices essential for rate improvement? The evidence is strongly against such a conclusion.

Cason,[12] for example, reports significant gains in rate among third-grade children whether a Metron-O-Scope or motivated free-reading was used. Westover (p. 65) [82] found that college students using ordinary printed materials made gains as great as students did who were using a Metron-O-Scope.

Andrews [3] reports a steady increase in reading speed using about fifty ten-minute practice sessions during a school year. The practice consisted of reading easy material as rapidly as possible for a minute and then counting the words read. The reading materials used were of a low level of difficulty. Andrews suggests that improvement was due to the heavy emphasis on rate. He writes (p. 355):

> I emphasize completely the aspect of speed in the early drills and encourage the students to ignore completely the aspect of understanding. I 'insist' from the second test on that all students read at least 350 words a minute 'whether you understand anything or not!'

Lewis,[42] using 27 college students, compared two methods for increasing speed. He found that mechanical devices combined with an emphasis on comprehension, meaning, and the structure of the material read were more effective than mechanical devices alone. Manolakes,[44] with two groups, each consisting of seventeen U. S. Marine Corps officers, failed to find the gains usually claimed for tachistoscopic training. He trained one group with a tachistoscope and a rate controller; the other group received training in vocabulary and comprehension skills and used a rate controller. The second group not only showed more rapid development of general reading skills than did the first but, in fact, they made greater rate gains as well.

Weber [79] found that a control group without special training showed gains in both rate and comprehension; however, its gains were not as great as those of his two experimental groups. His experimental group using the Pressey Manual of Reading Exercises obtained about the same amount of improvement in reading skill as did the group given tachistoscopic exercises. Cardwell [10] reports that an adult reading program had significant success without using any machines. The average words per minute before the program began were 297; after the 24 one-hour sessions, the average was 417 w.p.m. Comprehension increased by 18.75 per cent.

Bellows and Rush,[4] Johnson,[36] and Thompson [74] also report gains in rate with book-centered approaches. Thompson's subjects were 438 U. S. Air Force officers. Using three groups—a book-group, a machine-group, and a control-group—he found that in the 21-hour course the book-centered approach resulted in speeds significantly higher than those attained by the machine approach. There were no significant differences in comprehension scores, but all groups seemed to lose slightly in flexibility.

EVALUATION OF READING IMPROVEMENT PROGRAMS AND DEVICES

How to interpret these findings is not clear. It seems safe to conclude that training on mechanical devices is frequently accompanied by rate improvement. It is also generally true that rate gains have an adequate degree of permanency. Cole,[13] Reed,[51] Cosper and Kephart,[14] Mullins and Mowry,[48] and Weber [79] have reported follow-up studies that indicated permanency in rate gains. In reviewing five such studies, Spache found that 51 to 84 per cent of the improvement in rate was reported to be retained six to twelve months after training.[68]

However, rate gains are also obtainable without mechanical aids in programs that are book-centered. We still have to answer two important questions: Are there dangers inherent in attempts to regulate the eye movements of the reader? And do machine-gains transfer to actual reading?

Gates (p. 26) [26] says that tachistoscopic training is unnatural. He points out that this is not the way reading ordinarily is done. He suggests that the reader actually can do more to improve his reading rate by sliding a piece of cardboard down a page than by using mechanical devices. He indicates that in evaluating any device used to develop rate we should consider the extent to which it introduces artificial factors, distorts the natural process, or lacks proper flexibility and adaptability to the reader's needs.

Vernon (p. 88) [78] suggests that "Devices which compel the reader's eyes to move at an even speed whatever the nature of the material read, or his intention in reading it, might in the long run destroy the flexibility necessary for intelligent reading."

Horn wrote: "The classroom teacher needs to be concerned with movements of the eyes little more than with the movement of the bones of the inner ear" (pp. 201–202).[31]

Tinker (p. 174) [76] is not so severe in his evaluation. He feels that "an *occasional* person may be benefited in reading by training the eyes to greater accuracy in sweeping from one fixation to another, such as the back sweep from the end of one line to the beginning of the next."

There are other data to be considered. The evidence indicates that the ordinary reader's tachistoscopic (visual) span is already much larger than the recognition span he commonly uses. Robinson,[54] studying 51 college students, found that their average reading (recognition) span was only 41 per cent as large as their tachistoscopic span. Buswell [9] suggests that a narrow recognition span becomes habitual with the reader, even though it may be far below his capabilities.

Studies generally have found that a wide divergence exists between visual span as measured on the tachistoscope and reading rate and that an increase in visual span fails to produce significant gains in reading rate. It may well be that the reader uses a different span during motivated training than during normal reading. As stated earlier in the chapter, the mind, not the vision, generally seems to be the limiting factor. The evidence suggests that the more meaningful the material is to the individual, the wider will be his recognition span.

What, then, is the real function of tachistoscopic training? Do mechanical devices actually have little to do with eye movement and merely motivate the mind to work closer to its capacity and at a faster rate (p. 257) [28]? Does an increase in mental activity also account for the fact that improvement in rate of reading (or rate of thinking?) may result in better comprehension and in a better retention of what is read? There seems to be evidence for this. Thurstone (p. 130) [75] concluded that fast and slow readers are differentiated on the basis of "central processes." He points out that reading is primarily a perceptual function. The reader learns to make quick associations with rapidly changing visual stimuli. Thurstone implies that rate of association could well be the critical factor in distinguishing the rapid reader from the slow reader. Buswell,[9] studying 77 college seniors, found some evidence that those who excelled in rate of thinking tended to be high in rate of comprehension.

Taylor [73] observes that improvement in rate of reading can result from an increase in the lateral amount of print that can be perceived and organized rapidly. He writes (p. 503):

> The primary value of short exposure training, therefore, in reading improvement, is to contribute to an increase in the size of the span of recognition, to increase the accuracy and precision of perception, and to develop the reader's ability to organize perceived material more rapidly. One of the more important results from short exposure work, however, is the improvement in the over-all personal organization of the pupil. Usually pupils who have had such training tend to become more alert and observant.

Certainly the mechanical devices have motivational values. Jones (p. 313) [38] points out that

> The inventors of these machines, dealing with more adult subjects in college laboratories, have not emphasized to the full the psychological effect of the purring of a little motor on the machine-conscious younger students, especially the boys.

Dearborn suggests that methods "which are intrinsically not even sound or sane may, because of the novelty of their appeal and their assurance of success, arouse the student to new hopes and efforts at improvement." Speaking of visual training devices he says: "What these methods may do is to increase perceptual span by offering the reader fresh motivation. That is, they succeed not by stretching the visual span, but by spurring the mind" (p. 6).[17]

Nevertheless, not all reading specialists believe that motivation is an adequate justification for their use. Gates (p. 354) [25] suggests that the elaborate mechanical devices should be used as last resorts when other methods have failed or, if they are used at an earlier stage, there should be some tangible reason for selecting them.

Although certain readers may be most easily motivated by mechanical devices, timed reading with comprehension checks generally leads to comparable results. Sommerfeld (p. 21),[66] after an extensive summary of the research prior to 1954, concludes:

> The principal conclusion to be drawn from this investigation is that no significant relationship has been found between measures of tachistoscopic span and the measures of reading ability employed. It follows by implication that quick-exposure training, in and of itself, cannot influence the process of reading except as certain secondary factors, such as motivation, are involved.

Spache (p. 22) [67] suggests that

> It would seem more logical to implement the diagnosis of slow reading by providing simpler materials . . . or to attack the problem more directly by trying to improve the poor vocabulary, word recognition, or word-analysis skills which may be directly causal.

He continues:

> More real and permanent growth in rate can be accomplished by teaching the student *how* and *when* to use rapid reading and by direct instruction in reading for ideas, scanning for single facts without actual reading, and skimming by reading only headings and topic and summary sentences. The student achieves flexibility in rate (which, after all, is the real aim of rate training) only by learning to vary his speed and reading techniques according to his purposes, the difficulty and style of the reading material, and his familiarity with the content of the reading matter.*

In a later evaluation, Spache (p. 118) [68] points out that "While the training devices do seem to contribute to rate increases, in more carefully controlled experiments this contribution is as often a reflection of teacher variance and perhaps motivation as it is an intrinsic result of the method." Studies by Freeburne [24] and Glock [27] both suggest that differences among teachers may be more significant than differences in method. And Schick [58] has emphasized that training aids are *teaching adjuncts,* not teacher replacements.

Spache's (pp. 126–129) [68] recent comments concerning the use of mechanical devices are worth careful consideration at this point. He writes:

> We should like to suggest that mechanical training is successful in accelerating rate because the student is in effect being taught to read with fewer cues, to guess more readily what he sees peripherally, to overcome the caution exhibited in slow or word-by-word reading, to be more confident in dealing with vague or indistinct portions of words. . . .
>
> We are suggesting then that mechanical devices should be used, first, to improve visual discrimination and perception and, secondly, to improve rate of reading. The principles and materials of this approach might be outlined somewhat as follows:
>
> 1. Practice with tachistoscopic exposure of simple geometric forms to sharpen visual discrimination. Students are to copy these forms and to avoid attempting to verbalize what they see. Exposure time should vary with age of students from half a second to one-fifth of a second. Shorter exposures are unnaturally faster than average pause duration.
> 2. As accuracy of discrimination increases, shift to gross word forms or shapes or incompletely printed words equal in span to 8–10 letters of

10-point type. Promote insight into what is occurring by discussion of the nature of the act of reading, the limitations of visual span, and the necessity of more accurate recognition of material seen peripherally. In introducing each group of word forms, identify the group, thus providing contextual clues. Use outlines of names of prominent people (politicians, movie stars, etc.), of geographical places (cities, states), of buildings and other proper names. Later use outlines of common nouns, verbs, adjectives, etc.

These exercises are pencil outlines of the shape of words, as Eisenhower 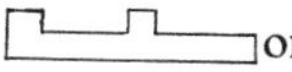 or incomplete words as  . Initial letters, tall letters, and other clues may be added as desired or necessary. The configurations chosen for practice should be common words well within the students' auditory and speech vocabularies.

3. As accuracy of recognition of word forms increases, increase span of recognition material gradually to 15–20 letters. Increase speed of exposure to one-tenth of a second, after high degree of accuracy is achieved. This training is not intended to increase perceptual span but rather to condition students to quick recognition of ideas or concepts expressed in more words than can actually be seen clearly.

   Discuss with class the lack of visual acuity in peripheral vision, and the need for confidence in dealing with the vague extremes of the span of material. Encourage guessing and use of context clues.

   At this stage, use related phrases drawn consecutively from continuous material.

4. Then shift to continuous material, such as the Harvard Films, Series Two, or the Perceptoscope training materials. If average reading rate of group permits the arbitrary rate increases present in the Harvard films, continue with them. If individual differences are to be met, or rate of reading is actually to be adapted to the present level and growing capabilities of the group, then use the Perceptoscope films. Use the three-fixations-per-line pattern first, then the two fixations. Gradually increase speed of these as accuracy of comprehension (70–80 per cent) is maintained. Shift to shade pattern after 360 words per minute is achieved by group with at least 70 per cent comprehension.

Spache suggests that the method be used with the following types of readers:

1. Those scoring low in rate, but distinctly higher in comprehension of the same material, *i.e.*, the slow, cautious, retentive reader.
2. Those scoring higher in an untimed power test of comprehension than in a timed test or in comprehension of timed material.
3. Those scoring distinctly higher in the untimed administration of a general vocabulary test than in timed administration.
4. Those clinically identified as habitually slow readers, lacking in flexibility, who tend to use the same rate in most materials, but show acceptable comprehension.

Educators frequently have asked: do rate-improvement programs improve school grades? Reed [51] suggests that it is quite possible that those personality characteristics that lead a student to seek reading improvement are the same traits that cluster to produce higher grades. He adds that even if improvement in grade points occurs, one cannot infer that the improvement necessarily resulted from the training, and he further suggests that grade point is not a *sole* nor necessarily even a useful criterion in evaluating a reading program. Sommerfeld,[66] calling attention to *post hoc, ergo propter hoc* fallacies, argues that even when rate improvement is observed following a rate-improvement program, it is not necessarily established that it is the result of the rate-improvement training. For example, the effect of increased motivation during training sessions is rarely controlled.

Robinson (p. 83) [57] reports that:

> A review of nearly one hundred studies . . . uncovers less than a dozen references to the effect of reading programs upon scholastic improvement. Of these only one study using control groups reports apparently significant gains in terms of academic grades for reading classes. Other investigators either report no significant improvement in academic standing as the result of remedial instruction, or without definitive findings take the hopeful and confident stand that reading instruction can improve academic work.

Kingston and George,[39] comparing the grade-point averages of 179 male college students who participated in a reading program in their freshman and junior years with 274 students who did not, found grade-point improvement among students whose curricula were linguistic in nature. Agricultural and engineering students did not show improvement. Humber [34] found that reading test scores correlated positively with final grades in English and music, but not with the grades in science.

Witty (p. 72) [85] concludes that:

> . . . one should anticipate improvement in grades in a particular subject only when the reading skills essential in that subject are stressed during the reading improvement program.

SUMMARY

In this chapter and in the preceding chapter we have been concerned with the basic reading skills of word recognition, comprehension, and rate. Reading skills, however, do not operate independently. They are modified by the attitudes and personality and by the sensory, perceptual, and intellectual processes of the reader. Few of the reading skills are so generalized that they are employed in all reading tasks. Frequently the reading skills required are specific to the reading act. The nature of each reading act is determined by the purposes and the abilities of the reader, the content and the level of difficulty of the material, and the reader's ability to apply the appropriate reading skills.

This chapter has identified certain principles governing comprehension and rate. The research suggests the following:

1. Drill and training in comprehension increases comprehension achievement rather than comprehension potential.
2. Comprehension is more directly dependent upon general intellectual ability than upon drill or training.
3. Poor readers are distinguished from good readers by their poorer comprehension abilities.
4. Rate of association may well be the critical factor in distinguishing the rapid from the slow reader.
5. Rate of reading has no meaning apart from rate of comprehension.
6. Rate of comprehension is dependent upon the difficulty of the material, the purposes of the reader, the organization of the material, the reader's intelligence, and the reader's skill.
7. Flexibility is an important criterion of reading excellence. (Good comprehenders adjust the rate of reading by slowing down as the material increases in difficulty, whereas poor comprehenders read both easy and difficult materials at much the same rate.)
8. The span of recognition generally is from one to two or, at most, two and one-half words. It depends on the reader's intelligence, comprehension abilities, and vocabulary.
9. The average adult's visual span as measured by tachistoscopic exposure is four to five unrelated words (16 to 25 letters) or five to six related words.
10. On meaningful materials the good reader has a wider recognition span than the poor reader. This does not hold true for nonsense materials.
11. The number of words recognized during a single fixation pause is dependent upon the reader's facility in word recognition, his familiarity with the material read, the physical characteristics of the material, and his ability to assimilate ideas.
12. By about the fourth grade, the child's rate of comprehension in silent reading generally surpasses his rate of comprehension in oral reading.
13. In oral reading the errors of the poor readers tend to change the meaning of the material but the errors of the good readers do not.

14. The slow reader of average or low intelligence comprehends better than the fast reader of average or low intelligence.
15. The more regressions, the slower is the reading; but this does not mean that the more regressions, the less effective is the reading. On certain materials regression is desirable.
16. Slower reading generally is positively associated with achievement in science, in medicine, in mathematics, and in Latin.
17. The more difficult the materials, the lower is the relationship between rate and comprehension and, vice versa, the easier the material, the higher is the relationship between rate and comprehension.
18. Rapid reading is positively associated with achievement in English and in languages.
19. The more interesting the materials to the reader, the better his comprehension tends to be.
20. Mechanical training devices motivate the reader to make better use of his abilities.
21. A valid appraisal of increase in reading rate must be based upon increase in *amount comprehended.*
22. Training on mechanical devices tends to result in an increased rate of reading, but is not significantly superior to book-centered approaches when motivation is held constant.
23. Overemphasis on speed tends to lead to poorer reading comprehension.

SUGGESTED READINGS

(Causey, *The Reading Teacher's Reader*)

Article 25, Grayum, Helen S. "What Is Skimming? What Are Its Uses at Different Grade Levels?" from *The Reading Teacher,* 7 (December, 1953), pp. 111–114.

Article 41, Gilbert, Doris Wilcox. "Fact and Fiction About Reading Improvement," from *Power and Speed in Reading,* Englewood Cliffs, New Jersey: Prentice-Hall, Inc., 1954, 1956, pp. 106–110.

Article 43, Cosper, Russell and Newell C. Kephart. "Retention of Reading Skills," from *Journal of Educational Research,* 49 (November, 1955), pp. 211–216.

Article 53, Larrick, Nancy. "How Many Words Does a Child Know?" from *The Reading Teacher,* 7 (December, 1953) pp. 100–104.

Article 78, Hamilton, George E. "Tachistoscopes and Their Use," from James S. Kinder and F. Dean McClusky, *The Audio-Visual Reader,* Dubuque, Iowa: William C. Brown, Co., 1954, pp. 151–154.

Article 81, Eller, William. "Evaluation of Reading Films," (from an unpublished paper).

QUESTIONS FOR DISCUSSION

1. What is meant by reading comprehension?
2. What are some of the most important comprehension skills?
3. What are some of the most important differences between "good" and "poor" readers?
4. How may word meanings best be developed?
5. How may you best define *rate of reading*?
6. What relationships commonly are found between *rate* and *comprehension*?
7. What methods are used to improve reading rate? What problems arise?
8. What is perceptual span? Peripheral vision?
9. What conclusions can you form concerning the place of mechanical devices in reading programs or various grade levels?
10. What study skills should a high school or college student possess? Discuss. How can we help the student acquire these skills?
11. Discuss the function of mechanical devices such as tachistoscopes and accelerators in the improvement of reading.
12. How can you train for intelligent reading?
13. Discuss the place of reaction and integration in effective reading.

BIBLIOGRAPHY

[1] Addy, M. L. "Development of a Meaning Vocabulary in the Intermediate Grades." *Elementary English Review,* 18 (January, 1941) 22–26, 30.

[2] Allen, Robert M. "Adult Reading Improvement at an Army Service School." *School and Society,* 74 (August, 1951) 72–76.

[3] Andrews, Joe W. "An Approach to Speed Reading." *English Journal,* 41 (September, 1952) 352–356.

[4] Bellows, Carol S., and Rush, Carl H., Jr. "Reading Abilities of Business Executives." *Journal of Applied Psychology,* 36 (February, 1952) 1–4.

[5] Blommers, Paul, and Lindquist, E. F. "Rate of Comprehension of Reading: Its Measurement and Its Relation to Comprehension." *Journal of Educational Psychology,* 35 (November, 1944) 449–473.

[6] Bond, Eva. *Reading and Ninth Grade Achievement.* Contributions to Education, No. 756, Bureau of Publications, Teachers College, Columbia University, New York, 1938.

[7] Bond, Guy L., and Tinker, Miles A. *Reading Difficulties: Their Diagnosis and Correction.* Appleton-Century-Crofts, Inc., New York, 1957.

[8] Brown, James I., and Wright, Eugene S. *Manual of Instruction for Use with the Minnesota Efficient Reading Series of Tachistoslides.* Keystone View Company, Meadville, Pennsylvania, 1957.

[9] Buswell, Guy T. "The Relationship between Rate of Thinking and Rate of Reading." *School Review,* 59 (September, 1951) 339–346.

[10] Cardwell, Irene. "Adult Reading Improvement Without Machines." *School and Society,* 82 (September, 1955) 71–72.

[11] Carlson, Thorsten R. "The Relationship between Speed and Accuracy of Comprehension." *Journal of Educational Research,* 42 (March, 1949) 500–512.

[12] Cason, Eloise B. *Mechanical Methods for Increasing the Speed of Reading.* Contributions to Education, No. 878, Bureau of Publications, Teachers College, Columbia University, New York, 1943.

[13] Cole, George K., Jr. "Adult Reading Clinic." *Library Journal,* 82 (February, 1957) 497–500.

[14] Cosper, Russell, and Kephart, Newell C. "Retention of Reading Skills." *Journal of Educational Research,* 49 (November, 1955) 211–216.

[15] Davis, Frederick B. "Fundamental Factors of Comprehension in Reading." *Psychometrika,* 9 (September, 1944) 185–197.

[16] Davis, Frederick B. "The Teaching of Comprehension in Reading in the Secondary School." *Education,* 76 (May, 1956) 541–544.

[17] Dearborn, Walter F. "Motivation versus 'Control' in Remedial Reading." *Education,* 59 (September, 1938) 1–6.

[18] Dolch, E. W. "Implications of the Seashore Vocabulary Report." *Elementary English,* 26 (November, 1949) 407–413.

[19] Durrell, Donald D. "Development of Comprehension and Interpretation." *Reading in the Elementary School,* Forty-eighth Yearbook of the National Society for the Study of Education, Part II, University of Chicago Press, Chicago, 1949, 193–204.

[20] Edwards, Thomas J. "Oral Reading in the Total Reading Process." *The Elementary School Journal,* 58 (October, 1957) 36–41.

[21] Fairbanks, Grant. "The Relation Between Eye Movements and Voice in the Oral Reading of Good and Poor Silent Readers." *Psychological Monographs,* 48 (No. 3, 1937) 78–107.

[22] Fay, Leo C. *Reading in the High School.* Department of Classroom Teachers, American Educational Research Association, Washington, 1956.

[23] Fink, August A. "The Effects of Tachistoscopic Training in Digit Perception on Eye Movements in Reading." Unpublished doctoral dissertation, Columbia University, 1956; (*Dissertation Abstracts,* 16 [2] (July, 1956), 1289.)

[24] Freeburne, Cecil Max. "The Influence of Training in Perceptual Span and Perceptual Speed Upon Reading Ability." *Journal of Educational Psychology,* 40 (October, 1949) 321–352.

[25] Gates, Arthur I. *The Improvement of Reading,* 3rd Edition. The Macmillan Company, New York, 1950.

[26] Gates, Arthur I. "Teaching Reading." *What Research Says to the Teacher,* Department of Classroom Teachers, and American Educational Research Association for the National Education Association, Washington, 1953.

[27] Glock, Marvin D. "The Effect Upon Eye-Movements and Reading Rate at the College Level of Three Methods of Training." *Journal of Educational Psychology,* 40 (February, 1949) 93–106.

[28] Gray, Lillian, and Reese, Dora. *Teaching Children to Read.* Ronald Press Company, New York, 1957.

[29] Harris, Albert J. *How to Increase Reading Ability,* 3rd Edition. Longmans, Green and Company, New York, 1956.

[30] Hartmann, George W. "Further Evidence on the Unexpected Large Size of Recognition Vocabularies Among College Students." *Journal of Educational Psychology,* 37 (October, 1946) 436–439.

[31] Horn, Ernest. *Methods of Instruction in the Social Studies.* Charles Scribner's Sons, New York, 1937.

[32] Hughes, Marie M., and Cox, Vivian K. "The Language of First Grade Children, I." *Elementary English,* 26 (November, 1949) 373–380, 406.

[33] Hughes, Marie M., and Cox, Vivian K. "The Language of First Grade Children, II." *Elementary English,* 26 (December, 1949) 468–474, 495.

[34] Humber, Wilbur J. "The Relationship Between Reading Efficiency and Academic Success in Selected University Curricula." *Journal of Educational Psychology,* 35 (January, 1944) 17–26.

[35] Jenkins, Marguerite. "Vocabulary Development: A Reading Experiment in Seventh Grade English." *Peabody Journal of Education,* 19 (May, 1942) 347–351.

[36] Johnson, Janet Bassett. "Reading Clinic for Adults." *Clearing House,* 24 (December, 1949) 195–198.

[37] Jones, Ernest A. "A Small College Reading Program." *Techniques and Procedures in College and Adult Reading Programs,* The Sixth Yearbook of the Southwest Reading Conference for Colleges and Universities, Texas Christian University Press, Fort Worth, 1957, 7–15.

[38] Jones, Nellie F. "A 'Motorized' Reading Project." *The English Journal,* 40 (June, 1951) 313–319.

[39] Kingston, Albert J., and George, Clay E. "The Effectiveness of Reading Training at the College Level." *Journal of Educational Research,* 48 (February, 1955) 467–471.

[40] Lanigan, Mary A. "The Effectiveness of the Otis, the A.C.E. and the Minnesota Speed of Reading Tests for Predicting Success in College." *Journal of Educational Research,* 41 (December, 1947) 289–296.

[41] Leary, Bernice E. "Developing Word Perception Skills in Middle and Upper Grades." *Current Problems of Reading Instruction,* Seventh Annual Conference on Reading, University of Pittsburgh Press, Pittsburgh, 1951, 22–27.

[42] Lewis, Norman. "An Investigation into Comparable Results Obtained From Two Methods of Increasing Reading Speed Among Adults." *College English,* 11 (December, 1949) 152–156.

[43] Luckiesh, Matthew, and Moss, Frank K. *The Science of Seeing.* D. Van Nostrand Company, Inc., New York, 1937.

[44] Manolakes, George. "The Effects of Tachistoscopic Training in an Adult Reading Program." *Journal of Applied Psychology,* 36 (December, 1952) 410–412.

[45] McKee, Paul. *The Teaching of Reading in the Elementary School.* Houghton Mifflin Company, Boston, 1948.

[46] Miles, Isadora W. "An Experiment in Vocabulary Building in a High School." *School and Society,* 61 (April 28, 1945) 285–286.

[47] Mills, Lloyd. "The Functions of the Eyes in the Acquisition of an Education." *Journal of the American Medical Association,* 93 (September, 1929) 841–845.

[48] Mullins, Cecil J., and Mowry, H. W. "How Long Does Reading Improvement Last?" *Personnel Journal,* 32 (April, 1954) 416–417.

[49] Paterson, Donald G., and Tinker, Miles A. "The Effect of Typography Upon the Perceptual Span in Reading." *American Journal of Psychology,* 60 (July, 1947) 388–396.

[50] Preston, Ralph C., and Botel, Morton. "Reading Comprehension Tested Under Timed and Untimed Conditions." *School and Society,* 74 (August, 1951) 71.

[51] Reed, James C. "Some Effects of Short Term Training in Reading Under Conditions of Controlled Motivation." *Journal of Educational Psychology,* 47 (May, 1956) 257–264.

[52] Renshaw, Samuel. "The Visual Perception and Reproduction of Forms by Tachistoscopic Methods." *Journal of Psychology,* 20 (October, 1945) 217–232.

[53] Rinsland, Henry D. *A Basic Vocabulary of Elementary School Children.* Macmillan Company, New York, 1945.

[54] Robinson, Francis P. "The Tachistoscope as a Measure of Reading Perception." *American Journal of Psychology,* 46 (January, 1934) 132–135.

[55] Robinson, Francis P. "An Aid for Improving Reading Rate." *Journal of Educational Research,* 27 (February, 1934) 453–455.

[56] Robinson, Francis P. *Effective Study.* Harper and Brothers, New York, Revised edition, 1961.

[57] Robinson, H. A. "A Note on the Evaluation of College Remedial Reading Courses." *Journal of Educational Psychology,* 41 (February, 1950) 83–96.

[58] Schick, George B. "New Frontiers in Teaching Reading to College Groups," *New Frontiers in Reading,* Conference Proceedings, International Reading Association, Scholastic Magazines, New York, 1960, 44–49.

[59] Seashore, Robert H., and Eckerson, Lois D. "The Measurement of Individual Differences in General English Vocabularies." *Journal of Educational Psychology,* 31 (January, 1940) 14–38.

[60] Shaw, Phillip. "Classroom Procedures in Correcting Reading Deficiencies in High School and College: Discussion." *Better Readers For Our Times,* Conference Proceedings, International Reading Association, Scholastic Magazines, New York, 1956, 146–147.

[61] Shores, J. Harland, and Husbands, Kenneth L. "Are Fast Readers the Best Readers?" *Elementary English,* 27 (January, 1950) 52–57.

[62] Smith, Henry P., and Tate, Theodore R. "Improvements in Reading Rate and Comprehension of Subjects Training with the Tachistoscope." *Journal of Educational Psychology,* 44 (March, 1953) 176–184.

[63] Smith, Madorah E. "An Investigation of the Development of the Sentence and the Extent of Vocabulary in Young Children." *University of Iowa Studies in Child Welfare,* 3 (No. 5, 1926) 1–92.

[64] Smith, Mary Katherine. "Measurement of the Size of General English Vocabulary Through the Elementary Grades and High School." *Genetic Psychology Monographs,* 24 (November, 1941) 311–345.

[65] Smith, S. Stephenson. *The Command of Words.* Thomas Y. Crowell Company, New York, 1949.

[66] Sommerfeld, Roy E. "An Evaluation of the Tachistoscope in Reading Improvement Programs." *What Colleges Are Doing in Reading Improvement Programs,* Third Yearbook of the Southwest Reading Conference for Colleges and Universities, Texas Christian University Press, Fort Worth, 1954, 7–25.

[67] Spache, George D. "Integrating Diagnosis with Remediation in Reading." *The Elementary School Journal,* 56 (September, 1955) 18–26.

[68] Spache, George D. "A Rationale for Mechanical Methods of Improving Reading." *Significant Elements in College and Adult Reading Improvement,* Seventh Yearbook of the National Reading Conference, Texas Christian University Press, Fort Worth, 1958, 115–132.

[69] Spache, George D., and Berg, Paul C. *The Art of Efficient Reading.* The Macmillan Company, New York, 1955.

[70] Stauffer, Russel G. "A Study of Prefixes in the Thorndike List to Establish a List of Prefixes That Should Be Taught in the Elementary School." *Journal of Educational Research,* 35 (February, 1942) 453–458.

[71] Stauffer, Russel G. "The Developmental Approach to Reading." *Educational Administration and Supervision,* 41 (October, 1955) 338–348.

[72] Sutherland, Jean. "The Relationship between Perceptual Span and Rate of Reading." *Journal of Educational Psychology,* 37 (September, 1946) 373–380.

[73] Taylor, Earl A. "The Spans: Perception, Apprehension, and Recognition." *American Journal of Opthalmology,* 44 (October, 1957) 501–507.

[74] Thompson, Warren Craig. "A Book-Centered Course Versus a Machine-Centered Course in Adult Reading Improvement." *Journal of Educational Research,* 49 (February, 1956) 437–445.

[75] Thurstone, L. L. *A Factorial Study of Perception.* University of Chicago Press, Chicago, 1944.

[76] Tinker, Miles A. "Motor Efficiency of the Eye as a Factor in Reading." *Journal of Educational Psychology,* 29 (March, 1938) 167–174.

[77] Traxler, Arthur E. "The Right to Read Rapidly." *Atlantic Monthly,* 190 (November, 1952) 88–96.

[78] Vernon, M. D. "The Improvement of Reading." *British Journal of Educational Psychology,* 26 (June, 1956) 85–93.

[79] Weber, C. O. "The Acquisition and Retention of Reading Skills by College Freshmen." *Journal of Educational Psychology,* 30 (September, 1939) 453–460.

[80] Weber, C. O. "Effects of Practice on the Perceptual Span for Letters." *Journal of General Psychology,* 26 (April, 1942) 347–351.

[81] Wedeen, Shirley Ullman. "Mechanical versus Non-Mechanical Reading Techniques for College Freshmen." *School and Society,* 79 (April 17, 1954) 121–123.

[82] Westover, F. L. *Controlled Eye Movements Versus Practice Exercises in Reading.* Contributions to Education, No. 917, Bureau of Publications, Teachers College, Columbia University, 1946.

[83] Wilson, Grace E. "The Comparative Value of Different Types of Developmental Reading Programs at the Tenth Grade Level." *Dissertation Abstracts,* 16 (April, 1956) 694.

[84] Witty, Paul A. *Reading in Modern Education.* D. C. Heath and Company, Boston, 1949.

[85] Witty, Paul A. "Problems in the Improvement and Measurement of Growth in Reading." *School and Society,* 78 (September, 1953) 69–73.

[86] Yoakam, Gerald A. "The Development of Comprehension in the Middle Grades." *Current Problems of Reading Instruction,* Seventh Annual Conference of Reading, University of Pittsburgh Press, Pittsburgh, 1951, 28–35.

9

READABILITY AND LEGIBILITY

We wish to put the right book in the right hands at the right time. To accomplish this, we need to know how to recognize the materials that best fit the needs of each child. A knowledge of readability formulas, which gauge the difficulty level of reading materials, will be useful to us. We also need to know the legibility factors which either promote or hinder reading. Readability and legibility have been studied extensively and the data that have accrued should be useful in detecting and eliminating some of the barriers to effective reading.

In the two preceding chapters our focus rests on how the child develops his basic reading skills. Here we focus on readability and legibility—those characteristics of the reading materials that are important determinants of both comprehension and rate. Thus far we have been concerned with the *who* of the reading process and the *how* of reading. Here we focus on the *what*—the materials that must be read.

Although writers frequently use the term readability to refer to a composite of understandability and legibility, in this chapter the term readability generally will refer to the perceptual problems of understandability. The sensory problems will be reserved for the latter portion of the chapter and will be discussed under the topic of legibility.

I. READABILITY

Concern with the problem of readability has not been limited to teachers. Readability formulas are now used also in industry and government. Publishers of all types of material have come to recognize that the difficulty level may be of critical importance in determining reader understanding and acceptance of their product. Consequently, readability checks of one kind or another have been applied to textbooks, magazines, newspapers, fictional materials, pamphlets, bulletins, income-tax forms, encyclopedias, instructional manuals, and standardized tests.

But teachers have an even more basic interest in the nature of readability and readability factors than have the publishers of the reading materials. A knowledge of readability is important to the teacher so that he will be able to organize reading activities and provide reading material that will meet the needs and capacities of each child in the classroom. The teacher must constantly ask: Should *this* pupil read *this* material? Is it appropriate to his abilities, is it *readable for him*?

THE NATURE OF READABILITY

Readability is not an easily identified concept. It depends on the interaction of a number of factors. Readability depends upon both the nature of the materials to be read and the nature of the reader. Because communication between writer and reader seldom, if ever, is perfect, readability cannot be absolute. Obviously, there are degrees of readability. Before we can say that a book is readable for the average child at a certain grade level, we must make certain practical decisions concerning the depth of understanding that is required. For example, *Gulliver's Travels* might be readable as an interesting tale at a much lower grade level than would be appropriate if we expected it to be understood as a political satire. And we recognize that when we say that a book is readable by the average child in a class, there are other children in the same class for whom the book is far too difficult and still others for whom it is too easy. What is readable thus depends not so much on the material to be read as on the background, abilities, and interests of the person doing the reading.

VARIATIONS IN READABILITY

A developmental reading program designed to start each student at an appropriate level and to lead him to progress at his own rate must be concerned with the difficulty level of the books that are being used. We recognize, of course, that there will be variations of from five to nine grades in the reading abilities of the children in a single class. This is one of the key reasons that the trend has been away from the use of single texts and toward the use of a variety of books and other materials chosen to meet the individual needs of various members of a class. However, any book considered for use as a basic text should be readable by all those who are to use it.

Research, following various readability formulas outlined in the next section, has shown that textbooks as well as other types of books are not always suited to the students for whom they are intended. Smith,[53] studying 20 fourth-grade textbooks in social studies, found that the readability average was 4.95 or almost fifth grade. Jones,[27] examining 32 health textbooks, found that these average from .5 to .7 of a grade too high. The fourth-grade books ranged from 4.0 to 5.6; the fifth-grade books from 5.9 to 6.4; the sixth-grade books from 6.1 to 7.7; the seventh-grade books from 7.1 to 9.6; and the eighth-grade books from 8.6 to 10.

Craig [11] reported on the difficulty level of a number of children's books. The grade-level difficulty of these is surprising, to say the least. The following are examples: *Pilgrim's Progress,* (6.6); *Aesop's Fables,* (6.0); *Robinson Crusoe,* (7.9); *Mother Goose,* (8.8); *Arabian Nights,* (9.9); *Tom Sawyer,* (9.0); *Treasure Island,* (8.8); *Alice in Wonderland,* (5.9); *Julius Caesar,* (7.9); *A Christmas Carol,* (10.5); *Heidi,* (5.7); and *Huckleberry Finn,* (7.3). Certainly this should lead us to consider carefully the difficulty level of the books we ask children to read.

Walchak,[72] analyzing 96 readers published since 1929, reported that 33 fourth-grade readers had a difficulty ranging from grade 4.3 to 7.2. Of the 31 fifth-grade readers, seven had a difficulty rating within the fifth-grade level, six within the sixth-grade level, 15 within the seventh-grade level, and 3 rated low eighth-grade level. The sixth-grade readers also varied widely in difficulty.

Mallinson and associates made a number of studies of the reading difficulty of science textbooks. They [42] examined five series designed for fourth, fifth, and sixth graders and found the readability level somewhat beyond the average reading ability for the grade levels for which they were intended and thus well beyond the ability of the below-average students. The fourth-grade books were relatively more difficult than the fifth- and sixth-grade books. In nine of the 15 books that composed the five series, passages taken from earlier portions of the text were more difficult than passages from later portions. They [41] found that there generally were wide variations of difficulty within the same high school text. Two texts were found to be too difficult even for the superior student. Another study by the group [40] indicated that the textbooks in science for grades seven, eight, and nine were reasonably well fitted for most students in those grades but that some of the texts would be difficult for all but the better students. The difficulty level was relatively higher on the seventh-grade level than on the eighth- or ninth-grade levels.

Dunlap [16] found that the median reading level of 38 samples from an eighth-grade reader was ninth grade. The reading levels of these samples ranged from grade five to twelve. Faison,[18] evaluating the readability of different textbooks used in grades five to eight, found that mathematics textbooks were most difficult. They were followed in order of difficulty by history, science, English, and literature. Burkey [6] analyzed 41 recently published elementary-science textbooks for readability. He found great internal variations within the textbooks. He suggested that if the vocabularies were more closely controlled, the textbooks would better fit the pupils' needs.

In a recent study at the University of Kansas, Wyatt and Ridgway [78] found that the average difficulty level of only one of nine state-adopted social-studies texts was higher than the grade level for which it was intended. Unfortunately, not all children are able to read materials that are appropriate for the *average* child in their grade. The study found that 14 per cent of a group of fifth-grade pupils could not read effectively any part of the adopted text. They concluded that nearly 85 per cent of the fifth-grade children could be expected to have some difficulty.

Even at the college level, books may not always be of appropriate difficulty. For example, Major,[39] investigating the readability of ten college biology textbooks, concluded that average students would have difficulty in reading 53.6 to 84.7 per cent of the text. He estimated that even the above average student would find from 32.8 to 70.8 per cent of the textbook difficult to understand. He concluded that the readability of passages could be improved by reducing the length of both words and sentences. When reading difficulty was decreased by one grade level, even the above average students showed a significant increase in comprehension; average students showed similar gains when the difficulty level was decreased by two grade levels. However, Witherington [76] studied eight textbooks in educational psychology published between 1948 and 1950. Using the Dale-Chall formula he concluded that the textbooks were on a tenth- to twelfth-grade level and hence should present no difficulty to the student using them.

Perhaps the fact that textbooks are frequently too difficult is not as significant as is the fact that in a developmental program the teacher must cope with *two* problems: the reading ability of each pupil and the readability of each book used. He dare not complacently use a "fifth-grade reader" for all fifth graders because not all fifth-grade readers are actually fifth grade in difficulty level, and not all fifth-grade children have fifth-grade reading skill.

Studies suggest that, typically, textbooks may be more "readable" in the upper- than in the lower-elementary grades. However, Chall (p. 132) [9] points out that some formulas may lead to higher estimates of difficulty at the primary level than are warranted because they are not specifically designed for that level. For example, the Flesch formula does not discriminate below the fifth grade and the Lorge formula does not do so below the third grade.

Recently there has been some concern lest primary readers become *too simple.* Stone,[56] for example, criticized a reading series of three preprimers, two primers, two first readers, two second readers, and two third readers that presented only 1,147 different words through the third grade. We know that children generally have a far larger speaking vocabulary than is used in these readers. Chall (p. 141) [8] indicates that basal readers now have approximately one-half the vocabulary load of the books published in the twenties, but suggests that it is impossible, at present, to say whether primary materials generally are too easy, too hard, or just right.

MEASURING READABILITY

In using the term readability we are assuming that it is possible to equate the reader and the reading material. We know that it is desirable to do so. We assume that there are identifiable and measurable factors that make reading materials too difficult or too easy to meet the needs and abilities of a given child.

One method a teacher can use to fit the book to the reader is to have the child read aloud from a book which is somewhat below his estimated level of reading ability. If he misses more than five words out of a hundred or has less than 85 to 95 per cent comprehension, the book should be considered too difficult.

Another approach to the study of readability is to examine the reading choice of children. Studies of reading interests sometimes give data concerning this. These have focused on what children do read or on what children say that they like to read. Knowing what books children choose to read gives us two important types of data concerning readibility. If a book is extremely popular among children of a certain grade level, not only do we know something specific about their interests, but we can feel sure that the book itself is readable at that grade level.

Studies have shown that teachers and others closely concerned with children's reading have not been too successful in making subjective judgments of the difficulty level of books. Russell and Merrill [52] report a study in which 63 librarians judged the reading difficulty of 60 juvenile books. Not one of the books was placed at the same grade level by all the librarians; only three were put at two adjacent grade levels. Twenty-one of the books were put at three consecutive grade levels. The difference among the ratings provided by librarians varied over a range of three to four grades. Such failures of subjective methods have increased our interest in finding objective ways for determining readability.

As Chall (p. 153) [8] points out, if we are to have a scientific basis for choosing curricular materials, we must have some means for quantifying our statements about difficulty. It is not enough to say that material is hard, average, or easy. We must have reference points and a scale, however rough, for measuring difficulty. Grade levels provide useful reference points and the formulas that have been developed for computing difficulty provide us with crude scales.

READABILITY FORMULAS

We are interested in readability formulas for a number of reasons. We recognize that reading is a chief tool for learning. We know that there is a relationship between the readability of instructional materials and frustrations shown by pupils in reading situations. Teachers have found vast discrepancies between grade scores achieved on standardized tests and the ability to read instructional materials.[3] We have seen that not all books with the same grade-level designation are equally readable; we have felt, for one thing, the need to control the vocabulary load of books, especially in the elementary grades. We have become aware that books that are readable are read and that improved readability leads to better retention, better recall, and to more economical, reading speeds.[29, 30]

Lively and Pressey [33] in 1923 made what may have been the earliest attempt to secure an objective estimate of the vocabulary difficulties of textbooks. Betts,[3] however, points out that the graded McGuffey readers, in about 1840, aroused professional interest in readability. Since 1923, more than 30 different formulas have been devised to measure the readability of printed materials. The best known of the early studies of readability is that developed by Vogel and Washburne [71] in 1928. They surveyed 37,000 children and published the Winnetka Graded Book List. This list contained 700 books that children from the second to the eleventh grade read and enjoyed. The average reading ability of the children who read and enjoyed each specific book determined its grade placement. Vogel and Washburne also developed a readability formula by analyzing 150 of these books. They identified ten factors which, in their opinion, determined the relative difficulty of reading materials. However, in a revision of the formula in 1938,[73] they retained but three of the factors:

(1) Number of different words in a sample of 1,000 words;
(2) Number of words (including duplicates) per 1,000 that were not in Thorndike's most common 1,500 words; and
(3) Number of simple sentences in 75 sample sentences.

Although some formulas have used this same general approach, others have emphasized different factors. For example, the Lorge formula [34] is based on (1) average sentence length; (2) the number of prepositional phrases; and (3) vocabulary. The Yoakam formula [79] estimates vocabulary difficulty only. The Dale-Chall formula [12] considers both average sentence length and vocabulary. Flesch's 1943 formula [19] was based on average sentence length, the relative number of words with prefixes, suffixes, and inflectional endings, and the number of personal references.* Spache,[55] noting that none of the three leading formulas (Flesch, Lorge, and Dale-Chall) is applicable for pupils reading below fourth-grade level, has proposed a formula for primary reading materials. His formula emphasizes vocabulary difficulty and sentence length. He suggests that for the primary grades sentence length may be a more significant determinant of readability than it is in the upper grades.

Betts [3] suggests that the major determinants of readability are the average number of words per sentence, the number of simple sentences, the number of prepositional phrases, the percentage of different words, the number of uncommon words, the number of words beginning with certain letters, the number of polysyllabic words, and the number of adjectives, adverbs, personal pronouns, and other words having a personal reference. He concludes that easy-to-read material generally has the following characteristics: personal references, a high percentage of common words, and short sentences. On the other hand, difficult material contains many uncommon words, different words, polysyllabic words, prepositional phrases, and complex and lengthy sentences.

Dale and Tyler [15] found that among adults of limited ability the following four factors were closely associated with comprehension difficulties: the number of different technical terms, the number of those non-technical terms known to but 10 per cent of sixth-grade pupils, the number of prepositional phrases, and, oddly enough, the number of words beginning with "i." Sochor [54] has suggested that the difficulty of materials depends largely on the number and unusualness of the facts that are presented, the vocabulary or terminology that is used to present them, and the context or language setting in which they are presented.

Peterson (pp. 4–5),[47] after reviewing the research on readability, suggests that the following factors deserve further study.

1. Density, or quantity of facts presented in a limited space.
2. Degree of directness with which ideas are presented.
3. Interest appeal.
4. Difficulties of ideas caused by remoteness of ideas from reader's experience and by lack of explanation.

---

* Personal references are names of persons, personal pronouns, and nouns such as mother, uncle, friend, people, lady, and child.

5. Abstractness of treatment.
6. Use of verbal or pictorial illustrations.
7. Patterns of organization.

Peterson mentions that the factors of interest and organization need to be explored. That both are important was indicated by Dale and Chall.[13] Bernstein,[2] for example, found that the more interesting story is read with greater comprehension. There is also some evidence that comprehension is best when the reading material is well-organized. Robinson (pp. 14–16) [48] found that comprehension was better when a paragraph contained topic headings, questions, enumerations, and summaries.

Wilson [75] reports that intermediate-grade children comprehend better when explanatory material is included in a reading selection. Longer versions of the same articles lead to better comprehension even though the same statements that are in the shorter versions are retained. The children seem to find the longer versions more interesting and they are able to discuss the content more logically.

Woody [77] compared the vocabulary, sentence length, and sentence structure in representative textbooks with the words listed in the Thorndike list and with the length and structure of sentences that the students used in their own compositions and suggested that they were not major factors contributing to reading difficulty. He found that the vocabulary was too difficult in the literature text, but not so in social studies. The sentences in the texts were no longer than those the students used in their own compositions, and there were actually more complex sentences in the compositions than in the texts. He concluded that the reader's lack of experience and background accounted for the seeming difficulty of the texts.

The teachers, librarians, and publishers who took part in the Gray and Leary [22] study deemed style, format, organization, and the reader's interest in the content most significant determinants of readability.

Leary (p. 280) [32] commenting on the Gray and Leary study notes:

> According to the combined opinion of these judges, then, if you give a reader a theme that interests him . . . you have made a strong attack upon the problem of readability. If, in addition, you discover what style of expression is best suited to the reader's needs and tastes, that is, the scope of vocabulary and the kind of sentences which he reads easily, and the type of approach that pleases him, you have the final solution of the problem close at hand. In the opinion of these judges the attractiveness of the book, its mechanical set-up, and its general plan of organization are matters of minor importance.

Dale and Chall [13] point out that the content must be interesting, that the style must be comprehensible, and that the format and organization should aid and permit understanding. Halbert [23] also reports that when the text is illustrated by pictures (improved format), children comprehend better.

As we examine the readability formulas and the factors on which they are based, it appears that readability generally is a function of the following factors:

1. Word length
2. Percentage of different words
3. Sentence length
4. Personal references *
5. Number of syllables
6. Number of pronouns
7. Number of affixes
8. Number of prepositional phrases
9. Number of difficult words according to word lists
10. The use of simple or complex sentences
11. Density and unusualness of the facts
12. Number of pictorial illustrations
13. Interest and purpose
14. Concept load—abstractness of words
15. Organization of the material and format
16. Interrelationship of the ideas

Actually, readability formulas generally have paid little attention to the last six of these factors. The goal in developing a formula, of course, is to get the highest degree of prediction with the smallest number of factors. And the factors that are chosen must be easy to measure. This latter point has tended to eliminate factors 11 to 16 from most studies. The Gray-Leary formula uses five factors; the Lorge and Flesch formula, three factors; and the Dale-Chall formula uses only two factors.

Some studies have indicated that vocabulary is the most significant determinant of readability. However, there is a complicating factor in attempting to determine vocabulary difficulty. The ordinary meaning of a word may be easily understood, yet in certain usages the word calls for unusual, and thus difficult, meanings. For example, dog, cow, run, and fall have common meanings but also frequently demand uncommon interpretations.

In evaluating vocabulary, Chall (p. 45) [9] writes:

> All measures of vocabulary difficulty are interrelated. The superiority of one or another measure of vocabulary difficulty depends upon the nature of the criterion, and the ease and reliability of its use. In general, the use of a short

---

* Flesch [19] uses this in his formula. He found a correlation of .27 between the number of "personal sentences" and comprehension. And Engelman [17] reported that children (particularly girls) definitely preferred conversational to expositional types of narrative.

list of easy words is a good predictor for materials at the lower ranges of difficulty. A longer list or a word-length measure has been found to discriminate better at the upper ranges of difficulty.

She says that several investigators have found that the conceptual difficulty of the text is probably of greater importance than is the difficulty of its vocabulary as measured by a word list.

Readability formulas certainly have not explored the full implications of diversities within the vocabulary. That it is an important consideration is readily apparent. For example, Bachmann [1] studied the various meanings of relatively common words found in two books chosen from the Juvenile Department of a city library. She concluded that the word *made* was used to designate 25 relatively distinct concepts and that *close* was used for 20 separate meanings. Among words used for ten or more meanings were: bear, time, end, way, give, command and light.

Sentence structure is another factor frequently related to the comprehensibility of the material. Furthermore, sentence length and the number of simple sentences as compared with the number of complex sentences must be considered. The number of phrases and clauses seems to be related positively to the ideational loading of the sentences, and thus is related to difficulty of reading material.

There are indications that the more verbs and nouns in the sentence, the harder materials are to comprehend. Chall (p. 47) [9] also points out that personal pronouns, proper names, and colorful words are related positively to ease of comprehension, but they add little to the over-all prediction of reading difficulty obtainable through other measures.

EVALUATION OF READABILITY FORMULAS

It is difficult to compare readability formulas because they have different bases and generally are intended for use only with specific materials. Formulas that have been used most widely are those of Flesch,[19] Dale-Chall,[12] Lorge,[34] Yoakam,[79] and Spache.[55] Formulas have been proposed by many others, including Gray-Leary,[22] Wheeler-Smith,[74] Washburne-Morphett,[73] and Dale-Tyler.[15]

The Flesch formula appears to be used primarily with adult, the Dale-Chall and Yoakam formulas with middle- and upper-grade, and the Spache and Wheeler formulas with primary materials. The Wilkinson and Lewerenz formulas also are used with primary-level materials, but are quite time-consuming in application. Hildreth (p. 374),[24] writing in 1958, suggested that the Washburne-Vogel formula remained the formula most valid for rating reading materials of elementary-school level.

Klare,[28] evaluating five readability formulas, concluded that the Gray-

Leary, Flesch, and the Dale-Chall approaches measured much the same thing. Russell and Fea [51] found that the Dale-Chall, Flesch, and Lorge formulas are about equally good measures, while Michaelis and Tyler [43] concluded that their use provided three quite different estimations of difficulty for the same material. However, Forbes and Cottle,[20] applying five formulas to 27 standardized tests, obtained significant correlations between the Dale-Chall, Flesch, Lorge, Lewerenz, and Yoakam formulas although they report substantial variation among the difficulty levels assigned by each.

Chall (pp. 95–96) [9] makes the following observations:

> Most studies show that, when used to appraise materials of intermediate-grade difficulty, the Lorge, Flesch, and Dale-Chall formulas assign similar grade-levels, which average well within one grade of each other. Above the seventh grade, however, the Lorge formula tends to give considerably lower indexes than the Flesch and Dale-Chall formulas, the discrepancy becoming larger as the difficulty of the material increases. However, it may be noted that at all ranges of difficulty the Flesch and Dale-Chall formulas tend to assign similar grade-levels.

Smith,[53] using social studies textbooks on the fourth-grade level, reports that the Lorge and the Dale-Chall formulas require more time than do other formulas tested. However, she implies that they also give a more reliable index. Wheeler and Smith [74] believe that the Flesch formula is the easiest to use on upper-grade and adult materials.

Although readability formulas generally emphasize similar factors, they alone cannot give a complete measurement of readability. Lorge [35] cautions that they tell us nothing about the kind of ideas expressed or the interrelationships among them. Dale and Chall [14] say that the readability formulas do not directly measure conceptual difficulty, organization, or abstractness of subject matter, though these factors are known to affect comprehensibility.

Chall (p. 96) [9] also points out that

> In the light of our present knowledge, it is questionable whether the grade-placement arrived at by the application of any one of these formulas can be used to make a definitive statement about the suitability of a particular piece of reading matter for a specific level of reading ability. . . .

She adds:

> It is even more questionable whether the grade-placement indexes of the various formulas can be used to make a definite statement about the suitability of a book for a particular school grade. Because of the wide range in reading

ability within one class, any book selected for the average reading ability of the class will almost invariably be too difficult for the children at the lower end of the scale. In addition, not all classes in the same grade average the same reading level. The average scores of some classes may be lower than the national norms, and hence they will need books lower in difficulty.

SUMMARY

Kress [31] has summarized the inadequacies of present reading formulas. He states (p. 98):

1. Different formulas yield different results and grade placement estimates, even when applied to the same material.
2. The formulas vary in relation to the level of material for which they were intended. The same formula is not adequate for measuring the reading level of all materials.
3. The formulas do not measure such factors as experience background, interest, and purpose in the reader.
4. The formulas do not measure 'concepts.' . . .
5. The formulas were not designed to provide rules for writing.

In the following summary the first two points are taken from Chall (p. 36) [7]; the last three, from Kress (p. 78).[31]

1. Readability formulas ". . . can give an estimate of relative difficulty of books."
2. "The predicted grade level alone cannot tell whether the book is suitable for children of a given grade or reading ability."
3. Readability formulas can be used for "determining the sequence in which books of varying content might be used in a reading program."
4. Readability formulas can be used for "determining which words in material would be most likely to cause difficulty for the reader."
5. Readability formulas can be used for "identifying long and involved sentences in the material which may need clarification for the reader."

Chall (pp. 156–158) [9] suggests that the following generalizations can be made from the research:

First, a variety of factors contribute to reading difficulty. . . .

Second, so far only stylistic elements have been amenable to reliable quantitative measurement and verification.

Third, of the diverse stylistic elements that have been reliably measured and found significantly related to difficulty, only four types can be distinguished: vocabulary load, sentence structure, idea density, and human interest.

Fourth, of the four types of stylistic elements, vocabulary load (diversity and difficulty) is most significantly related to all criteria of difficulty so far used. . . .

Fifth, almost every study found a significant relationship between sentence structure and comprehension difficulty. . . . All sentence measures are interrelated and significantly related to difficulty, but, once a vocabulary measure is included in a prediction formula, sentence structure does not add very much to the prediction.

Sixth, readability formulas measure idea intensity only indirectly through the percentage of prepositional phrases and, less often, through the percentage of different content words. . . . Prepositional phrases have less potent influence on difficulty than either vocabulary difficulty or sentence structure. They add little to the over-all prediction of difficulty, once some measure of these two factors is included in a formula.

Seventh, human interest has been measured by the number of personal pronouns, persons' names, and nouns denoting gender. It has also been estimated by the number of personal sentences—dialogue and sentences addressed to the reader. . . . However, these measures add little to a readability formula, once vocabulary difficulty and sentence structure are used.

II. LEGIBILITY

Legibility refers to the physical appearance of the printed materials. It involves such factors as line length, type size, style of type face, space between lines and between letters, margins, and physical format. Closely related to legibility are certain visibility factors. Among these are color of print, color and finish of the paper, and the contrast between the print and the paper. In a sense the visibility factors form the "setting" for the legibility factors. Legibility and visibility are determinants of the ease and speed with which the sensory phase of the reading act may be accomplished. Thus they reflect the relative suitability of printed materials for reading.

SOME VOCABULARY TERMS

The reports of studies on legibility and visibility contain a number of special vocabulary terms employed in typography. To understand the reports we need to know the meaning of some of these terms.* The printer has certain special units of measurement. His unit for measuring type height is the point which is approximately one seventy-second of an inch. Though faces (styles) of type vary in boldness and design, the type size is measured in points based on the height of the letter from the top of the highest ascender to the bottom of the lowest descender.

* Vocabulary terms used by printers, as well as illustrations of type faces and sizes, can be found in David Hymes, *Production in Advertising and the Graphic Arts,* Holt, Rinehart and Winston, Inc., New York, 1958. (In addition, most dictionaries contain information on many of these terms.)

The *pica,* which is equivalent to 12 typographical points (or one-sixth of an inch) is used as a measurement for line width. The term *pica* is used also to designate twelve-point type.

The spacing of type may refer to space between letters, words, lines, or paragraphs. All of these, of course, occur within the framework of the margin. *Leading* refers to the space that may be placed between lines of print. One-point leading would be one seventy-second of an inch. Spaces between lines normally appear larger than their actual leading measurements would indicate because the type line itself is high enough to accommodate ascenders and descenders even though they may be infrequent. Space between letters is dependent on several factors: type size, line length, the syllabification of the words to be set in type, and the means used for setting the type. Hand-set type uses spacers of blank type termed em quad (a square of the point size of the type) or smaller spacers such as en quad (same height as em quad but half as wide). These spacers, and other still narrower ones, permit equated spacing between words and letters within a line of print. Automatically-set type utilizes wedge-shaped spacebands to adjust the spacing.

There are numerous other special vocabulary terms that are found in the research on legibility. However, most of them are either known by most readers (italics, bold face, glossy paper, off-white paper, etc.) or their meanings are incorporated in the research reports. For example, there are many designs or styles of type face (Gothic, Spartan, Garamond, Caslon, etc.) and the specific design used ordinarily will be mentioned in describing a research study but a detailed knowledge of these generally lies somewhat outside the professional interest of the reading teacher. The special terms used in measuring light will be discussed in the section on illumination.

EXPERIMENTAL PROCEDURE

Before we consider the factors governing the legibility of printed materials, let us examine some of the experimental procedures used for studying legibility and the closely related problems of visibility and illumination. In any experiment a major task is to hold constant all factors except the one being studied. Thus if one wishes to determine the relative legibility of various type sizes, other aspects of legibility and visibility such as distance between lines (leading), length of line, style and boldness of type, and color and finish of the paper, usually will be kept the same. And, of course, the difficulty (readability) of the materials being compared must be held constant.

One experimental procedure is the distance method. The assumption in using this procedure is that the relative legibility of different printed materials may be determined by the distance at which they can be read. Another procedure is to use reading rate as the criterion. When this method is used those materials which can be read at the most rapid rate are considered most legible. A third approach uses rate of blinking as the criterion of legibility.

Another approach is to use accuracy of reading as the gauge of legibility. The fewer the number of errors made, the more legible the materials are judged to be. The tachistoscope presenting two or three words or four to eight letters during a very short exposure, perhaps one-hundredth of a second, has been used to study legibility. Still another procedure is to photograph eye movements. The assumption here is that, with the more legible materials, the reader will make fewer fixations and regressions and shorter pauses.

EVALUATIONS OF EXPERIMENTAL PROCEDURE

Each procedure has had its advocates. Unfortunately, different results often are obtained by using different experimental methods. For example typewritten materials rank high in legibility when the distance method is used but rank low when studied by the method of comparative rate of reading.

While this has something to do with the particular problems of the typewriter mechanism and the equidistant letter-spacing peculiar to it, to an extent it illustrates a difference between legibility and visibility and points to a weakness in the distance method for studying legibility. Larger type or type of the same size but with additional leading and linear spacing between the letters may be visible at greater distances and yet is not necessarily more legible at ordinary reading distances. Paterson and Tinker [44] point out that when using about a three-inch line, type sizes ranging from eight to twelve point were about equally legible although the twelve-point type certainly would be much more visible.

The differences in results of different experimental procedures have led to some controversy among experimenters as to the best procedures for studying the determinants of legibility. For example, for comparing various type faces, Luckiesh and Moss [36, 37] have suggested that rate of involuntary blinking is the superior measure of legibility; Tinker [60] has advocated rate of reading as the criterion. He argues that the blink rate is not a valid measure of readability nor an index of ease of reading.[62] He says that there is less blinking in newspaper reading than in book reading and suggests that, since other evidence indicates that newsprint is less readable than bookprint, this makes the blink technique appear to be invalid as a measure of legibility.

Tinker [61] found that 60 university students showed no significant difference in rate of blinking while reading text in capitals in comparison with lower case letters. And yet, text in all-capitals was read much more slowly than text in lower case. In another study Tinker [60] compared the two procedures of perceptability at a distance and speed of reading. He concluded that speed of reading is the best criterion of legibility.

On the other hand Hoffman [25] studied 30 college students while they were reading for a four-hour period. He found that blinking increased significantly after one hour, but there were no significant changes in the number of fixations and the number of regressions per line. Thus it may be that blinking as a criterion of legibility is not particularly valid when the reading experiment is of short duration, and yet it could be quite valid if the duration of the experiment is sufficiently long to make fatigue effects noticeable.

Additional problems in the study of legibility stem from the fact that a number of the determinants of legibility have interacting effects. Thus optimal line length depends on size of type and amount of leading.

Obviously in choosing materials for our students to read, we are concerned with legibility under typical classroom conditions. Thus the tests of legibility using reading rate for actual classroom-type materials, relative absence of fatigue, and accuracy of reading, seem to be closer to classroom conditions than do methods using a distance technique or a tachistoscope. We are particularly concerned that the materials chosen continue to be legible after prolonged reading and are not merely "seeable" under the short intensive effort that may be typical of some laboratory procedures.

With these points in mind let us examine some of the evidence concerning legibility factors.

KINDS OF TYPE

Considerable interest has been shown in the legibility of various type faces. Newspaper and magazine publishers frequently spend large sums of money to change to a more legible type face. Textbook publishers are greatly concerned with this same problem. However, detailed knowledge of specific differences in type faces and their effect on legibility may have little professional interest for the teacher. Probably the teacher's major interest will be in readability of materials. However, he should have enough knowledge of the determinants of legibility so that he makes his choice of readable materials from those that also rank high in legibility. And perhaps the furthest he can expect to go in his concern for legibility is to be aware that the type should be of an appropriate size and that each letter should be clear, definitely distinguishable from each other letter, and not too different in form from that with which the child is likely to be most familiar. In short, he will wish to choose plain rather than fancy type—type that is easy to read rather than stylized or "arty."

However, some of the studies of legibility of type are worth considering. Tinker [64] reports that italic type results in about a three per cent reduction in speed when compared with roman print. Paterson and Tinker (p. 16 ff) [44] report that typewritten type reduces speed by about five per cent when compared with ordinary book type and that capital letters (upper case) require about twelve per cent more time to read than do lower case letters. They also found that students prefer to read lower case rather than upper case letters and prefer a lightface to a boldface type. Paterson and Tinker [46] also found that when using material that was printed in all-capital letters 12.5 per cent fewer words were read per fixation. Comparing two type styles, Old English and Scotch Roman, they found that the former resulted in fewer words read per fixation.

Breland and Breland,[5] observing the newspaper-headline reading of 22 senior and graduate students at the University of Minnesota, also found that lower case was more easily read than capitals. In another study Tinker [66] found that all-capital material retarded reading rate by about the same amount whether a short four-minute test was used or a much longer (sixteen minutes) test was used.

TYPE SIZE

One of the determinants of legibility is type size. Paterson and Tinker (p. 148) [44] conclude that most adult readers prefer an eleven-point type, with ten-, twelve-, nine-, and eight-point types next in order of preference. Russell (p. 76),[50] however, notes that, whereas adults do prefer ten- to twelve-point type, children read best with fourteen- to eighteen-point type.

In general it has been observed that as the size of type is either increased or decreased from the optimum, more eye fixations per line are required, the fixation pause becomes longer, and there are more regressions. It may be that the disruption in eye movements accompanying the smaller type is primarily a result of reduced visibility. On the other hand the larger type may be less readable because a lesser number of characters can be seen at normal reading distance during each fixation.

Using a different approach to the problem of legibility, Glanville, Kreezer, and Dallenbach [21] found that it is easier to locate words in dictionaries set in twelve-point type than in dictionaries set in six-point type.

SPACING

As noted earlier, there are several aspects of spacing that are related to legibility—spacing between letters, words, lines (leading), and paragraphs. Probably the most commonly studied is leading.

Leading increased above the zero point improves legibility. However, optimum leading depends on the type size used and the length of the line. It also depends somewhat on the style of the type (the length of the ascenders and descenders and the height differences between upper and lower case letters vary with type style). Additional leading between paragraphs generally is considered an aid to legibility. It helps break visual monotony and points up the introduction of new ideas. The recommended spacing between paragraphs is that it be from two to four points greater than the lines within the paragraph (p. 79).[26]

The addition of spacing between letters in a word normally will not improve legibility. However, titles or other material composed of upper case letters, and material set in large-sized lower case letters, are made more legible by adding some space. Generally, the space between words should be about the same as the apparent space between the lines.

Now let us examine a few of the studies of legibility that are related to spacing. Paterson and Tinker,[45] using eight groups of 85 college students each, found that newspaper type with increased leading was read faster, and that 4- and 5-point leading produced the most significant differences. In an earlier study (p. 150) [44] they had found that for ten-point type and 19-pica line width, two-point leading seemed to be optimal. Although they indicated that size and style of type, the visual efficiency of the reader, and the quality and quantity of light are more important for legibility than leading, Luckiesh and Moss [38] stress that leading is significant. Using the frequency of blinking as a criterion, they concluded that three-point leading represented a practical optimum of readability. Since both of these studies used adult subjects, their findings are primarily applicable to adult materials. Most preprimers, for example, use approximately a twelve-point leading.

LENGTH OF LINE

Tinker and Paterson,[70] experimenting with 20 college students, found that very short or very long lines of print resulted in longer fixation pauses and less words read per fixation. There were fewer regressions with short lines than with long lines. The long lines made it more difficult to make the proper return sweep. On the other hand short lines necessitate more return sweeps and lead to "choppy" reading partly because the eye is unable to make effective use of peripheral vision.

Experimenting with ten-point type with two-point leading, Paterson and Tinker (p. 148) [44] report that line lengths of from 14 to 31 picas were equally good. Tinker and Paterson [69] also state that for an eight-point type an 18-pica line with one- or two-point leading is optimal. In a study [70] using nine-point type they found that for college students the optimal line length was from 14 to 30 picas with 1 to 4 points leading.

Hymes (p. 87) [26] says that line length must depend on size of type and that a line should contain about 40 characters.

ILLUMINATION

Authorities differ somewhat in the levels of illumination that they suggest. Russell (pp. 75–76) [50] says that for efficient work in ordinary reading, lighting of from 15 to 20 foot-candles * is required, whereas Luckiesh and Moss (p. 345) [37] recommend 20 to 50 foot-candles for ordinary reading and 50 to 100 foot-candles for difficult reading.

Tinker (p. 13),[58] in a summary of numerous studies, points out that:

> There is a rapid rise in acuity from low intensity up to about 5 foot-candles. From 5 foot-candles on, the rise in acuity becomes slower and slower and almost reaches a maximum at about 20 foot-candles. In fact, the improvement in visual acuity from about 15 foot-candles to higher intensities for the normal eye is scarcely noticeable and of doubtful significance. . . . [With] 20 to 100 foot-candles the increase in acuity was slight.

Rose and Rostas [49] found that for college students increased illumination does not necessarily lead to better comprehension or to a more rapid rate of reading. They concluded that so long as there is sufficient light to distinguish print (2 or 3 foot-candles), illumination seems to be one of the least important determinants of reading efficiency. They add, however, that even though they do not affect reading efficiency, such low intensities as

---

* One foot-candle is the amount of illumination produced by a one-inch-thick candle measured at a distance of one foot. The amount (intensity) of light on a surface depends upon candle power and the distance from source of light to the receiving surface. It varies inversely with the square of the distance from source to surface. If candle power is 100 and distance is 10 feet the intensity is 1 foot-candle. That is, 100 (candle power) divided by 10×10 (square of distance) equals 1 foot-candle.

A hundred-watt bulb usually gives an illumination of about 100 foot-candles one foot away; 25 foot-candles, two feet away; and approximately 11 foot-candles three feet away.

2 to 3 foot-candles should not be used because they lead to poor postural habits. Tinker (p. 571) [59] suggests that with ten-point type an intensity of from 10 to 15 foot-candles is sufficient for ordinary reading conditions. He concluded also that

> . . . the critical level of illumination for reading ten-point type is approximately 3 foot-candles. That is, speed of reading is not increased and clearness of seeing (fatigue) after two hours reading is not significantly changed when the intensity is raised above 3.1 foot-candles.

The amount of illumination provided in the classroom by the light from the sun varies both with the weather outside and with the location of the room and of the child within the room. Natural illumination creates unequal distribution of illumination among the classroom members and may even result in strong contrast of illumination for individuals within the room. Obviously, artificial lighting, if used correctly, is at least a partial remedy for these problems.

CONTRAST

Illumination is merely a means to an end. The letters receive as much light as does the paper. They are made visible because of the difference in the amount of light that they reflect to the reader. Thus black letters reflect only about one-fortieth as much light as does the white paper (p. 306).[37]

Various studies [57, 68] have shown that black print on a light background is a good combination for ease of readability. Generally a white paper with a slight tint of gray or cream is recommended (p. 76).[50] Tinker [67] points out that the brightness contrast between the ink and the paper, rather than the specific colors of the ink and paper, determine the legibility of printed material.

INTERACTING EFFECTS

As was mentioned earlier, one difficulty in determining the relative effect of certain factors on legibility is that one factor may depend upon another. For example, optimum spacing depends on size of type and length of line and optimum illumination depends on glossiness of paper and color of type. An experiment by Tinker has illustrated the dependence of one factor on another. He [63] reports that neither eight-point type, italic type, nor as little as three foot-candles of illumination reduced speed of reading significantly but that when all three were combined, speed was reduced by about ten per cent.

SUMMARY

This chapter has dealt with two related but somewhat distinct topics: the *readability* and the *legibility* of printed materials.

The term *readability* has been used in reference to those textual factors that either aid or hinder the understandability of reading materials. We have considered also the presentational or *legibility* factors that either promote or hinder reading. Sometimes these are referred to as elements in the "hygiene of reading."

The visibility factors form a "setting" for legibility. And to an extent legibility and visibility form a setting for readability. Legibility and visibility allow the sensory process to operate efficiently and thus form a basis for the perceptual process of comprehensibility or readability.

As we know, children generally come to school with a favorable attitude toward reading. They desire to learn to read. Because they are willing, they are easily stimulated. But this attitude is not enough to assure a persisting interest in reading. The best materials must be readable and legible if they are to prove satisfying to the reader.

SUGGESTED READINGS

For a comprehensive discussion of the measurement of readability and the application of readability formulas together with a survey of experimental studies and extensive bibliography:

Chall, Jeanne S. *Readability: An Appraisal of Research and Application,* Columbus: Ohio State University, Bureau of Educational Research Monographs, Number 34, 1958.

***

Practical suggestions on the elements of readability and instructions for using a readability formula may be found in:

Flesch, Rudolf, *The Art of Plain Talk.* New York: Harper & Brothers, 1946.

***

A detailed discussion of legibility factors, printer's vocabulary, and type faces has been published in:

Hymes, David, *Production in Advertising and the Graphic Arts.* New York: Holt, Rinehart and Winston, Inc., 1958.

***

For short abridged and adapted articles on readability and its prediction by George Spache, Irving Lorge, Edgar Dale and Jeanne S. Chall, Henry D. Rinsland, Mary K. Smith, and R. H. Seashore, see:

Chapter 7, "What Makes It Readable?" pp. 176–238 in C. W. Hunnicutt and

William J. Iverson, *Research in the Three R's,* New York: Harper & Brothers, 1958.

QUESTIONS FOR DISCUSSION

1. What is meant by readability? Legibility? How are they related?
2. What use may a teacher make of a knowledge of readability and legibility?
3. What are the determinants of readability? of legibility? Which determinants are of most importance? Which are and which are not measurable?
4. Why is the concept of readability of particular interest when reading instruction emphasizes a developmental approach?
5. Suggest evidence that there are wide variations in the readability of various textbooks designed for use in the same school grade. Suggest evidence that the same book may show wide variations.
6. What evidence is there that in certain school subjects the books frequently are too difficult?
7. Describe and criticize some of the more commonly used formulas for measuring readability.
8. What methods other than formulas are used to determine readability?
9. What are the most important weaknesses of readability formulas?
10. Describe and criticize experimental procedure for determining legibility.
11. List and define some of the more important special vocabulary terms used in a discussion of legibility.
12. How are interest and readability interrelated?
13. What is meant by a developmental reading program?
14. What are the determinants of interest? Which of these vary with the nature of the individual rather than with the nature of the situation or object?

BIBLIOGRAPHY

[1] Bachmann, Helen Marie. "A Semantic Study of the Books of Two Authors Dealing with Classical Antiquity." *The Graduate School Abstracts of Theses,* University of Pittsburgh, Bulletin No. 3, 40 (January, 1944) 16–27.

[2] Bernstein, Margery R. "Relationship between Interest and Reading Comprehension." *Journal of Educational Research,* 49 (December, 1955) 283–288.

[3] Betts, Emmett A. "Readability: Its Application to the Elementary School." *Journal of Educational Research,* 42 (February, 1949) 438–459.

[4] Bitterman, M. E., and Soloway, E. "The Relation between Frequency of Blinking and Effort Expended in Mental Work." *Journal of Experimental Psychology,* 36 (April, 1946) 134–136.

[5] Breland, Keller, and Breland, Marion Kruse. "Legibility of Newspaper Headlines Printed in Capitals and in Lower Case." *Journal of Applied Psychology,* 28 (April, 1944) 117–120.

[6] Burkey, Jacob E. *"The Readability Levels of Recently Published Elementary Science Textbooks."* Unpublished doctoral thesis, University of Pittsburgh, 1954; *Dissertation Abstracts,* 14 [5] (No. 9, 1954) 1328.

[7] Chall, Jeanne S. "The Measurement of Readability." *Readability: Finding Readable Material For Children,* Tenth Annual Conference on Reading, University of Pittsburgh, 1954, 26–37.

[8] Chall, Jeanne S. "Locating, Introducing and Using Easy-to-Read, High-Interest Reading Matter." *Reading in Action,* International Reading Association, Conference Proceedings, Scholastic Magazines, New York, 1957, 54–57.

[9] Chall, Jeanne S. *Readability: An Appraisal of Research and Application.* Bureau of Educational Research Monographs, Ohio State University, No. 34, 1958.

[10] Cleeton, G. U., and Pitkin, C. W. *General Printing.* McKnight and McKnight Publishing Company, Bloomington, Ill., 1953.

[11] Craig, James C. "The Readability of Children's Literature." *Readability: Finding Readable Material for Children,* Tenth Annual Conference on Reading, University of Pittsburgh, 1954, 113–124.

[12] Dale, Edgar, and Chall, Jeanne S. "A Formula for Predicting Readability." *Educational Research Bulletin,* Ohio State University, 27 (January, 1948) 11–20.

[13] Dale, Edgar, and Chall, Jeanne S. "The Concept of Readability." *Elementary English,* 26 (January, 1949) 19–26.

[14] Dale, Edgar, and Chall, Jeanne S. "Techniques for Selecting and Writing Readable Materials." *Elementary English,* 26 (May, 1949) 250–258.

[15] Dale, Edgar, and Tyler, Ralph W. "A Study of the Factors Influencing the Difficulty of Reading Materials for Adults of Limited Reading Ability." *The Library Quarterly,* 4 (July, 1934) 384–412.

[16] Dunlap, Carolyn C. "Readability of Newspaper Items and of Basic Reading Material." *Elementary School Journal,* 51 (May, 1951) 499–501.

[17] Engleman, F. E. "The Relative Merits of Two Forms of Discourse When Applied to Children's Factual Content Reading Material." *Journal of Educational Research,* 29 (March, 1936) 524–531.

[18] Faison, Edmund, W. J. "Readability of Children's Textbooks." *Journal of Educational Psychology,* 42 (January, 1951) 43–51.

[19] Flesch, Rudolf. "A New Readability Yardstick." *Journal of Applied Psychology,* 32 (June, 1948) 221–233.

[20] Forbes, F. W., and Cottle, W. C. "A New Method for Determining Readability of Standardized Tests." *Journal of Applied Psychology,* 37 (June, 1953) 185–190.

[21] Glanville, A. Douglas, Kreezer, George L., and Dallenbach, Karl M. "The Effect of Type-Size on Accuracy of Apprehension and Speed of Localizing Words." *American Journal of Psychology,* 59 (April, 1946) 220–235.

[22] Gray, William S., and Leary, B. E. *What Makes a Book Readable.* University of Chicago Press, Chicago, 1935.

[23] Halbert, Marie Goodwin. "The Teaching Value of Illustrated Books." *American School Board Journal,* 108 (May, 1944) 43–44.

[24] Hildreth, Gertrude. *Teaching Reading.* Holt, Rinehart and Winston, Inc., New York, 1958.

[25] Hoffman, Arthur C. "Eye-Movements during Prolonged Reading." *Journal of Experimental Psychology,* 36 (April, 1946) 95–118.

[26] Hymes, David, *Production in Advertising and the Graphic Arts.* Holt, Rinehart and Winston, Inc., New York, 1958.

[27] Jones, Harold. "Readability and the Results of Applying a Readability Formula to Health Textbooks." *Readability: Finding Readable Material for Children,* Tenth Annual Conference on Reading, University of Pittsburgh, 1954, 56–66.

[28] Klare, George R. "Measures of the Readability of Written Communication: An Evaluation." *Journal of Educational Psychology,* 43 (November, 1952) 385–399.

[29] Klare, George R., Mabry, James E., and Gustafson, Levarl M. "The Relationship of Style Difficulty to Immediate Retention and to Acceptability of Technical Material." *Journal of Educational Psychology,* 46 (May, 1955) 287–295.

[30] Klare, George R., Shuford, Ener H., and Nickols, William H. "The Relationship of Style Difficulty, Practice, and Ability to Efficiency of Reading and to Retention." *Journal of Applied Psychology,* 41 (August, 1957) 222–226.

[31] Kress, Roy A. "Finding Readable Materials For Remedial Reading." *Readability: Finding Readable Material for Children,* Tenth Annual Conference on Reading, University of Pittsburgh, 1954, 94–112.

[32] Leary, B. E. "Difficulties in Reading Material." *Reading in General Education,* American Council on Education, Washington, 1940, 272–306.

[33] Lively, Bertha A., and Pressey, S. L. "A Method for Measuring the 'Vocabulary Burden' of Textbooks." *Educational Administration and Supervision,* 9 (October, 1923) 389–398.

[34] Lorge, Irving. "Predicting Readability." *Teachers College Record,* 45 (March, 1944) 404–419.

[35] Lorge, Irving. "Readability Formulae—An Evaluation." *Elementary English,* 26 (February, 1949), 86–95.

[36] Luckiesh, Matthew. *Light, Vision, and Seeing.* D. Van Nostrand Company, Inc., New York, 1944.

[37] Luckiesh, Matthew, and Moss, Frank K. *The Science of Seeing.* D. Van Nostrand Company, Inc., New York, 1937.

[38] Luckiesh, Matthew, and Moss, Frank K. "Effects of Leading on Readability." *Journal of Applied Psychology,* 22 (April, 1938) 140–160.

[39] Major, Alexander G. "Readability of College General Biology Textbooks and the Probable Effect of Readability Elements on Comprehension." *Dissertation Abstracts,* 15 (September, 1955) 1573–1574.

[40] Mallinson, George G., Sturm, Harold E., and Mallinson, Lois M. "The Reading Difficulty of Textbooks in Junior High School Science." *School Review,* 58 (December, 1950) 536–540.

[41] Mallinson, George G., Sturm, Harold E., and Mallinson, Lois M. "The Reading Difficulty of Textbooks for High School Physics." *Science Education,* 36 (February, 1952) 19–23.

[42] Mallinson, George G., Sturm, Harold E., and Patton, Robert E. "The Reading Difficulty of Textbooks in Elementary Science." *Elementary School Journal,* 50 (April, 1950) 460–463.

[43] Michaelis, John U., and Tyler, Fred T. "A Comparison of Reading Ability and Readability." *Journal of Educational Psychology,* 42 (December, 1951) 491–498.

[44] Paterson, Donald G., and Tinker, Miles A. *How to Make Type Readable.* Harper and Brothers, New York, 1940.

[45] Paterson, Donald G., and Tinker, Miles A. "Influence of Leading upon Readability of Newspaper Type." *Journal of Applied Psychology,* 31 (July, 1947) 160–163.

[46] Paterson, Donald G., and Tinker, Miles A. "The Effect of Typography Upon the Perceptual Span in Reading." *American Journal of Psychology,* 60 (July, 1947) 388–396.

[47] Peterson, Eleanor M. *Aspects of Readability in the Social Studies.* Bureau of Publications, Teachers College, Columbia University, New York, 1954.

[48] Robinson, Francis P. *Effective Study,* Harper and Brothers, New York, Revised edition, 1961.

[49] Rose, Florence C., and Rostas, Steven M. "The Effect of Illumination on Reading Rate and Comprehension of College Students." *Journal of Educational Psychology,* 37 (May, 1946) 279–292.

[50] Russell, David H. *Children Learn To Read.* Ginn and Company, Boston, 1949.

[51] Russell, David H. and Fea, Henry R. "Validity of Six Readability Formulas as Measures of Juvenile Fiction." *Elementary School Journal,* 52 (November, 1951) 135–144.

[52] Russell, David H., and Merrill, Anne F. "Children's Librarians Rate the Difficulty of Well-Known Juvenile Books." *Elementary English,* 28 (May, 1951) 263–268.

[53] Smith, Ruth I. "Readability of Social Studies Books and Materials." *Readability: Finding Readable Material For Children,* Tenth Annual Conference on Reading, University of Pittsburgh, 1954, 18–25.

[54] Sochor, Elona E. "Readiness and the Development of Reading Ability at All School Levels." *Education,* 74 (May, 1954) 555–560.

[55] Spache, George. "A New Readability Formula for Primary-Grade Reading Materials." *Elementary School Journal,* 53 (March, 1953) 410–413.

[56] Stone, Clarence R. "A Vocabulary Study Based on 107 Primary-Grade Books," *Elementary School Journal,* 42 (February, 1942) 452–455.

[57] Taylor, Cornelia D. "The Relative Legibility of Black and White Print." *Journal of Educational Psychology,* 25 (November, 1934) 561–578.

[58] Tinker, Miles A. "Illumination Standards for Effective and Comfortable Vision." *Journal of Consulting Psychology,* 3 (February, 1939) 11–20.

[59] Tinker, Miles A. "The Effect of Illumination Intensities upon Speed of Perception and upon Fatigue in Reading." *Journal of Educational Psychology,* 30 (November, 1939) 561–571.

[60] Tinker, Miles A. "Criteria for Determining the Readability of Type Faces." *Journal of Educational Psychology,* 35 (October, 1944) 385–396.

[61] Tinker, Miles A. "Validity of Frequency of Blinking as a Criterion of Readability." *Journal of Experimental Psychology,* 36 (October, 1946) 453–460.

[62] Tinker, Miles A. "Readability of Book Print and Newsprint in Terms of Blink-Rate." *Journal of Educational Psychology,* 39 (January, 1948) 35–39.

[63] Tinker, Miles A. "Cumulative Effect of Marginal Conditions upon Rate of Perception in Reading." *Journal of Applied Psychology,* 32 (October, 1948) 537–540.

[64] Tinker, Miles A. "The Effect of Intensity of Illumination upon Speed of Reading Six-Point Italic Print." *American Journal of Psychology,* 65 (October, 1952) 600–602.

[65] Tinker, Miles A. "The Effect of Typographical Variations Upon Eye Movement in Reading." *Journal of Educational Research,* 49 (November, 1955) 171–184.

[66] Tinker, Miles A. "Prolonged Reading Tasks in Visual Research." *Journal of Applied Psychology,* 39 (December, 1955) 444–446.

[67] Tinker, Miles A. "Recent Studies of Eye Movements in Reading." *Psychological Bulletin,* 55 (July, 1958) 215–231.

[68] Tinker, Miles A., and Paterson, Donald G. "Studies of the Typographical Factors Influencing Speed of Reading: VII. Variations in Color of Print and Background." *Journal of Applied Psychology,* 15 (October, 1931) 471–479.

[69] Tinker, Miles A., and Paterson, Donald G. "Effect of Line Width and Leading on Readability of Newspaper Type." *Journalism Quarterly,* 23 (September, 1946) 307–309.

[70] Tinker, Miles A., and Paterson, Donald G. "Speed of Reading Nine Point Type in Relation to Line Width and Leading." *Journal of Applied Psychology,* 33 (February, 1949) 81–82.

[71] Vogel, Mabel, and Washburne, Carleton. "An Objective Method of Determining Grade Placement of Children's Reading Material." *The Elementary School Journal,* 28 (January, 1928) 373–381.

[72] Walchak, Frank A. "Trends in the Readability of School Readers." *Readability: Finding Reading Material for Children,* Tenth Annual Conference on Reading, University of Pittsburgh, 1954, 138–148.

[73] Washburne, Carleton, and Morphett, Mabel Vogel. "Grade Placement of Children's Books." *Elementary School Journal,* 38 (January, 1938) 355–364.

[74] Wheeler, Lester R., and Smith, Edwin H. "A Practical Readability Formula for the Classroom Teacher in the Primary Grades." *Elementary English,* 31 (November, 1954) 397–399.

[75] Wilson, Mary Caroline. "The Effect of Amplifying Material Upon Comprehension." *Journal of Experimental Education,* 13 (September, 1944) 5–8.

[76] Witherington, H. Carl. "Readability of Textbooks in Educational Psychology." *Journal of Educational Research,* 46 (November, 1952) 227–230.

[77] Woody, Clifford. "Intrinsic Difficulties of Certain Reading Materials." *Peabody Journal of Education,* 17 (November, 1939) 149–160.

[78] Wyatt, Nita M., and Ridgway, Robert W. "A Study of the Readability of Selected Social Studies Materials." *Bulletin of Education,* University of Kansas, 12 (May, 1958) 100–105.

[79] Yoakam, Gerald A. "Determining the Readability of Instructional Materials." *Current Problems of Reading Instruction,* Seventh Annual Conference on Reading, University of Pittsburgh, 1951, 47–53.

10

MOTIVATION AND READING INTERESTS

We know that performance is closely dependent upon motivation. Without motivation learning seldom, if ever, occurs. The reading teacher employs his knowledge of motivated learning to direct children first toward learning to read and later toward reading to learn. Interests are closely related to motivation: they develop from attempts to satisfy basic motives. The teacher wants to know the factors that direct interest toward reading and that attract the child to specific reading content. Effective reading not only creates interests but it can be a product of interest as well.

In the preceding chapters we were concerned with how children learn to read. We have examined the perceptual nature, the learning principles, the basic skills, and some of the psychological and physiological bases of reading and reading readiness, and finally the readability and legibility of printed materials. We now return to consider additional factors that have a bearing on reading and achievement.

Here we will examine motivation and interests. We wish to know *why* children read and why they choose the specific materials that they do read. We wish to know what basic needs, if any, reading satisfies. We are concerned also with the type of reading material that will do most to encourage reading and, as an additional value, the materials that will do most to raise the general level of reading taste.

THE FRAMEWORK OF MOTIVATION

Numerous attempts have been made to form an ordered understanding of the structure of human motivation. One approach is to consider human motives as falling into three general categories—physiological motives, psychological motives, and habit motives.

PHYSIOLOGICAL MOTIVES

The physiological motives are sometimes spoken of as the primary motives or drives. They are the motives, including hunger, thirst, and the sex drive, that have provided for the very survival of man. Drive-reduction theories and Freudian and Lewinian psychologists have emphasized the physiological motives. In these theories needs are understood to be tensions related to organic disturbances.

Cannon [12] suggests that the organism strives to maintain a balance within the bodily tissues: the temperature of the body, the acidity and the sugar concentration of the blood, and the water and salt balance of the body can deviate only slightly without threat to the life of the organism. Cannon called this internal self-regulatory system "homeostasis." Whenever the body deviates from these "steady states," the organism is "motivated" to action.

We know, of course, that much of an infant's behavior is controlled by his visceral hungers. A child cries when he is hungry or thirsty. Even an adult is subject to physiological motivation. Under certain circumstances the need for air, water, or food may dominate behavior. Physical defects such as bad vision, poor hearing, endocrine disturbances, malnutrition, or illness of any kind may prevent a child from becoming interested in the educational tasks that we provide for him. Generally a normal child will not be lackadaisical, indifferent, and unconcerned; but we cannot expect a child who is faced with elemental threats to his survival to be interested in classroom learning.

Data gained from experiments demonstrate the responsiveness of animals to physiological needs. Removal of the parathyroid gland is followed by a sharp reduction in the calcium content of the blood. After such an operation a rat almost immediately seeks solutions containing large amounts of calcium. Experimenters have remarked that the animal's behavior seems to be governed by changes in his taste organs directing him to a food required for his survival. Similarly, loss of the pancreas is followed by avoidance of sugar, loss of the thyroid by building larger nests, and loss of the adrenal by seeking salt.[60, 81]

PSYCHOLOGICAL MOTIVES

Although much of man's basic animal behavior is governed by his physiological motives, fortunately behavior does not depend on physiological motives alone. Even though some psychologists suggest that all motives are reducible to organic needs and that tension reduction serves as an adequate explanation of human motivation,[64] we can best gain an understanding of human behavior by examining the so-called psychological motives. We know that children continue playing after their physiological need for exercise is adequately satisfied. Man does not always work to eat, as drive reduction theory might suggest; perhaps more often he eats to work. Nuttin [57] points out that the chief characteristic of the dynamic development of man is his inability to resign himself to rest and equilibrium. Even in the animal world physiological drive reduction seems inadequate to explain all behavior. Harlow [31] reports that rhesus monkeys learn even though they are fed prior to the experiment and are munching food during both right and wrong responses. He concludes that learning efficiency is much more closely related to tensions in the brain than in the belly.

As teachers we are likely to be far more interested in the psychological than in the physiological aspects of motivation. We are concerned with the conscious direction of a person's activity. Psychologists stress man's desire for self-actualization and realization of his potentialities (pp. 196–207).[25] Man wishes to use his abilities and his organs. If he can see, he is motivated to look. And if he can read, he is motivated to read. Man finds pleasure in the efficient use of his mind and hands.

Often an external object seems to exert a positive attraction. The child sometimes eats ice cream, not because he is hungry, but because of the peculiar qualities possessed by the ice cream. Thus objects sometimes appear to have valences of their own. They attract the individual. The task itself appeals: it challenges the individual; it upsets his mental equilibrium; it creates an anxiety that prompts him to give it his attention. Harlow [31] is convinced that the key to human learning is motivation aroused by external stimuli. This has important implications for reading instruction. Certainly high interest value is as important as constant repetition and drill.

As we examine the topic of motivation, we come to see the importance of psychological motives. Self-esteem, self-realization, curiosity, security, and a need to be adequate, successful, and to belong are the motives that most commonly energize human behavior. These needs and drives sometimes are referred to as secondary or learned motives, and it is assumed that they are extensions of the primary or unlearned motives. To teachers the importance of psychological motives lies not so much in how they become motives in their own right or whether or not they are derived from primary needs. Rather, we are interested in the fact that they function like primary drives in energizing and directing learning (p. 348).[69]

The psychological motives are particularly powerful because, unlike the physiological motives, they seldom if ever can be completely satisfied. For example, an individual may become satiated with food and water, but few persons have ever had all they desired of security, self-esteem, and the esteem of others. Curiosity, too, seems ever available as an energizer of classroom learning.

HABIT MOTIVES

It is well recognized that habits are formed through the repetition of some act that satisfies a motivating condition. However, once well formed, habits no longer need draw on other motives for energy. They acquire their own ability to energize. A child learns to read because he is motivated by basic, personal needs. But gradually, as he becomes skilled in reading, reading acquires a motivating force of its own. Allport (p. 201) [2] points out that a skill learned for some extraneous reason can turn into an interest and become self-propelling, even though the original reason for acquiring it has been lost.

INTEREST IN READING

As teachers, we are concerned with two somewhat distinct relationships of interest to reading—*interest in reading* and *reading interests*. First, let us examine interest in reading. Reading interests will be examined later in the chapter.

Interests are learned. They arise from the interaction of our basic needs and the means that we discover for satisfying them. Interest in reading parallels learning how to read. As William James suggested, "Only what we partly know already inspires us with a desire to know more" (p. 111).[41]

ATTITUDES AND INTERESTS

Attitudes and interests are closely related. Attitudes represent general predispositions, and specific interests operate within this broader sphere.

Sometimes interests are defined as positive attitudes toward objects or classes of objects to which we are attracted (p. 213).[22]

Ryans (p. 312) [63] says:

> An interest may be classified either as a trait or as an attitude, depending, largely, on whether it is broad or narrow in its reference. At any rate, interests are *learned* responses which predispose the organism to certain lines of activity and which definitely facilitate *attention.* A trait or an attitude may favor activity of a given sort without involving the clear awareness and concentrated activity involved when we are 'paying attention' to something.

Getzels (p. 7) [24] defines an interest as ". . . *a characteristic disposition, organized through experience, which impels an individual to seek out particular objects, activities, understanding, skills, or goals for attention or acquisition.*" *

Interest is closely related to meaning. The interest value of an object or event closely depends upon its meaning to the child. A book, "if it has no meaning—if it does not signify something to be picked up, handled, examined, avoided, played with, or otherwise used—creates no mental disturbance, and hence no interest . . ." (pp. 46–47).[79] Learning may be motivated by an "anxiety"—by a need to know. Interest is aroused only if something causes a mental disturbance. Only if the book disturbs is the child ready to "attend" to the book. It has then acquired meaning for him.

INFLUENCE OF INTEREST

Each child's intellectual, sensory, and physical capabilities and limitations are unique and they are powerful determinants of interest. To an extent his interest pattern will be determined by his special fitness. The agile child may turn to physical competition for enhancing his self-esteem, the manually adept may achieve his successes in arts or crafts, the intellectually favored may realize prestige in scholastic pursuits.

Lack of interest in reading may be an important cause of poor reading. Witty [87] reports a study of 100 boys and girls at the Northwestern University Laboratory. All were poor readers. Eighty-two showed a lack of interest in reading, and of these, 43 actually disliked reading. Other than lack of interest, he found few reasons for the poor reading. Only 14 had defective vision, three had defective hearing, and but four were left handed.

Nemoitin [53] studied the performance of 150 high school seniors and found a "substantial and marked relationship" between ability and interest.

---

* Copyright 1956 by the University of Chicago, reprinted by permission.

High interest in a subject tended to be associated with high ability in that subject, and low interest with low ability. Bernstein [8] reports that high interest in a subject often is associated with superior reading comprehension in that subject. She concluded that higher interest results in more creative responses or responses that show that pupils are reading actively and thinking about the material.

If the child is to learn to read, his interest somehow must be captured. He must need to learn to read. And, further, his interest must be retained. He must continue to need to read. Finally, however, reading itself can become a habitual activity and thus acquire a motivational force of its own. Wheat (pp. 57–58) [79] points out:

> As a person learns to read, reading enters his mental make-up as a permanent mode of behavior. . . . Henceforth he uses reading as a means of enjoyment and as a means of studying and thinking. To the extent that he can read with ease, reading is a major factor in the control of his behavior. He will often arrange his daily schedule of work and play in order to provide time for reading. He will make sacrifices in order to provide himself with books to read. He will turn to reading as a means of discovering new interests and of losing himself for a time from the actualities of the external world. It is at this point that we see the employment of advanced spontaneous attention. No longer is reading an end on the outside that conflicts with other tendencies. It is now a dominating interest that is within.

We now recognize that ". . . to increase reading skill, promote the reading habit, and produce a generation of book-lovers, there is no other factor so powerful as interest" (p. 536).[54]

With the advent of radio, movies, and television, teachers have become greatly concerned lest these reduce the amount that children will read. Almost universally, however, studies have shown a constant increase in the number of books that are being sold and the number that are being checked out from libraries.

Mauck and Swenson [49] in 1949 studied the leisure-time activities of 364 pupils in grades four through eight. Among all grades reading was found to rank fourth as a recreational interest. Sports, games, and radio received higher ratings. Sister Mary Edith and Sister Mary Amatora [21] report that children between the ages of seven and thirteen spend much of their leisure time in reading.

Studies at the adult level, however, indicate that there is less reason for optimism. In fact, beginning with the high-school years, other interests begin to take the place of reading. Barbe [6] reports that children with I.Q.'s of 130 and above do less reading after the age of twelve than they did before that age. We also know that persons differ greatly in the amount that they read. Rose [62] indicates that in the United States perhaps 75 per cent of adults read no books, and that only about one per cent read as many as five books a year. Link and Hopf [47] found that 21 per cent of the population read almost 70 per cent of the books and 50 per cent read 94 per cent of all books read.

If we are to expect children to maintain an interest in reading, we must be concerned with the literature we require them to read. In 1946, after a twelve-year study of children's interests, Norvell [54] suggested that three-fourths of the reading selections used in the schools should be replaced with equal-quality selections that are endorsed by children.

This raises some questions. Do our basal readers generally appeal to children or are they composed of such "pallid, insipid stuff" that it prompts the six-year-old to say: "The story sounds just like my little two-year-old brother talks" (p. 23).[36] Do the free-reading materials that we offer best fit our pupils' interest patterns? Why do young people tend to choose certain kinds of reading material at certain periods in their lives? Is the pupil's choice dictated by his age, his sex, his intelligence, his environment, or by combination of these and perhaps other factors? In short, what are the major determinants of reading interest?

DETERMINANTS OF READING INTEREST

Many writers have emphasized the importance of the reader's interests in promoting ability to read and encouraging and directing reading. First, of course, we must assume that a child can read at a level somewhat appropriate to his mental age before a discussion of reading interests is apropos. However, acquiring an ability to read is pointless unless that ability is used. As Strickland has said, a reader ". . . is not a person who can read; he is a person who does read" (p. 240).[68] Although in the primary grades the teacher's concern is fostering interest in developing basic reading skills, once children have acquired ability to read, the teacher's concern shifts to promoting reading development through a continuing interest in reading. Consequently, he makes use of each child's special interests to promote voluntary reading. Interests determine not only the area within which the child will make his reading choices but, more important, they determine how much he will read or even whether he will become a "reader" at all.

In the past 20 or so years much of the psychological research on interests has been concerned with their *stability* and *permanence* for predicting and guiding vocational choice. The educational psychologist, however, is more concerned with how interests develop and *change* through experience.

We know that the child's curiosity and his tendency to explore lead him to acquire certain of his interests. But his capabilities may play an even more significant role in the development of his interests. The boy who is skilled in crafts may be an avid reader of books dealing with scouting or camping but find most historical novels or biography boring. His capabilities affect both his *interest* and his *interests.*

Cultural factors, too, play an important role in determining our interests. We are directed toward certain interests through our membership in a particular culture, by specific religious affiliation, and by living in a certain country or specific area within a country. To a great extent society decides what interests are appropriate to our age and sex. Society does not expect the girl of 16 to engage in the doll play of the six-year-old. And 16-year-old girls do not enhance their self-esteem by being the neighborhood tomboys.

The schools likewise channel our interests toward certain ends. In general our schools emphasize middle-class attitudes, ideals, and standards of behavior. The pressures to do well in school, to seek social approval, and to obey adult authority are more peculiar to middle-class homes than to homes of either the upper or the lower socio-economic classes.

Numerous studies have shown that social factors are important directors of interest. Kaplan,[44] for example, reports that 45 University of Idaho students ascribed the origin of their vocational interest to school subjects; 43 mentioned the influence of their parents and friends; 36 were influenced by persons within the occupation; 29 had had work experience in the chosen occupation; and 27 were influenced by their teachers. And Dyer,[20] studying 101 University of Kansas juniors, seniors, and graduate students, found that 31 ascribed their choice of college majors to family influences, 14 to prior occupational experience, 10 to hobbies, and 12 to the influence of a teacher or course of studies.

Social influences also have been shown to be important determinants of reading choice. Wightman [80] long ago found that teachers exert a strong influence on children's preferences. The pupils generally preferred books that the teacher was enthusiastic about. He concluded that a teacher's enthusiasm was a vital determinant of reading preferences. Gray and Munroe (p. 162) [27] reported that adult interest in magazines and periodicals stemmed from home influences. They found that 98 per cent attributed their interest in newspapers to family influences; 84 per cent gave similar reasons for their interest in magazines; and 80 per cent felt that the home influenced their book-reading habits. The authors found that 60 per cent listed school experience as influencing their reading of books, but only 28 per cent as influencing their reading of magazines. College students, especially, felt that their school work had been a major determinant of their reading habits.

SOCIO-ECONOMIC FACTORS

The exact nature of the role of socio-economic status in determining whether a child will become a "reader" and his choice of reading matter is not clear. In an urban school system, Havighurst [33] classified children in grades five, six, and seven according to socio-economic status. Investigating the leisure-time activities of four socio-economic groups he found that reading books was ranked either sixth or seventh in each. A total of twelve different leisure-time activities was reported. This seems to indicate that the proportion of time spent in book reading is not highly related to socio-economic status but that the specific type of reading done may be highly related.

Witty and Moore,[93] compared the reading interests of Negro and white children in grades four, five, and six and found that Negro children read the same type of comic magazines as do white children, but read nearly 50 per cent more of them. No racial differences were found in the reading of comic strips. Link and Hopf,[47] however, besides showing that about 58 per cent of the books that are read are fictional in nature, report that the more years of formal education an individual has, the more books he tends to read. A positive, but not as significant, correlation exists between the number of books read and personal income or socio-economic status.

INTELLIGENCE AS A FACTOR

The influence of intelligence on the reading interests of children also is worth our attention. Barbe,[6] in a questionnaire study of the reading interests and habits of 103 ninth- and tenth-grade pupils with I.Q.'s of 130 or more, found that these children read about six hours weekly. And in general their areas of interest were on a slightly higher level than those of other children. The boys read mystery, biography, history, historical fiction, comics, science, sports, humor, and westerns; the girls read historical fiction, modern novels, biography, mystery, teen-age books, sports, animal stories, science, history, and books treating social problems. The magazine reading done by this group was very much like that of the groups of average intelligence. In newspaper reading, the sports pages, the funnies, and the front page received most attention.

Jordan,[43] analyzing a study by Lazar, concluded that in the intermediate grades "dull" boys like fairy tales, stories of school life, poetry, and mystery stories whereas bright boys prefer adventure stories and science magazines. Günzburg's [29] study of 30 below-normal students between the ages of twelve and fifteen indicates that these children choose books with familiar scenes and persons. They prefer homely and familiar settings and reject "an obtrusive historical or foreign canvas" beyond their comprehension. They seek materials with settings in which they feel secure.

Witty [86] found that the "Quiz Kids" showed a wide variety of interests. They read novels, biography, autobiography, drama, and Greek plays. In another study Witty and Lehman [92] found that children with an I.Q. of about 140 tend to choose books that are of a "high type."

Generally the studies indicate that children with a high I.Q. read books that are more difficult and more adult than do low I.Q. children of the same age. Mental age rather than the intelligence quotient appears to be the major factor and it seems to direct interest toward specific areas of content rather than toward reading as distinguished from other activities.

SEX DIFFERENCES

The play activities of six-year-old boys and six-year-old girls generally are quite different. The girl spends time with her dolls, her puzzles, coloring books, and her jacks. Her physical activities, which include rope jumping, hopscotch, and skating, emphasize skill rather than direct physical competition. The boy wrestles, plays tag, kick-the-can, hide-and-seek, and engages in other simple competitive games. Social pressures certainly promote early differences in play activity. Do they also promote later differences in reading interests?

Generally, it is found that girls are more interested in reading than are boys. Some writers suggest that the books used in the classroom are more in accord with girls' than with boys' interests.

Norvell made extensive studies of the reading interests of children in grades three through six [56] and seven through twelve.[55] He found that changes were more rapid during the elementary than during the junior or senior high school grades. He says that whereas during the primary and elementary school years increased maturity seems about as important as sex in determining reading choice, during the high school years the most powerful determinant is the sex of the reader. Unfortunately, from grades seven through twelve about two-thirds of the literature selections commonly used in the classroom are better liked by girls than by boys. We do not know how this affects general reading development. It seems likely that it contributes to the tendency for fewer boys than girls to be interested in reading.

On the basis of his study of children in grades four to twelve, Thorndike (p. 36) [70] felt that the sex of the reader is "conspicuously more important" than are age or intelligence in determining what children will read.

Norvell (p. 532) [54] found that in grades seven through twelve "Both sexes react favorably to adventure; humorous poems, stories, and essays. . . ; poems and stories of patriotism; stories of mystery, of games and of animals. Boys are more favorably inclined than are girls to strenuous adventure, including war, to stories of wild animals, to science, and to speeches. Girls react very favorably to romantic love, to sentiment in general, and to poems and stories of home and family life."

Butterworth and Thompson,[11] reporting a questionnaire study of the interests of 1,256 boys and girls in grades six to twelve, found that boys prefer the sports, crime, and humor comics whereas girls prefer comics dealing with the activities of adolescents and with humor. Boys seem to be attracted by action—girls by people.

In general we may conclude that girls read more than boys, but that among children below the third grade sexual differences in choice of reading interest are negligible. Gradually, however, the differences in interests between boys and girls diverge and this divergence is particularly prominent after the age of nine. From this point on boys tend to become increasingly interested in sports and adventure and girls in stories of a sentimental nature.

AGE AND INTERESTS

Some writers have suggested that interests are an expression of the child's stage of development. In adolescence, for example, the child has a strong need for success, and the characters of his books must be successful, be they athletes or romantic lovers. Carlsen [13] proposes that interests result from an emerging self-concept. It appears that books can help to build the self-concept: by strengthening the child's feeling of importance and confidence; by letting him see himself and his feelings and emotions as part of the normal pattern of all human life; and by helping him identify, accept, and prepare for the role that he is to assume in society as an adult.

Tyler has made a unique suggestion about how interests develop. After a longitudinal study [74, 75] of children's interests, she concluded that generally the younger child's attitude is favorable toward everything and his later interests are selected through his acquisition of dislikes!

Gray and Munroe summarized a number of early studies of reading interests. From their work the following trends may be identified (pp. 105–107) [27]:

1. At each age and grade level reading preferences vary widely.
2. Among both children and youth fiction is the favorite reading material, informational books are not widely read, and prose is chosen over poetry.
3. There are few sex differences in reading choice prior to ages eight or nine. Substantial differences appear after age ten.

4. Ages twelve to fifteen are a critical period in developing reading habits because of the rapid physical development and variety of potential activities and interests.
5. Reading interests are closely related to level of mental ability and the amount and type of material read depends closely upon the individual's skill in reading.

Wilson,[82] studying kindergarten, first-, and second-grade levels, found that children liked how-to-do-it books, comics, fairy tales, animal stories, nature stories, and adventure stories. Witty, Coomer, and McBean,[89] studying the interests of kindergarten and first-, second- and third-grade children, found that animal stories were enjoyed most. Fairy tales and humor were also prominent choices. Dunn,[19] studying first, second, and third graders, reports that boys preferred stories that provided surprise and those that included animal characters. Girls liked stories with child characters and with familiar experiences, repetition, and conversation. In general their reading interests and their understanding of the materials is promoted by plot, surprise, familiar experiences, liveliness, and a strong narrative element.

In the intermediate grades the interests of boys and girls become differentiated. Boys become more interested in "true to life" adventure stories; girls prefer stories of school and home. Prose is liked better than poetry by both boys and girls, and fiction is the dominant choice of prose.[49] However, informational materials are chosen if they are written to suit the child's age and mental level. Comics become especially popular. The theme of the fictional story or book is the most important factor in influencing the child's selection.

Sister Mary Edith and Sister Mary Amatora,[3, 21] in a four-year study of the interests of 724 elementary school children, report that age is an important determinant of theme interest. Second- and third-grade children are greatly interested in stories with child characters or animals. In grades five and six they become more interested in adventure, and by grade eight it is the dominant interest. Witty, Coomer, and McBean [89] studied the reading interests of 7,879 school children from kindergarten through grade eight. In the intermediate grades children selected books of a humorous nature, books of adventure, and books about children in other lands. In grades seven and eight action and adventure stories are preferred.

A study [30] of the reading interests of 300 boys and 266 girls in grades four to six of an elementary school in Jerusalem indicated that the boys preferred adventure, legends, historical stories, child life, fiction, humor, and science; the girls enjoyed child life, legends, historical stories, adventures, fiction, and humor.

It is during the junior high years that interest in reading reaches a peak;

the end of these years marks the beginning of a drop in interest in reading.

Zeller [97] studied 2,052 girls and 1,995 boys and found that the factors of "action" and "humor" exerted the greatest influence on the reading choices of junior high school students. Anderson,[4] studying 686 seventh- and eighth-grade children, found that comic books, fiction, animal stories, biography, and western stories were the most commonly read materials. In order of preference boys ranked comic books, animal stories, fiction, western stories, mechanical, and biography; girls preferred fiction, comic books, biography, animal stories, western stories, and music. McCarty [51] studied the reading records of 4,814 pupils, grades seven through twelve, and found that approximately 40 per cent of all reading was general fiction; 17 per cent, adventure; and 8 per cent, animal stories. Vandament and Thalman,[76] studying 1,034 children in grades six and ten, found a general preference for story books, with comics and magazines in second and third place. The sixth grade group read comics more frequently than magazines but the tenth-graders preferred magazines to comics. Boys preferred aggressive content and girls preferred social content.

Studies indicate that the interests of the adolescent are different from those of the pre-adolescent. Punke [59] studied the interests in newspapers and periodicals of boys and girls from eleven Georgia and eleven Illinois high schools. Girls preferred romance, society, and fashion; the boys liked sports, adventure, travel, mechanics, and politics.

Sterner (p. 60),[65] studying the interests of 372 high school pupils, found that the three most commonly chosen themes were adventure, humor, and love. Girls preferred romance themes. He observed that adventure is the favorite with adolescents, humor is a close second, and the love theme is especially popular with high school girls. In summarizing fifteen studies he found that boys like adventure, mystery, and action; girls prefer romance and stories about family life, but also like adventure and mystery (pp. 90–93).[65]

Helen M. Robinson,[61] summarizing the research of reading interests from the primary grades through high school, points out that primary children like stories about children and animals. In the intermediate grades interests diverge along sexual lines. The pre-adolescent boy prefers adventure stories, descriptions of "how-to-do-it," hero-worship, hobbies, and science. The pre-adolescent girl revels in fantasy adventure and stories about home and family life. During adolescence the boys turn to sports, mysteries and comics; girls like romance and stories dealing with teen-agers' problems.

Jordan,[43] too has pointed out that at the junior high school level war, humor, mischief, and tales about animals and new places interest the boys, whereas the girls prefer mystery, stories about home life, humor, and romance. In high school both sexes grow more interested in magazines, newspapers, and current affairs, but also keep their interest in science, adventure, and romance. Huddleston,[38] using as a point of reference the Teen-Age Book Club, discovered that the 90,000 members generally chose novels of adventure and romance.*

Jones,[42] on the basis of a questionnaire concerning the reading habits of 498 college students, reports that they had formed their reading interests long before they reached college. He identifies family background, social and economic circumstances, intellectual level, and previous school experience as determinants of these tastes. He adds that, according to this particular study, for most of the students college did not appear to have altered extracurricular-reading interests to an appreciable extent.

Using two stories of equal difficulty, one of which was full of suspense and youthful action and the other made up of paragraphs from a famous novel with long description of adult action, Bernstein [8] found that ninth graders comprehended the first type of story much more readily. She suggests that if the child is interested in what he reads, his comprehension is improved. The implications are obvious.

COMICS AND READING INTERESTS

In attempting to discover the typical reading interests of children we may gain some information from a study of their reading of comics. The fact is that over 90% of boys and girls between eight and thirteen do read comics.[95] There is a predominance of comic reading in the fourth, fifth, and sixth grades, but comics remain popular through high school. In fact, one study [88] indicates that at least one-fourth of the total number of magazines read are comics. It also has been shown that boys read slightly more comics than do girls.[83]

What causes this tremendous interest? Why is it that some 40 million comics were read each month in 1946 and some 90 to 95 million in each month in 1954 [94]?

Strang [66] interviewed 30 children in grades one through twelve and studied 150 written reports of comic-strip readers from high school and college classes. She found that comics provided adventure, suspense, plot, humor, escape, romance, and relaxation. They were cheap and the pictures aided in understanding the story. Frank [23] points out that comics are up-to-date, are full of action, are in colloquial language, and are easy to read.

---

* It is worth noting that five of the ten leading selections appeared at one time or another as motion pictures.

Murrell [52] calls attention to the action, pictures, excitement, and the adventure in comics. Malter [48] analyzed the themes of 185 comic magazines published in the first two months of 1951. Approximately eleven per cent of the space was allotted to westerns; next came adventure with 10.7 per cent; animal stories with 10.3 per cent; love stories, 10.2 per cent; detective stories, 9.3 per cent; and superman stories, 6.9 per cent.

Comics obviously have interest value. Many an adult finds it enjoyable to read, in comic book form, stories that he normally would not select if they were presented in ordinary book form or style. As teachers we are inclined to ignore their interest and bemoan the comics' lack of literary quality, their unreality, their use of slang, their unattractiveness and impermanence, and their possible degradation of taste and morals.

Actually we are not so much concerned that children read comics as we are that, as a result of their reading of comics, they may read less that is "educational" and has "social value." But, are comics completely lacking in educational value?

Hutchinson (p. 244),[39] in a questionnaire study of teachers who used the comic strips in Puck in a thirteen-week experimental program, makes the following statement:

> In general, the more frequent criticisms of using comics in the classroom were that current strips do not fit into the sequence of work going on in the classroom; education is serious business and should not be approached through levity; comics introduce improper language; they make learning too easy; parents misunderstand and misinterpret the purpose of comics in the classroom; teachers do not have time to do these extra things.

Incidentally, 79 per cent of the 438 teachers felt that the comic strips increased individual participation; 58 per cent thought they helped pupil-teacher relations; and 42 per cent felt they increased interest in reading. Certainly, these are desirable outcomes.

Thorndike,[71] after a study of *Superman, Batman, Action Comics,* and *Detective Comics,* found that each contained approximately 10,000 words. He concluded that although comics may have other vices or virtues, they *do* provide a substantial amount of reading experience at about the level of difficulty appropriate for the upper elementary school or even junior high school child.

The reading of comics does not seem to be a totally bad thing educationally. We can be grateful that the child wants to *read.* For some children comics may offer a first happy experience with reading.

Heisler, comparing children in grades two through eight who read comic books, attended movies, and listened to radio serials with those who did not, reported (p. 464) [35] that:

> . . . the reading of comic books seemed to have no effect educationally on the children. . . .
>
> The results of the study give very little help in determining just why some children are attracted to the comics while others are not. Intelligence seems to be ruled out as a factor since there were bright, average, and dull children among those of both the Comic and Non-Comic groups. Reading ability and size of the home library, too, seemed to have no influence. Personality was the only area where a difference appeared and this difference was not significant.

Both teachers and parents have expressed concern about the social and emotional effects of reading comics. Wertham (p. 10) [78] writes:

> Slowly, and at first reluctantly, I have come to the conclusion that this chronic stimulation, temptation, and seduction by comic books, both their content and their alluring advertisements of knives and guns, are contributing factors to many children's maladjustment.

Thomas Hoult,[37] studying 235 boys and girls, ages 10 to 17, who had been arrested for some reason and a comparable non-delinquent group of 235 boys and girls, found that the delinquent group read more comic books of a harmful, or at least questionable, content.

However, not all writers report a relationship between comic reading and maladjustment. Lewin,[46] studied a group of boys and reported that those with a high interest in comics were as well adjusted as those who showed little interest in comics.

Witty and Sizemore [95] point out that throughout history many different explanations of anti-social behavior have been advanced. At one time sociologists spoke of criminal types. Mental deficiency, poverty, broken homes, and lately, motion pictures and TV have been suggested as the major causes of delinquency. And, Thrasher [73] writes: "The current alarm over the evil effects of comic books rests upon nothing more substantial than the opinion and conjecture of a number of psychiatrists, lawyers, and judges." It seems possible that, instead of contributing to maladjustment, the excessive reading of comics may be, as Lewin [46] has suggested, merely a *symptom* of maladjustment.

The reading of violent comics need not necessarily be harmful. Comics may give the child a vicarious expression for his aggressive impulses. Abrahamsen has suggested that the performance of a criminal act in fantasy may tend to prevent the actual performance of it (pp. 31–32).[1]

Although there is no clear cut agreement concerning the relationship between the reading of comics and maladjustment, comics probably should be read with moderation. Arbuthnot [5] has said that, as long as children are also enjoying good books, there probably is little cause to worry about their reading comic strips. However, the fact remains that the various comics are not equally wholesome. There are some that may tend to disarm the child morally. If we accept the premise that reading can foster personal and social development and encourage children to mold their lives after persons portrayed in literature, then it is unwise to ignore the possibility that unwholesome comic books may pose a threat to the child's wholesome development. Some psychologists have lamented (p. 418) [26] that harm may be done:

> . . . by the stereotypes concerning race, nationality, morality, and ethics in comics, which popularize such assumptions as the following: people are either all good or all bad; oriental people are sinister villains; white people are superior; it is natural to seek revenge; foreign customs are inferior to American customs; education and serious books are dull business.

As teachers we must help the child to locate stimulating content that is free from these dangers. Perhaps we can begin by aiding the child to discriminate between the poorer and the better comics. And our awareness of the popularity of comics with children can be extremely useful. If we will identify the elements that make the comic attractive to children and then supply literature of good quality that contains those elements that catch and hold reader attention, the comics will have provided a force contributing toward improved interest in reading.

DEVELOPING INTERESTS AND TASTES

Before we can do much to improve a child's reading interests and tastes, we should know what his present interests and tastes are. We need more than a general knowledge of the interests of children. We can never be certain that any one child has the same interests as does the "average" child. Various methods have been developed for finding out what interests an individual child may have. Interest blanks or inventories are found in Harris (pp. 479, 482–483) [32]; Witty (pp. 302–307) [85]; Dolch (pp. 444–446) [17]; (pp. 121–123) [18] *; Witty and Kopel (pp. 185–188, 316–321) [90]; Witty, Kopel, and Coomer [91]; and Thorpe, Meyers, and Sea.[72]

DEVELOPING READING INTERESTS

If a child has an interest in reading, a major step has been taken toward developing reading interests. However, this is not the end of our concern for his reading development.

---

* Dolch reproduces an inventory from Witty and Kopel.[90]

We wish to guarantee that his interest in reading will persist and that his reading will be directed to materials that best appeal to his basic needs. By knowing what he now reads, we may gain clues to his special interests. We can then provide him with reading materials that appeal to his present interests and at the same time may prepare him for newer and more mature interests.

Jacobs (pp. 23–24) [40] has suggested that teachers can promote reading interests in a number of ways: *

1. Keep immediately available an attractive and well-balanced collection of reading matter that is just right in content, form, and readability for this particular group of children.
2. Help the individual child find the reading content that he cannot resist. . . .
3. Encourage children to share their reflections of the reading which they have done. . . .
4. Relate school reading experiences to other communication arts, particularly television, radio, motion pictures, recordings, the comics, and picture magazines. . . .
5. Read to children. . . .
6. Develop with the children suggested reading lists on topics that relate either to content areas or to special interests or to human relations or to personality development. . . .
7. Encourage children to interpret what they have read in other forms of symbolism—dramatics, painting, dioramas, sculpturing, puppetry, for example.
8. Utilize the facilities of book exhibits and book fairs for extending children's awareness of the great variety of stimulating reading matter available to them.
9. Have children keep informal records of their independent reading. . . .
10. Use only those evaluating procedures that concretely aid the child to assess realistically his present reading accomplishments and his blocks to even greater reading prowess.

We know that interests are developed through learning, imitation, and conscious emulation. Getzels [24] has suggested that need for identification also plays an important part in developing interests: *

> The original and most important objects of identification are the mother or mother-surrogate and the father or father-surrogate. If reading is important to these figures, reading will ordinarily also be important to the child. For in making his identifications, the child attempts to incorporate their values and interests.

The teacher, as a parent-substitute, serves as an object of identification.

> By means of the identification process the child incorporates the expectations, values, and interests of the teacher, and of course, if the teacher has a genuine interest in reading himself (I do not mean only *teaches* reading), the child will interiorize this interest. One cannot so much *teach* interests as *offer appropriate models for identification* (p. 9).[24]

The development of interests has been described as a lure and ladder procedure.[15] A child must be lured to new interests and then he must be offered a ladder of suitable materials. There is a great deal of similarity between methods for promoting reading interests and methods for promoting an interest in learning to read. The parent helps by providing an environment that stimulates the child to read. Magazines, books, story telling, and story reading are important. Reading projects in co-operation with school and community libraries may help to advance reading as a leisure-time interest. Bookmobiles may increase the availability of good books. A television program may provide a basis for interests that both lead to further reading and broaden present interests, increase vocabularies, and generally help children to understand the world about them. DeBoer [16] says that television may help children to improve their level of taste as well as their judgment of what they see and hear.

Bond and Tinker (p. 399) [10] suggest still other methods of stimulating interest. These include

> . . . (1) displays of book jackets and book advertisements, (2) a book club with its own pupil officers, (3) carefully organized and regularly changed book exhibits in a corridor case, (4) an attractive wall chart on which each pupil can list books he has read, and (5) *very brief* book reports.

Adults do not directly teach the child his interests so much as they provide opportunities for the pursuit of interests. Identification with parents and teachers may be an important determinant of the child's interests. In general, however, the adults' responsibility is to open all possible doors to appropriate reading material and try to provide situations that stir the child to action. McCallister (p. 154) [50] describes some of the ways this may be done.*

1. Introduce topics by means of films, visual aids, recordings, and other devices that will arouse interest and lead to voluntary reading.
2. Review or refer to books and articles that are relevant to the immediate assignment.

---

3. Display books, periodicals, and bulletins, that are appropriate to the interests and reading levels of students.
4. Provide class time for reading from the room library. . . .
5. Compare the treatment of a subject by two or more authors to excite curiosity.
6. Permit one or more students to discuss books or other references that are not assigned to all members of the class.
7. Arrange for students to report reading experiences in panels or round-table discussions.
8. Permit friends to work together; sometimes better readers may help poor readers.

Yoakam [96] has said that the teacher must be aware of the fundamental interests of children. These interests are the result of experience and are susceptible to nurture. This is an important point of view. The teacher should not feed the student only what he already likes. He must stimulate the child's appetite for other fare and thus increase the variety of his interests.

DEVELOPING READING TASTES

Developing reading tastes is a step beyond developing an interest in reading. We frequently hear that children do not read, that the quality of what they read is exceedingly inferior, and that schools are failing to promote a persisting interest in reading.[84] In 1937 Betzner and Lyman [9] suggested that the preference for inferior reading material among secondary-school and college students as well as among adults might be a rebellion against the extensive amounts of uninteresting reading they were required to do in various school subjects.

To offer the child maximum help in improving his reading tastes, we need as much knowledge as possible in each of two areas: we must know the child and we must be well acquainted with the books to which we lead him. We must know his general ability and the level of his reading ability. We must know his interests and the time he has available for reading. When we suggest a book we must know that it is appropriate to his abilities and interests.

Unfortunately we frequently suggest books that are too difficult. Painter and Franzen [58] report that most of 22 junior and senior high school books they examined had higher difficulty placement than interest placement. We must remember that a child's liking for a book is dependent upon his understanding of it. Moreover

> . . . the most carefully chosen book may do little for a child unless, first, his motivation for reading is strong; and, second, our motivation for recommending it is the belief that it will help him get understanding, meet quandaries,

solve problems, face impending defeat, and live a fuller and happier life in today's world (p. 39).[45]

Still another point may be considered. Interest in reading usually leads to more reading and generally this promotes a growth in reading tastes. Harris (p. 491) [32] makes a pertinent observation:

> Children do not develop discrimination by being allowed contact only with superior reading matter; on the contrary, it is often found that the brightest children and most voracious readers read much that is of a trashy nature, as well as much that is good. Taste develops through comparison and contrast, not from ignorance.

As taste improves, interest in reading is likely to be still further stimulated. And the more proficient a child becomes in reading the better are his chances for developing more refined tastes. Through intelligent direction progression can be from narrower to broader interests, from lower levels of taste to higher levels. But basic to all progress in reading is this: the child must learn to read and he must find reading enjoyable.

SUMMARY

The development of a habit of reading for all normal children may well be one of the most important objectives of the school. Our educational goal is children who *will* read rather than merely children who *can* read.

To become a "reader" the child must first find in reading a satisfaction for his needs for self-esteem, the esteem of others, security, and new experiences. We know that reading proficiency builds reading interest and, in turn, reading interest fosters reading proficiency. One must understand to be interested, and when one is interested he strives to understand.

In guiding the child's interests in reading we must lure him to want to read and we must offer him a ladder of materials that lead him to become a more competent and discriminating reader.

SUGGESTED READINGS

For a background discussion of motivation and interests:

Smith, Henry P., Chapter 7, "Motivation: The Why of Human Behavior," pp. 185–207 in *Psychology in Teaching*. Englewood Cliffs, N. J.: Prentice-Hall, Inc., 1954.

***

For a review of the literature on types, determinants, and stability of interests (with bibliography):

Super, Donald E. "Interests," pp. 728–733 in *Encyclopedia of Educational Research,* Chester W. Harris (Ed.), 3rd Ed. New York: The Macmillan Company, 1960.

***

For detailed discussions of various aspects of the problem of promoting and guiding reading interests from kindergarten to adult level with professional references and book lists for different grades.

Robinson, Helen M. (Ed.), *Developing Permanent Interest in Reading.* Supplementary Educational Monographs, No. 84, University of Chicago Press, Chicago (December, 1956), 224 p.

***

(Causey, *The Reading Teacher's Reader*)

Article 34, Schubert, Delwyn G., "Interest—A Key to Reading Retardation," from *Elementary English,* 30 (December, 1953) pp. 518–520.

Article 35, Dolch, E. W., "Success in Remedial Reading," from *Elementary English,* 30 (March, 1953) pp. 133–137.

QUESTIONS FOR DISCUSSION

1. What is meant by *motivation?* How is it related to an effective learning situation?
2. Suggest reasons for the presence of physiological motives in man. Psychological motives. Habit motives.
3. Is there any evidence as to which types of motives are stronger? Discuss.
4. What advantages may psychological motives have over physiological motives for energizing and directing classroom learnings?
5. How does an interest differ from a motive? How are interests acquired?
6. How are attitudes and interests alike? How are they different? How are interests related to abilities?
7. What factors determine whether or not a child will have an interest in reading?
8. How are reading interests measured? What is known about reading interests of school-age persons?
9. What are some of the most important correlates of interest in reading and of special reading interests? Discuss.
10. What may the school do to encourage the development of reading interests and raise the level of reading tastes?
11. What are some of the relationships between interest and attitude?
12. What are the arguments for and against children's reading comic books?
13. Discuss the correlates of interests.

BIBLIOGRAPHY

[1] Abrahamsen, David. *Crime and the Human Mind.* Columbia University Press, New York, 1941.

[2] Allport, Gordon W. *Personality: A Psychological Interpretation.* Henry Holt and Company, New York, 1937.

[3] Amatora, Sister Mary, and Edith, Sister Mary. "Children's Interest in Free Reading." *School and Society,* 73 (March 3, 1951) 134–137.

[4] Anderson, Esther M. "A Study of Leisure-Time Reading of Pupils in Junior High School." *Elementary School Journal,* 48 (January, 1948) 258–267.

[5] Arbuthnot, Mary Hill. "Children and the Comics." *Elementary English,* 24 (March, 1947) 171–183.

[6] Barbe, Walter B. "A Study of the Reading of Gifted High-School Students." *Educational Administration and Supervision,* 38 (March, 1952) 148–154.

[7] Bender, Lauretta, and Lowrie, Reginald S. "The Effect of Comic Books on the Ideology of Children." *American Journal of Orthopsychiatry,* 11 (July, 1941) 540–550.

[8] Bernstein, Margery R. "Relationship between Interest and Reading Comprehension." *Journal of Educational Research,* 49 (December, 1955) 283–288.

[9] Betzner, Jean, and Lyman, R. L. "The Development of Reading Interests and Tastes." *The Teaching of Reading: A Second Report,* Thirty-sixth Yearbook of the National Society for the Study of Education, Part I, Public School Publishing Co., Bloomington, Ill., 185–205.

[10] Bond, Guy L., and Tinker, Miles A. *Reading Difficulties: Their Diagnosis and Correction.* Appleton-Century-Crofts, Inc., New York, 1957.

[11] Butterworth, Robert F., and Thompson, George G. "Factors Related to Age-Grade Trends and Sex Differences in Children's Preferences for Comic Books." *Journal of Genetic Psychology,* 78 (March, 1951) 71–96.

[12] Cannon, Walter B. *The Wisdom of the Body.* W. W. Norton and Company, New York, 1939.

[13] Carlsen, G. R. "Behind Reading Interests." *The English Journal,* 43 (January, 1954) 7–12.

[14] Chase, W. Linwood. "Subject Preferences of Fifth-Grade Children." *Elementary School Journal,* 50 (December, 1949) 204–211.

[15] Committee of the Upper Grades Study Council. "Developing the Reading Interests of Children." *Elementary English Review,* 20 (November, 1943) 279–286.

[16] DeBoer, John J. "Reading the Mass Media of Communication." *Mass Communication: A Reading Process,* Sixteenth Yearbook of the Claremont College Reading Conference, Claremont, 1951, 27–36.

[17] Dolch, E. W. *A Manual For Remedial Reading,* 2nd Edition. The Garrard Press, Champaign, 1945.

[18] Dolch, E. W. *Psychology and Teaching of Reading,* Revised, 2nd Edition. The Garrard Press, Champaign, 1951.

[19] Dunn, Fannie Wyche. *Interest Factors in Primary Reading Material.* Contributions to Education, No. 113, Bureau of Publications. Teachers College, Columbia University, 1921.

[20] Dyer, John Ruskin. "Sources and Permanence of Vocational Interests of College Men—101 Cases over Five Year Period." *Journal of Applied Psychology,* 16 (June, 1932) 233–240.

[21] Edith, Sister Mary, and Amatora, Sister Mary. "The Age Factor in Children's Interest in Free Reading." *Education,* 71 (May, 1951) 567–571.

[22] Eysenck, H. J. *The Structure of Human Personality.* Methuen and Company, Ltd., London, 1953.

[23] Frank, Josette. "What's in the Comics." *The Journal of Educational Sociology,* 18 (December, 1944) 214–222.

[24] Getzels, Jacob W. "The Nature of Reading Interests: Psychological Aspects." *Developing Permanent Interest in Reading,* Supplementary Educational Monographs, No. 84, University of Chicago Press, Chicago, 1956, 5–9.

[25] Goldstein, Kurt. *The Organism.* American Book Company, New York, 1939.

[26] Gray, Lillian, and Reese, Dora. *Teaching Children to Read.* Ronald Press Company, New York, 1957.

[27] Gray, William S., and Munroe, Ruth. *The Reading Interests and Habits of Adults.* The Macmillan Company, New York, 1929.

[28] Gunderson, Agnes G. "What Seven-Year-Olds Like in Books." *Elementary English,* 30 (March, 1953) 163–166.

[29] Günzburg, H. C. "The Subnormal Boy and His Reading Interests." *Library Quarterly,* 18 (October, 1948) 264–274.

[30] Haramati, Sh. "Hitany 'nutam shel y'ladim Bikria." "Reading Interests of Children." *Hahinuh,* 26 (1953–1954) 401–420; *Psychological Abstracts,* 30 (February, 1956) 1510.

[31] Harlow, H. F. "Mice, Monkeys, Men, and Motives." *Psychological Review,* 60 (January, 1953) 23–32.

[32] Harris, Albert J. *How to Increase Reading Ability,* 3rd Edition. Longmans, Green and Company, New York, 1956.

[33] Havighurst, Robert J. "Relations Between Leisure Activities and the Socio-Economic Status of Children." *Growing Points in Educational Research,* Official Report, American Educational Research Association, 1949, 201–208.

[34] Hebb, Donald O. "Drives and the C. N. S. (Conceptual Nervous System)." *Psychological Review,* 62 (July, 1955) 243–254.

[35] Heisler, Florence. "A Comparison of Comic Book and Non-Comic Book Readers of the Elementary School." *Journal of Educational Research,* 40 (February, 1947) 458–464.

[36] Hester, Kathleen B. "The Nature and Scope of Reading Programs Adapted to Today's Needs: Discussion." *Better Readers For Our Times.* International Reading Association, Conference Proceedings, Scholastic Magazines, New York, 1956, 23.

[37] Hoult, Thomas F. "Comic Books and Juvenile Delinquency." *Sociology and Social Research,* 33 (March–April, 1949) 279–284.

[38] Huddleston, Martha. "Teen-Age Reading Habits." *Wilson Library Bulletin,* 22 (September, 1947) 53, 68.

[39] Hutchinson, Katherine H. "An Experiment in the Use of Comics as Instructional Material." *The Journal of Educational Sociology,* 23 (December, 1949) 236–245.

[40] Jacobs, Leland B. "Goals in Promoting Permanent Reading Interests." *Developing Permanent Interest in Reading,* Supplementary Educational Monographs, No. 84, University of Chicago Press, Chicago, 1956, 20–25.

[41] James, William. *Principles of Psychology,* Vol. 2. Henry Holt and Company, 1890.

[42] Jones, Harold D. "The Extracurricular Reading Interests of Students in a State College." *School and Society,* 72 (July 15, 1950) 40–43.

[43] Jordan, A. M. "Children's Interests in Reading." *High School Journal,* 25 (November–December, 1942) 323–330.

[44] Kaplan, Oscar J. "Age and Vocational Choice." *Pedagogical Seminary and Journal of Genetic Psychology,* 68 (March, 1946) 131–134.

[45] Leary, Bernice E. "Meeting the Needs of Children Through Literature." *Current Problems of Reading Instruction,* Seventh Annual Conference on Reading, University of Pittsburgh Press, Pittsburgh, 1951, 36–39.

[46] Lewin, Herbert S. "Facts and Fears About the Comics." *Nation's Schools,* 52 (July, 1953) 46–48.

[47] Link, Henry C., and Hopf, Harry A. *People and Books,* Book Manufacturers' Institute, New York, 1946. Abridged in Hunnicutt, C. W., and Iverson, William J. *Research in the Three R's.* Harper and Brothers, New York, 1958, 6–9.

[48] Malter, Morton S. "The Content of Current Comic Magazines." *Elementary School Journal,* 52 (May, 1952) 505–510.

[49] Mauck, Inez L., and Swenson, Esther J. "A Study of Children's Recreational Reading." *Elementary School Journal,* 50 (November, 1949) 144–150.

[50] McCallister, James M. "Using the Content Subjects to Promote Reading Interests: In Grades Ten Through Fourteen." *Developing Permanent Interest in Reading,* Supplementary Educational Monographs, No. 84, University of Chicago Press, Chicago, 1956, 153–157.

[51] McCarty, Pearl S. "Reading Interests Shown by Choices of Books in School Libraries." *School Review,* 58 (February, 1950) 90–96.

[52] Murrell, Jesse L. "Annual Rating of Comic Magazines." *Parent's Magazine,* 27 (November, 1952) 48.

[53] Nemoitin, Bernard O. "Relation Between Interest and Achievement." *Journal of Applied Psychology.* 16 (No. 1, 1932) 59–73.

[54] Norvell, George W. "Some Results of a Twelve-Year Study of Children's Reading Interests." *English Journal,* 35 (December, 1946) 531–536.

[55] Norvell, George W. *The Reading Interests of Young People.* D. C. Heath and Company, Boston, 1950.

[56] Norvell, George W. *What Boys and Girls Like to Read,* Silver Burdett Company, Morristown, N. J., 1958.

[57] Nuttin, Joseph. "Personality." *Annual Review of Psychology,* Vol. 6, ed. by C. P. Stone and Q. McNemar, Annual Reviews Inc., Stanford, 1955, 161–186.

[58] Painter, Helen Welch, and Franzen, Carl G. F. "A Synthesis of Research on the Placement of Reading Material in Secondary School Literature." *Journal of Educational Research,* 39 (December, 1945) 304–306.

[59] Punke, Harold H. "The Home and Adolescent Reading Interests." *School Review,* 45 (October, 1937) 612–620.

[60] Richter, Curt P., and Eckert, John F. "Mineral Appetite of Parathyroid-

ectomized Rats." *American Journal of the Medical Sciences,* 198 (July, 1939) 9–16.

[61] Robinson, Helen M. "What Research Says to the Teacher of Reading: Reading Interests." *The Reading Teacher,* 8 (February, 1955) 173–177.

[62] Rose, Elizabeth. "Literature in the Junior High." *English Journal,* 44 (March, 1955) 141–147.

[63] Ryans, David G. "Motivation in Learning." pp. 289–331 in *Psychology of Learning.* Forty-first Yearbook of the National Society for the Study of Education, Part II, University of Chicago Press, Chicago, 1942.

[64] Scheerer, Martin. "Cognitive Theory." *Handbook of Social Psychology,* Vol. I, ed. by Gardner Lindzey, Addison-Wesley Publishing Company, Cambridge, 1954, 91–142.

[65] Sterner, Alice P. *Radio, Motion Picture, and Reading Interests: A Study of High School Pupils.* Contributions to Education, No. 932, Bureau of Publications, Teachers College, Columbia University, 1947.

[66] Strang, Ruth. "Why Children Read the Comics." *Elementary School Journal,* 43 (February, 1943) 336–342.

[67] Strang, Ruth. "Interest as a Dynamic Force in the Improvement of Reading." *Elementary English,* 34 (March, 1957) 170–176.

[68] Strickland, Ruth G. "Children, Reading, and Creativity." *Elementary English,* 34 (April, 1957) 234–241.

[69] Stroud, James B. *Psychology in Education.* Longmans, Green and Company, New York, 1956.

[70] Thorndike, Robert L. *Children's Reading Interests.* Bureau of Publications, Teachers College, Columbia University, New York, 1941.

[71] Thorndike, Robert L. "Words and the Comics." *Journal of Experimental Education,* 10 (December, 1941) 110–113.

[72] Thorpe, L. P., Myers, C. E., and Sea, M. R. *What I Like to Do; An Inventory of Children's Interests, Grades 4–6.* Science Research Associates, Chicago, 1954.

[73] Thrasher, Frederic M. "The Comics and Delinquency: Cause or Scapegoat." *Journal of Educational Sociology,* 23 (December, 1949) 195–205.

[74] Tyler, Leona E. "The Relationship of Interests to Abilities and Reputation Among First-Grade Children." *Educational and Psychological Measurement,* II (No. 3, 1951) 255–264.

[75] Tyler, Leona E. "The Development of Vocational Interests: I. The Organization of Likes and Dislikes in Ten-Year-Old Children." *Journal of Genetic Psychology,* 86 (March, 1955) 33–44.

[76] Vandament, William E., and Thalman, W. A. "An Investigation into the Reading Interests of Children." *Journal of Educational Research,* 49 (February, 1956) 467–470.

[77] Vandeberg, Ethyl. "Readiness for Language Arts Begins in the Kindergarten." *Elementary School Journal,* 53 (April, 1953) 447–453.

[78] Wertham, Fredric. *Seduction of the Innocent.* Holt, Rinehart and Winston, Inc., New York, 1954.

[79] Wheat, H. G. *Foundations of School Learning.* Alfred A. Knopf, New York, 1955.

[80] Wightman, H. J. "A Study of Reading Appreciation." *American School Board Journal,* 50 (June, 1915) 42.

[81] Wilkins, Lawson, and Richter, Curt P. "A Great Craving for Salt by a Child with Cortico-Adrenal Insufficiency." *Journal of American Medical Association.* 114 (March, 1940) 866–868.

[82] Wilson, Frank T. "Reading Interests of Young Children." *Journal of Genetic Psychology,* 58 (June, 1941) 363–389.

[83] Witty, Paul. "Reading the Comics—A Comparative Study." *Journal of Experimental Education,* 10 (December, 1941) 105–109.

[84] Witty, Paul. "Current Role and Effectiveness of Reading Among Youth." *Reading in the High School and College,* Forty-seventh Yearbook of the National Society for the Study of Education, Part II, University of Chicago Press, Chicago, 1948, 8–26.

[85] Witty, Paul. *Reading in Modern Education.* D. C. Heath and Company, Boston, 1949.

[86] Witty, Paul. "A Study of Graduates of the 'Quiz Kids' Program." *Educational Administration and Supervision,* 38 (May, 1952) 257–271.

[87] Witty, Paul. "Interest and Success—The Antidote to Stress." *Elementary English,* 32 (December, 1955) 507–513.

[88] Witty, Paul, and Coomer, Anne. "Reading the Comics in Grades IX to XII." *Educational Administration and Supervision,* 28 (May, 1942) 344–353.

[89] Witty, Paul, Coomer, Anne, and McBean, Dilla. "Children's Choices of Favorite Books: A Study Conducted in Ten Elementary Schools." *Journal of Educational Psychology,* 37 (May, 1946) 266–278.

[90] Witty, Paul, and Kopel, David. *Reading and the Educative Process.* Ginn and Company, Boston, 1939.

[91] Witty, Paul, Kopel, David, and Coomer, Anne. *The Northwestern Interest Inventory.* Psycho-Educational Clinic, Northwestern University, 1949.

[92] Witty, Paul, and Lehman, Harvey C. "The Reading and the Reading Interests of Gifted Children." *Pedagogical Seminary,* 45 (December, 1934) 466–481.

[93] Witty, Paul, and Moore, Dorothy. "Interest in Reading the Comics Among Negro Children." *Journal of Educational Psychology,* 36 (May, 1945) 303–308.

[94] Witty, Paul, and Sizemore, Robert A. "Reading the Comics: A Summary of Studies and an Evaluation, I." *Elementary English,* 31 (December, 1954) 501–506.

[95] Witty, Paul, and Sizemore, Robert A. "Reading the Comics: A Summary of Studies and an Evaluation, III." *Elementary English,* 32 (February, 1955) 109–114.

[96] Yoakam, Gerald A. "Fundamental Principles Concerning Reading and the Teaching of Reading." *Current Problems of Reading Instruction,* Seventh Annual Conference of Reading, University of Pittsburgh Press, 1951, 11–21.

[97] Zeller, Dale. *Relative Importance of Factors of Interest in Reading Materials for Junior High School Pupils.* Contributions to Education, No. 841, Bureau of Publications, Teachers College, Columbia University, 1941.

11

PERSONALITY FACTORS IN THE READING PROCESS

The children in our classroom differ greatly in personality. To plan appropriate educational experiences, we must understand the nature of personality development and become able to recognize the common emotional and maturational deviations. We are especially concerned with the personality patterns that are related to success or failure in reading. We must know what adjustments can be made for personality differences and, further, how reading may be used to influence personality development.

The teacher of reading needs to understand the facts and principles of personality development and the symptoms of adjustment problems. He needs to be able to interpret pupil behavior. Although recently teacher-preparation programs have put increasing emphasis on educational psychology and mental hygiene, many teachers recognize that they need to know still more about the nature of personal adjustment and maladjustment. Wickman [62] and Sparks,[52] in separate studies, found that teachers are likely to be more concerned with behaviors that result in classroom problems or that are related to moral issues than they are with behaviors indicating a threat to the child's long-range emotional health. For example, teachers were especially concerned with lying, stealing, and cheating. They tended to judge the child's adjustment by his obedience, truthfulness, and amenability to the imposed requirements of study and classroom order (p. 77).[62] Psychologists, on the other hand, generally recommend that symptoms of withdrawal should be of most concern since withdrawal is more likely to lead to mental illness.

Stouffer and Owens,[53] also, have studied teachers' attitudes toward children's behavior. They analyzed the questionnaire responses of 232 teachers who had indicated that they were not familiar with Wickman's study. These teachers considered stealing, cheating, lying, and exhibition of disrepect to be signs of serious maladjustment. They were more concerned with carelessness, laziness, and truancy than with discouragement, resentfulness, unsociability, nervousness, unhappiness, depression, and shyness. It was the writers' conclusion that today's teachers still consider annoying, disorderly, irresponsible, aggressive, untruthful, and disobedient behavior the chief symptoms of maladjustment. Certainly some teachers have not become sufficiently aware that withdrawal may be a symptom of serious threat to the child's emotional health and that, actually, a certain amount of aggressive behavior is normal—not abnormal.

READING AND ADJUSTMENT

We wish to know how a child's personality traits may influence his reading and how reading failure or success may influence the development of the child's personality. We are concerned particularly with individual differences in emotional reactions. Studies have shown that the incidence of maladjustments among poor readers is significantly greater than among good readers. Why is this so? Does proficiency in reading tend to promote good adjustment? Does reading deficiency contribute to emotional deviation? In short, does maladjustment tend to cause reading failure or does reading failure tend to cause maladjustment? Or does the cause–effect relationship vary from case to case? Actually, we may find it difficult to establish whether personality maladjustment is the cause, the effect, or a concomitant circumstance.

Everyone needs security, success, and social acceptance. Failure of any kind threatens both one's self-esteem and the esteem he receives from others. Failure in reading may pose a large and continuing block to the child's normal emotional development. The child who cannot read is deprived of a means for widening his interests, for satisfying his needs for new experiences, for filling his leisure time, and for promoting his emotional and social adjustment. Thus reading failure blocks the child from adequate communication with an important portion of his world.

Psychologists recognize that we are attracted to the persons and the situations that serve to satisfy our motives. When we say that something is rewarding we mean that it is satisfying to one or more of our basic motives (p. 562).[57] For him to find it rewarding the reading situation must prove satisfying to the child. And only if it is rewarding will he identify himself positively with it. Not only does inadequate achievement in reading lead to negative identification with reading itself, but it makes other aspects of the school, including persons identified with it, unattractive.

Because, in our culture, reading is an essential developmental task, failure in reading prevents adequate adjustment. There is no satisfactory substitute for success in reading. A reading disability is a disability in almost every area of learning.

To the extent that reading failure blocks the child's attempts to satisfy his needs, reading failure may be said to cause the emotional disturbances that accompany an inability to satisfy these needs.

The human individual is a unified organism. His various needs and drives are not independent subdivisions but are interrelating aspects of his total personality. As we study the human personality we see that the individual's conception of himself is the unifying force.[9] How he views himself will determine how he views his world and to a large extent how his world views him. White points out that without the self-concept we can find no point of anchorage for an interpretation of the pattern of tendencies that is characteristic of each individual. The self-concept functions as an integrating force and each person's self-concept is different from that of any other person (p. 156).[61] Although the self-concept is the unifying force within the individual's personality, nevertheless it is ever changing and growing. The self-concept cannot remain static, but change and growth derive direction from the existing self-concept. The self has needs that demand satisfaction. Let us examine the relationship between reading and the satisfaction of some of these basic needs.

SELF-ESTEEM

We all strive for self-esteem. We acquire and nurture it through success in dealing with our environment. It is closely related to our need for the esteem of others but it goes beyond that.

Silverberg (p. 29) [46] writes:

> Throughout life self-esteem has these two sources: an inner source, the degree of effectiveness of one's own aggression; and an external source, the opinions of others about oneself. Both are important, but the former is the steadier and more dependable one. . . .

Because of their necessary dependence and their domination by others, particularly their parents, many children come to school with very little self-confidence. The school must help these children acquire feelings of success and achievement. Unfortunately, our academic program tends to emphasize intelligence and intellectual pursuits, and the child who is lacking in these areas constantly feels threatened. White has pointed out that high intelligence favors adjustment and low intelligence obstructs it (p. 167).[61] He indicates that those with I. Q.'s ranging from 50 to 90 have a particularly difficult problem in achieving self respect.

Inferiority feelings develop when the child can find no way of acquiring a sufficient amount of self-esteem. A child needs to feel adequate. To do so he must find success in some area. Slavson (p. 20) [47] emphasizes this when he points out that:

> Success gives one the sense of self-worth which is essential to wholesome character formation. The need for success and achievement is . . . derivative from our culture, and is determined by comparison with others in the group. When this comparison is unfavorable, feelings of inferiority and intrapsychic tensions are set up which frequently find release in dissocial behavior or neurotic symptoms or both.

Even though a child is well-endowed intellectually, his school experiences may prove frustrating. A special reading disability may place a child in this situation and result in conflict with his environment. Blanchard (p. 787) [11] indicates that:

> When the reading disability persists over a period of years, it leads to failures in school and thus sets up a feeling of inferiority in the individual.
>
> Unless adequate and socially acceptable compensations for the feelings of inferiority are developed, personality and behavior deviations are apt to arise.

ESTEEM OF OTHERS

The child's personality is developed also through his interactions with others. He needs social acceptance, but full social acceptance seldom is extended to those considered "stupid," "slow learners," or "remedial cases."

Abel and Kinder (pp. 51–52) [1] mention some of the problems encountered by the subnormal adolescent girl:

> When a child's intellectual limitations become unmistakably apparent, she is generally placed in one of two situations, depending on the type of school system to which she belongs. If no special classes are available for the mentally retarded, the girl remains in the regular classes, usually repeating grades and acquiring a reputation of being both dull and the perennial despair of teachers. If a school system provides special classes, the subnormal girl may find the work she is expected to do much easier and more in keeping with her interests. But she still has to combat the disapprobation of more intelligent girls, who remain in the regular classes and make her feel inferior in some way. Either course lessens her possibilities for later adjustment by emphasizing her feeling of inferiority.

The psychologist recognizes that each experience affects the entire organism. Poor reading ability not only contributes directly to a sense of inadequacy but it threatens social acceptance. It makes the child an object of bad publicity as it were. Such a child suffers social humiliation and hurt. He is bound to feel ashamed. He is likely to become shy and withdrawn. Reading failure frequently is interpreted as a sign of stupidity, both by other students and by the poor reader himself. Failure tends to breed more failure, just as success tends to lead to more success. In such circumstances the reading failure seems likely to precipitate emotional maladjustment. This may be reason enough for the personal problems that frequently accompany serious reading problems.

And in numerous ways parents create problems for their children. If a child is somewhat retarded mentally, parents may easily stifle any possible interest in reading and promote maladjustment by a too-ambitious program. They may compound his problem by comparing him with his more fortunate brothers or sisters or, by convincing him that his slowness is all the teacher's fault, they may block the teacher from helping him.

As Gray and Reese have pointed out, if a child is already confused by reading, an anxious, nagging parent may be the last straw (p. 221).[26] Parents of a retarded child too frequently show their discouragement, worry, or anger. They may make it clear to the child that they feel he is stupid, idiotic, or feeble-minded. Young (p. 247)[67] describes cases in which parental and teacher attitudes hampered the treatment of reading disability cases. He found that in

> . . . two-thirds of these cases [41 in number, of which 37 were boys and four were girls] misunderstandings of psychological and physiological factors on the part of parents and teachers caused emotional difficulties in the children. Unfavorable comparison with other children and attempts to coerce the children to read, as well as an overemphasis of the importance of reading did, in individual instances, give the child a sense of inferiority and insecurity to which he responded by neurotic behavior such as stammering, nervous twitching, tics, enuresis, thumbsucking, and the like, or, in the most aggressive behavior of stealing, lying and truanting from school.

When we consider the special pressures placed on a child who fails, a causal relationship between reading failure and personal maladjustment not only is possible; it seems likely. In today's school, reading success is so vital to personal esteem and social acceptance, that failure almost invariably forces the child to behavioral deviations of one form or another. Obviously, the teacher must make every attempt to help each child achieve social acceptance. Although some children will need little special help from the teacher, others will require close attention.

BEHAVIORAL SYMPTOMS OF READING FAILURE

Studies generally have indicated that there are many behavioral symptoms that tend to accompany poor reading. Among these are apparent laziness, antagonism, tenseness, self-consciousness, nervousness, inattentiveness, and shyness. Poor readers may compensate by increased effort in other areas such as in arithmetic or manual skills. On the other hand their defeat in reading may predispose them to defeat in other areas. They may be defensive or truant; they may stutter or bite their nails; they may be irritable and easily discouraged. Robinson (p. 116) [41] says:*

> The manifestations listed by most writers might be summarized in one of four categories: aggression, withdrawal, loss of emotional effectivity, and general tenseness. Such reactions are evidenced if the failing pupil refuses to accept failure, accepts it and loses all confidence, or rationalizes his failure.

Siegel [45] found that disability in reading frequently is accompanied by personality maladjustments, but he also suggests that there is no 'typical' personality pattern which is characteristic of reading failure. Wiksell [63] reported that about 50 per cent of the poor readers in a college freshmen class had "emotional difficulties." And Johnson reports that of thirty-four clinical reading cases studied, all exhibited some form of personal maladjustment.[30]

Bouise,[14] studying retarded readers, reported that teachers felt that 21 of the 30 cases had serious personal problems. She concluded that there was a greater tendency toward introversion among poor readers than among good readers. Gann (pp. 131–135) [20] administered the Rorschach Ink-Blot Test to children in grades three to six and concluded that, as a group, those children with reading age one or more years below their mental age were less stable, less secure, less well-adjusted emotionally, and probably were less socially acceptable than average or superior readers of the same mental age.

Witty and Kopel (p. 231) [65] report that about one-half of the seriously retarded readers coming to the Northwestern University Psycho-Educational Clinic have "fears and anxieties so serious and so far-reaching that no program of re-education could possibly succeed which did not aim to re-establish self-confidence and to remove anxieties." Sherman (p. 132) [43]

---

notes that reading difficulties frequently lead to emotional disturbances. He points out that: *

> The emotional disturbances which result from the failure situation in reading must be evaluated from two standpoints. First, the failures involve frustration, accompanied by emotional disorganization and conflict formation. The result may be aggressive, defensive reactions, not only toward the learning situation itself, but also toward all situations associated with school work and especially reading problems. Second, the constant failures of a child decrease the intensity of his motivation to learn in a given situation.

Gates (p. 205),[21] in 1936, prepared a summary of the symptoms exhibited by 100 retarded readers. They are worth considering both from the standpoint of helping us to recognize emotional symptoms and for showing the importance of reading failure as a threat to the child's mental health.

(1) Nervous tensions and habits, such as stuttering, nail-biting, restlessness, insomnia, and pathological illness—10 cases.
(2) Putting up a bold front as a defense reaction, loud talk, defiant conduct, sullenness—16 cases.
(3) Retreat reactions such as withdrawal from ordinary associations, joining outside gangs, and truancy—14 cases.
(4) Counterattack; such as making mischief in school, playing practical jokes, thefts, destructiveness, cruelty, bullying—18 cases.
(5) Withdrawing reactions; including mind-wandering and daydreaming—26 cases.
(6) Extreme self-consciousness; becoming easily injured, blushing, developing peculiar fads and frills and eccentricities, inferiority feelings—35 cases.
(7) Give-up or submissive adjustments, as shown by inattentiveness, indifference, apparent laziness—33 cases.

Robinson (p. 122) [41] has reported on a number of reading disability cases. Some showed no evidence of emotional problems but her conclusions concerning retarded readers and emotional deviations are worth considering: **

1. A higher percentage of seriously retarded readers exhibited emotional problems, whereas fewer slightly retarded readers showed such problems.
2. The symptoms manifested could usually be classified as aggressive reactions, withdrawn tendencies, or general insecurity and apprehension. Within the framework of these general classifications, there were many specific symptoms. A few of these were: irritability, extreme criticism, attack on materials and the tutor, active refusal to attempt the job, evasive

---

behavior, short span of attention, unusual speed or lethargy in carrying on activities, extreme shyness, fear of and the reluctance in attacking a problem, over-anxiety in relation to success and failure, and over-dependence on other persons.

Spache [50] gave the *Rosenzweig Picture-Frustration Test* to 50 retarded readers, ages six to fourteen, whose mean verbal I.Q. on the Wechsler was 93.2. He concluded that retarded readers were more aggressive and cocky, less insightful, less apt to accept blame or admit fault, less tolerant, and more negativistic. These tendencies were less pronounced in their relations toward adults than toward other children. They tended to avoid open conflict with adults, either assuming a passive attitude or venting their aggression on the environment. Spache says (pp. 190–191) that since the retarded reader

. . . cannot achieve recognition by performance in academic areas, he achieves it by cockiness, exaggerated self-confidence, and refusal to accept blame or to arbitrate. This compensatory type of adjustment is evidenced in the tendency of retarded readers to secure recognition in non-academic areas such as sports and outdoor activities, carpentry and similar manual skills.

In another study Spache tested 125 children who were retarded in reading development. He used the *Children's Form* of the *Rosenzweig Picture-Frustration Test*. This consists of 24 cartoon-like drawings depicting conflict among several children or between a child and an adult. Certain generalizations applicable to the entire group were: these children were less insightful; had a greater tendency to self-blame; were more defensive and negativistic; had less social-conforming tendencies; manifested less solution-seeking behavior; were hypersensitive; showed less tolerance; and were more aggressive. However, he identified five major personality patterns among the retarded readers (p. 468) [51]:

1. An aggressive or hostile group in conflict with authority figures.
2. An adjustive group which seeks only to be inoffensive.
3. A defensive group that is sensitive and resentful.
4. A solution-seeking or peace-making type.
5. The autistic group characterized by blocking or withdrawal.

As we examine the numerous behavioral symptoms of reading retardation, we see that some are easily observable whereas others generally require the use of clinical tests for identification. In the following section we shall attempt to identify the possible cause and effect relationships between the behavioral symptoms and reading retardation. But, whatever the direction of the relationship, teachers need to acquire as much skill as possible in identifying the child who is having or is likely to have reading difficulty. In addition, a knowledge that certain behaviors are likely to accompany reading failure makes us both more likely to try to remedy weakness in reading and to strive for a better understanding of children with emotional problems.

We have seen that various anti-social and asocial behaviors tend to accompany failure in reading. Gray and Reese (p. 110) [26] have listed some of the more readily observable symptoms of such behavior.

1. Unable to make friends
2. Always quarreling
3. Immediately on the defensive
4. Excessively, self-righteously good
5. Overconcerned about the behavior of others
6. Apt to cry too easily
7. Too noisy
8. Shy and withdrawn
9. Nervous and fearful.*

CAUSE AND EFFECT RELATIONSHIPS

Writers generally have concluded that there are many possible causes of reading disability and that emotional disorders are not always present either before or after the failure. Actually some studies of groups of children have failed to find a positive correlation between reading failure and personality maladjustment. On the other hand, some writers take the stand that at least in certain cases, the personality maladjustment is the cause of the reading disability.

Robinson (p. 225) [40] states that in 32 per cent of her 22 reading disability cases the emotional difficulties may have caused the reading difficulties. Writing in 1941, Gates (p. 83) [22] concluded that 75 per cent of poor readers with marked specific disability show some maladjustment. He notes that "Of these, the personality maladjustment is the cause of the reading defect in a quarter of the cases and an accompaniment or result in three-quarters."

And other studies have emphasized that reading failures frequently are of emotional origin. Even when there is no evidence of personality maladjustment, a child's failure in reading might have an emotional origin.

* Lillian Gray and Dora Reese, *Teaching Children to Read,* 2nd ed., (New York: The Ronald Press Company, 1957).

Harris [27] suggests that painful emotional events occurring during a child's early efforts at reading may turn him against reading. Second, in certain cases a reader may be transferring a feeling of resistance from his mother to his teacher or from his eating to his reading. Third, a child may seek gang approval through not reading. And fourth, he may be fighting so hard to repress hostile impulses that he has little energy left for intellectual effort. Blanchard,[12] studying 73 reading disability cases of which 63 were boys and ten were girls, made a somewhat unique suggestion. She said that reading disability may satisfy a child's need for punishment and thus relieve a guilt feeling. She suggested that some children may actually seek failure in school and its resultant criticism.

Tulchin [58] points out that the child's first reading experiences may be so charged emotionally as to taint all his subsequent reactions and make him resistant to reading. In the same way, a physical defect, even though it did not directly interfere with reading, could lead to emotional difficulties that would interfere with reading success.

Castner [16] and Bird [10] suggest that personality disorders contribute to learning failure generally. Studying thirteen cases, Castner points out that numerous factors are related to reading disability. He notes especially (1) weaknesses in drawing tests, (2) tendency to left-handedness and cross laterality, (3) slow development in language and speech, and (4) emotional instability. These factors are present frequently before children begin school and are possibly prognostic of the reading difficulties that are developed later. Bird (p. 59) [10] states that:

> In the last analysis the same affective disturbances handicapping . . . children function largely in the failure of adults to achieve to the extent of their mental ability. The over-timid, the anti-social, the chronic introvert, the braggart, the annoying egotist, the excessively sociable are all victims of habits that divert the attention from the task at hand.

Missildine [36] studied 30 disabled readers who were under psychiatric care. All had I.Q.'s of 91 or better and normal eyesight and hearing. He concluded that all these children "harbored a serious affect disturbance" toward one or more members of their family. All except one were acutely ill emotionally! In these cases the reading disability is but another expression of each child's underlying emotional problems.

Certainly the studies that we have examined stress the emotional concomitants of poor reading. However, Bond and Tinker have concluded that the evidence generally indicates that emotional maladjustment is more frequently an effect than a cause (p. 107).[13] According to this viewpoint early diagnosis is emphasized and alleviation of all possible reading difficulties is extremely important. In those cases where poor reading is the cause, early diagnosis and remediation should reduce the number of children that will develop emotional difficulties.

Some studies have indicated that a general insecurity and lack of confidence may be a more important contributor to reading disability than are specific emotional deviations. Using matched pairs of average and poor readers in grades two, three, and four, Bennett [6] found no marked emotional abnormality in poor readers, but rather a lack of persistence and of capacity for sustained and concentrated attention. As a group the poor readers preferred inactive pursuits, felt lonely and indecisive, and made inadequate and insecure responses. Karlsen [31] reports that word-by-word readers generally are low in motivation, have difficulty attending, and lack social confidence. Wolfe [66] compared a group of nine-year old boys who were about two years retarded in reading with a group of boys of the same age who were normal readers. She found that the retarded readers were more lethargic, less attentive, and less persistent than those of the normal group.

Robinson (p. 222) [40] reports that unfavorable home conditions are frequently related to reading disability. Strang (p. 315) [54] points out that "A neurotic constitution may be a direct cause of reading disability inasmuch as it makes impossible the sustained effort and co-operation required in learning to read."

Kunst (pp. 133–135) [32] emphasizes the emotional origin of reading difficulties. She concludes that:*

> . . . reading failure, in a child of normal intelligence, who has had good teaching, is a neurotic symptom indicating emotional conflict. It may be quite true that these children wish to read. It is equally true that they simultaneously, though often unconsciously, wish to fail to read. . . .
>
> I think of reading failure, not as a passive inability to learn, but as an active, though usually unconscious, protection *against* learning to read. I have come to believe that this resistance stems from anxiety that is aroused by curiosity. . . .
>
> I view marked reading failure as a *symptom* of a general personality disturbance, and I attempt to treat the child for the emotional disturbance. I do not deny the success and appropriateness in some cases of treating the symptom. I believe, however, that success often comes because the tutor has intuitively met some of the basic needs of the child. I believe that in the long run, the individual child will be better helped, and we shall learn more about preventing reading failure, if we try to understand why reading failure is utilized as a protective symptom.

Mann (p. 199) [34] suggests that:

Reading problems are symptoms and as such respond to some extent to symptomatic treatment but the real causes lie embedded in the early life experiences of the individual which have created a fear factor which becomes associated with the act of learning to read.

She concludes that reading behavior provides a cross-section view of the person's general behavior. Because expression of the symptoms exhibited by the person with a reading problem may help him to adjust to his other problems, there is a serious danger in merely treating the symptoms.

Since the introduction of the Wechsler-Bellevue [59] with its eleven subtests, there have been several attempts to use the subscales to diagnose personality disorders. Some studies have been made of the relationship between the sub-test profiles and retarded reading.

Graham [24] has hypothesized that the similarity of the profiles of unsuccessful readers and adult hysterics indicates that reading may serve as a symbol for repressed resistance to oppressive or hostile emotional climates encountered by the child. He also found that the scattergrams of 96 unsuccessful readers obtained from the *Wechsler-Bellevue* and the *Wechsler Intelligence Scale for Children* (WISC) approximated those of adolescent psychopaths.[25] His group consisted of pupils between the ages of eight and seventeen and had an I.Q. of 90 or higher. He found that the unsuccessful reader tends to do better on performance than on verbal scales, but this pattern does not hold in all cases. On arithmetic, digit span, information, digit symbol, and vocabulary the poor readers were below the mean. He hypothesizes that perhaps both the psychopath and the unsuccessful reader may be unconsciously resisting the emotional climate of the school.

Altus,[2] studying 25 retarded readers from 12 elementary schools, found that severe disability cases had a distinct pattern on the WISC. Of the 25, 24 were boys, all had an I.Q. of 80 or above, and all were retarded at least two years. The mean I.Q. of the group on the full scale was 98.6. She found that performance in both the Digit Symbol and Arithmetic tests was significantly lower than on the Vocabulary, Digit Span, Picture Completion, Object Assembly, and Picture Arrangement tests. The score on the Information test was significantly lower than on the Picture Completion, Vocabulary, and Digit Span tests.

Certainly not all emotionally disturbed children are poor readers, nor are all poor readers emotionally disturbed. Challman,[17] for example, suggests that about one-fourth of the poor readers adjust successfully to their reading failure and develop no emotional problems.

The studies suggest that both success and failure in reading may be related to numerous emotional factors. Poor parent-child relationships, sibling rivalry, lack of encouragement from the home, and negative attitudes of parents toward learning in general may lead to failure. On the other hand these same factors could lead the child to so direct his attention toward reading that he might become an excellent reader. Although the teacher must be aware of the possibility that emotional factors are causing a child's reading failure, nevertheless, he must not conclude that all reading difficulties are rooted in emotional problems.

EVALUATION

The direction of the relationship between reading and personality is difficult to establish from group studies. Whether reading failure causes maladjustment or maladjustment causes reading failure must be established for each specific case. Berkowitz and Rothman [7] point out emotional maladjustment can cause academic retardation, and academic retardation can contribute considerably to a child's emotional problems. Bond and Tinker (p. 108) [13] conclude that the relationship frequently is circular in nature. Early reading failure may lead to maladjustment, and this maladjustment in turn may deter further growth in reading. As Challman [17] has suggested, however, even when the child is both emotionally maladjusted and a disabled reader, it is quite possible that one complex of factors caused the emotional maladjustment whereas a different set of factors caused the reading disability.

In summarizing the evidence, Bond and Tinker (pp. 110–111) [13] make the following suggestions:

1. In a relatively small proportion of the cases, children are emotionally upset and maladjusted when they arrive at school. . . .
2. In a relatively large proportion of reading cases, the children will have formed well-adjusted personalities before they arrive at school. The frustration from failure to learn to read results in some degree of personality maladjustment. In these cases, reading disability causes the emotional difficulty.
3. Emotional maladjustment may be both an effect and a cause of reading disability in many cases. The emotional disturbance produced by failure to learn to read may then become a handicap to further learning. . . .
4. If the personal and social maladjustment is due to reading disability, it tends to disappear in most cases when the child becomes a successful reader.
5. A few children need to be referred to a psychiatric social worker, a clinical psychologist, or a psychiatrist for psychotherapy. . . .
6. Adverse attitudes toward reading, the teacher, and school activities are due frequently to failure in reading.

Smith,[48] surveying the literature, found that many emotional maladjustments stem from the home; that the period in which the child is introduced to school life is also the period during which the emotions develop; that there is a high incidence of emotional maladjustment in children who have trouble in learning to read; and that many children who overcome their reading problems also change for the better emotionally. She recommends that the teacher try to acquaint himself with the child's fears and worries so he may help to reduce some of the pressures that otherwise could result in maladjustment.

Holmes (p. 14),[29] elaborating on Gates' [22] discussion of the relationships between reading and the emotions, writes:

1. Personality difficulties are frequently but not universally associated with reading difficulties.
2. In cases where they occur together personality difficulties may be causes, concomitants, or results of reading difficulties.
3. Emotional difficulties usually appear as part of a constellation of difficulties causing reading retardation.
4. There is no single personality pattern characteristic of reading failure and there is no proved one-to-one relationship between type of adjustment difficulties and type of reading disabilities. . . .
5. Symptoms associated with reading difficulties are commonly aggressive reactions, withdrawing tendencies or general insecurity and apprehension.
6. If emotional adjustment disturbances are one of a group of primary causes of reading difficulties, retardation in other academic learnings often occurs.
7. If reading difficulties are a cause of emotional difficulties, skilled remedial work in reading may clear up rather easily a considerable number of difficulties. If deep-seated personality difficulties are a cause of reading difficulties, ordinary remedial work is likely to be ineffective and more intensive therapy is required.

Holmes points out that in discussing reading and personality difficulties with children and their parents, phrases such as *reading diagnosis and treatment* are often more acceptable than *personality maladjustment and therapy*.

TYPES OF TREATMENT

Because of the intimate relationship between emotional adjustment and reading, therapy and remedial reading frequently are combined in dealing with reading disability cases. Burfield (p. 129) [15] reports that 32 of 116 students coming to the reading clinic had fairly pronounced symptoms of emotional maladjustment. Most of these had scholastic difficulties also. She concluded: *

1. Each emotional pattern was unique, and called for distinctive treatment.
2. The most common cause of emotional disturbance was the difficulty experienced in making adjustments to the scholastic requirements of the College.
3. The most frequent manifestations of an emotional disturbance were anxiety, fear, and withdrawal.
4. Before substantial progress can be made in reading, emotional stresses must be alleviated.
5. In general, the greater the intensity of the emotional problem, the more is individual instruction necessary, . . .
6. The reading problem of the mature student was often one of morale. Self-assurance was frequently restored by the revitalization of study techniques. Heightened morale resulted from attention to the individual problems, the solution of which enabled the student to adjust to his environment.

Various therapeutic techniques, such as art therapy, language therapy, play therapy, psychodrama, group interview therapy, sociodrama, and individual interview therapy have been tried. Art therapy has been used in The Reading Institute of New York University. Smith [49] writes of this program: "We have found . . . that a period of progress in overcoming an emotional problem as indicated by a sequence of free paintings usually coincides with a period of rapid progress in reading."

McGann [35] reports that the reading of dramatic dialogues involving two people, the teacher and the pupil, has the effect of emotional release, of establishing rapport, and of developing motivation and interest in reading. Osburn [38] claims success for substitution, catharsis, and psychodrama. In substitution, reading is disregarded temporarily and some activity that the child can perform successfully is substituted. In catharsis and psychodrama the child is allowed to talk out or to act out his problem. Roman,[42] working with 21 delinquent and retarded readers between the ages of 13 and 16 whose I.Q.'s ranged from 65 to 95, reports greatest success with the group utilizing both group therapy and remedial teaching during the same session.

Bills [8] selected eight children from a class of 22 third-grade retarded readers. Four of the children were of above 130 I.Q.; the others were of high-average intelligence. Six of the children were rated by judges as emotionally maladjusted. Each of the eight children received from four to six individual and from one to three group therapy sessions in addition to regular remedial reading class work during a 30-day period. There was judged to be a significant improvement in personal adjustment for six of the children. The average improvement in reading also was more rapid than it had been before the therapy was introduced.

Redmount [39] worked with 24 retarded readers ages eight to eighteen. A twenty-four-hour schedule of rest, therapy, recreation, individual counseling, and reading instruction was maintained for six weeks. As measured by Rorschach testing at the beginning and at the end of the program, 39 per cent appeared to show significant personality improvement. Unfortunately, 26 per cent appeared to show adverse effects. Forty-eight per cent of the group showed significant reading improvement.

Axline [3] used non-directive therapy with 37 second-grade pupils, all of whom were either non-readers or poor readers. She reports that therapy prepared the pupil for reading readiness and resulted in better personal adjustment.

Fisher [19] divided 12 deliquent boys, each at least three years retarded in reading, into two groups of six each. The remedial teacher was the same for both groups, and each pupil received remedial instruction for three hours each week. One of the groups also received group, non-directive therapy for one hour a week. Both the experimental and the control groups participated in a six-month program. The non-therapy group gained on the average 8.25 months in reading; the therapy group gained 11.5 months.

Berkowitz and Rothman [7] report on a reading program at Bellevue Psychiatric Hospital. Disturbed children were encouraged to express their phantasies. The younger children tended to do this first in drawing but finally they became able to verbalize them. Children were allowed to dictate sentences like "He saved the whales and the fish by killing the lions and the German submarine." The older children were encouraged to select words they wished to know by questions such as: "If you could learn only five or six words in your whole life, which words would you want to learn most of all?" The authors give three lists of typical words suggested by non-readers, aged 9, 12, and 14.

I	II	III
Mother	girl	Wolfman
grandmother	stupid	Zombie
Jesus	institution	wife
Christ	electricity	weight-lifting
cat	interplanetary	Atlas
pig		

These certainly are not easy words, but the children learned them. After a child had learned enough words, he dictated a phantasy booklet that was then typewritten for him to read. After a child had developed a large enough reading sight vocabulary, he was able to reliquish his own phantasy material in favor of textbooks.

It seems likely that there are various forms of therapy that help the child to overcome emotional difficulties and to achieve in reading. For many children therapy combined with the remedial reading program appears to be highly successful. Therapy may remove pressures and tensions and clear the way for attentive concentration on the reading material. In some cases it may remove a fear of reading and allow the child to develop attitudes favorable to reading. Thus the child may be led from a negative to a positive identification with reading. Strang (p. 315),[54] discussing the emotional concomitants of reading failure, states:

> Such affective factors as fear of reading, a profound feeling of inadequacy when faced with a situation requiring reading, a general lack of satisfactions in life, and the pull of other interests must be considered in remedial work on every educational level.

Obviously, many of the special intensive treatments that have been tried with seriously retarded children can not be used in the typical classroom. Some of them are far too time-consuming and others require clinical training beyond that possessed by most teachers. They have been mentioned here as illustrations of what can be done and has been done in the way of remediation. However, from a knowledge of these special methods the classroom teacher may encounter ideas or find certain techniques that he can adapt for children in his classroom who are encountering reading problems.

Gann (p. 140) [20] indicates that recognizing the involvement of the child's total personality in his learning activities leads the teacher to:

> A better appreciation of the problems of retarded readers.
>
> A better understanding of possible behavior deviations and disorders in the classroom.
>
> A more sympathetic rapport with the pupils.
>
> And encourages a growing sense of security within the retarded reader, himself, through:
>
> > Greater acceptance of him as a personality, regardless of achievements.
> >
> > Providing satisfaction in recognition of his other school achievements.
> >
> > Stimulating wholesome group relationships.
>
> Gann also suggests that reading improvement may foster improvement in the child's general personality.

Although therapy designed to alleviate underlying emotional disturbances will not be a cure-all for reading problems, Strang (p. 456) [56] has suggested that "When the individual is not accessible to reading instruction because of emotional disturbance, he should be treated by someone who is expert in psychotherapy." And the more severe the emotional maladjustment,* the greater is the need for therapy.

Since most forms of therapy require special training that few classroom teachers possess, what is the major role of the teacher in dealing with the problem of emotional disturbance? Perhaps it is in the direction of prevention of school-engendered difficulties and the detection of maladjustment so that proper steps may be taken for its early correction.

The classroom is a competitive locale despite the teacher's best efforts to dispel this atmosphere. And frequently, a competitive atmosphere contributes to the creation of an effective learning situation. But for some pupils such an atmosphere results in harmful pressures that block them from full participation and thus from optimal development. What can the teacher do about this? Stroud suggests that the teacher can make

> . . . a genuine contribution to mental hygiene in the school by providing rich and varied ways for pupils, *all* pupils, to achieve success and recognition. Ideally, every pupil, but especially those most in need of it, should have the opportunity to make contributions to the learning activities, contributions that others will recognize. Some pupils will require help in this. There is always the danger that the good pupil will get the lion's share of praise and recognition.[57] (p. 552)

READING FOR ADJUSTMENT

Reading can and often does have a great influence on personality; it may be used as a tool for promoting personal growth and, indeed, it has been advocated as a means of furthering personal adjustment.

Gates (p. 4) [23] suggests that "In wholehearted reading activity the child does more than understand and contemplate; his emotions are stirred; his attitudes and purposes are modified; indeed, his innermost being is involved."

Shrodes (p. 24) [44] has pointed out that:

> Reading, like other human behavior, is a function of the total personality. When we read fiction or drama, no less than when we work, meet people, teach, create, or love, we perceive in accordance with our needs, goal, defenses, and values.[44]

---

* Ellis [18] suggests that the greater the child's emotional disturbance, the less will be his reading improvement. (The severity of the psychiatric diagnosis is inversely related to the patient's reading gains.)

She says that reading induces "(1) identification, including projection and introjection, (2) catharsis and (3) insight." The reader may "introject meaning that will satisfy his needs and reject meaning that is threatening to his ego."

As we know, each child reads with his store of knowledge rather than merely with his eyes. He takes his own needs and his own problems to the reading experiences. He reads himself into the characters that he meets there. This in itself can be a kind of therapy. Shrodes has used the term *bibliotherapy* in referring to reading as a means for furthering personal adjustment and says that it is successful because of the "shock of recognition" that comes when the reader sees himself and his problems in a piece of literature. Reading can mirror life and the reader may come to see himself as others see him but it may be superior to a life situation in that he can better accept unsavory appraisals of his weaknesses since the mirror image does not so directly threaten his ego.

> If a character strongly arrests his attention, an identification may be made which, in effect, represents a transference of emotion from a previous experience to the vicarious experience. A positive identification is one that tends to enhance the reader's self-regard and may provide a model for emulation. A negative identification is usually engendered because of threat to his image of himself and takes the form of projection on to the character the feelings which have been repressed because they are unacceptable to the ego. However, in inducing these projections, the reading process may serve as a catalyst to free his emotions from their unconscious roots.[44]

An identification with the characters of literature allows the individual to relive elements of his own past experience and attain new understandings of them. For example, it may allow him to look at fictional mothers and fathers and thus gain a better understanding of his own parents. Or he sees, through a character portrayal, the reactions (and the reasons for those reactions) of other persons to his own personality traits.

Reading also may give the child vicarious experiences. Through these he becomes better prepared to meet life's problems. In effect he is better prepared to meet real problems because, through reading, he already has met similar problems.

Lind [33] says that children get four values from reading: escape; temporary diversion; an organizing influence on personality; and certain instrumental effects. This latter refers to reading's value as an aid to solving practical problems such as getting better grades in all school subjects.

Bailey [4] points out that reading can help the child to overcome five general types of insecurity:

1. Those based on his relations with his peers.
2. Those based on family relationships.
3. Those resulting from repeated failures.
4. Those based on economic factors.
5. Those based on physical factors.

Moore (pp. 216–232) [37] agrees that reading materials carefully selected to meet the needs of the specific individual can have a therapeutic effect. Weingarten,[60] in a questionnaire study involving 1,256 students from 17 colleges, reports the following: 28.2 per cent of those responding felt that their reading had led to self-understanding; 32.6 per cent, to finding the ideal self; 19.9 per cent, to solving a problem; 10 per cent, to selecting a vocation; 34.3 per cent, to changing their behavior; 60.5 per cent, to finding a way of life; and 29.9 per cent, to imitating a character read about. Remember, too, that percentages cannot include those students who were unconsciously affected by their reading.

Reading certainly can influence personality. Whether the teacher will have the skill to guide the child to use books therapeutically is another matter. The high level of professional skill called for by other forms of therapy—play therapy, for example—are needed for bibliotherapy.

Reading may have special therapeutic values for the gifted child. He is likely to have certain special problems in the area of social relations and in meeting frustrations constructively (pp. 133–134).[55] Frequently he is rejected or feels rejected by the large group of less gifted children with whom he is associated.[5] In some cases his intellectual superiority makes the companionship of his age mates dull and uninteresting to him. He may respond by attempting to "bully" others with his intellect and thus compound his problems. Fortunately, he likes to read and can gain a great deal from reading. Through vicarious experiences gained in his reading, he may be able to see himself in the actions of book characters: he may see how his own actions have affected others and are interpreted by others.

There are numerous books that appear to offer help to a child in overcoming a difficulty, in accepting himself for what he is, in re-living and evaluating past experiences, and in glimpsing from pages of print an insight into his problems. Through the experiences of the characters that he meets in books, he becomes better acquainted with himself and his own strengths and weaknesses. Thus he may better identify and develop his own self-concept.

A list containing a few of the many books that are built on themes that conceivably could serve the purposes of reading for adjustment may be found at the end of this chapter.

SUMMARY

Not all poor readers are emotionally maladjusted and not all emotionally maladjusted children are poor readers. Children are attracted to things that satisfy their basic needs of security, success, self-esteem, and social acceptance. To the extent that reading failure blocks the satisfaction of these needs, it may be said to cause emotional disturbances. And to the extent that emotional disturbances block adequate learning, they interfere with normal reading development. On the other hand, it is quite conceivable that for some children reading results in satisfactions that may improve emotional adjustment and in turn result in more reading and in improved reading.

Reading failure poses an important problem to any child. Even though reading failure may sometimes be attributed to attempted adjustment to emotional problems, persistant reading failure, whatever its cause, is certain to block the child from performing a basic developmental task. Thus reading failure serves to increase his emotional maladjustment. Emotional maladjustment, in turn, makes reading achievement more difficult because it interferes with all types of learning.

In short, maladjustment may lead to early failure in reading and this may result in further maladjustment. Or failure in reading may lead to maladjustment and this in turn may hinder further achievement in reading. Personal development and the learning of reading are so intertwined that the weakness of one may sap the strength and prevent the growth of the other.

***

The following list contains examples of the various types of books that may have therapeutic values. The majority of these books are most appropriate at the elementary school level, but many of them prove interesting to junior or senior high school students.

I. *Responsibility to Family and to Others—Responsibility and Cooperation*

1. Agle. *Three Boys and a Lighthouse* (responsibility).
2. Archibald. *Double Play Rookie* (baseball and co-operation).
3. Baker. *The Friendly Beasts* (giving according to one's means).
4. Bothwell. *Little Flute Player* (responsibility for family).
5. Burton. *Katy and the Big Snow* (co-operation, helpfulness).
6. Clark. *Magic Money* (family love).
7. Clymer. *Trolley Car Family* (family co-operation).
8. Dana. *Sugar Bush* (co-operation between an "old and a new" family).
9. Enright. *The Melendy Family* (family co-operation).

10. Estes. *The Hundred Dresses* (consideration of others).
11. Felson. *Crash Club* (responsibility on the race track).
12. Freeman. *Fly High, Fly Low* (family responsibility).
13. Garst. *Wish on An Apple* (family co-operation).
14. Harkins. *Southpaw from San Francisco* (pitcher and co-operation).
15. Harkins. *Touchdown Twins* (football and sportsmanship).
16. Ilsley. *The Pink Hat* (responsibility in the home).
17. Knapp. *Sink the Basket* (girl's athletics and human relations).
18. Kubes. *King Solomon's Horses* (kindness to others).
19. Lipkind and Mordvinoff. *Finders Keepers* (two dogs share a bone).
20. Meigs. *Dutch Colt* (boy takes care of horse).
21. Paull. *Some Day* (to be "somebody" we must work for it).
22. Rhoads. *The Corn Grows Ripe* (responsibility).
23. Sawyer. *Maggie Rose* (relationship with neighborhood).
24. Taylor. *All-of-a-Kind Family* (co-operation among five Jewish girls).
25. Tunis. *All-American* (football and co-operation).
26. Tunis. *City for Lincoln* (baseball coach does something about juvenile delinquency).
27. Ungerer. *The Mellops Go Diving for Treasure* (family co-operation).
28. White. *Lion's Paw* (three children in a boat).
29. Wilson. *The Owen Boys* (family relations).
30. Woolley. *Ginnie and Geneva* (relationship with friends).
31. Woolley. *Ginnie Joins In* (becoming a member of the group).
32. Woolley. *Holiday on Wheels* (responsibility for chores).
33. Yates. *Place for Peter* (physical strength and manly responsibility).

II. *Emotional Conflicts*

1. Bannon. *Red Mittens* (fear).
2. Bannon. *The Tide Won't Wait* (cowardliness).
3. Batchelor. *Tim and the Purple Whistle* (fear and courage).
4. Behn. *The Two Uncles of Pablo* (winning friends).
5. Beim. *Time for Gym* (jealousy and resentment).
6. Beim. *With Dad Alone* (broken home).
7. Bemelmans. *Madeline* (fear).
8. Bialk. *The Horse Called Pete* (fear).
9. Bialk. *Taffy's Foal* (stepchild).
10. Bischoff. *The Wonderful Poodle* (loneliness).
11. Bontemps. *Lonesome Boy* (loneliness).
12. Breck. *Hoofbeats on the Trail* (inferiority).
13. Brenner. *Dumb Juan and the Bandits* (stupidity).
14. Brown. *Little Frightened Tiger* (fear).
15. Burnett. *The Secret Garden* (discontent).
16. Carpenter. *The Blossoming Year* (shy girl).
17. Cavanna. *Going on Sixteen* (shyness and loneliness).
18. D'Aulaire and D'Aulaire. *Nils* (ridicule).
19. Dennis. *Flip* (fear).
20. DeWitt. *The Littlest Reindeer* (inconsolable reindeer).
21. Elkin. *Six Foolish Fishermen* (fear).
22. Eppenstein. *Sally Goes Traveling Alone* (fear).
23. Felsen. *Hot Rod* (speed-crazy boy).
24. Felt. *Contrary Woodrow* (contrariness).
25. Fisher. *Understood Betsy* (pampered girl).
26. Flack. *Wag Tail Bess* (dog overcomes shyness).
27. Friedman. *Carol from the Country* (sensitive girl).
28. Friedman. *Dot for Short* (friendship and success).
29. Gates. *Little Vic* (orphan boy).
30. Gilbert. *Dr. Trotter and His Big Gold Watch* (fear).

31. Goodenow. *The Bashful Bear* (bashfulness).
32. Gunther. *Death Be Not Proud* (death).
33. Hader and Hader. *Pancho* (fear).
34. Hawkins. *Don't Run-Apple* (fear).
35. Haywood. *Here's a Penny* (adoption).
36. Hinkle. *Shag* (no-account stag-hound).
37. Hogner. *Winky* (fear).
38. Howell. *Who Likes the Dark* (fear).
39. Kiser. *Sunshine for Merrily* (adoption).
40. Latham. *Perrito's Pup* (sibling rivalry).
41. Leinhauser. *Patricia's Secret* (motherless girl).
42. Lent. *Straight Down* (fear of high places).
43. Lewiton. *The Divided Heart* (broken home).
44. Lones. *Peggy's Wish* (orphaned child).
45. MacDonald. *Little Frightened Tiger* (fear).
46. MacDonald. *Little Lost Lamb* (fear).
47. Marshall. *The Unwilling Heart* (broken home).
48. Mason. *The Middle Sister* (fear).
49. McCullough. *Dark is Dark* (fear).
50. McKean. *David's Bad Day* (sibling rivalry).
51. Moody. *Man of the Family* (broken home).
52. Murphy. *Runaway Alice* (orphan).
53. Otto. *The Little Brown Horse* (security, friendship).
54. Paradis. *Timmy and the Tiger* (fear).
55. Paullin. *No More Tonsils* (fear).
56. Petersham and Petersham. *The Boy Who Had No Heart* (selfish boy).
57. Pont. *Sally on the Fence* (broken home).
58. Randall. *Tumbleweed Heart* (seeing fine qualities in others).
59. Sayers. *Bluebonnets for Lucinda* (fear).
60. Schneider. *While Susie Sleeps* (fear).
61. Schurr. *The Shy Little Kitten* (shyness).
62. Scott. *Judy's Baby* (sibling rivalry).
63. Singmaster. *The Isle of Que* (fear).
64. Slobodkin. *Magic Michael* (sibling rivalry).
65. Slobodkin. *Melvin, the Moose Child* (loneliness).
66. Smith. *He Went for a Walk* (broken home).
67. Sorensen. *Plain Girl* (underprivileged shy girl).
68. Sperry. *Call It Courage* (fear of the sea).
69. Spyri. *All Alone in the World* (loneliness, belongingness).
70. Stuart. *The Beatinest Boy* (broken home).
71. Summers. *Girl Trouble* (boy's trouble with opposite sex).
72. Tarkington. *Seventeen* (boy's first love).
73. Treffinger. *Li Lun, Lad of Courage* (fear of the sea).
74. Urmston. *New Boy* (teasing).
75. Wasson. *The Chosen Baby* (adoption).
76. Williams. *Timid Timothy* (fear).
77. Woolley. *Ginnie and the New Girl* (loneliness).
78. Woolley. *Schoolroom Zoo* (fear).
79. Yashima. *Grow Boy* (stupidity).

III. *Physical Handicaps*

1. Andersen. *The Ugly Duckling* (ugliness).
2. Barber. *The Trembling Years* (polio).
3. Beim. *The Smallest Boy in Class* (size).
4. Beim. *Triumph Clear* (physical handicaps).
5. Bialk. *The Horse Called Pete* (size).

6. Boynick. *Champions by Setback* (sports champions overcome physical handicaps).
7. De Angeli. *The Door in the Wall* (crippled boy).
8. Eager. *Red Head* (red-headed boy).
9. Evans. *Skookum* (size).
10. Felt. *Rosa-Too-Little* (size).
11. Forbes. *Johnny Tremain* (physical injury).
12. Foster. *Abraham Lincoln* (ugliness).
13. Frick. *Five Against the Odds* (polio).
14. Gag. *Millions of Cats* (ugliness).
15. Garfield. *Follow My Leader* (loss of eyesight).
16. Gates. *Sensible Kate* (plain girl).
17. Hogner. *Daisy, a Farm Fable* (size).
18. Jackson. *Giant in the Midget League* (tall and awkward boy).
19. Johnson and Johnson. *The Smallest Puppy* (size).
20. Krauss. *The Growing Story* (size).
21. Lasson. *Orang Oliver: The Kitten Who Wore Glasses* (eye defect).
22. Mason. *The Grey-Nosed Kitten* (ugliness).
23. Sayers. *Tag Along Too-Loo* (size).
24. Snyder. *Too Little* (size).
25. Tresselt. *The Smallest Elephant in the World* (size).
26. Vance. *Windows for Rosemary* (blind girl).
27. Wagoner. *Jane Addams* (crippled girl).
28. Walker. *Rise Up and Walk* (polio).
29. Wilson. *Half Pint* (size).

IV. *Intergroup Relations*

1. Beim. *Carol's Side of the Street* (Jewish girl).
2. Beim. *Swimming Hole* (tolerance).
3. Beim. *Two is a Team* (Negro and white boy).
4. Cavanah. *We Came to America* (young people who came to America).
5. D'Aulaire and D'Aulaire. *Nils* (Norwegian boy).
6. De Angeli. *Bright April* (tolerance of Negroes).
7. De Angeli. *Thee Hannah!* (Quaker girl).
8. De Angeli. *Up the Hill* (Polish family).
9. Eichelberger. *Bronko* (a Polish boy).
10. Estes. *The Hundred Dresses* (Polish girl).
11. Foster. *Ginger Box* (Quaker girl).
12. Fox. *Mountain Girl* (Kentucky mountain girl).
13. Frank. *Diary of a Young Girl* (prejudice).
14. Golden. *Only in America* (prejudice).
15. Graham. *South Town* (racial tensions).
16. Hayes. *Skid* (Negro boy).
17. Hoff. *Johnny Texas* (German boy comes to Texas).
18. Jackson. *Call Me Charley* (Negro boy).
19. Judson. *The Lost Violin—They Came from Bohemia* (Bohemian girl).
20. Judson. *Michael's Victory—They Came from Ireland* (Irish boy).
21. Lattimore. *Bayou Boy* (Negro boy).
22. Lattimore. *Junior, A Colored Boy of Charleston* (Negro boy).
23. Levy. *Corrie and the Yankee* (Negro girl helps wounded soldier).
24. Lide. *Wooden Locket* (Polish family).
25. Liu. *Little Wu and the Watermelons* (Chinese boy).
26. Long. *Hannah Courageous* (Quaker ideals).
27. MacAlvay. *Cathie Stuart* (gypsies).
28. Means. *Shuttered Windows* (Negro girl).
29. Means. *The Moved-Outers* (Japanese in California).

30. Phillips. *Chucho, The Boy with the Good Name* (life in Mexico).
31. Schiekey. *The House at the City Wall* (German family).
32. Seymour. *When the Dikes Broke* (family life in Holland).
33. Taylor. *All-of-a-Kind Family* (Jewish family life).
34. Thorson. *Keeko* (Indian boy).
35. Tunis. *The Keystone Kids* (Jewish—tolerance from team activities).
36. Whitney. *Willow Hill* (race problem).
37. Yates. *Prudence Grandall: Woman of Courage* (woman opens academy to Negro girl).

V. *Pioneers and Others Who Achieved Through Hardship*

1. Blackstock. *Songs for Sixpence* (story of John Newberry).
2. Brown. *Louisa—A Biography of Louisa May Alcott.*
3. Bulla. *Song of St. Francis.*
4. Curie. *Madame Curie.*
5. D'Aulaire and D'Aulaire. *Abraham Lincoln.*
6. D'Aulaire and D'Aulaire. *Benjamin Franklin.*
7. Dempsey. *Round by Round.*
8. Dougherty. *Daniel Boone.*
9. Foster. *George Washington.*
10. Garst. *Buffalo Bill.*
11. Judson. *Abraham Lincoln, Friend of the People.*
12. Judson. *Andrew Jackson, Frontier Statesman.*
13. Judson. *Theodore Roosevelt, Fighting Patriot.*
14. Keller. *The Story of My Life.*
15. Meadowcroft. *Boy's Life of Edison.*
16. Mills. *Three Together* (the Wright brothers and their sister).
17. Nolan. *Florence Nightingale.*
18. Pace. *Clara Barton.*
19. Pace. *Juliette Low.*
20. Paine. *Girl in White Armour* (Joan of Arc).
21. Schoor. *Red Grange: Football's Greatest Halfback.*
22. Woodham-Smith. *Lonely Crusader: The Life of Florence Nightingale.*

SUGGESTED READINGS

For a general background discussion of emotional development and of adjustment problems:

Smith, Henry P., Chapter 3, "Emotional Growth and Development," pp. 52–84 and Chapter 13, "The Goals and Problems of Human Adjustment," pp. 357–385 in *Psychology in Teaching.* Englewood Cliffs, N.J.: Prentice-Hall, Inc., 1954.

***

For a detailed review of studies in personality development with an extensive bibliography, see:

Mussen, Paul, "Developmental Psychology," pp. 439–478 in *Annual Review of Psychology,* Paul R. Farnsworth and Quinn McNemar (Ed.) Palo Alto, Calif.: Annual Reviews, Inc., 1960.

***

(Causey, *The Reading Teacher's Reader*)

Article 40, Weingarten, Samuel. "Reading as a Source of the Ideal Self," from *The Reading Teacher,* 8 (February, 1955), pp. 159–164.

Article 63, Zolkos, Helena H. "What Research Says about Emotional Factors in Retardation in Reading," from *Elementary School Journal*, 52 (May, 1951) pp. 512–518.
Article 70, Shrodes, Caroline "Bibliotherapy," from *The Reading Teacher*, 9 (October, 1955) pp. 24–29.

QUESTIONS FOR DISCUSSION

1. What types of child behavior generally cause teachers most concern? Which are generally of most concern to psychologists? Discuss.
2. How may a child's reading affect and be affected by his personality?
3. Identify and discuss the important psychological or *ego* motives. How do they differ from the biological motives in development, persistence, and strength?
4. What are some of the behaviors that seem to accompany reading failure?
5. Discuss the cause-and-effect relationship between emotional symptoms and reading difficulty.
6. Identify, discuss, and evaluate some of the types of treatment that have been suggested for children with emotional problems.
7. What is meant by bibliotherapy? How is it used? What are its values and its limitations?
8. Identify and discuss some of the clinical means that are used to identify personality deviations.
9. Discuss some ways in which the self-concept may (a) affect the learning of reading, and (b) be affected by the learning of reading.
10. What can be done to avoid undesirable attitudes and detrimental procedures by parents when their child has a reading disability?
11. Discuss the cause-and-effect relationships of emotional disturbances and reading disability.
12. How does one adjust? How are anger and fear related?

BIBLIOGRAPHY

[1] Abel, Theodora M. and Kinder, Elaine F. *The Subnormal Adolescent Girl.* Columbia University Press, New York, 1942.

[2] Altus, Grace T. "A WISC Profile for Retarded Readers." *Journal of Consulting Psychology,* 20 (April, 1956) 155–156.

[3] Axline, Virginia Mae. "Nondirective Therapy for Poor Readers." *Journal of Consulting Psychology,* 11 (March–April, 1947) 61–69.

[4] Bailey, Matilda. "A Candle of Understanding." *Education,* 76 (May, 1956) 515–521.

[5] Barbe, Walter B. "Differentiated Guidance for the Gifted." *Education,* 74 (January, 1954) 306–311.

[6] Bennett, C. C. *An Inquiry Into the Genesis of Poor Reading.* Contributions to Education, No. 755, Bureau of Publications, Teachers College, Columbia University, 1938.

[7] Berkowitz, Pearl, and Rothman, Esther. "Remedial Reading for the Disturbed Child." *The Clearing House,* 30 (November, 1955) 165–168.

[8] Bills, Robert E. "Nondirective Play Therapy with Retarded Readers." *Journal of Consulting Psychology,* 14 (April, 1950) 140–149.

[9] Bills, Robert E. "Believing and Behaving: Perception and Learning," pp. 55–73 in Alexander Frazier (Ed.), *Learning More About Learning,* Association for Supervision and Curriculum Development, National Educational Association, Washington, D.C., 1959.

[10] Bird, Grace E. "Personality Factors in Learning." *Personnel Journal,* 6 (No. 1, 1927) 56–59.

[11] Blanchard, Phyllis. "Reading Disabilities in Relation to Maladjustment." *Mental Hygiene,* 12 (October, 1928) 772–788.

[12] Blanchard, Phyllis. "Reading Disabilities in Relation to Difficulties of Personality and Emotional Development." *Mental Hygiene,* 20 (July, 1936) 384–413.

[13] Bond, Guy L., and Tinker, Miles A. *Reading Difficulties: Their Diagnosis and Correction.* Appleton-Century-Crofts, Inc., New York, 1957.

[14] Bouise, Louise M. "Emotional and Personality Problems of a Group of Retarded Readers." *Elementary English,* 32 (December, 1955) 544–548.

[15] Burfield, Leone M. "Emotional Problems of Poor Readers Among College Students." *Clinical Studies in Reading,* I, Supplementary Educational Monographs, No. 68, University of Chicago Press, Chicago, 1949, 123–129.

[16] Castner, Burton M. "Prediction of Reading Disability Prior to First Grade Entrance." *American Journal of Orthopsychiatry,* 5 (October, 1935) 375–386.

[17] Challman, Robert. "Personality Maladjustments and Remedial Reading." *Journal of Exceptional Children,* 6 (October, 1939) 7–11, 35.

[18] Ellis, Albert. "Results of a Mental Hygiene Approach to Reading Disability Problems." *Journal of Consulting Psychology,* 13 (February, 1949) 56–61.

[19] Fisher, Bernard. "Group Therapy with Retarded Readers." *Journal of Educational Psychology,* 44 (October, 1953) 354–360.

[20] Gann, Edith. *Reading Difficulty and Personality Organization.* King's Crown Press, New York, 1945.

[21] Gates, Arthur I. "Failure in Reading and Social Maladjustment." *Journal of the National Education Association,* 25 (October, 1936) 205–206.

[22] Gates, Arthur I. "The Role of Personality Maladjustment in Reading Disability." *Journal of Genetic Psychology,* 59 (September, 1941) 77–83.

[23] Gates, Arthur I. "Character and Purposes of the Yearbook." *Reading in the Elementary School,* Forty-eighth Yearbook of the National Society for the Study of Education, Part II, University of Chicago Press, Chicago, 1949, 1–9.

[24] Graham, E. E. *An Exploration of a Theory of Emotional Bases for Reading Failure.* Unpublished doctoral thesis, University of Denver, 1951.

[25] Graham, E. E. "Wechsler-Bellevue and WISC Scattergrams of Unsuccessful Readers." *Journal of Consulting Psychology,* 16 (August, 1952) 268–271.

[26] Gray, Lillian, and Reese, Dora. *Teaching Children to Read.* Ronald Press Company, New York, 1957.

[27] Harris, Albert J. "Unsolved Problems in Reading: A Symposium II." *Elementary English,* 31 (November, 1954) 416–430.

[28] Hebb, Donald O. *A Textbook of Psychology.* W. B. Saunders Company, Philadelphia, 1958.

[29] Holmes, J. A. "Emotional Factors and Reading Disabilities." *The Reading Teacher,* 9 (October, 1955) 11–17.

[30] Johnson, Marjorie Seddon. "A Study of Diagnostic and Remedial Procedures in a Reading Clinic Laboratory School." *Journal of Educational Research,* 48 (April, 1955) 565–578.

[31] Karlsen, Bjorn. *A Comparison of Some Educational and Psychological Characteristics of Successful and Unsuccessful Readers at the Elementary School Level.* Unpublished doctoral thesis, University of Minnesota, 1954.

[32] Kunst, Mary S. "Psychological Treatment in Reading Disability." *Clinical Studies in Reading,* I, Supplementary Educational Monographs, No. 68, University of Chicago Press, Chicago, 1949, 133–140.

[33] Lind, Katherine Niles. "The Social Psychology of Children's Reading." *American Journal of Sociology,* 41 (January, 1936) 454–469.

[34] Mann, Helene P. "Some Learning Hypotheses on Perceptual and Learning Processes with Their Applications to the Process of Reading: A Preliminary Note." *The Journal of Genetic Psychology,* 90 (June, 1957) 167–202.

[35] McGann, Mary. "Dramatic Dialogues for Simultaneous Treatment of Reading and Personality Problems." *Journal of Educational Psychology,* 38 (February, 1947) 96–104.

[36] Missildine, W. H. "The Emotional Background of Thirty Children with Reading Disabilities with Emphasis on its Coercive Elements." *Nervous Child,* 5 (July, 1946), 263–272.

[37] Moore, Thomas Verner. *The Nature and Treatment of Mental Disorders,* Grune and Stratton, New York, 1944.

[38] Osburn, Worth J. "Emotional Blocks in Reading." *The Elementary School Journal,* 52 (September, 1951) 23–30.

[39] Redmount, Robert S. "Description and Evaluation of a Corrective Program for Reading Disability." *Journal of Educational Psychology,* 39 (October, 1948) 347–358.

[40] Robinson, Helen M. *Why Pupils Fail in Reading.* University of Chicago Press, Chicago, 1946.

[41] Robinson, Helen M. "Manifestations of Emotional Maladjustments." *Clinical Studies in Reading,* I, Supplementary Educational Monographs, No. 68, University of Chicago Press, 1949, 114–122.

[42] Roman, Melvin. "Tutorial Group Therapy: A Study of the Integration of Remedial Reading and Group Therapy in the Treatment of Delinquents." *Dissertation Abstracts,* 15[3] (October, 1955) 1761.

[43] Sherman, Mandel. "Emotional Disturbances and Reading Disability." *Recent Trends in Reading,* Supplementary Educational Monographs, No. 49, University of Chicago Press, Chicago, 1939, 126–134.

[44] Shrodes, Caroline. "Bibliotherapy." *The Reading Teacher,* 9 (October, 1955), 24–29.

[45] Siegel, Max. "The Personality Structure of Children with Reading Disabilities as Compared with Children Presenting Other Clinical Problems." *The Nervous Child,* 10 (No. 3–4, 1954) 409–414.

[46] Silverberg, W. V. *Childhood Experience and Personal Destiny.* Springer Publishing Company, New York, 1952.

[47] Slavson, S. R. *An Introduction to Group Therapy.* Commonwealth Fund, New York, 1943.

[48] Smith, Nila Banton. "Readiness for Reading II." *Elementary English,* 27 (February, 1950) 91–106.

[49] Smith, Nila Banton. "Therapy as a Part of Remediation." *The Reading Teacher,* 9 (October, 1955) 18–23.

[50] Spache, George D. "Personality Characteristics of Retarded Readers As Measured by the Picture-Frustration Study." *Educational and Psychological Measurement,* Supplement on Reading Research, 14 (Spring, 1954) 186–192.

[51] Spache, George D. "Personality Patterns of Retarded Readers." *Journal of Educational Research,* 50 (February, 1957) 461–469.

[52] Sparks, Jack Norman. "Teachers' Attitudes toward the Behavior Problems of Children." *Journal of Educational Psychology,* 43 (May, 1952) 284–291.

[53] Stouffer, George A. W., Jr., and Owens, Jennie. "Behavior Problems of Children as Identified by Today's Teachers and Compared with those Reported by E. K. Wickman." *Journal of Educational Research,* 48 (January, 1955) 321–331.

[54] Strang, Ruth. "Diagnosis and Remediation." *Reading in General Education,* William S. Gray (Ed.), American Council on Education, Washington, 1940, 307–356.

[55] Strang, Ruth. "Mental Hygiene of Gifted Children." *The Gifted Child,* ed. by Paul Witty, D. C. Heath and Company, Boston, 1951, 131–162.

[56] Strang, Ruth. "Interrelations of Guidance and Reading Problems." *Education,* 75 (March, 1955) 456–461.

[57] Stroud, James B. *Psychology in Education.* Longmans, Green and Company, New York, 1956.

[58] Tulchin, Simon H. "Emotional Factors in Reading Disabilities in School Children." *Journal of Educational Psychology,* 26 (September, 1935) 443–454.

[59] Wechsler, David. *Measurement of Adult Intelligence.* The Williams and Wilkins Company, Baltimore, 1944.

[60] Weingarten, Samuel. "Developmental Values in Voluntary Reading." *School Review,* 62 (April, 1954) 222–230.

[61] White, Robert W. *The Abnormal Personality.* Ronald Press Company, New York, 1956.

[62] Wickman, E. K. *Children's Behavior and Teacher's Attitudes.* The Commonwealth Fund, New York, 1928.

[63] Wiksell, Wesley. "The Relationship Between Reading Difficulties and Psychological Adjustment." *Journal of Educational Research,* 41 (March, 1948) 557–558.

[64] Wilking, S. V. "Personality Maladjustment as a Causative Factor in Reading Disability." *Elementary School Journal,* 42 (December, 1941) 268–279.

[65] Witty, Paul and Kopel, David. *Reading and the Educative Process.* Ginn and Company, Boston, 1939.

[66] Wolfe, Lillian S. "Differential Factors in Specific Reading Disability: I. Laterality of Function." *Journal of Genetic Psychology,* 58 (March, 1941) 45–56.

[67] Young, Robert A. "Case Studies in Reading Disability." *American Journal of Orthopsychiatry,* 8 (April, 1938) 230–254.

12

READING IN THE LEARNING PROCESS

Learning to read is not an end in itself. Reading must become a tool for learning. Much is known about reading for effective learning which includes a composite of special skills beyond those commonly labeled basic reading skills. Among these are locating and organizing information and planning for its retention.

We cannot assume that once children have learned to read they automatically have acquired the skills and attitudes needed for reading to learn. Teaching children how to study is a distinct responsibility of teachers; it is a special responsibility of content-area teachers. Yoakam (p. 184) [38] points out that teachers

> . . . must come to regard themselves as directors of the study process. They must be as interested in the development and the improvement of study habits as in the imparting of knowledge to children. They must learn that, unless pupils form the habit of reading and studying, they have missed a large part of the purpose of education.*

Traxler (p. 290) [34] suggests that classroom teachers will have best results if they *"regard the improvement of study skills as a continuous objective in all their teaching. . . ."* ** Fay [9] says that "Responsibility for developing effective reading-study habits must be accepted as part of the job in content-area teaching. . . ."

Teachers frequently focus too little attention on the best methods of effective learning. And there is evidence that, for their full development,

---

* Copyright 1935 by the University of Chicago, reprinted by permission.
** Copyright 1945 by the University of Chicago, reprinted by permission.

study skills and habits do require direct teaching. Actually, effective study habits go beyond reading for understanding. An ability to understand fully what is on a printed page offers no guarantee that the understanding will be retained and applied. As a student, the most able reader may perform far below his capabilities if he has never learned how to study effectively.

But, specifically, how does the study process go beyond effective reading? Perhaps we might begin with what reading and study have in common. Certainly, one of the elements of good reading comprehension is integration. In this sense all reading is study. Gray [15] points out that integration is the heart of the learning act. The reading act is complete only when that which is read becomes assimilated. Thus what is read is changed by the reader and the reader is changed by what he reads. This process of integration is an essential element of effective study.

THE CHARACTERISTICS OF EFFECTIVE STUDY

When we examine the characteristics of effective study, in a sense we are examining the characteristics of effective teaching. We have merely shifted our view from the teacher-guided learning situation to the student-guided learning situation. Thus we can use our knowledge of teaching procedure to guide the student toward acquiring an effective study procedure. Also we find that we can transfer the knowledge we gain from our examination of the elements of effective study to the improvement of our teaching techniques.

Developing effective pupil study habits should be an important goal of all teachers at all grade levels. The student of low ability should be helped to make the best use of his capabilities. And the high-ability child should never become a weak student because he has not learned to study effectively.

Effective study is dependent on a number of factors. Among these are the child's intelligence, his out-of-school experience, his general educational development, his desire and motivation for learning, his ability to use time efficiently, and his proficiency in specific study skills. Let us examine three of these factors: motivation, habit formation, and study skills.

MOTIVATION

Motivation is essential for learning. Schlesser and Young,[26] studying the work habits of 498 male freshmen at Colgate University, concluded that it is less important to teach the student the techniques of study than it is to help him develop the motives for and habits of vigorous, persistent effort. They identified

> . . . steady, vigorous, highly motivated effort as the outstanding trait of the student whose achievement is high relative to his abilities. Whatever the techniques he employs in study, the studious individual is a *good worker*. He gets down to work quickly, he enjoys his work, and he persists until he has achieved his goals.*

Not every child with a background rich in experience and with high academic potential learns or studies effectively. Needs, drive, persistence, and desire are crucial elements.[4, 13] Uninterested children may find study

> . . . so disagreeable that they will make numerous mental excuses and waste much time before they get up the courage to plunge in, and even then they frequently think it necessary to try to neutralize the unpleasant feeling by introducing simultaneously something they regard as pleasant, such as a favorite radio program.[34] **

The application of intelligence to learning is so dependent on motivation that some writers include motivation as an essential part of intelligence. Wechsler (p. 3) [36] points out that drive and incentive enter directly into intelligent behavior. Alexander [1] concluded that ability to learn is determined not only by a general intelligence factor (G) and a verbal factor (V) but also by such special traits as the person's persistence and his interest, zeal, and desire. He called these special traits "X" and "Z" and he wrote (p. 128): [1]

> . . . we are suggesting that X must be interpreted as a character factor which exercises an important influence on success in all school subjects. If we were to attach a name to this factor, we should be inclined to call it persistence.

Persistence (pp. 284–285) [8] correlates to some extent with general intelligence, but it correlates even more closely with school grades. And variations in both degree and direction of interest may be a major cause of achievement differences between children of the lower socio-economic classes and children of higher socio-economic status.

Actually, intelligent behavior has many of the characteristics that are shown by the application of physical forces of various kinds. For example, the amount accomplished by a simple machine is dependent not only upon its basic power but upon its leverage or gears, and how long it remains at a task. Likewise the effectiveness of a light bulb is determined not only

---

by its wattage but by its focus and its duration or persistence. Children seem to differ thus in their application to a task. Although their basic powers vary greatly from one to another, so also do their abilities to focus on the task and their tendencies to persist until it is completed.

HABIT FORMATION

Persistent study requires more than a constant motivation. No one can expect to find his work intrinsically rewarding at all times. Well formed *habits* of attention and persistence are crucial to intelligent behavior.

The efficient student has a sense of system. He plans his activities. A written study schedule may help him to systematize his work. Assigning a time and place for study eliminates much dilatory behavior. The time schedule helps to develop a mental set or readiness for the task. Less time is likely to be wasted on achieving full-speed. When the student has an active set to learn and to remember he learns and retains better. Brown, Abeles, and Iscoe [5] found that poor students typically engage in delay activity. They lack decisiveness, tend to procrastinate, and seem unwilling to conform to academic routine.

Schubert [27] compared fifty college students who scored below the twenty-fifth percentile on the *Iowa Silent Reading Test* with 50 randomly selected college students. The poor readers generally were slower to begin study, were less interested, and felt that they were unable to do college work. They were nervous when taking part in class discussions, when reading aloud before the class, and during examinations. They also tended to interrupt their study more frequently. The unselected readers did more skimming and summarizing, and they more frequently raised questions while reading. Generally they liked their course-work.

It appears that the weak student, especially, needs to plan his work carefully and systematically. Frequently he is deprived of the rewards of day-to-day success in school work. If lack of routine is combined with lack of reward, he is certain to adopt dilatory behavior.

In preparing a time schedule and in appraising it the student may need the teacher's guidance. A time schedule should not result in slavery to routine, but it should represent an orderly plan for activities. A schedule is not an end in itself; for time alone does not guarantee learning. Nevertheless, it encourages the student to begin study promptly. In this way, it helps him to shorten the warm-up period for effective study.

Successful use of a time schedule depends on the student's ability to anticipate his own needs. Book reports, oral reports in class, examinations, term papers, and other long-term projects will demand a portion of his time, and the schedule must be adjusted to include them as the need arises.

Various writers have suggested principles that should guide the student in making a time schedule. Let us examine some of them.

1. Study periods should follow class periods as soon as possible. This has distinct advantages for the student:
   a. He is more interested.
   b. His memory of the class materials is still adequate.
   c. He requires less review time.
   d. He is better oriented to the study materials.
2. Study periods on a specific subject should be neither too short nor too long. One to two hours is the recommended length of an uninterrupted study period. Within the study period, breaks should be brief.
3. The student should include time for review in his schedule.
4. The student should learn to develop a balance between study, work, and recreation. His schedule should make provisions for classes, laboratories, work, study, meetings, meals, recreation, social activities, and sleep. Evening study should be held to a minimum.
5. The student should have a regular place for study with all needed equipment at hand. For building effective study habits a regular place for study is as important as a regular time.

STUDY SKILLS

In addition to motivation and organization, the student needs certain basic study skills and techniques. Recently special study-skills classes have become common in colleges and are beginning to appear in high schools. Numerous printed study aids are being published.

The major reason that study-skill classes now are being offered in many colleges is that it is at the college level, when the student is put on his own, that the grievous lack of training in the skills of independent learning becomes obvious to both the student and his teachers.

Some high schools now offer short, intensive courses in study skills for those students who plan to attend college. Actually, a substantial beginning in developing the skills of independent learning should have been made in the elementary school.

To teach study skills effectively, we must know which study skills are needed. Many specific plans and concrete suggestions for improving study skills have been devised by those directing special classes in this area. Let us examine some of these and hope to find applications to all grade levels. There seems to be general agreement that the following skills are basic to effective study:

1. Ability to identify and state the specific purposes for the reading
2. Ability to locate information

3. Ability to select the correct and needed information
4. Ability to comprehend what is read
5. Ability to organize the information
6. Ability to utilize the information
7. Ability to remember the information
8. Ability to adjust the method and rate of reading to the purposes and the nature of the materials.

As we examine this list we see that both the basic reading skills that were discussed in Chapter 7 and numerous special study techniques are included. The close relationship between reading and study skills is even more apparent when we examine the aims of a reading-study program. Yoakam (pp. 148–149) [39] lists these as the following:

1. To teach pupils to use textbooks and other curricular materials of a factual type effectively.
2. To promote the application of basal reading skills to curricular reading materials.
3. To discover any difficulties in study-reading and to correct them as rapidly as possible.
4. To teach pupils the special reading skills needed in curricular areas; for example, the use of maps and graphs, the use of indexes, atlases, and other books of reference.
5. To make the child familiar with source materials in a given area and to teach him how to find and use them.
6. To teach the child to adjust his rate and method of reading to materials of different levels of difficulty and variety of content.
7. To teach the use of aids to study, such as notebooks, notetaking, the use of outlines, bibliographies, etc.

Before discussing the study skills of location and organization, let us examine one frequently recommended method of study.

A METHOD OF STUDY

Robinson's (pp. 13–48) [25] study method is one of the best known. It appears to be applicable to study at all grade levels. He identifies five steps which he refers to as SQ3R: Survey, Question, Read, Recite, and Review.

SURVEY

The first step in Robinson's study method is the process of becoming familiar with the broad outlines, the chapter title, the headings, the topic sentences, and the summary. Spache and Berg (p. 30) [29] refer to this phase as "previewing." The reader tries to see the general outline of the study task. In doing this he may read the topic sentences and the headings. The student should not rush through this first step but should preview rather thoughtfully, trying to relate each heading to its main ideas and to relate each section to the rest of the chapter. In this phase of good study the student "warms-up" to the task ahead.

Skimming may be used in previewing. Skimming is selective reading rather than speeded reading. The reader wishes to get an over-all view of the material, is after certain information, or perhaps wishes to decide whether or not to read the selection more intensively. In skimming, the reader looks for specific clues, such as topic sentences, summaries, italicized words, and key transitional and inferential words, as he seeks to obtain a quick glimpse of the organization of the printed materials.

QUESTION

Robinson's second step calls for questioning. Sometimes the author poses questions at the beginning or at the end of the chapter. The teacher may suggest questions as a part of the assignment. The teacher uses questions of various types. These may require memorization, evaluation, recall, recognition, comparison, summarization, discussion, analysis, decision-making, outlining, illustration, refutation, and inductive or deductive thinking (p. 253).[14] And the student should become able to make his own questions. In doing this he may turn the main headings or italicized words into questions.

A student should readily see the value of this process. Generally, after he takes an examination and checks back with what he has read, he finds that he now knows and will remember the answers to those questions that he had missed. These questions now have become significant to him. The examination created a special need to attend to them. After all, memory is largely a matter of selective attention. Formulating questions encourages him to seek their answers as he reads. Many writers suggest that students write down these questions as a basis for review. Additional questions may be added as the student reviews or re-reads the chapter.

The value of asking and attempting to answer questions has been established by research. Holmes,[18] equating two groups of college students, presented one group with questions based on the material to be read. Both groups read the same English literature and science materials. Not only did the group with the list of questions learn better, but a re-test two weeks later indicated that they retained better. As early as 1922 Judd and Buswell (p. 44) [19] referred to the value of questions. They suggested that waiting for the teacher to raise questions at examination time frequently does not lead to any well-ordered plan of attack on the content of the passage read. Students should be encouraged to ask themselves intelligent questions and be shown how to find appropriate answers for them.

READ

A third phase of an effective study procedure is purposeful reading. Let us examine some of the objectives of purposeful reading. The reader should:

1. Have a definite reason for his reading
2. Define clearly the problem that he wishes to solve
3. Focus his attention on the main points
4. Try to group the supporting details with the main idea
5. Keep in mind the nature of the assignment
6. Pay special attention to illustrations of all kinds: graphs, maps, charts
7. Be a flexible reader—adjust his rate to the purpose of the reading and the nature of the material
8. Try to remember that he is seeking to answer questions.

Study-type reading often is called intensive reading. It is "very careful, rather slow reading with considerable emphasis upon remembering details. This is the kind of reading that is necessary when studying for immediate, detailed tests or recitations." (p. 29) [29] Intensive reading requires that, upon reaching the end of the chapter, the reader recognize the main ideas expressed by the author. He should know where the author was heading and how he got there. The reader tends to form an outline of what he has read. He identifies the major and supporting points.

Nevertheless, not all reading in a textbook needs to be, nor even should be, intensive reading. Gates [12] calls for greater stress on a flexible approach to reading. Reading should vary in speed from very slow, to moderate, to very fast—from detailed study to skimming and scanning. The student should become able to shift from reading to recall and vice versa. If he has learned to adapt his reading to the nature of the specific problem being met, his purposes and the nature of the paragraph or chapter will determine the type of reading that he will use. Even in comprehension there must be flexibility. Certain parts of a textbook chapter, perhaps most of it, must be read intensively, but frequently much can profitably be skimmed. The flexible reader reads rapidly or even skips those parts that are trivial, familiar, or unrelated to his goals and purposes.

RECITE

The fourth phase of Robinson's SQ3R study method is a self-recitation or a self-examination. Without referring to his notes or other aids, the student attempts to answer the questions that he has posed. He consults his notes or refers to the book only after he has answered or attempted to answer the questions. When we recite we recall, and recall is a powerful aid to retention. Recitation also directs our attention to specific questions, thereby aiding concentration. Concentration is a by-product of having a goal that challenges the mind.[23]

Generally it is recommended that the recitation should occur as soon as possible after the reading. Weigand and Blake (p. 39) [37] emphasize two other aspects of effective recitation and study:

> . . . (a) whenever possible substitute understanding for rote memorization and *recite in your own words,* and (b) if you *must* memorize (formulas, poetry, etc.) overlearn at once, that is, repeat the piece of material several times after you have proved to yourself that you know it.

Self-recitation makes a number of contributions to effective learning. The student immediately is aware of how well he read, how accurately he accomplished his purposes, and whether he can express his new-found knowledge in his own words. If he can verbalize his knowledge to his own satisfaction, generally he can also explain or recite to another's. Recitation is the heart of effective study. It is the seeking of answers to self-imposed questions and the putting of new learnings into one's own words.

Self-recitation also can be justified by what we know about transfer of training. Transfer has special significance when tasks are similar. Self-recitation tends to be similar to the use of the learnings the child later makes in examinations, in other learning tasks, and meeting life situations. Studies show that the closer the learning situation is to the test situation or the life situation, the greater are the chances that the training will be used.

REVIEW

The fifth and final phase of Robinson's method is review. Study is not complete until it includes a plan for retention. If learning is to be of any use in later situations, the child must remember what he has learned. Actually, remembering itself is defined in various ways. We say that one remembers facts if he can recall them, can relearn them more quickly, can recognize them, can use them in test situations, or can use them to learn something else more easily. Perhaps the most important criterion of retention is the transfer that is made from the school situation to the life situation, to future acquisition of knowledge, and to future behavior.

Since the goal of review is retention, review will be discussed in more detail under the topics of retention and forgetting.

PARALLELS WITH EFFECTIVE TEACHING

In Chapter 3 we saw that Herbart's five "formal" steps of teaching remain a basic part of current educational method. This has occurred because they contain the essential elements of effective learning procedure. Let us examine here their parallel with Robinson's five "formal" steps of effective study.

Herbart suggested that the child must be *prepared* for learning. In short his interest must be aroused; he must have a mental set or readiness for learning; he must see the goals of his learning. Robinson suggests that the student prepare and orient himself for learning by a *survey* of the material to be read. As an additional step in preparation he suggests that the student form questions to be answered in his study. Herbart's second step is *presentation;* Robinson also suggests that now is the time to read the material. Herbart next suggests *association;* Robinson suggests recitation or recall of the material learned and integration of this material with previous learnings. Herbart suggests finally we *systematize* and *apply.* Effective study, also, recognizes that finally we organize and review and, if possible, we review by applying our knowledge to new problems.

FACTORS AFFECTING RETENTION

We have seen that plans for effective study make specific recommendations designed to encourage both learning and retention. Now let us discuss those determinants of retention that should be considered as we guide the child to use reading for learning.

In attempting to guarantee that our students will retain as much as possible of what they learn, we become interested in any factors that affect retention. What are some of these factors? Most frequently mentioned are: intelligence, prior experience, age, review, degree of learning, the meaningfulness of the material, the learner's set to remember, the learner's emotional involvement with the material, the method of learning, the activities of the learner between learning and the time of testing, and the way retention is tested. Let's examine some of these.

FACTS VERSUS UNDERSTANDING

There is considerable evidence that retention is not the same for all types of learning. For example, Frutchey [10] found that for a chemistry course the retention after a year varied from 66 per cent for terminology,

70 per cent for symbols and formulas, 84 per cent for facts, and 92 per cent for the application of principles. And Tyler [35] reports that fifteen months after they had finished a course in zoology, college students had lost 77 per cent of what they had learned about the names of animal structures, 25 per cent of their ability to interpret new experiments, and less than one per cent of their ability to apply principles to new situations. These findings certainly encourage us to emphasize principles and generalization rather than isolated facts.

INDIVIDUAL DIFFERENCES

There are substantial differences in retentive ability among learners. Unfortunately the slow learner generally retains less than the rapid learner. McGeoch and Irion (p. 375) [22] conclude that, generally, individual differences in learning are reflected in individual differences in retention. Possibly this is because the rapid learner is better able to see the relationships and principles that are involved in whatever he learns. Long ago Pyle [24] reported that the fast learner remembers words, objects, pictures, syllables, and connected thought passages better than the slow learner and is more accurate. However, individual differences usually are not great when time required for relearning is compared with time required for initial learning. Thus experiments have indicated that individuals tend to differ less in retention than in the ability to learn. However, even this minor point in favor of the slow learner may be due to the fact that, in requiring much longer to learn, he overlearns certain portions of the task before he learns the entire task. Certainly the slow learner gains no general advantage in retention from his slowness (p. 376–377).[22]

REVIEW

Review becomes a relatively simple process if study has been done correctly. Any one of the following methods of study may serve as a basis for review: the student-developed outline, questions that he prepared for himself, or careful note-making either in a separate notebook or through identification of special points in the textbook itself.

Stroud (p. 469) [32] has pointed out that review should be more than a re-view or re-reading of materials. It should result in an extension and organization of what has been learned. Review should be a *critical re-examination* with a goal of integrating the content and acquiring useful generalizations. Review may serve to relate material studied at one time to material studied at another with the result that both sets of material are better understood and better remembered.

Review, whether through notes or through re-reading, should be an exercise in critical reading and thinking. Basically there are two methods of review: review by reimpression and symbolical review. Reimpression is the type of review we do when we re-read. Symbolical review is done through recall, self-recitation, class discussions, tests, and summaries. A re-reading of carefully made lecture notes can involve both reimpression and symbolic review. Symbolic review encourages thinking, assimilation, integration, and organization. It tends to be review with a purpose and with an eye toward application.

Gray and Reese (p. 255) [14] point out that, especially in the intermediate and upper grades, children will require a reason for re-reading a selection. They suggest that the following are valid purposes:

1. To prepare a dramatization, puppet show, or simulated television or radio broadcast. . . .
2. To select beautifully worded passages to share with others.
3. To memorize the apt phraseology and particularly the nub of a joke or anecdote in order to tell it to someone.
4. To select points relevant to the topic heading or to select new topic heading in a passage read.
5. To judge the suitability of a title of a story or poem.
6. To reread a passage in order to settle a point in controversy.
7. To reread to verify a point only partially grasped.
8. To reread to get a set of directions straight.*

Unless we do something to slow it, forgetting proceeds at a rapid pace immediately after learning. Thus review should come as soon as possible. And, generally, we need more than one review. The first reviews should follow each other rather closely with the interval of time between reviews gradually increasing. Lyon (p. 161) [21] suggested that

> . . . when associations have once been formed they should be recalled before an interval so long has elapsed that the original associations have lost their 'color' and cannot be recalled in the same 'shape', time, and order. . . . For similar reasons the student is advised to review his 'lecture notes' shortly after taking them, and if possible, to review them again the evening of the same day. Then the lapse of a week or two does not make nearly so much difference. When once he has forgotten so much that the various associations originally made have vanished, a considerable portion of the material is irretrievably lost.

Studies generally have emphasized that frequent and continued review is desirable. Robinson (p. 50) [25] points out that:

---

* Lillian Gray and Dora Reese, *Teaching Children to Read,* 2nd Ed. (New York: The Ronald Press Company, 1957).

Several review times, rather than one lengthy session, should be scheduled. A review time should be scheduled separately from study time. A definite segment of the lesson should be assigned to each review time so the task looks possible of completion and does not lead to procrastination.*

RECALL

In Chapter 3 we discussed the effect of practice in learning. We found that practice or repetition itself does not *cause* learning. Practice is important only because of conditions that operate during practice. That practice alone is not enough has been shown by numerous studies. In one study,[7] 134 educational psychology students were divided into five groups. Group I heard a passage just once; group II heard it twice; group III heard it three times; group IV heard it four times, and group V heard it five times. Testing ten minutes after completion of the experiment revealed a small gain from the second exposure but no advantages from additional repetitions. Generally similar results have been obtained when students have been asked to re-read the same material several times without intervening questions or re-direction of any kind.

However, there is a condition that has been found extremely powerful in making reading an effective means for learning. Gates [11] found that learning is improved when a part of the study time is devoted to recall or recitation rather than when all the available time is given to reading. Generally he obtained best results when about forty per cent of the time was devoted to reading and the remainder to recitation. Recitation was most important when used by third and fourth graders. And they profited more when a greater percentage of time was devoted to it. One of Gates' observations in connection with the value of recall is particularly important. Recall not only speeds learning; it enhances the permanency of learning. Thus the effect of recall is most clearly shown when the results of the learning are measured after some time has elapsed.

We cannot of course conclude from these observations that a specific percentage of study time should be spent on recall. The percentage of time used for recall will depend on the type of materials to be learned. In highly condensed, factual materials it is profitable to use much, perhaps most, of our time recalling. In other materials we may need most of our time for exposure—for reading. However, in all kinds of learning, recall

---

* Francis P. Robinson, *Effective Study,* Rev. Ed. (New York: Harper & Bros., 1961).

time is extremely worthwhile and its greatest value is in its contribution toward permanence in learning.

We have discussed at some length the general values of recitation and recall. Since recall has such obvious significance for learning, let's examine some of the specific benefits that may accrue from it. The following five points (pp. 221 ff.) [28] are suggested:

1. . . . the conscious use of recall during the process of study demands that the acts of reading be effortful. . . . It obliges him [the student] to set specific goals and to make an immediate evaluation of his progress towards them. (Studies show that this immediate evaluation of knowledge of one's success is a positive incentive to learning.)
2. . . . recall that is followed by a re-reading gives the learner a chance to check immediately on the accuracy of his learning. Correct information is confirmed and incorrect information is rejected.
3. . . . when the learner recalls material by himself he builds up confidence in his ability to recall it at a later time. There is less chance that panic will rob him of his learning when he tries to draw on it for an examination or a real-life situation.
4. Recall lets the learner assess what he has learned, and thus prevents useless practice on what he already knows.
5. Recall helps the learner to organize his knowledge into meaningful relationships.

EXAMINATIONS

Too often the examination or test is thought of as merely a basis for grading. This is one of its least important values. The well-planned examination is most important for motivating, directing, and reviewing learnings. It encourages the student to read to *learn.* It causes review and it is a review. It requires recall or an attempt to recall and thus facilitates permanency and organization of learnings.

Numerous studies have indicated that testing aids the retention of what is learned. We know that for this purpose the value of tests decreases as the time between learning and testing increases and that weekly tests better promote retention than do monthly tests. Tiedeman,[33] for example, studying 1055 fifth-grade pupils, found that review tests aided in the retention of geography materials learned in the classroom. When tests were delayed, the amount forgotten was greatest during the first day following learning; and best results were obtained when the review tests were given immediately after learning and then at less frequent intervals as time elapsed.

FORGETTING

Whenever we examine the determinants of learning, we find that we must be concerned with the topic of failure of retention, or, simply, forgetting. We forget while we learn as well as after we have learned.

Much of what we know about the general rate of forgetting comes from the early experimentation of Ebbinghaus.[6] The Ebbinghaus curve shows the amount remembered at the end of various periods of time. Ebbinghaus demonstrated that the most rapid forgetting occurs soon after learning. His findings help us to identify certain of the rules that govern forgetting.

However, Ebbinghaus obtained his data under conditions that have since been demonstrated to lead to very low retention. For example, he used nonsense syllables for his learning material, he learned many such lists during each learning period, and he learned each list to a rather low level of mastery (two errorless repetitions). His curve, then, tends to show a maximum rather than a typical rate of forgetting. His experiments have shown us the *shape* of the typical curve rather than the *amounts* typically forgotten per unit of time. Although Ebbinghaus demonstrated that a greater amount is forgotten soon after learning than is forgotten later, his data do not show us what *percentage* of material will be forgotten when meaningful materials are learned either in laboratory experiments or in classroom situations.

THE CAUSES OF FORGETTING

Some things are forgotten because they are too unpleasant to remember. Also some persons, at least on certain occasions, forget because in some way forgetting satisfies their needs better than does remembering. Perhaps it brings them attention they would not otherwise receive; perhaps they have no interest in remembering and, since forgetting is easier than remembering, they forget.

As an explanation of what happens during learning and forgetting we should be aware that neurologists have offered various theories of the physical process that is involved. Hebb has written extensively concerning this. A quotation from Hebb (p. 147) [17] contains interesting suggestions:

> . . . it is known that if the human subject has had vision long enough its effects do not disappear. If the child does not become blind until the age of four or five, the learning becomes more "ingrained" and disuse has little or no effect. . . .
>
> As to an explanation of these facts, which otherwise might seem very puz-

zling: the synaptic changes that are the basis of learning may consist of a fluid ("ameboid") outgrowth of the cell wall, making a closer connection with another cell. The growing neuron certainly acts in this way, sending out "pseudopods" as an ameba does; if learning also depends on such protrusions, it is possible that with disuse the cell wall slowly retracts, to produce forgetting; and it is possible also that if the connection is maintained for very long periods some further change (like the calcification that makes a child's bones more rigid) may occur to prevent retraction. The learning then would be permanent. But this of course is speculative.

For many years *disuse* was considered to be an acceptable explanation of forgetting. Although it is well recognized that, if there is no practice, forgetting occurs during a lapse of time, today no one considers disuse an adequate explanation of forgetting. Lapse of time is never an effector. Time is important to forgetting only because whatever does cause forgetting transpires *during* the passage of time.

Today, most psychologists agree that forgetting most generally results from the interference effects of past and subsequent learning.* Although as we have noted in certain types of forgetting other factors must be considered, it is these interference effects that are of most concern as we plan for effective classroom learning.

Since both past and subsequent learnings interfere with retention, we have two major determinants of forgetting. The interfering effect of prior learning may be called proactive inhibition; the interfering effect of later learning is called retroactive inhibition.

Thus we find that if a child first learns poem A and then learns poem B, his later retention of poem B is less than it would have been had he not first learned poem A (proactive inhibition). And if a child learns poem X and then learns poem Y, his retention of poem X is less than it would have been had he not later learned poem Y (retroactive inhibition).

As we study the causes of forgetting, we encounter a difficult problem. Perhaps if in a lifetime a child had but one learning experience, he could expect to retain it clearly until death, but this is scarcely a practical solution. Because of the importance of the problem to human learning, numerous experimenters have been concerned with ways to reduce interference and thus make learning more permanent.

THE DETERMINANTS OF INTERFERENCE

Although all those activities that fill the interval between the learning and the using of the learned material (as well as all activities that took

---

* As early as 1894, Bigham (p. 459) [2] theorized that "filling of the interval hinders the memory."

place before the learning occurred) interfere somewhat with memory, not all activities have the same effect on retention.

Numerous experiments have been directed toward identifying the determinants of interference. It is important that we know the conditions under which two learnings interfere most with each other. We can thus hope to evolve methods for minimizing interference. It has been found that the activities that are most *similar* interfere most with one another. This, of course, is true only up to a certain point. When two learnings become so similar that they are identical or have a substantial portion of identical elements, the interference tends to cease and memory is aided. In that case we have what is known as positive transfer of learning.

Psychologists have observed that similarities (and, consequently, differences) among learning tasks have numerous determinants and dimensions. For example, there are similarities of form or content. Two biographic paragraphs would result in more interference than a biographic paragraph and a biographic poem. And two poems of the same rhythm pattern would tend to cause more interference with learning than would two dissimilar poetry forms such as a sonnet and a limerick. Also, patriotic content in a poem leads to more interference with another poem of patriotic content than with a poem of a different theme.

Another dimension of similarity occurs in the sensory mode of learning. A motion picture about a country is likely to be more similar to a motion picture about another country than it would be to a written or an oral discussion of the second country. Two lectures by the same person might result in more interference than lectures by different persons. The number of senses used for learning can be an element in reducing the interference that is caused by similarity. Two poems each read *and* heard are less likely to cause interference through similarity than are two poems studied only by reading *or* hearing.

Time of learning is another determinant of interference. Learnings near each other in time might well interfere more than those set apart in time and even learning at night might interfere more with other learning done at night than with learning done during the day.

Although similarity is one of the major determinants of interference, there are other factors to be considered. Lester [20] had five groups of persons learn a list of syllables. Each group was given different instructions concerning the task. One group was merely told to learn the list. The second, third, and fourth groups were told that they would have to learn a second list the following day. The third group, however, was told that learning the new list might interfere with the recall of the present list. And the fourth group was informed of the effects of interference and was asked to resist them. A fifth group was told to learn the list but, unlike the other four groups, was not required to learn a new list. Lester found that knowledge of the effects of interference and an attempt to resist these resulted in better retention, but all groups that learned a new list on the second day retained less than did the group that was not required to learn a new list.

One important determinant of interference is the degree or thoroughness of learning. The better the materials are learned the less is the loss resulting from later learnings. And, generally, the better materials are learned, the less they will interfere with the learning and retention of other materials. It is only natural that materials that are not learned well will be more easily forgotten than those that are learned well, and that interpolated materials will interfere more with the retention of poorly-learned materials than of well-learned materials. However, when we recognize that not only do we fail to retain poorly-learned materials but, in addition, that poor learnings pose a threat to our retention of other learnings, we see a strong reason for learning well whatever is worth learning.

EDUCATIONAL IMPLICATIONS

As we study the determinants of interference and thus the basic causes of forgetting, we see that similar materials and, particularly, poorly-learned materials are the greatest threat to memory. However, some of the conditions of effective learning that have been discussed earlier in the chapter should also be considered as we attempt to identify the methods that we may use to minimize forgetting:

1. Meaningful learnings are easiest to remember. We have seen that Ebbinghaus used nonsense materials as he studied rate of forgetting. We know that understandings developed in areas such as the natural sciences and the social sciences are much better remembered than are isolated bits of factual information. Thus meaningful material seems to be less subject to interference and, probably, contributes less interference to other materials than does relatively meaningless material.

2. An active intention to remember aids memory. Lester's finding that a group of subjects could reduce interference effects by attempting to do so illustrates this. Even a set to remember for the purpose of doing well on an examination reduces interference.

3. It has been found that material is easiest to remember if it is well organized in the learner's mind. Thus procedures of outlining, summarizing, and making notes tend to reduce interference and aid retention.

4. We know that review is a powerful aid to retention. Review seems to make materials less subject to interference and, again, may make such materials less likely to interfere with other learnings.

5. We know that recall and self-examination are powerful aids to remembering. Such procedures lead to more rapid learning and far better retention than do reading and re-reading alone.

6. Finally, and perhaps most important, well-learned materials are less subject to interference and generally interfere least with other learnings.

Possibly it is to this last point that all other rules for efficient and permanent learnings most directly contribute. The basic determinant of interference may well be similarity; but the better we learn anything the less is it similar to anything else we learn. Familiar, well-learned things assume identities of their own and to us are *unlike* other things.

It is only when we know little about them that two rocks, two bugs, two trees, two persons, two poems, two nations, two events in history, or two physical skills seem similar and thus easily confused. Well-known things are not confused nor are they confusing.

Thus our knowledge of the causes of forgetting may finally be summarized in one simple rule: If a thing is worth learning at all it should be well-learned. In learning, whenever we must choose between quantity and quality, our choice must be quality. For the child of limited ability, it will be far better to learn well a carefully selected one-half of a curriculum than to receive a minimal exposure to all of it.

SOME RECOMMENDATIONS FOR EFFECTIVE STUDY

In using reading for learning, the locating and organizing of information are important skills. The library and its reference materials are important study tools and the student must be taught to use them well. We must show him how to *locate* and *organize* available information and we must help him to form bases for evaluating what he reads.

LOCATING AND EVALUATING INFORMATION

Effective study, particularly at the higher grade levels, requires that indices, periodical literature and its guides, atlases, almanacs, yearbooks, encyclopedias, and dictionaries be used efficiently.

Effective study requires some skill in evaluating books. The student should know what to look for on the title page. Frequently he needs to be concerned with the copyright date, the author's name, and perhaps the author's professional status. The student should use the preface as an indication of the purpose of the book. He should consider the table of contents as an outline of the book. He should be able, when the need arises, to get a still better conception of the book by reading the introductions, the summaries of each chapter, and the final summary at the end of the book. He should know that if he wants a closer look, he may check the main headings and subheadings of each chapter. The student should use the glossary, if one is provided, to find the special meanings of certain words. And he should know how to interpret and use the pictures, diagrams, charts, and graphs that are provided.

For locating specific information in a book or article the student should learn to rely heavily on scanning. This procedure will enable him to look over a paragraph or several pages very rapidly to locate special data or to find the answer to a question. Scanning may also give the reader the general tone of the material and the style and organization used by the writer.

ORGANIZING INFORMATION

Certainly the organizing of knowledge is an important part of effective study. There are various approaches to this task. Summarizing, outlining, underlining, notemaking, and combinations of these have been recommended. The specific approach used is not important. The goal is to perceive the interrelationship and organization of the material and to preserve for future use what has been found most important. However, the organization of material is of such importance that we shall examine here some of the recommended procedures and discuss the values of various organizational methods.

Summaries help to preserve the essential facts and the main ideas in capsule form. They are especially necessary when the student is not using his own book. We have seen that review is important; summaries prepare for review. Summarizing becomes most significant to students at the higher grade levels where the large amount of extra-class required reading demands the summarizing or outlining of materials for review.

Summarizing offers the student additional benefits in that it necessitates his identifying the main ideas and their supporting points. This should aid him to clarify meanings. It should enable him to see both the entire picture and its various parts in their proper perspective.

Outlining is closely related to summarizing. When the reader owns the book, he sometimes outlines by underlining and using letters and numbers to designate main and subordinate points. Weigand and Blake (p. 41),[37] however, suggest that underlining in the textbook should be followed, at the end of the reading session, by going back over the material to make a set of good notes from the underlined material. This latter step has certain values. It acts as an immediate review and encourages the student to put the ideas into his own words. Whatever the exact procedure, the purpose is to identify and organize the material as a step toward efficient learning. In outlining, the student must search for the organization. He focuses on the important points.

The outline should identify the major ideas and show the relation of supporting details in a logical, sequential order. The first step in teaching children to outline is to adopt some formal procedure. Use of identification visually distinguishes the major headings from the less important elements. The outline itself may be in word, phrase, or sentence form.

The outline has certain limitations. For example, it never includes the detail nor flavor of the original material. Weigand and Blake (p. 41) [37] list other limitations:

1. Students too frequently list a series of headings and consider they have outlined the text. Remember that a mere series of words is not a set of notes.
2. Outlining as you go tends to break up the continuity of thought in reading.
3. Too frequently, students use the author's words and headings rather than their own.
4. There is less opportunity for you to tie ideas together in a form which is meaningful to you.

There are certain types of reading materials that are not well suited either to summarizing or to outlining. *Notemaking* may be the most desirable approach for narrative materials and for some topical references that the teacher may assign. The student may find it helpful to skim-read these materials before beginning to take notes so that he will have a preview of the scope of the material and the author's purpose and direction. Note-making skill is of critical importance when it is necessary to use listening as the avenue of learning. During the reading of narrative material and topical references and while listening to lectures it is often necessary to make notes that are in neither summary nor outline form. Perhaps the notes will consist of hastily sketched words or phrases. However, the later re-casting of those notes into a summary or outline form is desirable and can serve as a review of the material read or heard.

Let us focus on the problem of note-making from lecture material. Certain elements of this high-level learning skill apply also to reading for learning.

Effective note-making from orally presented materials requires far more than stenographic skill. It requires attention, concentration, skillful listening and selection, and a certain proficiency in writing. Selecting and organizing are as important as recording and, ideally, these occur simultaneously with a considerable amount of digestion and learning. Although there is nothing wrong with recording the teacher's words verbatim, the student should learn to listen for and to record meanings rather than mere words. His goal should be note-making rather than note-taking.

Weigand and Blake (p. 32) [37] suggest that the student

> Listen carefully, putting into note form those items which have been (a) emphasized, (b) repeated several times, (c) referred to as items you will be expected to learn and will be examined on, (d) written on the blackboard or graphed for emphasis.

If the lecture is well organized—if the main ideas stand forth from the supporting elements and details—the student may be able to make notes in outline form. If he misses an essential element of the lecture he should learn to skip it temporarily in favor of keeping pace with the lecturer. He may later be able to obtain the missing element from another student.

There are certain general rules of note-making that the student should learn. Let's examine some of them. Generally he should do more listening or reading than writing. His notes should be brief but accurate. Effective students have learned to recognize certain cue words such as *first, second, finally, moreover, however, therefore;* they know, further, that books often indicate important details by underlining, by boldface type, italics, or capital letters. And numbered points often indicate important interrelationships. Formulas, statistics, and definitions often must be recorded exactly as given. He should decide on one method of note-making and use it until it becomes habitual.

For example, he may find it desirable to use the page on the right side of his notebook for recording points as they are given and later use the page on the left for identifying questions and major and minor topics from the notes he has taken. And certainly he should adopt a size and style of paper and notebook that he will use regularly so that his notes for each class or topic can be organized and kept available for future use.

Finally, notes must be reworked. It may not be necessary for him to rewrite them, but as soon as possible they should be organized and points that are vague should be made clear. The closer in time that the reworking is to the original learning event, the better he will be able to recall the original learning and the better he can organize his notes. The reworking of notes also provides for that first and most important review period.

Although notes left without reworking and review do not change physically, they suffer considerable loss of flavor. The student loses the associations that he has attached to his written cues. In short, his notes become "cold." The early reworking of notes preserves their freshness.

Note-making provides a *means* for organizing information, for learning, and for fostering retention. It is not an end in itself. As in the case of all the study skills, training and practice are required for its development.

GENERAL RECOMMENDATIONS

Gray and Reese (p. 304) [14] offer a number of suggestions as to how teachers may help the student to strengthen his skill in organizing information. These are:

1. Have students prepare outlines with the topical and marginal headings employed by the author. Then direct them to fill in subordinate ideas and details.
2. Ask students to find the topic sentence of each paragraph and state points which develop its theme in the sentences that follow.
3. Have the students state the theme of a paragraph and list from memory ideas related to it.
4. Ask the students to list key words in a selection, then review the material to note how key words are related to topic sentences.
5. Direct the students to find out the main purpose of the chapter. . . . Then have the class read the chapter through to discover how the author developed the theme. . . .
6. Have the students outline the main points of a chapter after a first reading. Then ask them to re-read the chapter and fill in supporting details.
7. Help the students identify transition words, such as moreover, clearly, hence, however, consequently, therefore.
8. Guide the students in recognizing transition sentences.
9. Give the students a lesson in previewing the contents of a textbook and chapter.*

Although psychologists and teachers generally are convinced that techniques for organizing information are tremendously important study skills, there have been few experimental studies of their importance. Certainly no form of underlining, outlining, summarizing, or making notes assures success. In fact Stordahl and Christensen [31] found that using these techniques does not automatically result in improved comprehension. The critical element is not the making of the summaries, outlines, or notes but the *use* that is made of them for seeing relationships, for identifying important points and for reviewing.

SUMMARY

This chapter has been concerned with reading for learning. Since effective listening differs little from effective reading, much that is known of the one process applies to the other. We have seen that the study methods

---

* Lillian Gray and Dora Reese, *Teaching Children to Read,* 2nd Ed. (New York: The Ronald Press Company, 1957).

required for effective learning closely parallel the steps used for effective teaching. We should expect this to be true. The criterion for judging both effective learning and effective teaching is the same.

With the younger child the teacher maintains a rather close supervision of the learning procedure. The teacher decides what should be learned and attempts to manipulate problems so that the learnings occur. He directs the child's process of study by surveying the lessons or the unit with the child and proposing questions to be answered through the child's reading. The teacher also directs the process of recitation and through tests and summaries he directs the child's review activities.

However, the child must be helped to grow from dependence to independence in his learning. A major goal of effective teaching is that the child become independent through the acquisition of effective work and study habits and the techniques for self-directed learning. The accomplishment of such a goal demands that not only the teachers of reading but *all* teachers employ methods that will help the student learn *and learn how to learn.* Of course motivation for learning is exceedingly important also, but motivation without direction rarely results in optimum learning.

SUGGESTED READINGS

For a brief discussion of learning theories and a helpful listing of principles of learning with applications to teaching, see:

Burton, William H., "Basic Principles in a Good Teaching-Learning Situation," *Phi Delta Kappan,* Vol. 39, Number 6 (March, 1958), pp. 242–248.

QUESTIONS FOR DISCUSSION

1. What factors in addition to intelligence enter into intelligent behavior? Discuss.
2. At about what grade level do children begin to read to learn? What opportunities and responsibilities do we have for teaching reading at the various grade levels?
3. What general study skills seem worth teaching? How may they be taught?
4. Describe and evaluate Robinson's SQ3R method of study.
5. What are some of the most important determinants of retention?
6. How are individual differences in learning ability related to individual differences in retention?
7. Discuss and evaluate review as a study procedure.
8. What is the cause of forgetting? Discuss the various factors that determine the degree of interference.
9. How may interference cause difficulties in learning to read?

10. Suggest methods for minimizing forgetting.
11. Discuss the process of location and organization of material. How would you teach this skill?

BIBLIOGRAPHY

[1] Alexander, William Picken. "Intelligence, Concrete and Abstract." *British Journal of Psychology,* Monograph Supplement, 6 (Number 19, 1935) 1–177.

[2] Bigham, John. "Memory." *Psychological Review,* 1 (September, 1894) 453–461.

[3] Bird, Charles and Bird, Dorothy M. *Learning More by Effective Study.* Appleton-Century-Crofts, Inc., New York, 1945.

[4] Bowman, Paul H. "Personality and Scholastic Underachievement," pp. 40–55 in *Freeing Capacity to Learn,* Alexander Frazier (Ed.), Association for Supervision and Curriculum Development, National Educational Association, Washington, D.C., 1960.

[5] Brown, William F., Abeles, Norman, and Iscoe, Ira. "Motivational Differences Between High and Low Scholarship College Students." *Journal of Educational Psychology,* 45 (April, 1954) 215–223.

[6] Ebbinghaus, Hermann. *Ueber das Gedaechtnis,* translated as *Memory* by H. A. Ruger and C. E. Bussenius. Teachers College, Columbia University, New York, 1913.

[7] English, Horace B., Welborn, E. L., and Killian, C. D. "Studies in Substance Memorization." *Journal of General Psychology,* 11 (October, 1934) 233–260.

[8] Eysenck, H. J. *The Structure of Human Personality.* Methuen and Company, Ltd., London, 1953.

[9] Fay, Leo. "Responsibility for and Methods of Promoting Growth in Reading in Content Areas." *Better Readers for Our Times,* International Reading Association, Conference Proceedings, Scholastic Magazines, New York, 1956, 88–92.

[10] Frutchey, F. P. "Retention in High-School Chemistry." *Journal of Higher Education,* 8 (April, 1937) 217–218.

[11] Gates, Arthur I. "Recitation as a Factor in Memorizing." *Archives of Psychology,* 6 (September, 1917) 1–104.

[12] Gates, Arthur I. "Developing Higher Levels of Reading Instruction." *Better Readers For Our Times,* International Reading Association, Conference Proceedings, Scholastic Magazines, New York, 1956, 95–98.

[13] Goldberg, Mirian L. "Studies in Underachievement Among the Academically Talented," pp. 56–73 in *Freeing Capacity to Learn,* Alexander Frazier (Ed.), Association for Supervision and Curriculum Development, National Educational Association, Washington, D.C., 1960.

[14] Gray, Lillian, and Reese, Dora. *Teaching Children to Read.* Ronald Press Company, New York, 1957.

[15] Gray, William S. "Is Your Reading Program a Good One?" *University of Kansas Conference on Reading,* International Reading Association, October 12, 1957.

[16] Harris, A. J. *How to Increase Reading Ability,* 3rd Edition. Longmans, Green and Company, New York, 1956.

[17] Hebb, Donald O. *A Textbook of Psychology.* W. B. Saunders Company, Philadelphia, 1958.

[18] Holmes, Eleanor. "Reading Guided by Questions Versus Careful Reading and Re-reading without Questions." *School Review,* 39 (May, 1931) 361–371.

[19] Judd, Charles H., and Buswell, G. T. *Silent Reading: A Study of Various Types.* Supplementary Educational Monographs, No. 23, University of Chicago Press, Chicago, 1922.

[20] Lester, Olive P. "Mental Set in Relation to Retroactive Inhibition." *Journal of Experimental Psychology,* 15 (December, 1932) 681–699.

[21] Lyon, Darwin Oliver. "The Relation of Length of Material to Time Taken for Learning and the Optimum Distribution of Time, Part III." *Journal of Educational Psychology,* 5 (March, 1914) 155–163.

[22] McGeoch, John A., and Irion, Arthur L. *The Psychology of Human Learning,* Longmans, Green and Co., New York, 1952.

[23] Perry, William G., Jr., and Whitlock, Charles P. "The Right to Read Rapidly." *Atlantic Monthly,* 190 (November, 1952) 88–96.

[24] Pyle, William H. "Retention as Related to Repetition." *Journal of Educational Psychology,* 2 (1911) 311–321.

[25] Robinson, Francis P. *Effective Study.* Revised Edition, Harper & Bros., New York, 1961.

[26] Schlesser, George E., and Young, C. W. "Study and Work Habits." *The School Review,* 53 (February, 1945) 85–89.

[27] Schubert, Delwyn G. "A Comparative Study of Retarded and Unselected College Readers with Respect to Certain Study Habits, Attitudes, and Personality Traits." *Journal of Educational Research,* 46 (February, 1953) 471–474.

[28] Smith, Henry P. *Psychology in Teaching.* Prentice-Hall, Inc., Englewood Cliffs, N.J., 1954.

[29] Spache, George D., and Berg, Paul C. *The Art of Efficient Reading.* Macmillan Company, New York, 1955.

[30] Staiger, Ralph C., and Bliesmer, Emery P. "Reading Comprehension in the High School." *Education,* 76 (May, 1956) 563–567.

[31] Stordahl, Kalmer E., and Christensen, Clifford M. "The Effect of Study Techniques on Comprehension and Retention." *Journal of Educational Research,* 49 (April, 1956) 561–570.

[32] Stroud, James B. *Psychology in Education.* Longmans, Green and Company, New York, 1956.

[33] Tiedeman, Herman R. "A Study in Retention of Classroom Learning." *Journal of Educational Research,* 41 (March, 1948) 516–531.

[34] Traxler, Arthur E. "The Improvement of Study." *The School Review,* 53 (May, 1945) 286–293.

[35] Tyler, Ralph W. "Permanence of Learning." *Journal of Higher Education,* 4 (April, 1933) 203–204.

[36] Wechsler, David. *Measurement of Adult Intelligence.* The Williams and Wilkins Company, Baltimore, 1944.

[37] Weigand, George, and Blake, Walter S., Jr. *College Orientation.* Prentice-Hall, Inc., Englewood Cliffs, New Jersey, 1955.

[38] Yoakam, Gerald A. "The Improvement of Reading and Study Habits." *Elementary School Journal,* 36 (November, 1935) 175–184.

[39] Yoakam, Gerald A. "The Reading-Study Approach to Printed Materials." *The Reading Teacher,* 11 (February, 1958) 146–151.

13

READING IN THE CONTENT AREAS

In each content area reading for learning requires certain specific skills. The teacher must know the unique reading demands of social studies, science, mathematics and the language arts. Special problems are posed by the vocabulary, symbolism, and concepts of each area.

Although reading in each of the content areas requires certain specific skills, this by no means reduces the importance of the general reading skills. However, it does mean that as the child advances through the school grades, it becomes increasingly difficult for him to be weak in reading and strong in the content subjects. We should expect this to be true. Good readers generally are more fortunate than poor readers in a number of ways. They have found reading interesting, they have good vocabularies, and, generally, they are of higher intelligence. These traits, as well as their better basic reading skills, should help them to become good readers in each content area. There is considerable evidence that this actually happens.

For example, Swenson [31] has pointed out that there are far more similarities than differences between general reading abilities and ability to read scientific materials. And she has concluded that if a group of pupils is found to be high in ability to read scientific materials, it is almost certain that the group average will be high also in vocabulary, rate, and comprehension skills when they read either scientific or general materials.

Writers have sought to identify those general reading abilities that are needed in all content-area reading. These include the ability to interpret facts and data, to apprehend the main idea, to organize ideas, to draw conclusions, and to appreciate the literary devices of the writer.

Spache (p. 159) [27] indicates that before high school and college students can read efficiently in the content areas, they must become skillful in the fundamental reading practices we have discussed in the preceding chapters. He stresses their need to become able to survey materials, choose appropriate reading techniques, and acquire a flexible reading rate.

W. S. Gray (pp. 11–12) [12] discusses an unpublished attempt by Jay to identify the common factors in about 30 reading tasks often assigned to fourth-grade pupils. The conclusions were that these tasks commonly require a purpose or "frame of reference," an ability to maintain an appropriate mental set, and an ability to shift as needed from one center of attention to another.

However, we are most concerned here with identifying the numerous specific comprehension skills that content-area reading requires. As Gray and Reese (p. 375) [11] point out:*

> Reading in the basic reader constitutes an easier task for children than reading in the content fields. Various important factors are controlled in the basic reader which cannot be similarly controlled in books dealing with subject-matter content. For example: vocabulary in the content fields is usually more difficult; new terms are introduced faster and with fewer repetitions; more facts are presented to the reader; greater retention is expected; and references to previous facts occur with more frequency in historical, geographical, and other such materials.

Each reader's background of vocabulary and experiences will vary from one content area to another. Consequently, in a given content area equally intelligent readers may differ greatly in readiness for reading. And each area poses its own problems. Specialized vocabulary, maps, tables, graphs, abbreviations, indices, diagrams, and footnotes are but a few of the new problems that the reader must deal with as he learns to read effectively in the content areas.

Studies have indicated that these specific demands of the content fields require special reading skills. Malter [20] found that children in grades four to eight had difficulty with diagrammatic materials. Hansen,[13] comparing sixth-grade children who were superior in solving verbal arithmetic problems with sixth-grade children who were inferior in this skill, found that general language ability and the ability to read graphs, charts, and tables were most closely related to the ability to solve arithmetic problems.

In the content areas the emphasis is on purposive reading. The specific purpose for reading should determine both the degree of comprehension that is required and the rate at which the reading is done. And a recognized

* Lillian Gray and Dora Reese, *Teaching Children to Read,* 2nd Ed. (New York: The Ronald Press Company, 1957).

purpose promotes concentration and attitudes favorable toward reading. "One of the bases for forming favorable attitudes toward reading is a perception of its inherent value" (p. 170).[10]

The content-area teacher helps the child to develop his reading and study skills by formulating questions that require the application of specific comprehension skills. Sometimes it is desirable that the child get only the general import of a selection; at other times he needs to get its literal meaning. Sometimes he must make inferences and applications, see implications and connotations, or understand the specific meaning of a word in context.[19] Through appropriate questions, the skillful teacher encourages the child to form summary statements, examine the authority of the writer, and bring to light misconceptions or gaps in knowledge that should be remedied.

In a unit plan all members of the class are working on the same broad topic. This can stimulate interest, encourage co-operation, and, at the same time, allow the teacher to help each pupil choose his specific subtopics and learn how to locate and organize the necessary reading material. The subtopics chosen by each pupil should fit his needs, abilities, and interests. Thus, to encourage effective learning, assignments are made a teacher-pupil co-operative activity. The class discussion, also, should be an effective learning situation rather than merely a testing period. And individual help or help to small groups can be given to those children who need it.

So far we have examined the general skills required by all content-area reading. However, each area—social studies, science, mathematics, and the language arts—makes specific as well as general demands. Let us examine some of these special requirements.

We will begin with the social studies since many of its special skills are required also by one or more of the other content areas.

READING IN THE SOCIAL STUDIES

Social studies commonly include history, geography, political science, economics, civics, sociology, anthropology, philosophy, and psychology. Effective reading in these subjects requires a number of special skills in addition to those that are common to all reading. The reader must have a purpose, and he must be skillful in identifying the main and subordinate ideas and in organizing his materials in an efficient manner. But he must also acquire the special vocabulary and understand the numerous special concepts of each subject. He must interpret maps, charts, diagrams, and pictures. He must read critically, and in certain circumstances he must become able to recognize and evaluate propaganda. Frequently he must apply both his present reading and his background knowledge to new problems.

Effective reading in the social studies presents three principal difficulties that require the development of specialized background and skills:

1. The vocabulary may be highly specialized and the reading material is likely to be heavily loaded with complex concepts.

2. The diagrammatic materials require considerable interpretive skill for their effective use.

3. The content frequently is emotionally loaded and controversial. A critical evaluation rather than blind acceptance is required.

VOCABULARY DIFFICULTY AND CONCEPT LOADING

One has only to try to define such terms as democracy, culture, law, political economy, and racial integration to experience the difficulty of putting abstractions into concrete terms. And one has only to examine a few paragraphs in a textbook in elementary-school social studies to find numerous vocabulary terms that call for special meaning although some other and more common meaning may be known to most of the readers. For example a child from an industrial area may get meanings from the word combinations "garden truck" and "truck farm" that are quite different from those intended by the author. In addition numerous words such as tall, broad, and heavy are well known to every child when used to describe tall men, broad streets, and heavy objects. However these same words require specialized knowledge when they are used to describe tall buildings, broad meaning, and heavy industry.

Horn (pp.157–158) [15] writes:

> Many of the ideas presented in typical textbooks in geography, history, or other social studies are so intrinsically complicated that they would be difficult to understand even if described in liberal detail, in untechnical language, and in a lucid attractive style. Actually, however, they are presented in the form of condensed and abstract statements that are readily understood only by those who have already formed the generalization for which the statements stand.

DIAGRAMMATIC MATERIALS

The symbolism employed in the social studies presents special difficulties. The student must learn to read maps, graphs, charts, tables, and pictures. And in many cases he must understand special vocabulary terms that accompany them. To read maps, for example, he must know such terms as longitude, latitude, equator, altitude, and hemisphere. The following discussion of the problems involved in reading a map illustrates the difficulties (pp. 194–195).[30] Just as a student must learn the vocabulary of a foreign language,*

> . . . so he has to learn the symbolic language of maps. Just as his impression of descriptive passages gains in vividness when he pictures the scenes described, so his reading of maps becomes more realistic if he visualizes the rivers, glaciers, and other features of the landscape indicated by maps. He needs to be taught to recognize that a map is a ground plan drawn to scale; to read a descriptive story from maps; to read different kinds of maps; to progress from simple to more complex maps; and to read maps in order to learn.

CRITICAL READING

Critical reading is a major reading demand in the social studies area. Spache and Berg (p. 58) [28] point out that a two-fold approach is required: identifying the facts and evaluating or appraising them. The critical reader is concerned both with *what* is being said and *why* it is being said. He wants to know the writer's qualifications. He is more than a literal reader. He is interested in the facts but he is even more interested in accurate *interpretations.* He sifts the ideas, organizes them, rejects some, questions some, and accepts others. Bond and Wagner (pp. 299–300) [3] describe critical reading as follows:**

> Critical reading is the process of evaluating the authenticity and validity of material and of formulating an opinion about it. It is essential for anyone dealing with controversial issues to be able to read critically. Because the social studies deal with human relationships, they naturally discuss many controversial issues. The child will get into difficulty in reading critically in the social studies if he is unable to understand the problem which faces him, remember the problem while reading, and hold himself to the problem. He must judge the pertinency of the material. He must understand the meanings implied as well as stated. He must evaluate the source from which he is reading. He must differentiate the important from the unimportant fact. He must detect statements of fact as opposed to statements of opinion. He must judge the relative accuracy of conflicting statements. He must be able to appraise the authoritativeness and accuracy of the material. He must be able to detect treatments warped by prejudice. He must keep in mind the author's percepts and intentions and judge whether in drawing his conclusions the author considered all the facts presented.

---

* Ruth Strang, Constance M. McCullough, and Arthur E. Traxler. *Problems in the Improvement of Reading* (New York: McGraw-Hill Book Company, 1955), reprinted by permission.

** Guy L. Bond and Eva Bond Wagner. *Teaching the Child to Read* (New York: The Macmillan Company, 1950), reprinted by permission.

In discussing the special skills required for reading critically in grades four to six, Fay says (p. 144) [6] that in addition to gaining a literal comprehension of his reading, the child must be able: *

1. To recognize the author's assumptions, biases, special interests, and general competence.
2. To evaluate the accuracy, adequacy, and appropriateness of what is presented.
3. To make judgments concerning the wisdom of action taken and of conclusions arrived at. This, in turn, brings into play the child's entire system of basic values, for he must rely on his values to make judgments and to reach conclusions.
4. To extend what has been read to other situations.

Huelsman (p. 149) [16] discussing the growth in ability to read critically in grades seven to ten, summarizes the skills of critical reading that he found mentioned in one or more of fifteen articles on the topic:**

1. To define and delimit a problem
2. To formulate hypotheses
3. To locate information bearing on specific problems
4. To determine that a statement is important for a given purpose
5. To distinguish the difference between facts and opinions
6. To evaluate the dependability of data
7. To recognize the limitations of given data even when the items are assumed to be dependable
8. To see elements common to several items of data
9. To make comparisons
10. To organize evidence that suggests relationships
11. To recognize prevailing tendencies or trends in the data
12. To judge the competency of a given author to make a valid statement on a given topic
13. To criticize data on the basis of its completeness and accuracy
14. To criticize a presentation on the basis of the completeness and logic of its reasoning
15. To suspend judgment until all evidence is assembled and evaluated

The statements by Spache and Berg, Bond and Wagner, Fay, and Huelsman provide a summary of what is meant by critical reading. Huelsman (p. 149) [16] goes on to describe the pitfalls that we seek to avoid by reading critically. These are:

---

1. Failure to detect errors in inductive and deductive reasoning
2. Failure to examine all the alternatives
3. Failure to detect false analogies
4. Failure to detect over-generalization
5. Failure to identify over-simplification
6. Failure to distinguish between observations and inferences
7. Failure to detect the shift in meaning of a term
8. Failure to detect distortion or suppression of the truth
9. Permitting emotions to anaesthetize critical powers

Newspapers, which Bowers (p. vii) [4] describes as rich mines of history in the rough, probably will be a major reading resource of the out-of-school adult. These, with radio, television, and magazines, are his primary avenues to information about current events and issues. These media convey information and furnish entertainment; but it is important that the reader or listener recognize that their advertisers have products to sell and their publishers or owners have opinions to purvey and positions to defend. He must learn to apply to these media the skills and attitudes of critical reading.

The critical reading skills developed in the social studies should enable the student to recognize propaganda. He should become able to detect materials that report but one side of the question, deal in prejudice and emotion, use misleading headlines, and confuse fact with opinion and misconstrue fact through opinions. He should become wary of publications that mislead the reader through dubious logic, questionable sampling, and the assumption that any relationship that may be found is a causal one.

Ferrell (p. 186) [8] has suggested that, to read critically, the child must acquire the following skills:*

1. To identify the purpose for which the article was written, namely, to discredit, to eulogize, to make news, or to give accurate information
2. To examine and evaluate the sources of information, distinguish between what is based upon observation and what is based upon inferences drawn from observations
3. To understand and identify the devices used to make the reader react according to a certain pattern:
   a) Appealing to emotion instead of reason
   b) Relating only one side
   c) Using glittering generalities
   d) Beginning with facts generally accepted and then introducing questionable points
   e) Getting indorsement from some prominent person

---

f) Calling names and using slanted words
g) Avoiding source of information
h) Encouraging one to join the band wagon.

SPECIAL SUBJECT REQUIREMENTS

The two social-study subjects most commonly studied throughout the elementary school and into the high-school years are geography and history. Attempts have been made to identify the specific reading skills demanded by these subjects.

Gray and Reese (pp. 379–380) [11] suggest that for effective reading of geography content, children need to be taught directly to:*

1. Sense space relations. A *thousand miles* is a distance difficult for children to understand even though they can easily read the words. . . . To teach directions, children must be taught the location and significance of *north,* and not conceive of it, for example, as the 'top of the map.'
2. Understand how geography influences people and events. . . .
3. Prepare detailed, well-organized reports for class discussion from materials read in different books.
4. Get the facts straight. . . .
5. Sense cause and effect relationships. . . .
6. Recognize generalities, such as the fact that increased altitude indicates a cooler climate.
7. Find the main ideas in an involved paragraph containing cross references and extraneous details.
8. Recognize supporting details.
9. Understand terminology. . . .
10. Classify geographical concepts according to basic human needs: food, shelter, clothing, occupations, recreation, communication, transportation, esthetic appreciation, government, education, and religion.
11. Compare statements and draw accurate conclusions.
12. Read graphs, maps. . . .

The same authors (pp. 387–388) [11] point out that in reading history, children should be taught to:

1. Read history as a true story, with implications important to the individual living today.
2. Sense cause and effect relationships. . . .
3. Become acquainted with sources of materials in this field.
4. Read historical materials voluntarily.

---

* Lillian Gray and Dora Reese, *Teaching Children to Read,* 2nd Ed. (New York: The Ronald Press Company, 1957).

5. Compare parallel materials in different books.
6. Know the difference between original source materials and secondary sources.
7. Compare the past and the present.
8. Distinguish between relevant and irrelevant materials.
9. Develop an interest in facsimilies of historical documents.
10. Understand "internal evidence" and its fascinating role in exposing historical hoaxes. . . .
11. Note the time of occurrence of events.
12. Pay attention to chronological sequence.
13. Apply old knowledge to new situations.
14. Select and organize materials for outlining.
15. Understand the significance of factual data.
16. Group items to be learned in a meaningful association, instead of memorizing them singly. . . .
17. Form the habit of associating personalities with events instead of attempting to remember isolated facts.
18. Understand the special vocabulary of this field.

McLendon (pp. 14–15) [21] points out that in the social studies, except for intentionally repetitious drill:

> The child, in learning, should be guided so that each additional experience . . . expands his conception. Each additional learning experience should not be approached as entirely new; it should contain or refer to some element of previous learning. Yet the additonal learning experiences must avoid complete repetition if they are to result in expanded concepts; another approach, a different point of view, or some variation in elements should be employed.

TEACHING TECHNIQUES

Critical reading can be taught, but a mere knowledge of the techniques of critical reading is not enough. The child needs training and guidance in their use. Critical reading requires critical thinking which is "essentially a matter of interpreting facts, applying generalizations, and recognizing errors in logic" (p. 463).[17] Training in critical reading should be directed toward critical thinking in all media of communication.

Huelsman [16] mentions three ways of teaching critical reading: the direct approach; the functional approach; and the incidental approach. In the direct approach, the pupils are taught the methods of logical reasoning and the devices used by writers and speakers to influence the reader or listener. Newspapers, magazines, editorials, and cartoons are then read critically to discover the presence of propaganda techniques in the materials read. In the functional approach, the pupils begin with the reading material and attempt to discover for themselves the pitfalls in logic as well as the essential features of good thinking. Huelsman concludes that the functional approach appears to offer the most promise if teachers throughout the school system co-ordinate their efforts. He says (p. 153) [16] :*

> Such a plan involves decisions regarding the sequential order in which the skills should be taught, plans for the continuity of practice after instruction, provision of increasing opportunity for pupils to use critical reading skills more and more independently, and constant appraisal of the effectiveness of the procedures.

An incidental approach to teaching critical reading assumes that it will occur as a mere by-product of learning in the social studies. Unfortunately, an incidental approach seems to be by far the least effective. The student must be encouraged to develop an attitude that results in critical reading and thinking. Taba (p. 45) [32] points out that:

> Critical thinking is not a simple gadget that can be taught and acquired on the spot in one lesson, unit, or even in one single subject. It is somewhat like a way of life . . . it is necessary to see critical thinking as a developmental process . . . in which there is a psychological learning sequence that students need to follow.

Certainly an important teaching goal is that pupils become adept in detecting propaganda, bias, and prejudice; that they recognize the reading materials and advertisements which make appeals to emotions but are not substantiated by fact or those which replace fact with opinion; that they detect questionable samplings and dubious logic. Such abilities in critical reading skills will enable pupils to become intelligent consumers and enlightened citizens.

READING IN THE SCIENCES

Each of the sciences, like each of the social studies, has its own special vocabulary and concepts. Though the vocabulary tends to be precise and definite, the concepts frequently are broad and extremely difficult to derive from concrete experiences. For example, valence, magnetism, atomic weights, and gravity are difficult to conceptualize. And, whereas one may readily learn terms such as hydrogen, oxygen, and elecricity, a full understanding of them is beyond immediate reach.

Science also shares with the social studies a basic need for critical read-

---

ing. Hypotheses are proposed and their acceptance or rejection requires critical evaluation. Johnson [18] suggests that the first step in developing critical thinking is the identification of problems that the individual feels a vital need to solve. Science as well as the social studies can be rich in such problems.

In science, more than in any other content area, the student needs to learn to follow directions precisely. The success of his experiments will depend on his ability to comprehend and to carry out instructions. Reading in science should be careful and analytical. There is a premium on detail. Each formula, chart, and graph is important.

SCIENTIFIC METHOD

The scientific method is well known as a method for solving scientific problems. The student must learn to identify the problem, search for the facts, formulate hypotheses, choose an hypothesis and test it, evaluate the results and finally, if necessary, reject the hypothesis and choose another for testing and evaluating. In the sciences purposive reading is frequently one phase of the active search for the facts.

The teacher has a dual responsibility in guiding students' problem-solving behavior. First, students must learn how to identify goals that are vital to them and second, they must acquire effective methods for identifying and solving the problems that bar progress to these goals. Properly used, the scientific method provides built-in guideposts to independent learning.

Although the scientific method is ideally suited to the solution of scientific problems, its applications extend far beyond the sciences. Its steps are followed by an intelligent person as he seeks to resolve many of his business and personal problems. For example, the professional teacher uses the scientific method as he decides how to handle behavior problems or special learning disabilities.

READABILITY OF MATERIALS

The readability of scientific materials presents numerous difficulties. Strang and Bracken (p. 247),[29] summarizing the research on the readability of science texts at the elementary- and high-school levels, say:

1. Reading levels of many [of the texts] are too advanced for students for whom they are written.
2. There are wide differences between levels of reading difficulty of the easiest and the most difficult science texts.
3. In some texts whose average level of reading difficulty seems satisfactory, there are passages that would be difficult for even some college students.

4. Many texts contain words—other than technical key words—that could be replaced with easier synonyms.

Teachers cannot expect the student to develop unaided the special skills and background needed for effective reading in the sciences. As we have seen, a major problem is the understanding of the vocabulary and concepts of each subject.

Schubert (p. 83) [24] suggests a

> . . . rotating, vocabulary-spotting committee whose job entails prereading chapters for difficult terms. Give this committee time to present new and unusual words before the class covers the assignment in which the words are involved.

The teacher, himself, can do much to make vivid the terms used in science textbooks. He can use laboratory demonstrations, films, filmstrips, science magazines, science fiction, and television.

TEACHING TECHNIQUES

The teaching method used also may direct the student's reading approach. Boeck (pp. 249–253) [2] compared the learning of students taught by the "inductive-deductive" and by the "deductive-descriptive" method in nine high-school chemistry classes. The essential difference in the two methods as studied by Boeck was in the laboratory approach. The inductive-deductive method used the laboratory to gather data for solving previously identified problems. The results then were used to formulate a general principle. Learning progressed from the particular to the general. In the deductive-descriptive method, the laboratory work followed exercises in a published manual. The general principle to be illustrated was first discussed in class and the laboratory experiment then provided an illustration of the principle. Under the inductive-deductive method the student had an important part in planning the experiment and in forming generalizations after the experiment was completed.

Boeck concluded that the methods led to equal attainment in general outcomes, but that the inductive-deductive method was ". . . significantly superior with respect to the crucial problem of attaining knowledge of and ability in the use of the methods of science with an accompanying scientific attitude. . . ."

As we examine the specific skills needed for effective reading in the sciences, we become particularly aware that the teacher who assigns reading must teach reading. The special vocabularies and concepts, the careful analytical approach, and the systematic scientific method of solving problems will not have been acquired from those courses in reading that were designed to develop general reading skills. To teach science effectively the teacher must help students to learn to read and to use the printed materials of science as surely as he must teach them to use the apparatus and materials of the scientific laboratory.

READING IN MATHEMATICS

Mathematics, too, has its own vocabulary and concepts. And its vocabulary and concepts tend to be even more peculiar to mathematics than are the vocabulary and concepts of the sciences.

In mathematics the student must acquire a special vocabulary of words and symbols which, generally, he will have no opportunity to use except as he applies them to mathematics. Few of the terms will become a part of his "working" vocabulary in the sense that they will be used in his other classes or in his every-day conversations.

The written material of mathematics differs from most written materials in that context clues are of little value. The terms and symbols are self-definitive; only rarely will embellishment of context aid in recalling their meanings. In well-written material every symbol is significant, concise, functional, and to the point. Reading in mathematics requires thought and deliberation. The rate of reading should be relatively slow and some of the material will need to be read several times. Shaw (p. 170),[25] speaking to the college student, says:*

> As you no doubt know from bitter experience, while working on mathematics problems you can make mistakes in *reading* as well as in *computation*. . . . In no other type of freshman reading is the single word so important as in mathematics problems.

Carter and McGinnis (p. 237) [5] advocate a rather specific procedure for reading a mathematics problem. They suggest that

> . . . the reader first read rapidly for an over-all view of a problem in mathematics; second, that he read in order to arrange the facts in their proper places with one another; and then, that he read to further test the organization of these relationships.

Many difficulties are encountered by the reader of mathematics. Among these are the following (pp. 198–203) [22] :

---

* Phillip B. Shaw. *Effective Reading and Learning* (New York: Thomas Y. Crowell Company, 1955).

1. . . . introduction and use of technical terms.
2. . . . unknown terms or phrases without definition or explanation.
3. . . . explanatory statements although correct are often expressed in language which is beyond the pupils' level of comprehension.
4. . . . explanatory statements which are vague, inadequate, or incomplete.
5. . . . statements which involve familiar words but which use these words in unfamiliar ways. . . .
6. . . . statements that are misleading or incorrect or that may lead the pupil to wrong conclusion.

Technical terms referring to difficult concepts are likely to be introduced quickly and without explanation. Terms such as minuend, product, vertical, divisor, proportion, subtrahend, average, multiplicand, and denominator are examples of such terms. Pressey and Moore (p. 453),[23] studying the mathematical vocabulary of grades three through twelve, wrote:

> The writers would like to offer the suggestion that inadequate mastery of fundamental terminology . . . is one of the most important reasons for the difficulty encountered by so many persons of all ages and social strata in dealing with anything of a mathematical nature.

In mathematics one must acquire meanings for a variety of symbols many of which designate important concepts; $+$, $-$, $\times$, $=$, sine, v_2 are just a few. Wren points out that the study of mathematics involves number concepts, algebraic concepts, geometric concepts, and trigonometric concepts. It includes the use of integers and fractions, computational tables, the use of measurements or estimates thereof, an understanding and construction of graphs, the use of formulas and equations, and an understanding of the decimal system. The student must be able to check his answers, interpret quantitative data, perceive relationships and make and apply generalizations. The student needs (p. 149) [33] :*

> . . . to learn a new form of sentence structure, which, in addition to the usual phraseology, combines symbols and words and, in many cases, uses only symbols to convey complete ideas. The type of reading required in mathematics is slow, intensive reading designed for such prosaic purposes as: following directions; obtaining, analyzing, and interpreting facts; recognizing and comprehending basic mathematical processes and quantitative relationships; drawing implications; and making applications.

Bond and Wagner (p. 317) [3] say that the child should know what the problem calls for, what facts are needed for the solution, what steps are appropriate in leading to a solution, and what is the probable answer. Thus,

---

in learning how to read a mathematical problem, the student should be taught to seek the answers for these questions:

What does the problem ask for?
What pertinent information is given?
What computations are required?
In what order should they be done?
And, how can I test the answer?

In mathematics more than in any other content field, learnings are built upon learnings. Although extra or accelerated work may be given to the advanced student, accommodation of pace to the slow student poses special problems. Whereas in the social studies and to some extent in elementary science courses we help him choose reading selections and topics that fit his abilities, such adjustment for ability levels is not practical in mathematics.

The reading skills needed in mathematics can and should be taught. Unfortunately, the very nature of the reading material often sets up a problem in the teaching process: the learning of new terms and concepts is often dependent upon previously acquired concepts and learnings. This necessity for building new learnings on old learnings means that in mathematics, possibly more than in any other area, what is worth teaching must be taught well.

READING IN THE LANGUAGE ARTS

The power and maneuverability for all reading tends to be derived from this last-discussed area, the language arts. The student's first steps toward becoming an able content-area reader are taken during his early experiences in language-arts reading. For example, his early recognition of word families and prefixes and suffixes will be a basis for his understanding of the social studies' more difficult words such as "excommunicate" or "insubordination." His early training in the use of reference materials from child-level dictionaries, encyclopedias, magazines, and the "how-to" books will serve as a natural approach for his later use of the more adult reference and research materials. He comes to know the library and he learns that there are many sources of information which can satisfy his curiosity or aid him in his search for information for classroom projects.

His early training in adapting his reading speed to the type of material or the purpose of the reading will continue to be a valuable skill as he progresses through the school grades. In fact all of his early training in reading and study skills will help him toward an economical use of his time spent in study and in his leisure-time reading.

However, if a teacher were to believe that these basic steps in the language arts could proceed without guidance and under their own momentum, he would be guilty of undue optimism. The child will need assistance and encouragement in these skills throughout every phase of his schooling. For example, his ability to locate information will have to progress toward evaluation of the authority of the purveyors of that information and toward the skills of assembling information from various sources, compiling it in usable form, and then making the best possible use of it for the problem at hand.

Here, too, his new learnings will be built on earlier learnings; his new skills will have as their foundations those that he has previously acquired.

Possibly the highest hope that a teacher holds for his pupils is that they will become able to *communicate*—if that word is interpreted as both receiving and giving information and ideas. If pupils are to maintain a storehouse of information and ideas from which they can *give,* they must be given opportunities to *receive*. Reading will be for them an important source of supply.

The goals in the teaching of literature are somewhat different from those of the other content areas. As our immediate goal we wish to have the child find that the reading act is rewarding so that for him reading becomes an end in itself rather than a means to an end. As an ultimate goal we wish to lead the child to enjoy literature. We hope that he will come to adopt reading as an important portion of his recreational program.

However, for greatest enjoyment, certain special skills, attitudes, and appreciations must first be learned. Thus in teaching literature, we teach it as a content area. We must teach the child the skills and approaches that will lead him to read for enlightenment and entertainment.

Gainsberg [9] has suggested that the child must be taught to read literature *critically* and that critical reading is *creative* reading. The reading of literature calls for an emotional involvement not generally demanded by other types of content-area reading. The effective reader is alert to shades of meaning and the interrelationships of details; he employs an active rather than a passive approach; he evaluates and questions as he reads; and his focus is less on what the author *says* than on what the author *means* by what he says.

The emotional and reading maturity of the reader will influence the depth of his understanding and appreciation of what he reads. Betts (p. 494) [1] says that ". . . the development, extension, and refinement of concepts is an important prerequisite to reading and a crucial outcome from reading." And it is well to remember that the appreciation of literature is much the same as the appreciation of all art forms—the more one knows of the techniques of any art, the more he will appreciate the art.

Generally we have specific purposes for the study of each selection in literature. Literature is chosen to develop the interests and tastes and to lead to the appreciation of moods, style, and meaning. It should activate the imagination, enrich personal living, and develop insights into man's ideals and experiences.[26] We should keep in mind that our ultimate goal is independent reading for enjoyment.

Assignments in literature should never be interpreted as just so many pages to be read. Instead, they should be expectations—adventures, thrills, excitement, and sorrows to share, characters to be met or to come to know better, new ideas and opinions to be challenged or shared.

Each literary form has its contributions to give to the reader and each requires a somewhat different reading approach. Collectively they offer character studies, a variety of new experiences, and the vitalization of opinions, sensations, and emotions.

Novels, short stories, and *plays* have many similarities in methods of presenting characters and settings and in the development of characters and plot. The short story might be referred to as "a telescoped novel" although there are technical differences in the development of characters and plot. The drama or play contains all the elements of the novel or short story, but there are differences in methods of presenting and developing characters and action and in indicating the settings. The reader or viewer of the play seems to be involved in the living, minute-by-minute unfolding of character and plot; the story- or novel-reader will achieve a different perspective through character discussion, flashbacks in memory and action, and sometimes a sort of author-reader sharing of plans for characters and plot.

These three forms of literature are rich in the possibilities of character study. They offer the reader a chance to meet and learn to judge people. The reader can study personality clues from the actions of the character, from what he says that he thinks and feels, what other characters say about him, how they react to him, and the causes of their reactions. In many cases the characters read about are identifiable by the reader. He may feel that he has met such a character and perhaps has formed a misjudgment because his reaction has been based on too few facets of character portrayal. Also, the reader may sometimes "identify with" a character and thus see how it is possible that his own actions and words may be misjudged by others.

The plots and settings of these literary forms offer the reader excitement, adventure, and new experiences. Many times the experiences gained through reading will be stepping stones to further reading in newly acquired fields of interest. And often the discovery or awareness of an author will lead to further reading of that author's works.

Essays are a literary form which may bear a close resemblance in style and purpose to the reading material usually found on the editorial pages of a modern newspaper. They may resemble either the editorials or the writings found under the by-lines of syndicated columnists. Many magazines, also, include similar reading materials. If the young reader develops an appreciation for the essay form in literature, it seems likely that as an adult he will seek out and find interest in similar materials in newspapers and magazines.

The essay is built around a central theme which is developed through a closely knit, though not necessarily obvious or pronounced, sequence of steps toward a logical conclusion.

Consideration of the author's mood, intent, and purpose will guide the reader in his approach to essay reading. There is a wide variety in essay types. They may be of a formal, pedantic, satiric, or political nature which will call for a careful following of the author's logic. The reader will need to consider the author's reasoning step by step and check its validity and fallaciousness. At the other end of the scale in essay types are the informal and humorous essays which are understood in a relaxed reading. The reader should be able to feel a communication with the author much like that which would be felt if he relaxed in an easy chair and listened to a friend who was "sounding off" on a topic dear to his heart.

Poetry is probably the least restricted of all literary forms. Its only requisite is that it have rhythm. But even that element may involve wide variations from poem to poem or within a poem. The rhythm may be both as uneven and as powerful as the play of lightning, thunder, rain, and hail during a storm. It may be as definite and easily identified as the beat of a bass drum or the ticking of a metronome. Or it may be as inconspicuous or ephemeral as the play of a breeze in the grass. The rhythm in certain poems is difficult to identify unless the poem is read aloud by one who understands its meanings and can feel and interpret the flow of words.

The interpretation of poetry is greatly dependent on the perceptual abilities of the reader. The poet's one word or phrase may evoke a paragraph-sized idea and the connotations of that word or phrase depend upon the past experiences of the reader. In many poems the sounds of the words themselves are important to the reader's interpretation. This means that the reader will interpret the poem through remembered sounds—a sort of reading by ear.

Restrictions in construction and scope are practically nonexistent in poetry. It may take the form of a couplet or a book-length play, narrative, or epic. It may have character delineations as deft and subtle or as profound as those in a play or psychological novel; it may express a point of view as gently, scathingly, or logically as the essay; it may contain adventure, emotional stimulation, and plot which rival short stories and novels. Its meanings may be completely obvious or they may be obscure or implied. Its appeal to the reader's emotions may be intense or its effect may be satiating, hypnotic, or soothing.

In the presentation of poetry to a class it is especially important that the readers have an opportunity to hear as well as to read aloud certain portions of the material. Young children are more impressed with a poem's sound and rhythmic appeal than with its thought content. Most of them have had experiences with rhythmic forms before they enter school. Their early responses to "Pat-a-cake" and "See-saw Margery Daw" and the later game-rhythms such as "Eenie, meenie, minie, mo" and "Tic-tac-toe, round I go" contain the basic qualities of poetry—sound and rhythm. It seems logical, then, that their interest in poetry should be caught and fostered through rhythm and sound.

The oral presentation of poetry has an important contribution to make at all grade levels. For one thing, even a dull child can appreciate and enjoy a poem well read even though he does not understand its full meaning. Listening to poetry read by a teacher, a guest reader, or through the playing of recordings will permit a degree of classroom cohesion.

In order to engender the greatest possible enjoyment, understanding, and appreciation of all forms of literature they must be presented in a manner which will arouse and then foster each child's interest. The teaching of literature is, fortunately, fairly adaptable to all intellectual levels in the classroom. The use of recorded selections and the wide variety of visual aids can be of great service to the teacher. For some of the slow readers or dull students the teacher may wish to employ simplified versions of a selection to serve as introductions to the original versions.

For some portions of literature study it will be advisable to have all the students working together. For example, the class will work as a unit during the introduction of new literary forms and new vocabulary terms and during the use of many of the audio and visual aids. However much of the time may be given to small-group or individualized instruction and to student-paced reading.

As was stated earlier in the chapter, the more one knows of the techniques of any art form, the more he will appreciate the art. Even a rudimentary knowledge of the mechanics of literary composition—techniques, terminology, devices, literary forms, types of rhythms—and actual practice in their use will assist the reader in understanding and appreciating what he reads. Within a class the extent of knowledge and practice of these mechanics may vary from an elementary to an extremely complex level. Individual readers may progress from simple identification of literary forms to the more complex levels of recognition: to the author's use of personification, allegory, flashback, satire, simile, onomatopoeia; poetic forms such as the ballad, the ode, and the sonnet; and the specific rhythms employed in poetry.

THE TEACHER AND THE CONTENT AREAS

Most educators have accepted the position that reading in the content areas demands careful guidance. This may be provided through supervised study, differential assignments, and the cultivation of the special reading skills required in the various content fields.

The content-area teacher must make definite attempts to assure the student's readiness for reading the materials that he assigns. First he makes a careful analysis of assignments to identify the skills needed for comprehension. To encourage effective reading in their subjects, teachers in any content area may profitably follow these general procedures (pp. 137–138) [30] :*

1. Provide a rich background of experience for the material to be read. . . .
2. Encourage wide reading of easy, popular material in the field by leaving magazines, pamphlets, and books where students can read them in their spare time. . . .
3. Ask for volunteers to look up additional information needed to answer the questions raised by the class.
4. Give practice and instruction in reading different kinds of material for different purposes—a news article, a literary description, a technical article. . . .
5. Build a vocabulary of key words in the field. . . .
6. Use as practice exercises passages from the books students are expected to read. . . .
7. Encourage students to analyze their own reading difficulties in the subject and to talk with the teacher about the kind of practice they need. If the whole class or a group within the class needs to improve particular reading skills, the teacher may use ten or fifteen minutes of the class period for this practice and instruction. In a work or study period the best readers may serve as tutors to individuals or to small groups. A few minutes at the end of the period may well be spent in discussing the best method of reading the assignment for the next day. . . .

---

* Ruth Strang, Constance M. McCullough, and Arthur E. Traxler, *Problems in the Improvement of Reading* (New York: McGraw-Hill Book Company, 1955), reprinted by permission.

Fay (p. 39–40),[7] in his nine point list, suggests, among other things, the following: *

Plan with your students the organization of the topics to be studied. . . . Organize your instruction about broad topics or problems rather than follow the presentation of a single textbook. . . . Give assignments that set purpose, that indicate specific methods of study, and that provide each student with material that he can read. . . . Always remember that reading is but one way to learn and that for some it is not the easiest way. . . . Teach study skills as well as information.

SUMMARY

Effective reading in the content areas demands all the general reading skills the student has been taught throughout the primary grades. However, each content-area course has its special vocabulary and concepts and requires its special reading skills.

The content-area teacher must assume full responsibility for teaching the special vocabulary, concepts, and reading skills required by his subject. To teach content effectively, he must teach reading effectively.

SUGGESTED READINGS

(Causey, *The Reading Teacher's Reader*)

Article 4, Eller, William, "Reading and Semantics," from Fifth Yearbook of the Southwest Reading Conference (1956), pp. 52–58.

Article 7, Eller, William, "Fundamentals of Critical Reading" (from an unpublished paper).

Article 37, Curry, James W., "Teaching Reading thru Social Studies," from *National Elementary Principal,* 35 (September, 1955), pp. 124–127.

Article 38, Sprague, Ellen J., "Science Teaches Reading," from *The Grade Teacher,* 72 (April, 1956), pp. 16, 122.

***

(Hunnicutt and Iverson, *Research in the Three R's*)

From Chapter V, "What We Read," the following three articles:

Bond, Eva, "Reading and Achievement in the Content Areas," adapted from *Reading and Ninth Grade Achievement,* Contributions to Education No. 756, Teachers College, Columbia University, New York, 1938.

Dewey, J. C., "Comprehension Difficulties in History," adapted from "A Case Study of Reading Comprehension Difficulties in American History," University of Iowa Studies in Education, 10 (1935) pp. 26–54.

Rudolf, Kathleen B., "Teaching Students How to Read Social Studies Mate-

---

rials," adapted from *The Effect of Reading Instruction on Achievement in Eighth Grade Social Studies,* Bureau of Publications, Teachers College, Columbia University, New York, 1949.

QUESTIONS FOR DISCUSSION

1. Apart from variations in the ability to read, what are the most important differences between good and poor readers?
2. Identify and discuss some of the specific skills needed for effective reading in general science, citizenship, world history, geography, and mathematics.
3. How may a teacher ensure that the child will acquire the skills he needs for content-area reading?
4. What special skills and attitudes are needed for critical reading?
5. How may critical reading be taught?
6. Show how the scientific method is used for solving problems outside the field of science.
7. What skills acquired during reading in the language arts are likely to make for better reading in the other content fields? And what skills acquired in other content fields contribute toward better reading in the language arts?
8. How do the goals of reading in the language arts differ from those of reading in other content fields?

BIBLIOGRAPHY

[1] Betts, Emmett Albert. *Foundations of Reading Instruction.* American Book Company, New York, 1957.

[2] Boeck, Clarence H. "The Inductive-Deductive Compared to the Deductive-Descriptive Approach to Laboratory Instruction in High School Chemistry." *Journal of Experimental Education,* 19 (March, 1951) 247–253.

[3] Bond, Guy and Wagner, Eva Bond. *Teaching the Child to Read,* Revised Edition. The Macmillan Company, New York, 1950.

[4] Bowers, Claude G. *Jefferson in Power.* Houghton Mifflin Company, Boston, 1936.

[5] Carter, Homer L. J., and McGinnis, Dorothy J. *Effective Reading for College Students.* The Dryden Press, New York, 1957.

[6] Fay, Leo C. "Promoting Growth in Ability to Interpret When Reading Critically: In Grades Four to Six." *Promoting Growth toward Maturity in Interpreting What is Read,* Supplementary Education Monographs, No. 74, University of Chicago Press, Chicago, 1951, 144–148.

[7] Fay, Leo C. "Adjusting Learning Activities and Reading Materials to Individual Differences: In Grades Seven to Nine." *Improving Reading in All Curriculum Areas,* Supplementary Educational Monographs, No. 76, University of Chicago Press, Chicago, 1952, 36–40.

[8] Ferrell, Frances Hunter. "Methods of Increasing Competence in Interpreting

Social-Studies Materials: In Grades Ten to Fourteen." *Improving Reading in All Curriculum Areas,* Supplementary Educational Monographs, No. 76, University of Chicago Press, Chicago, 1952, 183–187.

[9] Gainsberg, Joseph C. "Critical Reading is Creative Reading and Needs Creative Teaching." *The Reading Teacher,* 6 (March, 1953) 19–26.

[10] Glock, Marvin D. "Developing Clear Recognition of Pupil Purposes for Reading." *The Reading Teacher,* 11 (February, 1958) 165–170.

[11] Gray, Lillian, and Reese, Dora. *Teaching Children to Read.* The Ronald Press Company, New York, 1957.

[12] Gray, William S. "Growth in Understanding of Reading and Its Development Among Youth." *Keeping Reading Programs Abreast of the Times,* Supplementary Educational Monographs, No. 72, University of Chicago Press, Chicago, 1950, 8–13.

[13] Hansen, Carl W. "Factors Associated with Successful Achievement in Problem Solving in Sixth Grade Arithmetic." *Journal of Educational Research,* 38 (October, 1944) 111–118.

[14] Hobson, Cloy S. and Haugh, Oscar M. "Reading Skills and Habits Needed in the Language Arts," *Teaching Reading in the High School,* Vol. 10, No. 1, Kansas Studies in Education, University of Kansas Publications, School of Education, Lawrence, Kansas (February, 1960) 3–4.

[15] Horn, Ernest. *Methods of Instruction in the Social Studies.* Scribner's and Sons, New York, 1937.

[16] Huelsman, Charles B., Jr. "Promoting Growth in Ability to Interpret When Reading Critically: In Grades Seven to Ten." *Promoting Growth Toward Maturity in Interpreting What is Read,* Supplementary Educational Monographs, No. 74, University of Chicago Press, Chicago, 1951, 149–153.

[17] Jelinek, James J. "Literature and the Development of Critical Thinking." *The Clearing House,* 30 (April, 1956) 462–463.

[18] Johnson, Marjorie Seddon. "Readiness for Critical Reading." *Education,* 73 (February, 1953) 391–396.

[19] Lorge, Irving. "Reading, Thinking, and Learning." *Reading in Action,* International Reading Association, Conference Proceedings, Scholastic Magazines, New York, 1957, 15–18.

[20] Malter, Morton S. "Children's Ability to Read Diagrammatic Materials." *Elementary School Journal,* 49 (October, 1948) 98–102.

[21] McLendon, Jonathon C. *Teaching the Social Studies.* What Research Says to the Teacher, Number 20, Prepared by the American Educational Research Association in Cooperation with the Department of Classroom Teachers, Washington, D. C.: National Education Association, April, 1960.

[22] Morton, R. L. "Language and Meaning in Arithmetic." *Educational Research Bulletin,* 34 (November, 1955) 197–204.

[23] Pressey, L. C., and Moore, W. S. "The Growth of Mathematical Vocabulary from the Third Grade Through High School." *School Review,* 40 (June, 1932) 449–454.

[24] Schubert, Delwyn G. "Science Teachers: What You Can Do To Help Your Students To Read More Efficiently." *The Clearing House,* 30 (October, 1955) 83–84.

[25] Shaw, Phillip B. *Effective Reading and Learning.* Thomas Y. Crowell Company, New York, 1955.

[26] Smith, Dora V. "The Goals of the Literature Period and the Grade Sequence of Desirable Experiences." *Improving Reading in All Curriculum Areas,* Supplementary Educational Monographs, No. 76, University of Chicago Press, Chicago, 1952, 188–194.

[27] Spache, George D. "Types and Purposes of Reading in Various Curriculum Fields." *The Reading Teacher,* 11 (February, 1958) 158–164.

[28] Spache, George D., and Berg, Paul C. *The Art of Efficient Reading.* Macmillan Company, New York, 1955.

[29] Strang, Ruth, and Bracken, Dorothy Kendall. *Making Better Readers.* D. C. Heath and Company, Boston, 1957.

[30] Strang, Ruth, McCullough, Constance M., and Traxler, Arthur E. *Problems in the Improvement of Reading.* McGraw-Hill Book Company, Inc., New York, 1955.

[31] Swenson, Esther J. "A Study of the Relationships among Various Types of Reading Scores on General and Science Material." *Journal of Educational Research,* 36 (October, 1942) 81–90.

[32] Taba, Hilda. "The Problems in Developing Critical Thinking." *Progressive Education,* 28 (November, 1950) 45–48, 61.

[33] Wren, F. Lynwood. "What are the Goals of Instruction in Arithmetic and Mathematics and the Grade Sequence of Understandings and Skills?" *Improving Reading in All Curriculum Areas,* Supplementary Educational Monographs, No. 76, University of Chicago Press, Chicago, 1952, 144–149.

14

READING IN THE DEVELOPMENTAL PROGRAM

Reading and the entire process of growth and development are interdependent. Data concerning the typical patterns of development of boys and girls, as well as individual differences among members of the same sex, are of particular interest to teachers. Differences among children of the same age in physical, social, emotional, and attitudinal development guarantee that we cannot successfully use a patent-medicine approach to teaching children to read. When we add to the problems generated by these divergences the tremendous problems stemming from differences in intellectual development, we see why the teaching of reading at all grade levels is so extremely complex and why we must make individual diagnoses and prescriptions for each child.

In this chapter we shall try to identify the bases of a reading program that interprets in practice the principles arising from a recognition that reading is both a *growth process* and a *developmental task.* This requires two steps: (1) We must identify the psychological principles underlying a developmental program; and (2) we must interpret and integrate these principles into educational applications.

Development, of course, is a function of both nature and nurture. The child is a product of these two interacting forces. Because of the vast differences among children in both nature and nurture, no two children at any time are identical in any given characteristic.

Development in reading closely parallels human development in general. It involves the child's *total growth.* A child's reading development is a product of his biology and his culture.

If we could divorce reading from other fundamental aspects of growth, we might hope to produce a standardized product.[52] But this is not possible. For example, the range in achievement levels by the second grade is commonly about four grades. By the sixth grade this range may have increased to as much as seven grades (p. 37).[9] Sheldon [59] reports that the reading levels of seventh-graders vary from the second to the eleventh grade. Foster [22] reports that out of 1,106 entering freshmen tested in the high schools of Phoenix, Arizona, 21.4 per cent had a reading ability of fifth grade or lower and 34 per cent could not read at the seventh grade level. On the other hand the best readers in a typical high school freshman class read better than the average senior.

This tremendous range of achievement calls for a reading program that provides all children at all levels with the special reading skills they need.[60] Obviously, a single-standard basal reading program fails to adjust to the wide variety of individual differences in reading development and reading needs. It is delimited by grade levels, although development is not and needs cannot be thus limited. Reading development is a life-long process. It is not completed with the ending of elementary school nor even with the ending of formal education.

THE NATURE OF THE DEVELOPMENTAL PROGRAM

In the past, reading programs tended to be classified as either "basal" or "remedial." Only within the past twenty years has our emphasis been on developmental reading programs. Let us examine their characteristics:

First, the developmental program recognizes that reading is an integral part of the much broader educational program. Reading shares the responsibility for communicative development with the other linguistic and artistic activities. It is a program in which parents, teacher, pupils, and administrators have a positive concern. It is flexible, continuous, and comprehensive. It encompasses diagnosis and remediation.

Second, the developmental reading program is distinguished from the reading programs of the past in that it is concerned with *every pupil* and continues from elementary through high school years. It is vitally concerned with maintaining maximum progress for the average, the slow, and the gifted learner and with locating and correcting the special problems of the retarded reader. Thus it focuses on the superior reader as well as on the one whose reading development lags behind his intellectual ability.

Third, the developmental program focuses on individual needs and individual differences. Reading experiences and pupil progress are not dictated by a calendar. Grade-limits disappear and mass instruction in reading is replaced by an emphasis on pupil needs. It begins at each learner's current level and attempts to lead him at his own success rate to his maximum achievement.

Fourth, the developmental program helps the child to fulfill his developmental needs and tasks as they appear.[69] In our reading program we recognize that, because the child is a developing organism, we must adjust our instruction to his developmental needs. We try to identify the most teachable moment for each specific reading skill. A child should not be rushed into walking; neither can we successfully rush him into reading. However, we can help him to become ready.

Fifth, the developmental program provides the child with the opportunities to learn the skills needed to satisfy his needs for reading as he advances through school. It includes what Harris (p. 13) [33] calls developmental reading, functional reading, and recreational reading.

Sixth, the developmental program satisfies, extends, and enriches the child's interests.[69] Indeed, to be successful, the reading program must be based on pupil interest.

The six characteristics that we have examined here provide a descriptive definition of the program. Developmental reading has many variables and does not lend itself to a short, all-inclusive definition. We must include all methods, skills, and techniques that help the individual pupil to progress at his own success rate. It is planned for both vertical and horizontal growth. New learnings are built on previous learnings and the base is broadened constantly.

THE PRINCIPLES OF A DEVELOPMENTAL PROGRAM

Various writers have attempted to identify basic principles that may guide teachers and supervisors as they strive to make the developmental program workable and effective. Here is a selection of principles on which there seems to be general agreement:

1. The developmental program must be an all-school program directed toward carefully identified educational goals. It must receive the support and co-operation of the entire school staff.
2. The developmental program must be concerned with the social and personal development of each student as well as his growth in the skills, understandings, and attitudes necessary for successful reading.
3. The developmental program co-ordinates reading with the pupil's other communicative experiences.
4. The developmental program must be a continuous program extending through the elementary and secondary grades and college. It

must provide instruction and guidance in basic reading skills, in content-area reading, in study skills, and in recreational reading.

5. The developmental program must be a flexible program that is adjusted at each level of advancement to the wide variations in student characteristics, abilities, and reading needs.
6. The developmental program must have a stimulating classroom setting in which attitudes, interests, and abilities are developed effectively.
7. The developmental program must provide plentiful reading materials that cover a wide range of difficulty and interest.
8. The developmental program must include continuous measurement and evaluation of the effectiveness of the program as a whole and of its more specific aspects.
9. The developmental program must provide for continuous identification and immediate remediation of deficiencies and difficulties encountered by any student.
10. The developmental program must include differentiated instruction to meet the needs of each child, but it cannot ignore the commonality of needs, interests, and abilities among children.
11. The developmental program must look upon reading as a process rather than as a subject. Reading is taught on all levels in all subject areas by all teachers.
12. The developmental program must emphasize reading for understanding and aim to develop flexibility in comprehension and rate in accordance with the student's abilities and purposes and the difficulty levels of the materials.
13. The developmental program must allow each student to progress at his own success rate to his maximum capacity.
14. The developmental program must seek to develop reading maturity. A mature reader reads all kinds of materials. He perceives words quickly and accurately and reacts with correct meaning. He reads both for information and recreation.

RETENTION VS. PROMOTION

An identification of the principles underlying an effective developmental program provides us with guides for establishing and evaluating such a program. However, good principles alone do not assure a good program. Principles must be implemented by numerous practical decisions.

For example we must decide whether to promote or retain the child whose reading level is well below the average for his grade. And we must decide whether or not to accelerate the gifted child. In planning our developmental program we must decide upon the best methods for grouping children for classroom instruction. We must also make numerous decisions concerning the most appropriate teaching methods and materials.

First, let us see what bases can be found for deciding whether to promote or retain the child of below average achievement. In years past the elementary school child who was even moderately unsuccessful in reading generally was required to repeat the grade. At one time perhaps 50 per cent of the pupils experienced one or more failures during the elementary grades. Recently our schools have leaned toward a policy of almost automatic promotion. Although policies concerning retention and promotion vary from school to school, the rate of non-promotion today generally is no more than an average of five per cent at each grade level with a somewhat higher rate being typical during the first three grades and a lower rate during the final three grades of the elementary school.

However, even though only about five per cent may be retained annually, retention (failure) of pupils has a cumulative effect with the result that during the six elementary-school years, as many as 20 per cent of the children may experience one or more failures. Stroud (p. 385),[63] for example, estimates that the total number of children experiencing failure during their elementary years may be approximately four times the average number failing yearly. Concerning the cause of failure, it has been estimated that 90 to 95 per cent or even more of the failures during the first three grades result from reading difficulties.

Numerous attempts have been made to determine the results of requiring the child to repeat a grade. Does retention result in improved achievement? Coffield,[15] comparing two matched groups of students one of which consisted of students who had been promoted and the other of students who had been retained, found that the non-promoted students did not reach the grade mean even after repeating the grade, although significant educational gains occurred. He also found that retention in grades three to six did not lead to better achievement in grade seven, that the variability of achievement in grade seven is just as great with non-promotion as with promotion, and that school-wide achievement was not affected by having either many or few retentions.

Retention, in and of itself, has no positive effect on the child's learning rate.[14, 28] It does not make the student a more rapid learner. It is common to find that a student who is retained in grade two, for example, will still not come up to the average attainment of the class when he gets to grade three.

Numerous studies have shown that repeating a grade frequently results in discouragement, antagonism, resentment, and aggression. Repetition tends to block rather than to satisfy the child's basic needs. Non-promoted children have difficulty in making satisfactory social adjustments. We are well aware that punishment is likely to reduce interest in learning, and the child who is retained almost certainly will sense reproval and guilt and feel that he has been punished. Even if teachers can avoid giving the impression of punishment, the child's family and friends are unlikely to do so.

Goodlad (p. 154),[27] in summarizing the findings, writes: *

> Throughout the body of evidence runs a consistent pattern: undesirable growth characteristics and unsatisfactory school progress are more closely associated with non-promoted children than with promoted slow-learning children. Conversely, slow-learning children who have been promoted tend to make more satisfactory progress and adjustment than do their peers who have been kept back.

Finally, although children of the same age differ greatly, generally they are much more alike than they are different. Retaining a child in the second grade because he has a second grade reading level does not make him a second grader emotionally, psychologically, and physically.

Unfortunately, automatic promotion seems to be no more of a solution than is retention. It fails to motivate where motivation is our greatest single need. Certainly, one of the most obvious dangers of automatic promotion is that both teachers and students tend to grow slack in their efforts. Automatic promotion encourages careless attitudes and poor study habits; it, too, may lead to frustration and disciplinary problems. Attempting to advance all at the same rate can only lead to failure for many.

Unquestionably, the student who is promoted from one grade to another without having acquired the skills needed at the higher level may be as likely to become discouraged and resentful as is the student who is retained. He may be forced into unjust competition. And in many ways he may not be with peers—his classmates may be intellectually, socially, and emotionally more mature.

Thus neither blanket promotion nor retention is alone a satisfactory answer. Each has its advantages and its disadvantages. Although with promotion disciplinary problems seem less and attitudes and adjustments toward teachers and schools seem more positive, one cannot condemn all retention. Stroud (pp. 385–386) [63] suggests that the teacher and others working most closely with individual pupils must make the individual decisions to retain or to promote. He suggests that administrators should provide broad

---

policies concerning retention but that the teacher is in the best position to make the specific decision as to whether retention will accomplish its purposes.

The teacher needs to know why a child is failing in his work. Underachievement is a symptom of a problem; it is not *the* problem (p. 270).[23] The teacher needs to ask: Does the pupil feel antagonistic toward the teacher? Does he work after school and consequently have insufficient time for study? Does he lack certain specific reading skills? Is class work uninteresting? Is he emotionally upset? Does he lack ability or readiness? Is the school program so rigid that it leaves no provision for his individual needs? Is he "coasting along" and if so, why?

It is hard to find a good reason for retaining a child who is working near his potential. It seems even more difficult to justify retaining a child who is underachieving because of home or school conditions that he cannot control.

We need an educational organization that allows for continuous progress by each child. Such an organization may require the complete removal of grade barriers. Some attempts have been made to do this. We will examine these in connection with the problem of grouping.

GROUPING

We must make two basic decisions concerning grouping: first, shall we form sub-groups within our reading classes and, second, if we do form groups, what criteria shall we use in determining group membership?

HISTORICAL NOTES

Originally the major adjustment made for individual differences in achievement was to fail the weak and accelerate the gifted students. Historically, the next approach was some form of homogeneous grouping. Homeogeneous grouping attempts to bring together those children who are most similar in age, ability, industry, previous experience, or other factors that affect learning. Age-groups were used initially, but children of the same age did not achieve alike. With ability grouping children are grouped on the basis of their performance on an intelligence test or on their achievement in a school subject, usually reading. In 1952 the *Encyclopedia of Educational Research* summarized the data on ability grouping that had accumulated up to that time. It stated (p. 378) [54]:*

The present status of ability grouping is: (a) Detroit was one of the large cities which introduced ability grouping as early as 1919; since that date Detroit has experimented with several variations of the plan; (b) the fetish about ability grouping which prevailed in educational circles between 1920 and 1935 has subsided; (c) no data have been gathered during the past 20 years to show the extent to which ability grouping is practiced in elementary schools in this country; no research studies on ability grouping have been reported during the past 15 years; (d) the interest of teachers and administrators has changed from the rather narrow issues involved in ability grouping to broader concerns for well-rounded development in which emotional, social, character, and personality development receive as much attention as scholastic development.

The first large-scale evaluation of homogeneous grouping by abilities was made in 1936, and was published under the title, *The Grouping of Pupils.*[50] It was found that ability grouping does not necessarily result in better achievement. Grouping based on reading ability alone seemingly fails to provide adequately for the maximal development of the interests and special capacities of individual children.

CRITERIA FOR GROUPING

Whatever basis we may choose for grouping children, we can never achieve complete homogeneity. Even among a group of children of the same chronological age and the same intelligence quotient there are certain to be wide differences in interests and experience. And even children of the same family develop at different rates in all or most of their characteristics. Homogeneity, then, is hardly feasible, but even if it were, it might be socially undesirable. Our teaching must give recognition to the individual differences among children. We cannot teach a class as a whole.

However, we always group students in one way or another. We group children by age in the elementary school. In high school and college, as a result of a system of electives, interests and abilities tend to direct similar students into groups. Let us examine some of the criteria to be considered in grouping. Grouping should be directed toward certain objectives:

1) It should foster desirable social relationships and attitudes.
2) It should help us to provide for the individual reading needs of each child.
3) It should promote facility and independence in reading and study.
4) It should help us to provide each child with satisfactory reading material.
5) It should reduce the need for remedial instruction.

Whatever grouping procedure we may use, our basic criterion must be that we give each child maximum opportunity to master the skills needed for each succeeding task that he will face. And, just as important, once he has mastered a skill, he must have opportunities to use it. With these objectives in mind we can attempt to evaluate the various grouping procedures that have been used.

BASES FOR GROUPING

Frequently, reading ability is used as the basis for forming instructional groups. Here classes or sub-groups within a class are organized on the basis of how well the child reads.

Dolch [17] identifies three kinds of grouping that are commonly used in the elementary school. In one the teacher works with the entire class but may use different materials for those of higher and lower reading ability. Generally, the emphasis is on free reading and individualized assignments rather than use of a single text. The entire class, however, is working on the same general topic and joins in the discussions. Another procedure is to divide the class into fast and slow learners. The basic readers are the same, but the slow group progresses at a slower pace. Unfortunately, it is impossible to make a fourth-grade textbook into third-grade difficulty by proceeding more slowly. Schools have tried to overcome this problem by using different readers for the slow and for the fast groups. A third approach extends the number of groups to three or more. Unfortunately, whatever approach is used there are numerous unsolved problems.

The major problem pervading all attempts to group homogeneously is that children in the same grade have many differences in addition to their differences in reading ability. Our search must be for grouping methods that emphasize the similarities among children but make adjustments for their differences. Grouping must be on the basis of achievement level and interest in special areas rather than on classifications by I.Q. or reading ability.

Strang, McCullough, and Traxler (p. 112) [62] suggest that effective teaching requires six types of grouping. The teacher remains constantly conscious of them and loses no opportunity to bring them into play when they serve his purposes. The six types are: achievement grouping, research grouping, interest grouping, special needs grouping, team grouping, and tutorial grouping.

Achievement grouping is based upon reading levels. For each group the difficulty of the material is such that a pupil is challenged to learn, but he is fairly comfortable. Research grouping takes place when two or more children are curious enough about a certain question to investigate it in books and to report their findings to their reading group or to the entire class. Team grouping is used to facilitate the accomplishment of a task by direction of more than one mind toward its completion. In tutorial grouping one pupil who knows a certain portion of material or has a specific skill helps other pupils who do not know and are trying to learn.

Blanchard [6] identifies four kinds of grouping: interest grouping, information grouping (equivalent to research grouping), grouping for the acquisition of special skills, and grouping for drill or practice. Recently, another approach, "Homorthic grouping," [58] has been suggested. Here children are divided into two groups: those who want to learn and those who require additional motivation. Canfield [13] adds that groups may also be formed on the bases of friendship patterns (sociometric techniques may be used to group on this basis). Also the varying work habits of the children may be used as a basis for grouping.

FLEXIBLE GROUPING

Gowan [30] suggests that homogeneous grouping in each case should be related to *the specific learning task.* This suggests that flexibility is perhaps the most significant attribute of effective grouping.

Flexible grouping seems to have more advantages and less disadvantages than other approaches. A flexible group is formed from time to time to satisfy a particular need such as for practice of word recognition skills, and the group is dissolved when the need has been satisfied. No rigid lines are formed differentiating the good from the poor reader. The child may advance from one group to another, and he may belong to more than one group at a time.

Under flexible grouping there is no need to limit the number of groups to two or three. The number of groups formed depends on such factors as the size of the class, the range of abilities and needs of the groups, the length of the reading period, the social maturity of the class, and the teacher's skill.[4]

EVALUATION OF GROUPING

Although most data concerning the effects of grouping come from studies of fixed or rigid ability grouping, some of these studies are worth examining.

Strang, McCullough, and Traxler (p. 19) [62] point out that the most common arguments for homogeneous grouping state that: *

(1) it makes it easier for the teacher to provide the experiences and materials of instruction which each level needs;

(2) it does not waste the time of the superior readers nor bore them; and

---

* Ruth Strang, Constance M. McCullough and Arthur E. Traxler, *Problems in the Improvement of Reading* (New York: Mc-Graw-Hill Book Company, 1955), reprinted by permission.

(3) it does not undermine the self-esteem of the poor readers by throwing them into constant comparison with the superior readers.

Arguments against homogeneous grouping declare that:

(1) poor readers need the stimulation of better readers;
(2) better readers need to learn to understand and to be of service to others;
(3) being in a "low" group may give students a feeling of inferiority; . . .

The authors summarize the above points by stating that the solution seems obvious. We should continue the ordinary heterogeneous class and introduce flexible sub-groups or classes to meet varied needs and interests. Let us examine some other points of view.

An advantage claimed for ability grouping is that it leads to greater variability in achievement. Those at the extremes may be encouraged to work at more nearly their own maturity and ability levels.[30] Russell,[57] studying a reading program in grades 4, 5, and 6, found no differences in achievement between homogeneous and hetereogeneous grouping. Nevertheless, a majority of the principals of the schools studied felt that the pupils in homogeneous groups became better readers. In fact, most teachers seem to prefer homogeneous groups, and many school systems are using some form of ability grouping.

Actually, studies have shown repeatedly that with any teaching procedure we must expect a wide range of differences in achievement. In fact, Hollingshead [37] has shown that ability grouping doesn't substantially reduce the ranges of achievement within the group. Grouping on the basis of one criterion does not necessarily make individuals more alike on other measures, nor is the particular trait chosen for the grouping necessarily the dominant determinant of his behavior in the group. Thus, a good reader may not act as a good reader in certain groups because other personal characteristics keep him from performing up to his potential. He may excel in word comprehension but be retarded in word attack.

Another advantage claimed for homogeneous grouping is that children find their work more interesting. It is suggested that the teacher is better able to adjust materials to pupil needs, and that pupils tend to identify themselves more closely with one another. A study by Lazarus, however, indicates that grouping promotes interest only if the group is organized on an interest basis. Certainly ability grouping of itself does not insure that each student will become interested in the group activity. Lazarus [43] reports that 20 high-school sophomore readers with a median I.Q. of 104 were given an enriched and intensive course designed to improve their reading and writing skills. All had volunteered for the class and were allowed to enroll because of their expressed high interest in improving their reading skills. A group of 20 non-volunteers also was "steered" into a similar class.

The median I.Q. of the latter group was 120. Test scores at the end of the training period on the *A.C.E. Co-operative Tests* indicated that the group with the higher interest and desire to develop its reading and writing skills excelled in mechanics of expression, in effectiveness of expression, and in literary appreciation.

One of the most obvious disadvantages of grouping is emotional in character. A study by Luchins and Luchins [45] in a New York elementary school illustrates this. Grouping in this school was on the basis of I.Q. and previous achievement. Interviews with 190 children in the fourth, fifth, and sixth grade revealed that a high percentage (above 75 per cent) of the pupils in the bright, average, and dull classes preferred to be in the "bright" class. More than 80 per cent of the children reported that they believed their parents would want them to be in the accelerated group. An interesting finding was that 94 per cent of the bright students said that they would not change to another group even if the teacher were better and kinder. Only 18 per cent of the average students said that they would not change to another group under similar circumstances; and only 23 per cent of the dull students said that they would not change.

Grouping of children into slow and fast sections seems to leave the slow learner with feelings of inadequacy, failure, and frustration. Flexible grouping may tend to prevent the stigma of failure. The pupil sees that the grouping is temporary and is to help him overcome a specific weakness. He is not set apart permanently from his peers. Even the slow pupil may come to understand that slowness in one area does not mean slowness in all areas.

Certainly there are difficulties involved in all grouping procedures. Providing stimulation to the individuals in each sub-group remains a problem. As Dolch [17] has pointed out, even the most careful grouping does not eliminate the need for teaching reading to several different levels at the same time.

The use of some form of flexible grouping has been reported by a number of schools. The Nathaniel Hawthorne School in University City, Missouri, the Cabool Elementary School in Missouri, and some schools in the Green Bay, Wisconsin, and the Fresno, California, systems have tried forms of flexible grouping.[29] Under flexible grouping reading level tends to replace grade placement as a basis for choosing reading materials. The Fresno system has divided its six grades into twenty-one reading levels. Other systems are operating ungraded classes in the primary grades. Hester [35] describes multiple-level grouping within the same classroom. She states that the multiple-level instructional program allows a pupil to join any groups that meet his needs. The underlying educational philosophy of these programs is to provide experiences leading to the continuous advancement of each child.

Unfortunately multiple-level programs still leave us with the need to make decisions as to whether or not to advance the child from one level to the next. In fact, they require more frequent decisions than does a grade system. However, a completely ungraded organization during the first three years appears to have important advantages. And it may be that grades four to six could profitably be changed into some form of ungraded organization. Although competition and failure experiences may be a necessary portion of adolescent and adult living, there seems to be no good reason for adopting an elementary school program that constantly emphasizes any child's inadequacies.

INDIVIDUALIZED READING

Teaching practice long ago progressed beyond the single-textbook approach. However, in adjusting for variations in ability two somewhat different procedures have been recommended. One of these involves some form of ability-group approach. The other is the so-called "individualized reading" plan.

Olson's [53] position concerning self-selection and pacing has been mentioned in Chapter 4 in connection with readiness but his theories have contributed also to an educational interest in the individualizing of reading instruction at all grade levels. Veatch [66] and Miel [46] have been active in publicizing the self-selection approach and gathering materials and suggesting methods for various grade levels. Basically, the idea is to pace the reading instruction, and for that matter all instruction, to the unique growth pattern of each child.

We have discussed the wide range of abilities that exist within each classroom. Perhaps equally important are the variations in skill development within each child. A special concern of the individualized approach is to help each child acquire the specific skills that he lacks and is ready to acquire and to avoid wasting his time on skills that he already has or is not ready to acquire. The proponents of self-selection claim that each child can be rewarded through knowing just when he is succeeding and his energies are best used when they are directed toward his specific needs.

Probably no one claims that "individualized instruction" will or should eliminate group instruction. Nor is individualized reading in itself a "method." And its advocates do not recommend that the child be left to his own devices to learn or not to learn. Careful diagnosis and skillful teaching are of critical importance in this approach as in any other.

THE SLOW LEARNER

A sound developmental program is concerned with children of all levels of ability—the average, the slow, and the gifted. Considerable information has been gathered about the special needs and potentialities of children in each of these general categories. Let's begin with the slow learner.

Generally, children with I.Q.'s of 50 to 89 are classed as slow learners. Kirk (pp. 172–173),[42] points out that *

> The term "slow learner" should be restricted to the child who does not have the capacity or potentiality to learn intellectual things, such as reading, at the same rate as average children. It should not be used to refer to educational retardation regardless of the cause.

Of the slow-learning children, those with I.Q.'s from 50 to 70 or 74 commonly are referred to as mentally retarded. However, even the mentally retarded children generally are considered educable and will be in our regular schools although frequently in special classes.

The slow learner and, especially, the mentally retarded child, frequently is inferior to the normal child in health and physique. Baker notes (p. 261) [1] that slow learners have more physical disabilities than do average children.**

> As a group, they are of smaller stature than the average . . . they tend to have more physical deviations than the average, with asymmetry of the head and face, unusual size of the head either in the direction of being large or small, crowded and poorly formed teeth, ears of many shapes, and various other unusual conditions. . . . In the case of the mentally retarded there are likely to be two or more of these abnormalities per child whereas the normal seldom have more than one.

Blair [5] points out that in both the junior and the senior high school, boys and girls with lower than average intelligence (70 to 95 I.Q.) seldom assume leadership and they participate in fewer school activities with the possible exception of sports and athletics. They read less and tend to confine their reading to wild west, detective, mystery, movie, and pulp magazines. Of the school subjects they prefer shop and home economics.

Dunn [18] studied mentally retarded boys, ages eight to ten, and found them to be inferior to children of average intelligence in the use of context clues. They made more vowel errors and omitted more sounds. He found no differences, however, between them and boys of average intelligence in reversal errors, in handedness, and in mixed lateral preference. They had an excessive number of vision and hearing difficulties. They were also retarded in spelling and arithmetic reasoning. Teacher ratings indicated that the mentally retarded were generally poorly adjusted and came from lower-class homes. Relationships with their parents were poor.

Certainly major adjustments must be made for the slow learner in the content of the developmental reading program and the rate at which he progresses through it. He requires a longer readiness program than does the average child. To begin reading instruction before the child has a mental age of six or more is to waste the time of both teacher and pupil and result in pupil discouragement. The extended readiness program of the slow-learner demands a variety of concrete experiences. It must progress slowly, with an emphasis on pupil activity. Films and filmstrips are important sources of materials. The program for the slow learner should emphasize social interaction, story telling, arts and crafts, dramatizing, music, and recreational activities. The education of the slow learner requires a large amount of repetition. Reading charts built from the direct experiences of the children are especially useful. Muller [48] points out that these charts will be read and re-read with pride and satisfaction by mentally retarded pupils at chronological ages considerably beyond those at which they can be used with normal children. In the early stages of their learning, listening will need to be stressed more than reading.

In the slow learner's reading program, we generally spend considerable time on phonetic and structural analysis and, frequently, we encourage lip movements, vocalization, and pointing at the word. We emphasize word knowledge and the mastery of simple comprehension skills.

The slow learner appears to have little need for rapid reading skills. He will not read many different materials. He has a difficult time reading for practical purposes. Groelle [31] suggests that the reading of the slow learner, especially when he is about ready to leave school, should be functional in nature. He needs to learn the working vocabulary required in his future job and how to read and fill out application blanks; he needs to be able to read telephone books, city directories, road maps, street guides, menus, recipes, directions, radio and theater programs, advertisements, catalogues, want-ads, and newspapers; and he should become thoroughly familiar with the dictionary and book tables of contents and indices.

From his experience with slow learners, Kirk (pp. 174–175) [42] suggests that the teacher should keep the following in mind: *

1. It should not be expected that the slow learner should learn to read at the life age of six when he enters the first grade. . . .
2. Their rate of learning to read is slower than that of other children. . . .
3. Throughout his school career the slow learner has not been able to succeed in reading like other children. . . .
4. Possible health and poorer environmental handicaps have been found more frequently in the slow learner, thus contributing to his reading retardation.

---

5. Other school subjects, like history, geography, and even arithmetic computation, have been difficult since they require efficient reading habits.
6. Due to difficulties in reading, lack of interest in recreational reading, and avoidance of an unpleasant task, reading does not become a part of the life of a slow learner.

Brueckner and Bond (pp. 188–190) [11] give a detailed discussion of principles that should be considered in teaching the slow learner (70–95 I.Q.). They advocate deferring reading instruction until the child reaches a mental age of about six and one-half years, using material that introduces new words slowly and provides for considerable repetition, giving detailed and simplified directions for all work, providing concrete illustrations and short-range projects resulting in frequent rewards, frequent re-reading of materials, more use of oral reading, and an emphasis on physical activity and specific, concrete projects in connection with the learning experiences.

THE GIFTED LEARNER

From the days of Aristotle and Plato to the present time, writers have recognized that the gifted child should and would, if properly guided, grow up to become a leader in his society. Obviously, such leadership is needed in political life, in education, in religion, in science, and in business. In recent years the need for a more conscious, deliberate, and intelligent direction of human affairs has become most glaringly evident.[19] As our need for leadership becomes greater, education's responsibility for identifying and developing the gifted child increases (p. 16) [25]:

> The gifted individual has become a national issue just because he has not sufficiently been considered an educational issue. Government, industry, and education itself are suffering from a dearth of able people—a dearth directly attributable to our profligate attitude toward the reservoir of talent represented by young able learners.*

The very strength of an educational system designed to offer maximum educational advantages to children of all levels of ability frequently results in a weakness in our education of the gifted. It is extremely difficult to help the gifted achieve maximum growth under a system that must frequently be geared to the needs of the average or even of the dull child. The large proportion of slow learners in our elementary school and even high school classes causes us to neglect the gifted. The education of the slow learner to a modest level of attainment consumes so much teacher attention that

---

we are likely to be satisfied and even highly pleased with attainments by the gifted that are sub-standard when considered in the light of his ability to achieve.

Helping the gifted to achieve the educational growth necessary for a position of intelligent leadership requires high-level professional skill: we must know how to identify the gifted, we must know his characteristics as a learner, and we must know how to guide and lead him to his full capabilities.

IDENTIFICATION OF THE GIFTED LEARNER

To identify the gifted learner, we must reach some agreement as to what we mean by *gifted.* In the case of the slow learner, our criterion was low I.Q. However the I.Q. as the criterion of giftedness is not completely satisfactory for at least two reasons: (1) although low I.Q. generally guarantees low accomplishment, high I.Q. does not guarantee high accomplishment; (2) although the gifted learner generally learns anything quite easily, frequently gifted children are highly successful in one area and less successful in others. Thus Witty [70] would consider a child gifted if his performance is consistently remarkable in *any* valuable line of human activity.

Generally, however, standardized intelligence test results have been used as criteria both to identify the gifted and to define giftedness even though tests are never completely reliable or valid and some types of gifted children do not express their full capabilities on intelligence tests. Even when we use high I.Q. as our criterion, we still must decide the specific range of I.Q. levels that is to mark giftedness. Sometimes educators consider only the top one per cent (I.Q. of 137+), to be gifted, but more frequently the educational program for the gifted is extended to the top ten per cent—those with an I.Q. of 120 and above.

In defining giftedness the recent trend has been to combine intelligence with other criteria. Guilford,[32] for example, suggests that we must look well beyond the boundaries of the I.Q. if we are to fathom the domain of creativity. Havighurst *et al.* (p. 1) [34] state: *

> Thinking, then, of the unusual child as the talented child or the gifted child, I suggest that we speak of four areas of talent. We have found this useful in our work: first, the area of intellectual talent—a child with high intelligence or high I.Q.; second, the area of artistic talent—talent in music, drawing, or dramatics, and so on; third, the area of social leadership—this is something we sometimes do not think of as a talent, but certainly in our society a gift for social leadership is an important and a precious thing; and, fourth, some-

---

thing which I cannot define so clearly but I like to call "creative intelligence" or ability to find new ways of doing things and solving problems.

Perhaps one should speak of the intellectually bright as the "gifted learners" and of those who show special excellence in a specific area such as in the arts and in social and political leadership as the "specially gifted." Certainly, some distinction is needed. The child with special abilities or aptitudes may or may not be superior in general academic areas such as reading.

CHARACTERISTICS OF THE GIFTED LEARNER

Even the most dedicated user of intelligence test results recognizes that children of the same general level of intelligence frequently differ greatly in specific strengths and weaknesses among the various areas sampled by the test. And such children may differ even more in traits that the intelligence test is not designed to appraise. This variability in characteristics is most marked among the gifted. Witty (p. 271),[68] for example, points out that

> Frequently, the social development of the gifted child does not keep pace with his rapid mental growth. For example, a gifted child of five may display the mental ability of an eight- or nine-year-old child. Physically he may be somewhat superior to other five-year-old children, but he may be by no means so well developed as children two or three years older. His social development, too, may be somewhat accelerated, but not in proportion to his mental growth. This condition accounts in some cases for the bright child's understanding of such words as *co-operation* and *loyalty* and his inconsistent behavior with regard to these traits.

As a group, children with superior I.Q.'s are less neurotic, less selfish, more self-sufficient, more mature socially, more self-confident, taller, heavier, and healthier than average children. Their major strength, however, is their academic prowess. They tend to learn through association rather than through rote memory. They perceive relationships and like to deal with abstractions. They are curious, creative, and imaginative. They tend to work individually but they enjoy preparing and giving oral and written reports and organizing and cataloguing materials and information, and sharing their experiences with their classmates. They tend to write both prose and poetry creatively and effectively. Frequently what they choose to read and learn is on an adult level and they are attracted to school subjects that require abstraction. Also, their social consciousness and responses indicate a higher degree of maturity than do those of average children.

Terman (p. 223) [64] suggests that children of 140 I.Q. or higher:

> . . . are, in general, appreciably superior to unselected children in physique, health, and social adjustment; markedly superior in moral attitudes as measured either by character tests or by trait ratings; and vastly superior in their mastery of school subjects as shown by a three-hour battery of achievement tests. . . . Moreover, their ability as evidenced by achievement in the different school subjects is so general as to refute completely the traditional belief that gifted children are usually one-sided.

He adds:

> Results of thirty years' follow-up of these subjects . . . show that the incidence of mortality, ill health, insanity, and alcoholism is in each case below that for the generality of corresponding age, that the great majority are still well adjusted socially, and that the delinquency rate is but a fraction of what it is in the general population.

Terman goes on:

> As for schooling, close to 90 per cent entered college and 70 per cent graduated. Of those graduating, 30 per cent were awarded honors and about two-thirds remained for graduate work.

Barbe (p. 308) [2] summarized what is known of the gifted child in this way:

1. The gifted child frequently learns to walk earlier than the average child.
2. His speech development begins earlier and develops more rapidly.
3. He is probably more active than average children, and more curious about new situations.
4. Chances are about 50-50 that if he is gifted he will learn to read before entering school.
5. He will probably like school, more because of his desire for knowledge than for the challenge presented to him.
6. He is more likely to participate in a larger number of extra-curricular activities.
7. When he is allowed to elect subjects, he will prefer the harder ones.
8. Physically, he will at least be as well developed as other children.

THE NEED FOR GUIDANCE OF THE GIFTED

The tremendous potentiality of the gifted child for academic achievement and social leadership carries with it a high challenge and responsibility for educational guidance. The individual gifted learner frequently shows marked variations in his talents.

As Terman and Oden (p. 57) [65] point out:

> Gifted children do not fall into a single pattern but into an infinite variety of patterns. One can find within the group individual examples of almost every type of personality defect, social maladjustment, behavior problem, and physical frailty; the only difference is that among gifted children the incidence of those variations is, in varying degrees, lower than in the general population.

Barbe and Williams [3] suggest that in working with the gifted we should lead them to feel that they are members of a group in which different contributions are to be expected from different individuals.

A major problem in teaching the gifted child is that the curriculum too frequently is geared to the slower learners. Strang [61] has pointed out that able learners are likely to become irritated by the repetition which slow learners need to reinforce their learning. What may be extremely interesting to some children becomes uninteresting to the gifted child. Often they have learned to read before coming to school and find the readiness program unchallenging; even if they have not learned, they learn in a fraction of the time that others require. Particularly children with exceptionally high I.Q.'s may come to regard school with indifference or with positive distaste because they find nothing interesting to do there.[38] Almost from the beginning the gifted child is ready to read to learn. We can see what the ordinary learning to read program may do to such a child.

Barbe [2] points out that when the material is too easy the gifted child may withdraw from the group, become a clown to gain attention, or even pretend not to know answers. We cannot permit the gifted child to develop his skills through personal initiative alone. He is likely to find that he need make little effort and consequently his educational development falls far short of what his intellectual endowment should promise. The end result, often, is that the gifted child's educational development frequently is retarded by as much as one to three years below his mental age level. Wheeler and Wheeler (pp. 230–231) [67] call attention to the

> . . . common observation of those experienced in clinical reading, and reading in the upper-grade levels, that low mentality is not a cause of the majority of reading difficulties. . . . The most seriously retarded readers in our schools and colleges are the mentally superior students.

The commonly observed fact that as a group gifted children underachieve in relation to their ability poses a critical challenge to the professional teacher. In our teaching of reading, the gifted child should obtain an early exposure to critical reading, rate improvement, use of the dictionary, and especially to content-area skills. He should be guided toward skill in appreciation, in detecting mood and tone, and in recognizing literary devices. He should learn to question and evaluate the authority of the source material. He must learn to identify the author's purpose, to understand inferences, to anticipate outcomes, and to analyze the author's style.[7]

The program for the gifted child should be on a higher, more adult level than would be practical for general class use. As Murphy (p. 418) [49] has pointed out, in teaching the gifted learner we can emphasize such things as abstracting principles and significant interrelationships, synthesizing facts and drawing conclusions, tracing themes and analyzing their importance to the selection as a whole, and criticizing on the basis of all the various forces involved. Murphy cautions that we must prevent the gifted child from associating learning with the accumulation of facts, memorization, and unproductive discussion.

A developmental program requires that we challenge and reward the fast and the slow learner as well as the child of average ability. It places high demands on our knowledge of methods and materials and requires close acquaintance with the abilities and interests of each student. This calls for a high level of professional skill.

The adjustment of instruction to individual differences is much more than a method. It is an attitude—an attitude in which the teacher assumes that each child has the right to progress as rapidly as he is capable, that each child can expect the school to provide for his rate of learning be it slow or fast, and that each child can expect the school to study him as an individual and to help him when he is in difficulty. Bond and Wagner (p. 61) [10] point out: *

EDUCATIONAL ADJUSTMENTS FOR THE GIFTED LEARNER

Various procedures have been suggested for adjusting instruction to the needs of the gifted child. Individualized instruction, acceleration, grouping, differentiation of assignments, a system of electives, and unit instruction are some of the more common approaches. Occasionally special classes are set up. Core curricula and broad-fields curricula are other methods for adjusting to individual needs.

Some attempt at individualization of instruction for the gifted have been reported in the literature. Holcomb,[36] using a tutoring and guidance program for children with an I.Q. of 130 or over, reports that third-grade children finished beginning courses in French and German. In Chicago's Lloyd School [12] students of all ability levels are together during the morning, but in the afternoon the more able participate in a special program. This form of organization is used with pupils in grades IA through IIIB. Mosso [47]

---

reports the use of seminars for selected seniors. The able learner follows the regular high school curriculum but also has an enriched program through additional reading and study.

Acceleration is probably the most controversial method used today for providing for the needs of the gifted. Let us examine the results of acceleration more closely. Terman [64] found that 29 per cent of his gifted group graduated from high school before the age of 16½ and about one-fifth of these graduated before age 15½. Comparing the 29 per cent that graduated before age 16½ with the 71 per cent that graduated at a later age, he concluded that a larger proportion of the accelerated group graduated from college and that they averaged higher in college grades and more often remained for graduate work.

Justman [39, 40] compared two groups of children with I.Q.'s of 130 or higher. One group completed junior high in two years and the other in the normal three years. He found that the accelerated group achieved as well as the non-accelerated group in senior high school. Pressey [56] reports that 50 per cent of the students entering Ohio State University at age 16 graduated; and only 38 per cent of those who entered college at 18 graduated. Recent studies [24] conducted through grants from the Ford Foundation for the Advancement of Education show that youths who were below 16½ upon entrance to college generally did very well in college. Almost 54 per cent of these achieved scores on verbal aptitude equal to or above the 84th percentile of all college applicants in the nation taking this test.

Pressey [55] found that as the age of graduation from college increases, the percentage of persons acquiring national renown decreases. He suggested that the productive career of an individual is a decreasing function of age of graduation. He notes that the outstanding discoveries in science, the finest books in literature, and the greatest inventions tend to be by relatively young men. Lehman [44] found that the peak of achievement in the scientific, mathematical, psychological, musical, educational, economical, and physical fields usually is reached between ages 25 and 40. Flesher,[20] comparing two groups of 79 graduates each, reports that younger college graduates, ages 19 or 20, were more likely to obtain advanced degrees, obtain better-paying positions, and show teaching ability rated higher by administrators than those graduating at age 22.

Thus studies suggest that acceleration has some definite advantages. However, objections to acceleration frequently are made on social and emotional grounds. Stroud says that such objections have

> . . . persisted and prevailed generally despite the fact that there has never been any evidence that the younger members of a class are less well adjusted than those of normal age. One suspects that there is in these United States a kind of implicit notion that it does not pay to be too different (p. 327).[63]

Studies have found few instances of emotional maladjustment that could be traced directly to acceleration. Keys,[41] reports that students from Oakland, California, who graduated from high school at an earlier age took more scholarship honors, participated in more activities, and held more school offices. The few cases of serious problem behavior proved to be either bright but non-accelerated pupils, or accelerated pupils of only average intelligence. Stroud (p. 328) [63] adds:

> It is just possible that any disadvantages, from the standpoint of mental hygiene, associated with the gifted students' being thrown with older students may be compensated for by the satisfactions connected with more interesting and challenging school experiences. . . . the interests of gifted children tend to conform to those of children older than themselves.

We have discussed individualized instruction and acceleration as possible methods for adjusting our school program to the needs of the gifted. Let's examine programs that keep the gifted child with his age mates, but attempt to enrich his program through other means.

Enrichment, whether in special groups, in special schools for the gifted learner, or even within a heterogeneous class, may be the most defensible approach to individualization of instruction.

Flory,[21] studying special classes for gifted children at Ontario, California, concludes that

> One needs to know the students to appraise the intangibles—the happiness in self-mastery, the self-confidence they have gained from association with students of similar interests and equally high motivation, the interest in scholarly achievement, the eagerness for learning, the assurance they have acquired through institutional recognition of their intellectual ability, the determination to serve through the utilization of the special talents which they have learned to exploit. These are strong arguments for the creation of special classes for the gifted.

Unit instruction or the unit plan has been found to work well in the middle grades and in high school even when the class is quite heterogeneous. The assignment covers work over an extended period of time, possibly a week, month, or semester. This program offers possibilities for work by the group as a whole, for sub-grouping along ability and interest lines, for individualized assignments, and for enrichment within the same class. Bond's description of how the class is organized under a unit plan shows the opportunities for challenging the gifted learner as well as the average and the slow learner:

1. The teacher has (a) a preplan which may include a choice of topics for the unit and (b) a bibliography of suggested materials to be read in relation to a topic. . . .

2. Pupils select area for study. . . .
3. Pupils and teacher outline types of possible readings in bibliography. . . .
4. Pupils and teacher build bibliography for selection; locate materials through use of tables of contents and indexes in room library books. In other libraries card catalogs and guides with which pupils are familiar are used. Librarians may suggest new sources and give information regarding them. . . .
5. Pupils select area in which they plan to read. . . .
6. Teacher, following principles underlying any reading situation, works with each group of pupils in developing their selected area within the unit.
7. *In the course of any unit there will be times when selections or passages are enjoyed by all class members.*
8. Unit is concluded by culminating activity (p. 31).[8]

SUMMARY

In this chapter we have tried to identify some problems relating to retention, promotion, and grouping. We have examined ways in which instruction might be adjusted to both the slow and the gifted learner. Certainly the problems of individualization of instruction are not, at present, completely solved. However, the developmental approach promises progress toward solutions. This approach is based on a recognition that there is nothing more unequal than equal education. Individual differences do exist and must be reckoned with.

A developmental program emphasizes the need for readiness at every stage of growth and for instruction suited to the needs and the rate of learning of every child. The ideal of the developmental approach is to help each individual to grow at his full-potential rate.

SUGGESTED READINGS

For a background discussion of differences in ability to learn and the use and interpretation of intelligence tests:

Smith, Henry P., Chapter 10, "Individual Differences in Ability to Learn," pp. 270–296 in *Psychology in Teaching.* Englewood Cliffs, N. J.: Prentice-Hall, Inc., 1954.

***

For a detailed discussion of the nature of intelligence, history of intelligence testing, validity of the I.Q. and M.A., and data concerning mental and physical growth:

Stroud, James B., Chapter 7, "The Nature and Measurement of Intelligence," pp. 207–240 and Chapter 8, "Mental and Physical Growth," pp. 241–287 in *Psychology in Education.* New York: Longmans, Green and Co., 1956.

***

For a detailed review of the literature concerning gifted children (with extensive bibliography):

Carter, Harold D., "Gifted Children," pp. 583–593 in *Encyclopedia of Educational Research,* Chester W. Harris, Ed., 3rd Ed. New York: The Macmillan Company, 1960.

***

For a general resource on the use of sociometric techniques, methods of sociometric testing, the constructing of sociometric devices and administering, interpreting and recording sociometric tests and test results:

Gronlund, Norman E., *Sociometry in the Classroom.* New York: Harper & Brothers, 1959.

***

For reports by a number of educators on the goals and methodology of "individualized" reading programs:

Jeannette Veatch, *Individualizing Your Reading Program: Self-Selection in Action.* New York: G. P. Putnam's Sons, 1959.

***

(Causey, *The Reading Teacher's Reader*)

Article 21, Dawson, Dan T., "Some Issues in Grouping for Reading," from *The National Elementary Principal,* 35 (September, 1955), pp. 48–52.

Article 22, Whipple, Gertrude, "Good Practices in Grouping," from *The Reading Teacher,* 7 (1953), pp. 69–74.

Article 27, Strang, Ruth, "Reading Development of Gifted Children," from *Elementary English,* 31 (January, 1954), pp. 35–40.

QUESTIONS FOR DISCUSSION

1. Why is it impossible to divorce reading achievement from other aspects of development?
2. What administrative implications do the following two principles have:
   (a) reading instruction begins at the level that the student has attained and
   (b) reading instruction should permit each student to advance at his own success rate?
3. Why is it incorrect to speak of a "Remedial Reading Program"?
4. What are the arguments for and against retaining in a grade a child whose achievement does not compare favorably with the average achievement of his class?
5. What problems are created by a policy of automatic promotion?
6. Explain how low achievement may be a symptom of the student's problem rather than the problem itself.
7. Distinguish between homogeneous grouping and ability grouping.
8. Why should one try to group homogeneously when, if teaching is adequate, the individuals almost certainly will be further apart at the end of a learning period than they were at the beginning?
9. Explain why equality of opportunity doesn't mean equal education.

10. What are some of the advantages and disadvantages of flexible subgrouping?
11. Discuss some of the special plans that have been proposed for adjusting for individual differences.
12. Distinguish between the slow learner and the retarded learner.
13. Compare the reading habits of the gifted and the slow learner.
14. What are some of the advantages and disadvantages of acceleration?
15. What adjustments can be made in the reading program for the gifted learner? Which do you consider to be most desirable?

BIBLIOGRAPHY

[1] Baker, Harry J. *Introduction to Exceptional Children.* The Macmillan Company, New York, 1953.

[2] Barbe, Walter B. "Differentiated Guidance for the Gifted." *Education,* 74 (January, 1954) 306–311.

[3] Barbe, Walter B., and Williams, Thelma E. "Developing Creative Thinking in Gifted Children Through the Reading Program." *The Reading Teacher,* 9 (April, 1956) 200–203.

[4] Betts, Emmett A. "Adjusting Instruction to Individual Needs." *Reading in the Elementary School,* Forty-eighth Yearbook of the National Society for the Study of Education, Part II, University of Chicago Press, Chicago, 1949, 266–283.

[5] Blair, Glenn Myers. *Mentally Superior and Inferior Children in the Junior and Senior High School.* Contributions to Education, No. 766, Bureau of Publications, Teachers College, Columbia University, 1938.

[6] Blanchard, Marjorie. "Adjusting Learning Activities and Reading Materials to Individual Differences: In Grades Four to Six." *Improving Reading in All Curriculum Areas,* Supplementary Educational Monographs, No. 76, University of Chicago Press, Chicago, 1952, 32–36.

[7] Bland, Phyllis. "Helping Bright Students Who Read Poorly." *The Reading Teacher,* 9 (April, 1956) 209–214.

[8] Bond, Guy L. "Teaching Selections in Reading." *The Road to Better Reading,* Bureau of Secondary Curriculum Development, The State Education Department, Albany, New York, 1953, 30–37.

[9] Bond, Guy L., and Tinker, Miles A. *Reading Difficulties: Their Diagnosis and Correction.* Appleton-Century-Crofts, Inc., New York, 1957.

[10] Bond, Guy L., and Wagner, Eva Bond. *Teaching the Child to Read,* Revised Ed., The Macmillan Company, New York, 1950.

[11] Brueckner, Leo J., and Bond, Guy L. *The Diagnosis and Treatment of Learning Difficulties.* Appleton-Century-Crofts, Inc., New York, 1955.

[12] Bulinski, Delores P. "Specific Patterns of Classroom Organization." *Promoting Maximal Reading Growth Among Able Learners,* Supplementary Educational Monographs, No. 81, University of Chicago Press, Chicago, 1954, 40–41.

[13] Canfield, James K. "Flexibility in Grouping for Reading." *The Reading Teacher,* 11 (December, 1957) 91–94.

[14] Cheney, W. Walker, and Boyer, Philip A. "Is Non-Promotion a Defensible Policy?" extract. *Elementary School Journal,* 33 (May, 1933) 647–651.

[15] Coffield, William H. "A Longitudinal Study of the Effects of Non-promotion on Educational Achievement in the Elementary School." Unpublished doctoral dissertation, State University of Iowa, 1954; *Dissertation Abstracts,* 14 (No. 12, 1954) 2291–2292.

[16] Cooke, Dorothy E., and Niles, Olive S. "Organizing and Administering a Twelve-year Developmental Reading Program." *The Road to Better Reading,* Bureau of Secondary Curriculum Development, The State Education Department, Albany, New York, 1953, 98–112.

[17] Dolch, E. W. "Groups in Reading." *Elementary English,* 31 (December, 1954) 477–484.

[18] Dunn, Floyd, M.D. "A Comparative Study of Mentally Retarded and Mentally Normal Boys of the Same Mental Age on Some Aspects of the Reading Process." Unpublished doctoral dissertation, University of Illinois, 1953; *Dissertation Abstracts,* 14 (No. 2, 1954) 300.

[19] Edwards, Newton. "Education of the Able Student: Social Significance and Goals." *Promoting Maximal Reading Growth Among Able Learners,* Supplementary Educational Monographs, No. 81, University of Chicago Press, Chicago, 1954, 1–5.

[20] Flesher, Marie A. "Did They Graduate Too Young?" *Educational Research Bulletin,* 24 (November, 1945) 218–221.

[21] Flory, Vera. "Special Classes for the Gifted." *The Clearing House,* 32 (September, 1957) 22–24.

[22] Foster, Guy L. "Freshman Problem: 44% Couldn't Read Their Tests." *The Clearing House,* 29 (March, 1955) 414–417.

[23] Froehlich, Clifford P., and Darley, John G. *Studying Students.* Science Research Associates, Inc., Chicago, 1952.

[24] Fund for the Advancement of Education. *Bridging the Gap Between School and College,* Research Division of the Fund for the Advancement of Education, Report No. 1, New York, 1953.

[25] Getzels, Jacob W. "Distinctive Characteristics of Able Learners." *Promoting Maximal Reading Growth Among Able Learners,* Supplementary Educational Monographs, No. 81, University of Chicago Press, Chicago, 1954, 16–21.

[26] Glock, Marvin D. "Principles for Selecting Methods and Materials to Promote Growth in Reading." *Promoting Maximal Reading Growth Among Able Learners,* Supplementary Educational Monographs, No. 81, University of Chicago Press, Chicago, 1954, 65–69.

[27] Goodlad, John I. "Research and Theory Regarding Promotion and Non-promotion." *The Elementary School Journal,* 53 (November, 1952) 150–155.

[28] Goodlad, John I. "To Promote or Not to Promote." *Childhood Education,* 30 (January, 1954) 212–215.

[29] Goodlad, John I., Brooks, Fred E., Larson, Irene M., and Neff, Neal. " 'Reading Levels' " Replace Grades in the Non-Graded Plan." *The Elementary School Journal,* 57 (February, 1957) 253–256.

[30] Gowan, May Seagoe. "Why Homogeneous Grouping." *California Journal of Secondary Education,* 30 (January, 1955) 22–28.

[31] Groelle, Marvin C. "Techniques and Adjustments for Slow Learners with Special Reference to Reading." *Classroom Techniques in Improving Reading,* Supplementary Educational Monographs, No. 69, University of Chicago Press, Chicago, 1949, 182–186.

[32] Guilford, J. P. "Creativity." *American Psychologist,* 5 (September, 1950) 444–454.

[33] Harris, Albert J. *How to Increase Reading Ability,* 3rd Edition. Longmans, Green and Company, New York, 1956.

[34] Havighurst, Robert J., Rogers, Virgil M., and Witty, Paul A. *Are the Community and the School Failing the Unusual Child?* The University of Chicago Round-Table, Chicago, Number 735, April 27, 1952.

[35] Hester, Kathleen B. "Every Child Reads Successfully in a Multiple-Level Program." *The Elementary School Journal,* 53 (October, 1952) 86–89.

[36] Holcomb, Paul H. "Tutoring: Decisive Plus for Bedford's Gifted Pupils." *The Clearing House,* 29 (January, 1955) 268–270.

[37] Hollingshead, Arthur D. *An Evaluation of the Use of Certain Educational and Mental Measurements for Purposes of Classifications.* Contributions to Education, No. 302, Bureau of Publications, Teachers College, Columbia University, New York, 1928.

[38] Hollingworth, Leta S. *Children Above 180 IQ.* World Book Company, Yonkers, N.Y., 1942.

[39] Justman, Joseph. "Academic Achievement of Intellectually Gifted Accelerants and Non-Accelerants in Junior High School." *School Review,* 62 (March, 1954) 142–150.

[40] Justman, Joseph. "Academic Achievement of Intellectually Gifted Accelerants and Non-Accelerants in Senior High School." *School Review,* 62 (November, 1954) 469–473.

[41] Keys, Noel. "Adjustments of Under-Age Students in High School." *Psychological Bulletin,* 32 (October, 1935) 539.

[42] Kirk, Samuel A. "Characteristics of Slow Learners and Needed Adjustments in Reading." *Classroom Techniques in Improving Reading,* Supplementary Educational Monographs, No. 69, University of Chicago Press, Chicago, 1949, 172–176.

[43] Lazarus, Arnold L. "Grouping Based on High Interest vs. General Ability: A Senior High School Teacher's Viewpoint." *California Journal of Secondary Education,* 30 (January, 1955) 38–41.

[44] Lehman, H. C. "Man's Most Creative Years." *Scientific Monthly,* 59 (November, 1944) 384–393.

[45] Luchins, Abraham S. and Luchins, Edith H. "Children's Attitudes Toward Homogeneous Groupings." *Journal of Genetic Psychology,* 72 (March, 1948) 3–9.

[46] Miel, Alice. Ed., *Individualizing Reading Practices.* Teachers College, Columbia University, Bureau of Publications, New York, 1958.

[47] Mosso, Asenath M. "A Seminar for Superior High-School Seniors." *School Review,* 53 (October, 1945) 464–470.

[48] Mullen, Frances A. "Distinctive Problems Presented by Poor Readers: The Slow Learner." *Improving Reading in All Curriculum Areas,* Supplementary

Educational Monographs, No. 76, University of Chicago Press, Chicago, 1952, 104–108.

[49] Murphy, Geraldine J. "The Education of Gifted Children: Suggestions for a Philosophy and a Curriculum." *The School Review,* 62 (October, 1954) 414–419.

[50] National Society for the Study of Education. *The Grouping of Pupils,* Thirty-fifth Yearbook, Part I. Public School Publishing Company, Bloomington, Illinois, 1936.

[51] Oliver, Albert I. "The Gifted Pupil—A Challenge to Educators." *Education,* 74 (January, 1954) 312–322.

[52] Olson, Willard C. "Child Growth and Development." *Reading,* Association for Childhood Education International, Washington, 1956, 2–5.

[53] Olson, Willard C. *Child Development.* 2nd Edition. D. C. Heath and Company, Boston, 1959.

[54] Otto, Henry J. "Elementary Education—III. Organization and Administration." *Encyclopedia of Educational Research,* Revised Edition, Walter S. Monroe, Ed., The Macmillan Co., New York, 1952, 367–383.

[55] Pressey, S. L. "Age of College Graduation and Success in Adult Life." *Journal of Applied Psychology,* 30 (June, 1946) 226–233.

[56] Pressey, S. L. "Concerning the Nature and Nurture of Genius." *The Scientific Monthly,* 81 (September, 1955) 123–129.

[57] Russell, David H. "Inter-Class Grouping for Reading Instruction in the Intermediate Grades," *Journal of Education Research,* 39 (February, 1946) 462–70.

[58] Shannon, J. R. "Homorthic Grouping—A New Proposal." *The Clearing House,* 32 (November, 1957) 133–134.

[59] Sheldon, William D. "The Nature and Scope of Reading Programs Adapted to Today's Needs: In the Upper Grades and Junior High School." *Better Readers For Our Times,* International Reading Association, Conference Proceedings. Scholastic Magazines, New York, 1956, 30–33.

[60] Stauffer, Russell G. "The Developmental Approach to Reading." *Educational Administration and Supervision,* 41 (October, 1955) 338–348.

[61] Strang, Ruth. "Basic Issues and Problems in Reading Instruction for Capable Students." *Promoting Maximal Reading Growth Among Able Learners,* Supplementary Educational Monographs, No. 81, University of Chicago Press, Chicago, 1954, 6–10.

[62] Strang, Ruth, McCullough, Constance M., and Traxler, Arthur E. *Problems in the Improvement of Reading.* McGraw-Hill Book Company, Inc., New York, 1955.

[63] Stroud, James B. *Psychology in Education.* Longmans, Green and Company, New York, 1956.

[64] Terman, Lewis M. "The Discovery and Encouragement of Exceptional Talent." *The American Psychologist,* 9 (June, 1954) 221–230.

[65] Terman, Lewis M., and Oden, Melita H. *The Gifted Child Grows Up.* Stanford University Press, Stanford, Calif., 1947.

[66] Veatch, Jeannette. *Individualizing Your Reading Program: Self-Selection in Action,* G. P. Putnam's Sons, New York, 1959.

[67] Wheeler, Lester R., and Wheeler, Viola D. "The Relationship Between Reading Ability and Intelligence Among University Freshmen." *Journal of Educational Psychology,* 40 (April, 1949) 230–238.

[68] Witty, Paul. ed. *The Gifted Child.* D. C. Heath and Company, Boston, 1951.

[69] Witty, Paul. "Unsolved Problems in Reading: A Symposium II." *Elementary English,* 31 (November, 1954) 416–430.

[70] Witty, Paul. "Reading and the Gifted Child." *The Reading Teacher,* 9 (April, 1956) 195–196.

15

DIAGNOSIS AND REMEDIATION IN THE DEVELOPMENT PROGRAM

We know that, in learning to read, all children do not progress at the same rate. Even among those of adequate ability, some meet problems that delay or block their learning. We must strive constantly to discover these deterrents to learning and plan individualized work to further each child's development. An effective developmental reading program is built on a foundation of early diagnosis of inadequacies, careful evaluation of needs and abilities, and the utilization of professionally designed materials and methods.

To a large extent, this chapter is an extension of the preceding chapter. But our emphasis here will be on the specific rôle of diagnosis and remediation as essential elements of a true developmental program. Such a program requires continuing diagnosis and both individual and group remediation. The chief concerns are the needs, abilities, and day-to-day progress of each child.

Diagnosis and remediation are no longer to be considered the special privileges of the slow learner; they are extended to the gifted and to the average learners as well. Each child deserves diagnosis in order that his abilities, inadequacies, disabilities, and progress can be determined. Then remediation may overcome his disabilities so that he can progress to the extent of his abilities.

A developmental program requires a high level of professional skill. Instructional objectives must be carefully and clearly formulated. Only thus can we estimate progress toward them. There must be proficiency both in the use of instruments that indicate advancement toward those objectives and in the instruments that tell us the level at which each child is capable of working.

Our evaluation, then, encompasses measurement of the child's present achievement and of his ability to progress toward definite educational objectives. If he fails to make progress commensurate to his abilities, we must have a means for identifying the areas and the causes of his failures. Thus we proceed from *objectives,* to *measurement,* to *diagnosis.* But these steps are of small value unless remediation is to be a part of the instructional process.

DIAGNOSIS

Diagnostic procedure begins with a study of the child's instructional needs based on the expectancies of his chronological age, mental age, and grade placement. We seek to discover why he reads as he does, what he can read, and what he does read successfully. We need to know if he is having problems in reading and, if so, what they are and what are their causes. We wish to know his general abilities and his reading potentiality and we must identify causal factors that have retarded his reading development. In short, we must know his strengths and his weaknesses. Our information about the child comes from a wide variety of sources.

Brueckner (p. 2) [5] states that educational diagnosis

> . . . relates to the techniques by which one discovers and evaluates both strengths and weaknesses of the individual as a basis for more effective guidance. Diagnosis is a logical process based on a consideration of all the available data concerning a particular individual or group of individuals. The analysis of these data and their interpretation in the light of knowledge gained from past experience enables the diagnostician to suggest necessary developmental or remedial measures.

Tiegs (p. 5) [39] adds that educational diagnosis

> . . . is the basis of intelligent teaching. Its function is to facilitate the optimum development of every pupil. The following activities should become routine: determining for each pupil (1) which of his factors of intelligence are strong and which are weak, (2) whether he learns better through language or non-language materials and situations, (3) what his unattained objectives are, and (4) the nature of his desires, his fears, and his frustrations.

Standardized tests are among our most important diagnostic tools. However, we use numerous other resources. For example, we may gain important information from the child's performance on examinations in various subject-matter areas and from our informal observations of his study habits and leisure-time activities. We examine the child's school records and the results of his medical and visual tests. At times we must seek information from his parents. In summary, we use any information that provides us with a better understanding of the child.

INTELLIGENCE AND READINESS TESTS

Frequently *intelligence* test scores are the first standardized test results that the teacher is called upon to interpret. Intelligence tests are of two types: individual and group. Each has its unique advantages and disadvantages. The group tests require less time for administration, but generally they are less valid than individual tests. This is true primarily because they measure the present level of development of a child's verbal skills. And in those cases where the child's reading development has been retarded through inadequate instruction, emotional problems, or other reasons, the group test may greatly underestimate the general level of achievement of which the child is capable. The individual intelligence test, on the other hand, includes measures of the child's memory span and ability to visualize and to abstract. Thus it is less dependent upon his present level of reading achievement and more accurately indicates his potential for educational development.

Some intelligence tests, both individual and group, arrive at both a verbal and a non-verbal score. This may furnish a clue for diagnosis. When the verbal score is substantially below the non-verbal score, we may suspect that the child has had a poor cultural, linguistic, and/or reading background. Hage and Stroud [17] have pointed out that both types of scores correlate with reading comprehension and rate but verbal scores correlate more closely.

Readiness tests are closely related to intelligence tests and, in general, measure much the same area of development. Although to some extent every intelligence test is a test of readiness for academic development, a reading readiness test is designed to measure directly the child's experiential background and general preparedness for reading, whereas an intelligence test is designed to predict his ability to learn.

There is some disagreement concerning the value of readiness tests. Do they predict the child's readiness for reading better than do intelligence tests? Some studies indicate that they do; others, that they do not.[14, 25] An important factor, of course, is the validity of the specific reading readiness and intelligence tests that are being compared. Thorndike and Hagen (p. 261) [38] point out that the readiness test

. . . undertakes to predict ability to profit from reading instruction in the near future and is not used to forecast ultimate level of reading achievement. It may well be that it is more effective as an indicator of progress in reading within the next few months, even though an intelligence test is a better indicator of ultimate level of reading achievement.*

ACHIEVEMENT TESTS

In addition to intelligence and readiness tests, the teacher has frequent need for the use or interpretation of reading achievement tests. There are two general types of these: survey tests and diagnostic tests. The *survey test* is concerned with general achievement and typically is the first reading achievement test that the teacher will use. Usually it emphasizes vocabulary knowledge, comprehension of sentences or paragraphs, and perhaps speed of comprehension. It gives a general picture by identifying broad areas in which the pupil excels or is weak. It may tell, for example, that a certain child is reading at a level typical of children one or more grades above or below his present grade level. It indicates the general level of pupil progress and provides data for determining a pupil's proper grade placement and the reading materials that he should be expected to use with understanding.

There is another kind of achievement test, usually termed a *diagnostic test,* which seeks to discover specific strengths and weaknesses. It furnishes at least three or four subscores. Because this test helps the teacher to identify specific areas of deficiency, it is especially helpful in planning remedial procedures (pp. 278–279).[38]

A survey reading test tells us that Johnny, who is starting the fourth grade, performs on our test of reading paragraphs at a level typical of the usual child beginning the second grade. A series of diagnostic tests indicates that Johnny has a fair sight vocabulary of common words but no skills for working out unfamiliar words, that he is unable to blend sounds to form words, that he does not recognize the sounds that correspond to letter combinations, and that he makes frequent reversal errors. These findings, together with others, provide the basis for planning remedial teaching of word analysis and phonic skills that are specifically directed toward Johnny's deficiencies.**

CHARACTERISTICS OF TESTS

Obviously, we have a vital concern with the reliability and validity of any tests that we use. There is no magic in tests. Their value depends on the accuracy with which they measure those traits about which we are seeking information. Let us examine a few of the common deficiencies of tests.

First, diagnostic tests frequently yield formidable arrays of subscores. Unfortunately, to shorten administration time, diagnostic tests rarely contain a sufficient number of items to allow these subscores to be highly reliable. In any type of measurement, a five-minute sample of a child's behavior is less likely to give a reliable picture of him than is a twenty-minute sample.

Second, although reading tests generally try to measure rate and comprehension as separate outcomes, the measures of comprehension often are obtained from timed tests. This in itself tends to lower their validity because what is supposed to be a measure of comprehension frequently becomes in part at least a measure of rate. Stroud (pp. 174–175) [37] points out that:

> By any intelligent construction of the term, rate of reading means the rate at which a person reads with understanding. No one is seriously interested, except for some experimental purpose, in ascertaining that rate at which isolated words may be perceived. Rate of reading, then, really means rate of comprehension.

Third, reading tests suffer from a number of other basic deficiencies. Two tests supposedly measuring the same thing frequently disagree on the level of pupil achievement. And a closely related problem is that children often score higher on tests than their actual reading level appears to justify. Wheeler and Smith [43] report that a child's grade-level score on a test is likely to be about one grade above that at which he can read books used for instructional purposes. This results, says Dolch,[9] from the fact that reading tests do not require complete understanding to get a correct answer. Reading tests, in other words, may permit the child to get correct answers with only partial understanding and even with only partial reading of a selection.

Kingston [23] notes that tests of comprehension frequently emphasize the recall of facts rather than the understanding and comprehension of what is read. Memory rather than true comprehension is rewarded and becomes a major determinant of the final score.

Fourth, the teacher, moreover, may be more interested in how the pupil approaches a reading problem and the specific nature of his misunderstandings rather than in his total numerical score. And he wishes to know what errors in the child's techniques cause him to misunderstand.

Finally, the very lack of agreement as to just what is meant by "reading" results in anything but uniformity in the construction of reading tests. This may make a choice of reading tests difficult. For example, Traxler analyzed 28 reading tests and concluded that these tests measured 49 different reading skills (pp. 195–200).[41] Let us examine his list to see the variety of outcomes with which such tests are concerned.

Traxler's list indicates that reading tests most frequently attempt to measure vocabulary, paragraph comprehension, rate of reading, sentence meaning, and story comprehension. Obviously, however, no one test measures all the desired outcomes of reading instruction. Unfortunately, many tests appear to emphasize relatively unimportant aspects of reading at the expense of important ones. Traxler (p. 197) [41] comments:

> . . . it is reasonable to think that ability to perceive relationships, which appeared in only one of the twenty-eight tests, is at least as important in the interpretation of reading materials as reading speed, which was measured by ten of the tests.*

Davis [6] has suggested that as a goal of test construction the amount that each reading skill contributes to the total score should be the same as that particular skill contributes to the total reading process. Unfortunately, tests have not yet reached this stage of refinement. We can see that this is not entirely the fault of the testmaker. Not only do reading specialists disagree somewhat as to the nature of reading, but, also, they have not been able to decide the relative importance of specific reading skills.

However, even though there does appear to be agreement that interpretation and perceiving relationships, for example, are more important reading goals than is speed, the testmaker finds it more difficult to measure these various aspects of comprehension than to measure rate. Therefore, too often, tests emphasize what is easiest to measure rather than what is most important.

Although we may conclude that diagnostic reading tests have many inadequacies, they remain our best available means for identifying the child's specific strengths and weaknesses. But such identification is only one part of diagnosis. From a study of his strengths and weaknesses we try to identify the causes of each child's disabilities. The reading teacher seeks to follow the method of clinical psychology—diagnosis requires a thorough study of the individual case.

USING TESTS IN DIAGNOSIS

Obtaining test data is not diagnosis; it is merely one of several steps preliminary to diagnosis. And, for that matter, so is the gathering of data from school records, intelligence tests, survey tests, interest inventories,

---

Table 1

TYPES OF READING ABILITY MEASURED BY TWENTY-EIGHT READING TESTS *

Type of Reading Ability	*Tests Measuring This Ability* *Number*	*Percent*
Word meaning or vocabulary	19	67.9
Paragraph comprehension or meaning	13	46.4
Sentence meaning (also questions)	11	39.3
Rate of reading	10	35.7
Story comprehension	7	25.0
Noting and retaining details	6	21.4
Reading directions	5	17.9
Use of index	4	14.3
Word and phrase recognition—auditory (primary grades)	3	10.7
Word and phrase recognition—visual (primary grades)	3	10.7
Maps, graphs, and charts	3	10.7
Interpretation or interpreting paragraphs	3	10.7
Technical vocabulary or vocabulary of special fields	3	10.7
Central thought or main idea	2	7.1
Organization	2	7.1
Fact material	2	7.1
Total meaning	2	7.1
Directed reading	2	7.1
Alphabetization	2	7.1
Drawing conclusions or inferences	2	7.1
Speed of comprehension	2	7.1
Level of comprehension	2	7.1
General significance of a passage	2	7.1
Prediction of outcome	2	7.1
Use of references	2	7.1
Comprehension efficiency or accuracy of comprehension	2	7.1
Poetry comprehension	1	3.6
Use of dictionary	1	3.6
Relevant and irrelevant statements	1	3.6
True and false deductions	1	3.6
Recognition of form-likenesses and differences	1	3.6
Reading capacity—word meaning	1	3.6
Reading capacity—paragraph comprehension	1	3.6
Word discrimination	1	3.6
Reading comprehension in biology	1	3.6
Reading comprehension in history	1	3.6
Reading comprehension in literature	1	3.6
Reading comprehension in science	1	3.6
Ability to perceive relationships	1	3.6
Range of general information	1	3.6
Integration of dispersed ideas	1	3.6
Comprehension—auditory	1	3.6
Recognition—auditory	1	3.6
Associated word meanings	1	3.6
Selecting and classifying information	1	3.6
Word attack—oral	1	3.6
Word attack—silent	1	3.6
Directory reading	1	3.6
Advertisement reading	1	3.6

and study skills inventories. Nevertheless, diagnosis begins with measurement and each test used must have a specific purpose. The intelligence test helps us to know the child's capabilities of development; the survey test helps us to locate his present general level of development; the diagnostic test helps us to identify his specific strengths and weaknesses.

In planning our diagnostic procedure and, later, in carrying out the desired remedial program, we attempt to be as economical of time and materials as possible. First, we attempt to identify the general strengths and weaknesses of the group. For many children a detailed diagnosis will not be necessary.

According to Bond and Tinker (pp. 129–130) [4] this general diagnosis serves three purposes.

> First, it gives information necessary to adjust instruction to meet the needs of groups of children in general. For example, a fifth-grade class as a whole may be found to be relatively weak in reading ability. If so, the conclusion may be reached that more attention should be given to reading instruction than had been given in the past. Second, the general diagnosis can give the information necessary for adjusting instruction to individual differences in reading found within the class. . . . Third, a general diagnosis can help to locate the children who are in need of a detailed analysis of their reading disability.*

As a second level of diagnosis, to be used for such members of our group as require it, we make a more detailed or analytical diagnosis. For a basis of remedial teaching we wish to know specifically what skills the child may lack. The diagnostic test is used for this purpose.

> Analytical diagnosis has two important contributions to make to the correction of reading disability. *First,* it locates those areas of limited ability that need to be explored more fully. *Second,* it is often sufficiently diagnostic to indicate by itself the instructional adjustments required.**

As a third level of diagnosis reserved for particularly difficult problems, we may wish to make a thorough case study. Here we will attempt to assemble and interpret all pertinent facts concerning the child. We examine his past history, his current environment, and his present abilities, interests, and achievements. For his past history, we may obtain information from his cumulative record, from parents, previous teachers, and others who have known him for some time. To understand his current environment and his interests, we need to know the special problems he faces at home and with his peers. We want to know how he is regarded and what status he generally enjoys. And we want to know how he sees himself and

---

what his interests and goals are. Thus, in the case study we make an intensive analysis of the present difficulty and its past and present causes so that we may help the child to realize his potentialities.

PROFILE INTERPRETATION

Profiles frequently are used to aid diagnosis. They help us to see differences among the various areas of a child's achievement. Profiles help us to compare the child's achievement with the achievement of others in the class; his achievement with his mental age; and his achievement in one content area or specific skill with that in another. Actually a profile is merely a set of scores expressed according to some common unit. However, for the profile to be meaningful, the norms of the various tests that we use must be comparable. For example, in the profile in the following figure, the mental age equivalent must be fitted to the grade norms or we have no meaningful comparison between the child's expected performance and his actual achievement. However, if our measures are comparable, the profile helps us to identify strengths and weaknesses. The mental age indicates that the child should be achieving at approximately the 3.7 grade level. In arithmetic our test indicates that he is achieving at the 2.5 grade level. This profile helps us to compare the pupil's achievement in certain areas with his ability and also allows us to compare his achievement in one area with his achievement in another area. The profile can be used also to compare the child with other children of similar mental age who took similar tests and can be used to compare the specific achievement levels of various children in the class.

The teacher sometimes prepares a profile for the class as a whole. This provides for an overview of the individual differences in the class. It can show how the class norms compare with the national norms. And it may indicate what subject-matter areas need special emphasis and even what areas are being overemphasized.

There is another type of profile of particular importance to the reading teacher. In diagnostic tests numerous sub-areas are tested. The *Bond-Clymer-Hoyt Silent Reading Diagnostic Tests,* for example, are concerned with eleven areas. And many survey tests provide separate measures of vocabulary, paragraph comprehension, sentence meaning, and rate of reading.

In interpreting profiles it is particularly important that we recognize that the test-score points are not absolutes but are merely probabilities. Actually a child's true level of development either of abilities or in a subject-matter area cannot be located. Because all tests are far from perfect in both reliability and validity and because children vary from day to day in how well they may perform on a test, we cannot determine accurately

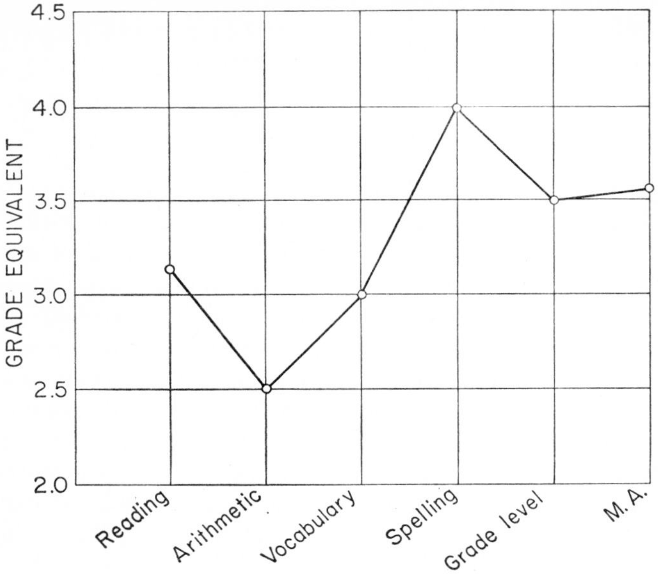

the actual point denoting a true score. We must be content to determine an *area* within which the true score lies. A profile drawn to show standard errors of measurement will indicate the range, surrounding the obtained test score, that almost certainly contains the true score. Such a profile, then, does not locate a specific point but, rather, an area or band.

On one typical test a child obtained a sentence-meaning score equivalent to the score obtained by the average third reader. Because this score is .5 of a grade below his current grade level, the teacher hypothesizes that a genuine difference exists and proceeds to test this prediction. He plots a band of scores. He goes out from the achieved score one standard error of measurement. He now can predict with 68 per cent of accuracy that the child's true score on sentence meaning lies somewhere between grades 2.5 and 3.5. By allowing two standard errors of measurement he can predict with 95 per cent of accuracy that the child's true score lies somewhere between 2.0 and 4.0. Ordinarily a teacher wishes to guarantee at least 95 per cent accuracy in his prediction.

INFORMAL PROCEDURES

In many cases we will not have available the detailed standardized test data that we might wish. Frequently we must rely on less objective techniques.

Betts suggests some general principles that can be used to guide our informal procedures. He (pp. 438 ff) [3] identifies three reading levels. For the extensive reading which we hope the child will do, the material must be readable at his *basal* or *independent* level. At his independent reading level a child should have 90% or better comprehension, be able to pronounce accurately 99% of the words, and read comfortably and rhythmically. However, short specific class assignments may offer a higher-level challenge to the child. Betts calls this the *instructional* reading level. To read at this level the child must have at least 75% comprehension and make no more than one error per 20 words. Material more difficult than this will be read at a *frustration* level. Betts recommends that the teacher determine for each child the grade-level of the material that he reads at each of the three reading levels.

Betts suggests also that the teacher determine the *capacity* level of the child—his ability to understand material that is read to him.

Wheeler and Smith [43] also discuss the *instructional* level. They indicate that for material to be appropriate for instructional purposes the child must understand from 95 to 98 per cent of the vocabulary and from 75 to 95 per cent of the main ideas. Material more difficult than this approaches the frustration level.

Informal oral reading is one of our best means for ascertaining how well the child reads and for identifying some of his problems. It permits us to learn something about how he attacks words. It acquaints us with his comprehension skills and his techniques for sounding and blending. It gives a clue to the child's willingness and desire to succeed.

As a part of our informal procedures, we look for discrepancies between silent and oral reading abilities. Frequently a child with high ability and an interest in reading understands words in his silent reading that he cannot pronounce. Also we may identify failures in understanding that are due to the child's ignorance of certain words that are important to sentence meaning. Actually, one of the most important uses of oral reading in our classroom is for the informal diagnosis of silent reading problems.

Observation of the child's oral reading, whether formal or informal in nature, has other advantages in diagnosis. It encourages us to find out why he pronounced a word in a peculiar way, why he reversed letters, or why he skipped a word. In diagnosing we are especially interested in the *causes* of errors. Our interest does not cease with a yes-no answer. We want to know why and how the child got his answer. It is, for example, quite common at the first-grade level for a child to recognize a word by means of irrelevant clues (e.g. identification of words with an erasure mark or a fly speck on the book or word card).

In using informal procedures we generally are trying to determine what books a child can read for enjoyment and how difficult an assigned reading can be and still be used as instructional materials. Although, unfortunately, grade-level designations furnished by the publishers of many books are far from accurate, the experienced teacher can select a suitable set of books and other materials for use in informal determinations of children's reading abilities. And at the very least a teacher should examine the class texts and supplementary readings to see if they are suitable for each child.

VALIDITY OF INFORMAL PROCEDURES

The question certainly arises as to how effective are the teacher's informal diagnostic procedures.

Hitchcock and Alfred (p. 422) [20] found that teachers' observations can be reliable and valid, and they suggest standards for guiding teacher observation. They report that a teacher of English, using eight criteria, attempted to judge the reading ability of 101 eighth-grade pupils. The teacher's ratings were then compared with standardized test results and correlations of .74 to .83 were obtained. It was concluded that carefully-made teacher estimates may be nearly as reliable as standardized test results. The criteria used by this teacher were these:

1. Pupil interest in school work that requires reading as a skill.
2. Pupil concentration on reading material—that is, his ability to resist distractions.
3. The degree of pupil vigor—or apathy—in attacking assignments involving reading.
4. Behavioral attitude—the pupil's interest, or lack of interest, in the work of the class.
5. Speed in completing work involving reading.
6. Willingness to read orally. (The poor reader is less likely than the good reader to volunteer.)
7. Desire to hear others read. (The poor reader is more likely to wish to hear others read than is the good reader.)
8. Ability to follow written directions.

Henig [19] found that teachers' forecast of the success of first-grade pupils in reading had about the same validity as a readiness test. In his study the teachers had observed the pupils for three weeks before making an evaluation. Kottmeyer [24] reported that a group of 142 teachers predicted the reading readiness of 3,156 children with 71.4 per cent accuracy. Kottmeyer found that the most experienced teachers made the most accurate predictions. And, in general, teacher prediction was more accurate than scores on the Metropolitan and Detroit Readiness tests.

Certainly, these studies suggest that the informal techniques of teachers possess considerable validity.

PRINCIPLES OF DIAGNOSIS

The techniques that are available and the problems involved in diagnosis suggest some general principles that the teacher may use as guides. Robinson (pp. 152–153),[31] for example, lists the following principles of diagnosis:

First, secure as much information as possible about the person and record it on a case history blank.
Second, obtain the most accurate measure possible of the level at which the person should be able to read.
Third, administer a standardized reading survey test. . . .
Fourth, analyze the data . . . to determine whether the person has a reading problem. . . .
Fifth, a detailed analysis of . . . the reading problem is made.
Sixth, an attempt is made to identify factors which may be inhibiting reading progress. . . .
[Seventh] . . . collate all of the data secured and . . . interpret the results as accurately as possible.
[Eighth] . . . make appropriate recommendations for remedial therapy. . . .

Bond and Tinker (p. 126) [4] list eight somewhat different aspects of diagnosis:

1. A diagnosis is always directed toward formulating methods of improvement.
2. A diagnosis involves far more than appraisal of reading skills and abilities.
3. A diagnosis must be efficient—going as far as and no farther than is necessary.
4. Only pertinent information should be collected and by the most efficient means.
5. Whenever possible, standardized test procedures should be used.
6. Informal procedures may be required when it is necessary to expand a diagnosis.
7. Decisions in formulating a diagnosis must be arrived at on the basis of patterns of scores.
8. A diagnosis should be continuous.*

Principles, unfortunately, are not enough. They must be applied. Strang, McCullough, and Traxler (pp. 256–257) [36] identify some of the difficulties in making a good diagnosis. In essence, the problems are these:

1. Not everyone has the same definition of reading.
2. No one knows exactly what comprehension is. How, then, can one measure it?
3. The part scores of many diagnostic tests are quite unreliable.
4. Vocabulary tests which form a part of reading tests do not restrict themselves to words of one meaning.
5. Tests of rate have not successfully combined evaluation of rate and comprehension.
6. The relationship of scores on a specific test with later achievement has not been evaluated.
7. Tests frequently lack sufficient validity and reliability to be useful.
8. Materials to help remedy deficiencies indicated by diagnosis are difficult to obtain.

READING RETARDATION

For a complete understanding of the problems of diagnosis and as a basis for our later discussion of remediation, we should examine the psychological principles involved in reading retardation. Certainly not all poor readers can properly be termed reading disability cases. Many poor readers are merely slow learners. In short, they have low I.Q.'s. There is no need for special reading instruction if the child is reading as well as his level of mental development justifies.

Retardation generally is defined in relation to level of general development with perhaps the greater emphasis being on mental development. A retarded reader is one who is reading below his present general level of development. This includes limits set by the pupil's physical, emotional, and social, as well as his mental, development. Austin [1] suggests several methods for identifying those children who can profit most from special help in reading. Among these are: noting the discrepancy between mental age and reading age, using the Monroe reading index,* applying the Olson and Hughes's split-growth analysis, and making a thorough case study. Whatever approach we use for identifying retardation, we retain a responsibility for defining the limits between satisfactory proficiency and reading retardation.

---

* The reading index is obtained by dividing the reading performance as expressed in school grade by the average of the child's chronological age, mental age, and arithmetic performance (these also are expressed in terms of school grade). Indices below .80 indicate severe reading disability.

Durrell (p. 279) [11] suggests applying a more rigid standard at the first grade level than in the later grades. He points out that a retardation of six months at the first grade level is more serious than is a retardation of a year or more at the sixth grade level. Harris (p. 299) [18] does not consider a first-grade child retarded unless his reading age is at least six months below his mental age. He suggests that in grades four and above, the discrepancy, to be significant, should be a year or more.

Certainly, retardation is a matter of degree. It has been suggested that there are general levels of retardation and that each level tends to be characterized by its own symptoms and requires its own remedial techniques. In discussing diagnosis, it was suggested that retardation could be general or specific. General retardation refers to a generally low level of reading ability as compared to mental age. Specific retardation is the term used to designate weaknesses in a specific area or areas of reading. Retardation also can be in the nature of a limiting disability or a complex disability. The child with limiting disability is one who has serious deficiencies in basic reading skills or abilities which impede his entire reading growth. In the case of a child with a complex disability there is severe reading retardation as shown by a marked discrepancy between his achievement and his ability and in addition he shows symptoms of personal problems, tension, and antipathy to reading.

Ordinarily our most immediate problem is to decide where the child can best receive help. In general, writers recommend that simple retardation cases be kept in the regular classroom. Some suggest, however, that on the secondary level such cases might best be helped in a reading clinic or special instructional group if such facilities are available. Cases of specific retardation also may be helped in regular classrooms by forming small groups of children having the same disabilities. The child with a limiting disability is perhaps best treated in the reading center and the severely disabled reader certainly needs the help of a specialist.

FACTORS CONTRIBUTING TO READING RETARDATION

There is no simple formula for identifying the causes of reading retardation. The correlates of failure in reading are many. For example, Schubert,[32] summarizing the descriptions of best and poor readers as listed by 80 teachers, concluded that as a group poor readers more frequently are male, have repeated a grade, give evidence of physical and emotional immaturity, have speech defects, evidence discipline problems, and frequently come from broken homes.

Johnson [21] studied 34 disability cases in the Temple University Reading Clinic Laboratory School. At the time of analysis the average age of the children was eleven years, four months. None of the children read above the second grade level and 76.5 per cent read at a pre-primer level. Of these 34 cases, 67.6 per cent showed social and emotional maladjustment; 41.2 per cent were retarded in language development; 64.7 per cent had had serious or recurring illness; and 20.6 per cent had suffered head injuries. Vision was inadequate in 61.8 per cent of the cases. Auditory acuity was unsatisfactory in 17.6 per cent of the cases. Performance on the *Van Riper Form Board* indicated that 93.8 per cent of the 32 cases tested had some confusion in dominance. Reversals occurred in 97.1 per cent of the cases.

Dolch [7] says that reading retardation may be caused by starting the child too early in reading, by absences from or frequent changes in school, by promotion into failure, by the use of too difficult reading material, and by poor methods of teaching. Sister Nila (p. 543) [29] suggests that the five major causes of reading retardation are:

> . . . a wrong start in grade one; advancement of the pupil from one reading level to the next higher level faster than his present ability and capacity permit; lack of adequate materials; lack of systematic instruction throughout all grades; and last, but not least, faulty teaching.

At one time or another reading difficulties have been attributed to any one or a combination of the "causes" listed by the above writers. Because of the tremendous array of factors that have been found related to reading development, two comprehensive lists are reproduced below. Betts' [2] listing emphasize the factors that may be related to reading disability. These flow from the five variables in reading: the pupil, the teacher, the parent, the teaching method, and the reading materials. The major problem areas as identified by Betts are as follows:

I. Maturation
   1. Defective cerebral development
   2. Delayed cerebral development
   3. Confusion of cerebral development
      a. Hand preference
      b. Eye preference
   4. Physiological and psychological readiness
      a. Maturation level
      b. Rate of maturation
   5. Interpupillary distance
   6. Background of information

II. Vision
   1. Acuity
   2. Refractive errors (such as farsightedness, nearsightedness, and astigmatism)

- 3. Anomalies of binocular co-ordination
  - a. Faulty fusion of small images
  - b. Convergence or adductive insufficiency or excess
  - c. Oculomotor and perception habits
  - d. Size and shape of ocular images
- 4. Lighting
- 5. Imagery (after, eidetic and memory)
- 6. Span

III. Audition
- 1. Acuity
- 2. Span
- 3. Perception
- 4. Blending or fusing sounds into words

IV. Kinesthesia
- 1. Poor eye co-ordination
- 2. Inappropriate eye-movement
- 3. Speech defects
- 4. Spatial orientation
- 5. Vocalization and lip-movement

V. Language
- 1. Meager vocabulary
- 2. Foreign language
- 3. Composition ability

VI. Emotional
- 1. Dislike for reading
- 2. Instability or lack of integration
- 3. Poor attention
- 4. Lack of motivation of work by the teacher
- 5. Conflict with teacher
- 6. Parental interference

VII. Sex Differences (boys outnumber girls)

VIII. Pedagogical
- 1. Inadequate instructional materials
  - a. Lack of variety of materials for each stage of reading
  - b. Sequence of reading materials not carefully graded
  - c. Vocabulary burden and rate of introduction of new words
  - d. Sentence structure and punctuation
  - e. Typography unsuitable
  - f. Size of type
  - g. Space between lines
  - h. Leading
- 2. Faulty teaching techniques
  - a. First teaching inadequate
  - b. Too much drill on words out of context
  - c. [Failure to] Establish efficient habits of work
  - d. Overemphasis on speed
  - e. Overemphasis on word analysis
  - f. Lack of attention to readiness
  - g. Insufficient maintenance drill
  - h. Lack of stress on reading for meaning

i. No provision for remedial drill
j. [Failure to identify] specific difficulties before drilling on next step in the hierarchy
k. . . . interference factors
l. Inadequate care of individual differences
m. [Lack of] Multi-sensory approach
n. [Lack of] Interest and ability
o. Classification and promotion . . .
p. Pupil [unaware of] achievement increments

IX. Psychological
1. Adequacy of concepts
2. Mental age
3. Rate of association of ideas
4. Anticipation of meaning
5. Perception of relationship

X. External
1. Attendance
2. Frequent changing of schools
3. Administrative policies
a. Size of class
b. Entrance age for first grade
c. [Lack of] Provision of quantities of supplementary instructional materials
d. Inadequate standards for promotion
e. Professional training of teachers
f. Clinical service

Betts' listing can help the teacher know where to look for possible causes of reading failure and, if used as a check list, it should form a basis for remedial reading prescriptions.

Wheeler's (p. 110) [42] listing emphasizes the behavioral clues to reading disability. He identifies the following specific indicators:

1. Lacks interest in reading tasks
2. Lacks independent study habits
3. Learns more readily through discussion and listening than through silent-reading assignments
4. Is unable to read materials that are on his grade level
5. Achieves much better in nonreading than in language subjects
6. Takes too long to complete reading tasks
7. Complains that reading is too difficult
8. May be poor in spelling
9. Shows symptoms of visual or hearing difficulties
10. Has difficulty remembering what he has read
11. Is unable to make practical applications of what he has read
12. Shows emotional disturbances and nervous tensions when reading materials on his normal grade level

13. Dislikes school, is socially maladjusted, or is a behavior problem
14. Shows reading difficulties on standard reading tests and/or informal checks
15. Makes academic progress below that expected of him in relation to his general mental alertness and the results of psychological tests.*

RECOMMENDATIONS

The skillful teacher uses every available means for making the best possible diagnosis. Lists of causes and of symptoms can help us to know where and when to look for specific difficulties. But identification, whether by tests or informal procedures, is not enough. Diagnosis is meant to lead to remediation. It must serve as a blueprint from which remediation is structured.

Somehow, either on our own or with specially skilled help if it is available, we must identify the child's problems and then plan and carry through the best possible corrective measures. This requires certain decisions based on particular information:

1. We must decide whether the child actually is a retarded reader rather than a child of low ability. If he is a retarded reader, we must identify the nature of his retardation.
2. We must decide what type of training is needed.
3. We must determine whether the needed remedial work can best be done in our own classroom or in separate facilities and, if in our classroom, whether individually or in groups.
4. We must determine the most efficient methods and materials that can be used.
5. We must be alert to the child's special interests and to any emotional or physical defects that may block his growth in reading.
6. We must acquire pertinent information concerning conditions in the child's home and community environment that may block his reading growth.

Unfortunately, it requires considerable skill and care to transfer the diagnostic data into an accurate prescription that can serve as the basis for remediation. In making the transfer we must recognize certain dangers. Sometimes the child's symptoms may lead us to take faulty steps toward his remediation. What may appear to be the cause of his difficulty may be quite unrelated to it or may even be a result or symptom of his problems. But skill and experience in the translation of diagnostic data and an earnest desire to help each child attain the highest goals that his capabilities permit should serve as a firm foundation for remediation.

REMEDIATION

In this book, the term "remedial reading program" has been avoided. However, to a certain extent, a modern developmental reading program is a remedial program in that it starts where the child stands and progresses with him. It seeks to satisfy his developmental needs and to remedy his inadequacies. Constant diagnosis and constant employment of remedial techniques are essential portions of the program.

Educational growth is rarely a unitary process. The child may "catch-on" quickly to one skill or in some areas of knowledge but lag in others. Thus, diagnosis and remediation must continually accompany all effective teaching.

In the past, remedial teaching was identified as a general process of re-teaching. In the developmental program remedial teaching is directed toward each child's specific needs and inadequacies.

The methods and principles of remedial teaching and developmental teaching are distinguishable, if at all, by the emphasis on individualization. Gates [13] points out that the primary characteristic of remedial instruction is individual prescription for individual needs. Actually remedial teaching is merely a phase of developmental teaching. Teaching that is remedial for one student will be developmental for others. Consequently, it is the nature of the child rather than the nature of the teaching that distinguishes the two procedures.

PRINCIPLES OF REMEDIATION

The reading teacher must understand the individual pattern of each case of reading disability. As Bond and Tinker (p. 205) [4] point out:

> . . . no two cases of reading disability result from the same set of circumstances, no two have exactly the same reading patterns, no two cases have the same instructional needs, and no two can be treated in exactly the same manner.*

A child in need of remedial teaching may have adequate development in certain skills and be deficient in others. We must depend on diagnosis to identify his adequacies and deficiencies and then tailor our remedial teaching to the pattern that is revealed.

The teacher must be aware that reading is but one aspect of the child's total development and that reading development influences and is influenced by those other aspects of development. Thus remedial teaching must take a different approach with the hard-of-hearing, the visually defective, the emotionally disturbed, or the slow learner even though the reading deficiencies of each may be the same.

As a first step in remediation we must prepare a plan and generally this plan should be put on paper and referred to frequently as the remediation progresses. All plans must be flexible. We must expect to re-evaluate our diagnosis and re-direct our remediation as needed. A remedial technique has value only if it works.

Motivation is important to all reading and especially to remedial reading. The teacher, by his own energetic and vigorous attack and interest, does much to instill in the student the desire to succeed. Sister Julitta [22] identifies the elements that make for success in a remedial program. The program must begin with short assignments, inspire confidence, and restore status to the child in the eyes of his peers. It should lead to the setting of definite goals. Dolch [8] says that for successful remedial reading, we must discover the child's *area of confidence*—those words of which he is certain. Advancement from this area requires pacing the materials to the interest and ability of the child so that he experiences a series of successes and avoids defeats.

Although we do everything possible to guide the child's reading development, we try to guarantee that the child will retain a feeling of responsibility for his own progress. Obviously we can not learn for him. Yet too frequently children and even adults cease trying to help themselves when others appear to take full responsibility for their problems.

REMEDIAL METHODS

Numerous specific remedial teaching techniques have been proposed. One which is valuable for work with severely disabled readers is the Fernald kinesthetic method.[12] The steps in her method vary from word tracing to word analysis and are determined somewhat by the ability and progress of the child. At the lower ranges of achievement, the child selects a word that he wishes to learn. The teacher writes the word on paper in large script or print. The child then traces the word with the forefinger, saying each part of the word as he does the tracing. The process continues until the child can write the word without the benefit of the copy. The child's fingers must make contact with the paper as he traces. Words thus learned are later typewritten and then included in stories for the child to read. As new words are learned they are collected by the pupil in an alphabetical file. As the child advances, tracing may cease entirely, but pronouncing the word while writing it is always an essential feature.

The kinesthetic method is time consuming, but it has many advantages. It teaches left-to-right orientation, and the sound of the word is associated with the visual stimulus. The child seems to acquire phonic skills without having formal training and he develops skills in syllabication. The method is designed especially for clinical use and requires almost constant direction from the teacher.

Harris (p. 386) [18] lists the strong points of this method:

(1) It enforces careful and systematic observation and study of words.
(2) It makes necessary a consistent left-to-right direction in reading.
(3) It provides adequate repetition.
(4) Errors are immediately noted and corrected.
(5) Progress can be noted by the child at practically every lesson.
(6) The sensory impressions from tracing, writing, and saying the words reinforce the visual impressions and seem to be of definite value to children whose visual memory is very poor.

Numerous writers have advocated phonetic methods both for remedial work and as a general portion of the developmental program. Monroe (pp. 111–136) [26] in 1932 evolved a phonetic approach using considerable repetition and drill. A basic emphasis was on the development of auditory discrimination. Pictures are mounted on cards and the child is taught to identify initial consonants and consonants followed by a vowel. After a few of these phonetic elements are known, blending is begun. Gradually, the child is initiated into the reading of specially written stories. Tracing is used in this method as the need arises, but the child uses a pencil rather than the forefinger for tracing. Monroe reports that this is highly successful with serious reading disability cases. With approximately 27 hours of remedial work spread over an average period of seven months, reading scores were raised by 1.39 year on the average. During the same time the control group made gains of only .14 year (pp. 139–145).[26]

Unfortunately, a heavy dependence on either a kinesthetic or a phonetic approach can be extremely time consuming. This may slow the progress unnecessarily for many members of a class. Gates (pp. 325, 489–503) [13] recommends that remedial teaching within the regular developmental program should ordinarily employ the more traditional methods of teaching skills. He suggests that special approaches such as the kinesthetic need be used only as last resorts.

PROBLEMS IN EVALUATING REMEDIAL METHODS

Although many quite different remedial procedures have been advocated, too few data actually are available concerning their relative effectiveness.

And for that matter, some writers actually challenge the effectiveness of special methods of remediation. Young,[45] for example, suggests that the personality of the teacher and his ability to enlist each child's active co-operation are more important than the specific method used. On the other hand, Tinker [40] concluded that a review of 54 studies on remedial and diagnostic methods indicated that reading difficulties can be either entirely or at least largely eliminated.

One problem in evaluating pupil improvement is that we often lack satisfactory tests for measuring progress in the skills that we teach. Murphy and Davis [28] have indicated that the tests used in experiments frequently do not measure the same skills that the teacher is seeking to develop.

Another problem in interpreting research findings is that the experimenters often fail to recognize the chance factors that intrude into test scores. Certain experimenters also have failed to consider the factor of regression in evaluating the possible progress of a group of disabled readers. As Sommerfeld (p. 24) [33] points out, regression means that

> . . . in a test–retest situation those people who score at the extremes of a distribution on the first test tend to score closer to the mean of the distribution on the second test; that is, the scores tend to regress toward the mean.

Although the research worker can use control groups or make statistical corrections to eliminate regression effects, frequently this is not done.

Sommerfeld's (p. 21) observations about the evaluation of rate–improvement programs identify still another problem:

> . . . should improvement be measured in terms of rate and comprehension on reading passages approximating normal reading materials or in terms of standardized tests? The question has often been raised as to whether we are actually improving reading ability, or whether we are merely improving reading-test performance with no meaningful transfer of the acquired skills to the academic situation.

Dolch (p. 80) [10] has cautioned that research can come up with the wrong answer unless it is carefully planned and watched. He recommends vigilance in these areas:

1. Compare equal teachers working equally hard.
2. Compare pupils of equal ability and equal home influences.
3. Compare equal school time and emphasis.
4. Watch carefully size of class.
5. Beware of misleading averages.
6. Watch for unmeasured results.

In discussing these points, Dolch emphasizes that the teacher using the method frequently is far more important than the method used. Numerous variables enter into any experiment. Sommerfeld (p. 56) [34] indicates that the reported results of experimental reading programs may be influenced by

> . . . the subjects involved, the techniques and materials used, the conditions specific to the study, the tests employed, the statistical devices used, and perhaps the bias or misinterpretations of the investigator. Further, most studies report results in terms of group means which obscure variations among the individuals in the group.

Studies often do not make allowance for the differences in both skill and motivation among teachers. Control groups are taught by the "regular" teachers; experimental groups are taught by teachers who have a special interest in the project and can give more time to their students. There may also be differences in motivation between the pupils in a control group using the regular methods and the experimental group using a new method.

Another problem in evaluating remedial teaching is that children should be expected to make some progress with good teaching regardless of what method is used. Thus progress in a remedial situation must be compared with progress by a control group or some statistical device must be used to estimate the effect of the special attention given to a group.

Mouly and Grant,[27] evaluating a program in which 30 minutes of remedial teaching was added to the regular reading sessions, proposed an equation to represent the gains that teachers using these same remedial methods might expect. They proposed that the equation $Y = 1.6476 + .0359X$ (where Y is the estimated monthly gain for a pupil of $I.Q. = 100$ and X is the retardation in months) represents the gains that might justifiably be expected if methods similar to those reported in their study were followed. They derived their equation from a study of the gains achieved by 989 pupils who had an average retardation of 17 months.

Probably most teachers use a much simpler formula for gauging a child's retardation and for predicting the advancement that can realistically be expected for him. Generally, the child's mental age is given important consideration. If his reading performance is found to be substantially below what may be expected of children of his mental age, remedial procedures are considered to be in order. Some writers suggest that in the first and second grades a lag of six months should be sufficient to cause concern, whereas in higher grades a differential of at least one year generally is considered to be substantial enough to call for planned remediation.

As the discussion has shown, valid standards for evaluating the effectiveness of remedial teaching are difficult to establish. However, there are various ways in which the child's progress will indicate his general improvement in reading. Witty (p. 73) [44] suggests the following:

. . . improvement on standard and informal tests of rate and comprehension, gains in amount and quality of reading, growth in ability to read for various purposes, gains in making personal and social adjustments, improvement in vocabulary, intensification or expansion of interests, and desirable changes in the student's pattern of reading.

SUMMARY

In this chapter we have examined some general principles of diagnosis and remediation and have proposed certain practical techniques. In diagnosis we must strive for accurate measurement. Numerous tests—intelligence, readiness, survey, and diagnostic—are at the teacher's disposal. But, for effective diagnosis, the teacher must rely on his own observations of the child and his reading skills and deficiencies.

We have seen that diagnosis is a continuous process designed to encourage the growth of all learners. The teacher must understand and be able to identify the numerous possible causes of retardation. Without this knowledge he cannot apply the appropriate remedial techniques nor, if the situation demands, can he be certain to make the appropriate referral to the specialist. And the reading teacher needs to familiarize himself with a variety of remedial methods. No one method is effective in all cases.

Finally, it is important that we recognize remediation to be an integral part of a developmental reading program. Diagnostic and remedial techniques are not reserved for "retarded" readers. Children of any level of ability, even those making normal or above-normal progress, may benefit from the identification and treatment of specific areas of weakness.

SUGGESTED READINGS

For general discussions of the essential aspects of evaluation, selecting tests and interpreting test results, and determining individual and group expectations for reading:

Robinson, Helen M., (Ed.) "Evaluation of Reading," *Supplementary Educational Monographs,* No. 88. Chicago: The University of Chicago Press, 1958.

Robinson, Helen M. "Corrective and Remedial Instruction," pp. 357–375, and Strang, Ruth. "Evaluation of Development in and through Reading," pp. 376–397, in *Development in and through Reading,* 60th Yearbook of the National Society for the Study of Education, Part I, 1961.

***

For a discussion of the determination of individual pupil goals and the importance of pupil maturity, background ability, and interests in evaluating pupil progress:

Chapter 11, "Evaluating and Reporting Pupil Progress," pp. 414–465 in McKim, Margaret G., Carl W. Hansen, and William L. Carter. *Learning to*

Teach in the Elementary School. New York: The Macmillan Company, 1959.

***

(Causey, *The Reading Teacher's Reader*)

Article 13, Dolch, E. W., "How to Diagnose Children's Reading Difficulties," from *The Reading Teacher,* 6 (January, 1953) pp. 10–14.

QUESTIONS FOR DISCUSSION

1. What are the objectives of a developmental reading program?
2. What are the relative advantages of intelligence and readiness tests?
3. What are the advantages and disadvantages of individual and of group intelligence tests?
4. Distinguish between survey and diagnostic reading tests. Why are both needed for adequate evaluation?
5. Discuss some of the most common inadequacies of tests.
6. What are the benefits of profile interpretation of test scores?
7. What is the meaning of "standard error of measurement"?
8. What factors must be considered in interpreting the child's test scores?
9. What is the purpose of Betts' three levels of reading proficiency?
10. What are the diagnostic values of the child's oral reading performance?
11. What are the advantages and disadvantages of subscores on tests?
12. How may reading retardation be defined? How can it be identified?
13. Discuss the Fernald kinesthetic method.
14. What criteria should be used for evaluating remedial methods?

BIBLIOGRAPHY

[1] Austin, Mary C. "Identifying Readers Who Need Corrective Instruction." *Corrective Reading in Classroom and Clinic,* Supplementary Educational Monographs, No. 79, University of Chicago Press, Chicago, 1953, 19–25.

[2] Betts, Emmett A. "Reading Disability Correlates." *Education,* 56 (September, 1935) 18–24.

[3] Betts, Emmett A. *Foundations of Reading Instruction.* American Book Company, New York, 1957.

[4] Bond, Guy L., and Tinker, Miles A. *Reading Difficulties: Their Diagnosis and Correction.* Appleton-Century-Crofts, Inc., New York, 1957.

[5] Brueckner, Leo J. "Introduction." *Educational Diagnosis,* Thirty-fourth Yearbook of the National Society for the Study of Education, Public School Publishing Company, Bloomington, 1935, 1–14.

[6] Davis, Fredrick B. "Comprehension in Reading." *Baltimore Bulletin of Education,* 28 (January–February, 1951) 16–24.

[7] Dolch, E. W. "Poor Readers are 'Made'." *Education,* 67 (March, 1947) 436–41.

[8] Dolch, E. W. "Success in Remedial Reading." *Elementary English,* 30 (March, 1953) 133–137.

[9] Dolch, E. W. "Complete Reading vs. Partial Reading." *Elementary English,* 33 (January, 1956) 11–12.

[10] Dolch, E. W. "School Research in Reading." *Elementary English,* 33 (February, 1956) 76–80.

[11] Durrell, Donald D. *The Improvement of Basic Reading Abilities.* World Book Company, Yonkers, N.Y., 1940.

[12] Fernald, Grace M. *Remedial Techniques in Basic School Subjects.* McGraw-Hill Book Company, Inc., New York, 1943.

[13] Gates, Arthur I. *The Improvement of Reading,* 3rd Edition. The Macmillan Company, New York, 1947.

[14] Gates, A. I., Bond, G. L., and Russell, D. H. *Methods of Determining Reading Readiness.* Bureau of Publications, Teachers College, Columbia University, 1939.

[15] Gray, William S. *Remedial Cases in Reading: Their Diagnosis and Treatment.* Supplementary Educational Monographs, No. 22, University of Chicago Press, Chicago, 1922.

[16] Gray, Lillian, and Reese, Dora. *Teaching Children to Read.* Ronald Press Company, New York, 1957.

[17] Hage, Dean S., and Stroud, James B. "Reading Proficiency and Intelligence Scores, Verbal and Nonverbal." *Journal of Educational Research,* 52 (March, 1959) 258–262.

[18] Harris, Albert J. *How to Increase Reading Ability,* 3rd Edition. Longmans, Green and Company, New York, 1956.

[19] Henig, Max S. "Predictive Value of a Reading-Readiness Test and of Teachers' Forecasts." *Elementary School Journal,* 50 (September, 1949) 41–46.

[20] Hitchcock, Arthur A., and Alfred, Cleo. "Can Teachers Make Accurate Estimates of Reading Ability?" *The Clearing House,* 29 (March, 1955) 422–424.

[21] Johnson, Marjorie Seddon. "A Study of Diagnostic and Remedial Procedures in a Reading Clinic Laboratory School." *Journal of Educational Research,* 48 (April, 1955) 565–578.

[22] Julitta, Sister Mary, O.S.F. "Classroom Methods in Correcting Reading Deficiencies in Elementary School." *Better Readers For Our Times,* International Reading Association, Conference Proceedings, Scholastic Magazines, New York, 1956, 134–138.

[23] Kingston, Albert J. "Cautions Regarding the Standardized Reading Test." *Evaluating College Reading Programs,* Fourth Yearbook of the Southwest Reading Conference for Colleges and Universities, Texas Christian University Press, Forth Worth, 1955, 11–16.

[24] Kottmeyer, William. "Readiness for Reading." *Elementary English,* 24 (October, 1947) 355–366.

[25] Lee, M. J., and Clark, W. W. *Lee-Clark Reading Readiness Test: Manual.* California Test Bureau, Los Angeles, 1951.

[26] Monroe, Marion. *Children Who Cannot Read.* University of Chicago Press, Chicago, 1932.

[27] Mouly, George J., and Grant, Virginia F. "A Study of the Growth to be Expected of Retarded Readers." *Journal of Educational Research,* 49 (February, 1956) 461–465.

[28] Murphy, Harold D., and Davis, Frederick, B. "A Note on the Measurement of Progress in Remedial Reading." *Peabody Journal of Education,* 27 (September, 1949) 108–111.

[29] Nila, Sister Mary, O.S.F. "Foundations of a Successful Reading Program." *Education,* 73 (May, 1953) 543–555.

[30] Robinson, F. P., and Hall, Prudence. "Studies of Higher-Level Reading Abilities." *Journal of Educational Psychology,* 32 (April, 1941) 241–252.

[31] Robinson, Helen M. "Clinical Procedures in Diagnosing Seriously Retarded Readers." *Better Readers For Our Times,* International Reading Association, Conference Proceedings, Scholastic Magazines, New York, 1956, 152–156.

[32] Schubert, Delwyn G. "Comparison Between Best and Poorest Classroom Readers." *Elementary English,* 33 (March, 1956) 161–162.

[33] Sommerfeld, Roy E. "Problems in Evaluating College Reading Programs." *Evaluating College Reading Programs,* Fourth Yearbook of the Southwest Reading Conference, for Colleges and Universities, Texas Christian University Press, Fort Worth, 1955, 17–27.

[34] Sommerfeld, Roy E. "Some Recent Research in College Reading." *Techniques and Procedures in College and Adult Reading Programs,* Sixth Yearbook of the Southwest Reading Conference, Texas Christian University Press, Fort Worth, 1957, 56–72.

[35] Spache, George. "Integrating Diagnosis with Remediation in Reading." *The Elementary School Journal,* 56 (September, 1955) 18–26.

[36] Strang, Ruth, McCullough, Constance M., Traxler, Arthur E. *Problems in the Improvement of Reading.* McGraw-Hill Book Company, Inc., New York, 1955.

[37] Stroud, James B. "A Critical Note on Reading." *The Psychological Bulletin,* 39 (March, 1942) 173–178.

[38] Thorndike, Robert L., and Hagen, Elizabeth. *Measurement and Evaluation in Psychology and Education.* John Wiley and Sons, Inc., New York, 1955.

[39] Tiegs, Ernest W. *Educational Diagnosis.* Educational Bulletin, No. 18, California Test Bureau, Los Angeles, 1956.

[40] Tinker, Miles A. "Trends in Diagnostic and Remedial Reading as Shown by Recent Publications in this Field." *Journal of Educational Research,* 32 (December, 1938) 293–303.

[41] Traxler, Arthur E. "Critical Survey of Tests for Identifying Difficulties in Interpreting What is Read." *Promoting Growth Toward Maturity in Interpreting What is Read,* Supplementary Educational Monographs, No. 74, University of Chicago Press, Chicago, 1951, 195–200.

[42] Wheeler, Lester R. "Distinctive Problems Presented by Poor Readers: The Retarded Reader." *Improving Reading in All Curriculum Areas,* Supple-

mentary Educational Monographs, No. 76, University of Chicago Press, Chicago, 1952, 109–114.

[43] Wheeler, Lester R., and Smith, Edwin H. "A Modification of the Informal Reading Inventory." *Elementary English,* 34 (April, 1957) 224–226.

[44] Witty, Paul. "Problems in the Improvement and Measurement of Growth in Reading." *School and Society,* 78 (September, 1953) 69–73.

[45] Young, Robert A. "Case Studies in Reading Disability." *American Journal of Orthopsychiatry,* 8 (April, 1938) 230–254.

16

THE SCOPE OF THE READING PROCESS

We have examined many areas of knowledge concerning reading and the reader. Now we must seek to identify some of the interrelationships that are involved. We wish to apply our knowledge to our professional tasks. To make wise application of our knowledge, its discriminate parts must be integrated.

Both educators and psychologists have devoted much attention to reading. This has resulted in a body of data and theory too complex to examine as a whole. Consequently, we have studied many seemingly unrelated areas of information about reading. However, to make the best use of this knowledge for more effective teaching, it should be unified and systemized.

This chapter's major task is to bring together the basic facts and general observations of the preceding chapters. As we discuss what is known of the psychology of reading, we must also consider what remains unknown, because an awareness of what is unknown helps the practitioner to recognize limitations and challenges the scientist to seek answers.

In Chapter 1 we identified eight aspects of the psychology of reading which have attracted the special attention of research workers. The data gathered in these areas have contributed greatly to our knowledge of the complex field of reading. The eight facets were as follows:

1. Reading as a sensory process
2. Reading as a perceptual process
3. Reading as a response
4. Reading as a learned process
5. Reading as a growth process
6. Reading as an interest

7. Reading as a tool for learning
8. Reading as a developmental task

At this point let us change our focus from the individual aspects of the psychology of reading to the *interrelationships* of those aspects. Although each facet has its own identity, it can never be isolated from the others. Information concerning each is dependent on research which may be pertinent to many or all of the other facets. For the teacher to utilize information from all of the areas, he must be able to see them as an entirety.

READING AS A SENSORY PROCESS

All knowledge comes to the individual through his senses. They provide his contact with the world about him. Both for building a background of experience and for the specific task of learning to read, adequate vision and hearing are of prime importance.

However, although the sensory process precedes the perceptual process by bringing the individual into contact with the world, the sensory process itself often is influenced by perception. For example, we saw that eye-movement patterns (the viewing) frequently are determined by comprehension (the perceptual factors). Faulty eye movements are usually symptoms, rather than causes, of inadequate understandings.

The sensory process has also been found related to the general growth process. We have seen that increased knowledge of the maturation of the eyes has resulted in serious questions concerning children's visual readiness for reading. We know that as children progress through the school grades an increasingly greater percentage have myopia. It has been suggested that this is due to a too early introduction to reading.

To become ready to read children need not only distance acuity but also adequate near-point vision and depth perception. Binocular co-ordination, ability to center, to focus, and to change fixation readily are skills that are important for reading. It is possible that some children are not ready for reading, at near point at least, before the age of eight. The tissues of the young eye are extremely plastic. One writer suggests that the sweep in reading from the end of one line to the beginning of the next causes pressures that may damage the immature eye.

Auditory factors also have a bearing on the child's readiness for accomplishing the developmental task of reading. To become a good reader the child must discriminate between the many sounds that form words. Inadequate hearing may make it impossible for the child to distinguish specific speech elements. And, since one can scarcely learn to pronounce distinctions that he does not hear, a child may fail to make correct associations or may come to associate the wrong sound with a graphic symbol.

The data indicate that the auditory acuity of six-year-old children as a group is lower than that of eight-year-old children. This may have a bearing on our decisions concerning when children are ready for reading instruction.

Sensory factors may also influence directly the methods that are most suitable for helping the child to learn to read. We have evidence that the quality of the child's sensory equipment may be a determinant of the method of instruction from which he can most benefit, and certainly it will have a direct bearing on our procedures in diagnosis and remediation.

Recent research findings indicate that proficiency in visual and auditory discrimination may be more significant than mental age in successfully accomplishing the developmental task of learning to read. We know that most first-grade children already know the meanings of the words that we wish to teach them to read. For this reason reading instruction in the first and second grades emphasizes word identification and recognition. To succeed here children must be able to see and hear differences in words. And they must learn to associate the visual differences with the auditory differences.

We can not be certain what interrelationships are connoted by observations that first-grade children who know the names of the letters of the alphabet generally have little trouble in learning to read. Perhaps knowledge of letters is merely an indication of intellectual maturity or it may be that a child who has learned to associate a name with a letter has already learned a basic reading skill—he has learned to discriminate between graphic symbols and to associate sounds with these symbols.

As another interrelationship between the sensory process and teaching method, it appears that auditory discrimination skills are more applicable to the learning of words that are spelled according to the way they sound and that visual discrimination skills are more significant in learning words that contain unusual letter combinations.

Ability in auditory and visual discrimination are necessary for reading progress but do not alone guarantee reading success. Because many children make slow progress in reading even though they are proficient in auditory and visual discrimination, we must search for other factors or combinations of factors that influence reading readiness and achievement.

READING AS A PERCEPTUAL PROCESS

Perhaps the most important characteristic of reading is that it is a *perception* of graphic symbols. Meaning is the essence of reading and graphic symbols are meaningful to us only if our fund of experience makes them meaningful. However, the extent of our fund of experience depends first upon our having possessed adequate sense organs. They were the bridge to whatever richness our environment has provided. And across this same bridge comes our present environmental stimulations to commune with our remembered experiences. This is the essence of perception.

As another interrelation between facets of the reading process, we are aware that our perceptions are acquired. The extent of our learned background of experiences is determined by our ability to interact with our environmental offerings. Since our background of experience is learned, the psychological research and theory from the entire field of learning has a bearing on the understanding of perception.

Although the quality of our experiential background is a major determinant of perception, other factors must be considered. Selections both from the data presently brought to us by our senses and from our background of experience are made on the basis of our needs and our need-determined interests. The perceptual process is indeed a complex one.

Words suggest rather than transmit meaning. The written symbol is a visible sign which represents something. Just what it will represent depends on the interpretation given to it by the observers. And those interpretations will be as various as are the qualities of sensory equipment and the experiential backgrounds of the interpreters. Communication always is imperfect. Its degree of perfection is dependent on the similarity of meanings that the reader and the writer (or the listener and the speaker) attach to the symbols used.

Generally the adequacy of communication between a child and a writer depends on the richness of the meanings that the child can bring to the written symbols. We find an interesting difference between children who are good readers and children who are poor readers. When the good reader makes a substitution error, he commonly keeps about the same meaning; the substitution of the poor reader typically distorts the meaning. Thus the perceptions of the good reader show a greater degree of veridicality than do those of the poor reader.

Too frequently we assume that accurate communication between writer and reader is taking place. We are inclined to assume that there is a direct connection between the symbols that are employed and the datum, object, or event which they represent. We forget that the experiences the symbol calls forth in the reader are always different from the experiences of the writer. Then, too, no two readers have had identical experiences. Thus not only does the writer and any one reader fail to communicate perfectly but each additional reader has a different type of discommunication. And discommunication tends to cumulate within a classroom. Each child gains different understandings even from those experiences offered to all children in the class.

Bright children, especially, tend to have great facility in manipulating symbols, but because of insufficient experience some of their symbols may have relatively little meaning for them and their manipulation becomes merely a verbalistic one. And as a group children are prone to identify symbols with concrete referents, and in manipulating these symbols they give the illusion that their level of conceptualization is higher than it actually is. It seems that very young children and, frequently, poor readers characteristically tend to react to a symbol in a specific rather than a general sense. Adequacy of communication is dependent on the reader's ability to conceptualize. In short, he must come to see individual objects as members of a class. Unfortunately not all persons become able to do this.

Successful reading is dependent on the formation and manipulation of concepts and thus the level of mental maturity is seen to be an important factor. Not only must the child develop certain concepts before he can be said to read but also there are numerous levels of interpretation, levels of abstraction, and levels of concept formation. And optimum communication at each higher level of reading development requires a corresponding growth in experiential readiness.

Somehow, we must discover more effective means for enriching children's lives with experiences that enhance their ability to communicate. The nursery school could contribute here. Unfortunately, we find that those children most in need of the rich experiences that would encourage concept formation are not the ones for whom nursery schools are most available.

Actually, the reading done in the first one or two grades presents fewer problems in concept development than does the reading of intermediate grades, high school, and college. As he progresses to higher educational levels, the student is required to relate one concept to another and to form many of his new concepts from vicarious experiences. Also he must learn to deal with units of increasing size.

There is a need for research on the problem of concept development. We would like to know what concepts are most necessary at each grade level. And we need more information on how to teach concepts such as size, space, number, and time. Reading should itself be a means for the development of the concepts needed for higher levels of reading. We need to know why certain children, especially boys, have particularly inadequate perceptual development. We need to know how to identify differences in perceptual development in the very young and how we can remedy inadequate development. We need better methods for measuring the reader's level of development in concept formation. Our measurements of a child's ability to reason with verbal concepts and to remember word meanings must be refined.

Certainly we do not know as much about the basic nature of meaning as we should like to know. Words are more than the tools with which we communicate. They are the basic materials with which we think. They are used to represent acquired concepts and they are important to the development of new concepts. We are rightfully concerned that, despite our emphasis on methods, the reading vocabularies of children develop slowly. Somehow, with little formal instruction, children learn to react to a far greater number of words orally than visually. Why? Is it possible that our emphasis on vocabulary control in our reading materials robs children of their interest in words? Or is it distinctly easier to discriminate orally than visually? We must know more about promoting vocabulary growth. We need to know how to make effective use of word-understanding skills, multi-sensory instructional aids, and the child's real and vicarious experiences. We need to know how and when to introduce the use of dictionaries, synonyms and antonyms, contextual clues, and structural analysis. To promote vocabulary growth we must base our methodology upon sound principles of learning and employ our knowledge of perception, concept development, readiness, remediation, and motivation.

Although the quality of our sense organs may be a restricting factor in perception, the mind—not the senses—seems to be the limiting factor. The visual span of the average reader is much larger than is his recognition span.

As we examine the use of mechanical devices for improving reading rate, we see that they do not improve the optic, retinal, and conductive processes. Their only effect can be on the perceptual aspects of reading. Improvements in reading that accompany the use of such equipment come from motivation including competition with self and others and the novelty of presentation plus an increased amount of practice and renewed concern about reading improvement. Such equipment may contribute to hastening the mind but it seems to do little stretching of the eye span.

READING AS A RESPONSE

When we focus upon reading as a response, we recognize that reading performance is closely related to motivation, physical well-being, fatigue, and habit.

Even children of the same age show wide variations in both stage and quality of physical and neurological development. Children with glandular or vitamin deficiencies, hemoglobin variation, heart disorders, nutritional and circulatory disorders, or with almost any debilitating condition may be handicapped in their ability to respond and thus to learn to read. In general, however, physical factors contribute to reading disability rather than cause it. This makes them no less important and, in fact, they may be more important than we have generally believed.

As we consider the child's ability to respond, we must include the possibility of emotionalized determinants of various kinds. Teacher-pupil rapport, general emotional climate of the classroom, the child's degree of self confidence, and his aspirational levels may be important factors.

Actually we do not know as much as we should like to about the relationship between reading disability and blocks to response such as speech defects, motor in-coordination, left-handedness, and ambidexterity. For example, speech defects frequently are associated with reading difficulties. Children with cleft palate tend to have difficulty with the letters, *p, b, t, d, k,* and *g*. Stuttering leads to confusion of the initial sounds of *b, p, w, t, k,* and *n*. Faulty articulation may result in a general confusion of word sounds. A child who hears a word one way when he says it and another way when someone else says it is bound to become confused.

But we must proceed beyond the identification of relationships. We wish to know more about the causes of blocks to responding. At present we can only surmise that certain children inherit a predisposition to them or that others have suffered minor brain injuries that give rise to them.

Language development in general and reading achievement in particular depend on the proper functioning of the brain. The brain may develop inadequately or it may suffer a specific injury. An injury to the brain, for example, may make it impossible for the person to recognize or to name what he sees or to recall what he has seen. Sometimes persons with brain injury cannot associate the printed word with meaning. The full significance of minor brain damage as it affects ability to respond needs clarification.

Numerous related questions confront us. We need to know what causes reversals and mirror writing. It is helpful to know that these conditions frequently are associated with left-handedness and ambidexterity, but we wish to know what causes such relationships to exist among these factors. Are reversals due to difficulties in differentiating among symbols, to inadequate brain maturation, to brain injuries, or to a combination of causes? Why do certain children find it difficult or impossible to note differences between symbols and between symbols and their backgrounds? We know that children are likely to reproduce forms without any apparent heed to the position they occupy in space. Shapes that point in opposite directions may appear alike to young children. And to some a word seems most recognizable when the letters are completely reversed. Why do some children and not others retain these tendencies?

Certainly if the child is unable to respond or to make a satisfactory response, he will be unable to learn at a normal rate. A knowledge of his problems and their causes will have a bearing on our plans for remediation, motivation, and also on the method of presentation.

READING AS A LEARNED PROCESS

Generally we define learning as changes in behavior that occur as the result of experience. To read, a child must make a response to the printed page, and the factors which affect and effect all responses apply to learning to read. Because this response must be learned, the same laws of learning that govern all other learned processes govern the child's learning to read. The principles which apply to effective learning must be employed for effective teaching.

Not only is reading itself a learned process, but much of what we call readiness for reading also is learned. This is easily seen when we consider the background of experiences that are the foundation of perception. It is less obvious that sensation, at least to an extent, is a learned process. From the vast array of stimuli that impinge upon our sense organs, we learn to "tune-in" what seems important to us and "tune-out" the unimportant. For example, in the case of vision we learn to focus on a restricted portion of the field and, to an extent, to magnify it. In reading a child learns how to see as well as how to interpret.

Learning to read requires more than the ability to make sensory responses. It involves the learned association of the spoken with the written word. Unfortunately, a child may learn wrong as well as right associations. He may not see the printed word clearly or may not hear the spoken word correctly. Children of above average intelligence frequently memorize word forms rather than identify the word forms with the meanings behind them. They fail to make the associations necessary for effective learning.

Learning to read includes even more than the ability to respond and to associate. It involves interpretation and at the higher levels it calls for some degree of organization, cognition, reasoning—in fact the elements we consider as necessary to thinking. At the level of interpretation there are many possibilities of inaccuracies because of the reader's lack of experience or the quality of his experiences. Even at the thinking level the reader's experiences, his biology, and his culture affect meanings.

We know that practice is a necessary condition for learning but generally we are agreed that practice without motivation is worthless. We know that children learn best when they find the learning rewarding. Learning also depends at least somewhat on the physical and emotional state of the learner. Defective vision or hearing, brain injury, bad health, generally low physical energy, and emotional maladjustment may deter learning or at the very least may require special teaching techniques.

Learning theorists have long been concerned with the exact nature of learning. In general, they have agreed that learning involves some form of association between the stimulus and the response. We say that a child has learned to read when he can make the same physical, emotional, and mental responses to the written word that he previously made to the spoken word. Stimulus substitution then has taken place. We find that with repeated and motivated association, meaning becomes attached to the written word.

READING AS A GROWTH PROCESS

When we focus on reading as a growth process, we are concerned with those areas of human growth and development that are most closely identified with the developmental task of learning to read.

As we examine the growth process of reading we see that it is dependent on both hereditary and environmental factors. And achievement in reading cannot be divorced from the vast range of individual differences that accompany other aspects of human growth and development. Each child's unique intellectual, emotional, physical, and social development, and his specific attitudes, ideals, and interests have a bearing on his growth in reading. Conversely, growth in reading is one expression of general human development.

Generally, mental age has been considered a most significant determinant not only of reading readiness but of readiness for all areas of educational achievement. We know that mental age places some ceiling on nearly all types of achievement and that level of mental development correlates even more highly with achievement in the later grades than it does in the earlier ones. However, a level of mental development generally considered sufficient for learning to read does not guarantee reading success. And, although a mental age of 6½ is generally recommended for beginning reading, many youngsters learn to read before they are 6½ years old. Actually, many—perhaps most—of our poor readers have I.Q.'s between 90 and 110 and we know that many children of high I.Q. are severely retarded in reading development.

The sex of the reader seems to play an important rôle both in the general growth process and in readiness for reading. Girls generally begin to read at an earlier age, achieve better reading, and show more interest in reading than do boys. Fewer girls become reading disability cases. Why? It may be because of their earlier readiness due to the generally more rapid physical maturation of girls. The fact that fewer girls are left-handed and fewer lisp or stutter may influence the discrepancy between boys and girls in achievement and readiness. There are factors in our culture that may incline girls toward reading; the schools' materials, activities, and the preponderance of women teachers may promote an atmosphere which favors the girls. Girls may learn to develop visual and auditory discriminatory skills as a result of their play activities. Are there other possible explanations? Is intelligence more variable among boys and consequently is reading achievement also more variable? Do girls have a natural interest in verbal activities or have they inherited a special facility in language?

The child's emotional growth also influences his readiness and achievement in reading. The incidence of maladjustment among poor readers is significantly greater than among good readers. Why is this so? Does proficiency in reading tend to promote good adjustment? Does personal maladjustment cause reading failure or does reading failure cause personal maladjustment?

Reading failure certainly makes it more difficult for a child to develop emotionally in a normal manner. Without success in reading, the child finds it difficult to satisfy his needs for security, success, social acceptance, and self-esteem. Also it is true that we are attracted to things that satisfy our basic needs and repelled by those that do not. Consequently, reading failure may lead not only to adjustment problems but also to dislike for reading.

Numerous explanations have been advanced for the behavioral deviations that frequently accompany reading failure. For example it has been suggested that reading failure sometimes satisfies a need for punishment and that children sometimes attempt to get recognition through aggressive behavior if they fail to receive it through success in reading. Painful emotional events during his early efforts at reading may turn the learner against reading. Or displaced resistance may result in unfavorable reaction toward his teacher or to reading. Frequently, a vicious spiral is set in motion: emotional maladjustment causes reading failure, and reading failure leads to a more serious maladjustment which may, in turn, lead to a complete rejection of reading.

Regardless of the causes or effects of reading failures, we will need to make certain decisions as to how to proceed with reading cases that have an emotional concomitant. We must decide whether the case warrants therapy and whether its treatment calls for skills beyond the range of our training. Some children have problems of such nature and magnitude that only a skilled clinician should work with them.

For those children who are less deeply disturbed, the teacher may be able to make use of at least certain therapeutic techniques that have been employed with the disturbed-disabled reader. These include art and play therapy, psychodrama, non-directive therapy, and group therapy. The teacher may also guide the child to obtain therapeutic help from books.

However, although the possible benefits of correctly employed therapy are rather obvious, the dangers of misdirected attempts to change the child's adjustment are great. Every professional person has a responsibility *not* to attempt certain tasks that are beyond his professional skills.

Frequently some form of therapy is used in combination with remedial teaching. Whether the reading disability caused or resulted from emotional maladjustment, an alleviation of the cause will not automatically remove its effect. Both remediation and therapy may be necessary for the removal of blocks to the child's readiness for further development.

READING AS AN INTEREST

We have recognized that reading not only can become an interest in its own right but that it may serve as a clue to the other interests of the individual. Interests are learned, they stem from motivation, and they reflect the individual's personality. They are related to level of maturity, state of health, and may even reflect the excellence of the individual's sensory equipment.

Motivation and interest are related both to reading readiness and to later reading achievement. We know that children learn to read when they are motivated by basic personal needs. Gradually, as they become more skilled in reading, reading becomes a motivating force in its own right. The reading skill turns into an interest that is self-propelling.

The reading teacher is especially concerned with why children read and why they choose the specific materials that they do read. The most significant determinants of interest seem to be sex, age, and intelligence, but environmental factors also are important.

Interest is a selective force; it directs attention to specific elements in the environment. And it directs the choice of reading materials. For example, we find that primary children like stories about children and animals. In the intermediate grades the boys turn toward adventure, how-to-do-it stories, hero-worship and science; the girls prefer fantasy and stories about home and family life. In adolescence, boys prefer sports, mystery and comics; girls like romance and teen-age problems stories.

There are many unanswered questions concerning how we may direct children both toward reading in general and toward specific types of reading. Unfortunately, we seem to have much better techniques for identifying children's interests than for developing them, and we know little about how the child acquires his wide variety of "untaught" interests.

There has been considerable educational focus on the "seeking" behavior of children. However, we retain an obligation to lead students beyond their immediate "felt" interests to a choice of literature of quality and to reading materials that will help them to expand understandings and to clarify and to pursue life goals.

Closely related to the facet of interest is the topic of readability of materials. Certainly a child will not retain an interest in material that for him is unreadable. We must make many decisions as to the readability of the texts we use, the supplementary reading materials provided for classroom use, and books we recommend for the purposes of therapy or for expanding interests. Readability formulas may help us choose readable books. Unfortunately, not all the determinants of readability have been identified or measured. We must make practical decisions concerning such factors as density and unusualness of the facts, illustrative content, suitability of vocabulary, abstractness of words, organization of the material, and interest for the reader. Also we will need to consider the desired levels of understanding. A level that is adequate for recreational reading may be inadequate for classroom study. Because no single text can meet the readability needs of every child in the classroom, we will need to make use of supplementary materials. As we strive to select readable materials, we must bear in mind that readability implies that the material be neither beyond nor *below* the capabilities of the reader. Materials that lack challenge are as inappropriate as are those that are too difficult.

Legibility factors also have significance. Certainly we should not use the same type-size with six-year-old children as we do with older individuals. Inadequacies in such visual factors as type-size, leading, line length, illumination, and contrast influence both rate of comprehension and the appeal of the printed material.

The development of reading as an interest is directly dependent on the child's interest in learning to read. And expansion of his interests through reading is dependent on both. In addition, improvement in general and special reading and study skills increases reading pleasure and results in further reading. With guidance toward new and challenging areas of study, interest in reading is maintained and enhanced. It is important that the teacher contribute to this cycle by helping the child develop reading skills and by extending the horizon of his interests. Motivation to explore through reading may come from classroom discussions, from visual aids, and from an adequate supply of readable materials for his classroom and home use.

READING AS A TOOL FOR LEARNING

Although originally the child learns to read, soon he reads to learn. In examining reading from this vantage point we are concerned with the particular reading and study skills demanded by the various learning tasks.

We know that each of the content areas requires certain reading skills. The child must know how to formulate his purposes for reading, survey the materials, utilize a flexible approach, understand graphic and illustrative materials, and become able to skim and scan as well as know when to read critically. Unfortunately, we do not know as much as we should like about the best methods for developing these skills.

The reader must also acquire the specific techniques that lead to best comprehension in each study task. In literature, for example, he reads for appreciation and for interpretation; in science reading is intensive, the vocabulary is precise, the reasoning is inductive, and a premium is put on detail. Reading for learning is dependent on the reader's familiarity with the concepts, the vocabulary, and the symbolism of the reading area. The tendency to verbalize without understanding is always a danger in content-area reading.

When we consider all the aspects of reading as a learning tool, we see that it has numerous relationships to the other facets of reading. The child's interests *direct* his reading choices and *make purposeful* his reading in the content areas.

Our knowledge of the principles of learning also apply here. An effective teaching situation is one in which children learn effectively. Our proper use of the assignment, of examinations to direct and encourage frequent review, and our use of discussion and summaries—in fact much of our methodology—are directed toward encouraging reading to learn and to remember.

READING AS A DEVELOPMENTAL TASK

From an eighth vantage point, we see that reading is not only a growth process but a developmental task as well—it is a task that the child must perform in order to satisfy his own needs and the demands imposed on him by his society.

We see an interdependence among all the aspects of the reading process that have been discussed previously. Unquestionably the performance of this developmental task depends on the prior accomplishment of many other goals. The child's sensory equipment, perceptual development, physical-emotional-social growth, interests, and his ability to respond must have advanced to a point of readiness for the accomplishment of this task. Learning to read is, in a sense, a culmination of the child's previous development. Until he is ready to read, he cannot learn to read; and until a child has learned to read, he cannot progress to reading to learn.

The fact that reading is a developmental task implies that there is a "teachable moment" for reading and, indeed, for each specific reading skill. And if a child does not learn to read at the appropriate time, other aspects of normal development are blocked and future success in reading becomes even more difficult.

As in the case of other developmental tasks, reading's successful accomplishment is determined by the child's state of progress in related areas of development. Thus there are numerous determinants of readiness for reading. Among these are the growth processes including mental age, visual and auditory development, and various phases of physiological and neurological development. And the child's general motivation, special interests, and level of aspiration will affect his readiness to read. These factors determine not only the child's initial readiness to undertake the task of learning to read but they also govern his degree of readiness for each succeeding phase of higher-level reading development.

RESEARCH AND DEVELOPMENT—THE FUTURE

It is always difficult to foresee the complete pattern or, indeed, the exact direction toward which an area of knowledge must develop during the future. However, research receives its general impetus and guidance from unsolved problems. In the psychology of reading many such problems are becoming identified and some of them already are attracting the attention of research workers. Let us examine some of the more obvious research needs.

NEED TO ORGANIZE AND INTEGRATE

As we have seen, the research in reading has been voluminous. This is true also of research in fields of knowledge that can contribute to our understanding of the reading process—psychology, physiology, sociology, medicine, and the various areas of educational methodology. However, volume of research frequently is not as important as is its wise direction toward important problems.

For research findings to be most helpful, general principles must be identified, abstracted, and organized. This is necessary both for the guidance of the practitioner and for the redirection of research workers. In this book some beginning may have been made toward the needed organization, but it has been little more than a beginning. However, let us examine for a moment how an organization of knowledge pertaining to the reading process might ultimately be brought about.

As a basic postulate, it seems clear that *reading is a perceptual process.* And whatever has been found true of perception in general should be found to hold true for reading. With this in mind, we proceed to identify a number of the principles or rules of perception. For example, perception may be regarded as a creative construction of meaning in response to external stimuli (in reading that response is made to the written symbol). This first-order principle can then be expanded by second-order principles: stimuli (and therefore the written symbol) (1) carry no direct meanings, (2) serve no purpose unless they evoke meaningful responses from the organism, (3) are dependent for interpretation on the biology and culture of the responder.

By identifying and organizing the known facts of perception, we also abstract a series of principles that should apply to reading. The reading specialist should be able to utilize most of the findings of research in the field of perception. Such sharing of knowledge may proceed from the other direction as well. An examination of the data acquired from research in reading may broaden knowledge of the perceptual process. Not only may such an approach promote a better understanding of reading and perception but it should help to identify those questions still in need of solution and can thus redirect research. There are other aspects of the reading process that allow for the formulation of postulates under which we may organize what is known and identify what remains to be determined. For example, we may propose that reading is a *response* and whatever affects ability to respond will similarly affect reading. Here we would utilize the co-ordinated information from such fields as learning, neurology, motivation, physiology, and experimental psychology. Similar co-ordination of information could be applied to the other facets of reading. Although only eight facets of reading have been emphasized in this book, no doubt there are still other possible vantage points from which the reading process may be viewed.

Now let us examine some further needs in the field of reading.

NEED TO MEASURE AND INTERPRET

The extent to which teaching can be directed to the unique needs of each pupil depends in large part on the accuracy with which we can measure his abilities and specific achievements. Much has been done to develop accurate instruments but much more remains to be accomplished. Our diagnostic instruments remain relatively unreliable. We are aware that in many—perhaps most—cases our error of measurement is so large that when applied to individual cases, our measuring gives us little more than gross estimates.

Our measurements lack also in validity. For example, in discussing the elements of effective reading, writers commonly say that ideal development is toward a *flexibility* of approach and that both rate and comprehension *should* vary with the goals of the reader and with the nature of the material read. And flexibility is assumed to apply not only to adjustments that should be made from one reading task to another but to adjustments within the accomplishment of any single reading task. However, as yet our tests go little beyond a single rate and a single comprehension score.

Perhaps an even greater need is to develop our diagnostic techniques so as to identify syndromes—those signs and symptoms that occur together and through whose *pattern* we may recognize a specific problem. We can use the field of medicine to illustrate our goal here. Although medicine constantly strives to improve its techniques for measuring bodily states—blood pressure, temperature, blood and urine chemistry, and the condition of the heart, lungs, and other organs—the emphasis in diagnosis is to interpret the pattern of bodily states rather than the meaning of the individual measures of discrete traits.

NEED TO COLLABORATE WITH OTHER AREAS

As we considered possibilities for organizing our knowledge of the reading process we saw that many values could be gained from integrating the findings and theories of various related fields of knowledge. Data concerning learning, individual differences, and motivation, for example, have contributed greatly to our knowledge of reading. However there appears to be a vast potential in as yet little-used fields. The concepts of social psychology such as those pertaining to group atmosphere, levels of aspiration, and morale have remained inadequately used. And the findings of biochemistry and of medical research in general are as yet given insufficient consideration. For example, variations in bodily chemistry are known to affect learning but so far we have taken little interest in the nature or direction of these effects.

NEED TO INCREASE LEARNING EFFICIENCY

An attempt to predict future research and development in the field of reading would be most inadequate without some attention to the so-called "teaching machine."

Psychology has long been aware of the importance of immediate reinforcement of desired learnings. And equally it has been aware that errors should immediately be made known to the learner. Many attempts have been made to apply these rather simple principles to various types of learning. The beginnings were made a number of years ago by the development of procedures through which a pupil could gain immediate knowledge of a right or wrong answer on each item in an examination over previously studied material.

More recently the principles of reinforcement have been applied to step-by-step classroom learning. Educational "programs" have been developed for specific portions of several subject-matter fields.* It is probable that similar programming, aimed at the reinforcement of correct behavior and the reteaching of inadequately learned behaviors, will be applied to various areas of reading. Many of the specific reading skills and understandings appear to be well-suited to such methods.

SUMMARY

A psychology of reading is made up of many discriminate parts. Reading is a product of man's culture and his biology. It is a complex process and its appearance is often determined by the vantage point from which we view it.

When we see reading as a perceptual process, we recognize that what we bring to the printed page may be a more important determinant of meaning than what the writer placed there. When we see reading as a learned process, we recognize that all the research in the psychology of learning becomes a part of the psychology of reading.

When we see reading as a developmental task, we recognize that all

---

* For discussions and descriptions of self-instructional devices and an overview of the theory and development of teaching machines see A. A. Lumsdaine and Robert Glaser (Eds.), *Teaching Machines and Programmed Learning: A Source Book.* Department of Audio-Visual Instruction, National Education Association, Washington, D. C., 1960.

areas of human development contribute to the psychology of reading; when we recognize that reading is a basic part of the learning process, we see the importance of reading to growth and development. And when we view reading as part of a developmental program we see that each child's present level of skills, backgrounds, interests, and abilities must be considered in each day's teaching plan.

The contributions to our knowledge of the reading process and to methods for improving reading come from many sources. The class-room teacher, the educational administrator, the oculist, the physician, the bio-chemist, the psychologist, the sociologist, the psychiatrist, the architect, and the engineer all have made contributions and all have potentialities for further contributions.

SUGGESTED READINGS

(Causey, *The Reading Teacher's Reader*)

Article 9, Smith, Nila Banton, "Looking Ahead in Teaching Reading," from *National Education Association Journal* (October, 1955) pp. 416–417.

Article 44, Artley, A. Sterl, "Some 'Musts' Ahead in Teaching Reading," from *National Elementary Principal,* 35 (September, 1955) pp. 2–6.

INDEX

C

D

E

S